W9-BZG-423

Ideas in America

Source
Readings
in
the
Intellectual
History
of
the
United
States

Ideas

in

America

Edited by **GERALD N. GROB** and **ROBERT N. BECK**

 The Free Press, New York
Collier-Macmillan Limited, London

The Free Press
A Division of The Macmillan Company
866 Third Avenue, New York, New York 10022

Collier-Macmillan Canada Ltd., Toronto, Ontario

Library of Congress Catalog Card Number: 71-99206

6-16-71

printing number
1 2 3 4 5 6 7 8 9 10

For Our Parents

CONTENTS

ONE: **THE PURITAN MIND**   1

FIVE: AMERICAN THOUGHT IN A
TROUBLED WORLD 351

PREFACE

Like most peoples, Americans have wondered about the nature and meaning of their national existence. Unlike other peoples, however, their questioning has been complicated by a number of unique circumstances, particularly the diversified national origins of the American people and their dependence on European traditions. Thus they have been led to ask whether America has an independent and indigenous intellectual tradition of its own, or whether American thought is simply a by-product of a larger and older European tradition, or, in either case, whether there is an identifiable American national purpose and goal.

This book is an attempt to deal with these important problems by presenting lengthy excerpts from the works of major American intellectual figures arranged in such a manner as to relate their ideas to the development of a native intellectual tradition. In addition, extensive introductions, connective commentaries, and headnotes provide the reader with the historical perspective and background that are so necessary to an understanding of America's intellectual heritage. The general point of view presented is that although America has borrowed much from Europe, it has always modified these borrowings in the light of its own experiences. The result has been the unique synthesis of ideas and attitudes that has characterized the American mind.

To illustrate the movement of American thought we have distinguished five major periods in the intellectual history of the United States: the Puritan era, the age of the Enlightenment, the Romantic period of the early nineteenth century, the reaction to industrialism, and finally the dilemmas of American society since the 1930's. We have conceived of our task in a broad manner and have attempted to take a representative cross-section of the American heritage, including the writings of theologians, philosophers, men of letters, political theorists, educators, statesmen, reformers, economists, jurists, and historians, in order to illustrate the predominant modes of thought in given historical epochs. Each generation has sought to give meaning and significance to its existence, and the way in which this has been accomplished has varied with the problems faced.

From the time of the Puritans until the coming of the Civil War, Americans looked to the future with optimism and eager expectation, firmly committed to the vision of a constantly improving society. They tended to interpret their experiences in religious terms, whether borrowed from the Puritan vocabulary, the creed of the Enlightenment, or the evangelical version of religious truth. Had not America been divinely blessed with abundant resources as well as immunization from a more corrupt and decadent Europe? Was not America destined to serve as a haven and model for all mankind, offering to the rest of the world a shining example of what human society could accomplish under the aegis of a generous Deity?

Indeed, the vision of a new society under a beneficent Deity provided much of the drive that constantly impelled Americans to improve their position and to build a better world. The Puritans underwent great hardships and deprivations in order to establish a society based on divine law, a society that would truly embody a religious ideal and serve as a beacon to all mankind. In many ways the Puritans set the tone for much of America's subsequent development, especially in the intellectual realm. Eighteenth-century Americans, while no longer influenced so profoundly by the God of the Puritans, nevertheless continued to uphold their belief in rights and duties that were derived from a divine source. Indeed, the natural rights argument was a primary issue in the important events that led to the American Revolution and ultimately to the establishment of a new nation that would be free to live according to its own ideals and to realize its own destiny. Finally, Americans during the first half of the nineteenth century tended to identify religion and progress, and their efforts to build a better society often were motivated by a mixture of spiritual zeal and social consciousness—this was particularly true in the abolitionist crusade against slavery. Thus, whatever the problems and difficulties they faced, Americans for the first two centuries of their existence looked hopefully toward a better and more humane world. It is this sense of optimism and destiny that helps to explain many of the intellectual patterns of the United States during this period.

After the Civil War, as technological developments swiftly transformed the United States from an agrarian and rural nation into an urban and industrial world power, new issues arose to challenge the American people. Since the traditional premises of the older Protestant individualistic ethic seemed less and less relevant to the changing times, a search began for a new rationale that would replace the older one and enable men to cope with the new and unfamiliar problems of a complex world. In formulating a new synthesis, Americans turned to contemporary advances in science, especially to evolutionary theory, in the hope of erecting a scientific ethical system. In so doing, however, they brought into question the whole religious basis of their society, creating an intellectual crisis of the first magnitude. Since the middle of the nineteenth century, therefore, Americans have continued to seek an adequate philosophical and ideological justification upon which their society could rest. After the Civil War there developed such intellectual systems as conservative Darwinism, reform Darwinism, pragmatism, and naturalism. In the present the search for national meaning and purpose continues amidst the troubles and dilemmas that confront all mankind. That Americans, despite the formal orthodoxy of a cold war era, still seek a faith for living is proven by the persistence of numerous and opposing intellectual movements, such as Protestant neo-orthodoxy and evangelical fundamentalism, the New Conservatism, the liberal-progressive ethic, and the New Left. Where the search will lead, however, few are willing to predict with any degree of authority.

We should like at this point to add a word of explanation. Any volume such as this must, by its very nature, be selective. In choosing the materials in this text, we have attempted not only to present a cross-section of major figures but also to arrange their thoughts in such a way as to provide a meaningful interpretation of the course of American thought. This being the case, we have included figures that seemed best to exemplify the climate of opinion, predominant interests, and modes of thought of the different generations. Because our selections are relatively long, the number of individuals that we have included has necessarily been limited; however, we feel that fewer but longer excerpts may provide the reader with deeper insights into the development of the American mind.

We have also attempted in all cases to reproduce the texts in their original version. In some cases, however, spelling and punctuation have been slightly modified to conform with more modern usage.

Last, but not least, we should like to thank Professor George A. Billias for his comments and suggestions, which have saved us from many errors. Our wives also provided that atmosphere which is so necessary for work of this kind.

G.N.G.
R.N.B.

ACKNOWLEDGMENTS

The editors gratefully acknowledge the kind permission of the following publishers, individuals, and organizations to reprint copyrighted material in this book:

The American Academy of Political and Social Science and Lawrence Dennis for selections from Lawrence Dennis, "Fascism for America," *Annals of the American Academy of Political and Social Science*, 180 (1935).

American Antiquarian Society for selections from Cotton Mather, "The Angel of Bethesda," in Otho T. Beall, Jr., and Richard H. Shryock, eds., "Cotton Mather: First Significant Figure in American Medicine," American Antiquarian Society, *Proceedings*, 63 (April, 1953).

Beacon Press for selections from Theodore Parker, *The World of Matter and the Spirit of Man* (1907), George Willis Cooke, ed.; Herbert Marcuse, "Repressive Tolerance" (copyright © 1965 by Herbert Marcuse) and "Postscript 1968" (copyright © 1969 by Herbert Marcuse), in *A Critique of Pure Tolerance* (1969), by Robert P. Wolff, Barrington Moore, Jr., and Herbert Marcuse; and Morton G. White, "Original Sin, Natural Law, and Politics," *Partisan Review*, 23 (Spring, 1956). The last selection is a shortened version of the "Epilogue for 1957" in Morton G. White, *Social Thought in America* (copyright © 1957 by Morton G. White).

Columbia University Press for selections from Sidney Hook, "Naturalism and Democracy," in Yervant H. Krikorian, ed., *Naturalism and the Human Spirit* (1944).

Commentary for selections from Nathan Glazer, "The New Left and Its Limits," *Commentary*, 46 (July, 1968) (copyright © 1968 by the American Jewish Committee).

Commentary and The Macmillan Company for selections from Michael Novak, "American Catholicism after the Council," *Commentary*, 40 (August, 1965) (copyright © 1965 by the American Jewish Committee). This article also appeared in a slightly amended form in Michael Novak, *A Time to Build* (The Macmillan Company, 1968).

Doubleday and Company, Inc., for selections from Billy Graham, *Peace with God* (copyright 1953 by Billy Graham).

Harper & Row for selections from Twelve Southerners, *I'll Take My Stand: The South and the Agrarian Tradition* (1930) (copyright renewed 1958 by Donald Davidson).

Holt, Rinehart and Winston, Inc., for selections from *The Influence of Darwin on Philosophy and Other Essays in Contemporary Thought* by John Dewey. (Copyright 1910 by Holt, Rinehart and Winston, Inc. Copyright 1938 by John Dewey. Reprinted by permission of Holt, Rinehart and Winston, Inc.)

Houghton Mifflin Company for selections from Arthur M. Schlesinger, Jr., *The Vital Center: The Politics of Freedom* (1949).

Walter Kaufmann for selections from Walter Kaufmann, "The Faith of a Heretic," *Harper's Magazine*, 218 (February, 1959).

Little, Brown and Company for selections from Walter Lippmann, *The Public Philosophy* (1955).

Massachusetts Historical Society for selections from John Winthrop, "A Modell of Christian Charity," *Winthrop Papers*, II (1931).

The Macmillan Company for selections from Henry Adams, *The Degradation of the Democratic Dogma* (1919, copyright renewed 1947 by The Macmillan Company); Herbert Croly, *The Promise of American Life* (1909, copyright renewed 1937 by The Macmillan Company); Michael Harrington, *Toward a Democratic Left: A Radical Program for a New Majority* (copyright © 1968 by Michael Harrington); and Walter Rauschenbusch, *A Theology for the Social Gospel* (1917, copyright renewed 1945 by Pauline E. Rauschenbusch).

The Nation for selections from Reinhold Niebuhr, "The Dilemma of Modern Man," *The Nation*, 164 (February 22, 1947).

The New Republic for selections from Lewis Mumford, "The Corruption of Liberalism," *The New Republic*, 102 (April 29, 1940).

Princeton University Press for selections from Elihu Root, *Experiments in Government and the Essentials of the Constitution* (copyright 1913 by Princeton University Press).

Harry N. Rosenfield (Estate of Morris Raphael Cohen) for selections from Morris Raphael Cohen, *The Faith of a Liberal* (1946).

Charles Scribner's Sons for selections from Reinhold Niebuhr, *The Children of Light and the Children of Darkness* (pages 1–2, 2–3, 5–7, 10–12, 16–19, 20, 21–22, 40–41, 70–71, 75–76, 77–78. Copyright 1944 Charles Scribner's Sons).

B. F. Skinner for selections from B. F. Skinner, "Freedom and the Control of Men," *The American Scholar*, 25 (Winter, 1955–1956).

D. G. Brinton Thompson and the trustees of the estate of Madison Grant for selections from Madison Grant, *The Passing of the Great Race* (1916).

University of Chicago Press for selections from Edward S. Ames, *The New Orthodoxy* (1918), and Friedrich A. von Hayek, *The Constitution of Liberty* (1960).

Peter Viereck for selections from Peter Viereck, *The Shame and Glory of the Intellectuals* (1953).

Yale University Press for selections from Thurman Arnold, *The Folklore of Capitalism* (1937).

Ideas in America

PART I

THE PURITAN
MIND

Puritanism, which dominated the intellectual life of colonial New England for nearly a century after its founding, has been a major force in shaping the development of the American mind. Not only did it influence the New England colonies, leaving a complex heritage of customs and ideas, but it also advanced with those pioneers who left New England to blaze a frontier to the West. Thus it became incorporated into the mainstream of American thought. As one authority had remarked, Puritanism "was firmly rooted in the American experience and in the emerging American mind of the eighteenth century, and from New England as a center it has radiated its influence in American civilization, for good or ill, from that day to this; and the end is not yet."[1] Indeed, it is probably safe to assert that without an understanding of Puritanism there can be no understanding of America.

Yet there is much less agreement on the precise manner in which Puritanism influenced that vague and shadowy complex often referred to as the "American character." To one group Puritanism stands for narrow-

[1] Max Savelle, *Seeds of Liberty: The Genesis of the American Mind* (New York, 1948), p. 27.

1

mindedness and intolerance, intellectual atrophy, a prohibition upon the enjoyment of life, a restricted and perhaps bigoted sectarianism coupled with a crippling and inhibiting sense of guilt, and an individualism that, by interpreting religion in terms of thrift and worldly success, has led to social selfishness and irresponsibility. On the other hand, there are those who credit the Puritans with planting the seeds of democracy in the New World, with founding the first college and public school system, and with preserving the intellectual and cultural heritage of Western civilization in a harsh frontier environment that in other areas led to cultural regression.

Any study of the cluster of ideas and beliefs that is loosely termed the "American mind" must, therefore, begin with an understanding of Puritanism and its influence during the formative years of seventeenth-century New England. In undertaking such a venture, however, we must not interpret Puritanism through the mood of revolt that marks much of twentieth-century intellectual history. During the 1920's, for example, it was fashionable for the opponents of the Eighteenth Amendment to characterize those in favor of Prohibition as "Puritans." Yet the Puritans of the seventeenth century never condemned the imbibing of alcoholic beverages; indeed, they consumed large amounts of spirits in their daily lives. What they did condemn was excessive rather than moderate drinking. Similarly, we must not only avoid defining Puritanism in modern terms, but we also must be careful to distinguish between the elements in original Puritanism and the beliefs that evolved from them in later years. Puritanism, after all, was a many-sided and complex force and, like many other philosophies, included elements of contradiction as well as unity. From its trunk, to illustrate again, could grow such different branches as Unitarianism, religious revivalism, and fundamentalism. Finally, we must recognize that Puritanism can be understood only when placed in its seventeenth-century English environment. While the Puritans came into conflict with some aspects of their native culture, most of their beliefs did not appreciably differ from those of the typical Englishman of that day.

Initially, Puritanism arose as an English movement of the late sixteenth and early seventeenth centuries. It sought to reform the Anglican Church by ridding it of all "popish" elements and restoring to it the simplicity of the early Christian Church. As such, it was intimately associated with the Protestant Reformation and all that movement implied. The English Puritans, although always maintaining that they were part of the Anglican Church, were nevertheless insistent in their belief that the English Reformation had not proceeded far enough, and they struggled to enforce their views upon the established Church. In an age when religion was perhaps the major force in human society, the conflict between the dissident sects and the Anglican Church had momentous repercussions, not only for religious life, but also for social, economic, political, and intellectual life. Thus, for well over a century, from the time of Henry VIII until the reign of William and Mary, religious struggles were to play a decisive role in English history.

The Puritans who migrated to New England in the 1630's and afterward were among the more radical, although not the most radical, of the Protestant sects. Unable to force their views upon the established Church in England, the Puritans chose to leave for the New World where they would be free to translate their beliefs into practice and establish their much cherished "Bible Commonwealth." In turn, the descendents of the Puritans, though no longer accepting the creed of their ancestors, nevertheless perpetuated many traits of Puritanism and preserved them within the framework of American culture.

At the heart of the Puritan creed lay the twofold assumption of the inherent sinfulness of man and the omnipotence of God. Man, according to Puritan theology, had fallen into a state of sin and could be saved only through the grace of God. Since God, however, has granted this grace to some and not to others, certain individuals were predestined to be saved while others were predestined to be damned. Yet the Puritans were not fatalists; and their emphasis upon predestination was more theoretical than real. They accepted the challenge of sin with enthusiasm, even though they recognized their inability to achieve perfection in this world. They insisted that God, in His infinite wisdom, was not a capricious deity, despite the fact that man did not always perceive His reason and logic. Mortal reason, after all, was not God's reason, and the Puritans never attempted to gloss over their shortcomings. To the typical Puritan, the sinfulness of man was a fact that could easily be verified through experience. Recognizing mankind's imperfections, the Puritans, as Perry Miller has so ably pointed out, "held on the one hand that men must act by reason and abide by justice, and strive for an inward communication with the force that controls the world, but on the other hand . . . they must not expect that force always to be cribbed and confined by their conceptions of what is reasonable and just."[2] Puritanism was a tough-minded philosophy, and the Puritan, because of his unquestioned faith in the grandeur and glory of God, could never be disillusioned by the transitory world in which he lived. Reconciling fate and freedom and accepting the omnipotence of God, the Puritans held that human life had value only insofar as man had the freedom to choose between good and evil.

Perhaps the feature that most distinguished Puritanism from other Protestant

[2] Perry Miller and Thomas H. Johnson, *The Puritans* (New York, 1938), p. 57.

sects was its belief that the Bible, as the revealed truth of God, was an absolute code of action that provided man with an infallible guide to life, not only in matters of religion and theology, but also in such diverse areas as politics, economics, ethics, and matters of art. The typical seventeenth-century Puritan never for a moment doubted that the universe was centered in God, and that religion constituted the very essence of life and could not be separated from it. Those who migrated to Massachusetts in the third and fourth decades of the seventeenth century, therefore, attempted to organize society along lines laid down in the Bible. Religious ideals played a dominant role in shaping the social and political institutions of the young colony. Only church members were permitted to vote; and since formal church membership was kept at a minimum, Massachusetts quickly became an oligarchy ruled by a small minority of ministers and elders. Regarding themselves as a chosen people, the Puritans vigorously worked to root out what they regarded as error, and they freely proclaimed themselves enemies of toleration. Any individuals or groups brave enough to dissent from the dictates of the ruling group—such as Roger Williams, Anne Hutchinson, or the Quakers—quickly found themselves in difficult and even dangerous positions.

In time, however, the theocracy established by the Puritans began to crumble, partly as a result of internal tensions and partly because of environmental factors. The English tradition of self-government slowly made its presence felt, and with the passage of time the power of the ministers was undermined. The breakdown of the compact Puritan village also weakened conformity. Internal discontent with the existing situation led to the migration of several groups to other areas, while the persecution of such minorities as the Quakers met with increasing opposition from within the colony. In addition, the authority of the English government was gradually reimposed upon Massachusetts, with a consequent reduction in the authority of the oligarchy. Finally, the rational and more liberal ideas of the Enlightenment, as well as the growth of a commercially oriented middle class, weakened the religious inclination of the Puritans in favor of a more secular outlook on life.

Puritanism, however, was more than simply an unsuccessful effort to organize society along Biblical lines. It was also an articulate philosophy growing out of the intellectual climate of opinion of its times. As such, Puritanism inherited not only the ideals and traditions of the Reformation and Renaissance but also those of medieval Christianity. Always adopting an intellectual rather than an intuitive or emotional approach to problems, the Puritans maintained that reason and faith were valuable allies, each reinforcing the other. Furthermore, no conflict existed between the natural world and the revealed word of God. On the contrary,

since each strengthened the other, the Puritan could easily accept
scientific knowledge as an adjunct to religion. Though man might be an
inherently evil being, he was also a rational creature and thus was capable
of understanding his actions and accepting reponsibility for them. The
Puritans therefore labored to unify religion and knowledge into a compatible system of thought, and they succeeded, according to their own
standards, in formulating a unified and coherent philosophy of life.

The Puritan emphasis on the harmony of faith and reason, moreover, was to
have a profound influence on the intellectual development of colonial
New England. It is undoubtedly true that in certain areas—notably the
drama, religious music, religious painting, religious sculpture, and
poetry—Puritanism acted as an inhibiting force by its insistence that
anything that prevented man from coming into direct communion with
God was a distraction and constituted a serious danger. Yet when the
intellectual level of colonial New England is compared with that of either
the middle or southern colonies, the unquestioned superiority of the
former is immediately noted. The establishment of a school system, a
college, and a printing press within a short time after the founding of the
Massachusetts Bay Colony, for example, bears witness to this fact. In
other areas, including literature, verse, science, and theology, the leadership of the Puritans is equally clear. The Puritans were adamant in their
opposition to ignorance, and their emphasis upon learning and education
constitutes one of their most important contributions to posterity.
While the harsh frontier environment in other areas led to a loss of
cultural values, the Puritans managed to keep a respect for learning and
ideas alive in hostile surroundings. Perhaps intellectual Puritanism was,
as Samuel Eliot Morison has commented, the only alternative to the
overwhelming materialism that marked the other newly settled regions,
whether English, French, Dutch, or Spanish.[3]

Not the least part of the intellectual and cultural legacy of the Puritans was
the literary tradition that they founded in seventeenth-century New
England. Like others oriented toward a religious conception of human
life, the Puritans were under the compulsion of justifying their beliefs
and actions. To accomplish this important task, they employed various
literary means, including the sermon, poetry, and history, and they also
developed a mode of expression peculiar to themselves. It is true that
their efforts, which resulted in a considerable body of writing, cannot in
any way match the productions of their English contemporaries. But to
judge the literary output of the New England Puritans by the same standards one might apply to John Donne or George Herbert is, of course, an

[3] Samuel Eliot Morison, *The Intellectual Life of Colonial New England* (New York,
1956), pp. 16–17.

unfair comparison, considering the differing environments. Viewed in its own setting, the literature of the Puritans still stands as an enduring monument to their intellectual and moral strength.

As in other areas, Puritan literature was closely entwined with religion. Broadly defining the function of literature, the Puritans maintained that it was not only a means of communication, but that it would also serve to teach and convince others of the true purposes of life. Literature, therefore, had to be written in a clear and concise manner, to enable all men to understand it. Such an attitude generally made for realism and simplicity, and this facet of the literary tradition of New England was to be perpetuated by such nineteenth-century writers as Henry David Thoreau, Ralph Waldo Emerson, Francis Parkman, and Henry Adams.

Being children of the Renaissance as well as of the Reformation, the Puritans inherited the poetic traditions of their mother country. Although they objected to certain forms of poetry that they considered blasphemous or impious, the Puritans never objected to poetry as such; they read and rejoiced in the religious poetry of the English language. While most critics agree that the quality of the Puritans' own poetry was not particularly high because their creed did not emphasize the poetic mode of expression, and certain of its tenets actually placed barriers in the way of writing verse, there are still passages in the poems of figures like Edward Taylor, Anne Bradstreet, and Michael Wigglesworth that show considerable merit.

It was in their historical writing, however, that the Puritans excelled. More than any other form of expression, history fulfilled the needs of religion. In the first place, history provided a defense against the claims of the Roman Catholic Church by establishing a case for Protestantism. Secondly, history would reawaken religious interest among the second and third generations by portraying the special interest that God had shown in the Bible Commonwealth. Thirdly, if the Puritans did not write their own history, it was probable that others less sympathetic to their cause would undertake this task. Finally, and undoubtedly most important, history provided man with a record of God's workings and intentions. The function of the historian, therefore, was not only to present all the facts but also to interpret them in the light of divine purpose. The Puritan faith in God was so complete, moreover, that they did not gloss over unfavorable events, for in such events important lessons could also be found.

Conceiving of this world in epic and heroic terms, the Puritans dramatized their own history. They were not simply a people who had migrated to a new home, but rather an army fighting on behalf of their God. The historiography of seventeenth-century New England thus effectively mirrored the Puritan attitude toward literature in general—namely, that literature was an art that could be put to work for a righteous cause. To the modern student such an attitude might appear to be archaic, but the historical and literary works of the Puritans hold up surprisingly well. In his own way the Puritan, too, was an artist who was depicting a heroic age when men "fought and suffered and died courageously, because they were committed, emotionally and intellectually, to a life of faith."[4]

Activistic, moralistic, even rationalistic, Puritanism began to develop in different directions on the American shores. One of its paths led to political intolerance and the suppression of dissent; another led to a comparatively high intellectual and literary level. Still another was to lead toward the relatively secular position of the next century, known as the American Enlightenment. Regardless of the distaste we might feel for certain aspects of Puritanism that may today be characterized as hypocritical, can we deny the strength of the Puritan ideal that character and nobility are values that man can achieve only by a personal struggle whereby he transcends his physical surroundings? In assessing the enduring influence of the Puritans, all of these conflicting elements must be taken into account.

The best way to study the mind of the Puritans and its influence on succeeding generations is to begin with their own writings. Fortunately, the Puritans were both articulate and prolific in putting their thoughts on paper, and they did not hesitate to express their opinions. The following pages contain a cross-section of leading Puritan pronouncements on a variety of seemingly unrelated topics. Taken together, however, they do suggest a picture of a people and an attitude whose influence and importance, whether good or bad, can scarcely be disputed.

[4] Kenneth B. Murdock, *Literature & Theology in Colonial New England* (Cambridge, Massachusetts, 1949), p. 97.

CHAPTER I

THE PURITAN AS
A RELIGIOUS TYPE

*T*hough it had many different facets, Puritanism was primarily a religious movement that sprang from the medieval conception that the meaning and purpose of human existence can be found only when men are related to God. Like their contemporaries of the Protestant Reformation, however, the Puritans rejected the doctrine that salvation could be achieved through man's efforts, and they resolutely maintained that it could be attained only through the grace of God, who freely granted it as a gift despite man's inherent sinfulness.

For the Puritan, therefore, salvation (often referred to as "regeneration") was the central element in human experience, one that far transcended all others in importance. Yet his conception of original sin and human depravity was by no means as categorical as some scholars have held. Though man might be a sinful creature, he was also a rational and responsible being, and in their theology the Puritans managed to reconcile these apparently conflicting views. Influenced by the teachings of the great French Protestant philosopher Petrus Ramus (1515–1572), they held that truth could be tested by the innate rationality of the human mind, within which dwelt a small measure of divine truth. Puritanism thus managed to combine the rising humanist tradition and a system of Christian thought in an all-embracing religious conception of the world.

Central to Puritan theology, furthermore, was the belief that the regenerate individual had undergone a concrete physical experience that was proof of his salvation. In turn, this religious experience manifested itself in the outward conduct of his life. The regenerate individual, although aware of his own shortcomings, was compelled to obey to the best of his imperfect abilities the moral ordinances of God. These ordinances served two important purposes: they provided a measure whereby man could judge the enormity of his sinfulness, and they also helped the regenerate to grow in sanctity. Thus the covenant of works, although having been invalidated by original sin, was to be construed as a practical guide, thereby applying religious values insofar as the natural world was concerned. The covenant of grace, on the other hand, introduced the individual to the mysteries of life and the unknown. So long as constituted authority, as exercised by the ministers and elders, had the power to unite religion as a way of life and as an emotional experience, the Puritan creed could remain pure and undiluted. But with the decline in the powers of the oligarchy, this restraint no longer operated, and Puritanism began to develop along divergent paths. One path led to Unitarianism, while the other led to a more emotional and revivalistic religion, both of which were to have important influences on America's intellectual and religious history.

Paradoxically, the Puritan emphasis on the covenant of grace did not lead to either a passive or a carefree conception of life, but rather to a highly activistic philosophy that was well suited to the rigors of a frontier environment. Blending together in a subtle and sophisticated manner the opposing ideas contained in the covenant of works and the covenant of grace, the typical Puritan emphatically opposed any form of monasticism or moral asceticism. Since man existed to glorify God, it followed logically that life was not tragic, despite all its difficulties and hardships. The Puritans looked at the world with a feeling of optimism rather than pessimism, with a sense of adventure rather than foreboding. They did not demand the elimination of all worldly pleasures and pursuits; they simply emphasized moderate rather than excessive indulgence, since the enjoyment of these pleasures would contribute toward the creation of a well-rounded and complete individual who would stand as living proof of the glory and omnipotence of God.

Samuel Willard

1640-1707

Born at Concord, Massachusetts, Samuel Willard graduated from Harvard in 1659. In 1678 he was called to the Old South Church in Boston, where he remained until his death. His fame also brought him the vice-presidency of Harvard in 1700, and between 1701 and 1707 he headed that institution in the absence of its president, Increase Mather. Refusing to gloss over the implications of Puritan theology, Willard argued against toleration even though he himself was moving toward a more liberal position in the practice of religion. A master of learning and logic, he delivered over the years a series of sermons outlining orthodox theology. These were published after his death in the largest volume ever to come from a colonial press.

The selection reprinted here is from Willard's sermons of April 24 and May 22, 1688, in which he attempted to show the essential difference between the covenant of grace and the covenant of works. The text is from A Compleat Body of Divinity in Two Hundred and Fifty Expository Lectures on the Assembly's Shorter Catechism (*Boston, 1726*).

Question II

*W*HAT RULE *hath God given to direct us, how we may glorify and enjoy Him?*

Answer

The WORD of God (which is contained in the Scriptures of the *Old & New Testament*) is the ONLY Rule to direct us, how we may glorify and enjoy Him. . . .

FOR a right Understanding, and full Explication of this Question and Answer; there are these things will call for our distinct Consideration. (1) That Man *must* have a *Rule* to direct him, or else he can never attain to his chief end. (2) That this Rule can be but *one.* (3) That the *Word of God* is the *only* Rule. (4) That this word, which is the Rule, is contained in the *Scriptures* of the *Old* and *New Testament.* . . .

Prop. III THAT *the* WORD *of* GOD *is this only Rule.* . . .

Q. 2. How *does it appear to be the only Rule?*

A. WE may here (to expedite this matter) call to mind, that there have been *two Covenants,* in which God hath traded with men about their happiness, *viz.* that of *Works,* and that of *Grace.* As to the *former,* or that of works, there needs no applying of this Consideration to it, because man is no longer to expect felicity by it. If fallen man could have attained his end according to the tenour of that, the second had been *super-fluous.* Gal. 3. 21. *Is the law then against the promises of God? God forbid: for if there had been a law given which could have given life, verily Righteousness should have been by the law.* That Covenant stands armed with *Curses,* and all that are under it can expect nothing else: Ver. 10. *For as many are of the works of the law, are under the curse: for it is written, Cursed is every*

10

one that continueth not in all things which are written in the book of the law to do them. And yet if there were need, it might be evidenced that God's *Word* was Man's only Rule there: but because *Adam's* apostate Children can expect Life & Salvation only according to the tenour of the Covenant of *Grace*, it will suffice to make it appear, that the Word of God is the only Rule, to direct us to glorify and enjoy him, in the ways of *this* Covenant. And this will be manifest by these Propositions.

1. THAT Man by his fall mis[sed] of the happiness offered in the first Covenant, & brought himself under a condition of *misery.* Man's happiness consists in the *glorifying* of God, & *enjoying* him: and the fall cut him off from both. From the former, Rom. 3. 23. *For all have sinned, and come short of the glory of God:* From the latter. Isa. 59. 2. *Your iniquities have separated between you and your God.* And hence he fell from Life into a state of Death: for therein did the Curse consist. Gen. 2. 17. *In the day that thou eatest thereof, thou shalt surely die.* So that all the Children of men are not only born *capable* of Misery: But they are born *actually* miserable. Hence this *Death* is said to be *past upon all men,* Rom. 5. 12.

2. THAT fallen man is *no longer capable* of being made *happy* by *that* Covenant. For, though his happiness be still in attaining his end, and his end be still the same that ever it was, yet it is not to be advanced by him *in that way* wherein it was at *first* prescribed: and this, not by reason of any default in the Law or Covenant, (that is holy, & just and good) but by reason of *his own Impotency.* . . . So that this Covenant speaks nothing but *terrour* and *despair* to all those that are held under the Conditions of it.

3. THAT hence, if ever the undone Creature be *restored* to happiness, by attaining his end, there must be *another way* found out for it. If blessedness can

be no longer *by the law,* then either man must *never* be blessed; Or, there must be a *new law* of blessedness provided for him; Or he must be made blessed *without any,* which cannot be; for, if he could not be happy when he was *innocent,* but by closing with his Rule, and reaching his End, much less can he be so now he is *miserable,* unless there be a way to rid him of his misery, and bring him back to felicity. If therefore the law of *works* cannot, something *else* must, or otherwise he must needs perish. And if there be another *way,* there must of necessity be another *Rule.* . . .

4. THAT the *Recovery* of fallen man from this Misery, is an act of *God's sovereign Pleasure.* It derives from hence, and hath its dependence here. If, when man had come short of his end, and lost his happiness, he had left him there without hopes forever, he could not have done him any *injury;* it had been but an Hell of *his own* procuring. Hence the Original of man's Recovery is referred to *God's Will.* Eph. 1. 5. *Having predestinated us to the adoption of children by Jesus Christ to himself, according to the good pleasure of his will.* God had once brought himself under an Obligation to give him life in case of Obedience; but he had not obliged himself to deliver him, if he should cast himself away.

5. THAT hence *the Way,* in which this recovery is to be obtained, *depends upon* that Pleasure of His. He that might have chosen, whether *ever* he would have saved us, hath the liberty of prescribing (as he sees meet) *how* he will bring it about, and upon what *Terms* we may expect it. If *he* do not restore us, none can: and if he do, it is *free Grace.* Who then shall prescribe to him? Or who shall make his terms for him? And for this reason it is, that *Salvation* is said to *belong to God.*

6. THAT as God *purposed* from Eternity to bring back a number of fallen Men, so he provided a *new Covenant-way*

to accomplish it in. God hath a company of Elect or chosen ones among the ruins of the fall, whom he appointed to felicity in the days of Eternity, before the World was, (*Eph.* 1. 6.) And when he appointed them to the *End*, he also allotted the *Means*, by which they should reach it. Eph. 1. 4. *According as he hath chosen us in him before the foundation of the world, that we should be holy, and without blame before him in love.* The new and living way was then fixed, & peremptorily resolved upon; and it was but *one* way that was then determined, unto the which the terms of the new Covenant are in the publication of it restrained. Mark 16. 16. *He that believeth and is baptized shall be saved; but he that believeth not, shall be damned.*

7. THAT *except God had revealed* this Way and Rule, it could *never* have been *known* in the World. Men nor Angels could not have so much as *published*

that good news, *that there is such a thing*, unless he had first declared it: much less could they have given a *draught* of it. . . .

8. THAT *in what way soever* God reveals this will of his, *that* is to be accounted *his Word.* For God's word is nothing else but his *making his mind known* to his Creature. . . .

9. THAT *nothing but what* GOD hath thus *revealed* to his People, doth or can belong to the *Rule.* That there *needs* no more, will be afterwards considered, when we come to observe the Perfection of Scripture: But here we observe, that there *can* be no more. We are therefore severely *forbidden* to add. . . . For any therefore of their own head to make any addition to this Rule, is a bold Intrusion upon the Divine Prerogative; an imposing upon God, which he will never admit of. . . .

John Cotton

1584-1652

Educated at Cambridge, John Cotton became a leading Anglican minister but was finally forced to resign because of his nonconformist views. In 1633 he migrated to New England. Upon his arrival in Boston, he was immediately chosen teacher of the local church, and for the next twenty years he played a leading role in the religious and political affairs of the colony. In 1636 Cotton prepared a body of laws, which was rejected by the General Court in favor of a somewhat more practical and slightly less Mosaic code. He also soon was engaged in a running controversy with Roger Williams, in which he argued against Williams' stand that only persons who had explicitly rejected the Church of England could be admitted to church membership. The two men also quarreled over the proper role of the civil authority in religious matters, with Cotton defending the orthodox position of the Puritan theocracy while Williams argued in favor of a complete separation of religious and secular affairs. Cotton was also a prolific writer, presenting in a forceful manner the major tenets of the Puritan creed.

The selection that follows is from The Covenant of Grace Discovering the Great Work of a Sinners Reconsiliation to God *(London, 1655), in which Cotton attempted to reconcile predestination with obedience to the laws of God.*

*I*f the Lord do give himself first in the Covenant of his grace, this may then be a doubt and a question in a Christian soul, If God give himself before any blessing, before any promise in order of nature (though he giveth himself always in a promise) if we cannot claim any blessing from God at the first in any conditional promise, therefore not by any condition in our selves, but as we received all things from God, so we claim all things from him in Jesus Christ, and so do first seek for him, and for all things in him: If thus, to what use then serveth the Law of God, which requireth such and such conditions in us, do we not abrogate the Law, & and make it of none effect, and root it out from having any power over Christians? And truly some, under pretence of the Covenant of grace, have thought it altogether bootless to bind Christians unto the Law of God, and to look at it as any part of the direction of their Course. Now because this is an imputation usually reflected upon the Covenant of Grace, let us Consider therefore and enquire to what use serveth the Law of God, if God gave himself first unto his people in the Covenant of his grace.

Answ. Though the Lord giveth himself freely to the soul, and his Son, and all the blessings of the Covenant of grace, without respect unto any work of the Law; yet the Law is of special and notable use unto all the sons of men, both unto them that are not yet brought home unto God by converting grace, and also to those that are regenerate in Jesus Christ. The Apostle *Paul* did observe that the question would arise upon the doctrine of the Covenant of grace, *Gal.* 3. 16, 17, 18. *For if the blessing of Abraham came upon the people of God by Jesus Christ, to what end then serveth the Law, which came* 430 *years after?* It cannot disannul grace, to make the promise of God of none effect? *to what end then serveth it?* Some say it is of no use, others say that it is of such use that they had rather renounce the Covenant of grace than it: but the Answer is, it is of especial use both unto spiritual and carnal men.

First, unto carnal men, and they are of two sorts, some belong unto the election of grace, though they be not yet called; others are not written in the Lambs book of life, but will in the end finally perish, and the Law is yet of use unto both sorts of them.

For the Elect, it is of use unto them; to aggravate their sin, and to multiply it unto them as it were, that is to say, to aggravate the apprehension of the heinousness of sin upon their Consciences, and to set home the burden of sin unto their souls, thereby to drive them to feel their great need of the Lord Jesus Christ, whom otherwise they should for ever have despised. Thus the Apostle answereth in the place afore-named, *The Law was added, because of transgressions;* that they might clearly appear, and be aggravated thereby, that a man might plainly discern how he hath made himself liable to the wrath of God, by so manifold breaches of so many Commandments in one kind or other: the Law giveth clear knowledge of sin, and so much the more doth it set on the weight of it upon the Conscience, working fear in the heart, *Rom.* 8. 15. And hence it is, that the Apostle telleth us, *Gal.* 3. 24. *The Law was our School-Master to Christ;* As a School-Master

driveth his Scholar through fear unto this or that duty, either to do it himself, or (if he cannot) to get others to do it for him; so the Law of God driveth the soul through fear unto Jesus Christ; not that it doth reveal Christ a Saviour of free-grace, but the soul being once more brought down under sense of sin by the terrors of the Law, will readily & willingly hearken unto the news of *Christ a Saviour;* for being once made sensible of his own inability to redeem himself, and unworthiness to be redeemed from the wrath of God; now is the soul fitted to hear the voice of the Gospel, now is the news of Christ beautiful and glad tidings: And of this use is the Law unto the Elect of God, before they come under the Covenant of the grace of God.

2. But of what use is the Law unto other men?

First, the Disobedience of it is of use. Secondly, the Obedience of it.

1. The *Disobedience;* for if men had not known sin, it had been some pretence, though they had committed sin, but when men have the knowledge of the Law, and yet commit sin willingly, now they have no cloak for their sin. . . . Thus there is use of the Law unto disobedient persons, their disobedience will leave them without excuse, when they sin against their consciences, & against the means which the Lord hath administered unto them: for though the Lord never gave them such grace as did accompany salvation, yet such Illumination he did give them, that they needed not to have broken his Law so many ways with such wicked hands as they have done: therefore when they have been enlarged to perform many duties, & might avoid much sin, & yet will sin against their consciences, and tread under foot those means of grace that were committed unto them, It is then most righteous with God, that they should be condemned.

2. Of what use is the Obedience of the Law unto such, whom Gods soul takes no pleasure in? Truly it is of sad and dreadful use unto them, for it serveth to harden them in their sins, (though that be but an accidental use thereof) their sins are thereby made out of measure sinful, *Rom.* 7. 13. They harden their hearts marvelously.

1. By their Obedience to the Law.
2. By the Comfort they find in that Obedience.

For the first of these; the Apostle *Paul, Acts* 23. 1. had kept so good a Conscience, that he knew not any sin against the Law that he had lived in, but though he was unrebukeable, he did count it all loss afterward, *Phil.* 3. 7, 8. *Those things that before he thought had been his gain, now he counteth them but dung that he may win Christ:* when a man attaineth unto outward conformity to the Law, he is then indeed ready to justify himself, and to think that it is indeed good for poor sinful men to look for salvation by Jesus Christ: but for himself he hopeth in his self-devotion, and that he is able to save himself; these are such as justify themselves before men, to whom our Saviour speaketh, *Luke* 16. 15. And of whom he saith, that *Publicans and harlots shall go into the kingdom of heaven before them. Mat.* 21. 31, 32. For many times you shall have the most debauched and prophane more humbled and readier to hearken to the voice of Christ, and sooner convinced of the necessity of the Covenant of grace, than those that are morally righteous by the law, *Rom.* 9. 30, 31, 32 & Chap. 10. 21. Thus the Law becometh a snare unto them, and that which is of singular and wholesome use unto the children of God, is made death unto them; So, secondly, the delight and comfort which they take in their obedience, is a greater snare than the other. . . . So long as a man findeth life and comfort in his own performances, what need can he see to be

grieved for the want of *Jesus Christ?* or at best, if he do grieve and find his heart comforted in grieving, and delighting in the Course of humiliation, he then thinketh he hath no need of being further solicitous about his spiritual estate. Thus we see that the Law of God is of marvelous use in the days of the Gospel; of great use unto those that belong unto God, to break their hearts for sin, and to drive them to *Jesus Christ;* and for others, the disobedience of the Law leaves them without excuse, that so disobey it. Again, the obedience of it and comfort in that obedience doth harden the hearts of others from Christ.

2. But what say you then unto men that are under a Covenant of grace, and brought unto fellowship with Christ therein? of what use is the Law of God unto such? is it utterly antiquated? or is there any more to be done about it?

Answ. The Apostle answereth this question, when he saith, *I am not without the Law to God, but under the Law to Christ,* 1 *Cor.* 9. 21. So that (mind you) the Law is of use unto the Apostle *Paul,* but how? As the Law cometh under Christ, so *Paul* cometh under the Law; this is the sum of the Answer, but that would be further explained. What meaneth he, when he sayeth, *I am under the Law to Christ?* In some sense a Christian is freed from the Law, in some sense he is under the Law; so far as the Law is any way besides or out of Christ, so far the Apostle is without the Law; so far as the Law is under Christ, so far he is under the Law; keep close to these two principles, and you shall safely avoid rocks on every hand, thus by the use of the Law shall you not go aside to a Covenant of works, nor by attendance unto grace, shall you neglect the Law. How far is the Law under Christ? When it hath brought the soul nearer unto Christ, and in a remote manner prepared him: the law is in Christ, and you subject to it in him. . . . Our Saviour Christ expoundeth the Law more spiritually, showing that *Anger* against a man's brother is a breach of the sixth Commandment, and *whosoever shall look on a woman to lust after her, hath committed Adultery with her already in his heart*, and broken the seventh Commandment. . . . Thus we see the Apostles of Jesus Christ put it upon Christians to keep the Law of God; and Christ himself beareth witness to the Law, *for God will never justify sin to be no sin, though he will justify the person of a sinner*.

Now as the Lord Jesus giveth the Law, and as it were reneweth it, so he doth also give his Spirit unto his servants, enabling them to keep it. . . . Now this Law would he not write in the hearts of his people, nor give unto them his holy Spirit, enabling them to keep it, were it not his will in *Jesus Christ*, that the Law should be the Rule of holiness and righteousness unto his people; hence it is that the children of God, though they be not under the Covenant of the Law, yet take themselves to be bound to the obedience of it, for if *Christ* have given the Law as well as *Moses*, and if he have ratified it by giving them his Spirit to teach and strengthen them to keep it, though not perfectly, yet sincerely, then they take themselves bound to obey the Law, though they be under the Covenant of grace; for *do we make void the Law through faith? God forbid; yea, we establish the Law;* for what need have Christians of free justification by Christ, if they were not bound unto the obedience of the Law by the Commandment of the Law? therefore the free justification of men under a free Covenant of grace doth establish the obedience of the Law; otherwise what need they run to Christ for the continuance of our Justification, but that we find our selves ungodly Creatures against the righteous and holy Law of God? Therefore if God have given men the Law, & his Holy Spirit to strengthen them in the obedience of it,

and his grace to save them from the curse of it, then Christians are to know, that they are bound to keep the Law, they lie under the authority of it, and dare not pluck their necks from under that yoke. . . . It is manifest, because a Christian man neither looketh for justification and salvation from his obedience to the Law, nor feareth condemnation, though he fail in his obedience; and this is a fruit of his exemption from under the Covenant of the Law; for if a man should look for life by his obedience to the Law, and fear condemnation by the breach of it, this would bring a man under the Covenant of the Law; for the sanction of the Covenant of the Law is *Life* to them that obey, and to them that disobey *death and the curse;* but a Christian looketh not for life by his obedience, and that is plain, *Psal.* 143. 2. *Rom.* 3. 20. Therefore no hope of salvation from our obedience to the Law.

But methinks (you will say) *a Christian may fear his condemnation, because of his disobedience to the Law?*

Truly this is a great snare, and this doctrine will be scandalous to many a poor soul, but without cause; indeed if God give a man to be under the Covenant of grace, and not to see it, then he may fear; but if a man know himself to be under the Covenant of grace, then he doth not fear condemnation from his disobedience. . . .

But will not this make a Christian wanton against God, and cause him to abuse his liberty to hardness of heart?

No, no, this is the kindly melting of a godly heart, to consider a Redeemers love, drawing him from the power of the grave, and that he should by his sins pierce the Lord Jesus Christ, this melteth him more than all his other sins, especially considering the abounding grace of God, *which where sin hath abounded, aboundeth much more.* Thus when a man doth not look for life by his own righteousness, but knoweth the Redemption of souls to be more precious than so, this showeth a man not be to under a Covenant of works, and then his very *iniquity* shall not make him afraid, there is such a state in Christianity, and let all men know it.

But will not all men think the worse of Christian profession?

No, *David* will have all men know it, that they may see the difference between all worldly confidences, and the confidence of Christians; all the glory of worldly men will leave them to be like the Beasts that perish, and cannot redeem their souls, that the Lord only might be exalted in his Redeemed.

2. As a Christian looketh not for salvation by his obedience to the Law, nor feareth condemnation by his disobedience: So neither doth he seek for any blessing from his obedience, nor fear any curse from his disobedience. . . .

3. This also is a third effect of the freedom from the Covenant of works, that a Christian doth not look for conjugal comfort from his obedience, nor fear conjugal divorce, from his disobedience. . . . he that is freed from the Covenant of works, is freed also from expecting salvation, or fearing damnation for what he doth: He knoweth the Lord will hide his face from him, if he do evil, but he knoweth the Lord will not cast him off for ever, yet he dares not commit sin, but being under grace, he is the more affected if he shall at any time displease God, and procure chastisement to himself, and by this means the Lord doth mortify his distempers. . . .

4. And finally, the soul doth not claim his right unto any Conditional Promise by his performance of the condition, nor doth he deny himself the blessing that the Promise may reach forth unto him, though he be wanting in obedience to this or that Commandment. . . . But this is not the manner of Gods people, and yet if they look for any mercy, it is in the way of God, but not for their own goodness, their hope is in the faithfulness and free grace of God; they may make mention to the praise of God, how he hath guided them, and carried them an end in his own ways, yet they challenge nothing for any thing that they have done, but put the Lord in mind of his free Promise; that as of his free grace he hath freely promised, so from the same grace he may make good what he hath promised.

Use 1. If any therefore shall accuse the Doctrine of the Covenant of free grace, of *Antinomianism*, and say it teacheth men freedom from the Law of *Moses*, and if they commit any sin, they plead they are not bound unto the Law; we see how false such an aspersion would be, for all the people of God know that *the Lord is an avenger of every such wickedness;* There is none under a Covenant of Grace that dare allow himself in any sin, for if a man should negligently commit any sin, the Lord will school him thoroughly, and make him sadly to apprehend how unworthily he hath made bold to abuse & embezzle the treasures of the grace of God. . . .

So that the children of the Covenant of grace will only tell you, that they are free from the Covenant of the Law, but not from the Commandment of it: for as it is given by *Jesus Christ*, and ratified in the Gospel, and as Christ hath given us his Spirit, enabling us to keep it, we are under it, so far as to take our selves bound by the Authority of it: and if we do transgress against it, we know it is sin in the sight of God, & therefore it is, that the soul in such a case is sensible of the wrath and displeasure of God, whether it be his own sin, or the sin of his brethren; therefore he runneth unto God for mercy, which he would not do, if he did not know that his desert according to the Law did utterly cut him off from mercy; else would he never pray for pardon of sin, nor rejoice when the Lord helpeth him to do that which is right and just in his sight, nor bless the Lord for strengthening him unto obedience, unless he thought it to be his duty. . . .

Jonathan Edwards

1703-1758

One of America's most important minds, Jonathan Edwards defies easy classification. He is often linked with the Puritans, and he was a staunch defender of such Calvinistic doctrines as God's sovereignty and man's utter dependence on Him. But Edwards was not simply a Calvinist, for he developed a philosophical idealism and a supernaturalistic empiricism of marked originality and depth.

Edwards was born in East Windsor, Connecticut, and was educated at Yale College. After his graduation he settled in Northampton, Massachusetts, as assistant to his grandfather, Reverend Solomon Stoddard, minister of the local Congregational Church. Edwards became the regular minister in 1729. A powerful preacher, he was instrumental in helping to set in motion the Great Awakening of the 1730's and 1740's, a religious revival of a type to be repeated many times in subsequent years. However, in 1750 a rupture occurred between Edwards and his congregation, and he was dismissed. He then settled as missionary to the Indians in Stockbridge, Massachusetts, where he wrote many of his important works. In 1757 he was called to the presidency of the College of New Jersey (now Princeton), but he died shortly after his move to Princeton.

The philosophical idealism developed by Edwards held that all reality is mental; that is, that the world is an ideal order of mental reality. This is a common assertion in idealistic systems, although Edwards' argument is closest to—though developed independently of—the English divine and philosopher Bishop George Berkeley. Edwards' supernatural empiricism taught that the Spirit of God acts on the mind of a believer as an indwelling principle, and what today might be considered emotionalism was for Edwards really an experiential response to the divine. These guiding ideas, together with his Calvinist theology, were developed by Edwards in his many books and sermons, of which the following selections are but a small sample.

Following Edwards' life, a strong stream of philosophical idealism persisted through American history down to the beginning of the twentieth century. German thought was especially influential in America; less than a century after Edwards' death, such

Americans as George Bancroft were studying in Germany and absorbing some of the ideals of European scholarship. Transcendentalism also had deep roots in idealism and in Plato's thought; and the famous St. Louis school of William T. Harris in the late nineteenth century continued the study of German thought. The last idealist of the tradition was Josiah Royce, who, with such students as William Ernest Hocking and Mary Whiton Calkins, gave idealism another major restatement. But for most Americans it was a final restatement: under the onslaughts of naturalism and realism the citadel of idealism toppled at the beginning of the twentieth century.

The selection that follows is a sermon preached in 1741 called "Sinners in the Hand of an Angry God." It is contained in S. E. Dwight, ed., The Works of President Edwards, *10 vols. (New York, 1830), vol. I.*

*I*n this verse [from Deuteronomy] is threatened the vengeance of God on the wicked unbelieving Israelites, who were God's visible people, and who lived under the means of grace; but who, notwithstanding all God's wonderful works towards them, remained (as ver. 28.) void of Counsel, having no understanding in them. Under all the cultivations of heaven, they brought forth bitter and poisonous fruit; as in the two verses next preceding the text.—The expression I have chosen for my text, *Their foot shall slide in due time* [Deut. 32: 35], seems to imply the following things, relating to the punishment and destruction to which these wicked Israelites were exposed.

1. That they were always exposed to *destruction;* as one that stands or walks in slippery places is always exposed to fall. This is implied in the manner of their destruction coming upon them, being represented by their foot sliding. The same is expressed, Psalm lxxiii. 18. "Surely thou didst set them in slippery places; thou castedst them down into destruction."

2. It implies, that they were always exposed to sudden unexpected destruction. As he that walks in slippery places is every moment liable to fall, he cannot foresee one moment whether he shall stand or fall the next; and when he does fall, he falls at once without warning: Which is also expressed in Psalm lxxiii. 18, 19. "Surely thou didst set them in slippery places; thou castedst them down into destruction: How are they brought into desolation as in a moment!"

3. Another thing implied is, that they are liable to fall *of themselves*, without being thrown down by the hand of another; as he that stands or walks on slippery ground needs nothing but his own weight to throw him down.

4. That the reason why they are not fallen already, and do not fall now, is only that God's appointed time is not come. For it is said, that when that due time, or appointed time comes *their foot shall slide.* Then they shall be left to

fall, as they are inclined by their own weight. God will not hold them up in these slippery places any longer, but will let them go; and then, at that very instant, they shall fall into destruction; as he that stands on such slippery declining ground, on the edge of a pit, he cannot stand alone, when he is let go he immediately falls and is lost.

The observation from the words that I would now insist upon is this. "There is nothing that keeps wicked men at any one moment out of hell, but the mere pleasure of God"—By the *mere* pleasure of God, I mean his *sovereign* pleasure, his arbitrary will, restrained by no obligation, hindered by no manner of difficulty, any more than if nothing else but God's mere will had in the least degree, or in any respect whatsoever, any hand in the preservation of wicked men one moment.—The truth of this observation may appear by the following considerations.

1. There is no want of *power* in God to cast wicked men into hell at any moment. Men's hands cannot be strong when God rises up. The strongest have no power to resist him, nor can any deliver out of his hands.—He is not only able to cast wicked men into hell, but he can most easily do it. Sometimes an earthly prince meets with a great deal of difficulty to subdue a rebel, who has found means to fortify himself, and has made himself strong by the numbers of his followers. But it is not so with God. There is no fortress that is any defence from the power of God. Though hand join in hand, and vast multitudes of God's enemies combine and associate themselves, they are easily broken in pieces. They are as great heaps of light chaff before the whirlwind; or large quantities of dry stubble before devouring flames. We find it easy to tread on and crush a worm that we see crawling on the earth; so it is easy for us to cut or singe a slender thread that any thing hangs by: thus easy is it for God, when

he pleases, to cast his enemies down to hell. What are we, that we should think to stand before him, at whose rebuke the earth trembles, and before whom the rocks are thrown down?

2. They *deserve* to be cast into hell; so that divine justice never stands in the way, it makes no objection against God's using his power at any moment to destroy them. Yea, on the contrary, justice calls aloud for an infinite punishment of their sins. Divine justice says of the tree that brings forth such grapes of Sodom, "Cut it down, why cumbereth it the ground?" Luke xiii. 7. The sword of divine justice is every moment brandished over their heads, and it is nothing but the hand of arbitrary mercy, and God's mere will, that holds it back.

3. They are already under a sentence of *condemnation* to hell. They do not only justly deserve to be cast down thither, but the sentence of the law of God, that eternal and immutable rule of righteousness that God has fixed between him and mankind, is gone out against them, and stands against them; so that they are bound over already to hell. John iii. 18. "He that believeth not is condemned already." So that every unconverted man properly belongs to hell; that is his place; from thence he is, John viii. 23. "Ye are from beneath:" And thither he is bound; it is the place that justice, and God's word, and the sentence of his unchangeable law assign to him.

4. They are now the objects of that very same *anger* and wrath of God, that is expressed in the torments of hell. And the reason why they do not go down to hell at each moment, is not because God, in whose power they are, is not then very angry with them; as he is with many miserable creatures now tormented in hell, who there feel and bear the fierceness of his wrath. Yea, God is a great deal more angry with great numbers that are now on earth; yea, doubtless, with many that are now in this

congregation, who it may be are at ease, than he is with many of those who are now in the flames of hell.

So that it is not because God is unmindful of their wickedness, and does not resent it, that he does not let loose his hand and cut them off. God is not altogether such an one as themselves, though they may imagine him to be so. The wrath of God burns against them, their damnation does not slumber; the pit is prepared, the fire is made ready, the furnace is now hot, ready to receive them; the flames do now rage and glow. The glittering sword is whet, and held over them, and the pit hath opened its mouth under them.

5. The *devil* stands ready to fall upon them, and seize them as his own, at what moment God shall permit him. They belong to him; he has their souls in his possession, and under his dominion. The scripture represents them as his goods, Luke xi. 12. The devils watch them; they are ever by them at their right hand; they stand waiting for them, like greedy hungry lions that see their prey, and expect to have it, but are for the present kept back. If God should withdraw his hand, by which they are restrained, they would in one moment fly upon their poor souls. The old serpent is gaping for them; hell opens its mouth wide to receive them; and if God should permit it, they would be hastily swallowed up and lost.

6. There are in the souls of wicked men those hellish *principles* reigning, that would presently kindle and flame out into hell fire, if it were not for God's restraints. There is laid in the very nature of carnal men, a foundation for the torments of hell. There are those corrupt principles, in reigning power in them, and in full possession of them, that are seeds of hell fire. The principles are active and powerful, exceeding violent in their nature, and if it were not for the restraining hand of God upon them, they would soon break out, they would

flame out after the same manner as the same corruptions, the same enmity does in the hearts of damned souls, and would beget the same torments as they do in them. The souls of the wicked are in scripture compared to the troubled sea. Isa. lvii. 20. For the present, God restrains their wickedness by his mighty power, as he does the raging waves of the troubled sea, saying, "Hitherto shalt thou come, but no further;" but if God should withdraw that restraining power, it would soon carry all before it. Sin is the ruin and misery of the soul; it is destructive in its nature; and if God should leave it without restraint, there would need nothing else to make the soul perfectly miserable. The corruption of the heart of man is immoderate and boundless in its fury; and while wicked men live here, it is like fire pent up by God's restraints, whereas if it were let loose, it would set on fire the course of nature; and as the heart is now a sink of sin, so if sin was not restrained, it would immediately turn the soul into a fiery oven, or a furnace of fire and brimstone.

7. It is no security to wicked men for one moment, that there are no visible means of death at hand. It is no security to a natural man, that he is now in health, and that he does not see which way he should now immediately go out of the world by any accident, and that there is no visible danger in any respect in his circumstances. The manifold and continual experience of the world in all ages, shows this is no evidence, that a man is not on the very brink of eternity, and that the next step will not be into another world. The unseen, unthought-of ways and means of persons going suddenly out of the world are innumerable and inconceivable. Unconverted men walk over the pit of hell on a rotten covering, and there are innumerable places in this covering so weak that they will not bear their weight, and these places are not seen. The arrows of death

fly unseen at noon-day; the sharpest sight cannot discern them. God has so many different unsearchable ways of taking wicked men out of the world and sending them to hell, that there is nothing to make it appear, that God had need to be at the expence of a miracle, or go out of the ordinary course of his providence, to destroy any wicked man, at any moment. All the means that there are of sinners going out of the world, are so in God's hands, and so universally and absolutely subject to his power and determination, that it does not depend at all the less on the mere will of God, whether sinners shall at any moment go to hell, than if means were never made use of, or at all concerned in the case.

8. Natural men's prudence and care to preserve their own lives, or the care of others to preserve them, do not secure them a moment. To this, divine providence and universal experience do also bear testimony. There is this clear evidence that men's own wisdom is no security to them from death; that if it were otherwise we should see some difference between the wise and politic men of the world, and others, with regard to their liableness to early and unexpected death: but how is it in fact? Eccles. ii. 16. "How dieth the wise man? even as the fool."

9. All wicked men's pains and *contrivance* which they use to escape hell, while they continue to reject Christ, and so remain wicked men, do not secure them from hell one moment. Almost every natural man that hears of hell, flatters himself that he shall escape it; he depends upon himself for his own security; he flatters himself in what he has done, in what he is now doing, or what he intends to do. Every one lays out matters in his own mind how he shall avoid damnation, and flatters himself that he contrives well for himself, and that his schemes will not fail. They hear indeed that there are but few saved,

and that the greater part of men that have died heretofore are gone to hell; but each one imagines that he lays out matters better for his own escape than others have done. He does not intend to come to that place of torment; he says within himself, that he intends to take effectual care, and to order matters so for himself as not to fail.

But the foolish children of men miserably delude themselves in their own schemes, and in confidence in their own strength and wisdom; they trust to nothing but a shadow. The greater part of those who heretofore have lived under the same means of grace, and are now dead, are undoubtedly gone to hell; and it was not because they were not as wise as those who are now alive: it was not because they did not lay out matters as well for themselves to secure their own escape. If we could speak with them, and inquire of them, one by one, whether they expected, when alive, and when they used to hear about hell, ever to be the subjects of that misery: we doubtless, should hear one and another reply. "No, I never intended to come here: I had laid out matters otherwise in my mind; I thought I should contrive well for myself: I thought my scheme good. I intended to take effectual care; but it came upon me unexpected; I did not look for it at that time, and in that manner; it came as a thief: Death outwitted me: God's wrath was too quick for me. Oh, my cursed foolishness! I was flattering myself, and pleasing myself with vain dreams of what I would do hereafter; and when I was saying, Peace and safety, then suddenly destruction came upon me."

10. God has laid himself under *no obligation*, by any promise to keep any natural man out of hell one moment. God certainly has made no promises either of eternal life, or of any deliverance or preservation from eternal death, but what are contained in the covenant of grace, the promises that are given in

Christ, in whom all the promises are yea and amen. But surely they have no interest in the promises of the covenant of grace who are not the children of the covenant, who do not believe in any of the promises, and have no interest in the Mediator of the covenant.

So that, whatever some have imagined and pretended about promises made to natural men's earnest seeking and knocking, it is plain and manifest, that whatever pains a natural man takes in religion, whatever prayers he makes, till he believes in Christ, God is under no manner of obligation to keep him a moment from eternal destruction.

So that, thus it is that natural men are held in the hand of God, over the pit of hell; they have deserved the fiery pit, and are already sentenced to it; and God is dreadfully provoked, his anger is as great towards them as to those that are actually suffering the executions of the fierceness of his wrath in hell, and they have done nothing in the least to appease or abate that anger, neither is God in the least bound by any promise to hold them up one moment; the devil is waiting for them, hell is gaping for them, the flames gather and flash about them, and would fain lay hold on them, and swallow them up; the fire bent up in their own hearts is struggling to break out: and they have no interest in any Mediator, there are no means within reach that can be any security to them. In short, they have no refuge, nothing to take hold of; all that preserves them every moment is the mere arbitrary will, and uncovenanted, unobliged forbearance of an incensed God.

Application

*T*he use of this awful subject may be for awakening unconverted persons in this congregation. This that you have heard is the case of every one of you that are out of Christ.—That world of misery, that lake of burning brimstone, is extended abroad under you. There is the dreadful pit of the glowing flames of the wrath of God; there is hell's wide gaping mouth open; and you have nothing to stand upon, nor any thing to take hold of; there is nothing between you and hell but the air; it is only the power and mere pleasure of God that holds you up.

You probably are not sensible of this; you find you are kept out of hell, but do not see the hand of God in it; but look at other things, as the good state of your bodily constitution, your care of your own life, and the means you use for your own preservation. But indeed these things are nothing; if God should withdraw his hand, they would avail no more to keep you from falling, than the thin air to hold up a person that is suspended in it.

Your wickedness makes you as it were heavy as lead, and to tend downwards with great weight and pressure towards hell; and if God should let you go, you would immediately sink and swiftly descend and plunge into the bottomless gulf, and your healthy constitution, and your own care and prudence, and best contrivance, and all your righteousness, would have no more influence to uphold you and keep you out of hell, than a spider's web would have to stop a fallen rock. Were it not for the sovereign pleasure of God, the earth would not bear you one moment; for you are a burden to it; the creation groans with you; the creature is made subject to the bondage of your corruption, not willingly; the sun does not willingly shine upon you to give you light to serve sin and Satan; the earth does not willingly yield her increase to satisfy your lusts; nor is it willingly a stage for your wickedness to be acted upon; the air does not willingly serve you for breath to maintain the flame of life in your vitals, while you spend your life in the service of God's enemies. God's creatures are good, and were made for men to serve God with, and do not willingly subserve to any other purpose, and groan when they are abused to purposes so directly contrary to their nature and end. And the world would spew you out, were it not for the sovereign hand of him who hath subjected it in hope. There are black clouds of God's wrath now hanging directly over your heads, full of the dreadful storm, and big with thunder; and were it not for the restraining hand of God, it would immediately burst forth upon you. The sovereign pleasure of God, for the present, stays his rough wind; otherwise it would come with fury, and your destruction would come like a whirlwind, and you would be like the chaff of the summer threshing floor.

The wrath of God is like great waters that are dammed for the present; they increase more and more, and rise higher and higher, till an outlet is given; and the longer the stream is stopped, the more rapid and mighty is its course, when once it is let loose. It is true, that judgment against your evil works has not been executed hitherto; the floods of God's vengeance have been withheld; but your guilt in the mean time is constantly increasing, and you are every day treasuring up more wrath; the waters are constantly rising, and waxing more and more mighty; and there is nothing but the mere pleasure of God, that holds the waters back, that are unwilling to be stopped, and press hard to go forward. If God should only withdraw his hand from the floodgate, it would immediately fly open, and the fiery floods of the fierceness and wrath of God, would rush forth with inconceivable fury, and would come upon you with omnipotent power; and if your strength were ten thousand times greater than it is, yea, ten thousand times greater than the strength of the stoutest, sturdiest devil in hell, it would be nothing to withstand or endure it.

The bow of God's wrath is bent, and the arrow made ready on the string, and justice bends the arrow at your heart, and strains the bow, and it is nothing but the mere pleasure of God, and that of an angry God, without any promise or obligation at all, that keeps the arrow one moment from being made drunk with your blood. Thus all you that never passed under a great change of heart, by the mighty power of the Spirit of God upon your souls; all you that were never born again, and made new creatures, and raised from being dead in sin, to a state of new, and before altogether unexperienced light and life, are in the hands of an angry God. However you may have reformed your life in many things, and may have had religious affections, and may keep up a form of religion in your families and closets, and in the house of God, it is nothing but his mere pleasure that keeps you from being this moment swallowed up in everlasting destruction. However unconvinced you may now be of the truth of what you hear, by and by you will be fully convinced of it. Those that are gone from being in the like circumstances with you, see that it was so with them; for destruction came suddenly upon most of them; when they expected nothing of it, and while they were saying, Peace and safety: now they see, that those things on which they depended for peace and safety, were nothing but thin air and empty shadows.

The God that holds you over the pit of hell, much as one holds a spider, or some loathsome insect over the fire, abhors you, and is dreadfully provoked: his wrath towards you burns like fire; he looks upon you as worthy of nothing else, but to be cast into the fire; he is of purer eyes than to bear to have you in his sight; you are ten thousand times more abominable in his eyes, than the most hateful venomous serpent is in ours. You have offended him infinitely more than ever a stubborn rebel did his prince; and yet it is nothing but his hand that holds you from falling into the fire every moment. It is to be ascribed to nothing else, that you did not go to hell the last night; that you was suffered to awake again in this world, after you closed your eyes to sleep. And there is no other reason to be given, why you have not dropped into hell since you arose in the morning, but that God's hand has held you up. There is no other reason to be given why you have not gone to hell, since you have sat here in the house of God, provoking his pure eyes by your sinful wicked manner of attending his solemn worship. Yea, there is nothing else that is to be given as a reason why you do not this very moment drop down into hell.

O sinner! Consider the fearful danger you are in: it is a great furnace of wrath, a wide and bottomless pit, full of the fire of wrath, that you are held over in the hand of that God, whose wrath is provoked and incensed as much against you, as against many of the damned in hell. You hang by a slender thread, with the flames of divine wrath flashing about it, and ready every moment to singe it, and burn it asunder; and you have no interest in any Mediator, and nothing to lay hold of to save yourself, nothing to keep off the flames of wrath, nothing of your own, nothing that you ever have done, nothing that you can do, to induce God to spare you one moment. —And consider here more particularly,

1. *Whose* wrath it is: it is the wrath of the infinite God. If it were only the wrath of man, though it were of the most potent prince, it would be comparatively little to be regarded. The wrath of kings is very much dreaded, especially of absolute monarchs, who have the possessions and lives of their subjects wholly in their power, to be disposed of at their mere will. Prov. xx. 2. "The fear of a king is as the roaring of a lion: Whoso provoketh him to anger, sinneth against his own soul." The subject that very much enrages an arbitrary prince, is liable to suffer the most extreme torments that human art can invent, or human power can inflict. But the greatest earthly potentates in their greatest majesty and strength, and when clothed in their greatest terrors, are but feeble, despicable worms of the dust, in comparison of the great and almighty Creator and King of heaven and earth. It is but little that they can do, when most enraged, and when they have exerted the utmost of their fury. All the kings of the earth, before God, are as grasshoppers; they are nothing, and less than nothing: both their love and their hatred is to be despised. The wrath of the great King of kings, is as much more terrible than theirs, as his majesty is greater. Luke xii. 4, 5. "And I say unto you, my friends, Be not afraid of them that kill the body, and after that, have no more that they can do. But I will forewarn you whom you shall fear: fear him, which after he hath killed, hath power to cast into hell; yea, I say unto you, Fear him."

2. It is the *fierceness* of his wrath that you are exposed to. We often read of the fury of God; as in Isaiah lix. 18. "According to their deeds, accordingly he will repay fury to his adversaries." So Isaiah lxvi. 15. "For behold, the Lord will come with fire, and with his chariots like a whirlwind, to render his anger with fury, and his rebuke with flames of fire." And in many other places. So, Rev. xix. 15. we read of "the wine press of the fierceness and wrath of Almighty God." The words are exceeding terrible. If it had only been said, "the wrath of God," the words would have implied that which is infinitely dreadful: but it is "the fierceness and wrath of God." The fury of God! the fierceness of Jehovah! Oh, how dreadful must that be! Who can utter what such expressions carry in them! But it is also "the fierceness and

wrath of *Almighty* God." As though there would be a very great manifestation of his almighty power in what the fierceness of his wrath should inflict, as though omnipotence should be as it were enraged, and exerted, as men are wont to exert their strength in the fierceness of their wrath. Oh! then, what will be the consequence! What will become of the poor worms that shall suffer it! Whose hands can be strong? And whose heart can endure? To what a dreadful, inexpressible, inconceivable depth of misery must the poor creature be sunk who shall be the subject of this! . . .

3. The *misery* you are exposed to is that which God will inflict to that end, that he might show what that wrath of Jehovah is. God hath had it on his heart to show to angels and men, both how excellent his love is, and also how terrible his wrath is. Sometimes earthly kings have in mind to show how terrible their wrath is, by the extreme punishments they would execute on those that would provoke them. Nebuchadnezzar, that mighty and haughty monarch of the Chaldean empire, was willing to show his wrath when enraged with Shadrach, Meshech, and Abednego; and accordingly gave orders that the burning fiery furnace should be heated seven times hotter than it was before; doubtless, it was raised to the utmost degree of fierceness that human art could raise it. But the great God is also willing to show his wrath, and magnify his awful majesty and mighty power in the extreme sufferings of his enemies. Rom. ix. 22. "What if God, willing to show his wrath, and to make his power known, endure with much long-suffering the vessels of wrath fitted to destruction?" And seeing this is his design, and what he has determined, even to show how terrible the unrestrained wrath, the fury and fierceness of Jehovah is, he will do it to effect. There will be something accomplished and brought to pass that

will be dreadful with a witness. When the great and angry God hath risen up and executed his awful vengeance on the poor sinner, and the wretch is actually suffering the infinite weight and power of his indignation, then will God call upon the whole universe to behold that awful majesty and mighty power that is to be seen in it. Isa. xxxiii. 12-14. "And the people shall be as the burnings of lime, as thorns cut up shall they be burnt in the fire. Hear ye that are far off, what I have done; and ye that are near, acknowledge my might. The sinners in Zion are afraid; fearfulness hath surprised the hypocrites," &c.

Thus it will be with you that are in an unconverted state, if you continue in it; the infinite might, and majesty, and terribleness of the omnipotent God shall be magnified upon you, in the ineffable strength of your torments. You shall be tormented in the presence of the holy angels, and in the presence of the Lamb; and when you shall be in this state of suffering, the glorious inhabitants of heaven shall go forth and look on the awful spectacle, that they may see what the wrath and fierceness of the Almighty is; and when they have seen it, they will fall down and adore that great power and majesty. Isa. lxvi. 23, 24. "And it shall come to pass, that from one new moon to another, and from one sabbath to another, shall all flesh come to worship before me, saith the Lord. And they shall go forth and look upon the carcasses of the men that have transgressed against me; for their worm shall not die, neither shall their fire be quenched, and they shall be an abhorring unto all flesh."

4. It is *everlasting* wrath. It would be dreadful to suffer this fierceness and wrath of Almighty God one moment; but you must suffer it to all eternity. There will be no end to this exquisite horrible misery. When you look forward, you shall see a long for ever, a boundless duration before you, which will swallow

up your thoughts, and amaze your soul; and you will absolutely despair of ever having any deliverance, any end, any mitigation, any rest at all. You will know certainly that you must wear out long ages, millions of millions of ages, in wrestling and conflicting with this almighty merciless vengeance; and then when you have so done, when so many ages have actually been spent by you in this manner, you will know that all is but a point to what remains. So that your punishment will indeed be infinite. Oh, who can express what the state of a soul in such circumstances is! All that we can possibly say about it, gives but a very feeble, faint representation of it; it is inexpressible and inconceivable: For "who knows the power of God's anger?"

How dreadful is the state of those that are daily and hourly in the danger of this great wrath and infinite misery! But this is the dismal case of every soul in this congregation that has not been born again, however moral and strict, sober and religious, they may otherwise be. Oh that you would consider it, whether you be young or old! There is reason to think, that there are many in this congregation now hearing this discourse, that will actually be the subjects of this very misery to all eternity. We know not who they are, or in what seats they sit, or what thoughts they now have. It may be they are now at ease, and hear all these things without much disturbance, and are now flattering themselves that they are not the persons, promising themselves that they shall escape. If we knew that there was one person, and but one, in the whole congregation, that was to be the subject of this misery, what an awful thing would it be to think of! If we knew who it was, what an awful sight would it be to see such a person! How might all the rest of the congregation lift up a lamentable and bitter cry over him! But, alas! instead of one, how many is it likely will remember

this discourse in hell? And it would be a wonder, if some that are now present should not be in hell in a very short time, even before this year is out. And it would be no wonder if some persons, that now sit here, in some seats of this meeting-house, in health, quiet and secure, should be there before to-morrow morning. Those of you that finally continue in a natural condition, that shall keep out of hell longest will be there in a little time! your damnation does not slumber; it will come swiftly, and, in all probability, very suddenly upon many of you. You have reason to wonder that you are not already in hell. It is doubtless the case of some whom you have seen and known, that never deserved hell more than you, and that heretofore appeared as likely to have been now alive as you. Their case is past all hope; they are crying in extreme misery and perfect despair; but here you are in the land of the living and in the house of God, and have an opportunity to obtain salvation. What would not those poor damned hopeless souls give for one day's opportunity such as you now enjoy! . . .

And let every one that is yet of Christ, and hanging over the pit of hell, whether they be old men and women, or middle aged, or young people, or little children, now hearken to the loud calls of God's word and providence. This acceptable year of the Lord, a day of such great favours to some, will doubtless be a day of as remarkable vengeance to others. Men's hearts harden, and their guilt increases apace at such a day as this, if they neglect their souls; and never was there so great danger of such persons being given up to hardness of heart and blindness of mind. God seems now to be hastily gathering in his elect in all parts of the land; and probably the greater part of adult persons that ever shall be saved, will be brought in now in a little time, and that it will be as it was on the great out-pouring of the Spirit upon the

Jews in the apostles' days; the election will obtain, and the rest will be blinded. If this should be the case with you, you will eternally curse this day, and will curse the day that ever you was born, to see such a season of the pouring out of God's Spirit, and will wish that you had died and gone to hell before you had seen it. Now undoubtedly it is, as it was in the days of John the Baptist, the axe is in an extraordinary manner laid at the root of the trees, that every tree which brings not forth good fruit, may be hewn down and cast into the fire.

Therefore, let every one that is out of Christ, now awake and fly from the wrath to come. The wrath of Almighty God is now undoubtedly hanging over a great part of this congregation: Let every one fly out of Sodom: "Haste and escape for your lives, look not behind you, escape to the mountain, lest you be consumed."

CHAPTER II

THE BEGINNINGS
OF AMERICAN
POLITICAL THEORY

Although largely a religious movement, Puritanism also had political implications that played an important role not only in shaping the development of seventeenth-century New England but also in preparing the ground for the revolutionary ideas of the 1760's and 1770's. This is not to imply that democracy was an outgrowth of Puritanism, for the Puritans always proclaimed themselves indefatigable foes of any form of democratic or popular government. Nevertheless, there is an unbroken line of thought from Puritan political theories to those of the eighteenth-century rationalist thinkers.

The Puritans, unlike their descendants, were never able to separate religion and politics, and they always treated the two as different sides of the same coin. Their political ideology rested on the assumption that government was necessary because of original sin. Had man been good, they argued, such an instrument of restraint and regulation would have been superfluous. But since man was inherently evil, God placed over him a government designed to check his evil and selfish impulses. Although the Puritans held that each person would eventually face his Maker alone, they did not extend this individualistic theory to society. Instead, they maintained that society was a unit that existed to further certain divinely inspired ideals.

This being the case, the Puritans then logically reasoned that their system left no room for toleration of other ideas, and that the function of government was to enforce conformity according to God's laws. They therefore defined liberty as the freedom to do what was just and right, which in turn was determined by God and interpreted by the ministers and regenerate of the colony. Hence, the government of Massachusetts was in effect a dictatorship by a small minority. Lest we be too critical of Puritan religious and political intolerance, however, we should remember that their ideals did not materially differ from those of the Western world of that time.

The Puritans who came to New England, furthermore, brought with them some other basic assumptions concerning government. They accepted the existence of a fundamental law that far transcended the importance of any human law or edict of divine right monarchs. All men, regardless of their position, were subject to this law. In Puritanism the fundamental law was to be found in the Scriptures; later Americans were to find it elsewhere. But, wherever found, the concept of a higher law was destined to occupy an important place in American thought, for from it proceeded the corollary of a limited government.

Equally important was the Puritan belief that their government was based on the consent of the governed. This did not mean, however, that all people had a share in the workings of government. The eminent Puritan leader, John Winthrop, for example, argued that mankind had two forms of liberty, natural and civil. Natural liberty included the freedom to sin, and it placed man in the same category as animals. Civil liberty, on the other hand, meant the coming together of the regenerate souls, who voluntarily submitted their will to God through a government that they themselves had formed. The Puritans always stressed the voluntary character of the social compact, for, although it included only the regenerate, others who were excluded had only their own sinfulness to blame.

In effect, the Puritans were basing their government on a religious and a civil foundation, using two forms of covenant theory to buttress their logic. One covenant had been made between man and God, the other among individual men. Since the two covenants together had committed human beings to the rule of law and the control of authority, it followed that the church and state existed on a reciprocal basis, each supporting and strengthening the other.

It cannot be denied that many of the basic ideas of seventeenth-century Puritanism were not peculiar to that group alone but were common to the age as a whole. Yet the Puritans took these ideas and combined them into a coherent system of thought, which they attempted to translate into reality when they established their "Bible Commonwealth." For various reasons this experiment failed, but the political theories that had inspired this undertaking, when divorced from a religious background, did not die or disappear; a century later, many of them were being reiterated in a secular form by the revolutionary generation.

John Winthrop

1588-1649

A prominent English Puritan, Winthrop became dissatisfied with the restrictions placed upon the nonconformist sects in England. He was one of the twelve signatories to the Cambridge Agreement of 1629, in which prominent Puritans pledged themselves to migrate to America provided the charter and government of the Massachusetts Bay Company could be transferred there. Elected the first governor of Massachusetts, he served in this position or as deputy governor for the remainder of his life.

Both of the following excerpts illustrate the Puritan interpretation of the religious and civil bases of the state.

The first selection is from Winthrop's sermon "A Modell of Christian Charity" delivered aboard the Arbella *in 1630 during the voyage to New England; the text is from the* Winthrop Papers (*Boston: Massachusetts Historical Society, 1931*), vol. II. *In the second selection, written in 1645, Winthrop was defending himself against the charge of having exceeded his powers. The text is from Winthrop's* The History of New England from 1630 to 1649, *James Savage, ed.* (*Boston, 1853*), vol. II.

1. . . . We are a Company professing ourselves fellow members of Christ, in which respect only though we were absent from each other many miles, and had our employments as far distant, yet we ought to account ourselves knit together by this bond of love, and live in the exercise of it, if we would have comfort of our being in Christ, this was notorious in the practice of the Christians in former times, as is testified of the Waldenses from the mouth of one of the adversaries Aeneas Sylvius *mutuo [solent amare] penè antequam norint* [that is,] they use to love any of their own religion even before they were acquainted with them.

2. For the work we have in hand, it is by a mutual consent through a special overruling providence, and a more than ordinary approbation of the Churches of Christ to seek out a place of Cohabitation and Consortship under a due form of Government both civil and ecclesiastical. In such cases as this the care of the public must oversway all private respects, by which not only conscience, but mere Civil policy doth bind us; for it is a true rule that particular estates cannot subsist in the ruin of the public.

3. The end is to improve our lives to do more service to the Lord the comfort and increase of the body of Christ whereof we are members that ourselves and posterity may be the better preserved from the common coruptions of this evil world to serve the Lord and work out our Salvation under the power and purity of his holy Ordinances.

4. For the means whereby this must be effected, they are twofold, a Conformity with the work and end we aim at, these we see are extraordinary, therefore we must not content ourselves with usual ordinary means whatsoever

31

we did or ought to have done when we lived in England, the same must we do and more also where we go: That which the most in their Churches maintain as a truth in profession only, we must bring into familiar and constant practice, as in this duty of love we must love brotherly without dissimulation, we must love one another with a pure heart fervently we must bear one anothers burdens, we must not look only on our own things, but also on the things of our brethren, neither must we think that the Lord will bear with such failings at our hands as he doth from those among whom we have lived, and that for three reasons.

1. In regard of the more near bond of marriage, between him and us, wherein he hath taken us to be his after a most strict and peculiar manner which will make him the more Jealous of our love and obedience so he tells the people of Israel, you only have I known of all the families of the Earth therefore will I punish you for your Transgressions.

2. Because the Lord will be sanctified in them that come near him. We know that there were many that corrupted the service of the Lord, some setting up Altars before his own, others offering both strange fire and strange Sacrifices also; yet there come no fire from heaven, or other sudden Judgment upon them as did upon Nadab and Abihu who yet we may think did not sin presumptuously.

3. When God gives a special Commission he looks to have it strictly observed in every Article, when he gave Saul a Commission to destroy Amaleck he indented with him upon certain Articles and because he failed in one of the least, and that upon a fair pretence, it lost him the kingdom, which should have been his reward, if he had observed his Commission: Thus stands the cause between God and us, we are entered into Covenant with him for this work, we have taken out a Commission, the Lord hath given us leave to draw our own Articles we have professed to enterprise these Actions upon these ends, we have hereupon besought him of favor and blessing: Now if the Lord shall please to hear us, and bring us in peace to the place we desire, then hath he ratified this Covenant and sealed our Commission, [and] will expect a strict performance of the Articles contained in it, but if we shall neglect the observation of these Articles which are the ends we have propounded, and dissembling with our God, shall fall to embrace this present world and prosecute our carnal intentions, seeking great things for ourselves and our posterity, the Lord will surely break out in wrath against us be revenged of such a perjured people and make us known the price of the breach of such a Covenant.

Now the only way to avoid this shipwreck and to provide for our posterity is to follow the Counsel of Micah, to do justly, to love mercy, to walk humbly with our God, for this end, we must be knit together in this work as one man, we must entertain each other in brotherly Affection, we must be willing to abridge ourselves of our superfluities, for the supply of others necessities, we must uphold a familiar Commerce together in all meekness, gentleness, patience and liberality, we must delight in each other, make others' Conditions our own, rejoice together, mourn together, labor, and suffer together, always having before our eyes our Commission and Community in the work, our Community as members of the same body, so shall we keep the unity of the spirit in the bond of peace, the Lord will be our God and delight to dwell among us, as his own people and will command a blessing upon us in all our ways, so that we shall see much more of his wisdom power goodness and truth than formerly we have been acquainted with, we shall find that the God of Israel is among us, when ten of us shall be able to resist a thousand of our enemies, when he shall make us a praise and glory, that men shall say of succeeding plantations: the Lord make it like that of New England: for we must Consider that we shall be as a City upon a Hill, the eyes of all people are upon us; so that if we shall deal falsely with our God in this work we have undertaken and so cause him to withdraw his present help from us, we shall be made a story and a by-word through the world, we shall open the mouths of enemies to speak evil of the ways of God and all professors for Gods sake; we shall shame the faces of many of Gods worthy servants, and cause their prayers to be turned into Curses upon us till we be consumed out of the good land whither we are going: And to shut up this discourse with that exhortation of Moses, that faithful servant of the Lord, in his last farewell to Israel. *Deut.* 30. Beloved there is now set before us life, and good, death and evil in that we are Commanded this day to love the Lord our God, and to love one another to walk in his ways and to keep his Commandments and his Ordinance, and his laws, and the Articles of our Covenant with him that we may live and be multiplied, and that the Lord our God may bless us in the land whither we go to possess it: But if our hearts shall turn away so that we will not obey, but shall be seduced and worship other Gods our pleasures, and profits, and serve them; it is propounded unto us this day, we shall surely perish out of the good Land whether we pass over this vast Sea to possess it;

Therefore let us choose life, that we, and our Seed, may live; by obeying his voice, and cleaveing to him, for he is our life, and our prosperity.

*F*or the other point concerning liberty, I observe a great mistake in the country about that. There is a twofold liberty, natural (I mean as our nature is now corrupt) and civil or federal. The first is common to man with beasts and other creatures. By this, man, as he stands in relation to man simply, hath liberty to do what he lists; it is a liberty to evil as well as to good. This liberty is incompatible and inconsistent with authority, and cannot endure the least restraint of the most just authority. The exercise and maintaining of this liberty makes men grow more evil, and in time to be worse than brute beasts: *omnes summus licentia deteriores* [we are all worse in liberty]. This is that great enemy of truth and peace, that wild beast, which all the ordinances of God are bent against, to restrain and subdue it. The other kind of liberty I call civil or federal, it may also be termed moral, in reference to the covenant between God and man, in the moral law, and the politic covenants and constitutions, amongst men themselves. This liberty is the proper end and object of authority, and cannot subsist without it; and it is a liberty to that only which is good, just, and honest. This liberty you are to stand for, with the hazard (not only of your goods, but) of your lives, if need be. Whatsoever crosseth this, is not authority, but a distemper thereof. This liberty is maintained and exercised in a way of subjection to authority; it is of the same kind of liberty wherewith Christ hath made us free. The woman's own choice makes such a man her husband; yet being so chosen, he is her lord, and she is to be subject to him, yet in a way of liberty, not of bondage; and a true wife accounts her subjection her honor and freedom, and would not think her condition safe and free, but in her subjection to her husband's authority. Such is the liberty of the church under the authority of Christ, her king and husband; his yoke is so easy and sweet to her as a bride's ornaments; and if through frowardness or wantonness, etc., she shake it off, at any time, she is at no rest in her spirit, until she takes it up again; and whether her Lord smiles upon her, and embraces her in his arms, or whether he frowns, or rebukes, or smites her, she apprehends the sweetness of his love in all, and is refreshed, supported, and instructed by every such dispensation of his authority over her. On the other side, ye know who they are that complain of this yoke and say, let us break their bands, etc., we will not have this man to rule over us. Even so, brethren, it will be between you and your magistrates. If you stand for your natural corrupt liberties, and will do what is good in your own eyes, you will not endure the least weight of authority; but will murmur, and oppose, and be always striving to shake off that yoke; but if you will be satisfied to enjoy such civil and lawful liberties, such as Christ allows you, then will you quietly and cheerfully submit unto that authority which is set over you, in all the administrations of it, for your good. Wherein, if we fail at any time, we hope we shall be willing (by God's assistance) to hearken to good advice from any of you, or in any other way of God; so shall your liberties be preserved, in upholding the honor and power of authority amongst you.

Nathaniel Ward

1578(?)-1652

Educated at Emanuel College, Cambridge, Ward migrated to Massachusetts in 1634 and became a minister of the church in Aggawam (Ipswich). In 1638 he was appointed by the General Court to assist in drawing up a legal code, which was adopted in 1641. According to John Winthrop, Ward himself composed these laws, known as "The Body of Liberties."

In 1645 Ward completed his most famous political work, The Simple Cobler of Aggawam in America, *first published in England in 1647 under the pseudonym of Theodore de la Guard. Supposedly the reflections of a self-exiled cobbler upon the political and religious dissensions of the times, the tract was really a protest against the idea of toleration. Written in a simple and homely style, it remains a landmark in the history of American letters.*

The text reprinted here is taken from the fifth edition, printed in London in 1713, and reproduced in Peter Force, ed., Tracts and Other Papers, Relating Principally to the Origin, Settlement, and Progress of the Colonies in North America, from the Discovery of the Country to the Year 1776, *4 vols. (Washington, D.C., 1836–1846), vol. III, No. 8.*

*I*f the Devil might have his free option, I believe he would ask nothing else, but liberty to enfranchise all false Religions, and to embondage. the true; nor should he need: It is much to be feared that lax Tolerations upon State-pretences and planting necessities, will be the next subtle Stratagem he will spread to distate the Truth of God, and supplant the Peace of the Churches. Tolerations in things tolerable, exquisitely drawn out by the lines of the Scripture, and pencil of the Spirit, are the sacred favours of Truth, the due latitudes of Love, the fair Compartments of Christian fraternity: but irregular dispensations, dealt forth by the facilities of men, are the frontiers of error, the redoubts of Schism, the perilous irritaments of carnal and spiritual enmity.

My heart hath naturally detested four things: The standing of the Apocrypha in the Bible; Foreigners dwelling in my Country, to crowd out Native Subjects into the corners of the Earth; Alchemized Coins; Tolerations of diverse Religions, or of one Religion in segregant shapes: He that willingly assents to the last, if he examines his heart by day-light, his Conscience will tell him, he is either an Atheist, or an Heretic, or an Hypocrite, or at best a captive to some Lust: Poly-piety is the greatest impiety in the World. True Religion is *Ignis probationis*, which doth *congregare homogenea & segregare heterogenea.*

Not to tolerate things merely indifferent to weak Consciences, argues a Conscience too strong: pressed uniformity in these, causes much disunity: To tolerate more than indifferents, is

35

not to deal indifferently with God: He that doth it, takes his Scepter out of his hand, and bids him stand by. Who hath to do to institute Religion but God. The power of all Religion and Ordinances, lies in their Purity: their Purity in their Simplicity: then are mixtures pernicious. I lived in a City, where a Papist Preached in one Church, a Lutheran in another, a Calvinist in a third; a Lutheran one part of the day, a Calvinist the other, in the same Pulpit: the Religion of that Place was but motly and meagre, their affections Leopard-like.

If the whole Creature should conspire to do the Creator a mischief, or offer him an insolency, it would be in nothing more, than in erecting untruths against his Truth, or by sophisticating his Truths with human medleys: the removing of some one iota in Scripture, may draw out all the life, and traverse all the Truth of the whole Bible: but to authorize an untruth, by a Toleration of State, is to build a sconce against the walls of Heaven, to batter God out of his Chair: To tell a practical lie, is a great Sin, but yet transient; but to set up a Theoretical untruth, is to warrant every lie that lies from its root to the top of every branch it hath, which are not a few. . . .

That State is wise, that will improve all pains and patience rather to compose, than tolerate differences in Religion. There is no divine Truth, but hath much Celestial fire in it from the Spirit of Truth: nor no irreligious untruth, without its proportion of Antifire from the spirit of Error to contradict it: the zeal of the one, the virulency of the other, must necessarily kindle Combustions. Fiery diseases seated in the Spirit, embroil the whole frame of the body: others more external and cool, are less dangerous. They which divide in Religion, divide in God; they who divide in him, divide beyond *Genus Generalissimum*, where there is no reconciliation, without atonement; that is, without uniting in him, who is One, and in his Truth, which is also one.

Wise are those men who will be persuaded rather to live within the pale of Truth, where they may be quiet, than in the purlieues, where they are sure to be hunted ever and anon, do Authority what it can. Every singular Opinion, hath a singular opinion of it self, and he that holds it a singular opinion of himself, and a simple opinion of all contrasentients: he that confutes them, must confute all three at once, or else he does nothing; which will not be done without more stir than the Peace of the State or Church can endure.

And prudent are those Christians, that will rather give what may be given, than hazard all by yielding nothing. To sell all Peace of Country, to buy some Peace of Conscience unseasonably, is more avarice than thrift, imprudence than patience: they deal not equally, that set any Truth of God at such a rate; but they deal wisely that will stay till the Market is fallen.

My Prognostics deceive me not a little, if once within three seven years, Peace prove not such a Penny-worth at most Marts in Christendom, that he that would not lay down his Money, his Lust, his Opinion, his Will, I had almost said the best flower of his Crown for it, while he might have had it; will tell his own heart, he played the very ill husband.

Concerning Tolerations, I may further assert.

That Persecution of true Religion, and Toleration of false, are the *Jannes* and *Jambres* to the Kingdom of Christ, whereof the last is far the worst. *Augustines* Tongue had not owed his Mouth one Penny-rent though he had never spake word more in it, but this, *Nillum malum pejus libertate errandi* [nothing is more evil than the liberty of error].

Frederick, Duke of *Saxon*, spake not one foot beyond the mark when he said,

He had rather the Earth should swallow him up quick, than he should give a toleration to any Opinion against any Truth of God.

He that is willing to tolerate any Religion, or discrepant way of Religion, besides his own, unless it be in matters merely indifferent, either doubts of his own, or is not sincere in it.

He that is willing to tolerate any unsound Opinion, that his own may also be tolerated, though never so sound, will for a need hang God's Bible at the Devils girdle.

Every toleration of false Religions, or Opinions hath as many Errors and Sins in it, as all the false Religions and Opinions it tolerates, and one sound one more.

That State that will give Liberty of Conscience in matters of Religion, must give Liberty of Conscience and Conversation in their Moral Laws, or else the Fiddle will be out of Tune, and some of the strings crack.

He that will rather make an irreligious quarrel with other Religions than try the Truth of his own by valuable Arguments, and peaceable Sufferings; either his Religion, or himself is irreligious.

Experience will teach Churches and Christians, that it is far better to live in a State united, though a little Corrupt, than in a State, whereof some Part is uncorrupt, and all the rest divided. . . .

I take Liberty of Conscience to be nothing but a freedom from Sin, and Error. *Conscientia in tantum libera, inquantum ab errore liberata* [conscience is so free insofar as it is free from error]. And Liberty of Error nothing but a Prison for Conscience. Then small will be the kindness of a State to build such Prisons for their Subjects.

The Scripture saith, there is nothing makes free but Truth, and Truth saith, there is no Truth but one: If the States of the World would make it their sumoperous Care to preserve this One Truth in its purity and Authority, it would ease you of all other Political cares. I am sure Satan makes it his grand, if not only task, to adulterate Truth; Falsehood is his sole Scepter, whereby he first ruffled, and ever since ruined the World. . . .

It is said, That Men ought to have Liberty of the Conscience, and that it is Persecution to debar them of it: I can rather stand amazed than reply to this: it is an astonishment to think that the brains of men should be parboil'd in such impious ignorance; Let all the wits under the Heavens lay their heads together and find an Assertion worse than this (one excepted) I will Petition to be chosen the universal Idiot of the World.

It is said, That Civil Magistrates ought not to meddle with Ecclesiastical matters.

I would answer to this so well as I could, did I not know that some Papers lately brought out of *New England*, are going to the Press, wherein the Opinions of the Elders there in a late Synod, concerning this point are manifested, which I suppose will give clearer satisfaction than I can.

John Wise

1652-1725

A Congregational clergyman born in Roxbury, Massachusetts, Wise graduated from Harvard in 1673 and spent most of his life as a minister in Ipswich. A frequent participant in public controversies, Wise protested against the witchcraft trials in the 1690's and argued in favor of inoculation against smallpox (which was opposed by most ministers).

Wise's historical importance, however, lies in the realm of political thought. His writings here were occasioned by a proposal to transfer control of the churches from the members to the clergy and end the independence of the several churches. In attacking this proposal, Wise also critically reviewed the fundamentals of all government, separating the Biblical and rational arguments. His system of democratic church government was based on reason and nature rather than on a theological foundation. Although Wise's work was primarily concerned with church government, his ideas were extended by a later generation to apply to all government.

The text is from Wise's comprehensive and important defense of democratic Congregationalism, A Vindication of the Government of New-England Churches (*Boston, 1717*).

Chapter I

I shall disclose several Principles of Natural Knowledge; plainly discovering the Law of Nature; or the true sentiments of Natural Reason, with Respect to Mans Being and Government. And in this Essay I shall peculiarly confine the discourse to two heads, *viz.*

1. Of the Natural [in distinction to the Civil] and then,

2. Of the Civil Being of Man. . . .

1. I shall consider Man in a state of Natural Being, as a Free-Born Subject under the Crown of Heaven, and owing Homage to none but God himself. It is certain Civil Government in General, is a very Admirable Result of Providence, and an Incomparable Benefit to Mankind, yet must needs be acknowledged to be the Effect of Human Free-Compacts and not of Divine Institution; it is the Product of Mans Reason, of Human and Rational Combinations, and not from any direct Orders of Infinite Wisdom, in any positive Law wherein is drawn up this or that Scheme of Civil Government. Government [says the Lord *Warrington*] is necessary—in that no Society of Men can subsist without it; and that Particular Form of Government is necessary which best suits the Temper and Inclination of a People. Nothing can be Gods Ordinance, but what he has particularly Declared to be such; there is no particular Form of Civil Government described in Gods Word, neither does Nature prompt it. The Government of the *Jews* was

changed five Times. Government is not formed by Nature, as other Births or Productions; If it were, it would be the same in all Countries; because Nature keeps the same Method, in the same thing, in all Climates. If a Commonwealth be changed into a Monarchy, is it Nature that forms, and brings forth the Monarch? Of if a Royal Family be wholly Extinct [as in *Noah's* Case, being not Heir Apparent from Descent from *Adam*] is it Nature that must go to work [with the King Bees, who themselves alone preserve the Royal Race in that Empire] to Breed a Monarch before the People can have a King, or a Government sent over them? And thus we must leave Kings to Resolve which is their best Title to their Crowns, whether Natural Right, or the Constitution of Government settled by Human Compacts, under the Direction and Conduct of Reason. But to proceed under the head of a State of Natural Being, I shall more distinctly Explain the State of Human Nature in its Original Capacity, as Man is placed on Earth by his Maker, and Clothed with many Investitures, and Immunities which properly belong to Man separately considered. As,

1. The Prime Immunity in Mans State, is that he is most properly the Subject of the Law of Nature. He is the Favourite Animal on Earth; in that this Part of Gods Image, *viz.* Reason is Congenial with his Nature, wherein by a Law Immutable, Instamped upon his Frame, God has provided a Rule for Men in all their Actions, obliging each one to the performance of that which is Right, not only as to Justice, but likewise as to all other Moral Virtues, the which is nothing but the Dictate of Right Reason founded in the Soul of Man. . . . That which is to be drawn from Mans Reason, flowing from the true Current of that Faculty, when unperverted, may be said to be the Law of Nature; on which account, the Holy

Scriptures declare it written on Mens hearts. For being endowed with a Soul, you may know from your self, how, and what you ought to act, Rom. 2. 14. *These having not a Law, are a Law to themselves.* So that the meaning is, when we acknowledge the Law of Nature to be the dictate of Right Reason, we must mean that the Understanding of Man is endowed with such a power, as to be able, from the Contemplation of human Condition to discover a necessity of Living agreeably with this Law: And likewise to find out some Principle, by which the Precepts of it, may be clearly and solidly Demonstrated. The way to discover the Law of Nature in our own state, is by a narrow Watch, and accurate Contemplation of our Natural Condition, and propensions. Others say this is the way to find out the Law of Nature. If a Man any ways doubts, whether what he is going to do to another Man be agreeable in the Law of Nature, then let him suppose himself to be in that other Mans Room; And by this Rule effectually Executed. A Man must be a very dull Scholar to Nature not to make Proficiency in the Knowledge of her Laws. But more particularly in pursuing our Condition for the discovery of the Law of Nature, this is very obvious to view, *viz.*

1. A Principle of Self-Love, & Self-Preservation, is very predominant in every Mans Being.

2. A Sociable Disposition

3. An Affection or Love to Mankind in General. And to give such Sentiments the force of a Law, we must suppose a God who takes care of all Mankind, and has thus obliged each one, as a Subject of higher Principles of Being, than mere Instincts. For that all Law properly considered, supposes a capable Subject, and a Superior Power; And the Law of God which is Binding, is published by the Dictates of Right Reason as other ways: Therefore says *Plutarch, To follow God and obey Reason is the*

same thing. But moreover that God has Established the Law of Nature, as the General Rule of Government, is further Illustrable from the many Sanctions in Providence, and from the Peace and Guilt of Conscience in them that either obey, or violate the Law of Nature. But moreover, the foundation of the Law of Nature with relation to Government, may be thus Discovered. Man is a Creature extremely desirous of his own Preservation; of himself he is plainly Exposed to many Wants, unable to secure his own safety, and Maintenance without the Assistance of his fellows; and he is also able of returning Kindness by the furtherance of mutual Good; But yet Man is often found to be Malicious, Insolent and easily Provoked, and as powerful in Effecting mischief, as he is ready in designing it. Now that such a Creature may be Preserved, it is necessary that he be Sociable; that is, that he be capable and disposed to unite himself to those of his own species, and to Regulate himself towards them, that they may have no fair Reason to do him harm; but rather incline to promote his Interests, and secure his Rights and Concerns. This then is a Fundamental Law of Nature, that every Man as far as in him lies, do maintain a Sociableness with others, agreeable with the main end and disposition of human Nature in general. For this is very apparent, that Reason and Society render Man the most potent of all Creatures. And Finally, from the Principles of Sociableness it follows as a fundamental Law of Nature, that Man is not so Wedded to his own Interest, but that he can make the Common good the mark of his Aim: And hence he becomes Capacitated to enter into a Civil State by the Law of Nature; for without this property in Nature, *viz.* Sociableness, which is for Cementing of parts, every Government would soon molder and dissolve.

2. The Second Great Immunity of Man is an Original Liberty Instampt upon his Rational Nature. He that intrudes upon this Liberty, Violates the Law of Nature. In this Discourse I shall waive the Consideration of Mans Moral Turpitude, but shall view him Physically as a Creature which God has made and furnished essentially with many Ennobling Immunities, which render him the most August Animal in the World, and still, whatever has happened since his Creation, he remains at the upper-end of Nature, and as such is a Creature of a very Noble Character. For as to his Dominion, the whole frame of the Lower Part of the Universe is devoted to his use, and at his Command; and his Liberty under the Conduct of Right Reason, is equal with his trust. Which Liberty may be briefly Considered, Internally as to his Mind, and Externally as to his Person.

1. The Internal Native Liberty of Mans Nature in general implies, a faculty of Doing or Omitting things according to the Direction of his Judgment. But in a more special meaning, this Liberty does not consist in a loose and ungovernable Freedom, or in an unbounded Licence of Acting. Such Licence is disagreeing with the condition and dignity of Man, and would make Man of a lower and meaner Constitution than Brute Creatures; who will in all their Liberties are kept under a better and more Rational Government, by their Instincts. Therefore as *Plutarch* says, *Those Persons only who live in Obedience to Reason, are worthy to be accounted free: They alone live as they Will, who have Learnt what they ought to Will.* So that the true Natural Liberty of Man, such as really and truly agrees to him, must be understood, as he is Guided and Restrained by the Ties of Reason, and Laws of Nature; all the rest is Brutal, if not worse.

2. Mans External Personal, Natural Liberty, Antecedent to all Human parts, or Alliances must also be con-

sidered. And so every Man must be conceived to be perfectly in his own Power and disposal, and not to be controlled by the Authority of any other. And thus every Man, must be acknowledged equal to every Man, since all Subjection and all Command are equally banished on both sides; and considering all Men thus at Liberty, every Man has a Prerogative to Judge for himself, *viz.* What shall be most for his Behoof, Happiness and Well-being.

3. The Third Capital Immunity belonging to Mans Nature, is an equality amongst Men; Which is not to be denied by the Law of Nature, till Man has Resigned himself with all his Rights for the sake of a Civil State; and then his Personal Liberty and Equality is to be cherished, and preserved to the highest degree, as will consist with all just distinctions amongst Men of Honour, and shall be agreeable with the public Good. For Man has a high valuation of himself, and the passion seems to lay its first foundation [not in Pride, but] really in the high and admirable Frame and Constitution of Human Nature. The Word Man, says my Author, is thought to carry somewhat of Dignity in its sound; and we commonly make use of this as the most proper and prevailing Argument against a rude Insulter, *viz. I am not a Beast or a Dog, but am a Man as well as your self.* Since then Human Nature agrees equally with all persons; and since no one can live a Sociable Life with another that does not own or Respect him as a Man; It follows as a Command of the Law of Nature, that every Man Esteem and treat another as one who is naturally his Equal, or who is a Man as well as he. There be many popular, or plausible Reasons that greatly illustrate this Equality, *viz.* that we all Derive our Being from one stock, the same Common Father of the human Race. On this Consideration *Boethius* checks the pride of the Insulting Nobility. . . .

And also that our Bodies are Composed of matter, frail, brittle, and liable to be destroyed by thousand Accidents; we all owe our Existence to the same Method of propagation. The Noblest Mortal in his Entrance on to the Stage of Life, is not distinguished by any pomp or of passage from the lowest of Mankind; and our Life hastens to the same General Mark: Death observes no Ceremony, but Knocks as loud at the Barriers of the Court, as at the Door of the Cottage. This Equality being admitted, bears a very great force in maintaining Peace and Friendship amongst Men. For that he who would use the Assistance of others, in promoting his own Advantage, ought as freely to be at their service, when they want his help on the like Occasions. . . . That it would be the greatest absurdity to believe, that Nature actually Invests the Wise with a Sovereignty over the weak; or with a Right of forcing them against their Wills; for that no Sovereignty can be Established, unless some Human Deed, or Covenant Precede: Nor does Natural fitness for Government make a Man presently Governor over another; for that as *Ulpian* says, *by a Natural Right all Men are born free;* and Nature having set all Men upon a Level and made them Equals, no Servitude or Subjection can be conceived without Inequality; and this cannot be made without Usurpation or Force in others, or Voluntary Compliance in those who Resign their freedom, and give away their degree of Natural Being. And thus we come,

2. To consider Man in a Civil State of Being; wherein we shall observe the great difference between a Natural, and Political State, for in the Latter State many Great disproportions appear, or at least many obvious distinctions are soon made amongst Men; which Doctrine is to be laid open under a few heads.

1. Every Man considered in a Natural

State, must be allowed to be Free, and at his own dispose; yet to suit Mans Inclinations to Society; And in a peculiar manner to gratify the necessity he is in of public Rule and Order, he is Impelled to enter into a Civil Community; and divests himself of his Natural Freedom, and puts himself under Government; which amongst other things Comprehends the Power of Life and Death over Him; together with Authority to Enjoin him some things to which he has an utter Aversion, and to prohibit him other things, for which he may have as strong an Inclination; so that he may be often under this Authority, obliged to Sacrifice his Private, for the Public Good. So that though Man is inclined to Society, yet he is driven to a Combination by great necessity. For that the true and leading Cause of forming Governments, and yielding up Natural Liberty, and throwing Mans Equality into a Common Pile to be new Cast by the Rules of fellowship; was really and truly to guard themselves against the Injuries Men were liable to Interchangeably; for none so Good to Man, as Man, and yet none a greater Enemy. So that,

2. The first Human Subject and Original of Civil Power is the People. For as they have a Power every Man over himself in a Natural State, so upon a Combination they can and do bequeath this Power unto others; and settle it according as their united discretion shall Determine. For that this is very plain, that when the Subject of Sovereign Power is quite Extinct, that Power returns to the People again. And when they are free, they may set up what species of Government they please; or if they rather incline to it, they may subside into a State of Natural Being, if it be plainly for the best. . . .

3. The formal Reason of Government is the Will of a Community, yielded up and surrendered to some other Subject, either of one particular Person, or more. . . .

1. The Forms of a Regular State are three only, which Forms arise from the proper and particular Subject, in which the Supreme Power Resides. As,

1. A Democracy, which is when the Sovereign Power is Lodged in a Council consisting of all the Members, and where every Member has the Privilege of a Vote. This Form of Government, appears in the greatest part of the World to have been the most Ancient. For that Reason seems to show it to be most probable, that when Men [being Originally in a condition of Natural Freedom and Equality] had thoughts of joining in a Civil Body, would without question be inclined to Administer their common Affairs, by their common Judgment, and so must necessarily to gratify that Inclination establish a Democracy; neither can it be rationally imagined, that Fathers of Families being yet Free and Independent, should in a moment, or little time take off their long delight in governing their own Affairs, & Devolve all upon some single Sovereign Commander; for that it seems to have been thought more Equitable, that what belonged to all, should be managed by all, when all had entered by Compact into one Community. . . .

A democracy is then Erected, when a Number of Free Persons, do Assemble together, in Order to enter into a Covenant for Uniting themselves in a Body: And such a Preparative Assembly hath some appearance already of a Democracy; it is a Democracy in *Embryo* properly in this Respect, that every Man hath the Privilege freely to deliver his Opinion concerning the Common Affairs. Yet he who dissents from the Vote of the Majority, is not in the least obliged by what they determine, till by a second Covenant, a Popular Form be actually Established; for not before then can we call it a Democratical Government, *viz.* Till the Right of Determining all matters relating to the public Safety, is actually placed in a

General Assembly of the whole People; or by their own Compact and Mutual Agreement, Determine themselves the proper Subject for the Exercise of Sovereign Power. And to complete this State, and render it capable to Exert its Power to answer the End of a Civil State: These Conditions are necessary.

1. That a certain Time and Place be Assigned for Assembling.

2. That when the Assembly be Orderly met, as to Time and Place, that then the Vote of the Majority must pass for the Vote of the whole Body.

3. That Magistrates be appointed to Exercise the Authority of the whole for the better dispatch of Business, of every days Occurrence; who also may with more Mature Diligence, search into more important Affairs; and if in case any thing happens of greater Consequence, may report it to the Assembly; and be peculiarly Serviceable in putting all Public Decrees into Execution. Because a large Body of People is almost useless in Respect of the last Service, and of many others, as to the more Particular Application and Exercise of Power. Therefore it is most agreeable with the Law of Nature, that they Institute their Officers to act in their Name, and Stead.

2. The Second Species of Regular Government, is an Aristocracy; and this is said then to be Constituted when the People, or Assembly United by a first Covenant, and having thereby cast themselves into the first Rudiments of a State; do then by Common Decree, Devolve the Sovereign Power, on a Council consisting of some Select Members; and these having accepted of the Designation, are then properly invested with Sovereign Command; and then an Aristocracy is formed.

3. The Third Species of a Regular Government, is a Monarchy which is settled when the Sovereign Power is confered on some one worthy Person. It differs from the former, because a Monarch who is but one Person in Natural, as well as in Moral account, & so is furnished with an Immediate Power of Exercising Sovereign Command in all Instances of Government; but the fore named must needs have Particular Time and Place assigned; but the Power and Authority is Equal in each. . . .

3. A Democracy. This is a form of Government, which the Light of Nature does highly value, & often directs to as most agreeable to the Just and Natural Prerogatives of Human Beings. This was of great account, in the early times of the World. And not only so, but upon the Experience of several Thousand years, after the World had been tumbled, and tossed from one Species of Government to another, at a great Expense of Blood and Treasure, many of the wise Nations of the World have sheltered themselves under it again; or at least have blandished, and balanced their Governments with it.

It is certainly a great Truth, That Mans Original Liberty after it is Resigned, [yet under due Restrictions] ought to be Cherished in all wise Governments; or otherwise a man in making himself a Subject, he alters himself from a Freeman, into a Slave, which to do is Repugnant to the Law of Nature. Also the Natural Equality of Men amongst Men must be duly favoured; in that Government was never Established by God or Nature, to give one Man a Prerogative to insult over another; therefore in a Civil, as well as in a Natural State of Being, a just Equality is to be indulged so far as that every Man is bound to Honour every Man, which is agreeable both with Nature and Religion. 1 Pet. 2. 17. *Honour all Men.*—The End of all good Government is to Cultivate Humanity, and Promote the happiness of all, and the good of every Man in all his Rights, his Life, Liberty, Estate, Honour, &c. without injury or abuse done to any. Then certainly it cannot easily be thought, that a company of

Men, that shall enter into a voluntary Compact, to hold all Power in their own hands, thereby to use and improve their united force, wisdom, riches and strength for the Common and Particular good of every Member, as is the Nature of a Democracy; I say it cannot be that this sort of Constitution, will so readily furnish those in Government with an appetite, or disposition to prey upon each other, or embezzle the common Stock; as some Particular Persons may be apt to do when set off, and Entrusted with the same Power. And moreover this appears very Natural, that when the aforesaid Government or Power, settled in all, when they have Elected certain capable Persons to Minister in their affairs, and the said Ministers remain accountable to the Assembly; these Officers must needs be under the influence of many wise cautions from their own thoughts [as well as under confinement by their Commission] in their whole Administration: And from thence it must needs follow that they will be more apt, and inclined to steer Right for the main Point, *viz.* The peculiar good, and benefit of the whole, and every particular Member fairly and sincerely.

And why may not these stand for very Rational Pleas in Church Order?

For certainly if Christ has settled any form of Power in his Church he has done it for his Churches safety, and for the Benefit of every Member: Then he must needs be presumed to have made choice of that Government as should least Expose his People to Hazard, either from the fraud, or Arbitrary measures of particular Men. And it is as plain as day light, there is no Species of Government like a Democracy to attain this End. There is but about two steps from an Aristocracy, to a Monarchy, and from thence but one to a Tyranny; an able standing force, and an Ill-Nature, *Ipso facto*, turns an absolute Monarch into a Tyrant; this is obvious among the Roman *Caesars*, and through the World. And all these direful Transmutations are easier in Church affairs [from the different Qualities of things] than in Civil States. For what is it that cunning and learned Men can't make the World swallow as an Article of their Creed, if they are once invested with an Uncontrollable Power, and are to be the standing Orators to Mankind in matters of Faith and Obedience?

CHAPTER III

PURITANISM AND CAPITALISM

Puritanism was largely a middle-class movement that had economic as well as political implications. In fact, some students—such as Max Weber and Ernst Troeltsch—have implied that Puritanism stimulated the growth of capitalism by breaking down certain medieval economic ideals, such as the limitation on usury. It is clear that the monastic and ascetic objectives of the medieval church were incompatible with the rise of the middle class and the gradual disintegration of feudalism, and hence the new class turned to Puritanism, which was much better suited to meet its needs.

There is little doubt that Puritanism was closer than medieval theory to the material goals and values of a growing middle class that was becoming prominent in England and Western Europe after the fifteenth century. While the Puritan never thought of his religion in economic terms, he did emphasize the fact that man could serve God not by withdrawing from the world, but rather by following an occupation or calling that served the world. The puritan emphasis on industry and enterprise appealed to the middle class in a way that could not appeal to the peasantry or nobility. Although it is difficult to show a causal relationship between capitalism and Puritanism,

it is probably safe to assert that both movements tended to move closer together because of the affinity and attraction of each toward the other.
Undoubtedly Puritan and capitalist ideas went into the formation of the
American doctrine of laissez-faire individualism, a theory that was destined
to have momentous repercussions for subsequent economic and social
development.

In spite of the proximity of certain Puritan values to the rising capitalistic ethic, Puritanism was more medieval than modern in its economic theory
and practice. The idea of unrestrained economic individualism would have
seemed a dangerous notion to any self-respecting Puritan. The statute books
and court records of seventeenth-century Massachusetts abound in examples
of price and wage controls instituted by the government of the colony. The
Puritans, furthermore, always looked upon wealth as a gift from God given in
the form of a trust; and they emphasized not only the benefits that accrued
from work and wealth, but also their duties and responsibilities. In 1639, for
example, one of the richest merchants in the colony was fined by the General
Court (the highest legislative body) for excessive profiteering, despite the
fact that there was no statute against this practice. The Puritans could never
separate religion and business, and they often reiterated the medieval conception of the "just price."

In the long run, however, the Puritan ethic, when divorced from its
religious background, did serve to quicken and stimulate the spirit of capitalism. The limitations placed by the Puritans on the individual and the freedom
of movement within society were subordinated as time went on in favor of
the enterprising and driving individual who possessed the ability and ambition to rise through his own exertions. Thus it is paradoxical that seventeenth-century Puritanism, which was diametrically opposed to economic
individualism, should have played a major part in the emergence of a laissez-
faire capitalistic ethic.

Cotton Mather

1663-1728

The eldest son of Increase Mather and the grandson of Richard Mather and John Cotton—three of the most eminent ministers of Massachusetts—Cotton Mather, after his graduation from Harvard, became a leading exponent of Puritan orthodoxy at a time when the ideals of the original founders had entered a period of decline. While taking a leading role in the affairs of the community, he was also a prodigious writer, the author of more than 450 volumes during his lifetime. Although generally conservative and orthodox in his views, he was always torn between the demands of a new age and the ideals of an older one. Most of his time was spent in an effort to reassert and strengthen the religious foundations of Puritanism in the New World.

The following selections illustrate the religious basis of Puritan economic thought and its affinity to medieval ideas. They are taken from Durable Riches *(Boston, 1695); the first is from "The True Cause of Loosing" and the second from "The True Way of Thriving."*

1. The first Counsel proper for them that have met with Losses, is that which we have, Repeated in our Context here. Thus saith the Lord of Hosts, Consider your Ways. Consideration under our Losses, is as needful as ready a way, to the Sanctification of those Losses. And there are especially two things to be thereupon Considered.

First, When we have met with Losses, we are to Consider the Hand from whence those Losses come upon us. Briefly, We are to Consider the Hand of God in all our Losses. It was well Considered and Confessed, by the Holy Job, when he had Lost a fair Estate. . . . It is the Lord that has taken away. We shall be very Fretful under our Losses, if we are not very Thoughtful under them. . . . This is the First Rule for us under our Losses; Let us acknowledge a Wise, and a just God as the First Cause of all. It has been sometimes the Good Speech of a Good Man, I can take any thing well at the Hand of God. As for

our Losses, they will all Prove well if we can Take them well. . . . Let us Consider, That when we Loose Wealth, we must Remember the Lord our God; for 'tis he who denies us the power of keeping our Wealth. Perhaps our Losses may rise from the Fraud or Force of our Enemies; but let us Consider, It was our God that let Loose those Devourers upon us. . . . 'Tis the Lord Almighty that Empties us, by all the Losses that come upon us. Mark what I say: A man will never be a Looser by any of his Losses, except he be Impatient under them. Now, the best Antidote against Impatience is, to Consider, 'Tis the Will of God, that I should meet with such Losses as I do.

Secondly, When we have met with Losses, we are to Consider the Ground for which those Losses come. The God of Heaven sent one Wasting Plague after another upon the poor Jews, till at last they Lost all they had in the World; but then said He, in Ezek. 14. 23. Ye shall know that I have not without a

47

Cause, done all that I have done in it, saith the Lord. Our Losses are usually the fruit and sign of Gods Quarrels. Ordinarily our God is managing of some Controversy with us, when He causes us to Loose those things that were Comfortable to us. . . . It would be a Profitable thing for us to Loose what is Comfortable, if we might be brought thereby to Mourn for, and to Turn from our Sins, and to Humble our selves before God, with a deep Repentance. . . .

Thirdly, Under our Losses we may do well to Consider, Whether our Unthankfulness and Unfruitfulness under our Enjoyments, have not given much of Reasonableness unto our Losses. All that we have, is but a Loan from the Great God unto us. Now, if we be so Unthankful, that we will not particularly and affectionately Recognize the Kindness of God unto us in such a Loan, is it not very Reasonable that we should come to have a Loss instead of a Loan? Is it famous Threatning of God, in Deut. 28, 47, 48. Because thou servest not the Lord thy God, with Joyfulness, and Gladness of Heart, for the Abundance of all things; therefore thou shalt Serve thine Enemies in Hunger and in Thirst, and in Nakedness, and in the want of all things. It seems, we come to the Want, and the Loss of our Former Abundance; Why? Because we do not Serve God with a due Thankfulness of Heart, in and for that Abundance. . . . Don't we know that as what we have, is the Gift of God, so it must be used for the Praise of God? Know we not, that our Corn, and Wine, and Oil, and Silver, and Gold, is to be Laid out only so as may be for the glory of God? If we don't know this, we shall know that He will Take it, and we must Loose it all. . . .

Fourthly, Under our Losses we may do well to Consider, How we Got what we have Lost. . . . Many a man has been such a Fool, as to augment his Riches in some ways of Dishonesty; he has either by Fraud or Force made himself a Master of Gold, whereto he had no Right, by that Golden Rule, Do as thou wouldest be done unto. . . . It is a Righteous Thing with God, That One Loss after another should snatch away from us, those Riches, whereat we have snatched more Greedily than Honestly. . . . Yea, There is many a Godly man, who through Ignorance, or Carelessness, never made a possible Restitution of Things unlawfully Obtained, if not by himself, yet by those that Left him what he has; and so a long Series of Losses is Entail'd upon him. Thus also, such as have once Broken, by their own Extravagancies, rather than by the Unavoidable Frowns of God upon them; and have after all, had more Fraudulence, than Fair-dealing, in their Compositions with their Creditors, do ordinarily so plunge themselves into further Losses, that (as we say) no Butter will ever stick upon their Bread afterwards. Yea, if any Thing have been Gotten by any Trade, offensive unto God; such a Trade, suppose, as that wherein by Strong Drink Sold unto our Indians, the Savages have been hastened unto Hell before their Time; 'tis well if it been't Lost, all in as little a while as it was Got; and it may be, that some Good men have made the Unwary and Unhappy Trial of it. . . .

*B*ehold, a Duty of our Christian Conversation, which according to the Divine Heraldry of the Scripture, has a very High Place in Christianity belonging to it; a Duty than which there are not many, more Acceptable to God, more Profitable to Us, more Honourable to our Profession, or more Neglected and Omitted by multitudes, that will yet wear the Name which was begun at Antioch. And it is Remarkable to see, what a broad Contradiction is herein given to the Dictates of that Common and Carnal Reason, which mankind is generally misguided by. The Ordinary

Notion of the World is, If I have Bread, my own Cupboard is the fittest place to keep it in. But the Holy Spirit of God will teach us otherwise, Cast thy Bread upon the Waters. The Customary Dialect of the World is, I'll keep what I have, because I know not what Evil I may Live to see, I may Live to want it all. But we are otherwise Advised by the Holy Spirit of God; Give a Portion, because thou knowest not what Evil may be upon the Earth. 'Tis the God of Heaven, to whom we are beholden, for our Estates; our Possessions and Enjoyments, by which we are furnished against the Natural Inconveniencies of Human Life, are all bestowed upon us, by that God, whose Providence disposeth of all our Affairs. . . . The Same Covenant in which we are to make a Surrender of our Spirits and our Bodies unto God, must by a parity of Reason also Devote our Estates unto Him; and All that we Have, as well as All that we Are, must come under a Dedication to the Lord. . . . It is therefore most highly Reasonable, That we should be at the Direction of the Eternal God, as to what we do with our Estates; esteeming our selves but Stewards of those Things, whereof our Neighbours call us the Owners, and preparing our selves for the Account which we must give of our Stewardship unto Him that is, The Lord of All. Now the Orders which our Lord has given us, about our Estates, are principally Two. The First, is in 1 Tim. 5. 8. If any provide not for his own, especially those of his own House, he hath Denied the Faith. Our Estates are in the first place, to Feed and Clothe and Cherish our own Families; and we may even Lay up for our Children a part thereof, if that may be done without the Defrauding of such other Objects as God has required us, as long as we live, to be helpful unto. But then there is Another part of our Estates, that must be Consecrated unto more Pious Uses. . . .

What are those Pious Uses, that a Proportion of our Estates must be Devoted unto? And under these Four Heads may they be Enumerated, Paying, Lending, Giving, and Forgiving.

First, then, The Paying of our Duties, to the Public Charges of the Place in which we Live, is one of those Pious Uses, which our Estates are to be put unto. Something must be paid by us, for the support of the Government, and of the Ministry. . . .

But, Secondly, The Ready Lending of what may Assist those that want Means and Helps for their Trades, is likewise one of the Pious Uses which our Estates are to be placed in. . . .

And Thirdly, The Giving of what may supply the Necessities, and Relieve the Calamities of the Indigent, is among the Pious Uses of our Estates. It was the Speech of the Apostle, in 1 John 3. 17. Whoso has this Worlds Goods, and see his Brother has Need, and shutteth up his Bowels of Compassion from him, how dwelleth the Love of God in him? We must Give of our Goods to our Brethren, when they have a manifest Need thereof. . . .

But, Fourthly, 'Tis among the Pious Uses of our Estates for us, to Forgive a Debt, when the Hand of God has made the Borrower unable to Discharge it.

Jonathan Mitchell

1624-1668

A Harvard graduate, Mitchell was selected for the important and influential post of minister of the church at Cambridge. He played a leading role in the adoption of the "Half-Way Covenant" (1662), which was an attempt to meet the problems arising from the declining religious enthusiasm of the second generation. Among the first generation the prerequisite for church membership had been a personal religious experience, a test that their children often could not pass. But under the new covenant children of the adults who were not communicants could be baptized if their parents did not dissent from the doctrines of the church. The result, therefore, was that church membership was made easier.

The selection that follows is from an election sermon preached in 1667, and it demonstrates the broad welfare functions that the Puritans assigned to government. The text is from Nehemiah on the Wall in Troublesom Times (*Cambridge, 1671*).

Quest. 1. *What is that good, or welfare of the people, which Rulers ought to seek? or Wherein doth it consist?*

Answ. Take it in the Example of *Nehemiah,* the improvement whereof the Text leads us unto. . . .

1. Consisting in their *Safety*; that *Nehemiah* taketh care for in the first place (the preservation and safety of their persons and enjoyments, both Public and Personal, Religious and Civil). To that end he builds the Wall of *Jerusalem,* for their safety, that they might not be a prey unto, or reproach amongst their Adversaries, *Nehem.* 2. 17. This is fundamentally necessary to the welfare, or well-being of a people, they cannot possibly have *well-being,* without the *preservation* of their *Being,* both Personal and Political. When *Nehemiah* came to seek the welfare of the children of *Israel,* his great business was to build the Wall of *Jerusalem,* in which place their principal Concernments, both of Religion and Government, were laid up, *Psal.* 122. 3, 4, 5. That

Jerusalem have a Wall for the safety and preservation of it, (and of what is contained in it) is requisite to the welfare of *Israel.*

2. Their *Honesty:* Rulers are to seek to maintain, cherish and preserve *Civil Honesty* amongst a people, by restraining and redressing Injuries between man and man, and other Crimes and Misdemeanours, by the Administration and Execution of Justice; by the free passage of *Righteousness,* which assigneth to every one his own; and of *Equity* also, abating the rigour and extremity of strict Justice, where need is. *Nehemiah* left an eminent Example of this, *Neh.* 5. 7–13. causing them to deal honestly, yea mercifully with their poor brethren, according as the distress of the time required, suppressing the biting *Usury* that was among them; he frees the oppressed from their oppressions, and taketh care that *Righteousness* and *Equity* may obtain amongst the people; this also is a part of his care for the good of *Israel.* That people may live together

50

in *all honesty* as well as *godliness*, is the care and the benefit of good Rulers, 1 *Tim.* 2. 1, 2. and so that *Judgment* and *Justice* may be faithfully administered, which is a main *Basis* of the welfare of a people, and a main part of the work of Rulers, 1 *Kings* 10. 9. *Jer.* 22. 3, 15, 16. *Amos* 5. 24. 1 *Pet.* 2. 14.

3. Their *Prosperity*, in matters of outward Estate and Livelihood, by such help as the care of Government may contribute to that end. That we commonly call (*Wealth*) is a part of the wealth or welfare of a people, though not the greatest part, as the world is apt to esteem it. Good Rulers will gladly be a furtherance thereunto, what in them lies, that the *Commonwealth* may flourish and prosper in that respect, but especially in reference to necessary livelihood, when it is a time of distress and poverty, or special scarcity in this or that, of food or clothing: when the people are in a low condition (or many of them at least) wrestling with many and great difficulties, or in a dearth, *Chap.* 5. 3. how careful is *tender-hearted Nehemiah* of the people at such a time, *Nehem.* 5. he took great care that things might be so carried on, that *poor people* might be provided of *necessaries*, and be able to sustain their Families, that they might not perish in a time of dearth and scarcity, *vers.* 2, 3, &c. this was part of the good he did for the people. . . .

4. Let people be friends and *Helpers* to their own welfare; or every one in your several places seek the common good of the whole. If Rulers are to *seek* the welfare of the people, then surely people themselves are not to *prejudice* or neglect their own welfare. The *Patient* must contribute Endeavours towards his own health, as well as the *Physician*, else there will be but little good done. It is the Rulers work eminently, as his Place is more eminent; but it is also the work of every one, according to the compass of his capacity and opportunity, to seek the welfare of the place and

people, where & among whom he lives, *Jer.* 29. 7. So the Lord speaks to Captives in *Babylon*, during the time of Gods patience with it; much more doth that duty lie on those that dwell in *Zion*, to seek the good and the peace of the place, both by Prayer to God, and by all other due means within their power. Love thy Neighbour, much more a whole *Community*, a multitude of thy Neighbours, is the Lords charge to every one. A little more particularly.

1. Be sure (every particular person, I now speak to even them that are in private capacity) to do no *hurt* to *Israel*, (to the Lords people among whom you live) either *directly*, or *indirectly;* either wilfully or carelessly: that is just contrary to seeking the welfare of the place and people where you live; which is a Moral and great duty lying upon every Soul. Woe to that person, whosoever he be, that shall be a willing or blameable cause of hurt or harm to the *Lords people* here, whom he that toucheth will be found to touch the *Apple of his Eye*, *Psal.* 34. 21. When God called *Abraham* forth to follow him in a way of Reformation, he gave that word along with him, *Gen.* 12. 3. and so to *Jacob* or *Israel*, *Gen.* 27. 29. and he did and will make it good. If you love your Souls, take heed of touching *Israel* to their hurt: yea even words that tend to the reproach or prejudice of the people of God, or Builders in *Jerusalem*, is not a small matter, *Neh.* 4. 2, 3, 4, 5. (such *Imprecations* tell us, what will be the portion of such except they repent, though not that ordinary and private Spirits should be forward to with that it might be so to particular persons) *They have provoked anger* (*Thee* is not in the Hebrew) irritated and raised spirits (by their Scoffs and Reproaches) *before*, or in respect of *the Builders*. The words may carry that meaning.

2. Think it not enough to do *no hurt*, but according to your place and opportunity do *good* to *Israel*, to that part of

it in special in which the Lord hath cast you. Be willing to put forth thy self for the public good according to thy *Talent.* Hast thou Estate which the Lord hath blessed thee with, (and gotten, it may be, here under the shadow of the Government?) let not the Public suffer for want, when as thou hast it by thee. Hast thou Ability to serve the Country any other way? be ready thereunto: Do not only *pray*, but put forth *endeavours* according to capacity and opportunity for the peace and good of *Jerusalem;* else you do but dally in praying, if you will do nothing for it, *Psal.* 122. 9. Seek it in the use of all due means. A *public* Spirit even in a *private* person is a precious thing; *i.e.* according to the compass of his place to be ready to do for the common good. Could the Heathen (the *Romans* and others) produce such Sayings as these; *That man was not born for himself, but for his Country; That even to die for it is sweet: Dulce & decorum pro Patria mori;* and boast of those among them that practised accordingly: and shall Christians be strangers to such a Public Spirit, or be backward to act for the common welfare. Here in *Nehemiahs* time every one set his hand to, to build up the Wall of *Jerusalem*, and the *particular* persons and companies that did their parts therein, are to their honour *recorded* in the holy story, *Neh.* 3. Oh that is a pleasant sight, to see all sorts contributing to the Safety, Peace, Welfare of *Jerusalem*, and joining *Hearts* and *Hands* therein, *Neh.* 4. 6. Oh! have you a mind to *build* or to save the Wall and Welfare of *Jerusalem?* Are you *cheerful, cordial, forward, industrious* therein? not a man to *talk* only, but to *work* when the case requires it. . . .

CHAPTER IV

REASON AND
SCIENCE IN
PURITAN
THOUGHT

*T*he popular image of the Puritan is often that of a narrow-minded individual whose preoccupation with religion served to limit his intellectual horizons and make him an enemy of any form of liberalism in learning. Yet in studying the Puritan attitude toward two intellectual disciples, education and science, a paradox emerges—namely, that Puritanism resulted in the raising of the intellectual level of New England to much greater heights than existed in the middle or southern colonies. In the midst of a primitive environment, the hardy pioneers of Massachusetts had by 1636 provided for the establishment of a college and a short time later passed the first public compulsory educational law in American history. Nor were the Puritans in any way opposed to the new scientific discoveries that were slowly bringing about a revolution in European thought. On the contrary, they were highly receptive to and interested in the new scientific theories of their day.

In the case of the Puritans, religion undoubtedly worked as a stimulant to intellectual ferment. Although emotion played a role in their theology, the Puritans emphasized above all that man, though he might be an evil creature, was also a rational and intelligent once. Since God was intelligible (up to a point), true knowledge would help rather than hinder man's understanding of His works and purposes. Ignorance was something to be feared, and thus the Puritans not only demanded an educated and literate clergy, but they also made provision for the general uplifting of the mass of the people. The famous law of 1647, for example, required that every town in the colony containing fifty families appoint a schoolmaster to teach the children to read and write, and that every town of 100 or more was to make provision for a grammar school to prepare youths for the college. In their curriculum, furthermore, the emphasis was not solely on religion, for the classical and humanistic standards of the English universities were taken as model examples.

Similarly, Puritanism acted as a stimulus rather than a barrier to the acceptance of new scientific discoveries. No less than eleven New Englanders were elected to membership by the Royal Society of London, the greatest English scientific body, as compared with only one from South Carolina and three each from Virginia and Pennsylvania. To the Puritans the natural world was God's creation in operation, and they felt that an understanding of this world would serve as an invaluable aid in discerning divine intentions. In general, their attitude toward science was typical of European thought. When the Puritans looked upon comets as portents of things to come, they were simply echoing a belief dating from antiquity, and when they held that comets operated according to natural law, they were expressing their belief in the new astronomical theories. Similarly, the Puritans were interested in witchcraft from a scientific point of view, for this phenomenon, in their eyes —and in the eyes of most Englishmen and Europeans—was a fact that could be empirically verified. The tragic Salem witchcraft trials in 1692 were simply a feature of the age and cannot be attributed to Puritan theology or practice. Finally, such an eminent Puritan divine as Cotton Mather could champion inoculation for smallpox, the clinical treatise on inoculation communicated in 1721 to the Royal Society of London (and published in their transactions)— a landmark in medical history—was, in fact, based on Boston's experience in inoculation against smallpox.

The record left by the Puritans in their educational and scientific strivings thus established a significant precedent for later generations. Although their individual contributions were relatively insignificant, they did provide for an institutional and intellectual framework that proved vital to scholarship in the New World.

Charles Chauncy

1592(?)-1671/2

A leading Puritan intellectual, Charles Chauncy migrated to New England in 1638, after having been involved in difficulties arising from his opposition to some of Archbishop Laud's regulations in England. His ideas on baptism made him somewhat unwelcome to the more orthodox; and, although he accepted the presidency of Harvard College in 1654, it was with the stipulation that he refrain from disseminating his views on this subject. Continuing in that position until his death, he seems to have been eminently successful in his career as a college president because of his acknowledged erudition.

The following selection is from Gods Mercy, Shewed to His People in Giving Them a Faithful Ministry and Schooles of Learning for the Continual Supplyes Thereof (*Cambridge, 1655*), *a commencement sermon defending a liberal education.*

. . . Schools of learning are approved and appointed of God, and of great importance for the benefit of Gods people: Seeing that the Lord works with, & blesseth this means, for the laying up of provision, & making of supplies for the work of the ministry; and the Lord here reckons it up as the chiefest of all the blessings mentioned: and this was always one way (even when there were extraordinary Prophets) of raising up of Prophets &c: And there is much more need of schools now, when those extraordinary Prophets are wanting.

Quest: What ground is there in the Scriptures, for Schools of learning?

Answ: Give me leave to show this as a matter called by many into question in these days. Now the Text, and the explication thereof before shows that the Lord did approve of them in the days of the old Testament, that is the intent of the frequent mentioning of the sons of the Prophets, that is their scholars that were trained up under them: besides 2 *Kings* 22. 14. There is mention of a College (where *Huldah* the Prophetess, and no doubt many others nurtured in a

way of learning lived,) and the Hebrews have an usual word where by they call their schools (*yeshibah*) a company of scholars that sit together to be taught. . . . But the example of our Saviour Christ is above all, that kept a school, first of his twelve disciples, then of the seventy disciples *Luke* 10 that he also sent forth to preach the Gospel. Yea there is a most clear and express Commandment, that Paul gives to Timothy 2 *Tim:* 2. 2. he saith *the things that thou hast heard of me before many witnesses, the same commit to faithful men, who shall be able to teach others also.* Where we see that Timothy had many school fellows that are called witnesses, and also that Timothy is commanded to teach others, so it concerns such as God enables to teach them that may be teachers of others, to instruct them in the things of God.

But now it will be very needful upon this occasion for us to consider what weight there is in the objections that diverse in these days have printed against them.

Object. 1. Mr. Dell in his answer to

Mr. S. Simpson allows schools of the prophets wherein Christian religion is taught, *but against schools of humane learning this is that that makes them Antichrists, seeing they are contrary to, and do oppose Christ, this makes the universities stews of Antichrist, houses of lies, and to stink before God with most loathsome abomination &c:* with a multitude of other reproachful terms which Luther & others have loaded Popish Universities withall.

Answ. 1. I do much desire that the opposers of schools & universities would speak plainly what they mean by humane learning, then we should easily come to some conclusion. Therefore let this distinction be premised, that humane learning may either be taken for all that learning that the heathen Authors or philosophers have delivered in their writings: or else all other Arts besides Theology, as they call *physics, ethics, politics &c:* take in also the grounds of language, *Latin Greek & Hebrew.* Now in the former sense, if *Mr. D.* do mean by humane learning, all that learning that the heathen men have uttered out of the light of nature: It will be a great oversight to pass such a sentence upon it. 1. Because we find in Scriptures, some testimonies out of humane writers, as *Tit:* 1. 12. *Acts* 17. 28. 1 *Cor:* 15. 33. &c: which the Spirit of God would not have alleged, if their writings had been utterly unlawful to read. 2. There are certain principles of truth written, even in corrupt nature, which heathen authors have delivered unto us, that do not cross the holy writ, 1 *Cor:* 11. 14. *doth not nature it self teach you &c:* and it cannot be denied that all truth, whosoever it be that speaks it, comes from the God of truth, as he is called several times. And who can deny but that there are found many excellent & divine moral truths in *Plato, Aristotle, Plutarch, Seneca &c:* and to condemn all pell-mell, will be an hard censure, especially to call universities Antichrists for reading

of them. Besides they have treated of the works of God, most excellently in many places, and the works of God ought to be *declared by parents to their children, Psal.* 78. 2–6. Besides they have delivered many excellent sayings of God, and have attested many Scripture histories, as might be showed by several instances, out of *Justine, Tacitus &c:* and *Mr. D.* is not ignorant of them, shall all these be thrown away as antiChristian, or as lies?

Object. But they have much profaneness and filthiness in them, and besides they are made idols of in our universities, when as *ipse, dixit,* and their authority goeth for current, as Scripture it self amongst them.

Answ. But 1. All heathenish writers, have not such profaneness in them. 2. Those that have, let them be condemned & abhorred, & let not youth be poisoned by them. 3. Let God be true & every man a liar, and let not man, especially any heathen be deified, or his authority be accounted on, or go cheek by jowl with the speaking in the Scriptures: this is indeed to be abhored wheresoever it is received, but *abusus non tollit usum.*

II. But now if humane learning be taken in the second sense, for all those Arts are commonly taught in Universities, as *Physics, Ethics, Politics, Oeconomics, Rhetoric, Astronomy &c:* or also for learned tongues of *Latin, Greek, and Hebrew &c:*

1. I will be bold to affirm, that these in the true sense and right meaning thereof are Theological & Scripture learning, and are not to be accounted of as humane learning. For who can deny, that the first and second chapters of *Genesis,* and many chapters in *Job,* and the *Psalms,* and diverse other places of holy Scripture, do afford excellent and sure grounds for natural Philosophy, and a just system thereof: which *Mr. Zanchy, Daneus,* and diverse other eminent Divines have opened & declared

unto us? And where are there to be found such *Ethical, Political,* or *Moral* precepts, as are to be found in holy Scriptures? or such principles for the ordering of our lives, families, or common weals? let any man declare it unto us. And where are there such high strains of all sorts of *Rhetorical Tropes, & figures,* to be found in any Author, as there are in the writings of the *Prophets & Apostles?* and who can imagine, but that the best & surest Chronology in the world, is to be found in holy Scriptures, upon which all the computation of times in all ages in the world depends? . . .

Object: But there is no necessity of Schools or Universities, or any humane learning to teach men Divinity, or to make able preachers of the Gospel: the teaching of the Spirit of God alone is sufficient: which Mr. Dell proves by the examples of our Saviour Christ & his Apostles, seeing Christ himself had only the unction of the Spirit. Isay 61. 1–4. Luke 4. Mat: 13. 54, 55. *Besides when he would send forth preachers into all the world, he chose Fishermen, Publican, Tent makers, plain men, and of ordinary employment in the world, and only put his Spirit upon them* Acts 2. 17. *This argument is much stood upon* by Mr. Horne, & Mr. Crandon *against* M. Baxter.

Answ. 1. It is a marvelous mistake to reason from our Savior Christ & his Apostles to these times: For our Saviour received the Spirit not by measure *John* 3. 24. and the Apostles had the miraculous & visible extraordinary gifts of the Spirit bestowed on them *Acts* 2. So the reason will stand thus. If our Saviour Christ and his Apostles, without other learning, by the miracu-

lous and extraordinary gifts of the Spirit, were enabled and furnished sufficiently for the ministry; Then other ministers in after times (that have no such extraordinary gifts) need no other learning, but the unction of the Spirit, as if he should say, if Aholiab & Bezaleel were filled with the Spirit of God in wisdom, and in knowledge, and all manner of workmanship, to devise cunning works, (as they were *Exod.* 31. 3, 4.) then no man need to be an apprentice to learn any Mechanical trade, seeing the teaching of the Spirit is sufficient for any cunning work, who is there that would not account this reasoning ridiculous? Surely if Mr. D. had not excluded Logic & reason out of Divinity he would never have made such collections: It is much like his reasoning in an other Sermon of his, the Scripture saith that Christ shall Baptise with the holy Ghost, & with fire, therefore there is no baptism with water to be used, or to be in force. But forsooth what ever he saith, ye must expect no reason from him, ye must take all from him as dictates of the Spirit, and so all Ordinances in the Church that the Spirit hath appointed, the Spirit shall also overthrow, yea I know no reason why Mr. Dell, or any other believer, upon this ground, may not make an other Scripture, for if the same Spirit that indighted or penned the Scripture, be in the same or the like measure in Mr. Dell or other believers, as it was in the holy men of God and penmen of the Scripture, then what Mr. D. and any other believers write or say, is of equal authority with the Canonical Scriptures. So Mr. Dell and every believer is made a Pope, that can not err &c: but here I will stop & spare.

Cotton Mather

1663-1728

Both of the following selections illustrate the modern as well as the medieval elements in Puritan scientific thought. The first is from The Christian Philosopher: A Collection of the Best Discoveries in Nature, With Religious Improvements (*London, 1721*), *and the second from* "The Angel of Bethesda," *written in the early 1720's but never published. The text of the latter is taken from Otho T. Beall, Jr., and Richard H. Shryock,* "Cotton Mather: First Significant Figure in American Medicine," *American Antiquarian Society*, Proceedings, *vol. 63 (April 1953), [For Mather's career, see p. 47.]*

Essay XVI

Of the Thunder and Lightning

*H*is *powerful Thunder, who can understand?* Yet our Philosophy will a little try to see and say something of it.

The Account of *Thunder*, given by Dr. *Hook*, is this. The Atmosphere of the Earth abounds with *nitrous Particles* of a spirituous nature, which are every where carried along with it. Besides which sort of Particles, there are also others raised up into the *Air*, which may be somewhat of the Nature of *sulphurous*, and *unctious*, and other combustible Bodies. We see Spirit of *Wine*, of *Turpentine*, of *Camphor*, and almost all other combustible Bodies, will by *Heat* be rarified into the Form of *Air*, or *Smoke*, and be raised up into the Air. All these, if they have a sufficient Degree of *Heat*, will catch *Fire*, and be turned into *Flame*, from the nitrous Parts of the Air mixing with them; as it has been proved by Thousands of Experiments. There are also other sorts of such Steams, that arise from *subterraneous* and *mineral* Bodies; which only by their coming to mix with the *Nitre* of the Air, though they have no sensible *Heat* in them, will so ferment and act upon one another, as to produce an actual *Flame*. Of this, the *Mines* are too frequent Witnesses and Sufferers. The *Lightning* seems to be very much of such an Original.

Dr. *Wallis* observes, That *Thunder* and *Lightning* have so much resemblance to *fired Gunpowder* in their *Effects*, that we may very well suppose much of the same *Causes*. The principal Ingredients in *Gunpowder*, are *Nitre* and *Sulphur*. Suppose in the Air, a convenient Mixture of *nitrous* and *sulphurous* Vapors, and those to take *fire* by accident, such an *Explosion*, and with such *Noise* and *Light* as that in the firing of *Gunpowder*, may well follow upon it; and being once kindled, it will run from place to place, as the Vapor leads it, like as in a Train of *Gunpowder*. This Explosion, high in the Air, and far from us, will do no considerable mischief. But, if it be very near us, it has terrible Consequences. The Distance of its *Place* may be estimated by the Distance of the *Time*, which there is between seeing the *Flash*, and hearing the *Clap:* For though in their Generation they be simultaneous, yet *Light* moving faster than *Sound*, they come successively to us. That there is a *nitrous* Vapor in it, we may reasonably judge, because we know of no other Body so liable to so sudden and furious Explosion. That there is a *sulphurous* one, is manifest from the Smell that attends it, and the sultry Heat, that is commonly a Forerunner of it.

The *natural Causes* of the *Thunder* do not at all release me from considering the *Interest* and *Providence* of the Glorious GOD, concerned in it. It is a Note prepared for the Songs of the Faithful, *The* GOD *of Glory thundereth.* It is He, who

Fulmina molitur dextra, quo maxima motu
Terra tremit, fugere Ferac, & mortalia Corda
Per Gentes humilis stravit Pavor.[1]

And indeed, as the *Thunder* has in it the *Voice of* God, . . . thus there are several Points of *Piety*, wherein I am, as with a *Bath Kol*, instructed from it.

There is this *Voice* most sensibly to be heard in the *Thunder*, *Power belongeth unto God.* There is nothing able to stand before those *Lightnings*, which are styled the *Arrows of God.* We see Castles fall, Metal melt, Bricks themselves vitrify; all flies, when *hot Thunderbolts* are scattered upon them. The very *Mountains* are torn to pieces, when— *Feriunt summos sua Fulmina Montes* [His lightning bolts strike the tops of the mountains]. It becomes me now to say, *The Thunder of his Power who can understand?* An haughty Emperor shrinks, and shakes, and hides his guilty Head, before the powerful *Thunder* of God.

How can I hear the *Voice* of the *Almighty Thunderer*, without such Thoughts as these? *Glorious God, let me, through the Blood of a sacrificed Saviour, be in good Terms with One so able to destroy me in a moment!* And, let me be afraid of offending Him, who is possessed of such an *irresistible Artillery!*

At the same time, do I not see the *Mercy* and *Patience* of a Good God to a sinful World? The Desolations of the World, how wonderfully would they be,

Si quoties peccant Homines sua Fulmina mittat [If whenever men sin, He were to send his lightnings]! It is no rare thing for the Children of Men to die by a *Thunderbolt;* A *King* has been so slain in the midst of his Army. There was a Punishment of old used upon Criminals, by pouring hot Lead into their Mouths, which was called *Combustio Animae* [burning of the soul], and used in imitation of God's destroying Men with *Lightning;* whereby the *inward* Parts are burnt without any visible Touch upon the *outward.* This *Combustio Animae*, a Death by *Lightning*, has been frequently inflicted. Their being *asleep* at the time has not preserved them, though there be a Fancy in *Plutarch* that it would; nor would a Tent of *Seal-Skin* have done it, though some great ones have repaired unto such an *Amulet* for their Protection. *My God, I adore thy Sovereign Grace, that such a Sinner as I have not yet been by Lightning turned into Dust and Ashes before thee!*

I take notice of one thing, That as Guilt lying on the Minds of Men, makes them startle at a *Thunder-Clap.* . . . So the Miscarriages about which our Hearts do first and most of all misgive us in a *Thunder-Storm*, are those which most of all call for a *thorough Repentance* with us. There are some Writings which I cannot read, except I hold them against the Fire; by having my Heart held up against the *Lightning*, I may quickly read *my own Iniquity.*

Impious People are *deaf to Thunder!* *Herlicius*, in his *Tractatus de Fulmine*, reckons up a considerable number of those, which might be called *Faelicia Fulmina.* Such will they be that make these Impressions upon us.

---

[1] [He wields the thunderbolts in his right hand, by which motion the mighty earth trembles, while beasts run away, and lowly trembling has laid low mortal hearts among the nations in the world.]

*T*here has been a wonderful Practice lately used in several Parts of the World, which indeed is not yet become common in our Nation.

I was first instructed in it, by a Guarantee-servant of my own, long before I knew that any Europeans or Asiatics had the least Acquaintance with it, and some Years before I was enriched with the Communications of the learned Foreigners, whose Accounts I found agreeing with what I received of my Servant, when he showed me the Scar of the Wound made for the Operation; and said, that no Person ever died of the Small-Pox, in their Country that had the Courage to use it.

I have since met with a considerable Number of these Africans, who all agree in one Story; that in their Country grandy—many die of the Small-Pox; but now they learn this Way: People take Juice of Small-Pox, and Cutty-Skin, and put in a Drop; then bye'nd bye a little sicky, sicky; then very few little Things like Small-Pox; and no body die of it; and no body have Small-Pox any more. Thus in Africa, where the poor Creatures die of the Small-Pox like rotten Sheep, a Merciful God has taught them an infallible Preservative. 'Tis a common Practice, and is attended with a constant Success.

But our Advice of this Matter, as it comes from Superior Persons in the Levant, is what may have most Attention given to it.

Our first Communication comes from Dr. Emanuel Timonius R.S.S. who writes from Constantinople, in December, 1713. To this Effect.

The Practice of procuring the Small-Pox, by a Sort of Inoculation, has been introduced among the Constantinopolitans, by the Circassions and Georgians, and other Asiatics; for about forty Years.

At the first, People were cautious and afraid. But the happy Success on thousands of Persons for eight years now past, has put it out of all Suspicion. The Operation has been performed on Persons of all Ages, both Sexes, differing Temperaments, and even in the worst Constitution of the Air; and none that have used it ever died of the Small-Pox; tho' at the same Time, it were so malignant, that at least half the People died, that were affected with it in the Common Way.

They that have this Inoculation practiced on them (he says) are subject unto very slight Symptoms, and hardly sensible of any Sickness; nor do what Small-Pox they have, ever leave any Scars or Pits behind them.

They make Choice of as healthy a young Person as they can find, that has the Small-Pox of the best Sort upon him; on the twelfth or thirteenth Day of his Decumibiture. With a Needle they prick some of the larger Pustules and press out the Matter coming from them into some convenient Vessel of Glass (or the like) to receive it; which ought first of all to be washed very clean with warm Water. A convenient Quantity of this Matter being thus collected, is to be stop'd close, and kept warm, in the Bosom of the Person that carries it (who ought rather to be some other Person than what visited the sick Chamber for it, lest the Infection of the Small-Pox be convey'd in the Garment as well as in the Bottle, and the intended Operation be hurt by the Infection being first convey'd another Way,) and so it should be convey'd as soon as may be, to the Person that is waiting to be the Patient.

The Patient being in a warm Chamber, is to have several small Wounds made with a Surgeons three-edged Needle, or with a Lancet, in two or more Places of the Skin; (the best Places are in the Muscles of the Arm:) till some Drops of Blood follow: and immediately let there be dropt out a Drop of the Matter in the Glass, on each of the Places; and mixed well with the Blood that is issuing out. The Wound should be covered with half a Walnut-Shell, or any such concave Vessel, and bound over, that the Matter may not be rubbed off by the Garments, for a few Hours. And now, let the Patient (having Fillets on the Wounds) keep House, and keep warm, and be careful of his Diet. The Custom at Constantinople is to abstain from Flesh and Broth, for twenty Days or more.

They choose to perform the Operation, either in the Beginning of the Winter, or the Spring.

The Small-Pox begins to appear sooner in some than in others, and with lesser Symptoms in some than in others: but, with happy Success in all. Commonly ten or twenty Pustules break out: here and there one has no more than two or three; few have an Hundred. There are some in whom no Pustule rises, but in the Places where the Incision was made, and here the Tubercles will be purulent. Yet even these, have never had the Small-Pox afterwards, tho' they have cohabited with Persons having of it. No small Quantity of Matter will run out for several Days, from the Places of the Incision. The Pocks arising from this Operation, are dried up in a short Time, and fall off; partly in thin skins, and partly vanishing by an insensible Wasting.

The Matter is hardly so thick a Pus, as in the common Small-Pox; but a thinner Kind of Sanies; whence it rarely Pits; except at the Place of the Incision, where the Cicatrices are never worn out, and where the Matter is more of the common Sort.

If an Apostem should break out in any, (which is more frequent in Infants,) yet there is no Fear, for tis heal'd safely by Suppuration. . . .

Hitherto you have Nothing but History. But a little Philosophy and Speculation may be now asked for; and an Inquiry into Causes a little endeavoured. No Doubt, among the wise Men of Inquiry, three may be found, so many Men so many Minds. Every Gentleman may form his own Hypothesis; and some of the later and more modern Curiosity will try how far the vermicular Scheme will carry them thro' a Solution of these and all Appearances in this Distemper.

I have seen the Point after this pothecary Manner talk'd about. The venomous Miasms (Let that Word serve at the present) of the Small-Pox, entering into the Body, in the Way of Inspiration, are immediately taken into the Blood of the Lungs: And, I pray, how many Pulses pass before the very Heart is pierced with them? And within how many more they are convey'd into all the Bowels, is easily apprehended by all that know Anything how the Circulation of the Blood is carried on. At the same Time, the Bowels themselves are enfeebled, and their Tone impaired, by the Venom that is thus insinuated. Behold, the Enemy at once got into the very Center of the Citadel. And the invaded Party must be very strong indeed, if it can struggle with him, and after all entirely expel and conquer him. Whereas, the Miasms of the Small-Pox being admitted in the Way of Inoculation, their Approaches are made only by the Outworks of the Citadel, and at a considerable Distance from the Center of it. The Enemy, 'tis true, gets in so far as to make some Spoil, yea, so much as to satisfy him, and leave no Prey in the Body of the Patient for him ever afterwards to seize upon. But the vital Powers are kept so clear from his Assaults, that they can manage the Combats bravely and, tho' not without a Surrender of those Humours in the Blood which the Invader makes a Seizure on, they oblige him to march out the same Way he came in, and are sure of never being troubled with him any more. But perhaps the few Words that I wrote in my introducing of the Story, may be as much to the Purpose as all of this Jargon. I'll have done with it.

I durst not engage that the Success of the Trial here will be the same that has been in all the other Countrys where it has been tried hitherto, tho' we have seen it succeed well in very different climates. Nor am I sure that if it should be made upon a Body, where the Blood is already nigh upon the Point of some unhappy Fever, this may not help to set Fire to such a Thing. But I am very confident no Person would miscarry in it, but what would most certainly have miscarried upon taking the Contagion in the common Way. Wherefore, if it be made at all, (and all the Scruples that some have about the Tempting of Providence be also got over) I advise, that it be never made but under the Management of a Physician, whose Conduct may be much relied upon, and who will wisely prepare the Body for it before he perform the Operation. I have done.

I am now able, as an Eyewitness (and more than so) to give a more full Account of the Practice, which until now I could only propose as a Matter at a greater Distance.

About the Month of May, 1721, the Small-Pox being admitted into the City of Boston, I proposed unto the Physicians of the Town, the unfailing Method of preventing Death, and many other grievous Miseries, from a tremendous Distemper, by receiving and managing the Small-Pox, in the Way of Inoculation. One of the Physicians had the Courage to begin the Practice upon his own Children and Servants; and another expressed his Good Will unto it. But the Rest of the Practitioners treated the Proposal with an Incivility and an Inhumanity not well to be accounted for. Fresh Occasion I saw for the Complaint of a great Physician, "*Heus, quanto Dolore auger, dum video Naturae ministrum medicum, hostem ejus devenisse* [Alas, how my grief is increased when I see a physician, a minister of nature, has become an enemy]." The vilest

Arts were used, and with such an Efficacy, that not only the Physician, but also the Patients under the Small-Pox inoculated were in Hazard of their very Lives from an infuriated People. But I myself had thrown into my House in the dead of the Night, a fired Granado, charged with combustible Matter, and in such a Manner, that upon its going off, it must probably have killed them that were near it, and would have certainly fired the Chamber and speedily have laid the House in Ashes. But the merciful Providence of God our Saviour so ordered it, that the Granado passing thro' the Window, had by the Iron in the Middle of the Casement such a Turn given to it, that in falling on the Floor, the fired Wild-fire in the Fuse, was violently shaken out some Distance from the Shell, and burnt out upon the Floor, without firing off the Granado.

The Opposition was carried on with a Folly, and Falsehood, and Malice, hardly ever known to be parallel'd on any Occasion. And in the Progress of the Distemper many hundreds of Lives were lost, which might have been saved, if the People had not been Satanically filled with Prejudices against this *Method of Safety*. However, the Practice went on, and tho' the Physician was under extreme Disadvantages on more Accounts than one, yet he was attended with vast Success. The Experiment has now been made on several hundreds of Persons; and upon both Male and Female, both old and young, both strong and weak, both white and black, at all Seasons, of Summer and Autumn and Winter: And they have generally professed, *they had rather undergo the Small-Pox inoculated once every Year, than undergo the Small-Pox once in their Lives after the common Way, tho' sure to live. . . .*

It has been unhappily given to some few, that have already newly received the Infection in the common Way. The Eruption has then been presently made in two or three Days after the Incision, and they have undergone the Small-Pox in the common Way; hardly escaping with their Lives; tho' some have thought, the Running of the Sores in these has been some Advantage to them.

Two or three have died under or soon after the Inoculation, from a Complication of other mortal Distempers. [An Indian Servant getting a violent Cold, fell into a pleuretic Fever, that killed her. Another Person that had long been under a crazy Melancholy and Consumption, utterly refused all Sustenance and starved herself to Death.]

But of all the Hundreds that have been under a regular Management, we know not of one but what rejoices in their having undergone the Operation.

John Winthrop, Jr.

1605/6-1676

The eldest son of Governor Winthrop of Massachusetts, young Winthrop was noted for his versatility. Educated at Trinity College in Dublin, he came to New England in 1631. Winthrop was responsible for the founding of Ipswich and New London, and also served as governor of Connecticut. He has been highly acclaimed for his scientific achievements and has sometimes been called the first American scientist.

The selection below, which illustrates Winthrop's broad scientific interests, is from a letter written by him to Sir Robert Moray, January 27, 1664, reprinted in the Proceedings of the Massachusetts Historical Society, *Vol. 16 (1878).*

HARTFORD, Jan. 27, 1664

HONORABLE SIR—

*I*n my former I gave your honor an account of the favor I had of your letter by the Honorable Colonel Richard Nicolls. I then omitted to acquaint your honor what now I will be bold to add: that having looked upon Jupiter with a Telescope, upon the 6th of August last, I saw 5 [?] Satellites very distinctly about that Planet: I observed it with the best curiosity I could, taking very distinct notice of the number of them, by several aspects with some convenient time of intermission; & though I was not without some consideration whether that fifth might not be some fixt star with which Jupiter might at that time be in near conjunction, yet that consideration made me the more carefully to take notice whether I could discern any such difference of one of them from the other four, yet might by the more twinkling light of it or any other appearance give ground to believe that it might be a fixed star, but I could discern nothing of that nature: & I consider that the tube with which I looked upon them, though so good as to show very clearly the Satellites, yet was but of three foot & half with a concave eyeglass; & I question whether by a far

better tube a fixt star can be discerned so near the body of that planet when in the ever bright activity of its light, for, if so, why are there not often if not always seen with the best tubes the like or more. Is not Jupiter often in near conjunction with them, especially *in via lactea?* I have been in much doubt whether I should mention this, which would possibly be taken from a single affirmation but a mistaken novelty: but I thought I would rather bear such censure than omit the notice of it to such worthy friends as might from the hint of it take occasion to cause more frequent observations to be made upon that planet, & at least this will at length be cleared, whether the light of Jupiter doth not take away the appearance of fixed stars so near in conjunction with it, as that they should appear within the periphery of that single *intuitus* by a tube which taketh in the body of Jupiter & that at the same unmoved aspect: & I am bold the rather to mention this as an inquiry whether any such number of Satellites or moons hath been seen by your honor or Mr. Rooke or any mathematicians or other gentlemen that have good tubes & often have the curiosity to view that planet, for possibly it may be new to me which hath been more usually known by others, though the notion of such a thing is not new to myself, for I remember I met with the like narration many years since in a little book entitled *Philosophia Natur-alis* by Joh. Phociliden, though then I thought that was but a mistake of some fixed stars. An other thing I make bold to mention, upon occasion of a relation which I had lately from an understanding Seaman, that hath been Master of some vessels & often been in the West Indies (Mr. John Blackleech), he affirmed confidently that being in the Gulf of Florida he saw a great Pillar of Water (such as Commonly called Spouts) rise up from the Sea & rise higher till it joined itself to a White cloud over it. I urged it to him to be a mistake, & that it was one of those spouts (usual in the Indies & other parts) that fall from the clouds above: he confidently affirmeth it could be no mistake, his ship was near & that both himself & all in the ship with one consent judged it to rise out of the Sea. I mention not this out of any credence that it was any other than a mistake, supposing it to have been an ordinary spout falling down; yet because of his confidence in the affirmation as before upon the occasion thereof, I thought fit to commend it to your honours consideration, & the Royal Society (if you think fit), that, if they please, inquiry may be made of several Captains or Masters of Ships or other understanding Seamen that have often visited the West Indies, what the true original & manner of those Spouts are, for, however, they are of a strange nature & wonderful, & possibly there will be something reported about them & the effects of them that will be worth the knowing. Since my former I have been again at New York to give the Honorable Governor Colonel Nicolls a visit there, & left him with all there in good health & peace, & have not long since received a letter from him which signified the continuance of the same. Not far from thence upon Long Island there was last summer, at an English Plantation called Gravesend, eighteen oxen killed at once all together with lightning: & at a plantation called Stratford, as I was going last to New York, I saw a great tall oak that was stripped of so much of the bark as the breadth of four fingers from the very uppermost small top of one of the highest bows to the very bottom of the tree at the ground—that breadth I measured by my hand as high as I could reach, but by the judgment of the eye it might be narrower upward according to the proportion of the body & bows upward, but no part of the other bark, nor the body of the tree hurt by it, & all that breadth that was taken off, it was in a kind of spiral line running at least six or eight times about the tree & bows from the top bow to the root of the tree.

But I have been too prolix in these discourses, for which I presume I may have your honors excuse, & shall not add further.

J.W.

PART II

THE MIND OF THE ENLIGHTENMENT

From the viewpoint of American intellectual history, the Revolutionary period begins with Britain's defeat of France in the Seven Years' War and ends with the adoption of the Constitution. These two and a half decades witnessed the crystallization of the American Revolutionary mind, the waging of the Revolution itself, and the formation of the Union. Such momentous events provide inexhaustible and exciting materials for those studying intellectual history. For it is in these years that the American mind formulated and articulated its presuppositions and, in turn, utilized them in the destruction of one political tie and the creation of another. Never before in American history, and perhaps never since—as Professor Herbert W. Schneider observes—have public interests been so intimately linked to philosophic issues.[1]

The signing of the peace treaty between Britain and France in 1763 was a welcome event in the American colonies. The threat of French competition in the rich western fur trade was ended and a vast continent seemed ready for the colonists. But colonial rejoicing was to be short

[1] Herbert W. Schneider, *A History of American Philosophy* (New York, 1946), p. 35.

lived. Saddled with debt and facing new colonial responsibilities, Britain was already designing a new policy toward the colonies. Before a decade was over, that policy was to bring disillusionment, bitterness, discontent, and revolution to the American shores.

The changed British imperial policy began with the Sugar Act of 1764 and Stamp Act of 1765, both directed at increasing the royal treasury in London. The reaction of the colonies was immediate and bitter. They rejected the idea of direct taxes being levied by Parliament and proclaimed their opposition to such taxation in a series of resolutions and declarations of rights. As a result Parliament repealed the Stamp Act but substituted a series of revenue measures known as the Townshend Acts of 1767, which further incensed the colonies. Parliament finally repealed the Townshend Act in 1770, but at the same time it maintained the duty on tea, and thus provoked continued colonial resentment.

Few if any colonists thought in terms of ultimate independence during the early years of grievance. Yet, in retrospect, the entire period was one of inexorable movement toward separation from Britain. Indeed, the Revolution was accomplished in the years prior to 1776. In the words of John Adams, "The Revolution was effected before the war commenced. The Revolution was in the hearts and minds of the people. . . . This radical change in the principles, opinions, sentiments, and affections of the people was the real American Revolution."

To achieve "radical change" in the public opinion of America required the continual use of all available means of communication and propaganda. And the patriots successfully employed all these means—including newspapers, pamphlets, verse and songs, speeches, and even to a small extent the theater. Nor were they above the use of directed violence (aimed primarily at property, not life); and at various commemorations, such as the fifth of March addresses in remembrance of the Boston massacre, they made effective use of all the methods of persuasion. The March addresses not only were heard by many, but also were widely read in pamphlet form. Adams wrote of them that they "were read, I had almost said, by every-body that can read, and scarcely ever with dry eyes." Many orators rose to the occasion of the day, and some of them, such as Patrick Henry and Richard Henry Lee, won renown throughout the colonies.

Many of the spokesmen of the rising revolutionary consciousness were members of the professions, a fact that tended early to give a middle-class direction to American society. The legal profession contributed many leaders to the cause. As they analyzed and stated the issues of the day, lawyers like John Adams, John Dickinson, Thomas Jefferson, and James Otis provided both active political leadership and the philosophical justification needed by the revolutionary movement. The clergy, too, particularly the New England Congregationalists, gave support to political home rule as well as to church home rule as they learned to practice politics from the pulpit. Artists and writers contributed to the movement in their own ways, and wrote patriotic songs and verses that were well received throughout the colonies, though both were more stirring than aesthetically satisfying. (Only Philip Freneau and John Trumbull were poets worthy of remembrance for their poetry.) Paul Revere is best known among the artists-craftsmen who gave expression to the ideas of the day. And patriotic writers turned out a series of almanacs, newspapers, pamphlets, and books that were important in molding public opinion. The volume, the scope, and the unanimity of thought in all this material was truly impressive.

What were the ideas and sentiments that found crystallization in this material? The answer to this question may be summed up in the phrase "the American Enlightenment." The American Enlightenment refers to a cluster of ideas, and the mentality that produced them, that became more and more dominant as the colonies moved toward nationhood and that found their consummate political expression in the Declaration of Independence and—perhaps to a lesser extent—in the Constitution.

The spirit of Enlightenment was in many ways a continuous outgrowth of Puritanism, even though it was essentially a rejection of the Puritan mind. For Puritanism had emphasized, together with its theocentrism, a form of rationalism in its ethics, politics, and theology. Nature is God's *techné*, and the ways of God (or some of them) are open to rational beings. The Enlightenment, while always acknowledging the existence of God, was to move from election to Arminianism and deism; from theocracy to Nature, rights, happiness, and tolerance; and from religious to more secular virtues. It was also to become even more worldly than Puritanism in its emphasis on progress, mission, and social justice (though Puritanism, too, unlike medieval piety, had come to grips with the world). Despite these differences, a basic continuity with the Puritans remained.

But the more direct source of the spirit of Enlightenment was the scientific writing of Sir Isaac Newton and the political philosophy of John Locke. Newton had proceeded by a rational, mathematical method to demonstrate truths, or "laws," about the physical universe. Both aspects of his work became widely influential, and in fact formed the basis of much of eighteenth-century thought on both sides of the Atlantic.

The mathematical systematization of scientific thought had been the means for Newton's synthesis, which offered a picture of nature as thoroughly orderly, lawful, and rational. The Enlightenment understandably drew the implication—with hints from Newton himself—that the mathematical-scientific method could and should be used to reach secure conclusions or laws in all fields of human concern. "The great object of human endeavor," writes Professor J. H. Randall, Jr., "was to discover what in every field was natural and reasonable, and to brush aside the accretions of irrational tradition that Reason and Nature might the more easily be free to display its harmonious order."[2]

The earliest spokesmen of the scientific revolution were quick to argue that science provided the clue and the tool for improving the human species. Francis Bacon defined knowledge as power, and his campaign for science was really one to make the satisfaction of human needs a principal criterion in the field of knowledge. Others made even more explicit the optimistic views of the first apologists of science. Although they were more realistic than present-day critics of the age of reason would admit, they nevertheless did believe, in the words of Priestley, that "the human powers will, in fact, be enlarged . . . men will make their situation in this world more easy and comfortable . . . [and] communicate happiness to others. Thus, whatever was the beginning of this world, the end will be glorious and paradisaical, beyond what our imaginations can now conceive."[3] Happiness was the norm of Enlightenment ethics, and the methods and conclusions of science were the primary means to that end.

In America, the Puritans helped prepare the way for the acceptance of science. Calvinists in theory but practical Arminians in fact, the Puritans had rejected otherworldliness for activity in this world. (Thus Yankee ingenuity and American technology, too, have roots in Puritanism.) And the men of the Enlightenment furthered the acceptance of science, and indeed purified the scientific impulse by removing the Puritan's theological concern. At any rate, during the Enlightenment science and invention became dominant interests. The list of contemporary American scientists was impressive, and although a utilitarian interest sometimes dampened the pursuit of pure science, the age was generally a scientifically productive one.

The Revolutionary War also gave the Enlightenment's sanction of science a special emphasis and a sense of urgency. The prophets of science as well as the men of science—the latter perhaps less optimistically than the former, however—believed that the causes of science and liberty were inseparable and that one depended upon the other. As Jeremy Belknap was to express it, the basic desire of the Enlightenment was to make America the "Mistress of the Sciences as well as the Asylum of Liberty."

[2] John Herman Randall, Jr., *The Making of the Modern Mind* (Boston, 1940), p. 276.
[3] Joseph Priestley, *An Essay on the First Principles of Government, and on the Nature of Political, Civil, and Religious Liberty* (2nd ed., London, 1771), pp. 4–5.

This desire led in fact to proposals to organize science on a federal basis, similar to America's political structure. One must conclude with Brooke Hindle that "science was so central to the thought of the Enlightenment and it lay so directly behind the Revolutionary argument, that the men who made the American Revolution were thoroughly committed to the pursuit of science. . . . The unprecedented richness of modern America is a monument to the faith of the Revolutionary generation in the power and beneficence of science, just as its form of government is a monument to their faith in man's capacity to govern himself."[4]

The search for the reasonable and the natural also led to a scientific study of man, including his history, his religion, his ethics, and his politics. Here, too, regularities and certainties seemed available to the rational mind. The rational was taken as the natural, and the natural was the lawful. In the field of politics—most immediately important to the American colonies—the search ended in the theory of natural law.

It was at this point that the American Enlightenment learned so much from Locke. Locke's importance for the history of ideas lies in the fact that he was one of the first philosophers to develop the philosophical consequences of modern science and to show its implications for morality, religion, and politics. So pervasive was his influence that John Adams was led to remark that the Declaration of Independence was simply a recapitulation of Locke's *Second Treatise on Government*. While today we cannot be as sure as Adams was of Locke's own meaning in his political writings, or of their relation to democratic theory, or even of the precise nature of his influence on the framers of revolutionary thought, he nevertheless remains a critical figure for an understanding of the American Enlightenment.

In developing a theory of the state in harmony with Enlightenment sympathies, Locke argued that man's life in society must be governed by those regularities called the "natural law." The natural law required that men abandon outworn traditional institutions and replace them with the rational institutions of the enlightened state. Locke went even further in applying the "law of reason" to society. He argued that since there is no natural positional relation among human beings (as, for example, there is a natural spatial relation among physical substances) "hierarchies" or political aristocracies are neither natural nor inevitable. All social and political relations, including those formalized by a framework of law, are conventions men have agreed to, and so they obtain their authority solely by the consent of the individual. Likewise, religion is properly the concern of the individual himself, hence toleration not

[4] Brooke Hindle, *The Pursuit of Science in Revolutionary America* (Chapel Hill, 1956), p. 385.

theocracy, democracy not divine right, should be the rule in human society.

As we turn to the writings of the Revolutionary period, we find these philosophical ideas of the American Enlightenment forming the background of Revolutionary thought. Even the earliest protests against British policy contained references to the natural rights of men, and such rights continued to be the basis of protest up to the Declaration of Independence itself. Perhaps even more useful historically was the derivation from natural-law theory of the right of revolution, the right to reject a political order and establish a new government. This derivation was primarily the work of Jonathan Mayhew and Thomas Paine. John Adams called Mayhew's *Discourse on Unlimited Submission and Passive Obedience* the "opening gun of the Revolution." In this work, Mayhew argued against political absolutism and the theory of divine right supporting it; as his own contribution he justified the right of revolution against any king who set himself above the law. Then Paine, the supreme pamphleteer, took over as the spokesman of revolution during the decisive events of 1776. The colonies had chosen, in their appeal to mankind's common sense, to bring all institutions, including government, before the bar of reason. Should reason demonstrate the threat of such institutions to the individual, they must be altered or overturned. The themes of the Enlightenment—reason, natural rights, progress, nature, social contract, consent, individualism, liberty and equality, rational virtue—were constantly invoked in the shaping of revolutionary opinion and revolutionary action.

And yet these ideas were not without their difficulties and ambiguities. This becomes apparent as we review the events between 1776 and the inauguration of Washington in 1789. Government during these years was centered in the Continental Congress. This group proposed and adopted the Declaration of Independence, undertook the duties of a legislative and executive body charged with conducting the war, and, in 1777, drew up the Articles of Confederation which formed the basis of government until 1789.

The achievements of the Continental Congress were impressive, but once Independence had been won many leaders of the day began to see the need for "a more perfect union." The final issue of this need was the Constitution. Once again, during the debates and the well-known compromises of the Constitutional Convention, the fundamental ideas of the Enlightenment were invoked to solve the problems of historical circumstance. Truly, the very idea that men could come together to create justice, almost to begin history anew, was itself a concept of the Enlightenment.

But did the Constitutional debates—and the Constitution—hold to the ideas of the Declaration? This continues to be a much disputed point, and even the contemporaries of the Founding Fathers were divided on their views of the Constitution. Conservatives were generally satisfied that the Constitution expressed the best political thought of the day. Other observers, such as Jefferson, were disturbed that it did not limit the tenure of office of the President or contain a bill of rights. More extreme dissent was expressed by men like George Mason, who believed it was setting up at best "a moderate aristocracy" that might devolve into monarchy or "corrupt, tyrannical aristocracy."

The Bill of Rights was soon appended to the Constitution, and before a generation had passed, most Americans had come to accept the document as a wise and effective instrument of government. The problem of relating the Constitution to the philosophy of the Enlightenment became in some ways almost an academic one—partly because that philosophy, as a philosophy, was never systematically developed, and partly because, whatever its philosophical justification, the Constitution was serving the nation effectively—and the emerging pragmatism of the American mind that was to become a dominant national characteristic soon found this sufficient justification. Yet the struggles of the day—political, economic, military, legal, even moral and religious—had produced a document truly worthy of the effort, and one that continues to serve the nation not only as a basis of law and unity but also as a national symbol.

CHAPTER V

REASON AND BENEVOLENCE

*T*he Enlightenment not only used the methods of the rising sciences for the study of nature but also, as we have seen, extended those methods to the areas of ethics, law, politics, and religion. Certainties were available in all these areas, and starting with sure premises, the enlightened mind could arrive at moral as well as scientific truths. Science had given man a new method: it only remained to apply it generally. "I am bold enough to think," wrote Locke, "that morality is capable of demonstration, as well as mathematics."

The promise of science, then, was one motivation for reconsidering the problems of ethics. A second motive was the search for an ethics (and, in turn, a politics) that would be independent of the theoretical sanctions of church and state. As a prominent political theorist has observed, "Morality associated with either Catholicism or Protestantism was vitiated by that dependence. . . . As soon as Toleration prevailed, orthodoxy faded. That followed—if persecution, sorcery, etc., were wrong, then the religions that promoted them were not to be trusted. Conscience must look elsewhere."[1]

[1] G. E. Fasnacht, *Acton's Political Philosophy* (London, 1952), p. 202.

74

And conscience did look elsewhere. During the eighteenth century Europeans were reviving the ancient philosophies of Stoicism and Epicureanism—ethical systems requiring no sanction of church or state—as well as developing such autonomous systems as Francis Hutcheson's theory of moral sense and the utilitarianism of Jeremy Bentham. The separation of religion and ethics was accomplished by the early leaders of the Enlightenment. And with the rising spirit of autonomous ethical values went toleration, an ideal that found its classic expression in Locke's *Essay on Toleration.*

The ethical thought of the Enlightenment was primarily derived from the Greeks, but not wholly so. It also worked within the Judaic-Christian tradition. Consequently, its philosophical heritage included the ideal of love or benevolence as well as the Greek virtues of courage, temperance, justice, and wisdom. The Enlightenment, inspired by the rationalism of science, adopted both the method of Greek ethics and the content of Christian morality, and its ethical thinking was aimed at harmonizing these two traditions.

The philosophy of the American Enlightenment was not that of traditional Christianity. There was, to be sure, continuity between Puritan and Enlightenment virtues—a continuity supported in part by the Puritan's insistence on the intelligibility of God in terms of art and contract. But Puritan virtues were in any case not entirely orthodox, and the secularism of the day made explicit the divorce from some of the major Christian moral traditions. Professor Schneider takes this divorce to be at the heart of the American Enlightenment in general.[2]

In the selections that follow, we find these motifs of the Enlightenment. Franklin's well-known autobiography expounds a secular humanitarianism quite true to Enlightenment ideals. President Witherspoon's lectures on moral philosophy are those of an eminent Presbyterian clergyman, yet they reflect Enlightenment influence. However, it is well to remember that the American Enlightenment, unlike the French Enlightenment, never became atheistic, though in some cases its deism bore little resemblance to traditional Christianity. In Jefferson's thought we find a lifelong struggle to formulate an ethical position that would be true to the spirit of the Enlightenment yet include the "ethics of Jesus." And in the writings of Palmer we find Enlightenment sentiments at their extreme.

[2] Schneider, *op. cit.*, p. 42.

Benjamin Franklin

1706-1790

The youngest boy in a family of ten, Franklin matured early and lived to become America's first world-renowned citizen. A true symbol of the Enlightenment, he was successful in many fields, ranging from business and public affairs to theoretical science. What also distinguishes him is the relative secularization of his mind. He sought to maintain the chief Puritan virtues but to drop their theological sanctions.

The selection reprinted here is from his discussion of his own moral discipline in his widely read Autobiography, *taken from the* Memoirs of the Life and Writings of Benjamin Franklin, *6 vols. (Philadelphia, 1808–1817), vol. I.*

*I*t was about this time I conceiv'd the bold and arduous project of arriving at moral perfection. I wish'd to live without committing any fault at any time; I would conquer all that either natural inclination, custom, or company might lead me into. As I knew, or thought I knew, what was right and wrong, I did not see why I might not always do the one and avoid the other. But I soon found I had undertaken a task of more difficulty than I had imagined. While my care was employ'd in guarding against one fault, I was often surprised by another; habit took the advantage of inattention; inclination was sometimes too strong for reason. I concluded, at length, that the mere speculative conviction that it was our interest to be completely virtuous, was not sufficient to prevent our slipping; and that the contrary habits must be broken, and good ones acquired and established, before we can have any dependence on a steady, uniform rectitude of conduct. For this purpose I therefore contrived the following method.

In the various enumerations of the moral virtues I had met with in my reading, I found the catalogue more or less numerous, as different writers included more or fewer ideas under the same name. Temperance, for example, was by some confined to eating and drinking, while by others it was extended to mean the moderating every other pleasure, appetite, inclination, or passion, bodily or mental, even to our avarice and ambition. I propos'd to myself, for the sake of clearness, to use rather more names, with fewer ideas annex'd to each, than a few names with more ideas; and I included under thirteen names of virtues all that at that time occurr'd to me as necessary or desirable, and annexed to each a short precept, which fully express'd the extent I gave to its meaning.

These names of virtues, with their precepts, were: (1) TEMPERANCE. Eat not to dulness; drink not to elevation. (2) SILENCE. Speak not but what may benefit others or yourself; avoid trifling conversation. (3) ORDER. Let all your things have their places; let each part of your business have its time. (4) RESOLUTION. Resolve to perform what you ought; perform without fail what you resolve. (5) FRUGALITY. Make no expense but to do good to others or yourself: *i.e.*, waste nothing. (6) INDUSTRY. Lose no time; be always employ'd in something useful; cut off all unnecessary actions. (7)

SINCERITY. Use no hurtful deceit; think innocently and justly, and, if you speak, speak accordingly. (8) JUSTICE. Wrong none by doing injuries, or omitting the benefits that are your duty. (9) MODERA-TION. Avoid extreams; forbear resenting injuries as much as you think they deserve. (10) CLEANLINESS. Tolerate no uncleanliness in body, cloaths, or habitation. (11) TRANQUILITY. Be not disturbed at trifles, or at accidents common or unavoidable. (12) CHASTITY. Rarely use venery but for health or offspring, never to dulness, weakness, or the injury of your own or another's peace or reputation. (13) HUMILITY. Imitate Jesus and Socrates.

My intention being to acquire the *habitude* of all these virtues, I judg'd it would be well not to distract my attention by attempting the whole at once, but to fix it on one of them at a time; and, when I should be master of that, then to proceed to another, and so on, till I should have gone thro' the thirteen; and, as the previous acquisition of some might facilitate the acquisition of certain others, I arrang'd them with that view, as they stand above. Temperance first, as it tends to procure that coolness and clearness of head, which is so necessary where constant vigilance was to be kept up, and guard maintained against the unremitting attraction of ancient habits, and the force of perpetual temptations. This being acquir'd and establish'd, Silence would be more easy; and my desire being to gain knowledge at the same time that I improv'd in virtue, and considering that in conversation it was obtain'd rather by the use of the ears than of the tongue, and therefore wishing to break a habit I was getting into of prattling, punning, and joking, which only made acceptable to trifling company, I gave *Silence* the second place. This and the next, *Order*, I expected would allow me more time for attending to my project and my studies. *Resolution*, once become habi-

tual, would keep me firm in my endeavors to obtain all the subsequent virtues; *Frugality* and *Industry* freeing me from my remaining debt, and producing affluence and independence, would make more easy the practice of *Sincerity* and *Justice*, etc., etc. Conceiving then, that, agreeably to the advice of Pythagoras in his *Golden Verses*, daily examination would be necessary, I contrived the following method for conducting that examination.

I made a little book, in which I allotted a page for each of the virtues. I rul'd each page with red ink, so as to have seven columns, one for each day of the week, marking each column with a letter for the day. I cross'd these columns with thirteen red lines, marking the beginning of each line with the first letter of one of the virtues, on which line, and in its proper column, I might mark, by a little black spot, every fault I found upon examination to have been committed respecting that virtue upon that day.

I determined to give a week's strict attention to each of the virtues successively. Thus, in the first week, my great guard was to avoid even the least offence against *Temperance*, leaving the other virtues to their ordinary chance, only marking every evening the faults of the day. Thus, if in the first week I could keep my first line, marked *T*, clear of spots, I suppos'd the habit of that virtue so much strengthen'd, and its opposite weaken'd, that I might venture extending my attention to include the next, and for the following week keep both lines clear of spots. Proceeding thus to the last, I could go thro' a course compleat in thirteen weeks, and four courses in a year. And like him who, having a garden to weed, does not attempt to eradicate all the bad herbs at once, which would exceed his reach and his strength, but works on one of the beds at a time, and, having accomplish'd the first, proceeds to a second, so I should have, I hoped, the encouraging pleasure of seeing on my pages the progress I made in virtue, by clearing successively my lines of their spots, till in the end, by a number of courses, I should be happy in viewing a clean book, after a thirteen week's daily examination. . . .

It may be well my posterity should be informed that to this little artifice, with the blessing of God, their ancestor ow'd the constant felicity of his life, down to his 79th year in which this is written. What reverses may attend the remainder is in the hand of Providence; but, if they arrive, the reflection on past happiness enjoy'd ought to help his bearing them with more resignation. To Temperance he ascribes his long-continued health, and what is still left to him of a good constitution; to Industry and Frugality, the early easiness of his circumstances and acquisition of his fortune, with all that knowledge that enabled him to be a useful citizen, and obtained for him some degree of reputation among the learned; to Sincerity and Justice, the confidence of his country, and the honorable employs it conferred upon him; and to the joint influence of the whole mass of the virtues, even in the imperfect state he was able to acquire them, all that evenness of temper, and that cheerfulness in conversation, which makes his company still sought for, and agreeable even to his younger acquaintance. I hope, therefore, that some of my descendants may follow the example and reap the benefit.

It will be remark'd that, tho' my scheme was not wholly without religion, there was in it no mark of any of the distinguishing tenets of any particular sect. I had purposely avoided them; for, being fully persuaded of the utility and excellency of my method, and that it might be serviceable to people in all religions, and intending some time or other to publish it, I would not have any thing in it that should prejudice any one, of any sect, against it. I purposed writing a little comment on each virtue, in which I would have shown the advantages of possessing it, and the mischief attending its opposite vice; and I should have called my book THE ART OF VIRTUE,[1] because it would have shown the means and manner of obtaining virtue, which would have distinguished it from the mere exhortation to be good, that does not instruct and indicate the means, but is like the apostle's man of verbal charity, who only, without showing to the naked and hungry how or where they might get clothes or victuals, exhorted them to be fed and clothed.—James ii, 15, 16.

But it so happened that my intention of writing and publishing this comment was never fulfilled. I did, indeed, from time to time, put down short hints of the sentiments, reasonings, etc., to be made use of in it, some of which I have still by me; but the necessary close attention to private business in the earlier part of my life, and public business since, have occasioned my postponing it; for, it being connected in my mind with *a great and extensive project*, that required the whole man to execute and which an unforeseen succession of employs prevented my attending to, it has hitherto remain'd unfinish'd.

In this piece it was my design to explain and enforce this doctrine, that vicious actions are not hurtful because they are forbidden, but forbidden because they are hurtful, the nature of man alone considered; that it was, therefore, every one's interest to be virtuous who wish'd to be happy even in this world; and I should, from this circumstance (there being always in the world a number of rich merchants, nobility, states, and princes, who have need of honest instruments for the management of their affairs, and such

[1] Nothing so likely to make a man's fortune as virtue.

being so rare), have endeavoured to convince young persons that no qualities were so likely to make a poor man's fortune as those of probity and integrity.

My list of virtues contain'd at first but twelve; but a Quaker friend having kindly informed me that I was generally thought proud; that my pride show'd itself frequently in conversation, that I was not content with being in the right when discussing any point, but was overbearing, and rather insolent, of which he convinc'd me by mentioning several instances; I determined endeavouring to cure myself, if I could, of this vice or folly among the rest, and I added Humility to my list, giving an excessive meaning to the word.

I cannot boast of much success in acquiring the *reality* of this virtue, but I had a good deal with regard to the *appearance* of it. I made it a rule to forbear all direct contradiction to the sentiments of others, and all positive assertion of my own. I even forbid myself, agreeably to the old laws of our Junto, the use of every word or expression in the language that imported a fix'd opinion, such as *certainly, undoubtedly*, etc., and I adopted, instead of them, *I conceive, I apprehend*, or *I imagine* a thing to be so or so; or it *so appears to me at present*. When another asserted something that I thought an error, I deny'd myself the pleasure of contradicting him abruptly, and of showing immediately some absurdity in his proposition; and in answering I began by observing that in certain cases or circumstances his opinion would be right, but in the present case there

appear'd or *seem'd* to me some difference, etc. I soon found the advantage of this change in my manner; the conversations I engag'd in went on more pleasantly. The modest way in which I propos'd my opinions procur'd them a readier reception and less contradiction; I had less mortification when I was found to be in the wrong, and I more easily prevail'd with others to give up their mistakes and join with me when I happened to be in the right.

And this mode, which I at first put on with some violence to natural inclination, became at length so easy, and so habitual to me, that perhaps for these fifty years past no one has ever heard a dogmatical expression escape me. And to this habit (after my character of integrity) I think it principally owing that I had early so much weight with my fellow-citizens when I proposed new institutions, or alterations in the old, and so much influence in public councils when I became a member; for I was but a bad speaker, never eloquent, subject to much hesitation in my choice of words, hardly correct in language, and yet I generally carried my points.

In reality, there is, perhaps, no one of our natural passions so hard to subdue as *pride*. Disguise it, struggle with it, beat it down, stifle it, mortify it as much as one pleases, it is still alive, and will every now and then peep out and show itself; you will see it, perhaps, often in this history, for, even if I could conceive that I had compleatly overcome it, I should probably be proud of my humility.

Elihu Palmer

1764-1806

A brilliant student, Palmer graduated from Dartmouth in 1787. He was a militant deist, and his extreme religious liberalism made it difficult for him to procure a position. He finally became a deistic preacher as well as founder of a deistic society in New York. Palmer also was a political liberal and he hailed the Revolution as the beginning of an age of reason. He lost his sight during a yellow fever epidemic and died a short time later, exhausted from opposing the religious opinion of his day, which found his deism too extreme even for its own liberal tendencies.

The selection here is from his Principles of Nature; or a Development of the Moral Causes of Happiness and Misery among the Human Species (*New York, 1801*).

Preface

*T*he following pages have been written with a view to aid the cause of moral virtue, and extend in some small degree, the empire of human felicity. The establishment of theological systems claiming a divine origin, it is conceived, has been among the most destructive causes by which the life of man has been afflicted. History furnishes an awful picture of the fatal effects of fanaticism among the nations of the earth; but history furnishes only the exterior; there is a deeper internal wound which superstition has inflicted in the bosom of society, subversive of all moral sympathy, and of the fairest traits in the character of man. The sincerity with which many upright minds are attached to the Christian religion, can force no substantial objection against an unqualified investigation into its truth or falsehood. If it be founded in truth, it will stand the test of every examination —it will stand the test of all future ages, and become immortal. It is a point of justice to observe, that this work has been written under the misfortune and embarrassment of a total loss of sight— this, in the estimation of candid minds,

will form at least a partial apology for, verbal incorrectness, or the want of better arrangement in the construction of sentences; but it is not offered as constituting any kind of apology for errors of opinion or principle. On this head, the fullest examination is invited, and if any one can point out in what respect the principles herein advanced are inconsistent and erroneous, the author will be amongst the first to reject and condemn them.

But this must be done upon the ground of evidence, and not of authority, as the latter bears no relation to truth. The great moral and political questions which now agitate the world, cannot be settled by an appeal to the authority of law books, theological books, or the decisions of ecclesiastical councils— they rest upon the broad basis of evidence, and by this principle alone they must be determined. The circumstance that the author was once a public speaker in the cause of Christianity, which is here opposed, so far from forming a reasonable objection against the perusal of this work, ought to become an additional motive of attention; for it was by a candid and attentive investigation into the character of revealed religion, that he became convinced that it was neither true nor divine. It was therefore a duty which he owed to the integrity of his own mind, and what was deemed the best interests of human society to abandon that system, and assume a higher and better ground, that of Nature, and the immutability of her laws. If any one should be disposed to censure on this account, let him remember that there is more honor, and much more utility in the relinquishment, than in the retention of errors.

The AUTHOR

NEW YORK, May 1st. 25th Year of American Independence.

Chapter I. *The Power of Intellect, Its Duty and the Obstacles That Oppose Its Progress*

*T*he sources of hope and consolation to the human race are to be sought for in the energy of intellectual powers. To these, every specific amelioration must bear a constant and ininvariable reference, and whatever opposes the progress of such a power, is unquestionable in most pointed opposition to the best and most important interests of our species. The organic construction of man, induces a strong conclusion that no limits can possibly be assigned to his moral and scientific improvements. The question relative to the nature and substance of the human mind is, of much less consequence than that which relates to the extent of force and capacity, and the diversified modes of beneficial application. The strength of the human understanding is incalculable, its keenness of discernment would ultimately penetrate into every part of nature, were it permitted to operate with uncontrouled and unqualified freedom. It is because this sublime principle

of man, has been constantly the object of the most scurilous abuse, and the most detestable invective from superstition, that his moral existence has been buried in the gulph of ignorance, and his intellectual powers tarnished by the ferocious and impure hand of fanaticism. Although we are made capable of sublime reflections, it has hitherto been deemed a crime to think, and a still greater crime to speak our thoughts after they have been conceived. The depotism of the universe had waged war against the power of the human understanding, and for many ages successfully combated its efforts; but the natural energy of this immortal property of human existence was incapable of being controuled by such extraneous and degrading restraints. It burst the walls of its prison; explored the earth; discovered the properties of its component parts; analyzed their natures and gave to them specific clasification and arrangement. Not content with terrestrial researches, intellect abandoned the earth and travelled in quest of science through the celestial regions. The heavens were explored, the stars were counted and the revolution of the planets subjected to mathematical calculation. All nature became the theatre of human action, and man in his unbounded and ardent desire attempted to embrace the universe. Such was the nature of his powers, such their strength and fervor, that hopes and anticipations were unqualified and unlimited. The subordinate objects in the great mass of existence were decompounded, and the essential peculiarieties of their different natures deliniated with astonishing accuracy and wonderful precision. Situated in the midst of a world of physical wonders, and having made some progress in the analytical decomposition of material substances, and the relative position of revolving orbs, man began to turn his powers to the nice disquisitions of the subtle properties of his mental existence. Here the force of his faculties was opposed by the darkness and difficulties of the subject, and superstition ever ready to arrest and destroy moral improvement, cast innumerable difficulties in the way, and the bewildered mind found this part of the system of nature less accessible than the physical universe whose prominent disparities struck the understanding and presented clear discrimination. The ignorance and barbarism of former ages, it is said, furnish an awful intimation of the imbecility of our mental powers and the hopeless condition of the human race. If thought be reflected back for the purpose of recognizing through a long night of time, the miseries and ignorance of the species, there will be found, no doubt, powerful causes of lamentation; but courage will be resuscitated when the energy of intellect is displayed and the improvement of the world which has already been made, shall be clearly exhibited to view. It is not sufficient that man acknowledge the possession of his intellectual powers, it is also necessary that these powers should be developed and their force directed to the discovery of correct principle, and the useful application of it to social life; errors, evils and vices, every where exist, and by these the world has been rendered continually wretched, and the history of mankind furnishes the most dreadful lessons, and shocks the sensibility of every human being. The savage ferocity of despotism has destroyed the harmony of society; the unrelenting cruelty of superstition has cut asunder the finest fibres that ever concreted the hearts of intelligent beings. It has buried beneath its gloomy vale all the moral properties of our existence, and entombed in the grave of ignorance and terror, the most sublime energies and the purest affections of the human mind. An important duty is therefore imposed upon intellect, and a departure from its faithful performance should be ranked among the crimes which have most disgraced and injured the felicity of the world. If the few philanthrophists who have embarked in the cause of humanity, have not been adequately rewarded, it is nevertheless true that the principle and force of duty remain the same, unbroken and incapable of being abrogated. It is the discovery and propagation of truth which ought to engage the attention of man, and call forth the powerful activity of his mind.

The nature of ancient institutions, instead of forming a reason against the activity of mind, should be considered as constituting a double stimulus; these institutions are such a complete abandonment of every just and correct principle; they have been so destructive in their operation and effects, that nothing but the strong and energetic movement of the human understanding will be capable of subverting them. The whole earth has been made the wretched abode of ignorance and misery—and to priests and tyrants these dreadful effects are to be attributed. These are the privileged monsters who have subjugated the earth, destroyed the peace and industry of society, and committed the most atrocious of all robberies—that which has robbed human nature of its intellectual property leaving all in a state of waste and barrenness. Moses, Zoroaster, Jesus, and Mahomet, are names celebrated in history; but what are they celebrated for? Have their institutions softened the savage ferocity of man? have they developed a clear system of principles either moral, scientific, or philosophical? Have they encouraged the free and unqualified operation of intellect, or rather by their institutions, has not a gloom been thrown over the clearest subjects and their examination prohibited under the severest penalties? The successors and followers of these men have adhered to the destructive lessons of their masters with undeviating tenacity. This has formed one of the most powerful obstacles to the progress of improvement, and still threatens with eternal *Damnation*, that man who shall call in question the truth of their dogmas, or the divinity of their systems.

The political tyranny of the earth, coalesced with this phalanx of religious despots, and the love of science and of virtue was nearly banished from the world. Twelve centuries of moral and political darkness in which Europe was involved, had nearly completed the destruction of human dignity, and every thing valuable or ornamental in the character of man. During this long and doleful night of ignorance, slavery and superstition, Christianity reigned triumphant—its doctrines and divinity were not called in question. The power of the Pope, the Clergy and the Church was omnipotent, nothing could restrain their frenzy, nothing could controul the cruelty of their fanaticism; with mad enthusiasm they set on foot the most bloody and terrific crusades, the object of which was to recover from infidels the *Holy Land.* Seven hundred thousand men are said to have perished in the two first expeditions which had been thus commenced and carried on by the pious zeal of the Christian church, and in the total amount, several millions were found numbered with the dead—the awful effects of religious fanaticism presuming upon the aid of Heaven. It was then that man lost all his dignity, and sunk to the condition of a brute; it was then that intellect received a deadly blow from which it did not recover till the fifteenth century. From that time to the present, the progress of knowledge has been constantly accelerated; the independence of mind has been ascerted and opposing obstacles have been gradually diminished. The Church has resigned a part of her power, the better to retain the remainder; civil tyranny has been shaken to its centre in both hemispheres; the malignity of superstition is abating and every species of *quackery*, imposture and imposition are yielding to the light and power of science. An awful contest has commenced which must terminate in the destruction of thrones and civil despotism; in the annihilation of ecclesiastical pride and domination; or on the other hand, intellect, science and manly virtue, will be crushed in one general ruin, and the world will retrograde towards a state of ignorance, barbarism and misery. The latter however is an event rendered almost impossible by the discovery of the art of printing, by the expansion of mind, and the general augmentation of knowledge. Church and State may unite to form an insurmountable barrier against the extension of thought, the moral progress of nations and the felicity of nature; but let it be recollected that the guarantee for moral and political emancipation is already deposited in the archives of every school and college, and in the mind of every cultivated and enlightened man of all countries. It will henceforth be a vain and fruitless attempt to reduce the earth to that state of slavery of which the history of former ages has furnished such an awful picture. The crimes of ecclesiastical despots are still corroding upon the very vitals of human society; the severities of civil power will never be forgotten. The destructive influence of ancient institutions will teach us to seek in nature and the knowledge of her laws for the discovery of those principles whose operation alone can emancipate the world from dreadful bondage. If in the succeeding chapters we shall be able to destroy any considerable portion of human errors, and establish some solid truths, our labours will bear a relation to the progressive improvement of the human race, which to intelligent minds, is of all considerations the most beneficial and important.

Chapter XXII. Conclusion: *Reason, Science, Virtue and Happiness*

*I*n surveying the history of man, it is clearly discovered that the miseries and misfortunes of his existence, are, in a high degree the result of his ignorance, and his vices. Ignorance renders him savage and ferocious: while science pours into his mind the benign sentiments of humanity, and gives a new colouring to his moral existence. Reason, which every kind of supernatural Theology abhors—Reason, which is the glory of our nature, is destined eventually in the progress of future ages, to overturn the empire of superstition, and erect upon its ruins, a fabric, against which, the storms of despotism may beat in vain—against which, superstition may reck her vengeance without effect, from which she will be obliged to retire in agonizing tortures. It has been the opinion of some honest and intelligent minds, that the power of intellect is inadequate to the moral and political emancipation of man. This opinion, though sometimes it is found to be operative upon benevolent hearts, seems however, to be at war with the intellectual structure of our existence, and the facts furnished by modern history. In the great question which relates to human improvement, the cause which is productive of thought, cannot, in any high degree, be included as influencing the final decision. It is probable, however, that the opinion which refers intellect to organic material combination, would favour most, an unlimited improvement of the human species. If thought be an effect of matter finely organized, and delicately constructed, the best method of augmenting its power, would be, to preserve the whole human system in the most pure, regular, and natural mode of operation. Parents and

instructors, in this respect, are capable of doing great injury, or of producing most important benefits to future ages.

The Science of the world has been, in some measure, diminished by the propagation of an opinion, that there are only a few human beings who are possessed of what is called genius, to the exclusion of all the rest. This looks too much like mystery, and seems to include in it the idea that mind is sent from heaven, to occupy for a short time, a miserable and material tenement, and then return to its native home. It ought to be recollected that earth is the abode of man, and that of this the materials of his existence are composed. His energies, his powers, his existence—all are confined to this place of residence, and to the amelioration of sensitive and intelligent life, all his labours ought to be directed. He should learn to respect, and not despise his reason. He should learn to consider moral virtue, as the greatest good, as the most substantial joy of his existence. In order, however, to be eminently good, a full scope must be given to the operation of intellectual powers, and man must feel an unqualified confidence in his own energies. The double despotism of Church and State, has borne so hard upon human existence, that man is sunk beneath its dreadful weight; but resuscitated nations are about to teach kings and tyrants, a lesson awfully impressive, in regard to the destiny which awaits the aggregate injustice of the world. The period is at hand, in which kings and thrones, and priests and hierarchies, and the long catalogue of mischiefs which they have produced, shall be swept away from the face of the earth, and burried in the grave of everlasting destruction. Then will arrive the era of human felicity, in which the heart of unfortunate man shall be consoled—then will appear the moment of national consolation, and universal freedom—then the empire of reason, of science, and of virtue, will extend over the whole earth, and man, emancipated from the barbarous despotism of antiquity, will assume to himself, his true predicament in nature, and become a standing evidence of the divinity of thought, and the unlimited power of human reason.

CHAPTER VI

LIBERAL RELIGION
AND THE THEORY
OF FREEDOM

Professor Morris R. Cohen has observed that the Enlightenment's appeal to reason or nature was "simply the effort of liberal thought to examine all traditional institutions; to bring them before the bar of reason to justify themselves."[1] The men of the Enlightenment re-examined not only the principles of ethics but also those of religion and—as we have seen in Palmer's writings—the relationship between religion and the state. The results of this re-examination were twofold: the development of deism and the secular or nondenominational theory of freedom.

The writings of Locke were here, as in so much of Enlightenment thinking, the platform from which subsequent developments began. In many ways, Locke's statements on religion were in the Christian tradition: he accepted the existence of God and believed in special revelation. It was rather his basic definitions of religion and the church that departed from tradition. A church, he wrote, is "a voluntary society of men, joining themselves together of their own accord, in order to the public worshipping of God, in such a manner as they may judge acceptable to him, and effectual to the salvation of their

---

[1] Morris R. Cohen, *American Thought* (New York, The Free Press of Glencoe, 1954), p. 124.

souls." From this Locke inferred that the "care of souls is not committed to the civil magistrate, any more than to other men"; and, further, that "the care of souls cannot belong to the civil magistrate, because his power consists only in outward force: but true and saving religion is the inward persuasion of the mind, without which nothing can be acceptable to God."

In bringing religion before the "bar of reason," the American Enlightenment was aware not only of European developments but also of certain concurrent tendencies in colonial thought. John Wise and Roger Williams had already argued against theocracy, and, although their general positions were much too theological for most of the Enlightenment, their conclusions were largely acceptable. There was also some continuity between the Puritan emphasis on reason, science, and God's intelligibility and the deism of the Enlightenment. But the emphasis here should be on continuity, not identity. Deism, as it evolved, was to reject most of the specifically theological doctrines of traditional Christian teaching and to base itself on natural reason as the source of religious truth. All denominations felt the liberalizing spirit of the day, even when they rejected an explicit deism. In its extreme forms, as in the belief of men like Ethan Allen, however, deism had little in common with traditional Christianity.

Deism developed partly as an outgrowth of the Enlightenment, partly as a reaction to the excessive enthusiasm of the religious revival (the so-called Great Awakening) of the 1730's and 1740's, and partly as a response to the political needs of the day. Deism began to have significant influence in America about 1760—although it did not attain its full stature until the 1780's. Its institutional development occurred within Unitarianism; King's Chapel, Boston, in 1782 became the first church officially to preach the Unitarian faith. However, the influence of deism had appeared earlier in the realm of political thought. The establishment of the new nation, in particular, gave substance to advanced political concepts, and these, in turn, reinforced the trend toward religious freedom and toleration. This trend is reflected in the Virginia Statute of Religious Liberty, Madison's *Memorial and Remonstrance*, the First Amendment, and Jefferson's many pronouncements on religious toleration. The Enlightenment thus hoped to establish political unity without religious conformity. Though some traditional Churchmen decried it, deism not only provided a rationalistic source of religion and values but also became a political theory and a defense of religious freedom.

Jonathan Mayhew

1720-1766

Educated at Harvard, Mayhew served as pastor of West Church in Boston all his life. A liberal theologian, he was noted for his learning and industry, his political liberalism, and his support of great causes. His Discourse *seeks to justify the right of revolution by an appeal to, and reconsideration of, Scripture. It is based on the thought of Locke, Milton, Sydney, Cudworth, Clarke, and Hutcheson.*

The text is from A Discourse Concerning Unlimited Submission and Non-Resistance to the Higher Powers (*Boston, 1750*).

Text: Romans, 13, 1-8

*T*he apostle's doctrine, in the passage thus explained, concerning the office of civil rulers, and the duty of subjects, may be summed up in the following observations;[1] *viz.*,

That the end of magistracy is the good of civil society, *as such:*

That civil rulers, *as such,* are the ordinance and minsters of God; it being by his permission and providence that any bear rule; and agreeable to his will, that there should be *some persons* vested with authority in society, for the well-being of it:

That which is here said concerning civil rulers, extends to all of them in common: it relates indifferently to monarchical, republican and aristocratical government; and to all other forms which truly answer the sole end of government, the happiness of society; and to all the different degrees of authority in any particular state; to inferior officers no less than to the supreme:

That disobedience to civil rulers in the due exercise of their authority, is not merely a *political sin*, but an heinous *offence against God* and *religion:*

That the true ground and reason[2] of our obligation to be subject to the *highest powers*, is the usefulness of magistracy (when properly exercised) to human society, and its subserviency to the general welfare:

That obedience to civil rulers is here equally required under all forms of government, which answer the sole end

[1] The several observations here only mentioned, were handled at large in two preceding discourses upon this subject.

[2] Some suppose the apostle in this passage inforces the duty of submission, with *two* arguments quite distinct from each other; one taken from this consideration, that rulers are the ordinance, and the ministers of God (ver 1, 2, and 4) and the other, from the benefits that accrue to society, from civil government (ver. 3, 4, and 6). And indeed these may be distinct motives and arguments for submission, as they may be separately viewed and contemplated. But when we consider that rulers are not the ordinance and the ministers of God, but only so far forth as they perform God's will, by acting up to their office and character, and so by being benefactors to society, this makes these arguments coincide, and run up into *one* at last: At least so far, that the former of them cannot hold good for submission where the latter fails. Put the supposition, that any man bearing the title of a magistrate, should exercise his power in such a manner as to have no claim to obedience by virtue of that argument which is founded upon the usefulness of magistracy; and you equally take off the force of the other argument also, which is founded upon his being the ordinance and minister of God. For he is no longer God's ordinance and minister than he acts up to his office and character, by exercising his power for the good of society. This is, in brief, the reason why it is said above, in the *singular* number, *that the true ground and reason,* &c. The use and propriety of this remark may possibly be more apparent in the progress of the argument concerning resistance.

of all government, the good of society; and to every degree of authority in any state, whether supreme or subordinate:

(From whence it follows,

That if unlimited obedience and non-resistance, be here required as a duty under any one form of government, it is also required as a duty under all other forms; and as a duty to subordinate rulers as well as to the supreme.)

And lastly, that those civil rulers to whom the apostle injoins subjection, are the persons *in possession; the powers that be;* those who are *actually* vested with authority. . . .

I now add, farther, that the apostle's argument is so far from proving it to be the duty of people to obey, and submit to, such rulers as act in contradiction to the public good,[3] and so to the design of their office, that it proves *the direct contrary.* For, please to observe, that if the end of all civil government, be the good of society; if this be the thing that is aimed at in constituting civil rulers; and if the motive and argument for submission to government, be taken from the apparent usefulness of civil authority, it follows, that when no such good end can be answered by submission, there remains an argument or motive to enforce it; if instead of this good end's being brought about by submission, a *contrary end* is brought about, and the ruin and misery of society effected by it, here is a plain and positive reason against submission in all such cases, should they ever happen. And therefore, in such cases, a regard to the public welfare, ought to make us with-hold from our rulers, that obedience and subjection which it would, otherwise, be our duty to render to them. If it be our duty, for example, to obey our king, merely for this reason, that he rules for the public welfare (which is the only argument the apostle makes use of) it

follows, by a parity of reason, that when he turns tyrant, and makes his subjects his prey to devour and to destroy, instead of his charge to defend and cherish, we are bound to throw off our allegiance to him, and to resist; and that according to the tenor of the apostle's argument in this passage. Not to discontinue our allegiance, in this case, would be to join with the sovereign in promoting the slavery and misery of that society, the welfare of which, we ourselves, as well as our sovereign, are indispensably obliged to secure and promote, as far as in us lies. It is true the apostle puts no case of such a tyrannical prince; but by his grounding his argument for submission wholly upon the good of civil society; it is plain he implicitly authorises, and even requires us to make resistance, whenever this shall be necessary to the public safety and happiness. Let me make use of this easy and familiar *similitude* to illustrate the point in hand—Suppose God requires a family of children, to obey their father and not to resist him; and enforces his command with this argument; that the superintendence and care and authority of a just and kind parent, will contribute to the happiness of the whole family; so that they ought to obey him for their own sakes more than for his: Suppose this parent at length runs distracted, and attempts, in his mad fit, to cut all his children's throats: Now, in this case, is not the reason before assigned, why these children should obey their parent while he continued of a sound mind, namely, their *common good*, a reason equally conclusive for disobeying and resisting him, since he is become delirious, and attempts their ruin? It makes no alteration in the argument, whether this parent, properly speaking, loses his reason; or does, while he retains his

---

[3] This does not intend, their acting so in *a few particular* instances, which the best of rulers may do through mistake, &c., but their acting so *habitually*; and in a manner which plainly shows, that they aim at making themselves great, by the ruin of their subjects.

understanding, that which is as fatal in its consequences, as any thing he could do, were he really deprived of it. This similitude needs no formal application—

But it ought to be remembered, that if the duty of universal obedience and non-resistance to our king or prince, can be argued from this passage, the same unlimited submission under a republican, or any other form of government; and even to all the subordinate powers in any particular state, can be found by it as well: which is more than those who allege it for the mentioned purpose, would be willing should be inferred from it. So that this passage does not answer their purpose; but really overthrows and confutes it. This matter deserves to be more particularly considered. The advocates for unlimited submission and passive obedience, do, if I mistake not, always speak with reference to kingly or monarchical government, as distinguished from all other forms, and with reference to submitting to the will of the king, in distinction from all subordinate offices, acting beyond their commission, and the authority which they have received from the crown. It is not pretended that any person besides kings, have a divine right to do what they please, so that no one may resist them, without incurring the guilt of factiousness and rebellion. If any other supreme powers oppress the people, it is generally allowed, that the people may get redress, by resistance, if other methods prove ineffectual. And if any officers in a kingly government, go beyond the limits of that power which they have derived from the crown, (the supposed original source of all power and authority in the state) and attempt, illegally, to take away the properties and lives of their fellow subjects, they may be *forcibly resisted*, at least till application can be made to the crown. But as to the sovereign himself, he may not be resisted in any case; nor any of his officers, while they confine themselves within the bounds which he has prescribed to them.

This is, I think a true sketch of the principles of those who defend the doctrine of passive obedience and non-resistance. Now there is nothing in scripture which supports this scheme of political principles. As to the passage under consideration, the apostle here speaks of civil rulers in *general;* of all persons in *common,* vested with authority for the good of society, without any particular reference to one form of government, more than to another; or to the supreme power in any particular state, more than to subordinate powers. The apostle does not concern himself with the different forms of government.[4] This he supposes left entirely to human prudence and discretion. Now the consequence of this is, that unlimited and passive obedience, is no more enjoined

---

[4] The essence of government (I mean *good* government; and this is the *only* government which the apostle treats of in this passage) consists in the *making* and *executing of good laws*— laws attempered to the common felicity of the *governed*. And if this be, *in fact*, done, it is evidently, in itself, a thing of no consequence at all, what the *particular* form of government is; whether the legislative and executive power be lodged in *one and the same* person, or in *different* persons; whether in *one* person, whom we call an *absolute monarch;* whether in a *few*, so as to constitute an *aristocracy;* whether in *many*, so as to constitute a *republic;* or whether in *three co-ordinate branches*, in such manner as to make the government *partake* something of *each* of these forms; and to be, at the same time, *essentially different* from them all. If the *end* be attained, it is enough. But no form of government seems to be so unlikely to accomplish this *end*, as *absolute monarchy*. Nor is there any one that has so little pretence to a *divine original*, unless it be in this sense, that God *first* introduced it into, and thereby overturned, the common wealth of *Israel*, as the curse upon that people for their *folly* and *wickedness*, particularly in desiring such a government. (See I Sam. viii. chap.) Just so God, before, sent *Quails* amongst them, as a *plague*, and a *curse*, and not as a *blessing. Numb.* chap. xi.

in this passage, under monarchical government, or to the supreme power in any state, than under all other species of government, which answer the end of government, or, to all the subordinate degrees of civil authority, from the highest to the lowest. Those, therefore, who would from this passage infer the guilt of resisting kings, in all cases whatever, though acting ever so contrary to the design of their office, must, if they will be consistent, go much farther, and infer from the guilt of resistance under all other forms of government; and of resisting *any petty officer* in the state, tho' acting beyond his commission, in the most arbitrary, illegal manner possible. The argument holds equally strong in both cases. All civil rulers, as such, are the *ordinance* and *ministers of God;* and they are all, by the nature of their office, and in their respective spheres and stations bound to consult the public welfare. With the same reason therefore, that any deny unlimited and passive obedience to be here injoined under a republic or aristocrasy, or any other established form of civil government; or to subordinate powers, acting in an illegal and oppressive manner; (with the same reason) others may deny, that such obedience is enjoined to a king or monarch, or any civil power whatever. For the apostle says nothing that is *peculiar to kings;* what he says, extends equally to *all* other persons whatever, vested with any civil office. They are all, in exactly the same sense, the *ordinance of God;* and the *ministers of God;* and obedience is equally injoined to be paid to them all. For, as the apostle expresses it, *there* is NO POWER *but of God:* And we are required to *render to* ALL *their* DUES; and not MORE than that DUES. And what these *dues* are, and to *whom* they are to be *rendered*, the apostle *sayeth not;* but leaves to the reason and conscience of men to determine.

Thus it appears that the common argument, grounded upon this passage, in favor of universal, and passive obedience, really overthrows itself, by proving too much, if it proves any thing at all; namely, that no civil officer is, in any case whatever, to be resisted, though acting in express contradiction to the design of his office; which no man, in his senses, ever did, or can assert.

Thomas Paine

1737-1809

The son of a Quaker staymaker, Paine came to America in 1774, largely at the encouragement of Franklin. In 1776 he published Common Sense, *a republican document that met with instant success and was a decisive event in the Revolutionary cause. His other political works include* The Crisis *and* The Rights of Man. *Paine served the patriot cause during the American Revolution; then in 1787 he went to France where his ideas were soon to play a prominent part in the French Revolution. In 1802, he returned to America, only to find his popularity greatly diminished because of his savage indictment of religion in* The Age of Reason.*

The following selection gives his view of the relation of religion and the state. (A subsequent selection will give his general political views). The excerpt here is from Common Sense (*Philadelphia, 1776*).*

*A*s to religion, I hold it to be the indispensable duty of government, to protect all conscientious professors thereof, and I know of no other business which government hath to do therewith: let a man throw aside that narrowness of soul, that selfishness of principle, which the niggards of all professions are so unwilling to part with, and he will be delivered of his fears on that head. Suspicion is the companion of mean souls and the bane of all good society. For myself I fully and conscientiously believe, that it is the will of the Almighty, that there should be diversity of religious opinions among us. It affords a larger field for our Christian kindness: were we all of one way of thinking, our religious dispositions would want matter for probation: and on this liberal principle I look on the various denominations among us, to be like children of the same family differing only in what is called their Christian names.

Ethan Allen

1738-1789

Revolutionary soldier, author, colonel commander of the Green Mountain Boys, Allen is Vermont's favorite son and patriot. His Oracle *has been referred to as the "Vermont Bible." It represents a deistic position (although Allen professed ignorance of the creed) very similar to Paine's—so similar indeed that Allen was charged with plagiarism. This book is particularly noteworthy, since it was one of the first works published in America to oppose the Christian religion.*

This selection is from that book, Reason, The Only Oracle of Man, or a Compendious System of Natural Religion (*Bennington, Vermont, 1784*).

Argumentative Reflections on Supernatural and Mysterious Revelation in General

*T*here is not any thing, which has contributed so much to delude mankind in religious matters, as mistaken apprehensions concerning supernatural inspiration or revelation; not considering, that all true religion originates from reason, and can no otherwise be understood, but by the exercise and improvement of it; therefore they are apt to confuse their minds with such inconsistencies. In the subsequent reasonings on this subject, we shall argue against supernatural revelation in general, which will comprehend the doctrine of inspiration or immediate illumination of the mind. And first; we will premise, that a revelation consists of an assemblage of rational ideas, intelligibly arranged and understood by those to whom it may be supposed to be revealed; for otherwise, it could not exist in their minds as such. To suppose a revelation, void of rationality or understanding, or of communicating rational intelligence to those, to whom it may be supposed to be given, would be a contradiction; for that it would contain nothing except it were unintelligibleness which would

be the same as to reveal and not to reveal; therefore, a revelation must consist of an assemblage of rational ideas, intelligibly communicated to those who are supposed to have been the partakers or receivers of it; from the first supposed inspiration, down to this or any other period of time. But such a revelation as this, could be nothing more or less than a transcript of the law of nature, predicated on reason, and would be no more supernatural, than the reason of man may be supposed to be. The simple definition of supernatural is, that which is "Beyond or above the powers of nature," which never was or can be understood by mankind; the first promulgators of revelation not excepted; for such revelation, doctrine, precept or instruction only, as comes within the powers of our nature, is capable of being apprehended, contemplated or understood by us, and such, as does not, is to us incomprehensible and unknown, and consequently cannot for us compose any part of revelation.

The author of human nature impressed it with certain sensitive aptitudes and mental powers, so that apprehension, reflection or understanding could no other wise be exerted or produced in the compound nature of man, but in the order prescribed by the creator. It would therefore be a contradiction in nature,

93

and consequently impossible for God to inspire, infuse, or communicate the apprehension, reflection or understanding of any thing whatever into human nature, out of, above, or beyond the natural aptitudes, and mental powers of that nature, which was of his own production and constitution; for it would be the same as to inspire, infuse, or reveal apprehension, reflection or understanding, to that which is not; inasmuch as out of, beyond, or above the powers of nature, there could be nothing to operate upon, as a prerequisite principle to receive the inspiration or infusion of the revelation, which might therefore as well be inspired into, or revealed to nonentity, as to man. For the essence of man is that, which we denominate to be his nature, out of or above which he is as void of sensation, apprehension, reflection or understanding, as nonentity may be supposed to be; therefore such revelation as is adapted to the nature and capacity of man, and comes within his powers of perception and understanding, is the only revelation, which he is able to receive from God or man. Supernatural revelation, is as applicable to beasts, birds and fishes, as it is to us; for neither we, nor they are capable of being acted upon supernaturally, as all the possible exertions and operations of nature, which respect the natural or moral world, are truly natural. Nor does God deviate from his rectitude of nature in matters of inspiration, revelation or instruction to the moral world, any more than in that of his government of the natural. Man is a species of being who belongs in part to both worlds, therefore, was God to reveal any particular thing to us, he must of course adapt his revelation to our bodies, as well as to our souls; or to our senses as well as to our reason: but a revelation so adapted would be natural instead of supernatural. Which truly is the case respecting all our sensations, reflections and understandings. We will premise that at a future time God should superadd a sixth sense to our sensorium, and that inconceivably diverse from our present five senses, and as mysterious to us at present, as the idea of colours are to persons born blind, by which, when superadded to the other senses, we might perceive and understand such things, as at present are mysterious or supernatural to us, and which without the beforementioned sixth sense would have eternally remained so, but that sense being once added to the sensorium, would become as natural as the other senses, and the premised additional knowledge acquired by it, would be as natural as that which is produced by the instrumentality of the other five senses; so that superaddition to nature, was it possible, and a fact, would not at all contribute to evince the possibility of a supernatural revelation: so likewise admitting that God should superadd mental ability to the principle of the human soul, by which, with the five senses only, it could form simple ideas, and extend its reasonings to a far greater progression than previous to or without such additional mental ability it could have done; still the extensiveness of such supposed reasonings would be as natural, as that which may be supposed to be acquired by the previous mental powers, or that which was supposed to be acquired by the instrumentality of the sixth sense before mentioned. For if it be supposed, that either sensation or reason, or both, be ever so much enlarged by a superaddition, or the mind ever so much improved and enlarged by any and all possible methods, still progression in knowledge would not be supernatural, whether in consequence of a supposed superaddition to nature, or by the improvement of our present compounded natural powers, of sensation or reason or both. Should the perception or knowledge of colours or of sound be communicated to those who are born blind or deaf, or both, and who ever after continue to be so, such discoveries would be supernatural: as, on this position, there could have been no pre-requisite sensitive power or aptitude, which the minds of those who were supposed to be born blind or deaf, could have made use of, in acquiring the premised knowledge of colours or of sound. Therefore, when such discoveries as these are made, we must admit them to be "beyond or above the powers of nature," which is the same as supernatural; so likewise should we extend our knowledge beyond the limits of our mental capacity, or, which is the same, to understand more than we do or can understand, it would be supernatural: and when such facts as these take place in the world, it will be time enough to credit supernatural revelation. The infinitude of the wisdom of God's creation, providence and moral government will eternally remain supernatural to all finite capacities, and for that very reason we can never arrive to the comprehension of it, in any state of being and improvement whatever: inasmuch as progression can never attain to that which is infinite, so that an eternal proficiency in knowledge could not be supernatural, but on the other hand would come within the limits and powers of our nature, for otherwise such proficiency would be impossible to us; nor is the infinite knowledge of God supernatural to him, for that his perfection is also infinite. But if we break over the limits of our capacity, so as to understand any one supernatural thing, which is above or beyond the power of our natures, we might by that rule as well understand all things, and thus by breaking over the confines of finite nature and the rank of being which we hold in the universe, comprehend the knowledge of infinity. From hence we infer, that every kind and degree of apprehension, reflection and understanding, which we can attain to in any state of improvement whatever, is no

more supernatural than the nature of man, from when perception and understanding is produced, may be supposed to be so: nor has or could God Almighty ever have revealed himself to mankind in any other way or manner, but what is truly natural.

All manner of inspiration, revelation, instruction or understanding must unavoidably be denominated to be natural or supernatural, as there is no third way or medium between these two; so that if instead of the word supernatural, we adopt the word immediate, special, instantaneous, or any other phrases, yet we must be careful to affix the same definition or ideas to those several words or phraseology, as we do to the word supernatural, when applied to revelation, viz. "that which is beyond or above the powers of nature." So that when we make use of any terms whatever to define revelation, we must be sure to mean supernatural, for otherwise we should define revelation to be no more than natural, which in the opinion of some people would spoil it, and divest it of all its charms, as most believers are fond of a revelation, which they unintelligibly imagine to be supernatural, though neither they nor any body else know any thing what it is. The word *mystery*, as applied to revelation, has the same impropriety as the word supernatural. To reveal, is to make known, but for a mystery to compose any part of a revelation, is abuse; for it is the same as to reveal and not reveal at the same time; for was it revealed, it would cease to be mysterious or supernatural, but together with other parts of our knowledge would become natural. Was a revelation, like other writings, adapted to our capacity, it might like them be instructive to us; but a mysterious or supernatural one would not. For such doctrine, precept or injunction, which is unintelligible to us, the terms, positions and inferences whereof exceed our comprehension, or "concerning which our ideas are inadequate'' (which is the very definition of a mystery) cannot be so much as examined into, or contemplated upon by us, nor could a state of improvement unfold those mysterious things, for which our ideas are altogether inadequate. Such knowledge as we acquire by improvement, is that to which our capacity is inadequate, or we could not attain it. But admitting that the knowledge of a mysterious revelation may be arrived at merely by improvement, still such a revelation (though it is improper to call it so) could not be instructive, which must be the end and design of a supposed revelation, for such a premised improvement would have comprehended it as well without it as with it. For if reason has to advance its progression of knowledge, independent of any assistance from the supposed mysterious revelation, untill it is supposed to comprehend it, it would render it altogether uninstructive and useless; inasmuch as the comprehension or understanding of it is supposed to be obtained by the exercise and improvement of reason, without any assistance from the hidden mystery itself, which could not be revealed until reason, by natural improvement, came upsides with it, and by thus exploring the knowledge of a mysterious revelation, would at the same time nullify the usefulness of it. And as reason is naturally progressive in its operations, having once rivaled such revelation, would still advance its improvement beyond it, which, when reason had once surpassed, could gain no instruction therefrom, any more than it did in its previous progression in rivalling it.

CHAPTER VII

OF MEN AND GOVERNMENT

*T*o establish a new nation, conceived in liberty, became the dominant motive of the American Enlightenment by the mid 1770's. By then the Stamp Act and its successors had caused widespread dissent and occasioned declarations of natural rights like the Virginia Stamp Act Resolutions and the Reverend Jonas Clarke's "Instructions of the Town of Lexington in Relation to the Stamp Act." At the same time the volume of protest literature grew and continued to spread the seeds of rebellion and the philosophy of independence.

The thought of the Enlightenment is in many ways stated most clearly in political documents of the period. The men of reason demanded political reforms, but they invoked reason and natural law to justify such action. At hand was the philosophy of Locke, with its theory of natural rights, its social contract, and its espousal of representative government. The result was that, modified and adapted to American uses, Locke provided the basic philosophy for the new nation.

Locke's thoughts on government belong to the moralistic tradition to which later thinkers like Rousseau, Marx, and, in our own time, John Dewey also belong, namely, that political doctrines reflect a moral position and are in fact designed to promote it. Thus, for Locke, the state of nature provides a norm for man's life in society, natural rights are specifications of that norm, and the social contract is a general *moral* agreement to establish a government that will have limited functions and seek to protect natural rights. Indeed, the contract is itself largely an expression of Enlightenment values.

America's actual political experience seemed to suggest and support these values. In many of the colonies, government had been based on royal charters, which seemed to confirm the social contract doctrine. The Virginians, with their quasi-aristocratic society, had practiced a kind of limited government akin to Locke's model. And the activities of pioneers, hunters, and trappers seemed to verify the individualism of Locke's state of nature. Finding Locke confirmed in experience, the Enlightenment believed he had divined political truth. The master assumption of American political thought, the reality of atomistic social freedom, soon ceased to be an assumption and became an absolute.[1]

Lord Bryce observed that American government "is the work of men who believed in original sin and were resolved to leave open for transgressors no door which they could possibly shut. . . . The aim of the constitution seems to be not so much to attain great common ends by securing a good government as to avert the evils which will flow not merely from a bad government but from any government strong enough to threaten the pre-existing communities and individual citizens."[2] Though they might seldom use the term "original sin," the Founding Fathers, unlike some of their European contemporaries, had not basically changed their view of human nature. Government was, after all, the work of men and men cannot fully be trusted. But even this hearty Puritanism was turned to republican uses; for if men need government to curb their unruly passions, men in government cannot be trusted too much because they also have the passions of men.

Despite its emphasis on progress and science, the American Enlightenment did thus maintain a sense of realism about human nature, primarily because it viewed human nature as a constant. Progress was essentially a teleological process aiming toward a rather fixed pattern of relations insuring happiness and was to be achieved by scientific reason in its study of nature, man, and human behavior. Perhaps the words of Jefferson—among the more optimistic believers in the perfectibility of man—can be taken as a summary of the Enlightenment's tempered belief in science and progress. He wrote: "Although I do not, with some enthusiasts, believe that the human condition will ever advance to such a state of perfection as that there shall no longer be pain or vice in the world, yet I believe it susceptible of much

[1] See further Louis Hartz, *The Liberal Tradition in America* (New York, 1955).
[2] James Bryce, *The American Commonwealth*, 2 vols. (New York, 1889), vol. I, p. 306.

improvement, and most of all, in matters of government and religion; and that the diffusion of knowledge among the people is to be the instrument by which it is to be effected."[3]

More like a lawyer's brief than the Declaration, and in the opinion of some authorities, representing a conservative trend away from the spirit of the Declaration, the Constitution was constructed in response to the problems of the day as much as to the demands of a philosophy. An implicit pragmatism in the American mind is evident in the Constitutional debates and compromises. Yet its doctrines of federalism and the separation of powers nevertheless reflect Enlightenment sentiments as directly as does the Declaration itself.

[3] To Pierre Samuel Dupont de Nemours, April 24, 1816.

James Otis

1725-1783

Graduated from Harvard in 1743, Otis became a member of the bar in Boston and held many political offices. A scholar in the law and a student of the classics, he had a quick mind and was an able pleader. His Vindication *brought him much abuse, yet he struck a high note of patriotism in it. His* Rights of the British Colonies Asserted and Proved *(1764) has been called "one of the earliest and ablest pamphlets written from the natural law point of view." Indeed, in the years before the Revolution his pamphlets had more influence than those of any other American except John Dickinson, and they were of unique importance in the formation of the revolutionary mind.*

The selection given here is from A Vindication of the Conduct of the House of the Province of Massachusetts-Bay *(Boston, 1762).*

*T*he Journal stand thus, "Read and Ordered, that Mr. Otis, Mr. Tyler, Captain Cheever, Col. Clap and Mr. Witt, take said message under consideration, and report an answer thereto."

Sept. the 15th, The committee reported the following answer and Remonstrance, Viz.

May it please your Excellency,
The House have duly attended to your Excellency's message of the 11th, Instant, relating to the Massachusetts *Sloop*, and are humbly of opinion that there is not the least *necessity* for keeping up her present complement of men, and therefore desire that your Excellency would be pleased to reduce them to six, the old establishment made for said Sloop by the General Court.

Justice to our selves, and to our constituents oblige us to remonstrate against the method of making or increasing establishments by the Governor and council.

It is in effect taking from the house their most darling privilege, the right of originating all Taxes.

It is in short annihilating one branch of the legislature. And when once the Representatives of a people give up this Privilege, the Government will very soon become arbitrary.

No Necessity therefore can be sufficient to justify a house of Representatives in giving up such a Privilege: *for it would be of little consequence to the people whether they were subject to George or Lewis, the King of Great*

Britain *or the French King, if both were arbitrary, as both would be if both could levy Taxes without Parliament.*

Had this been the first instance of the kind, we might not have troubled your Excellency about it; but lest the matter should grow into precedent; we earnestly beseech your Excellency, as you regard the peace and welfare of the Province, that no measures of this nature be taken for the future, let the advice of the council be what it may.

Which being read, was accepted by a large majority, and soon after sent up and presented to his Excellency by Captain Goldthwait, Mr. Otis, Captain Taylor, Mr. Cushing and Mr. Bordman.

The same day the above remonstrance was delivered, the Town was alarmed with a report that the House had sent a message to his Excellency reflecting upon his Majesty's person and government, and highly derogatory from his crown and dignity, and therein desired that his Excellency would in no case take the advice of his majesty's council. About five of the clock P.M. the same day Mr. *Speaker* communicated to the house a Letter from the Governor of the following purport.

SIR,
I have this morning received a message from the house, which I here inclose, in

which the King's name, dignity, and cause, are so improperly treated, that I am obliged to desire you to recommend earnestly to the house, that it may not be entered upon the Minutes in the terms it now stands. For if it should, I am satisfied that you will again and again wish some parts of it were expunged; especially if it should appear, as I doubt not but it will, when I enter upon my vindication, that there is not the least ground for the insinuation under colour of which that sacred and well-beloved name is so disrespectfully brought into Question.

Your's, &c.
Fra: Bernard

September 15th. To the Honourable Speaker of the House of Representatives

Upon the reading of this letter, it was moved to insert these words, to wit, "with all due reverence to Majesty's sacred Person and Government, to both which we profess the sincerest attachment and loyalty be it spoken" "it would be of little importance," &c. But a certain member crying "*Rase them*," "*Rase them*,"[1] the proposed amendment was dropped, it being obvious, that the

remonstrance would be the same in effect, with or without the words excepted against. These dreadful words, under which his Excellency had placed a black mark, were accordingly erased and expunged, and the Message returned to the Speaker.

In the course of the debate a new and surprizing doctrine was advanced. We have seen the times when the majority of a council by their words and actions have seemed to think themselves obliged to comply with every Thing proposed by the Chair, and to have no rule of conduct but a Governor's will and pleasure. But now for the first time, it was asserted that the Governor in all cases was obliged to act according to the advice of the council, and consequently would be deemed to have no Judgment of his own.

In order to excuse if not altogether justify the offensive Passage, and clear it from ambiguity, I beg leave to premise two or three *data*.[2] (1) God made all men naturally equal. (2) The ideas of earthly

[1] Meaning that part of the remonstrance which is in Italic.

[2] The natural liberty of man is to be free from any superior power on earth, and not to be under the will or legislative authority of man; but to have only the law of nature for his rule. The liberty of man in society, is to be under no other legislative power, but that established by consent in the common wealth; nor under the dominion of any will, or restraint of any law, but what that legislature shall enact according to the trust put in it. Freedom is not what Sir *Robert Filmer* tells us, O. A. 55. A liberty for every one to do what he lists, to live as he pleases, and not to be tied by any laws. But freedom of men under government, is to have a standing rule to live by, common to every one of that society, and made by the legislative power erected in it; a liberty to follow my own will in all things where that rule prescribes not, and not to be subject to the unknown, unconstant, uncertain, arbitrary will of another man; a freedom of nature is to be under no restraint but the law of nature. This freedom from absolute arbitrary power, is so necessary to, and closely joined with a man's preservation, that he cannot part with it but by what forfeits his preservation & life together. For a man not having power over his own life, cannot by compact or his own consent enslave himself to any one, nor put himself under the absolute, arbitrary power of another, to take away his life when he pleases: no body can give more power than he has himself. He that cannot take away his own life, cannot give another power over it. Locke's *Discourse on Govern't.* Part II. Ch. IV.

The legislative, whether placed in one or more, whether it be always in being, or only by intervals, though it be the supreme power in every common-wealth, yet in the utmost bounds of it, it is limited to the public good of the society, it is a power that hath no end but preservation; and those can never have a right to destroy, enslave or designedly to impoverish the subjects.

These are the bounds to which the trust that is put in them, by the Society, and the laws of God and nature, have set to the legislative power of every common wealth, in all forms of government.

First, They are to govern by established promulgated laws, not to be varied in particular cases; but to have one rule for rich and poor, and for the favourite at court, and the countryman at plough.

superiority, pre-eminence and grandeur are educational, at least acquired, not innate. (3) Kings were (and plantation Governor's should be) made for the good of the people, and not the people for them. (4) No government has a right to make hobby horses, asses and slaves of the subject, nature having made sufficient of the two former, for all the lawful purposes of man, from the harmless peasant in the field, to the most refined politician in the cabinet; but none of the last, which infallibly proves they are unnecessary. (5) Tho' most governments are *de facto* arbitrary, and consequently the curse and scandal of human nature; yet none are *de jure* arbitrary. (6) The British constitution of government as now established in his Majesty's person and family, is the wisest and best in the world. (7) The King of Great Britain is the best as well as most glorious Monarch upon the Globe, and his subjects the happiest in the universe. (8) It is most humbly presumed the King would have all his plantation Governors follow his royal example, in a wise and strict adherence to the principles of the British constitution, by which in conjunction with his other royal virtues, he is enabled to reign in the hearts of a brave and generous, free and loyal people. (9) This is the summit, the *ne plus ultra* of human glory and felicity. (10) The French King is a despotic arbitrary prince, and consequently his subjects are very miserable.

Let us now take a more careful review of this passage, which by some out of doors has been represented as seditious,

Secondly, These laws ought to be designed for no other end ultimately, but the good of the people.

Thirdly, They must not raise taxes on the property of the people, without the consent of the people, given by themselves or deputies.

Fourthly, The legislature neither must nor can transfer the power of making laws to any body else, nor place it any where but where the people have. *Id*. Ch. XI.

Where the legislative and executive power are in distinct hands, as they are in all moderated monarchies and well formed governments, there the good of the society requires that several things should be left to the discretion of him that has the supreme executive power. This power to act according to discretion for the public good, without the prescription of Law, and sometimes even against it, is that which is called PREROGATIVE.

This power, while employed for the benefit of the community, and suitably to the trust and ends of government, is undoubted Prerogative, and never is questioned. For the people are very seldom or never scrupulous or nice in the point, they are far from examining Prerogative whilst it is in any tolerable degree employed for the use it was meant, that is, for the good of the people, and not manifestly against it. But if there comes to be a question between the executive power and the people, about a thing claimed as a prerogative, the tendency of the exercise of such prerogative to the good or hurt of the people, will easily decide the question. Prerogative is nothing but the power of doing public good without a rule. The old question will be asked in this matter of Prerogative, but who shall be judge when this power is made a right use of? I answer, between an executive power in being with such prerogative, and a legislative, that depends upon his will, for their convening, there can be no judge on earth, as there can be none between the legislative and the people. Should either the executive or legislative, when they have got this power in their hands, design or go about to destroy them, the people have no other remedy in this, as in other cases, when they have to judge upon earth, but to appeal to heaven. Nor let any one think that this lays a perpetual foundation for disorder, for this operates not 'till the inconveniency is so great that the majority feel it, and are weary of it, and find a necessity to have it amended. But this the executive power or wise Princes never need come in the danger of; and it is the thing of all others, they have most need to avoid; as of all others the most perilous. *Id*. Ch. XIV.

"Fatherly authority, or a right of fatherhood in our Author's sense (i.e. Sir *Robert Filmer*) is a divine unalterable right of sovereignty, whereby a Father, or a Prince, (and a Governor might have been added) hath an absolute, arbitrary, unlimited, & unlimitable power over the lives, liberties and estates of his children and subjects: so that he may take or alienate their estates, sell, castrate or use their persons as he pleases, they being all his slaves, and he Lord Proprietor of every thing, and his unbounded will their law." *Locke on Govt.* B. I. Ch. II.

rebellious and traiterous. I hope none however will be so wanting to the interests of their country, as to represent the matter in this light on the east side of the Atlantic, tho' recent instances of such a conduct might be quoted, wherein the province has after its most strenuous efforts, during this and other wars, been painted in all the odious colours that avarice, malice and the worst passions could suggest.

The house assert, that "it would be of little consequence to the people, whether they were subject to George or Lewis, the King of Great Britain or the French King, if both were arbitrary, as both would be, if both could levy taxes without parliament." Or in the same words transposed without the least alteration of the sense.

It would be of little consequence to the people whether they were subject to George the King of Great Britain, or Lewis the French King, if both were arbitrary, as both would be, if both could levy taxes without parliament.

The first question that would occur to a philosopher, if any question could be made about it, would be whether the position were true. But truth being of little importance with most modern politicians, we shall touch lightly upon that topic, and proceed to inquires of a more interesting nature.

That arbitrary government implies the worst of temporal evils, or at least the continual danger of them is certain. That a man would be pretty equally subjected to these evils under every arbitrary government, is clear. That I should die very soon after my head should be cut off, whether by a sabre or a broad sword, whether chopped off to gratify a tyrant by the christian name of

---

"He that will not give just occasion to think that all government in the world is the product only of force and violence, and that men live together by no other rules but that of beasts, where the strongest carries it, and so lay a foundation for perpetual disorder, mischief, tumult, sedition and rebellion, (things that the followers of that hypothesis, i.e. *Filmer*, and the advocates for passive obedience, so loudly cry out against) must of necessity find out another rise of government, another original of political power, and another way of designing and knowing the persons that have it, than what Sir *R. Filmer* hath taught us." *Locke on Govt.* B. II. Ch. II.

This other original Mr. *Locke* has demonstrated to be the consent of a free people. It is possible there are a few, and I desire to thank God there is no reason to think there are many among us, that can't bear the names of LIBERTY and PROPERTY, much less that the things signified by those terms, should be enjoyed by the vulgar. These may be inclined to brand some of the principles advanced in the vindication of the house, with the odious epithets *seditious* and *levelling*. Had any thing to justify them been quoted from Col. *Algernon, Sidney*, or other British Martyrs, to the liberty of their country, an outcry of rebellion would not be surprising. The authority of Mr. *Locke* has therefore been preferred to all others, for these further reasons, (1) He was not only one of the most wise, as well as most honest, but the most impartial man that ever lived. (2) He professedly wrote his discourses on Government, as he himself expresses it, "To establish the throne of the great restorer king *William*, to make good his title in the consent of the people, which being the only one of all lawful governments, he had more fully and clearly, than any Prince in christendom, and to justify to the world, the people of England whose love of liberty, their just and natural rights, with the resolution to preserve them, saved the nation when it was on the brink of slavery and ruin." By this title, our Illustrious Sovereign GEORGE the III. (whom GOD long preserve) now holds. (3) Mr. *Locke* was as great an ornament, under a crown'd head, as the church of England ever had to boast off. Had all her sons been of his wise, moderate, tolerant principles, we should probably never have heard of those civil dissensions that have so often brought the nation to the borders of perdition. Upon the score of his being a Churchman however, his sentiments are less liable to the invidiuous reflections and insinuations that High flyers, Jacobites, and other stupid Bigots, are apt too liberally to bestow, not only upon Dissenters of all denominations, but upon the moderate; and therefore infinitely the most valuable part of the Church of England itself.

Tom, Dick or *Harry* is evident. That the name of the tyrant would be of no more avail to save my life than the name of the executioner, needs no Proof. It is therefore manifestly of no importance what a prince's christian name is, if he be arbitrary, any more, indeed, than if he were not arbitrary. So the whole amount of this dangerous proposition may at least in one view be reduced to this, viz. *It is of little importance what a King's christian name is.* It is indeed of importance that a King, a Governor, and all other good christians should have a christian name, but whether Edward, Francis or William, is of none, that I can discern. It being a rule to put the most mild and favourable construction upon words that they can possibly bear, it will follow that this proposition is a very harmless one, that cannot by any means tend to prejudice his Majesty's Person, Crown, Dignity or Cause, all which I deem equally sacred with his Excellency.

If this proposition will bear an hundred different constructions, they must all be admitted before any that imports any bad meaning, much more a treasonable one.

It is conceived the house intended nothing disrespectful of His Majesty, his Government or Governor, in those words. It would be very injurious to insinuate this of a house that upon all occasions has distinguished itself by a truly loyal spirit, and which spirit possesses at least nine hundred and ninety-nine in a thousand of their constituents throughout the province. One good natured construction at least seems to be implied in the assertion, and that pretty strongly, viz. that in the present situation of Great Britain and France, it is of vast importance to be a Briton, rather than a Frenchman; as the French King is an arbitrary despotic Prince; but the King of Great Britain is not so *de jure, de facto,* nor by *inclination;* a greater difference on this side the *Grave* cannot be found, than that which sub-

sists between British subjects, and the slaves of tyranny.

Perhaps it may be objected that there is some difference even between arbitrary Princes in this respect at least, that some are more rigorous than others. It is granted, but then let it be remembered, that the life of man is as a vapour that soon vanisheth away, and we know not who may come after him, a wise man or a fool; tho' the chances before and since Solomon, have ever been in favour of the latter. Therefore it is said of little consequence. Had it been *No* instead of *little,* the clause upon the most rigid stricture might have been found barely exceptionable.

Some fine Gentlemen have charged the expression as indelicate. This is a capital impeachment in politics, and therefore demands our most serious attention. The idea of delicacy in the creed of some politicians, implies that an inferior should at the peril of all that is near and dear to him (i.e. his interest) avoid every the least trifle that can offend his superior. Does my superior want my estate? I must give it him, and that with a good grace, which is appearing, and if possible being really obliged to him that he will condesend to take it. The reason is evident; it might give him some little pain or uneasiness to see me whimpering, much more openly complaining at the loss of a little glittering dirt. I must according to this system not only endeavour to acquire my self, but impress upon all around me a reverence and *passive obedience* to the sentiments of my superior, little short of adoration. Is the superior in contemplation a king, I must consider him as God's vicegerent, cloathed with unlimited power, his will the supreme law, and not accountable for his actions, let them be what they may, to any tribunal upon earth. Is the superior a plantation governor? he must be viewed not only as the most excellent representation of majesty, but as a viceroy in his department, and *quoad* provincial administration, to all intents and purposes vested with all the prerogatives that were ever exercised by the most absolute prince in Great Britain.

The votaries of this sect are all Monopolizers of offices, Peculators, Informers, and generally the Seekers of all kinds. It is better, say they, "to give up any thing, and every thing quietly, than contend with a superior, who by his prerogative can do, and (as the vulgar express it) right or wrong, will have whatever he pleases." For you must know, that according to some of the most refined and fashionable systems of modern politics, the ideas of right and wrong, and all the moral virtues, are to be considered only as the vagaries of a weak or distempered imagination in the possessor, and of no use in the world, but for the skilful politician to convert to his own purposes of power and profit.

With these,

The Love of Country is an empty Name,
For Gold they hunger: but n'er thirst for Fame.

It is well known that the least "patriotic spark" unawares "catched," and discovered, disqualifies a candidate from all further preferment in this famous and flourishing order of knights errant. It must however be confessed they are so catholic as to admit all sorts from the knights of the post to a garter and Star; provided they are thoroughly divested of the fear of God, and the love of mankind, and have concentrated all their views in *dear self*, with them the only "sacred and well-beloved name," or thing in the universe. See Cardinal Richlieu's *Political Testament*, and the greater Bible of the Sect, Mandeville's *Fable of the Bees*. Richlieu expressly in solemn earnest, without any sarcasm or irony, advises the discarding all honest men from the presence of a prince, and from even the purlious of a court. According to Mandeville, "*The* moral virtues are the political offspring which flattery begot upon pride." The most darling principle of the great Apostle of the order, who has done more than any mortal towards diffusing corruption, not only thro' the three kingdoms, but thro' the remotest dominions, is, "that every man has his price, and that if you bid high enough, you are sure of him."

To those who have been taught to bow at the name of a King, with as much ardor and devotion as a papist at the sight of a crucifix, the assertion under examination may appear harsh; but there is an immense difference between the sentiments of a British house of commons remonstrating, and those of a courtier cringing for a favour. A house of Representatives here at least, bears an equal proportion to a Governor, with that of a house of Commons to the King. There is indeed one difference in favour of a house of Representatives; when a house of Commons address the King they speak to their Sovereign, who is truly the most august Personage upon earth: When a house of Representatives remonstrate to a Governor, they speak to a fellow subject; tho' a superior, who is undoubtedly entitled to decency and respect; but I hardly think to quite so much Reverence as his master.

It may not be amiss to observe, that a form of speech may be, in so sort improper, when used *arguendo*, or for illustration, speaking of the King, which same form might be very harsh, indecent and even ridiculous, if spoken to the King.

The expression under censure has had the approbation of diverse Gentlemen of sense, who are quite unprejudiced by any party. They have taken it to imply a compliment rather than any indecent reflection, upon his Majesty's wise and gracious administration. It seems strange therefore that the house should be so suddenly charged by his Excellency with *Impropriety*, *groundless Insinuations*, &c.

What cause of so bitter Repentance, *again* and *again*, could possibly have taken place, if this clause had been printed in the Journal, I can't imagine. If the case be fairly represented, I guess the province can be in no danger from a house of Representatives daring to speak plain English, when they are complaining of a grievance. I sincerely believe the house had no disposition to enter into any contest with the Governor or Council. Sure I am that the promoters of this address had no such view.

On the contrary, there is the highest reason to presume that the house of Representatives will at all times rejoice in the prosperity of the Governor and Council, and contribute their utmost assistance, in supporting those two branches of the legislature, in all their just rights and preheminence. But the house is and ought to be jealous and tenacious of its own priviledges; these are a sacred deposit intrusted by the people, and the jealousy of them is a godly jealousy.

Samuel Adams

1722-1803

Revolutionary statesman and author, Sam Adams was said to have had but one occupation, public business. A graduate of Harvard, he soon became a leading figure in Massachusetts politics, and represented that colony as a delegate to the Continental Congress. He was a skillful polemic writer and continued the natural law philosophy that began in America with John Wise and found consummate expression in the Declaration of Independence. He has been called "the Father of the American Revolution."

This selection is from The Rights of the Colonists (*Old South Leaflets: n. p., n. d.*), *vol. VII.*

Report of the Committee of Correspondence to the Boston Town Meeting, Nov. 20, 1772

I. Natural Rights of the Colonists as Men

*A*mong the natural rights of the Colonists are these: *First, a right* to life; *Secondly*, to liberty; *Thirdly*, to property; together with the right to support and defend them in the best manner they can. These are evident branches of, rather than deductions from, the duty of self-preservation, commonly called the first law of nature.

All men have a right to remain in a state of nature as long as they please; and in case of intolerable oppression, civil or religious, to leave the society they belong to, and enter into another.

When men enter into society, it is by voluntary consent; and they have a right to demand and insist upon the performance of such conditions and previous limitations as form an equitable *original compact.*

Every natural right not expressly given up, or, from the nature of a social compact, necessarily ceded, remains.

All positive and civil laws should conform, as far as possible, to the law of natural reason and equity.

As neither reason requires nor religion permits the contrary, every man living in or out of a state of civil society has a right peaceably and quietly to worship God according to the dictates of his conscience.

"Just and true liberty, equal and impartial liberty," in matters spiritual and temporal, is a thing that all men are clearly entitled to by the eternal and immutable laws of God and nature, as well as by the law of nations and all well-grounded municipal laws, which must have their foundation in the former.

In regard to religion, mutual toleration in the different professions thereof is what all good and candid minds in all ages have ever practised, and, both by precept and example, inculcated on mankind. And it is now generally agreed among Christians that this spirit of toleration, in the fullest extent consistent with the being of civil society, is the chief characteristic mark of the Church.[1] Insomuch that Mr. Locke has asserted and proved, beyond the pos-

[1] See Locke's Letters on Toleration.

sibility of contradiction on any solid ground, that such toleration ought to be extended to all whose doctrines are not subversive of society. The only sects which he thinks ought to be, and which by all wise laws are excluded from such toleration, are those who teach doctrines subversive of the civil government under which they live. The Roman Catholics or Papists are excluded by reason of such doctrines as these, that princes excommunicated may be deposed, and those that they call heretics may be destroyed without mercy; besides their recognizing the Pope in so absolute a manner, in subversion of government, by introducing, as far as possible into the states under whose protection they enjoy life, liberty, and property, that solecism in politics, *imperium in imperio*, leading directly to the worst anarchy and confusion, civil discord, war, and bloodshed.

The natural liberty of man, by entering into society, is abridged or restrained, so far only as is necessary for the great end of society, the best good of the whole.

In the state of nature every man is, under God, judge and sole judge of his own rights and of the injuries done him. By entering into society he agrees to an arbiter or indifferent judge between him and his neighbors; but he no more renounces his original right than by taking a cause out of the ordinary court of law, and leaving the decision to referees or indifferent arbitrators. In the last case, he must pay the referees for time and trouble. He should also be willing to pay his just quota for the support of government, the law, and the constitution; the end of which is to furnish indifferent and impartial judges in all cases that may happen, whether civil, ecclesiastical, marine, or military.

The *natural* liberty of man is to be free from any superior power on earth,

² Locke on Government.

and not to be under the will or legislative authority of man, but only to have the law of nature for his rule.²

In the state of nature men may, as the patriarchs did, employ hired servants for the defence of their lives, liberties, and property; and they should pay them reasonable wages. Government was instituted for the purpose of common defence, and those who hold the reins of government have an equitable, natural right to an honorable support from the same principle that "the laborer is worthy of his hire." But then the same community which they serve ought to be the assessors of their pay. Governors have no right to seek and take what they please; by this, instead of being content with the station assigned them, that of honorable servants of the society, they would soon become absolute masters, despots, and tyrants. Hence, as a private man has a right to say what wages he will give in his private affairs, so has a community to determine what *they* will give and grant of their substance for the administration of public affairs. And, in both cases, more are ready to offer their service at the proposed and stipulated price than are able and willing to perform their duty.

In short, it is the greatest absurdity to suppose it in the power of one, or any number of men, at the entering into society, to renounce their essential natural rights, or the means of preserving those rights; when the grand end of civil government, from the very nature of its institution, is for the support, protection, and defence of those very rights; the principal of which, as is observed, are Life, Liberty, and Property. If men, through fear, fraud, or mistake, should in terms renounce or give up any essential natural right, the eternal law of reason and the grand end of society would absolutely vacate such renunciation. The right to freedom being the gift of God Almighty, it is not in the power of man to alienate this gift and voluntarily become a slave.

II. *The Rights of the Colonists as Christians*

*T*hese may be best understood by reading and carefully studying the institutes of the great Law Giver and Head of the Christian Church, which are to be found clearly written and promulgated in the New Testament.

By the act of the British Parliament, commonly called the Toleration Act, every subject in England, except Papists, &c., was restored to, and re-established in, his natural right to worship God according to the dictates of his own conscience. And, by the charter of this Province, it is granted, ordained, and established (that is, declared as an original right) that there shall be liberty of conscience allowed in the worship of God to all Christians, except Papists, inhabiting, or which shall inhabit or be resident within, such Province or Territory.[3] Magna Charta itself is in substance but a constrained declaration or proclamation and promulgation in the name of the King, Lords, and Commons, of the sense the latter had of their original, inherent, indefeasible natural rights,[4] as also those of free citizens equally perdurable with the other. That great author, that great jurist, and even that court writer, Mr. Justice Blackstone, holds that this recognition was justly obtained of King John, sword in hand. And peradventure it must be one day, sword in hand, again rescued and preserved from total destruction and oblivion.

III. *The Rights of the Colonists as Subjects*

A commonwealth or state is a body politic, or civil society of men, united together to promote their mutual safety and prosperity by means of their union.[5]

The absolute rights of Englishmen and all freemen, in or out of civil society, are principally personal security, personal liberty, and private property.

All persons born in the British American Colonies are, by the laws of God and nature and by the common law of England, exclusive of all charters from the Crown, well entitled, and by acts of the British Parliament are declared to be entitled, to all the natural, essential, inherent, and inseparable rights, liberties, and privileges of subjects born in Great Britain or within the realm. Among those rights are the following, which no man, or body of men, consistently with their own rights as men and citizens, or members of a society, can for themselves give up or take away from others.

First, "The first fundamental, positive law of all commonwealths or states is the establishing the legislative power. As the first fundamental *natural* law, also, which is to govern even the legislative power itself, is the preservation of the society."[6]

Secondly, The Legislative has no right to absolute, arbitrary power over the lives and fortunes of the people; nor can mortals assume a prerogative not only too high for men, but for angels, and therefore reserved for the exercise of the Deity alone.

"The Legislative cannot justly assume to itself a power to rule by extempore

---

[3] See 1 Wm. and Mary, St. a, c. 18, and Massachusetts Charter.

[4] Lord Coke's inst. Blackstone's Commentaries, VI. p. 122. The Bill of Rights and the Act of Settlement.

[5] See Locke and Vattel.

[6] Locke on Government. *Salus populi suprema lex esto.* [Let the welfare of the people be the supreme law.]

arbitrary decrees; but it is bound to see that justice is dispensed, and that the rights of the subjects be decided by promulgated, standing, and known laws, and authorized *independent judges*"; that is, independent, as far as possible, of Prince and people. "There should be one rule of justice for rich and poor, for the favorite at court, and the country-man at the plough."[7]

Thirdly, The supreme power cannot justly take from any man any part of his property, without his consent in person or by his representative.

These are some of the first principles of natural law and justice, and the great barriers of all free states and of the British Constitution in particular. It is utterly irreconcilable to these principles and to many other fundamental maxims of the common law, common sense, and reason that a British House of Commons should have a right at pleasure to give and grant the property of the Colonists. (That the Colonists are well entitled to all the essential rights, liberties, and privileges of men and free-men born in Britain is manifest not only from the Colony charters in general, but acts of the British Parliament.) The statute of the 13th of Geo. 2, c. 7, naturalizes even foreigners after seven years' residence. The words of the Massachusetts charter are these: "And further, our will and pleasure is, and we do hereby for us, our heirs, and succes-sors, grant, establish, and ordain, that all and every of the subjects of us, our heirs, and successors, which shall go to, and inhabit within our said Province or Territory, and every of their children, which shall happen to be born there or on the seas in going thither or returning from thence, shall have and enjoy all liberties and immunities of free and natural subjects within any of the dominions of us, our heirs, and suc-cessors, to all intents, constructions, and purposes whatsoever, as if they and every one of them were born within this our realm of England."

Now what liberty can there be where property is taken away without consent? Can it be said with any color of truth and justice, that this continent of three thousand miles in length, and of a breadth as yet unexplored, in which, however, it is supposed there are five millions of people, has the least voice, vote, or influence in the British Parlia-ment? Have they all together any more weight or power to return a single mem-ber to that House of Commons who have not inadvertently, but deliberately, assumed a power to dispose of their lives, liberties, and properties, than to choose an Emperor of China? Had the Colonists a right to return members to the British Parliament, it would only be hurtful; as, from their local situation and circumstances, it is impossible they should ever be truly and properly repre-sented there. The inhabitants of this country, in all probability, in a few years, will be more numerous than those of Great Britain and Ireland together; yet it is absurdly expected by the promoters of the present measures that these, with their posterity to all generations, should be easy, while their property shall be disposed of by a House of Commons at three thousand miles' distance from them, and who cannot be supposed to have the least care or concern for their real interest; who have not only no natural care for their interest, but must be *in effect* bribed against it, as every burden they lay on the Colonists is so much saved or gained to themselves. Hitherto, many of the Colonists have been free from quit rents; but if the breath of a British House of Commons can originate an act for taking away all our money, our lands will go next, or be subject to rack rents from haughty and relentless landlords, who will ride at ease, while we are trodden in the dirt. The Colonists have been branded with the odious names of traitors and rebels only for complaining of their grievances. How long such treatment will or ought to be borne, is submitted.

[7] Locke.

Thomas Paine

1737-1809

The popular influence of Paine's Common Sense *can hardly be over-estimated. It presented the revolutionary arguments with moving force and brought the young nation some unanimity of opinion. Arguing that society is a good but government a necessary evil, Paine moves to the Enlightenment ideals of consent of the governed and natural rights. He seeks also to show the impossibility of the colonies remaining under the rule of the British monarch.*

The text of the selection is from Common Sense (*Philadelphia, 1776*). [*For Paine's career, see p. 92.*]

Of the Origin and Design of Government *in General, with Concise Remarks on the* English Constitution

Some writers have so confounded society with government, as to leave little or no distinction between them; whereas, they are not only different, but have different origins. Society is produced by our wants, and government by our wickedness; the former promotes our happiness *positively* by uniting our affections, the latter *negatively* by restraining our vices. The one encourages intercourse, the other creates distinctions. The first is a patron, the last a punisher.

Society in every state is a blessing, but Government even in its best state is but a necessary evil; in its worst state an intolerable one: for when we suffer, or are exposed to the same miseries by *a Government*, which we might expect in a country *without Government*, our calamity is heightened by reflecting that we furnish the means by which we suffer. Government like dress is the badge of lost innocence, the palaces of kings are built on the ruins of the bowers of paradise. For were the impulses of conscience clear, uniform, and irresistibly obeyed, man would need no other law-giver; but that not being the case, he finds it necessary to surrender up a part of his property to furnish means for the protection of the rest; and this he is induced to do, by the same prudence which in every other case advises him, out of two evils to choose the least. *Wherefore*, security being the true design and end of government, it unanswerably follows, that whatever *form* thereof appears most likely to ensure it to us, with the least expence and greatest benefit, is preferable to all others.

In order to gain a clear and just idea of the design and end of government, let us suppose a small number of persons settled in some sequestered part of the earth, unconnected with the rest; they will then represent the first peopling of any country, or of the world. In this state of natural liberty, society will be their first thought. A thousand motives will excite them thereto, the strength of one man is so unequal to his wants, and his mind so unfitted for perpetual solitude, that he is soon obliged to seek assistance and relief of another, who in his turn requires the same. Four or five united would be able to raise a tolerable dwelling in the midst of a wilderness, but *one* man might labour out the common period of life without accomplishing any thing; when he had felled his timber he could not remove it, nor erect it after it was removed; hunger

111

in the mean time would urge him from his work, and every different want call him a different way. Disease, nay even misfortune would be death; for tho' neither might be mortal, yet either would disable him from living, and reduce him to a state in which he might rather be said to perish, than to die.

Thus necessity like a gravitating power would soon form out newly arrived emigrants into society, the reciprocal blessings of which, would supersede, and render the obligations of law and government unnecessary while they remained perfectly just to each other; but as nothing but Heaven is impregnable to vice, it will unavoidably happen that in proportion as they surmount the first difficulties of emigration, which bound them together in a common cause, they will begin to relax in their duty and attachment to each other: and this remissness will point out the necessity of establishing some form of government to supply the defect of moral virtue.

Some convenient Tree will afford them a State-House, under the branches of which the whole Colony may assemble to deliberate on public matters. It is more than probable that their first laws will have the title only of REGULATIONS and be enforced by no other penalty than public disesteem. In this first parliament every man by natural right will have a seat.

But as the colony increases, the public concerns will increase likewise, and the distance at which the members may be separated, will render it too inconvenient for all of them to meet on every occasion as at first, when their number was small, their habitations near, and the public concerns few and trifling. This will point out the convenience of their consenting to leave the legislative part to be managed by a select number chosen from the whole body, who are supposed to have the same concerns at stake which those have who appointed them, and who will act in the same manner as the whole body would act were they present. If the colony continues increasing, it will become necessary to augment the number of the representatives, and that the interest of every part of the colony may be attended to, it will be found best to divide the whole into convenient parts, each part sending its proper number: and that the *elected* might never form to themselves an interest separate from the electors, prudence will point out the propriety of having elections often: because as the elected might by that means return and mix again with the general body of the electors in a few months, their fidelity to the public will be secured by the prudent reflexion of not making a rod for themselves. And as this frequent interchange will establish a common interest with every part of the community, they will mutually and naturally support each other, and on this (not on the unmeaning name of king), depends the *strength of government; and the happiness of the governed.*

Here then is the origin and rise of government; namely, a mode rendered necessary by the inability of moral virtue to govern the world; here too is the design and end of government, viz. Freedom and security. And however our eyes may be dazzled with show, or our ears deceived by sound; however prejudice may warp our wills, or interest darken our understanding, the simple voice of nature and of reason will say, 'tis right.

I draw my idea of the form of government from a principle in nature which no art can overturn, viz. That the more simple any thing is, the less liable it is to be disordered, and the easier repaired when disordered; and with this maxim in view I offer a few remarks on the so much boasted constitution of England. That it was noble for the dark and slavish times in which it was erected, is granted. When the world was over-run with tyranny the least remove therefrom was a glorious rescue. But that it is imperfect, subject to convulsions, and incapable of producing what it seems to promise is easily demonstrated.

Absolute governments, (tho' the disgrace of human nature) have this advantage with them, that they are simple; if the people suffer, they know the head from which their suffering springs; know likewise the remedy; and are not bewildered by a variety of causes and cures. But the constitution of England is so exceedingly complex, that the nation may suffer for years together without being able to discover in which part the fault lies, some will say in one and some in another, and every political physician will advise a different medicine.

I know it is difficult to get over local or long standing prejudices, yet if we will suffer ourselves to examine the component parts of the English constitution, we shall find them to be the base remains of two ancient tyrannies, compounded with some new Republican materials.

First. The remains of Monarchical tyranny in the person of the King.

Secondly. The remains of Aristocratical tyranny in the persons of the Peers.

Thirdly. The new Republican materials, in the persons of the Commons, on whose virtue depends the freedom of England.

The two first by being hereditary are independent of the People; wherefore in a *constitutional sense* they contribute nothing towards the freedom of the State.

To say that the constitution of England is an *union* of three powers reciprocally *checking* each other, is farcical, either the words have no meaning or they are flat contradictions.

To say that the Commons are a check upon the King, presupposes two things.

First. That the King is not to be trusted without being looked after; or in other words, that a thirst for absolute power is the natural disease of Monarchy.

Secondly. That the Commons by being appointed for that purpose, are either wiser or more worthy of confidence than the Crown.

But as the same constitution which gives the Commons a power to check the King by with-holding the supplies, gives afterwards the King a power to check the Commons by empowering him to reject their other bills; it again supposes that the King is wiser than those, whom it has already supposed to be wiser than him. A mere absurdity!

There is something exceedingly ridiculous in the composition of Monarchy; it first excludes a man from the means of information, yet empowers him to act in cases where the highest judgment is required. The state of a king shuts him from the World, yet the business of a King requires him to know it thoroughly; wherefore, the different parts by unnaturally opposing and destroying each other, prove the whole character to be absurd and useless.

Some writers have explained the English constitution thus; the King say they is one, the People another; the Peers are an house in behalf of the King: the Commons in behalf of the People; But this hath all the distinctions of an house divided against itself; and tho' the expressions be pleasantly arranged, yet when examined they appear idle and ambiguous: and it will always happen, that the nicest construction that words are capable of, when applied to the description of some thing which either cannot exist, or is too incomprehensible to be within the compass of description, will be words of sound only, and tho' they may amuse the ear, they cannot inform the mind: for this explanation includes a previous question, viz. *how came the King by a power which the People are afraid to trust and always obliged to check?* Such a power could not be the gift of a wise People, neither can any power *which needs checking* be from God: yet the provision which the constitution makes, supposes such a power to exist.

But the provision is unequal to the task, the means either cannot, or will not accomplish the end, and the whole affair is a *Felo de se:* for as the greater weight will always carry up the less, and as all the wheels of a machine are put in motion by one, it only remains to know which power in the constitution has the most weight, for that will govern: and tho' the others, or a part of them, may clog, or check the rapidity of its motion, yet so long as they cannot stop it, their endeavours will be ineffectual: the first moving power will at last have its way, and what it wants in speed will be supplied by time.

That the crown is this overbearing part in the English constitution needs not be mentioned, and that it derives its whole consequences merely from being the giver of places and pensions is self-evident, wherefore, tho' we have been wise enough to lock the door against absolute Monarchy, we at the same time have been foolish enough to put the Crown in possession of the key.

The prejudice of Englishmen in favour of their own government by King, Lords and Commons, arises as much or more from national pride than reason. Individuals are undoubtedly safer in England than in some other Countries: but the *will* of the King is as much the *law* of the land in Britain as in France, with this difference, that instead of proceeding directly from his mouth, it is handed to the People under the more formidable shape of an act of Parliament. For the fate of Charles the first, hath only made Kings more subtle—not more just.

Wherefore laying aside all national pride and prejudice in favour of modes and forms, the plain truth is, that *it is wholly owing to the constitution of the People, and not to the constitution of the Government* that the Crown is not as oppressive in England as in Turkey.

An inquiry into the *constitutional errors* in the English form of government, is at this time highly necessary; for as we are never in a proper condition of doing justice to others, while we continue under the influence of some leading partiality, so neither are we capable of doing it to ourselves while we remain fettered by any obstinate prejudice. And as a man who is attached to a prostitute is unfitted to choose or judge of a wife, so any prepossession in favour of a rotten constitution of government will disable us from discerning a good one.

Of Monarchy and Hereditary Succession

*M*ankind being originally equals in the order of creation, the equality could only be destroyed by some subsequent circumstance: the distinctions of rich and poor may in a great measure be accounted for, and that without having recourse to the harsh ill-sounding names of oppression and avarice. Oppression is often the *consequence*, but seldom or never the *means* of riches: and tho' avarice will preserve a man from being necessitously poor, it generally makes him too timorous to be wealthy.

But there is another and greater distinction for which no truly natural or religious reason can be assigned, and that is, the distinction of Men into KINGS and SUBJECTS. Male and female are the distinctions of nature, good and bad the distinctions of Heaven; but how a race of Men came into the World so exalted above the rest, and distinguished like some new species, is worth enquiring into, and whether they are the means of happiness or of misery to mankind.

In the early ages of the World according to the Scripture chronology there were no Kings; the consequence of which was there were no wars; it is the pride of Kings which throws mankind into confusion. Holland without a King hath enjoyed more peace for this last century, than any of the Monarchical governments in Europe. Antiquity favours the same remark; for the quiet and rural lives of the first Patriarchs hath a happy something in them, which vanishes away when we come to the history of Jewish royalty.

Government by Kings was first introduced into the World by the Heathens, from whom the children of Israel copied the custom. It was the most prosperous invention the Devil ever set on foot for the promotion of idolatry. The Heathens paid divine honors to their deceased Kings, and the Christian World hath improved on the plan by doing the same to their living ones. How impious is the title of sacred Majesty applied to a worm, who in the midst of his splendor is crumbling into dust!

As the exalting one man so greatly above the rest cannot be justified on the equal rights of nature, so neither can it be defended on the authority of scripture: for the will of the Almighty as declared by Gideon and the prophet Samuel, expressly disapproves of Government by Kings. All anti-monarchical parts of scripture have been very smoothly glossed over in monarchical governments, but they undoubtedly merit the attention of Countries which have their governments yet to form. *"Render unto Caesar the things which are Caesar's"* is the scripture doctrine of Courts, yet it is no support of monarchical government, for the Jews at that time were without a King and in a state of vassalage to the Romans.

John Adams

1736-1826

Adams graduated from Harvard in 1755 and began his career as a lawyer. He became a leading patriot during the Revolution and later served as second President of the United States. He had few of the qualities of personal leadership that marked his cousin, Sam Adams; it was rather through his skills as a constitutional lawyer that he influenced American events. He held many political offices and was the author of scores of important political papers and documents.

The following selection, advancing the republican theory of separation of powers in government, clearly represents the climate of opinion of the day. It is taken from Thoughts on Government, in a Letter from a Gentleman to his Friend (*Boston, 1776*).

MY DEAR SIR:

*I*f I was equal to the task of forming a plan for the government of a colony, I should be flattered with your request and very happy to comply with it because, as the divine science of politics is the science of social happiness, and the blessings of society depend entirely on the constitutions of government, which are generally institutions that last for many generations, there can be no employment more agreeable to a benevolent mind than a research after the best.

Pope flattered tyrants too much when he said,

For forms of government let fools contest,
That which is best administered is best.

Nothing can be more fallacious than this. But poets read history to collect flowers, not fruits; they attend to fanciful images, not the effects of social institutions. Nothing is more certain from the history of nations and nature of man than that some forms of government are better fitted for being well administered than others.

We ought to consider what is the end of government before we determine which is the best form. Upon this point all speculative politicians will agree that the happiness of society is the end of government, as all divines and moral philosophers will agree that the happiness of the individual is the end of man. From this principle it will follow that the form of government which communicates ease, comfort, security, or, in one word, happiness to the greatest number of persons and in the greatest degree is the best.

All sober inquiries after truth, ancient and modern, pagan and Christian, have declared that the happiness of man, as well as his dignity, consists in virtue. Confucius, Zoroaster, Socrates, Mahomet, not to mention authorities really sacred, have agreed in this.

If there is a form of government, then, whose principle and foundation is virtue, will not every sober man acknowledge it better calculated to promote the general happiness than any other form?

Fear is the foundation of most governments: but it is so sordid and brutal a passion and renders men in whose breasts it predominates so stupid and miserable that Americans will not be likely to approve of any political institution which is founded on it.

Honor is truly sacred but holds a lower rank in the scale of moral excellence than virtue. Indeed, the former is but a part of the latter and consequently has not equal pretensions to support a frame of government productive of human happiness.

The foundation of every government is some principle or passion in the minds of the people. The noblest principles and most generous affections in our nature, then, have the fairest chance to support the noblest and most generous models of government.

A man must be indifferent to the sneers of modern Englishmen to mention in their company the names of Sidney, Harrington, Locke, Milton, Nedham, Neville, Burnet, and Hoadly. No small fortitude is necessary to confess that one has read them. The wretched condition of this country, however, for ten or fifteen years past has frequently reminded me of their principles and reasonings. They will convince any candid mind that there is no good government but what is republican. That the only valuable part of the British constitution is so because the very definition of a republic is ''an empire of laws, and not of men.'' That, as a republic is the best of governments, so that particular arrangement of the powers of society or, in other words, that form of government which is best contrived to secure an impartial and exact execution of the laws is the best of republics.

Of republics there is an inexhaustible variety because the possible combinations of the powers of society are capable of innumerable variations.

As good government is an empire of laws, how shall your laws be made? In a large society inhabiting an extensive country, it is impossible that the whole should assemble to make laws. The first necessary step, then, is to depute power from the many to a few of the most wise and good. But by what rules shall you choose your representatives? Agree upon the number and qualifications of persons who shall have the benefit of choosing or annex this privilege to the inhabitants of a certain extent of ground.

The principal difficulty lies, and the greatest care should be employed, in constituting this representative assembly. It should be in miniature an exact portrait of the people at large. It should think, feel, reason, and act like them. That it may be the interest of this assembly to do strict justice at all times, it should be an equal representation, or, in other words, equal interests among the people should have equal interests in it. Great care should be taken to effect this and to prevent unfair, partial, and corrupt elections. Such regulations, however, may be better made in times of greater tranquility than the present; and they will spring up themselves naturally when all the powers of government come to be in the hands of the people's friends. At present, it will be safest to proceed in all established modes to which the people have been familiarized by habit.

A representation of the people in one assembly being obtained, a question arises whether all the powers of government—legislative, executive, and judicial—shall be left in the body? I think a people cannot be long free, nor ever happy, whose government is in one assembly. . . .

But shall the whole power of legislation rest in one assembly? Most of the foregoing reasons apply equally to prove that the legislative power ought to be more complex, to which we may add that if the legislative power is wholly in one assembly and the executive in another or in a single person, these two powers will oppose and encroach upon each other until the contest shall end in war, and the whole power, legislative and executive, be usurped by the strongest.

The judicial power, in such case, could not mediate or hold the balance between the two contending powers because the legislative would undermine it. And this shows the necessity, too, of giving the executive power a negative upon the legislative; otherwise this will be continually encroaching upon that.

To avoid these dangers, let a distinct assembly be constituted as a mediator between the two extreme branches of the legislature, that which represents the people and that which is vested with the executive power.

Let the representative assembly then elect by ballot, from among themselves or their constituents or both, a distinct assembly which, for the sake of perspicuity, we will call a council. It may consist of any number you please, say twenty or thirty, and should have a free and independent exercise of its judgment and consequently a negative voice in the legislature. . . .

The dignity and stability of government in all its branches, the morals of the people, and every blessing of society depend so much upon an upright and skillful administration of justice that the judicial power ought to be distinct from both the legislative and executive, and independent upon both, that so it may be a check upon both, as both should be checks upon that. The judges, therefore, should be always men of learning and experience in the laws, of exemplary morals, great patience, calmness, coolness, and attention. Their minds should not be distracted with jarring interests; they should not be dependent upon any man, or body of men. To these ends, they should hold estates for life in their offices; or, in other words, their commissions should be during good behavior and their salaries ascertained and established by law. For misbehavior the grand inquest of the colony, the house of representatives, should impeach them before the governor and council, where they should have time and opportunity to make their defense; but, if convicted, should be removed from their offices and subjected to such other punishment as shall be thought proper. . . .

A constitution founded on these principles introduces knowledge among the people and inspires them with a conscious dignity becoming freemen; a general emulation takes place which causes good humor, sociability, good manners, and good morals to be general. That elevation of sentiment inspired by such a government makes the common people brave and enterprising. That ambition which is inspired by it makes them sober, industrious, and frugal. You will find among them some elegance, perhaps, but more solidity; a little pleasure, but a great deal of business; some politeness, but more civility. If you compare such a country with the regions of domination, whether monarchical or aristocratical, you will fancy yourself in Arcadia or Elysium. . . .

You and I, my dear friend, have been sent into life at a time when the greatest lawgivers of antiquity would have wished to live. How few of the human race have ever enjoyed an opportunity of making an election of government—more than of air, soil, or climate—for themselves or their children! When, before the present epoch, had three millions of people full power and a fair opportunity to form and establish the wisest and happiest government that human wisdom can contrive? I hope you will avail yourself and your country of that extensive learning and indefatigable industry which you possess to assist her in the formation of the happiest governments and the best character of a great people. For myself, I must beg you to keep my name out of sight; for this feeble attempt, if it should be known to be mine, would oblige me to apply to myself those lines of the immortal John Milton in one of his sonnets:

I did but prompt the age to quit their clogs
By the known rules of ancient liberty,
When straight a barbarous noise environs me
Of owls and cuckoos, asses, apes, and dogs.

Thomas Jefferson

1743-1826

Educated at William and Mary, Jefferson remained a man of scholarly habits and interests throughout his life. Elected a member of the Virginia House of Burgesses in 1769, he rose to fame as a champion of the Revolution and as the author of the Declaration of Independence. He later served as third President of the United States. His accomplishments, like Franklin's, ranged over the whole of human learning, and his mind was an almost complete embodiment of Enlightenment sympathies. His epitaph indicates the activities most dear to him: "Author of the Declaration of Independence; of the Statute for Religious Liberty in Virginia; and Founder of the University of Virginia."

In addition to separation of powers, democratic theory placed great emphasis on the doctrine of the "consent of the governed." A just government, the men of the Enlightenment believed, can have its only legitimate foundation in the will of the people. In the following selections, Jefferson states his convictions on consent as the true sanction of all good government. To some of his contemporaries, these beliefs seemed somewhat extreme; yet the basic principle they reflect was accepted by the Enlightenment as essential to republican government.

The selections reprinted here are taken from the third and fourth volumes of Memoir, Correspondence, and Miscellanies from the Papers of Thomas Jefferson, T. J. *Randolph, ed., 4 vols. (Boston, 1830).*

To Governeur Morris

PHILADELPHIA,
November 7, 1792

. . . It accords with our principles to acknowledge any government to be rightful which is formed by the will of the nation substantially declared. The late government was of this kind and was accordingly acknowledged by all the branches of ours. So any alteration of it, which shall be made by the will of the nation substantially declared, will doubtless be acknowledged in like manner.

To John W. Eppes

MONTICELLO,
June 24, 1813

. . . But what limits, it will be asked, does this prescribe to their powers? What is to hinder them from creating a perpetual debt? The laws of nature, I answer. The earth belongs to the living, not to the dead. The will and the power of man expire with his life, by nature's law. Some societies give it an artificial continuance, for the encouragement of industry; some refuse it, as our aboriginal neighbors, whom we call barbarians.

119

The generations of men may be considered as bodies or corporations. Each generation has the usufruct of the earth during the period of its continuance. When it ceases to exist, the usufruct passes on to the succeeding generation, free and unincumbered, and so on, successively, from one generation to another for ever. We may consider each generation as a distinct nation, with a right, by the will of its majority, to bind themselves, but none to bind the succeeding generation, more than the inhabitants of another country.

To John Adams

MONTICELLO,
October 28, 1813

. . . I agree with you that there is a natural aristocracy among men. The grounds of this are virtue and talents. Formerly, bodily powers gave place among the *aristoi*. But since the invention of gun powder has armed the weak as well as the strong with missle death, bodily strength, like beauty, good humor, politeness, and other accomplishments, has become but an auxiliary ground of distinction. There is also an artificial aristocracy, founded on wealth and birth, without either virtue or talents; for with these it would belong to the first class. The natural aristocracy I consider as the most precious gift of nature for the instruction, the trusts, and government of society. And, indeed, it would have been inconsistent in creation to have formed man for the social state and not to have provided virtue and wisdom enough to manage the concerns of the society. May we not even say that that form of government is the best which provides the most effectually for a pure selection of these natural *aristoi* into the offices of government? The artificial aristocracy is a mischievous ingredient in government, and provision should be made to prevent

its ascendency. On the question what is the best provision, you and I differ, but we differ as rational friends, using the free exercise of our own reason and mutually indulging its errors. You think it best to put the pseudo-*aristoi* into a separate chamber of legislation, where they may be hindered from doing mischief by their co-ordinate branches and where, also, they may be a protection to wealth against the agrarian and plundering enterprises of the majority of the people. I think that to give them power in order to prevent them from doing mischief is arming them for it and increasing instead of remedying the evil.

To John Taylor

MONTICELLO,
May 28, 1816

. . . If, then, the control of the people over the organs of their government be the measure of its republicanism (and I confess I know no other measure), it must be agreed that our governments have much less of republicanism than ought to have been expected; in other words, that the people have less regular control over their agents, than their rights and their interest require. And this I ascribe, not to any want of republican dispositions in those who formed these constitutions, but to a submission of true principle to European authorities, to speculators on government, whose fears of the people have been inspired by the populace of their own great cities, and were unjustly entertained against the independent, the happy, and therefore orderly citizens of the United States. . . .

On this view of the import of the term *republic*, instead of saying, as has been said, "that it may mean any thing or nothing," we may say with truth and meaning, that governments are more or less republican, as they have more or less of the element of popular election and control in their composition: and believing, as I do, that the mass of the citizens is the safest depository of their own rights, and especially, that the evils flowing from the duperies of the people, are less injurious than those from the egoism of their agents, I am a friend to that composition of government which has in it the most of this ingredient. And I sincerely believe, with you, that banking establishments are more dangerous than standing armies; and that the principle of spending money to be paid by posterity, under the name of funding, is but swindling futurity on a large scale.

James Madison
1751-1836

Madison was a prominent participant in the major events of the Revolution, one of the most important authors of the Constitution, and later served as the fourth President of the United States.

Unlike their European counterparts, the men of the American Enlightenment did not adopt a facile optimism about human nature. But even their "realism" was turned to republican purposes. Madison is an instructive example, for though his analysis of behavior in terms of self-interest and faction is within the tradition that sees government as a necessary evil, he himself was totally committed to federal republicanism.

The selection here is from the famous Federalist *No. 10, first printed in the* New York Packet, *Friday, November 23, 1787.*

To the People of the State of New York

*A*mong the numerous advantages promised by a well-constructed Union, none deserves to be more accurately developed than its tendency to break and control the violence of faction. The friend of popular governments never finds himself so much alarmed for their character and fate, as when he contemplates their propensity to this dangerous vice. He will not fail, therefore, to set a due value on any plan which, without violating the principles to which he is attached, provides a proper cure for it. The instability, injustice, and confusion introduced into the public councils, have, in truth, been the mortal diseases under which popular governments have everywhere perished; as they continue to be the favorite and fruitful topics from which the adversaries to liberty derive their most specious declamations. The valuable improvements made by the American constitutions on the popular models, both ancient and modern, cannot certainly be too much admired; but it would be an unwarrantable partiality, to contend that they have as effectually obviated the danger on this side, as was wished and expected. Complaints are everywhere heard from our most considerate and virtuous citizens, equally the friends of public and private faith, and of public and personal liberty, that our governments are too unstable, that the public good is disregarded in the conflicts of rival parties, and that measures are too often decided, not according to the rules of justice and the rights of the minor party, but by the superior force of an interested and overbearing majority. However anxiously we may wish that these complaints had no foundation, the evidence of known facts will not permit us to deny that they are in some degree true. It will be found, indeed, on a candid review of our situation, that some of the distresses under which we labor have been erroneously charged on the operation of our governments; but it will be found, at the same time, that other causes will not alone account for many of our heaviest misfortunes; and, particularly, for that prevailing and increasing distrust of public engagements, and alarm for private rights, which are echoed from one end of the continent to the other. These must be chiefly, if not wholly, effects of the unsteadiness and injustice with which a factious spirit has tainted our public administrations.

By a faction, I understand a number of citizens, whether amounting to a majority or minority of the whole, who are united and actuated by some common impulse of passion, or of interest, adverse to the rights of other citizens, or to the permanent and aggregate interests of the community.

There are two methods of curing the mischiefs of faction: the one, by removing its causes: the other, by controlling its effects.

There are again two methods of removing the causes of faction: the one by destroying the liberty which is essential to its existence: the other, by giving to every citizen the same opinions, the same passions, and the same interests.

It could never be more truly said than of the first remedy, that it was worse than the disease. Liberty is to faction what air is to fire, an element without which it instantly expires. But it could not be less folly to abolish liberty, which is essential to political life, because it nourishes faction, than it would be to wish the annihilation of air, which is essential to animal life, because it imparts to fire destructive agency.

The second expedient is as impracticable as the first would be unwise. As long as the reason of man continues fallible, and he is at liberty to exercise it, different opinions will be formed. As long as the connection subsists between his reason and his self-love, his opinions and his passions will have a reciprocal influence on each other; and the former will be objects to which the latter will attach themselves. The diversity in the faculties of man, from which the rights of property originate, is not less an insuperable obstacle to a uniformity of interests. The protection of these faculties is the first object of government. From the protection of different and unequal faculties of acquiring property, the possession of different degrees and kinds of property immediately results; and from the influence of these on the sentiments and views of the respective proprietors, ensues a division of the society into different interests and parties.

The latent causes of faction are thus sown in the nature of man; and we see them everywhere brought into different degrees of activity, according to the different circumstances of civil society. A zeal for different opinions concerning religion, concerning government, and many other points, as well of speculation as of practice; an attachment of different leaders ambitiously contending for pre-eminence and power; or to persons of other descriptions whose fortunes have been interesting to the human passions, have, in turn, divided mankind into parties, inflamed them with mutual animosity, and rendered them much more disposed to vex and oppress each other than to co-operate for their common good. So strong is this propensity of mankind to fall into mutual animosities, that where no substantial occasion presents itself, the most frivolous and fanciful distinctions have been sufficient to kindle their unfriendly passions and excite their most violent conflicts. But the most common and durable source of factions has been the various and unequal distribution of property. Those who hold and those who are without property have even formed distinct interests in society. Those who are creditors, and those who are debtors, fall under a like discrimination. A landed interest, a manufacturing interest, a mercantile interest, a moneyed interest, with many lesser interests, grow up of necessity in civilized nations, and divide them into different classes, actuated by different sentiments and views. The regulation of these various and interfering interests forms the principal task of modern legislation, and involves the spirit of party and faction in the necessary and ordinary operations of the government.

No man is allowed to be a judge in his own cause, because his interest would certainly bias his judgment, and, not improbably, corrupt his integrity. With equal, nay with greater reason, a body of men are unfit to be both judges and parties at the same time; yet what are many of the most important acts of legislation, but so many judicial determinations, not indeed concerning the rights of single persons, but concerning the rights of large bodies of citizens? And what are the different classes of legislators but advocates and parties to the causes which they determine? Is a law proposed concerning private debts? It is a question to which the creditors are parties on one side and the debtors on the other. Justice ought to hold the balance between them. Yet the parties are, and must be, themselves the judges; and the most numerous party, or, in other words, the most powerful faction must be expected to prevail. Shall domestic manufactures be encouraged, and in what degree, by restrictions on foreign manufactures? are questions which would be differently decided by the landed and the manufacturing classes, and probably by neither with a sole regard to justice and the public good. The apportionment of taxes on the various descriptions of property is an act which seems to require the most exact impartiality; yet there is, perhaps, no legislative act in which greater opportunity and temptation are given to a predominant party to trample on the rules of justice. Every shilling with which they overburden the inferior number, is a shilling saved to their own pockets.

It is in vain to say that enlightened statesmen will be able to adjust these clashing interests, and render them all subservient to the public good. Enlightened statesmen will not always be at the helm. Nor, in many cases, can such an adjustment be made at all without taking into view indirect and remote considerations, which will rarely prevail over the immediate interest which one party may find in disregarding the rights of another or the good of the whole.

The inference to which we are brought is, that the *causes* of faction cannot be removed, and that relief is only to be sought in the means of controlling its *effects.*

If a faction consists of less than a majority, relief is supplied by the republican principle, which enables the majority to defeat its sinister views by regular vote. It may clog the administration, it may convulse the society; but it will be unable to execute and mask its violence under the forms of the Constitution. When a majority is included in a faction, the form of popular government on the other hand, enables it to sacrifice to its ruling passion or interest both the public good and the rights of other citizens. To secure the public good and private rights against the danger of such a faction, and at the same time to preserve the spirit and the form of popular government, is then the great object to which our inquiries are directed. Let me add that it is the great desideratum by which this form of government can be rescued from the opprobrium under which it has so long labored, and be recommended to the esteem and adoption of mankind.

By what means is this object attainable? Evidently by one of two only. Either the existence of the same passion or interest in a majority at the same time must be prevented, or the majority having such coexistent passion or interest, must be rendered, by their number and local situation, unable to concert and carry into effect schemes of oppression. If the impulse and the opportunity be suffered to coincide, we well know that neither moral nor religious motives can be relied on as an adequate control.

They are not found to be such on the injustice and violence of individuals, and lose their efficacy in proportion to the number combined together, that is, in proportion as their efficacy becomes needful.

From this view of the subject it may be concluded that a pure democracy, by which I mean a society consisting of a small number of citizens, who assemble and administer the government in person, can admit of no cure for the mischiefs of faction. A common passion or interest will, in almost every case, be felt by a majority of the whole; a communication and concert result from the form of government itself; and there is nothing to check the inducements to sacrifice the weaker party or an obnoxious individual. Hence it is that such democracies have ever been spectacles of turbulence and contention; have ever been found incompatible with personal security or the rights of property; and have in general been as short in their lives as they have been violent in their deaths. Theoretic politicians, who have patronized this species of government, have erroneously supposed that by reducing mankind to a perfect equality in their political rights, they would, at the same time, be perfectly equalized and assimilated in their possessions, their opinions, and their passions.

A republic, by which I mean a government in which the scheme of representation takes place, opens a different prospect, and promises the cure for which we are seeking. Let us examine the points in which it varies from pure democracy, and we shall comprehend both the nature of the cure and the efficacy which it must derive from the Union.

The two great points of difference between a democracy and a republic are: first, the delegation of the government, in the latter, to a small number of citizens elected by the rest; secondly, the greater number of citizens, and greater sphere of country, over which the latter may be extended.

The effect of the first difference is, on the one hand, to refine and enlarge the public views, by passing them through the medium of a chosen body of citizens, whose wisdom may best discern the true interest of their country, and whose patriotism and love of justice will be least likely to sacrifice it to temporary or partial considerations. Under such a regulation, it may well happen that the public voice, pronounced by the representatives of the people, will be more consonant to be public good than if pronounced by the people themselves, convened for the purpose. On the other hand, the effect may be inverted. Men of factious tempers, of local prejudices, or of sinister designs, may, by intrigue, by corruption, or by other means, first obtain the suffrages, and then betray the interests, of the people. The question resulting is, whether small or extensive republics are more favorable to the election of proper guardians of the public weal; and it is clearly decided in favor of the latter by two obvious considerations:

In the first place, it is to be remarked that, however small the republic may be, the representatives must be raised to a certain number, in order to guard against the cabals of a few; and that, however large it may be, they must be limited to a certain number, in order to guard against the confusion of a multitude. Hence, the number of representatives in the two cases not being in proportion to that of the two constituents, and being proportionally greater in the small republic, it follows that, if the proportion of fit characters be not less in the large than in the small republic, the former will present a greater option, and consequently a greater probability of a fit choice.

In the next place, as each representative will be chosen by a greater number of citizens in the large than in the small republic, it will be more difficult for unworthy candidates to practise with success the vicious arts by which elections are too often carried; and the suffrages of the people being more free, will be more likely to centre in men who possess the most attractive merit and the most diffusive and established characters.

It must be confessed that in this, as in most other cases, there is a mean, on both sides of which inconveniences will be found to lie. By enlarging too much the number of electors, you render the representative too little acquainted with all their local circumstances and lesser interests; as by reducing it too much, you render him unduly attached to these, and too little fit to comprehend and pursue great and national objects. The federal Constitution forms a happy combination in this respect; the great and aggregate interests being referred to the national, the local and particular to the State legislatures.

The other point of difference is, the greater number of citizens and extent of territory which may be brought within the compass of republican than of democratic government; and it is this circumstance principally which renders factious combinations less to be dreaded in the former than in the latter. The smaller the society, the fewer probably will be the distinct parties and interests composing it; the fewer the distinct parties and interests, the more frequently will a majority be found of the same party; and the smaller the number of individuals composing a majority, and the smaller the compass within which they are placed, the more easily will they concert and execute their plans of oppression. Extend the sphere and you take in a greater variety of parties and interests; you make it less probable that a majority of the whole will have a common motive to invade the rights of other citizens; or if such a common motive exists, it will be more difficult

for all who feel it to discover their own strength, and to act in unison with each other. Besides other impediments, it may be remarked that, where there is a consciousness of unjust or dishonorable purposes, communication is always checked by distrust in proportion to the number whose concurrence is necessary.

Hence, it clearly appears, that the same advantage which a republic has over a democracy, in controlling the effects of faction, is enjoyed by a large over a small republic—is enjoyed by the Union over the States composing it. Does the advantage consist in the substitution of representatives whose enlightened views and virtuous sentiments render them superior to local prejudices and to schemes of injustice? It will not be denied that the representation of the Union will be most likely to possess these requisite endowments. Does it consist in the greater security afforded by a greater variety of parties, against the event of any one party being able to outnumber and oppress the rest? In an equal degree does the increased variety of parties comprised within the Union, increase this security. Does it, in fine, consist in the greater obstacles opposed to the concert and accomplishment of the secret wishes of an unjust and interested majority? Here, again, the extent of the Union gives it the most palpable advantage.

The influence of factious leaders may kindle a flame within their particular States, but will be unable to spread a general conflagration through the other States. A religious sect may degenerate into a political faction in a part of the Confederacy; but the variety of sects dispersed over the entire face of it must secure the national councils against any danger from that source. A rage for paper money, for an abolition of debts, for an equal division of property, or for any other improper or wicked project, will be less apt to pervade the whole body of the Union than a particular member of it; in the same proportion as such a malady is more likely to taint a particular county or district, than an entire State.

In the extent and proper structure of the Union, therefore, we behold a republican remedy for the diseases most incident to republican government. And according to the degree of pleasure and pride we feel in being republicans, ought to be our zeal in cherishing the spirit and supporting the character of Federalists.

PUBLIUS

CHAPTER VIII

THE
ENLIGHTENMENT

"The present age is an enlightened one," observed the Rev. Charles Backus in 1788.[1] Self-consciously enlightened it was, and little wonder that it bequeathed to America a sense of mission and national greatness. "It is impossible not to be sensible that we are acting for all mankind," Jefferson wrote Joseph Priestley in 1802. This belief in America stemmed from the Enlightenment's view of the drama of history—a sense that history was starting anew and that the future would fulfill mankind's dream of freedom and happiness. The introduction of the new principle of representative democracy, wrote Jefferson to J. H. Tiffany in 1816, "has rendered useless almost everything written before on the structure of government," and, we might add, on civilization. It was to remain for the next generation of Americans to create the past and mold the tradition necessary to hold the nation together.

Benevolence, natural rights, happiness, reason, deism, freedom, individualism, utilitarianism, progress, science, republicanism—these were the major ideas of the Enlightenment. The following selections—one a sermon, the other a poem—are summary statements of the *Weltanschauung* and values

[1] See the following selection.

of the Enlightenment. It is hoped they will bring together for the reader the many themes of the preceding pages.

The Enlightenment had produced a nation, yet its creative force seemed to decline with this very achievement. Nor did it produce any major philosophers to act as its spokesmen. Perhaps such men as Jefferson or Madison could have risen to the task, but they were too engaged in the political affairs of the day. Perhaps, as Professor Joseph Blau has written, the Enlightenment's failure to develop a theory of human nature spelled its doom. Perhaps it was inevitable that the expanding nation would find Enlightenment ideas partial and inadequate. Indeed, the infant pragmatism of the American mind may have found philosophical justifications unnecessary. Whatever the reasons, the Enlightenment gave the nation a vision of greatness but failed to hold the hearts of men.

Charles Backus
1749-1803

Born in Norwich, Connecticut, Backus graduated from Yale in 1769, where he showed special proficiency in science. He studied theology there under the Rev. Dr. Hart, and after his ordination in 1773 he became pastor of the Congregational church in Somers. He developed a reputation both as a preacher and theologian and was given an honorary Doctor of Divinity degree from Williams College in 1801.

Just as Backus' education reflected his scientific and religious interests, the following selection is an expression of Enlightenment sympathies, together with a pervasive ''sense of sin.'' It is from A Sermon Preached in Long-Meadow at the Publick Fast, April 17, 1788 (*Springfield, 1788*).

Ecclesiastes VII. 10

Say not thou, what is the cause that the former days were better than these? for thou dost not enquire wisely concerning this.

*C*omplaints under those sufferings, which are inseparable from the present state of man, evidence a bad temper of mind. Invectives against the wickedness of the times, are apparently designed in some instances, as an apology, to quiet the conscience of the exclaimer in sin, and to keep off the home enquiry *what have I done*. Corrupt as the world may be, we are not driven by any fatal necessity, to follow bad examples: *Lot* kept his garments undefiled even in *Sodom*.

It is not so easy, as it may seem to a superficial observer, to determine what particular ages are most corrupt. It hurts our feelings, and endangers our reputation, to speak evil of the dead, who were held but in moderate esteem, while they were living: As a natural consequence, we magnify their virtues, and draw a veil over their faults. Besides, those impressions which we receive in early life, are commonly the strongest. When discernment is small, and the passions are warm, we are liable to think too highly of the characters then in repute. Hence, we find that old people in general, give the preference to the manners of the times, which they saw when they were young. Add to this, we are more shock'd with vice in new than in ancient forms. Mode and fashion will have influence on vicious conduct: wickedness will vary it's manner of expression. These new appearances alone, are sometimes taken for a worse heart; whereas, human nature is always essentially the same. *As in water face answereth to face; so the heart of man to man.*

Preferring former days to the present, is a very ancient practice. *Solomon* takes notice of the custom in his time, and declares, that the *cause* of the supposed degeneracy was not wisely sought. It cannot be his design, to forbid all comparisons betwixt the faith and the manners of different ages. The inspired writers abound with such comparisons, and found many of their reproofs and warnings upon them. The reproof in the text, is pointed against a murmuring temper, under those calamities which the present generation feel: And against all those, who while they smart under the rod, never search after the apparent *moral causes* of their punishment. If we are governed by such a spirit of blindness, when enquiring *why the former days were better than these*, our decisions will be rash and ill-founded, and the charge of folly will be patient under the frowns of Providence, in the worst times; to practice self-examination, and to be humbled under the mighty hand of God.

That the present times are bad, needs no formal proof to any one, whose senses are exercised to discern good and evil. The badness of the times, will certainly be acknowledged by every religious assembly, which can be collected within the United States of America. My present design, is, to advert to some of the obvious causes which render the present days evil.

In the first place, we have had too high expectations from the world. This temper has been in man's heart ever since the fall; but it rises to a higher pitch, and shows itself more, on some occasions than on others. We were lately placed in a situation, which gave unusual scope to all our wishes. The ardour, which glow'd in almost every breast, in the beginning of the war with Britain, we may remember, but we can never describe. In effecting the late memorable Revolution, the generality of all ranks vied with each other, in their zeal and exertions. Their motives indeed were very different; but happening to fix upon the same general object, a very great apparent union existed. In the day when our hopes were brightest, the imagination of the Poet knew no bounds, in describing what America *would* be. The Philosopher became a Rhapsodist, in contemplating the importance of the American Revolution. After a perilous and bloody conflict, we have obtained our Independence. A vast and fertile country, comprising a great variety of soils and climates, has been ceded to us by the late treaty of peace. We have had the very rare privilege, of deliberately forming a plan of government for ourselves. Fortunate Usurpers have given law to most other nations. The few who

have escaped so hard a lot, have obtained a partial security of their nobles or kings. But in America; *the People* have had an opportunity of forming a compact *betwixt themselves;* from which alone, their rulers derive all their authority to govern.

In looking forward to those events, which enraptured our minds in prospect, we raised our expectations of happiness from the world, beyond what it can afford. In the most eligible and promising state of human society, man is still born to trouble. Disappointments will increase, in proportion as we calculate too highly for enjoyment, on this side the grave. Human depravity will show itself in a thousand forms. The greatest outward blessings may be awfully abused; and a country, the first for privileges since the deluge, may become the most wretched spot on the globe— which Heaven avert! Whereever our lot is cast, we must be joined in society with those, who are characterized in the Book of God, as *hateful, and hating one another.* As though the necessary evils of life, were not enough to embitter our days, mankind rack their inventions, and exert their malice, to add to each other's misery. It should seem, that companions in danger, would maintain the closer friendship, when the danger is past; but it is too often the case, that with the return of prosperity, all fraternal love is done away. Contentions with a foreign enemy, are frequently followed with domestic broils. How vain is it for us in a world like this, to look for a paradise? Man has seen none upon the earth, since he was banished from the Garden of *Eden.* He will never see another, except in the New Jerusalem. Pride, or ignorance, will prevent an acknowledgment from most persons, that they ever expected to be made completely happy by any situation in life. But from comparing our present temper with our past high professions, it becomes very evident, that we once felt, that to be an *American*, was but another name for *a happy man*.

Countries, like individuals, commonly enjoy most quiet when they are young. Their public expences are small; and less personal liberty need be sacrificed, to secure the public good. Before they are brought into notice, ambition and intrigue can have but small scope, in hurrying them on to dangerous enterprises, or in fomenting divisions. We are grown numerous; our colonial relation has come to an end;—it can never return. Our youth is over. We are called in Providence, to take rank with the kingdoms of the world. We have a national character to support, and national dangers to encounter. The present era is highly critical and important. It must extend vast influence, to the happiness or misery of unborn millions. . . .

The present age is an enlightened one.

Theories capable of being corrected and improved by experiment, have been greatly elucidated. Principles, venerable for their antiquity, have been freely examined, and absurdities exposed. Few, if any, can be found, who will seriously maintain, that the first discovery of a Pagan country, by a Christian prince or state, gives the latter a right to the soil; and to crush or expel the natives, in case of opposition to their usurped claim. The principles of civil liberty were never better understood. Conviction has generally obtained, that all mankind, of whatever colour or descent, are by nature, equally entitled to freedom: That voluntary associations are the only equitable origin of civil government; and that rulers as well as subjects are limited by the constitution. The rights of conscience, have been set in a clear and convincing light.[1] The idea of

[1] The religious toleration in the United States, is without a precedent, in the history of mankind. It will probably never be abridged, whatever changes may take place in our political system. It must be followed with great consequences. Had it happened a few centuries ago, in any single place, of much importance, it would, in all probability, have paved the way for some unfeeling, merciless establishment. The endless variety of opinionists, may enjoy their respective modes of worship, in this land, without the least controul from the ruling powers. Ignorance joined with wildness, is much emboldened to vent itself in it's usual tremendous vociferation. Teachers of this stamp may flourish for a time, in their proper soil. But their influence cannot be lasting, in any great extent, in a country of such religious freedom, and where science is making such rapid advances. It will be nothing new or strange, should indifference to all religion, follow in those places, where the enthusiastic tribes have gained many adherents. Superstition paves the way for infidelity. The raving fanaticism in *Cromwel's* time, fitted the English nation for the licentiousness which came like a flood, in the reign of *Charles* the second. Infidelity threatens to take a wide spread in our young empire. But gloomy as the prospect is, we may derive consolation from the assurance, that *the wrath of man praises God*, and that *the remainder of wrath he will restrain*. God may improve infidelity to destroy all remaining superstition. The general course of events in *Christendom*, for the last hundred years, leads us to this conclusion.

All the friends of the REDEEMER, especially his Ministers, are loudly called upon, to see that their faith *does not stand in the wisdom of men, but in the power of God*. The public teachers of the church will do much to support religion, or to bring it into contempt. It becomes them to act with great caution, in introducing persons into the Ministry. Let dullness, ignorance, and characters whose piety is doubtful, receive no encouragement of entering into the sacred employment. A well-grounded union amongst Ministers, would add much to the reputation and influence of their order. It is ardently to be desired, that such as are agreed in the great essentials of Christianity, and have it's real glory at heart, might be more closely united together. To promote so benevolent a design, it will be necessary, to discriminate betwixt blind zealots on the one hand, and time-serving latitudinarians on the other; to encourage a spirit of free enquiry; and above all, to put on much more of that *charity, which is the bond of perfectness*. Should we behold, evangelical, enlightened, pious teachers, firmly knit together in love, we might indulge the pleasing hope, that the day was dawning, when the prediction of Isaiah, shall receive it's full accomplishment. *Thy watchmen shall lift up the voice, with the voice together shall they sing; for they shall see eye to eye, when the Lord shall bring again Zion.*

attempting an uniformity of faith and worship by *coercion*, is generally acknowledged, to have a much more direct tendency, to make martyrs or hypocrites, than to convince the world that Christianity is from God.

Reason is to be reckoned amongst the choicest gifts of the beneficent Creator. We cannot be sufficiently thankful to the God of Providence, for granting us opportunity to cultivate and improve our rational powers. But this kind of liberty is often used for *an occasion to the flesh*. Self-evident moral principles are treated as great uncertainties: Attempts are made to take off the restraints of the self-denying lessons of Christianity; and infidelity lifts up it's head. . . .

Improvement

*H*aving pointed out the leading causes of the present bad times, we are admonished, on a review of our subject,

I. To put our trust in the living God. In Him *there is everlasting strength.* He will never disappoint the hope of those, who submit to his government, and rest upon his promises. The higher our expectations are raised by earthly prospects, the more poignant sorrow shall we feel, by the unavoidable disappointments of human life. Happy are they, who have learned to treat all objects according to their worth. Such alone are living to good purpose, and shall finally triumph over all the evils of time. If our minds are stayed on God, he will keep them in peace. We shall, under all our trials, maintain the fortitude of the Psalmist, *God is our refuge and strength, a very present help in trouble. Therefore we will not fear, though the earth be removed, and though the mountains be carried into the midst of the sea; though the waters thereof roar and be troubled, though the mountains shake with the swelling thereof.*

II. WE may see the necessity of great circumspection in our conduct, at the present time. We are surrounded with temptations. There are some, whose selfish interest prompts them, to use every artifice to deceive. Such may be known, by their addressing the passions rather than the reason of their fellowmen. Let us *judge not according to the appearance, but judge righteous judgment.* A candid, impartial temper, is the only proper frame of mind for interesting decisions. Should we throw this aside, we shall be towed upon those rocks of perdition, which prove the ruin of the presumptuous.

If *America* should lose sight of the principles of the late Revolution, she will become wretched in the extreme. In that case, dire necessity would control all the enlightened speculations of the closet, on the rights and liberties of mankind. The sage and the patriot, would give way to established absurdities, from motives similar to those which have shut their mouths, in other countries and ages. Should we crumble in pieces, despotism will follow; and those who had been the first, to detest any former usurpation, will be the last to alarm the fears of the multitude. To guard against such evils, let our temper and conduct correspond, with the present important stage of our national existence. Let us, in our respective spheres of action and influence, countenance and support such measures, as shall tend to give union and prosperity to our infant empire.

While the good man is anxious for the political salvation of his country, his heart trembles yet more for the ARK OF GOD. Should the means of grace be taken away, *the glory will depart from our Israel.* No miracle is necessary, to remove our candlestick out of it's place. Let Christianity be treated with general neglect and contempt, it will soon cease to enlighten any people.

That Divine religion which we enjoy,

is not now opposed by the secular arm, as it was in former ages. But the feelings of the heart towards it, are not altered; it's native enmity remains. The indifference which prevails, and the skepticism and ridicule, which are at present employed against the cause of the REDEEMER, are doing the work of the bloody persecutors of former times. Mankind are, at least, in as great danger of being laughed out of religion, as of being deterred from it, by fire and faggots. What holy zeal and vigilance become us, that we be not carried down the torrent of licentiousness and infidelity. Let us *receive a kingdom which cannot be moved; and watch and pray, that we enter not into temptation.*

Lastly, let us all be awakened to unfeigned repentance, and a thorough amendment of life. When God's hand is lifted up in wrath, we are solemnly warned, to search and try our ways, and turn unto him. If we forget the mighty works of our great REDEEMER, we provoke him to cast us out of his holy protection. Nothing will make real good times but reformation. Let us reverence the name and attributes of God. If we have any regard for sacred things, or any desire that Christian ordinances might be continued to us, we must *call the Sabbath a delight, the holy of the Lord, honourable.*

Let us resolve, that as for us and our houses, *we will serve the Lord.* Our holy religion requires us to make a dedication of our all unto God. If public religous bonds be omitted, or degenerate into *mere ceremony,* we may justly fear, that the rising generation will be ignorant of God. Let us not forget any of the duties belonging either to the first or the second table of the Law. While we are pious towards God, let us be just, beneficent and merciful towards men. *Thus speaketh the* LORD OF HOSTS, *saying, execute true judgment, and shew mercy and compassion, every man to his brother: and oppress not the widow, nor the fatherless, the stranger nor the poor; and let none of you imagine evil against his brother in your heart.*[2]

Every man may promote the good of society. Every member has it's office in the body politic, as in the natural body. A truly benevolent mind will be as willing to hold a lower as a higher station, when it appears necessary to promote the general good. Let us imitate the meekness of the great Founder of our religion; and prove by our behaviour, that we are more zealous to be found citizens of the heavenly Zion, than to obtain the plaudit of capricious mortals. We have here no continuing city. May we look for one, which cannot be shaken by the broils and tumults of this world.

With holy happiness in view, how ardently shall we desire, that the spirit of the gospel might spread throughout our land, and the whole habitable globe? If we are true Christians, we are sincere friends to mankind. We are unworthy of the name, if we do not fervently pray, that wars might cease, and that all the nations and tribes of men, might be united together in the bonds of love. May the period soon commence, when *the kingdoms of this world, shall become the kingdoms of our Lord, and of his Christ.*

To God only wise, be glory through Jesus Christ forever. AMEN.

[2] *Zecha.* vii, 9, 10.

Joel Barlow
1754-1812

Joel Barlow was a poet, statesman, and one of the most liberal thinkers of his age. After he received his B.A. from Yale in 1778, he led a varied career that included the study of philosophy, the practice of law, and participation in French politics.

Barlow penned many political pieces in addition to his more formal literary efforts. His best-known poem, Columbiad, *was envisioned by Barlow as early as 1779. Its purpose was clearly stated in its preface: "My object is altogether of a moral and political nature. I wish to encourage and strengthen, in the rising generation, a sense of the importance of republican institutions; as being the great foundation of public and private happiness, the necessary aliment of future and permanent ameliorations in the condition of human nature." The poem made Barlow one of the new nation's leading literary figures. The following selection is from* Columbiad (*Philadelphia, 1808*).

Thro Europe's wilds when feudal nations spread,
The pride of conquest every legion led.
Each fur-clad chief, by servile crowds adored,
O'er conquer'd realms assumed the name of lord,
Built the proud castle, ranged the savage wood,
Fired his grim host to frequent fields of blood,
With new made honors lured his subject bands,
Price of their lives, and purchase of their lands;
For names and titles bade the world resign
Their faith, their freedom and their rights divine.
Contending baronies their terrors spread,
And slavery follow'd where the standard led;
Till, little tyrants by the great o'erthrown,
The spoils of nobles build the regal crown;
Wealth, wisdom, virtue, every claim of man
Unguarded fall to consummate the plan.
Ambitious cares, that nature never gave,
Torment alike the monarch and the slave,
Thro all degrees in gradual pomp ascend,
Honor, the name, but tyranny the end.
Far different honors here the heart shall claim,
Sublimer objects, deeds of happier fame;
A new creation waits the western shore,
And moral triumphs o'er monarchic power.
Thy freeborn sons, with genius unconfined,
Nor sloth can slacken nor a tyrant bind;

With self-wrought fame and worth internal blest,
No venal star shall brighten on their breast,
Nor king-created name nor courtly art
Damp the bold thought or desiccate the heart.
Above all fraud, beyond all titles great,
Truth in their voice and sceptres at their feet,
Like sires of unborn states they move sublime,
Look empires thro and span the breadth of time,
Hold o'er the world, that men may choose from far
The palm of peace, or scourge of barbarous war;
Till their example every nation charms,
Commands its friendship and its rage disarms.
Here social man a second birth shall find,
And a new range of reason lifts his mind,
Feed his strong intellect with purer light,
A nobler sense of duty and of right,
The sense of liberty; whose holy fire
His life shall temper and his laws inspire,
Purge from all shades the world-embracing scope
That prompts his genius and expands his hope.
When first his form arose erect on earth,
Parturient nature hail'd the wondrous birth,
With fairest limbs and finest fibres wrought,
And framed for vast and various toils of thought.
To aid his promised powers with loftier flight,
And stretch his views beyond corporeal sight,

135

Prometheus came, and from the floods of day
Sunn'd his clear soul with heaven's internal ray,
The expanding spark divine; that round him springs,
And leads and lights him thro the immense of things,
Probes the dense earth, explores the soundless main,
Remoulds their mass thro all its threefold reign,
O'er great, o'er small extends his physic laws,
Empalms the empyrean or dissects a gaz,
Weighs the vast orbs of heaven, bestrides the sky,
Walks on the windows of an insect's eye:
Turns then to self, more curious still to trace
The whirls of passion that involve the race,
That cloud with mist the visual lamp of God,
And plunge the poignard in fraternal blood.
Here fails his light. The proud Titanian ray
O'er physic nature sheds indeed its day;
Yet leaves the moral in chaotic jars,
The spoil of violence, the sport of wars,
Presents contrasted parts of one great plan,
Earth, heaven subdued, but man at swords with man;
His wars, his errors into science grown,
And the great cause of all his ills unknown.
    But when he steps on these regenerate shores,
His mind unfolding for superior powers,
FREEDOM, his new Prometheus, here shall rise,
Light her new torch in my refulgent skies,
Touch with a stronger life his opening soul,
Of moral systems fix the central goal,
Her own resplendent essence. Thence expand
The rays of reason that illume the land;
Thence equal rights proceed, and equal laws,
Thence holy Justice all her reverence draws;
Truth with untarnish'd beam descending thence,
Strikes every eye, and quickens every sense,
Bids bright Instruction spread her ample page,
To drive dark dogmas from the inquiring age,
Ope the true treasures of the earth and skies,
And teach the student where his object lies.
    Sun of the moral world! effulgent source
Of man's best wisdom and his steadiest force,
Soul-searching Freedom! here assume thy stand,
And radiate hence to every distant land;
Point out and prove how all the scenes of strife,
The shock of states, the impassion'd broils of life,
Spring from unequal sway; and how they fly
Before the splendor of thy peaceful eye;
Unfold at last the genuine social plan,
The mind's full scope, the dignity of man,

Bold nature bursting thro her long disguise,
And nations daring to be just and wise.
    Yes! righteous Freedom, heaven and earth and sea
Yield or withhold their various gifts for thee;
Protected Industry beneath thy reign
Leads all the virtues in her filial train;
Courageous Probity with brow serene,
And Temperance calm presents her placid mien;
Contentment, Moderation, Labor, Art,
Mould the new man and humanize his heart;
To public plenty private ease dilates,
Domestic peace to harmony of states.
Protected Industry, careering far,
Detects the cause and cures the rage of war,
And sweeps, with forceful arm, to their last graves,
Kings from the earth and pirates from the waves. . . .
Equality of Right is nature's plan;
And following nature is the march of man.
Whene'er he deviates in the least degree,
When, free himself, he would be more than free,
The baseless column, rear'd to bear his bust,
Falls as he mounts, and whelms him in the dust.
    See Rome's rude sires, with autocratic gait,
Tread down their tyrant and erect their state;
Their state secured, they deem it wise and brave
That every freeman should command a slave,
And, flusht with franchise of his camp and town,
Rove thro the world and hunt the nations down;
Master and man the same vile spirit gains,
Rome chains the world, and wears herself the chains.
    Mark modern Europe with her feudal codes,
Serfs, villains, vassals, nobles, kings and gods,
All slaves of different grades, corrupt and curst
With high and low, for senseless rank athirst,
Wage endless wars; not fighting to be free,
But *cujum pecus*, whose base herd they'll be.
    Too much of Europe, here transplanted o'er,
Nursed feudal feelings on your tented shore,
Brought sable serfs from Afric, call'd it gain,
And urged your sires to forge the fatal chain.
But now, the tents o'erturn'd, the wars dogs fled,
Now fearless Freedom rears at last her head
Matcht with celestial Peace—my friends, beware
To shade the splendors of so bright a pair;
Complete their triumph, fix their firm abode,

Purge all privations from your liberal code,
Restore their souls to men, give earth repose,
And save your sons from slavery, wars and
woes.
　　Based on its rock of Right your empire lies,
On walls of wisdom let the fabric rise;
Preserve your principles, their force unfold,
Let nations prove them and let kings behold.
EQUALITY, your first firm-grounded stand;
Then FREE ELECTION; then your FEDERAL
BAND;
This holy Triad should forever shine
The great compendium of all rights divine,
Creed of all schools, whence youths by
millions draw
Their themes of right, their decalogues of
law;
Till men shall wonder (in these codes inured)
How wars were made, how tyrants were
endured.
　　Then shall your works of art superior rise,
Your fruits perfume a larger length of skies,
Canals careering climb your sunbright hills,
Vein the green slopes and strow their nur-
turing rills,
Thro tunnel'd heights and sundering ridges
glide,
Rob the rich west of half Kenhawa's tide,
Mix your wide climates, all their stores
confound,
And plant new ports in every midland mound.
Your lawless Mississippi, now who slimes
And drowns and desolates his waste of climes,
Ribb'd with your dikes, his torrent shall
restrain,
And ask your leave to travel to the main;
Won from his wave while rising cantons
smile,
Rear their glad nations and reward their toil.
　　Thus Nile's proud flood to human hands of
yore
Raised and resign'd his tide-created shore,
Call'd from his Ethiop hills their hardy
swains,
And waved their harvests o'er his newborn
plains;
Earth's richest realm from his tamed current
sprung;
There nascent science toned her infant
tongue,
Taught the young arts their tender force to
try,
To state the seasons and unfold the sky;
Till o'er the world extended and refined,
They rule the destinies of humankind. . . .
Great without pomp their modest walls
expand,
Harvard and Yale and Princeton grace the
land,
Penn's student halls his youths with gladness
greet,

On James's bank Virginian Muses meet,
Manhattan's mart collegiate domes command,
Bosom'd in groves, see growing Dartmouth
stand;
Bright o'er its realm reflecting solar fires,
On yon tall hill Rhode Island's seat aspires.
　　Thousands of humbler name around them
rise,
Where homebred freemen seize the solid
prize;
Fixt in small spheres, with safer beams to
shine,
They reach the useful and refuse the fine,
Found, on its proper base, the social plan,
The broad plain truths, the common sense of
man,
His obvious wants, his mutual aids discern,
His rights familiarize, his duties learn,
Feel moral fitness all its force dilate,
Embrace the village and comprise the state.
Each rustic here who turns the furrow'd soil,
The maid, the youth that ply mechanic toil,
In equal rights, in useful arts inured,
Know their just claims, and see their claims
secured;
They watch their delegates, each law revise,
Its faults designate and its merits prize,
Obey, but scrutinize; and let the test
Of sage experience prove and fix the best.
　　Here, fired by virtue's animating flame,
The preacher's task persuasive sages claim.
To mould religion to the moral mind,
In bands of peace to harmonize mankind,
To life, to light, to promised joys above
The soften'd soul with ardent hope to move.
No dark intolerance blinds the zealous
throng,
No arm of power attendant on their tongue;
Vext Inquisition, with her flaming brand,
Shuns their mild march, nor dares approach
the land.
Tho different creeds their priestly robes
denote,
Their orders various and their rites remote,
Yet one their voice, their labors all combined,
Lights of the world and friends of humankind.
So the bright galaxy o'er heaven displays
Of various stars the same unbounded blaze;
Where great and small their mingling rays
unite,
And earth and skies exchange the friendly
light.
　　And lo, my son, that other sapient band,
The torch of science flaming in their hand!
Thro nature's range their searching souls
aspire,
Or wake to life the canvass and the lyre.
Fixt in sublimest thought, behold them rise
World after world unfolding to their eyes,
Lead, light, allure them thro the total plan,
And give new guidance to the paths of man.

Yon meteor-mantled hill see Franklin tread,
Heaven's awful thunders rolling o'er his head;
Convolving clouds the billowy skies deform,
And forky flames emblaze the blackening storm.
See the descending streams around him burn,
Glance on his rod and with his finger turn;
He bids conflicting fulminants expire
The guided blast, and holds the imprison'd fire.
No more, when doubling storms the vault o'erspread,
The livid glare shall strike thy race with dread,
Nor towers nor temples, shuddering with the sound,
Sink in the flames and shake the sheeted ground.
His well tried wires, that every tempest wait,
Shall teach mankind to ward the bolts of fate,
With pointed steel o'ertop the trembling spire,
And lead from untouch'd walls the harmless fire;
Fill'd with his fame while distant climes rejoice,
Wherever lightning shines or thunder rears its voice.

And see sage Rittenhouse, with ardent eye,
Lift the long tube and pierce the starry sky;
Clear in his view the circling planets roll,
And suns and satellites their course control.
He marks what laws the widest wanderers bind,
Copies creation in his forming mind,
Sees in his hall the total semblance rise,
And mimics there the labors of the skies.
These student youths without their tubes behold
The spangled heavens their mystic maze unfold,
And crowded schools their cheerful chambers grace
With all the spheres that cleave the vast of space.

To guide the sailor in his wandering way,
See Godfrey's glass reverse the beams of day.
His lifted quadrant to the eye displays
From adverse skies the counteracting rays;
And marks, as devious sails bewilder'd roll,
Each nice gradation from the stedfast pole. . . .

Tis thus Society's small sources rise;
Thro passions wild her infant progress lies;
Fear, with its host of follies, errors, woes,
Creates her obstacles and forms her foes;
Misguided interest, local pride withstand,
Till long tried ills her growing views expand,
Till tribes and states and empires find their place,
Whose mutual wants her widest walks embrace;
Enlighten'd interest, moral sense at length,
Combine their aids to elevate her strength,
Lead o'er the world her peace-commanding sway,
And light her steps with everlasting day.

From that mark'd stage of man we now behold,
More rapid strides his coming paths unfold;
His continents are traced, his islands found,
His well taught sails on all his billows bound,
His varying wants their new discoveries ply,
And seek in earth's whole range their sure supply.

First of his future stages, thou shalt see
His trade unfetter'd and his ocean free.
From thy young states the code consoling springs,
To strip from vulture War his naval wings;
In views so just all Europe's powers combine,
And earth's full voice approves the vast design.
Tho still her inland realms the combat wage,
And hold in lingering broils the unsettled age,
Yet no rude shocks that shake the crimson plain
Shall more disturb the labors of the main;
The main that spread so wide his travell'd way,
Liberal as air, impartial as the day,
That all thy race the common wealth might share,
Exchange their fruits and fill their treasures there,
Their speech assimilate, their counsels blend,
Till mutual interest fix the mutual friend.
Now see, my son, the destined hour advance;
Safe in their leagues commercial navies dance,
Leave their curst cannon on the quay-built strand,
And like the stars of heaven a fearless course command.

PART III

THE MIND
OF A NATION

At the beginning of the nineteenth century America faced the task of creating
a nation. The events of 1776 and 1787 had produced a body of principles
that—however much historical experience would change—were to set the
fundamental cast of the American mind. But a nation with a central
sovereignty, a common past and traditions, and common cultural aspirations still had to be brought into being. Three factors—events, ideas, and
environment—were involved in the making of the American nation; and,
though most of the ideas were part of Western tradition, as Professor
Gabriel observes, "the configuration of the cluster was unique."[1]

The new nation was soon confronted by events that threatened its survival.
Just before 1800, two of them posed the problem of national union in a
particularly striking way. In 1793 an alliance with France dating from
1778 nearly drew the United States into war with Britain. The alliance
was ended in 1800, but not before Americans had received many warnings
about the evils of "entangling alliances." In 1794 the Whiskey Rebellion,
though unsuccessful, was a serious challenge to the authority of the new

[1] Ralph H. Gabriel, *The Course of American Democratic Thought*, 2nd ed. (New York,
1956), p. 14.

central government. The years following 1800 also saw many important and challenging events, but perhaps the most crucial was the War of 1812. This engagement produced, it is true, internal dissensions that threatened the nation's very existence. But what is more important, it also produced new national heroes and a sense of unity and national purpose. At the conclusion of this war, America turned its back on Europe, and set its face westward. As the frontier expanded, the nation seemed to achieve a clearer sense of its own identity. In 1823 the Monroe Doctrine formalized America's isolation from Europe into a foreign policy. From this date onward, America still faced crucial problems—even that supreme test of democratic principles, the Civil War—but these were problems of an expanding, industrializing country rather than those of a nation at birth.

By 1815 Americans had restated their republican heritage in terms of three beliefs: individualism, the higher law, and the humane ends of government. To be sure, there were Federalists who still tried to interpret these ideas in terms of an older, more aristocratic persuasion (as late as 1837 Noah Webster wanted to eliminate the popular election of presidents), yet they were heard more out of respect for their past contributions than for their present ideas. But within a few more years Federalism was dead, and in the center of the stage stood the American democrat and "the common man." The presidency of Andrew Jackson, with its "equal rights for all, special privilege for none," marked the culmination of the hopes and fears, aspirations and, sometimes disappointments, of a nation of democrats.

The democratic interpretation of the heritage of the golden past, which for Americans now meant the era of the Revolution, was an idealized one. As Vernon Parrington[2] interpreted the Romantic period, Americans glorified the ideal of individualism in every area of human concern—political, economic, and cultural. From this ideal, in turn, came a number of important implications. The first and most immediate concerned independence and its corollary, self-reliance. Born an individual, the American was born free, and in fact his freedom seemed to him less a consequence of political theory than a political fact. Self-reliance, understood in a Puritan sense even after Emerson gave it a Transcendentalist context, was the moral ideal for the freedom the American had. Secondly, Americans felt themselves duty-bound to explore the providential theme of equality. Again, it was the Jacksonians who waged battle for this ideal; and they contributed a special meaning to it—namely, equality of opportunity. Walt Whitman was to sing the praises of equality and individualism even after the end of the Romantic era. Thirdly, such

[2] See volume II of his *Main Currents in American Thought* (New York, 1927), *passim.*

equality, combined with Puritan virtues and a republican order, helped to create a feeling of optimism, a sense of a nation being called to greatness. "Perhaps no theme," writes Professor Burns in his study of the idea of mission, "has ever dominated the minds of the leaders of this nation to the same extent as the idea that America occupies a unique place and has a special destiny among the nations of the earth."[3] Longfellow's verse, "Humanity with all its fears/With all its hopes of future years/ Is hanging breathless on thy fate," expressed the thought in a way that, if it displeased critics, yet brought the sense of America's mission even to the child. The idea of mission, concludes Professor Gabriel, is "the culminating doctrine of the American democratic faith,"[4] and—as the circle completes itself—this same idea reinforced that of nationalism.

Another formative factor in the American experience has been the American environment, with its sense of spaciousness, its isolation from Europe, and its developing frontier. All three of these features tended to reinforce individualism and to provide an experiential basis for the American dream. Professor Louis Hartz has commented extensively on this reinforcement, attempting to show that the American environment tended to confirm John Locke's analysis to such a degree that Locke seemed less to be proposing a political theory than to be describing political actuality.[5] Professor Richard Hofstadter has also quipped that "it is our fate as a nation, not to have ideologies but to be one." America's isolation from Europe allowed her to pursue internal development in a way impossible for other Western nations, and the rich resources of a virgin continent provided the materials for individuals to practice their individualism in an unprecedented way. "It was not, in short," writes Professor Commager, "particular environments that determined the American character or created the American type but the whole of the American environment— the sense of spaciousness, the invitation to mobility, the atmosphere of independence, the encouragement to enterprise and to optimism."[6]

But in many ways it was the frontier that provided Americans with their unique confirmation of individualism. Lord Bryce wrote that "the West may be called the most distinctively American part of America because the points in which it differs from the East are the points in which America as a whole differs from Europe."[7] The frontier, as de Tocqueville observed more than a century ago, placed men, at least initially, in a condition of equality. The actions of the hunter, trapper, trader, and frontier

[3] Edward McNall Burns, *The American Idea of Mission* (New Brunswick, N.J., 1957), p. 5.
[4] Gabriel, *op. cit.*, p. 80.
[5] Louis Hartz, *The Liberal Tradition in America* (New York, 1955), *passim*.
[6] Henry Steele Commager, *The American Mind* (New Haven, 1952), pp. 4–5.
[7] James Bryce, *The American Commonwealth*, 2 vols. (New York, 1888), vol. II, p. 311.

farmer were those of individualists of the mold of the rural farmer that many of the Founding Fathers—particularly, Jefferson—had in mind when they dreamed of an agrarian society.

The famous American historian Frederick J. Turner viewed the frontier as the fundamental cause of America's unique historical development. Lord Bryce, too, believed that the American environment, with its free land and advance of settlement westward, was the feature that most distinguished American from European civilization. Of special importance was the "safety-valve" function of the frontier in relieving pressures of discontent in the East. Turner and his followers also related the frontier to a number of emerging American characteristics: nationalism, individualism, inventiveness, and materialism. More recent historical judgment has modified Turner's thesis, and holds that the frontier did not originate these characteristics but rather helped to strengthen them once they began to crystallize as important features of the American mind. Along the same line, Professor Billington has stated, "most historians today would agree that political institutions have been altered but not completely transformed by the frontier process."[8]

But, while the actual frontier was not as formative a feature in America's development as Turner believed, the imagined frontier—the frontier of story, saga, and song—cast its spell over the American mind. Thus, a "frontier mentality" became a further characteristic of the American. And with this mentality went a frontier faith, a faith in common humanity that was rooted and expressed in the spontaneous and autonomous strivings of the individual. Recognizing man as a creative agent, this mentality sensed the ultimate value of man as an individual member of society; and in fact this insight into individualism often compensated for the cultural sterility that sometimes accompanied pioneering life. Thus the frontiersman found in action what Locke and the Founding Fathers had divined in theory.

In two areas especially, politics and economics, the individualistic dreams of the American democrat were especially sympathetic to the Romantic mind. The hopes of political individualism centered on the ideas of equal rights and universal suffrage—the former to be achieved, of course, by the latter. By the early nineteenth century most property qualifications for voting had been dropped, though suffrage was not extended without controversy. Fisher Ames spoke of democracy as "an illuminated Hell," Noah Webster declared that a pending bill to democratize Massachusetts suffrage would prostrate the wealth of individuals "to the rapaciousness of a merciless gang who had nothing to lose," and Chancellor James Kent used his every talent to prevent the extension of suffrage in New York.

---

[8] Ray A. Billington, *The American Frontier* (Washington, D.C., 1958), p. 18.

But the efforts of these Federalists were futile, and by the time of Jackson male suffrage was almost universal. The real issue in the struggle, as Federalists saw it, had been the conflict between the rich and poor, though in a broader sense it was also a question of democracy versus aristocracy. But the Federalists failed to perceive that in a nation of individualists the poor would strive to achieve riches themselves rather than to oppose the accumulation of wealth. This shared individualistic view helped Americans solve the classic problem of democracy, majority rule and minority rights, for when a nation is united in an individualistic vision, the majority will not destroy it for a minority. Americans willingly came to accept the principle of majority rule, and it was to fail them only once—during the Civil War.

In the economic sphere, also, individualism found unique expression. In 1789 America had an agrarian and mercantile economy, rather than an industrial one. Among the controversial issues of the day was that of America's economic future. Jeffersonians held largely to the agrarian ideal, believing that a nation of farmers best insured the future of republican principles. The vision of industrial greatness for America was reserved for Alexander Hamilton, who not only labored to strengthen the authority of the federal government but also espoused an economic nationalism as the basis for American capitalism. The promotion of manufacturing, a balanced economy, a protective tariff, and a policy of internal improvements sponsored by the federal government were among the ideas proposed by Hamilton for the nation's growth.

Hamilton's views thus raised another debated issue, that of the role of the federal government in the nation's economic development. Some Americans favored individual enterprise without federal interference or aid. Others like Henry Clay and John Quincy Adams continued to favor Hamiltonian ideas, as embodied in their "American Plan" for national economic development.

The Jacksonian era, however, with its struggle over the tariff, the Bank, and chartered privilege, marked an attempt to halt governmental action in economic affairs. Yet the Jacksonians were related to emerging American capitalism in a paradoxical way. They had achieved power partly because the nation's expanding commerce, industry, and urbanization had undermined aristocratic ideas and furthered the spread of the democratic belief. The Jacksonian movement thus grew out of these changes in the economy, and out of a common desire to promote economic opportunity still further by removing restrictions and privileges. Yet many of their policies supported the cause of America's emerging capitalism even as they questioned it. Chief Justice Taney's decision in *Charles River Bridge* opened wider doors of economic opportunity. The journalist William

Leggett, an ardent Jacksonian, in his concern with rights and power, demanded economic liberty within the republican framework, and thus became a spokesman of unconditional laissez faire. The conservative Federalism of Hamilton and John Adams was dead in the 1830's, but the economic development they foresaw had become reality. Herein lies the paradox of Jacksonianism. It traced its political beliefs to the earlier ideals of the republic but at the same time it helped advance economic trends that clearly prefigured future American capitalism.

The result of these political ideals and economic changes was a laissez-faire capitalism. Economic democracy in America came to mean that individuals should participate in economic processes as they participate in political affairs (though later generations of Americans were to wonder about the reality of this participation). Add to this the Puritan virtues of work, thrift, inconspicuous consumption, simplicity, order, and the belief that property is an outward and visible sign of an inner and invisible state, and the basis for America's mobile, acquisitive, and productive economic order was complete. "During the thirty-odd years between the Peace of Paris and the end of the War of 1812," Parrington writes of these economic changes, "that older America was dying. The America that succeeded was a shifting, restless world, youthfully optimistic, eager to better itself."[9]

Actually, the development of the American economy soon outdistanced the ideas Americans had formulated in the realm of economics. Economic activity—"materialism" some critics called it—soon changed the fate of the nation. The continent's rich resources were discovered and exploited, canals, turnpikes, and railroads were built, vast tracts of land were opened up, and immigrant labor from Europe arrived in growing numbers to man the new mills and factories that sprang up everywhere in the East. Economic expansion brought many serious problems as well: the use of child labor, the low wages and long hours in the new mines and factories, the suffering caused by depressions and unemployment, to name but a few. A few individuals like Robert Owen (1771–1858) and Albert Brisbane (1809–1890) tried unsuccessful utopian experiments to solve these problems. Most Americans, however, were confident that the wonders of the new economy would bring its own solutions. Not always fully understood, the emerging capitalism seemed almost inevitable. Indeed, to many Americans an attack on their economic system (and this system was frequently defined in terms of individual enterprise, free competition, and nationalism) was regarded as an attack on a fundamental tenet of American democracy.

What were the characteristics of the nineteenth-century American? No

---

[9] Parrington, *op. cit.*, II, viii.

listing can be fully adequate, but some generalization can be made. The American's optimism grew out of his fortitude, his energy, and his confidence in a future that seemed limitless in its promise. "Go west, young man," referred both to the frontier, as a safety valve that solved some of the problems of life, and to the future promise of America in which, it was sanguinely believed, solutions would be found to all problems. The American's "common sense" led him to a practical ethics, to a conduct based on religion but not always devout. His quantitative cast made him practical and material: even his culture was built on and out of material, not necessarily because his reality was material but because his interests were practical. His individualism led him to experiment and innovate, to distrust and sometimes to disregard authority, and to be tolerant. Lest he be seen as a man of only virtues, mention should also be made of the American's romantic view of sex, his sentimentalism, and his provincialism.

A romanticized Lockianism—if such it may be called—remained the dominant cast of the American mind through mid-century. It is Professor Hartz's ably argued thesis[10] that the Lockian view constituted the basic problem of American society. The chief danger to that society was not the tyranny of the majority but the pressure of unanimity. The European world of the Enlightenment, Hartz writes, had shaped the political and philosophic thought of the founders of the Republic. America did not have to throw off the shackles of feudalism or wage the social revolutions of Europe, and consequently Locke's theories often were regarded less as premises of political behavior than as absolutes. Hence, as de Tocqueville pointed out, the danger to America was that, lacking a feudal past, equality here would lead to a tyranny of the majority. America, it seemed, had begun its existence as Locke had indicated, in a state of nature, and by contractual arrangements instituted government. This pattern in turn shaped the American mind in all its expressions (here the mind of the South may be the exception). America in the nineteenth century retained its liberal— that is, Lockian—inheritance, responded to an expanding frontier and changing economic conditions, and established a political, economic, and to some extent cultural nationalism. The accomplishments of this half-century were substantial though less dramatic than the splendor of the preceding era.

[10] Hartz, *op. cit., passim.*

CHAPTER IX

AN AMERICAN NATIONALISM

A number of emerging characteristics of the American mind have been noted in earlier sections, but for the first half of the nineteenth century none is more important or central than those of nationalism and its corollary, national mission. When Washington assumed office, the American people faced the crucial task of giving reality to the hopes for national greatness expressed in the Constitution. The task was not an easy one, for Americans were still divided over the kind of nation they wanted to create—a division that reached its climax in the presidential campaign of 1800. Yet a sense of national identity and national pride were gradually developing among the people. Nationalism soon passed beyond patriotism and became America's abiding ideal.

Conscious efforts to awaken the nationalistic spirit were undertaken in all the major areas of national endeavor. Under Washington attempts to develop a national economy were begun by Alexander Hamilton, and an avowed economic nationalism was later promoted by such men as Mathew Carey and Henry Clay. The decisions of Chief Justice John Marshall, often criticized and sometimes bitterly attacked by the Jeffersonians, not only strengthened federal authority but also helped to write nationalism into the law. Achievements of the federal government also helped to strengthen national pride; the Louisiana Purchase, the War of 1812, and the Monroe Doctrine marked major steps in this direction.

Among the most important efforts in creating American nationalism, however, were those of writers and artists. Even as these groups had contributed greatly to the Revolutionary cause, so they now turned to the problems of the nation. Noah Webster wrote of the necessity of a national language as a bond of union, and he called on writers and Americans generally to create a national instrument of expression and communication. Literary artists in particular accepted Webster's challenge—especially those in New York and New England, such as Washington Irving, William Cullen Bryant, and Henry Wadsworth Longfellow. These writers produced a "literary nationalism." So important was their work that they may be ranked among the founding fathers of American nationalism. They posed the question of a national literature (see the selection on page 151 from Longfellow's novel *Kavanagh*), and then endeavored to create it. But before the young republic could become a nation in fact as well as name, Americans had to gain a sense of a common past, and a common body of experiences and ideals. From Joel Barlow at the beginning of the period to Herman Melville and Walt Whitman at its end, American writers were concerned with this national problem.

Nationalism, of course, was not peculiar to America; pride of country is experienced by all peoples. Yet American nationalism was unique in that it was part of the larger national mystique of America's mission to embody freedom for all mankind. The eyes of the world were on the American experiment in democracy. But could men be trusted to govern themselves? Were the republican principles that Jefferson hoped would be eternal adequate for the government of men? Americans voiced clear, affirmative answers to all such questions, for themselves and for mankind. For was not America's mission to be the repository of political truths and the political hope of the world? An abiding faith in this mission and destiny has marked the American mind from its inception to the present day.

Noah Webster

1758-1843

Graduating from Yale after a short period of military service, Noah Webster began a career as a writer and lecturer that was to earn him the title "Schoolmaster to America." In a series of lectures and books he emphasized the necessity of an American language and an American system of education, both for national unity and national character. America, he believed, "must be as independent in literature *as she is in* politics, *as famous for* arts *as for* arms." *His zeal on behalf of the* Constitution, *his long humanitarian career, and his concern with America's cultural development earned him a place among the major figures of his day.*

This selection, one of Webster's many pleas for a national language, is from his Dissertations on the English Language *(Boston, 1789).*

A regular study of language has, in all civilized countries, formed a part of a liberal education. The Greeks, Romans, Italians and French successively improved their native tongues, taught them in Academies at home, and rendered them entertaining and useful to the foreign student.

The English tongue, tho' later in its progress towards perfection, has attained to a considerable degree of purity, strength and elegance, and been employed by an active and scientific nation to record almost all the events and discoveries of ancient and modern times.

This language is the inheritance which the Americans have received from their British parents. To cultivate and adorn it, is a task reserved for men who shall understand the connection between language and logic, and form an adequate idea of the influence which a uniformity of speech may have on national attachments.

It will be readily admitted that the pleasures of reading and conversing, the advantage of accuracy in business, the necessity of clearness and precision in communicating ideas, require us to be able to speak and write our own tongue with ease and correctness. But there are more important reasons why the language of this country should be reduced to such fixed principles as may give its pronunciation and construction all the certainty and uniformity which any living tongue is capable of receiving.

The United States were settled by emigrants from different parts of Europe. But their descendants mostly speak the same tongue; and the intercourse among the learned of the different States, which the revolution has begun and an American Court will perpetuate, must gradually destroy the differences of dialect which our ancestors brought from their native countries. This approximation of dialects will be certain; but without the operation of other causes than an intercourse at Court, it will be slow and partial. The body of the people, governed by habit, will still retain their respective peculiarities of speaking; and for want of schools and proper books, fall into many inaccuracies, which, incorporating with the language of the state where they live, may imperceptibly corrupt the national language. Nothing but the establishment of schools and some uniformity in the use of books, can annihilate differences in speaking and preserve the purity of the American tongue. A sameness of pronunciation is of considerable consequence in a political view, for provincial accents are disagreeable to strangers and sometimes have an unhappy effect upon the social affections. All men have local attachments, which lead them to believe their own practice to be the least exceptionable. Pride and prejudice incline men to treat the practice of their neighbors with some degree of contempt. Thus small differences in pronunciation at first excite ridicule—a habit of laughing at the singularities of strangers is followed by disrespect—and without respect friendship is a name, and social intercourse a mere ceremony.

These remarks hold equally true with respect to individuals, to small societies, and to large communities. Small causes, such as a nick-name or a vulgar tone in speaking, have actually created a dissocial spirit between the inhabitants of the different states, which is often discoverable in private business and public deliberations. Our political harmony is therefore concerned in a uniformity of language.

As an independent nation, our honor requires us to have a system of our own, in language as well as government. Great Britain, whose children we are and whose language we speak, should no longer be *our* standard, for the taste of her writers is already corrupted and her language on the decline. But if it were not so, she is at too great a distance to be our model and to instruct us in the principles of our own tongue.

It must be considered further that the English is the common root or stock from which our national language will be derived. All others will gradually waste away—and within a century and a half North America will be peopled with a hundred millions of men, *all speaking the same language*. Place this idea in comparison with the present and possible future bounds of the language in Europe—consider the Eastern (that is, European) Continent as inhabited by nations, whose knowledge and intercourse are embarrassed by differences of language; then anticipate the period when the people of one quarter of the world will be able to associate and converse together like children of the same family. Compare this prospect, which is not visionary, with the state of the English language in Europe, almost confined to an island and to a few millions of people; then let reason and reputation decide how far America should be dependent on a transatlantic nation for her standard and improvements in language.

Let me add, that whatever predilection the Americans may have for their native European tongues, and particularly the British descendants for the English, yet several circumstances render a future separation of the American tongue from the English necessary and unavoidable. The vicinity of the European nations, with the uninterrupted communication in peace and the changes of domination in war, are gradually assimilating their respective languages. The English with others is suffering continual alterations. America, placed at a distance from those nations, will feel, in a much less degree, the influence of the assimilating causes; at the same time numerous local causes, such as a new country, new associations of people, new combinations of ideas in arts and science, and some intercourse with tribes wholly unknown in Europe, will introduce new words into the American tongue. These causes will produce in a course of time a language in North America as different from the future language of England as the modern Dutch, Danish, and Swedish are from the German or from one another: Like remote branches of a tree springing from the same stock; or rays of light, shot from the same center, and diverging from each other in proportion to their distance from the point of separation.

Whether the inhabitants of America can be brought to a perfect uniformity in the pronunciation of words, it is not easy to predict; but it is certain that no attempt of the kind has been made, and an experiment, begun and pursued on the right principles, is the only way to decide the question. Schools in Great Britain have gone far towards demolishing local dialects—commerce has also had its influence—and in America these causes, operating more generally, must have a proportional effect. . . .

Rapid changes in language proceed from violent causes, but these causes cannot be supposed to exist in North America. It is contrary to all rational calculation that the United States will ever be conquered by any one nation, speaking a different language from that of the country. Removed from the danger of corruption by conquest, our language can change only with the slow operation of the cause before-mentioned and the progress of the arts and sciences, unless the folly of imitating our parent country should continue to govern us and lead us into endless innovation. This folly however will lose its influence gradually, as our particular habits of respect for that country shall wear away and our *amor patriœ* acquire strength and inspire us with a suitable respect for our own national character.

We have therefore the fairest opportunity of establishing a national language and of giving it uniformity and perspicuity in North America that ever presented itself to mankind. Now is the time to begin the plan. The minds of the Americans are roused by the events of a revolution; the necessity of organizing the political body and of forming constitutions of government that shall secure freedom and property, has called all the faculties of the mind into exertion; and the danger of losing the benefits of independence has disposed every man to embrace any scheme that shall tend, in its future operation, to reconcile the people of America to each other and weaken the prejudices which oppose a cordial union. . . .

A *national language* is a bond of *national union*. Every engine should be employed to render the people of this country *national*, to call their attachments home to their own country, and to inspire them with the pride of national character. However they may boast of Independence and the freedom of their government, yet their *opinions* are not sufficiently independent; an astonishing respect for the arts and literature of their parent country and a blind imitation of its manners are still prevalent among the Americans. Thus an habitual respect for another country, deserved indeed and once laudable, turns their attention from their own interests and prevents their respecting themselves. . . .

Now is the time, and *this* the country, in which we may expect success in attempting changes favorable to language, science, and government. Delay, in the plan here proposed, may be fatal; under a tranquil general government, the minds of men may again sink into indolence; a national acquiescence in error will follow; and posterity be doomed to struggle with difficulties which time and accident will perpetually multiply.

Let us then seize the present moment and establish a *national language* as well as a national government. Let us remember that there is a certain respect due to the opinions of other nations. As an independent people our reputation abroad demands that in all things we should be federal, be *national*; for if we do not respect *ourselves*, we may be assured that *other nations* will not respect us. In short, let it be impressed upon the mind of every American that to neglect the means of commanding respect abroad is treason against the character and dignity of a brave independent people.

Henry Wadsworth Longfellow

1807-1882

Educated at Bowdoin College, Longfellow became one of the most popular poets of the nineteenth century. His writing ranged from the overfluent "Hymn to the Night" and "A Psalm of Life" to his fine sonnets, which are deepened by the scholarship also revealed in his translations of Dante. Longfellow was one of the major literary spokesmen of America's growing sense of national greatness. This selection, a discussion of national literature, is from Chapter XX of his novel Kavanagh *(Boston, 1849).*

*M*eanwhile, things had gone on very quietly and monotonously in Mr. Churchill's family. Only one event, and that a mysterious one, had disturbed its serenity. It was the sudden disappearance of Lucy, the pretty orphan girl; and, as the booted centipede, who had so much excited Mr. Churchill's curiosity, disappeared at the same time, there was little doubt that they had gone away together. But whither gone, and wherefore, remained a mystery.

Mr. Churchill, also, had had his profile, and those of his wife and children, taken, in a very humble style, by Mr. Bantam, whose advertisement he had noticed on his way to school nearly a year before. His own was considered the best, as a work of art. The face was cut out entirely; the collar of the coat velvet; the shirt collar very high and white; and the top of his head ornamented with a crest of hair turning up in front, though his own turned down,— which slight deviation from nature was explained and justified by the painter as a license allowable in art.

One evening, as he was sitting down to begin, for at least the hundredth time, the great Romance,—subject of so many resolves and so much remorse, so often determined upon but never begun,— a loud knock at the street door, which stood wide open, announced a visitor. Unluckily, the study door was likewise open; and consequently, being in full view, he found it impossible to refuse himself; nor, in fact, would he have done so, had all the doors been shut and bolted,—the art of refusing one's self being at that time but imperfectly understood in Fairmeadow. Accordingly, the visitor was shown in.

He announced himself as Mr. Hathaway. Passing through the village, he could not deny himself the pleasure of calling on Mr. Churchill, whom he knew by his writings in the periodicals, though not personally. He wished, moreover to secure the cooperation of one, already so favorably known to the literary world, in a new Magazine he was about to establish, in order to raise the character of American literature, which, in his opinion, the existing reviews and magazines had entirely failed to accomplish. A daily increasing want of something better was felt by the public, and the time had come for the establishment of such a periodical as he proposed. After explaining, in rather a florid and exuberant manner, his plan and prospects, he entered more at large into the subject of American literature, which it was his design to foster and patronize.

151

"I think, Mr. Churchill," said he, "that we want a national literature commensurate with our mountains and rivers,—commensurate with Niagara, and the Alleghenies, and the Great Lakes!"

"Oh!"

"We want a national epic that shall correspond to the size of the country; that shall be to all other epics what Banvard's Panorama of the Mississippi is to all other paintings,—the largest in the world!"

"Ah!"

"We want a national drama in which scope enough shall be given to our gigantic ideas, and to the unparalleled activity and progress of our people!"

"Of course."

"In a word, we want a national literature altogether shaggy and unshorn, that shall shake the earth, like a herd of buffaloes thundering over the prairies!"

"Precisely," interrupted Mr. Churchill; "but, excuse me!—are you not confounding things that have no analogy? Great has a very different meaning when applied to a river, and when applied to a literature. Large and shallow may perhaps be applied to both. Literature is rather an image of the spiritual world, than of the physical, is it not?—of the internal, rather than the external. Mountains, lakes, and rivers are, after all, only its scenery and decorations, not its substance and essence. A man will not necessarily be a great poet because he lives near a great mountain. Nor, being a poet, will he necessarily write better poems than another, because he lives nearer Niagara."

"But, Mr. Churchill, you do not certainly mean to deny the influence of scenery on the mind?"

"No, only to deny that it can create genius. At best, it can only develop it. Switzerland has produced no extraordinary poet; nor, as far as I know, have the Andes, or the Himalaya mountains, or the Mountains of the Moon in Africa."

"But, at all events," urged Mr. Hathaway, "let us have our literature national. If it is not national, it is nothing."

"On the contrary, it may be a great deal. Nationality is a good thing to a certain extent, but universality is better. All that is best in the great poets of all countries is not what is national in them, but what is universal. Their roots are in their native soil; but their branches wave in the unpatriotic air, that speaks the same language unto all men, and their leaves shine with the illimitable light that pervades all lands. Let us throw all the windows open; let us admit the light and air on all sides; that we may look towards the four corners of the heavens, and not always in the same direction."

"But you admit nationality to be a good thing?"

"Yes, if not carried too far; still, I confess, it rather limits one's views of truth. I prefer what is natural. Mere nationality is often ridiculous. Every one smiles when he hears the Icelandic proverb. 'Iceland is the best land the sun shines upon.' Let us be natural, and we shall be national enough. Besides, our literature can be strictly national only so far as our character and modes of thought differ from those of other nations. Now, as we are very like the English,—are, in fact, English under a different sky,—I do not see how our literature can be very different from theirs. Westward from hand to hand we pass the lighted torch, but it was lighted at the old domestic fireside of England."

"Then you think our literature is never to be anything but an imitation of the English?"

"Not at all. It is not an imitation, but, as some one has said, a continuation."

"It seems to me that you take a very narrow view of the subject."

"On the contrary, a very broad one. No literature is complete until the language in which it is written is dead. We may well be proud of our task and of our position. Let us see if we can build in any way worthy of our forefathers."

"But I insist upon originality."

"Yes; but without spasms and convulsions. Authors must not, like Chinese soldiers, expect to win victories by turning somersets in the air."

"Well, really, the prospect from your point of view is not very brilliant. Pray, what do you think of our national literature?"

"Simply, that a national literature, is not the growth of a day. Centuries must contribute their dew and sunshine to it. Our own is growing slowly but surely, striking its roots downward, and its branches upward, as is natural; and I do not wish, for the sake of what some people call originality, to invert it, and try to make it grow with its roots in the air. And as for having it so savage and wild as you want it, I have only to say, that all literature, as well as all art, is the result of culture and intellectual refinement."

"Ah! we do not want art and refinement; we want genius,—untutored, wild, original, free."

"But, if this genius is to find any expression, it must employ art, for art is the external expression of our thoughts. Many have genius, but, wanting art, are forever dumb. The two must go together to form the great poet, painter, or sculptor."

"In that sense, very well."

"I was about to say also that I thought our literature would finally not be wanting in a kind of universality. As the blood of all nations is mingling with our own, so will their thoughts and feelings finally mingle in our literature. We shall draw from the Germans, tenderness; from the Spaniards, passion; from the French, vivacity,—to mingle more and more with our English solid sense. And this will give us universality, so much to be desired."

Joseph Story

1779-1845

Joseph Story attended the academy at Marblehead, Massachusetts, shortly after its founding and later studied at Harvard. He then practiced law in Marblehead and became active in Massachusetts affairs, where he served in the legislature and held other political posts. When in 1811 he was appointed associate justice of the United States Supreme Court, he was the youngest appointee in the history of the Court. During his years on the high bench his opinions showed great breadth of learning. He became particularly well known for his dissent in Charles River Bridge v. Warren Bridge, *in which he opposed the majority's emphasis on the social responsibility of private property. In 1842 he drew up the rules of equity practice for the Court.*

Of Story's many writings, his Commentaries *(1833) were the most immediately successful, and they earned him an international reputation. His praise of republican principles and his hopes for America's future are expressed in the following selection, which is from the "Concluding Remarks" of his* Commentaries on the Constitution of the United States, *2 vols. (Boston, 1891), vol. II.*

§ 1910. We have now reviewed all the provisions of the original constitution of the United States, and all the amendments which have been incorporated into it. And here the task originally proposed in these Commentaries is brought to a close. Many reflections naturally crowd upon the mind at such a moment,—many grateful recollections of the past, and many anxious thoughts of the future. The past is secure. It is unalterable. The seal of eternity is upon it. The wisdom which it has displayed and the blessings which it has bestowed, cannot be obscured; neither can they be debased by human folly or human infirmity. The future is that which may well awaken the most earnest solicitude, both for the virtue and the permanence of our republic. The fate of other republics—their rise, their progress, their decline, and their fall—are written but too legibly on the pages of history, if indeed they were not continually before us in the startling fragments of their ruins. They have perished, and perished by their own hands. Prosperity has enervated them, corruption has debased them, and a venal populace has consummated their destruction. Alternately the prey of military chieftains at home, and of ambitious invaders from abroad, they have been sometimes cheated out of their liberties by servile demagogues; sometimes betrayed into a surrender of them by false patriots; and sometimes they have willingly sold them for a price to the despot who has bidden highest for his victims. They have disregarded the warning voice of their best statesmen; and have persecuted and driven from office their truest friends. They have listened to the fawning sycophant, and the base calumniator of the wise and the good. They have reverenced power more in its high abuses and summary movements than in its calm and constitutional energy, when it dispensed blessings with an unseen but liberal hand. They have surrendered to faction what belonged to the country. Patronage and party, the triumph of a leader, and the discontents of a day, have outweighed all solid principles and institutions of government. Such are the melancholy lessons of the past history of republics down to our own.

§ 1911. It is not my design to detain the reader by any elaborate reflections addressed to his judgment, either by way of admonition or of encouragement. But it may not be wholly without use to glance at one or two considerations, upon which our meditations cannot be too frequently indulged.

§ 1912. In the first place, it cannot escape our notice, how exceedingly difficult it is to settle the foundations of any government upon principles which do not admit of controversy or question. The very elements out of which it is to be built are susceptible of infinite modifications; and theory too often deludes us by the attractive simplicity of its plans, and imagination by the visionary perfection of its speculations. In theory, a government may promise the most perfect harmony of operations in all its various combinations. In practice, the whole machinery may be perpetually retarded, or thrown out of order by accidental mal-adjustments. In theory, a government may seem deficient in unity of design and symmetry of parts, and yet in practice it may work with astonishing accuracy and force for the general welfare. Whatever, then, has been found to work well in experience should be rarely hazarded upon conjectural improvements. Time and long and steady operation are indispensable to the perfection of all social institutions. To be of any value they must become cemented with the habits, the feelings, and the pursuits of the people. Every change discomposes for a while

the whole arrangements of the system. What is safe is not always expedient; what is new is often pregnant with unforeseen evils and imaginary good.

§ 1913. In the next place, the slightest attention to the history of the national constitution must satisfy every reflecting mind how many difficulties attended its formation and adoption, from real or imaginary differences of interest, sectional feelings, and local institutions. It is an attempt to create a national sovereignty, and yet to preserve the State sovereignties; though it is impossible to assign definite boundaries in every case to the powers of each. The influence of the disturbing causes which, more than once in the convention, were on the point of breaking up the Union, have since immeasurably increased in concentration and vigor. The very inequalities of a government confessedly founded in a compromise were then felt with a strong sensibility; and every new source of discontent, whether accidental or permanent, has since added increased activity to the painful sense of these inequalities. The North cannot but perceive that it has yielded to the South a superiority of representatives, already amounting to twenty-five, beyond its due proportion; and the South imagines that with all this preponderance in representation, the other parts of the Union enjoy a more perfect protection of their interests than her own. The West feels her growing power and weight in the Union; and the Atlantic States begin to learn that the sceptre must one day depart from them. If, under these circumstances, the Union should once be broken up, it is impossible that a new constitution should ever be formed embracing the whole territory. We shall be divided into several nations or confederacies, rivals in power and interest, too proud to brook injury, and too close to make retaliation distant or ineffectual. Our very animosities will, like those of all other kindred nations, become more deadly, because our lineage, laws, and language are the same. Let the history of the Grecian and Italian republics warn us of our dangers. The national constitution is our last and our only security. United we stand, divided we fall.

§ 1914. If these Commentaries shall but inspire in the rising generation a more ardent love of their country, an unquenchable thirst for liberty, and a profound reverence for the Constitution and the Union, then they will have accomplished all that their author ought to desire. Let the American youth never forget that they possess a noble inheritance, bought by the toils and sufferings and blood of their ancestors, and capable, if wisely improved and faithfully guarded, of transmitting to their latest posterity all the substantial blessings of life, the peaceful enjoyment of liberty, property, religion, and independence. The structure has been erected by architects of consummate skill and fidelity; its foundations are solid; its compartments are beautiful as well as useful; its arrangements are full of wisdom and order; and its defences are impregnable from without. It has been reared for immortality, if the work of man may justly aspire to such a title. It may, nevertheless, perish in an hour by the folly or corruption or negligence of its only keepers—THE PEOPLE. Republics are created by the virtue, public spirit, and intelligence of the citizens. They fall when the wise are banished from the public councils, because they dare to be honest; and the profligate are rewarded, because they flatter the people in order to betray them.

William Leggett

1801-1839

*After attending Georgetown College,
Leggett spent a short time in the Navy as a
midshipman. Then, under William Cullen
Bryant, he became part owner and assistant
editor of the New York* Evening Post.
*From 1836 until his death he was editor of
the* Plaindealer. *A warm Jacksonian, he
discussed the political issues of his day with
vigor and insight. Fearless in his writings,
he championed many liberal causes. His
support of individual rights against special
privilege in the economic field served as a
healthy guidepost for America's rising
capitalism.*

*The selection here is from Theodore
Sedgwick, Jr., ed.,* A Collection of the
Political Writings of William Leggett,
2 vols. (New York, 1840), vol. I.

Since the organization of the Government of the United States the people of this country have been divided into two great parties. One of these parties has undergone various changes of name; the other has continued steadfast alike to its appellation and to its principles, and is now, as was at first, the DEMOCRACY. Both parties have ever contended for the same opposite ends which originally caused the division—whatever may have been, at different times, the particular means which furnished the immediate subject of dispute. The great object of the struggles of the Democracy has been to confine the action of the General Government within the limits marked out in the Constitution: the great object of the party opposed to the Democracy has ever been to overlap those boundaries, and give to the General Government greater powers and a wider field for their exercise. The doctrine of the one party is that all power not expressly and clearly delegated to the General Government, remains with the States and with the People: the doctrine of the other party is that the vigor and efficacy of the General Government should be strengthened by a free construction of its powers. The

one party sees danger from the encroachments of the General Government; the other affects to see danger from the encroachments of the States.

This original line of separation between the two great political parties of the republic, though it existed under the old Confederation, and was distinctly marked in the controversy which preceded the formation and adoption of the present Constitution, was greatly widened and strengthened by the project of a National Bank, brought forward in 1791. This was the first great question which occurred under the new Constitution to test whether the provisions of that instrument were to be interpreted according to their strict and literal meaning; or whether they might be stretched to include objects and powers which had never been delegated to the General Government, and which consequently still resided with the states as separate sovereignties.

The proposition of the Bank was recommended by the Secretary of the Treasury on the ground that such an institution would be "of primary importance to the prosperous administration of the finances, and of the greatest utility in the operations connected with the support of public credit.'' This scheme, then, as now, was opposed on various grounds; but the constitutional objection constituted then, as it does at the present day, the main reason of the uncompromising and invincible hostility of the democracy to the measure. They considered it as the exercise of a very important power which had never been given by the states or the people to the General Government, and which the General Government could not therefore exercise without being guilty of usurpation. Those who contended that the Government possessed the power, effected their immediate object; but the controversy still exists. And it is of no consequence to tell the democracy that it is now established by various precedents, and by decisions of the Supreme Court, that this power is fairly incidental to certain other powers expressly granted; for this is only telling them that the advocates of free construction have, at time, had the ascendancy in the Executive and Legislative, and, at all times, in the Judiciary department of the Government. The Bank question stands now on precisely the same footing that it originally did; it is now, as it was at first, a matter of controversy between the two great parties of this country— between parties as opposite as day and night—between parties which contend, one for the consolidation and enlargement of the powers of the General Government, and the other for strictly limiting that Government to the objects for which it was instituted, and to the exercise of the means with which it was entrusted. The one party is for a popular Government; the other for an aristocracy. The one party is composed, in a great measure, of the farmers, mechanics, laborers, and other producers of the middling and lower classes (according to the common gradation by the scale of wealth), and the other of the consumers, the rich, the proud, the privi-

leged—of those who, if our Government were converted into an aristocracy, would become our dukes, lords, marquises and baronets. The question is still disputed between these two parties—it is ever a new question—and whether the democracy or the aristocracy shall succeed in the present struggle, the fight will be renewed, whenever the defeated party shall be again able to muster strength enough to take the field. The privilege of self-government is one which the people will never be permitted to enjoy unmolested. Power and wealth are continually stealing from the many to the few. There is a class continually gaining ground in the community, who desire to monopolize the advantages of the Government, to hedge themselves round with exclusive privileges, and elevate themselves at the expense of the great body of the people. These, in our society, are emphatically the aristocracy; and these, with all such as their means of persuasion, or corruption, or intimidation, can move to act with them, constitute the party which is now struggling against the democracy, for the perpetuation of an odious and dangerous moneyed institution.

Putting out of view, for the present, all other objections to the United States Bank—that it is a monopoly, that it possesses enormous and overshadowing power, that it has been most corruptly managed, and that it is identified with political leaders to whom the people of the United States must ever be strongly opposed—the constitutional objection alone is an insurmountable objection to it.

The Government of the United States is a limited sovereignty. The powers which it may exercise are expressly enumerated in the Constitution. None not thus stated, or that are not ''necessary and proper'' to carry those which are stated into effect, can be allowed to be exercised by it. The power to establish a bank is not expressly given; neither is incidental; since it cannot be shown to be "necessary" to carry the powers which are given, or any of them, into effect. That power cannot therefore be exercised without transcending the Constitutional limits.

This is the democratic argument stated in its briefest form. The aristocratic argument in favour of the power is founded on the dangerous heresy that the Constitution says one thing, and means another. That *necessary* does not mean *necessary*, but simply *convenient*. By a mode of reasoning not looser than this is would be easy to prove that our Government ought to be changed into a Monarchy, Henry Clay crowned King, and the opposition members of the Senate made peers of the realm; and power, place, and prerequisites given to them and their heirs forever. . . .

But it is in relation to his course with regard to the Bank of the United States, that he [President Jackson] appears most emphatically as the champion of the Constitution and the EQUAL RIGHTS of the people. Fully aware of the great truth, that monopolies, whether of rank or privilege, whether possessed by virtue of hereditary descent or conferred by legislative folly or legislative corruption, were the most sly and dangerous enemies to equal rights ever devised by the cunning of avarice or the wiles of ambition, he saw in the vast accumulation of power in that institution, and its evident disposition to exercise, as well as perpetuate it, the elements of destruction to the freedom of the people and the independence of their government. He, therefore, with the spirit and firmness becoming his character and station as the ruler of a free people, determined to exercise his constitutional prerogative in arresting its usurpations, and preventing their being perpetuated.

The child, the champion, and the representative of the great democracy of the United States, he felt himself identified with their interests and feelings. He was one of themselves, and as such had long seen and felt the oppressions which a great concentrated money power, extending its influence, nay, its control over the currency, and consequently the prosperity of the country throughout every nook and corner of the land, had inflicted or might inflict upon the people. He saw in the nature, and in the acts, of this enormous monopoly, an evident tendency, as well as intention, to subjugate the states and their government to its will; and like himself, and in conformity with the whole tenor of his life, he resolved to risk his place, his popularity, his repose, in behalf of the EQUAL RIGHTS of the people.

He saw, moreover, as every true democrat must see, who interprets the Constitution upon its true principles, that the creation of a Bank with the privilege of establishing its branches in every state, without their consent, was not delegated by the states to the general government; and he saw that by one of the first declaratory amendments of the Constitution, that "*The powers not delegated to the United States by the Constitution, nor prohibited to it by the states, are reserved to the states respectively, or to the people.*"

But there is, unfortunately, a clause in the Constitution, which is somewhat of the consistency of India rubber, and by proper application can be stretched so as to unite the opposite extremes of irreconcilable contradictions. It is somewhat like the old gentleman's will in the Tale of a Tub, about which Lord Peter, Martin and Jack disputed so learnedly, and which at one time was a loaf of brown bread, at another a shoulder of mutton. It admits of a wonderful latitude of construction, and an ingenious man can find no great difficulty in interpreting it to suit his own particular interests. We allude to the following, which will be found among the enumeration of the powers of Congress:

"To make all laws which shall be *necessary and proper* for carrying into execution the foregoing powers, and all other powers vested in the government of the United States, or in any department or officer thereof."

The sticklers for state rights in the Convention which adopted the Constitution, and in the State Conventions to which it was referred for acceptance or rejection, did not much relish this saving clause. They imagined they saw in it a sort of Pandora's box, which if only fairly opened, would cast forth a legion of constructive powers and constructive usurpations. They thought they perceived in these two little words "NECESSARY PROPER" a degree of elasticity which might be expanded so as to comprehend almost any thing that a majority of Congress might choose to ascribe to them. They were, in our opinion, not much mistaken in their anticipations, although probably they scarcely dreamed that the constructive ingenuity of the times would find that to be indispensably "necessary" which the country was enabled for many years to dispense with, during which time it enjoyed a degree of prosperity which excited the envy and admiration of the world!

However this may be, the people of the United States will do well to bear in mind, when they hear General Jackson denounced as a tyrant and usurper for the course he has pursued in relation to the Bank, that this institution has no other legs in the Constitution to stand upon than those two, little words "necessary and proper." If it is necesary and proper, then it may be recharted under the Constitution; but it has no right to demand a recharter. If it is not necessary and proper, then it ought never to have been chartered, and ought not to be continued one moment longer than the faith of the nation is pledged.

As this is one of those points which rests on the nice interpretation of words, it naturally depends for its decision on the general bias of the two parties in the controversy. The party attached by habit, education, interests, or prejudice to a consolidated or strong government, will interpret "necessary and proper" one way, and the party opposed to any accumulation of constructive powers in the federal government, will interpret them the other way. General Hamilton, for example, considered a Bank of the United States "necessary and proper," while Mr. Jefferson believed, and has repeatedly denounced it, to be the most dangerous infraction of the constitution ever attempted under the cloak of constructive power. Such has always been the opinion of the great leaders of the democracy of the United States, although some of them have yielded to the voice of a majority of Congress, mistaking it for that of the people.

We have premised thus much in order to show that the course pursued by General Jackson, in regard to the Bank of the United States, is in perfect consonance with the known principles of the democracy, the people of the United States. When the Democratic Party had the ascendency, they took the first opportunity that offered to put an end to the First Bank of the United States, and now they avail themselves of a similar occasion to give a like demonstration of their settled principles and policy. General Jackson would not have been re-elected by that party, against all the corruptions of the Bank, combined with the whole force of all the disjointed, incongruous elements of opposition, *after* he had placed his Veto on its recharter, had he not acted in this instance in strict conformity with the sentiments of a great majority of the democracy of the United States. Here as in every other act of his administration, they saw in him the great opponent of monopolies, the stern, inflexible champion of EQUAL RIGHTS.

With regard to the other alleged acts of despotism charged upon this true unwavering patriot, such as the removal of Mr. Duane from office, and the appointment of one of the very ablest and purest men of this country in his stead; the subsequent removal of the deposits from the Bank of the United States, and the protest against the ex parte condemnation of the "Independent Aristocratic Body," more has already been said in his defence than such charges merited. We do not believe the Senators making them believed one word they themselves uttered on the subject, because, though tainted to the core by personal antipathies and personal ambition, they are men of too clear intellect, seriously to cherish such ideas of the constitution as they have lately put forth to the people. These speeches and denunciations, like those on the subject of universal distress and bankruptcy, were merely made for effect. They certainly could not believe that what the constitution expressly delegates was intended to be withheld; that what was expressly conceded by the charter of the Bank of the United States was intended to be denied; or that the exercise of a privilege inherent in human nature, to wit, that of self-defence, was an outrage on the privileges of the Senate. Real honest error may sometimes be combated successfully by argument; but we know of no way of convincing a man who only affects to be in the wrong in order to deceive others, and shall therefore spare ourselves and our readers any further discussion with opponents who are not in earnest, but who have so high an opinion of the sagacity of the people, that they think they can make them believe what they do not believe themselves.

It will be perceived from this brief analysis of the leading measures of General Jackson's administration, that all his "tyranny" has consisted in successfully interposing the Constitution of the United States in defence of the EQUAL RIGHTS of the people; and that all his "usurpations" have been confined to checking those of the advocates of consolidation, disunion, monopolies, and lastly a great consolidated moneyed aristocracy, equally dangerous to liberty from the point it legally possesses, and those it has usurped. Yet this is the man whom the usurpers themselves denounce as a usurper. This is the man against whom the concentrated venom of disappointed ambition and baffled avarice is vainly striving to contend in the heads and hearts of the American people, and bury under a mass of wilful calumnies. This is the very man whose whole soul is wound up to the great and glorious task of restoring the EQUAL RIGHTS of his fellow-citizens, as they are guaranteed by the letter and spirit of the constitution. May Providence send us a succession of such usurpers as Andrew Jackson, and spare the people from such champions of liberty as Henry Clay, John C. Calhoun, Daniel Webster, George Poindexter, and Nicholas Biddle! . . .

"DO NOT GOVERN TOO MUCH," is a maxim which should be placed in large letters over the speaker's chair in all legislative bodies. The old proverb "too much of a good thing is good for nothing," is most especially applicable to the present time, when it would appear, from the course of our legislation, that common sense, common experience, and the instinct of self-preservation, are utterly insufficient for the ordinary purposes of life; that the people of the United States are not only incapable of self-government, but of taking cognizance of their individual affairs; that industry requires protection, enterprise bounties, and that no man can possibly find his way in broad day light without being tied to the apron string of a legislative dry-nurse. The present system of our legislation seems founded on the total incapacity of mankind to take care of themselves or to exist without legislative enactment. Individual property must be maintained by invasions of personal rights, and the "general welfare" secured by monopolies and exclusive privileges.

The people of the United States will discover when too late that they may be enslaved by laws as well as by the arbitrary will of a despot; that unnecessary restraints are the essence of tyranny; and that there is no more effectual instrument of depriving them of their liberties, than a legislative body, which is permitted to do anything it pleases under the broad mantle of THE PUBLIC GOOD—a mantle which, like charity, covers a multitude of sins, and like charity is too often practised at the expense of other people.

CHAPTER X
THE RISE OF
THE COMMON MAN

One of the most serious problems confronting the new nation had been the conflict between aristocracy and democracy. Generally, the struggle had been waged between the Federalists, who supported the aristocratic view, and the Jeffersonians, who favored an appeal to the people. By 1828 the republican philosophy of Jefferson had won the victory. By then the suffrage had been extended so that nearly all male citizens had gained the right to vote.

The election of Andrew Jackson in 1828 symbolized the final defeat of Federalist values and institutionalized America's democratic premises. The "common man" had come into his own even before 1828, but the election of Jackson was symbolic of his triumph. That election made many conservative Americans question whether the republic could survive the rule of the people. "The reign of 'King Mob' seemed triumphant," as one Federalist put it. And Jackson's two terms did bring with them republican rule. The spoils system, though decried by conservatives, served the immediate purpose of ridding government of an entrenched aristocracy of civil servants and of bringing government closer to the people. In this respect, the crucial importance of Jackson's war against the Second Bank of the United States cannot be overestimated. The Bank, headed by Nicholas Biddle, had come to exert tremendous power over the American economy, and symbolized all the older aristocratic values of power, privilege, and inequality. In Jackson's eyes, the Bank was a "money power," a monopoly which wealthy eastern aristocrats used to advance their own fortunes. The Bank was for him a veritable "monster,"[1] threatening the independence of republican government, creating a monied elite, and destroying equality of opportunity for the masses. Jackson saw (though not always too clearly) the Bank as a portent of a changing economic order, in which credit and finance capital would play a leading role in economic change and development. His own appeal to hard money, enterprise, and the simple republican virtues reflected the older, Puritan values of thrift, hard work, and self-reliance. Thus Jackson was caught in the dilemma of seeking to conserve the old republican order without impeding the development of emerging capitalism.

Historians, reflecting the period's turmoils, interpret the crosscurrents and complexities in a variety of ways. Charles M. Wiltse denies that Jackson was a liberal democrat at all, and regards him, rather, as a president bent on consolidating personal and political power. Bray Hammond sees business —especially the independent entrepreneurs—as the driving force behind Jacksonianism; Richard Hofstadter, too, interprets it as a nation-wide movement favoring the middle class. Arthur M. Schlesinger, Jr., sees a class struggle rather than sectional differences underlying Jacksonianism, and views its mainsprings as an eastern working-class movement that foreshadowed the New and Fair Deals. Finally, Marvin Meyers finds the basic impulse of Jacksonianism to be an effort to restore the old republican virtues that were being lost in the changing social and economic conditions of the day.

However much historians disagree about Jackson, there is little question that his presidency climaxed a revolution in political values. As Schlesinger puts it, "It destroyed neo-Federalism as a public social philosophy and restated fundamentally the presuppositions of American political life. No one ever again could talk with hope of success in the language of Fisher Ames, of Chancellor Kent, of Jeremiah Mason."[2] Thus, ironically enough, what began as an attempt to restore the virtues of republicanism, in the end produced a profound social transformation in American life. Few periods indeed are as appealing to the student of American history as Jacksonian democracy.

[1] See Marvin Meyers, *The Jacksonian Persuasion* (Stanford, California, 1957), Chapter 5.
[2] Arthur M. Schlesinger, Jr., *The Age of Jackson* (Boston, 1945), p. 267.

Kent–Sanford Debates

1821

From 1800 to the election of Jackson, the franchise was gradually extended to include most male citizens. However, in every state there were those who opposed this trend. New York provides a good example. In 1821 a Constitutional Convention dropped substantially all property qualifications for voting. The leader of the opposition in New York was Chancellor James Kent (1763–1847).

Kent graduated from Yale in 1781 and was elected three times on the Federalist ticket to the New York State Assembly. He was appointed Chief Justice of the New York Supreme Court and Chancellor of the New York Court of Chancery. Throughout his career he remained a steadfast conservative.

One of the chief supporters of the measure to drop property qualifications for voting in New York was Nathan Sanford (1777–1838), a legislator and jurist who succeeded Kent as Chancellor. Sanford later served as United States Senator, and was an unsuccessful candidate for Vice-President.

Part of the Kent–Sanford debates is given in the following selection. The text used here is from Reports of the Proceedings and Debates of the Convention of 1821 Assembled for the Purpose of Amending the Constitution of the State of New York *(Albany, 1821).*

[*C*HANCELLOR KENT]: By the report before us, we propose to annihilate, at one stroke, all those property distinctions and to bow before the idol of universal suffrage. That extreme democratic principle, when applied to the legislative and executive departments of government, has been regarded with terror by the wise men of every age because, in every European republic, ancient and modern, in which it has been tried, it has terminated disastrously and been productive of corruption, injustice, violence, and tyranny. And dare we flatter ourselves that we are a peculiar people who can run the career of history, exempted from the passions which have disturbed and corrupted the rest of mankind? If we are like other races of men, with similar follies and vices, then I greatly fear that our posterity will have reason to deplore, in sackcloth and ashes, the delusion of the day. . . .

Now, sir, I wish to preserve our senate as the representative of the landed interest. I wish those who have an interest in the soil to retain the exclusive possession of a branch in the legislature as a stronghold in which they may find safety through all the vicissitudes which the state may be destined, in the course of Providence, to experience. I wish them to be always enabled to say that their freeholds cannot be taxed without their consent. The men of no property, together with the crowds of dependents connected with great

165

manufacturing and commercial establishments, and the motley and undefinable population of crowded ports, may, perhaps, at some future day, under skilful management, predominate in the assembly, and yet we should be perfectly safe if no laws could pass without the free consent of the owners of the soil. That security we at present enjoy; and it is that security which I wish to retain.

The apprehended danger from the experiment of universal suffrage applied to the whole legislative department is no dream of the imagination. It is too mighty an excitement for the moral constitution of men to endure. The tendency of universal suffrage is to jeopardize the rights of property and the principles of liberty. There is a constant tendency in human society, and the history of every age proves it; there is a tendency in the poor to covet and to share the plunder of the rich; in the debtor to relax or avoid the obligation of contracts; in the majority to tyrannize over the minority and trample down their rights; in the indolent and the profligate to cast the whole burdens of society upon the industrious and the virtuous; and *there is a tendency in ambitious and wicked men to inflame these combustible materials.* It requires a vigilant government, and a firm administration of justice, to counteract that tendency. Thou shalt not covet; Thou shalt not steal, are divine injunctions induced by this miserable depravity of our nature. Who can undertake to calculate with any precision how many millions of people this great state will contain in the course of this and the next century, and who can estimate the future extent and magnitude of our commercial ports? The disproportion between the men of property and the men of no property will be in every society in a ratio to its commerce, wealth, and population. We are no longer to remain plain and simple republics of farmers like the New England colonists or the

Dutch settlements on the Hudson. We are fast becoming a great nation, with great commerce, manufactures, population, wealth, luxuries, and with the vices and miseries that they engender. One-seventh of the population of the city of Paris at this day subsists on charity, and one-third of the inhabitants of that city die in the hospitals; what would become of such a city with universal suffrage? France has upwards of four, and England upward of five millions of manufacturing and commercial laborers without property. Could these kingdoms sustain the weight of universal suffrage? The radicals in England, with the force of that mighty engine, would at once sweep away the property, the laws, and the liberties of that island like a deluge. . . .

Liberty, rightly understood, is an inestimable blessing, but liberty without wisdom, and without justice, is no better than wild and savage licentiousness. The danger which we have hereafter to apprehend is not the want, but the abuse, of liberty. We have to apprehend the oppression of minorities and a disposition to encroach on private right—to disturb chartered privileges—and to weaken, degrade, and overawe the administration of justice; we have to apprehend the establishment of unequal and, consequently, unjust systems of taxation and all the mischiefs of a crude and mutable legislation. A stable senate, exempted from the influence of universal suffrage, will powerfully check these dangerous propensities, and such a check becomes the more necessary, since this Convention has already determined to withdraw the watchful eye of the judicial department from the passage of laws. . . .

Mr. N. SANFORD took the floor. The question before us is the right of suffrage—who shall, or who shall not, have the right to vote. The committee have presented the scheme they thought best; to abolish all existing distinctions and make the right of voting uniform. Is this not right? Where did these distinctions arise? They arose from British precedents. In England they have their three estates, which must always have their separate interests represented. Here there is but one estate—the people. To me the only qualifications seem to be the virtue and morality of the people; and if they may be safely intrusted to vote for one class of our rulers, why not for all? In my opinion, these distinctions are fallacious. We have the experience of almost all the other states against them. The principle of the scheme now proposed is that those who bear the burdens of the state should choose those that rule it. There is no privilege given to property as such; but those who contribute to the public support we consider as entitled to a share in the election of rulers. The burdens are annual, and the elections are annual, and this appears proper. To me, and the majority of the committee, it appeared the only reasonable scheme that those who are to be affected by the acts of the government should be annually entitled to vote for those who administer it. Our taxes are of two sorts, on real and personal property. The payment of a tax on either, we thought, equally entitled a man to a vote, and thus we intended to destroy the odious distinctions of property which now exist. But we have considered personal service, in some cases, equivalent to a tax on personal property, as in work on the high roads. This is a burden and should entitle those subject to it to equivalent privileges. The road duty is equal to a poll tax on every male citizen, of twenty-one years, of 62½ cents per annum, which is about the value of each individual's work on the road. This work is a burden imposed by the legislature—a duty required by rulers, and which should entitle those subject to it to a choice of those rulers. Then, sir, the militia next presents itself; the idea of personal service, as applicable to the road duty, is, in like manner, applicable here; and this criterion has been adopted in other states. In Mississippi mere enrolment gives a vote. In Connecticut, as is proposed here, actual service, and that without the right of commutation, is required. The duty in the militia is obligatory and onerous. The militia man must find his arms and accoutrements and lose his time. But, after admitting all these persons, what restrictions, it will be said, are left on the right of suffrage? 1st. The voter must be a citizen. 2d. The service required must be performed within the year, on the principle that taxation is annual, and election annual; so that when the person ceases to contribute or serve, he ceases to vote.

A residence is also required. We propose the term of six months, because we find it already in the constitution; but we propose this residence in the state and not in the county or town, so that, wherever a voter may be at the time of election, he may vote there, if he has been a resident of the state for six months. The object of this was to enable those who move, as very many do, in the six months preceding an election, out of the town or ward in which they have resided, to retain the right of voting in their new habitations. The term of six months is deemed long enough to qualify those who come into our state from abroad to understand and exercise the privileges of a citizen here. Now, sir, this scheme will embrace almost the whole male population of the state. There is perhaps no subject so purely matter of opinion as the question how far the right of suffrage may be safely carried. We propose to carry it almost as far as the male population of the state. The Convention may perhaps think this too broad. On this subject we have much experience; yet there are respectable citizens who think this extension of suffrage unfavorable to the rights of property. Certainly this would be a fatal objection, if well founded; for any government, however constituted, which does not secure property to its rightful owners is a bad government. But how is the extension of the right of suffrage unfavorable to property? Will not our laws continue the same? Will not the administration of justice continue the same? And if so, how is private property to suffer? Unless these are changed, and upon them rest the rights and security of property, I am unable to perceive how property is to suffer by the extension of the right of suffrage. But we have abundant experience on this point in other states. Now, sir, in many of the states the right of suffrage has no restriction; every male inhabitant votes. Yet what harm has been done in those states? What evil has resulted to them from this cause? The course of things in this country is for the extension and not the restriction of popular rights. I do not know that in Ohio or Pennsylvania, where the right of suffrage is universal, there is not the same security for private rights and private happiness as elsewhere. Every gentleman is aware that the scheme now proposed is derived from the law calling this Convention, and in the constitution of this body we have the first fruits of the operation of the principle of extensive suffrage—and will anyone say that this example is not one evincing the discretion with which our people exercise this right? In our town meetings too, throughout the state, we have the same principle. In our town elections we have the highest proof of the virtue and intelligence of our people; they assemble in town meetings as a pure democracy and choose their officers and local legislatures, if I may so call them; and if there is any part of our public business well done, it is that done in town meetings. Is not this a strong practical lesson of the beneficial operation of this principle? This scheme has been proposed by a majority of the committee; they think it safe and beneficial, founded in just and rational principles, and in the experience of this and neighboring states. The committee have no attachment, however, to this particular scheme and are willing to see it amended or altered if it shall be judged for the interest of the people.

Timothy Flint

1780-1840

Graduated from Harvard in 1800, Flint became a preacher and writer. In 1815 he undertook, partly for reasons of health, a missionary tour of the West. Frontier life provided him with materials for his voluminous writings, which included a number of novels. Flint held a romantic and idealized notion of the frontier settler, and undoubtedly he experienced frequent disillusionment. Yet he continued to soften frontier harshness and vulgarity and to praise heroism and nobility. Eastern writers were frequent borrowers from Flint when they wrote on the West.

The selection below is from Letter XVII of Flint's Recollections of the Last Ten Years *(Boston, 1826).*

*T*he people in the Atlantic states have not yet recovered from the horror, inspired by the term "backwoodsman." The prejudice is particularly strong in New England, and is more or less felt from Maine to Georgia. When I first visited this country, I had my full share, and my family by far too much for their comfort. In approaching the country, I heard a thousand stories of gougings, and robberies, and shooting down with the rifle. I have travelled in these regions thousands of miles under all circumstances of exposure and danger. I have travelled alone, or in company only with such as needed protection, instead of being able to impart it; and this too, in many instances, where I was not known as a minister, or where such knowledge would have had no influence in protecting me. I never have carried the slightest weapon of defense. I scarcely remember to have experienced any thing that resembled insult, or to have felt myself in danger from the people. I have often seen men that had lost an eye. Instances of murder, numerous and horrible in their circumstances, have occurred in my vicinity. But they were such lawless rencounters, as terminate in murder every where, and in which the drunkenness, brutality, and violence were mutual. They were catastrophes, in which quiet and sober men would be in no danger of being involved. When we look round these immense regions, and consider that I have been in settlements three hundred miles from any court of justice, when we look at the position of the men, and the state of things, the wonder is, that so few outrages and murders occur. The gentlemen of the towns, even here, speak often with a certain contempt and horror of the backwoodsmen. I have read, and not without feelings of pain, the bitter representations of the learned and virtuous Dr. Dwight, in speaking of them. He represents these vast regions, as a grand reservoir for the scum of the Atlantic states. He characterizes in the mass the emigrants from New England, as discontented coblers, too proud, too much in debt, too unprincipled, too much puffed up with self-conceit, too strongly impressed that their fancied talents could not find scope in their own country, to stay there. It is true there are worthless people here, and the most so, it must be confessed, are from New England. It is true there are gamblers, and gougers, and outlaws; but there are fewer of them, than from the nature of things, and the character of the age and the world, we ought to expect. But it is

169

unworthy of the excellent man in question so to designate this people in the mass. The backwoodsman of the west, as I have seen him, is generally an amiable and virtuous man. His general motive for coming here is to be a freeholder, to have plenty of rich land, and to be able to settle his children about him. It is a most virtuous motive. And notwithstanding all that Dr. Dwight and Talleyrand have said to the contrary, I fully believe, that nine in ten of the emigrants have come here with no other motive. You find, in truth, that he has vices and barbarisms, peculiar to his situation. His manners are rough. He wears, it may be, a long beard. He has a great quantity of bear or deer skins wrought into his household establishment, his furniture, and dress. He carries a knife, or a dirk in his bosom, and when in the woods has a rifle on his back, and a pack of dogs at his heels. An Atlantic stranger, transferred directly from one of our cities to his door, would recoil from a rencounter with him. But remember, that his rifle and his dogs are among his chief means of support and profit. Remember, that all his first days here were passed in dread of the savages. Remember, that he still encounters them, still meets bears and panthers. Enter his door, and tell him you are benighted, and wish the shelter of his cabin for the night. The welcome is indeed seemingly ungracious. "I reckon you can stay," or "I suppose we must let you stay." But this apparent ungraciousness is the harbinger of every kindness that he can bestow, and every comfort that his cabin can afford. Good coffee, corn bread and butter, venison, pork, wild and tame fowls are set before you. His wife, timid, silent, reserved, but constantly attentive to your comfort, does not sit at the table with you, but like the wives of the patriarchs, stands and attends on you. You are shown to the best bed which the house can offer. When this kind of hospitality

has been afforded you as long as you choose to stay, and when you depart, and speak about your bill, you are most commonly told with some slight mark of resentment, that they do not keep tavern. Even the flaxen-headed urchins will turn away from your money.

In all my extensive intercourse with these people, I do not recollect but one instance of positive rudeness and inhospitality. It was on the waters of the Cuivre of the upper Mississippi; and from a man to whom I had presented bibles, who had received the hospitalities of my house, who had invited me into his settlement to preach. I turned away indignantly from a cold and reluctant reception here, made my way from the house of this man, who was a German and comparatively rich, through deep and dark forests, and amidst the concerts of wolves howling on the neighbouring hills. Providentially, about midnight, I heard the barking of dogs at a distance, made my way to the cabin of a very poor man, who arose at midnight, took me in, provided supper, and gave me a most cordial reception.

With this single exception, I have found the backwoodsmen to be such as I have described; a hardy, adventurous, hospitable, rough, but sincere and upright race of people. I have received so many kindnesses from them, that it becomes me always to preserve a grateful and affectionate remembrance of them. If we were to try them by the standard of New England customs and opinions, that is to say, the customs of a people under entirely different circumstances, there would be many things in the picture, that would strike us offensively. They care little about ministers, and think less about paying them. They are averse to all, even the most necessary restraints. They are destitute of the forms and observances of society and religion; but they are sincere and kind without professions, and have a coarse, but substantial morality, which is often rendered more striking by the immediate contrast of the graceful bows, civility, and professions of their French Catholic neighbours, who have the observances of society and the forms of worship, with often but a scanty modicum of the blunt truth and uprightness of their unpolished neighbours.

George Bancroft

1800-1891

*One of America's first accomplished
historians, Bancroft was also one of the
first Americans to submit himself to the
rigors of German university training. After
unsuccessful attempts to transplant that
rigor to American education, he became a
publicist and an active Jacksonian partisan.
He also began work on his* History of the
United States, *the first volume of which
appeared in 1834. After an active life in
politics and government, Bancroft retired in
1874 to spend his last years revising and
completing his* History.

*A basic democratic faith underlies all
Bancroft's writing; indeed, it is fashionable
to remark that every line of his* History
*voted for Andrew Jackson. Bancroft's
discourse on the "Office of the People"
is a summary statement of that faith.*

*The text here is from "The Office of the
People in Art, Government, and Religion
(An Oration Delivered Before the Adelphi
Society of Williamstown College, in August,
1835),"* in Literary and Historical
Miscellanies (*New York, 1855*).

*T*he material world does not
change in its masses or in its powers.
The stars shine with no more lustre
than when they first sang together in the
glory of their birth. The flowers that
gemmed the fields and the forests, before
America was discovered, now bloom
around us in their season. The sun that
shone on Homer shines on us in unchanging lustre. The bow that beamed
on the patriarch still glitters in the
clouds. Nature is the same. For her no
new forces are generated; no new capacities are discovered. The earth turns on
its axis, and perfects its revolutions,
and renews its seasons, without increase
or advancement.

But a like passive destiny does not
attach to the inhabitants of the earth.
For them the expectations of social
improvement are no delusion; the hopes
of philanthropy are more than a dream.
The five senses do not constitute the
whole inventory of our sources of knowledge. They are the organs by which
thought connects itself with the external
universe; but the power of thought is
not merged in the exercise of its instruments. We have functions which connect
us with heaven, as well as organs which
set us in relation with earth. We have
not merely the senses opening to us the
external world, but an internal sense,
which places us in connexion with the
world of intelligence and the decrees of
God.

There is a *spirit in man:* not in the
privileged few; not in those of us only
who by the favor of Providence have
been nursed in public schools. *It is in
man:* it is the attribute of the race. The
spirit, which is the guide to truth, is the
gracious gift to each member of the
human family.

Reason exists within every breast. I
mean not that faculty which deduces
inferences from the experience of the
senses, but that higher faculty, which
from the infinite treasures of its own
consciousness, originates truth, and

assents to it by the force of intuitive evidence; that faculty which raises us beyond the control of time and space, and gives us faith in things eternal and invisible. There is not the difference between one mind and another, which the pride of philosophers might conceive. To them no faculty is conceded, which does not belong to the meanest of their countrymen. . . .

In like manner the best government rests on the people and not on the few, on persons and not on property, on the free development of public opinion and not on authority; because the munificent Author of our being has conferred the gifts of mind upon every member of the human race without distinction of outward circumstances. Whatever of other possessions may be engrossed, mind asserts its own independence. Lands, estates, the produce of mines, the prolific abundance of the seas, may be usurped by a privileged class. Avarice, assuming the form of ambitious power, may grasp realm after realm, subdue continents, compass the earth in its schemes of aggrandizement, and sigh after other worlds; but mind eludes the power of appropriation; it exists only in its own individuality; it is a property which cannot be confiscated and cannot be torn away; it laughs at chains; it bursts from imprisonment; it defies monopoly. A government of equal rights must, therefore, rest upon mind; not wealth, not brute force, the sum of the moral intelligence of the community should rule the State. Prescription can no more assume to be a valid plea for political injustice; society studies to eradicate established abuses, and to bring social institutions and laws into harmony with moral right; not dismayed by the natural and necessary imperfections of all human effort, and not giving way to despair, because every hope does not at once ripen into fruit.

The public happiness is the true object of legislation, and can be secured only by the masses of mankind themselves awakening to the knowledge and the care of their own interests. Our free institutions have reversed the false and ignoble distinctions between men; and refusing to gratify the pride of caste, have acknowledged the common mind to be the true material for a commonwealth. Every thing has hitherto been done for the happy few. It is not possible to endow an aristocracy with greater benefits than they have already enjoyed; there is no room to hope that individuals will be more highly gifted or more fully developed than the greatest sages of past times. The world can advance only through the culture of the moral and intellectual powers of the people. To accomplish this end by means of the people themselves is the highest purpose of government. If it be the duty of the individual to strive after a perfection like the perfection of God, how much more ought a nation to be the image of Deity. The common mind is the true Parian marble, fit to be wrought into likeness to a God. The duty of America is to secure the culture and the happiness of the masses by their reliance on themselves.

The absence of the prejudices of the old world leaves us here the opportunity of consulting independent truth; and man is left to apply the instinct of freedom to every social relation and public interest. We have approached so near to nature, that we can hear her gentlest whispers; we have made Humanity our lawgiver and our oracle; and, therefore, the nation receives, vivifies and applies principles, which in Europe the wisest accept with distrust. Freedom of mind and of conscience, freedom of the seas, freedom of industry, equality of franchises, each great truth is firmly grasped, comprehended and enforced; for the multitude is neither rash nor fickle. In truth, it is less fickle than those who profess to be its guides. Its natural dialectics surpass the logic of the schools. Political action has never been so consistent and so unwavering, as when it results from a feeling or a principle, diffused through society. The people is firm and tranquil in its movements, and necessarily acts with moderation, because it becomes but slowly impregnated with new ideas; and effects no changes, except in harmony with the knowledge which it has acquired. Besides, where it is permanently possessed of power, there exists neither the occasion nor the desire for frequent change. It is not the parent of tumult; sedition is bred in the lap of luxury, and its chosen emissaries are the beggared spendthrift and the impoverished libertine. The government by the people is in very truth the strongest government in the world. Discarding the implements of terror, it dares to rule by moral force, and has its citadel in the heart.

Such is the political system which rests on reason, reflection, and the free expression of deliberate choice. There may be those who scoff at the suggestion, that the decision of the whole is to be preferred to the judgment of the enlightened few. They say in their hearts that the masses are ignorant; that farmers know nothing of legislation; that mechanics should not quit their workshops to join in forming public opinion. But true political science does indeed venerate the masses. It maintains, not as has been perversely asserted, that "the people can make right," but that the people can DISCERN right. Individuals are but shadows, too often engrossed by the pursuit of shadows; the race is immortal: individuals are of limited sagacity; the common mind is infinite in its experience: individuals are languid and blind; the many are ever wakeful: individuals are corrupt; the race has been redeemed: individuals are time-serving; the masses are fearless: individuals may be false, the masses are ingenuous and sincere: individuals claim the divine sanction of truth for the

deceitful conceptions of their own fancies; the Spirit of God breathes through the combined intelligence of the people. Truth is not to be ascertained by the impulses of an individual; it emerges from the contradictions of personal opinion; it raises itself in majestic serenity above the strifes of parties and the conflict of sects; it acknowledges neither the solitary mind, nor the separate faction as its oracle; but owns as its only faithful interpreter the dictates of pure reason itself, proclaimed by the general voice of mankind. The decrees of the universal conscience are the nearest approach to the presence of God in the soul of man.

Thus the opinion which we respect is, indeed, not the opinion of one or of a few, but the sagacity of the many. It is hard for the pride of cultivated philosophy to put its ear to the ground, and listen reverently to the voice of lowly humanity; yet the people collectively are wiser than the most gifted individual, for all his wisdom constitutes but a part of theirs. When the great sculptor of Greece was endeavoring to fashion the perfect model of beauty, he did not passively imitate the form of the loveliest woman of his age; but he gleaned the several lineaments of his faultless work from the many. And so it is, that a perfect judgment is the result of comparison, when error eliminates error, and truth is established by concurring witnesses. The organ of truth is the invisible decision of the unbiased world; she pleads before no tribunal but public opinion; she owns no safe interpreter but the common mind; she knows no court of appeals but the soul of humanity. It is when the multitude give counsel, that right purposes find safety; theirs is the fixedness that cannot be shaken; theirs is the understanding which exceeds in wisdom; theirs is the heart, of which the largeness is as the sand on the seashore.

It is not by vast armies, by immense

natural resources, by accumulations of treasure, that the greatest results in modern civilization have been accomplished. The traces of the career of conquest pass away, hardly leaving a scar on the national intelligence. The famous battle grounds of victory are, most of them, comparatively indifferent to the human race; barren fields of blood, the scourges of their times, but affecting the social condition as little as the raging of a pestilence. Not one benevolent institution, not one ameliorating principle in the Roman state, was a voluntary concession of the aristocracy; each useful element was borrowed from the Democracies of Greece, or was a reluctant concession to the demands of the people. The same is true in modern political life. It is the confession of an enemy to Democracy, that *"All the great and noble institutions of the world have come from popular efforts."*

It is the uniform tendency of the popular element to elevate and bless Humanity. The exact measure of the progress of civilization is the degree in which the intelligence of the common mind has prevailed over wealth and brute force; in other words, the measure of the progress of civilization is the progress of the people. Every great object, connected with the benevolent exertions of the day, has reference to the culture of those powers which are alone the common inheritance. For this the envoys of religion cross seas, and visit remotest isles; for this the press in its freedom teems with the productions of maturest thought; for this the philanthropist plans new schemes of education; for this halls in every city and village are open to the public instructor. Not that we view with indifference the glorious efforts of material industry; the increase in the facility of internal intercourse; the accumulations of thrifty labor; the varied results of concentrated action. But even there it is mind that achieves the triumph. It is the genius of the archi-

tect that gives beauty to the work of human hands, and makes the temple, the dwelling, or the public edifice, an outward representation of the spirit of propriety and order. It is science that guides the blind zeal of cupidity to the construction of the vast channels of communication, which are fast binding the world into one family. And it is as a method of moral improvement, that these swifter means of intercourse derive their greatest value. Mind becomes universal property; the poem that is published on the soil of England, finds its response on the shores of Lake Erie and the banks of the Missouri, and is admired near the sources of the Ganges. The defence of public liberty in our own halls of legislation penetrates the plains of Poland, is echoed along the mountains of Greece, and pierces the darkest night of eastern despotism.

The universality of the intellectual and moral powers, and the necessity of their development for the progress of the race, proclaim the great doctrine of the natural right of every human being to moral and intellectual culture. It is the glory of our fathers to have established in their laws the equal claims of every child to the public care of its morals and its mind. From this principle we may deduce the universal right to leisure; that is, to time not appropriated to material purposes, but reserved for the culture of the moral affections and the mind. It does not tolerate the exclusive enjoyment of leisure by a privileged class; but defending the rights of labor, would suffer none to sacrifice the higher purposes of existence in unceasing toil for that which is not life. Such is the voice of nature; such the conscious claim of the human mind. The universe opens its pages to every eye; the music of creation resounds in every ear; the glorious lessons of immortal truth, that are written in the sky and on the earth, address themselves to every mind, and claim attention from every human being. God has made man upright, that he might look before and after; and he calls upon every one not merely to labor, but to reflect; not merely to practise the revelations of divine will, but to contemplate the displays of divine power. Nature claims for every man leisure, for she claims every man as a witness to the divine glory, manifested in the created world.

CHAPTER XI

AMERICAN REVIVALISM

merica's religious concern, noted in earlier periods of its history, continued into the nineteenth century. Unlike some of their European counterparts, Americans invoked religious premises for their thought and action. They sought to provide religious justification for their most cherished beliefs—individualism, human rights, liberty, and equal opportunity (and even, in the South, for the institution of slavery). This concern was also expressed in a number of religious trends.

The deism of the preceding generation that had so often been called upon to sanction revolutionary purposes was now a much weakened force, partly because of the excesses of the French Revolution, which had become identified with deism and even atheism, and partly because of the failure of deism to satisfy the religious and emotional needs of Americans. In its place came a revival of religious fervor known as the Second Great Awakening. Led by such men as President Timothy Dwight of Yale, it inspired a nationwide religious zeal that was reflected in renewed missionary activities among the Indians, and, more importantly, in the increased religious fervor in nearly all sects and denominations, whether rural or urban. In the East a new Uni-

177

tarianism sought to liberalize Christianity and relate it to the advances of science. Roman Catholicism, organized under Bishop John Carroll, continued its growth as immigration increased after 1815. Finally, a bewildering number of new religious sects sprang up, fostered perhaps by the expanse and individualism of America.

The camp meeting, America's unique contribution to religion, also developed during this period. As the frontier moved westward, evangelical Protestantism accompanied it, especially that of the Baptists and Methodists. It was to meet the peculiar needs of the frontier, with its scattered population, its lack of established churches and clergy, and its isolated and emotionally deprived circumstances that the camp meeting arose. To the tents of the evangelical preachers, settlers came from miles around. The camp meeting often lasted for several days. Revival services stressing the themes of heaven and hell, sin and salvation, were interspersed with periods of social get-togethers where families could visit with neighbors and friends. In this way, the camp meeting provided at least a minimum of social and religious fulfillment. It brought the frontier both religious idealism and social fellowship.

By mid-century the fervor underlying renewed Christian faith permeated American life, supporting and sustaining it. Evangelical Protestantism especially seemed to support the basic American ideals of liberty, individualism, and mission: liberty, for redemption from sin freed the believer; individualism, for the call of the Gospel was to the individual believer; and mission, for evangelicalism fostered the millennial hope. Even America's emphasis on the practical found support in evangelicalism, for revival meetings served emotional needs in a direct, pragmatic way, and later were to issue in a variety of reform movements.

This chapter in the history of American religion has often been criticized. And it is true that the religion of the period sometimes led to an excessive emotionalism that developed few theological interests. It is also true that it fostered anti-intellectualism, and produced individuals who were religious but not always devout, and sometimes confused the religious mission with practical human wishes. Yet revivalism played an important, even a necessary, role in the development of the nation. American life, and especially the frontier, was, as Professor Gabriel observed, "crude, turbulent, and godless. Evangelical Protestantism, more than any other force, tamed it."[1]

---

[1] Ralph H. Gabriel, *The Course of American Democratic Thought* (2nd ed., New York, 1956), p. 33.

Charles G. Finney

1792-1875

Long associated with Oberlin College, Finney served as its president from 1851 to 1866. He began his career as a lawyer in New York, but his own reading of the Bible and certain personal experiences resulted in an emotionally intense religious conversion. In 1824 he was licensed to preach by the St. Lawrence Presbytery, and he began to conduct revival services throughout the middle and eastern states. Finney was masterful in portraying man's guilt and disobedience and he had a remarkable appeal to all classes of Americans.

Finney was the outstanding evangelist of the early nineteenth century. His theology was that of a New England Calvinist, but his emphasis on the efficacy of individual repentance was unique.

The selection reprinted here is from his Lectures on Systematic Theology (*Oberlin, 1846*), *which were delivered during his tenure at Oberlin, where he was called after his revival work.*

How Moral Depravity Is to Be Accounted For

1. It consists, remember, in the committal of the will to the gratification or indulgence of self—in the will's following or submitting itself to be governed by the impulses and desires of the sensibility instead of submitting itself to the law of the intelligence.

2. This definition of the thing shows how it is to be accounted for namely: The sensibility acts as a powerful impulse to the will from the moment of birth, and secures the consent and activity of the will to procure its gratification, before the reason is at all developed. The will is thus committed to the gratification of feeling and appetite, when first the idea of moral obligation is developed. This committed state of the will is not moral depravity, and has no moral character until the idea of moral obligation is developed. The moment this idea is developed, this committal of the will to self-indulge must be abandoned or it becomes selfishness, or moral depravity. But as the will is already in a state of committal, and has to some extent already formed the habit of seeking to gratify feeling, and as the idea of moral obligation is at first but feebly developed, unless the Holy Spirit interferes to shed light on the soul, the will, as might be expected retains its hold on self-gratification. Here moral character does and must commence. Let it be remembered that selfishness consists in the supreme and ultimate choice, or in the preference of self-gratification as an end, or for its own sake, over all other interests. Now, as the choice of an end implies and includes the choice of the means, selfishness of course, causes all that outward life and activity that makes up the entire history of sinners.

This selfish choice is the wicked heart —the sinful nature—the propensity to sin—the sinful appetite—the craving for sin, and all that causes what is generally termed actual transgression. This sinful choice, is properly enough called indwelling sin. It is the latent, standing,

179

controlling preference of the mind, and the cause of all the outward and active life. It is not the choice of sin, but the choice of self-gratification, which choice is sin.

Again. It should be remembered that the physical depravity of our race has much to do with our moral depravity. A diseased physical system renders the appetites, passions, temper, and propensities more clamorous and despotic in their demands, and of course confirms and strengthens selfishness. It should be distinctly understood that physical depravity has no moral character in itself. But yet it is a source of fierce temptation to selfishness. The human sensibility is, manifestly, deeply physically depraved, and as sin or moral depravity consists in committing the will to the gratification of the sensibility, its physical depravity will mightily strengthen moral depravity. Moral depravity is then universally owing to temptation. That is, the soul is tempted to self-indulgence, and yields to the temptation, and this yielding, and not the temptation, is sin or moral depravity. This is manifestly the way in which Adam and Eve became morally depraved. They were tempted, even by undepraved appetite, to prohibited indulgence, and were overcome. The sin did not lie in the constitutional desire of food, or of knowledge, nor in the excited state of these appetites or desires, but in the consent of the will to prohibited indulgence. . . .

The Universal Necessity of Regeneration

1. The necessity of regeneration as a condition of salvation must be coextensive with moral depravity. This has been shown to be universal among the unregenerate moral agents of our race. It surely is impossible that a world or a universe of unholy or selfish beings should be happy. It is impossible that

heaven should be made up of selfish beings. It is intuitively certain that without benevolence or holiness no moral being can be ultimately happy. Without regeneration a selfish soul can by no possibility be fitted either for the employments or for the enjoyments of heaven.

2. The scriptures expressly teach the universal necessity of regeneration. "Jesus answered and said unto him, Verily, verily, I say unto thee. Except a man be born again, he cannot see the kingdom of God."—Jon. 3: 3. "For in Christ Jesus neither circumcision availeth any thing, nor uncircumcision but a new creature."—Gal. 6: 15.

Agencies Employed in Regeneration

1. The scriptures often ascribe regeneration to the Spirit of God. "Jesus answered, Verily, verily, I say unto Thee, Except a man be born of water and of the Spirit, he cannot enter into the Kingdom of God. That which is born of the flesh is flesh; and that which is born of the Spirit is spirit."—Jon. 1: 15.

2. We have seen that the subject is active in regeneration, that regeneration consists in the sinner changing his ultimate choice, intention, preference; or in changing from selfishness to love or benevolence; or in other words in turning from supreme choice of self-gratification to the supreme love of God and the equal love of his neighbor. Of course the subject of regeneration must be an agent in the work.

3. There are generally other agents, one or more human beings concerned in persuading the sinner to turn. The bible recognizes both the subject and the preacher as agents in the work. Thus Paul says: "I have begotten you through the gospel." Here the same word is used which is used in another case where regeneration is ascribed to God. . . .

Instrumentalities Employed in the Work

1. Truth. This must from the nature of regeneration be employed in effecting it, for regeneration is nothing else than the will being duly influenced by truth.

2. There may be and often are many providences concerned in enlightening the mind and in inducing regeneration. These are instrumentalities. They are means or instruments of presenting the truth. Mercies, judgments, men, measures, and in short all those things that conduce to enlightening the mind, are instrumentalities employed in affecting it.

Those who hold to physical or constitutional moral depravity must hold of course to constitutional regeneration, and of course consistency compels them to maintain that there is but one agent employed in regeneration, and that is the Holy Spirit, and that no instrument whatever is employed, because the work is according to them an act of creative power; that the very nature is changed and of course no instrument can be employed, any more than in the creation of the world. These theologians have affirmed over and over again that regeneration is a miracle; that there is no tendency whatever in the gospel however presented, and whether presented by God or man, to regenerate the heart. Dr. Griffin in his Park Street Lectures maintains that the gospel in its natural and necessary tendency creates and perpetuates only opposition to and hatred of God until the heart is changed by the Holy Spirit. He understands the carnal mind to be not a voluntary state, not a minding of the flesh, but the very nature and constitution of the mind, and that the enmity against God is a part, attribute, or appetite of the nature itself. Consequently he must deny the adaptability of the gospel to regenerate the soul. It has been proclaimed by this class of theologians times without number that there is no philosophical con-

nection between the preaching of the gospel and the regeneration of sinners, no adaptedness in the gospel to produce that result; but on the contrary that it is adapted to produce an opposite result. The favorite illustrations of their views have been Ezekiel's prophesying over the dry bones and Christ's restoring sight to the blind man by putting clay on his eyes. Ezekiel's prophesying over the dry bones had no tendency to quicken them they say. And the clay used by the Savior was calculated rather to destroy than to restore sight. This shows how easy it is for men to adopt a pernicious and absurd philosophy and then find or think they find it supported by the bible. What must be the effect of inculcating the dogma that the gospel has nothing to do with regenerating the sinner? Instead of telling him that regeneration is nothing else than his embracing the gospel to tell him that he must wait and first have his constitution recreated before he can possibly do any thing but oppose God? This is to tell him the greatest and most abominable and ruinous of falsehoods. It is to mock his intelligence. What! call on him on pain of eternal death to believe, to embrace the gospel; to love God with all his heart and at the same time, represent him as entirely helpless and constitutionally the enemy of God and of the gospel and as being under the necessity of waiting for God to regenerate his nature before it is possible for him to do otherwise than to hate God with all his heart? O Orthodoxy, falsely so called, how absurd and false thou art! What an enemy of God; what a stumbling block to man; what a leaven of unrighteousness and of hell is such a dogma as this! But a few years have elapsed since almost the entire church were settled down in the delusion of a passive regeneration.

In regeneration the subject is both passive and active.

1. That he is active is plain from what

has been said and from the nature of the change.

2. That he is at the same time passive is plain from the fact that he acts only when and as he is acted upon. That is, he is passive in the perception of the truth presented by the Holy Spirit. I know that this perception is no part of regeneration. It is the condition and the occasion of regeneration. Therefore the subject of regeneration must be a passive recipient or percipient of the truth presented by the Holy Spirit at the moment and during the act of regeneration. The Spirit acts upon him through or by the truth. Thus far he is passive. He closes with the truth. Thus far he is active. What a mistake those theologians have fallen into who represent the subject as altogether passive in regeneration! This rids the sinner at once of the conviction of any duty or responsibility about it. It is wonderful that such an absurdity should have been so long maintained in the church. But while it is maintained, it is no wonder that sinners are not converted to God. Why, while the sinner believes this, it is impossible if he has it in mind that he should be regenerated. He stands and waits for God to do what God requires him to do, and which no one can do for him. Neither God nor any other being can regenerate him if he will not turn. If he will not change his choice, it is impossible that it should be changed. Sinners who have been taught thus and have believed what they have been taught, would never have been regenerated had not the Holy Spirit drawn off their attention from this error, and ere they were aware, induced them to close in with the offer of life.

What is Implied in Regeneration

1. The nature of the change shows that it must be instantaneous. It is a change of choice or of intention. This must be instantaneous. The preparatory work of conviction and enlightening the mind may have been gradual and progressive. But when regeneration occurs, it must be instantaneous.

2. It implies an entire present change of moral character, that is, a change from entire sinfulness to entire holiness. We have seen that it consists in a change from selfishness to benevolence. We have also seen that selfishness and benevolence cannot co-exist in the same mind; that selfishness is a state of supreme and entire consecration to self; that benevolence is a state of entire and supreme consecration to God and the good of the universe. Regeneration then surely implies an entire change of moral character.

Again: The bible represents regeneration as a dying to sin and becoming alive to God. Death in sin is total depravity. This is generally admitted. Death to sin and becoming alive to God, must imply entire present holiness.

3. The scriptures represent regeneration as the condition of salvation in such a sense that if the subject should die immediately after regeneration and without any further change, he would go immediately to heaven.

Again: The scripture requires only perseverance in the first love as the condition of salvation, in case the regenerate soul should live long in the world subsequent to regeneration.

4. When the scriptures require us to grow in grace and in the knowledge of the Lord Jesus Christ, this does not imply that there is yet sin remaining in the regenerate heart which we are required to put away only by degrees. But the spirit of the requirement must be that we should acquire as much knowledge as we can of our moral relations, and continue to conform to all truth as fast we know it. This and nothing else is implied in abiding in our first love, or abiding in Christ, living and walking in the Spirit, etc. . . .

5. The true saint is distinguished by

his firm adherence to all the principles and rules of the Divine government. He is a reformer from principle, and needs not the gale of popular excitement or of popular applause to put and keep him in motion. His intellect and conscience have taken the control of his will, or the will has renounced the impulses of the sensibility as its law, and voluntarily committed itself to the demands of the reason. This fact must appear both on the field of his consciousness, and also in most instances be very manifest to others. His zeal does not wax and wane with every breeze of excitement. He is not carried away by every change in the effervescing sensibility. The law of reason being written in his heart, he does not at one time appear reasonable and to be influenced by conscience and a regard to the law of love, and at another to be infinitely unreasonable and to have little or no regard to God or his laws. He fears and shuns popular excitements as he does all other temptations. He loathes and resists them. The excitements of politics and business and amusements are regarded by him with a jealous eye. He dreads their influence on his sensibility, and when he feels them, it causes a deep struggle and groaning of spirit, because the will, adhering to the law of conscience, steadfastly resists them. Such like excitements instead of being his element and the aliment of his life, are a grief and a vexation to him. Instead of living, and moving, and having his being as it were in the midst of them and by them, he is only annoyed by them. They are not the moving spring of his activity, but only embarrass his spiritual life. His spiritual life is founded in the law of the intelligence, and supported by the light of the Holy Spirit poured upon his intellect through the truth. He steadily resists the flood tides of mere feeling on every subject and abides truth and principle and moral law whatever may be the circumstances of worldly or religious excitement around

him. Be it ever remembered, it is moral law, moral principle, the law of love, and not mere feeling that governs him.

The sinner or deceived professor, for they are one, is right over against this. Excitement is his element and his life. He has truly no moral principle except in theory. He is never truly influenced by truth, law, reason, but always by excitement of some kind. His activity is based on this; hence he is not disturbed and embarrassed in his movements by excitements of any kind, any longer than it takes to put down one form of excitement and take on another. If when he is much interested and excited and carried away in one direction, a counter influence or excitement comes in his way, he is taken aback for the time being. He is disconcerted and embarrassed, perhaps displeased. But you will soon see him go about and fill away to the new excitement. Excitement is his life, and although like a ship at sea, he is thrown into temporary confusion by a sudden change of the winds and waves, so, like her whose life and activity are the breezes and gale and the ocean wave, he readily accommodates his sails and his course to the ever changing breeze and currents of excitement in the midst of which he loves to live, and on the foaming surface of which he is borne along. If you wish to move him, you must strongly appeal to his feelings. Reason does not, can not govern him. 'Tis not enough to say to him, Thus saith the Lord. He will admit the right, but surely will not do it. He will not go that way, unless you can first make his feelings move in that direction. He holds the truth only in theory and in unrighteousness. It is not the law of his life, his heart, his warmest affections and sympathies. Present considerations to his intelligence: unless they excite his sensibility, and arouse his hopes, or fears, or feelings in some direction, you might as well attempt to change the course of the winds by your words. His imagination must be aroused and set on fire. His sensibility must be reached, enkindled. The gales of excitement must be awaked, and the mainspring of his action must be touched and directed to impel his will, before you can quicken him into life. His feelings are his law.

The saint is justified, and he has the evidence of it in the peace of his own mind. He is conscious of obeying the law of reason and of love. Consequently he naturally has that kind and degree of peace that flows from the harmony of his will with the law of his intelligence. He sometimes has conflicts with the impulses of feeling and desire. But unless he is overcome, these conflicts, though they may cause him inwardly and perhaps audibly to groan, do not interrupt his peace. There are still the elements of peace within him. His heart and conscience are at one, and while this is so, he has thus far the evidence of justification in himself. That is, he knows that God can not condemn his present state. Conscious as he is of conformity of heart to the moral law he can not but affirm to himself that the lawgiver is pleased with his present attitude. But further, he has also within the Spirit of God witnessing with his spirit that he is a child of God, forgiven, accepted, adopted. He feels the filial spirit drawing his heart to exclaim, Father, Father. He is conscious that he pleases God and has God's smile of approbation.

He is at peace with himself because he affirms his heart to be in unison with the law of love. His conscience does not upbraid, but smile. The harmony of his own being is a witness to himself that this is the state in which he was made to exist. He is at peace with God, because he and God are pursuing precisely the same end and by the same means. There can be no collision, no controversy between them. He is at peace with the universe in the sense that he has no ill-will and no malicious feelings or wish

to gratify in the injury of any one of all the creatures of God. He has no fear but to sin against God. He is not influenced on the one hand by the fear of hell, nor on the other by the hope of reward. He is not anxious about his own salvation, but prayerfully and calmly leaves that question in the hands of God and concerns himself only to promote the highest glory of God and the good of being. "Being justified by faith he has peace with God through our Lord Jesus Christ." "There is now no condemnation to them that are in Christ Jesus, who walk not after the flesh, but after the Spirit."

The sinner's experience is the opposite of this. He is under condemnation, and seldom can so far deceive himself, even in his most religious moods, as to imagine that he has a consciousness of acceptance either with his own conscience or with God. There is almost never a time in which he has not a greater or less degree of restlessness and misgiving within. Even when he is most engaged in religion as he supposes, he finds himself dissatisfied with himself. Something is wrong. There is a struggle and a pang. He may not exactly see where and what the difficulty is. He does not after all obey reason and conscience, and is not governed by the law and will of God. Not having the consciousness of this obedience, his conscience does not smile. He sometimes feels deeply, and acts as he feels, and is conscious of being sincere in the sense of feeling what he says and acting in obedience to deep feeling. But this does not satisfy conscience. He is more or less wretched after all. He has not true peace. Sometimes he has a self-righteous quiet and enjoyment. But this is neither peace of conscience nor peace with God. He after all feels uneasy and condemned, notwithstanding all his feeling and zeal and activity. They are not of the right kind. Hence they do not satisfy the conscience. . . .

God's will is not his law; but his own sensibility is his law. With him it is not enough to know the will of God; he must also have his sensibility excited in that direction before he goes. He does not mean or expect to avoid every form and degree of iniquity. His heart has not renounced sin as sin. It has not embraced the will of God from principle, and of course has not embraced the whole will of God. With him it is a small thing to commit what he calls little sins. This shows conclusively where he is. If the will of God were his law—as this is as really opposed to what he calls little as to what he calls great sins, he would not expect and intend to disobey God in one thing more than in another. He could know no little sins, since they conflict with the will of God. He goes about to pick and choose among the commandments of God, sometimes yielding an outward obedience to those that conflict least with his inclinations, and which therefore will cost him the least self-denial, but evading and disregarding those that lay the ax to the root of the tree and prohibit all selfishness. The sinner or deceived professor does not in fact seriously mean or expect wholly to obey God. He thinks that this is common to all Christians. He as much expects to sin every day against God as he expects to live, and does not think this at all inconsistent with his being a real though imperfect Christian. He is conscious of indulging in some sins, and that he has never repented of them and put them away, but he thinks that this also is common to all Christians, and therefore it does not slay his false hope. He would much sooner indulge in gluttony than in drunkenness because the latter would more seriously affect his reputation. He would not hesitate to indulge wanton thoughts and imaginations when he would not allow himself in outward licentiousness because of its bearing upon his character, and as he says, upon the cause of God. He will not hesitate to take little advantages of his neighbor, to amass a fortune in this way while he would recoil from robbing on the highway or on the high seas; for this would injure his reputation with man, and as he thinks, more surely destroy his soul. Sinners sometimes become exceedingly self-righteous and aim at what they call perfection. But unless they are very ignorant they soon become discouraged and cry out, O wretched man that I am, who shall deliver me from the body of this death? They, however, almost always satisfy themselves with a mere outward morality and that, as I have said, not descending to what they call little sins.

Peter Cartwright

1785-1872

Peter Cartwright was one of the most notable camp-meeting preachers of the Middle West. Born in Kentucky, he was converted to Methodism at the age of sixteen during a camp meeting. He then began to proselytize among his acquaintances and, although he had little schooling, he was given a license to preach in 1802. For fifty years he rode Methodist circuits in Kentucky, Tennessee, Indiana, Illinois, and Ohio. His descriptions of the circuit rider's life and experiences provide an excellent portrait of the emotional yet muscular Christianity practiced among the midwesterners.

This selection is from one of his autobiographical works, The Backwoods Preacher *(New York, 1857).*

*M*y appointment, during 1805–6, was on the Scioto Circuit, Ohio State and District. John Sale was presiding elder, and James Quinn was senior preacher, or preacher in charge. The reader will see how greatly I was favoured the first two years of my regular itinerant life, to be placed under two such men as Benjamin Lakin and James Quinn, and more, two such presiding elders as William M'Kendree and John Sale. These four men were able ministers of Jesus Christ, lived long, did much good, witnessed a good confession, died happy, and are all now safely housed in heaven. Peace to their memory for ever!

Scioto Circuit extended from the Ohio River to Chillicothe, situated on that river; and crossed it near the mouth, at what is now called Portsmouth. It was a four-weeks' Circuit, and there were 474 members on it. Dr. Tiffin, who was governor of the State, was a local preacher; and both he and his wife were worthy members of our Church. He lived at Chillicothe, then the seat of government for the State.

There were two incidents happened while I was on the east end of this Circuit, which I will relate.

We had an appointment near Eagle Creek. Here the Shakers broke in Mr. Dunlevy, whom we have mentioned elsewhere as having been a regular Presbyterian minister, who had left that Church and joined the New Lights. His New Light increased so fast, that he lost what little sense he had, and was now a ranting Shaker. He came up here, and roared and fulminated a while, led many astray, flourished for some time, and then his influence died away, and he left for parts unknown.

On the south-eastern part of the Circuit, we took in a new preaching place, at a Mr. Moor's. We gave them Sunday preaching. Mr. Moor had built a large hewn log-house, two stories high. There was no partition in the second story; but it was seated, and he gave it to us to preach in. Not far from this place lived a regularly educated Presbyterian preacher, who had a fine family, and was in many respects a fine man, but, unhappily, he had contracted a love for strong drink. He had preached in this neighborhood, and was much beloved, for he was withal a very good preacher.

In making my way on one occasion to Mr. Moor's, to my Sunday appointment, I got lost and was belated, and when I arrived, there was a large assembly collected, and this minister was preaching to them, and he preached well, and I was quite pleased with the sermon so far as I heard it. When he was done, he undertook to make a public apology for a drunken spree he had got into a few days before. "Well," thought I, "this is right; all right, I suppose!" But to excuse himself for his unaccountable love of whiskey, he stated that he had been informed by his mother that before he was born she longed for whiskey; and he supposed that this was the cause of his appetite for strong drink, for he had loved it from his earliest recollection. This was the substance of his apology.

I felt somewhat indignant at this; and when I rose to close after him, I stated to the congregation that I thought the preacher's apology for drunkenness was infinitely worse than the act of drunkenness itself; that I looked upon it as a lie, and a downright slander on his mother; and that I believed his love of whiskey was the result of the intemperate use of it, in which he had indulged until he formed the habit; and that I, for one, was not willing to accept or believe the truth of his apology; that I feared the preacher would live and die a drunkard, and be damned at last; and that I hoped the people there would not receive him as a preacher until he gave ample evidence that he was entirely cured of drunkenness.

After I made these statements, I felt that God was willing to bless the people there and then; and, raising my voice, gave them as warm an exhortation as I could command. Suddenly an awful power fell on the congregation, and they instantly fell right and left, and cried aloud for mercy. I suppose there were not less than thirty persons smitten down; the young, the old, the middle-aged, indiscriminately, were operated on in this way. My voice at that day was strong and clear; and I could sing, exhort, pray, and preach almost all the

time, day and night. I went through the assembly, singing, exhorting, praying, and directing poor sinners to Christ. While I was thus engaged, the Presbyterian minister left.

There were a few scattered members of the Church around this place, who got happy and shouted aloud for joy, and joined in and exhorted sinners, and they helped me very much. Indeed, our meeting lasted all night, and the greater part of next day. Between twenty and thirty professed religion, and joined the Church; and fully as many more went home under strong conviction and in deep distress. Many of them afterward obtained religion, and joined the Church.

There was a very remarkable case that I will mention here. There was one lady about forty-five years old, who was a member of the Presbyterian Church, and a very rigid predestinarian. Her husband was a Methodist, and several of their children had obtained religion among the young converts. This lady got powerfully convicted, and concluded that she never had any religion. She had fallen to the floor under the mighty power of God. She prayed and agonized hard for days. At length the devil tempted her to believe that she was a reprobate, and that there was no mercy for her. She went into black despair under this temptation of the devil, and such was the desperate state of her mind, that at length she conceived that she was Jesus Christ, and took it upon her, in this assumed character, to bless and curse any and all that came to see her.

The family were, of course, greatly afflicted, and the whole neighbourhood were in great trouble at this afflictive dispensation. Her friends and all of us used every argument in our power, but all in vain. She at length utterly refused to eat, or drink, or sleep. In this condition she lingered for thirteen days and nights, and then died without ever returning to her right mind. A few

persecutors and opposers of the Methodists tried to make a great fuss about
this affair, but they were afraid to go far
with it, for fear the Lord would send the
same affliction on them.

The Hockhocking River lay immediately north of us, the Scioto River
between us. John Meek and James
Axley were assigned to that circuit. The
Circuit reached from Scioto to Zanes-
ville, on the Muskingum River. It was a
hard and laborious Circuit. Brother
Meek's health failed, and Brother Sale,
our presiding elder, moved me from
Scioto, and placed me on this Circuit
with Brother Axley. I was sorry to
leave the Brethren on the Scioto
Circuit, and especially Brother Quinn,
whom I dearly loved; but Brother Sale
was still my presiding elder, and Brother
Quinn's family lived in Hockhocking
Circuit, and a precious family it was.

I got to see Brother Quinn every
round. Brother Axley and myself were
like Jonathan and David. There were
no parsonages in those days, and
Brother Quinn lived in a little cabin on
his father-in-law's land. He had several
children, and his cabin was small. When
the preachers would come to see him,
they would eat and converse with
Brother Quinn and family, but would
sleep at old Father Teel's, Brother
Quinn's father-in-law. The first time I
came round, I spent the afternoon with
Brother Quinn. He made some apologies,
and told me I could sleep better at
Father Teel's. "But," said he, "I will
tell you how you must do. You will
sleep, at Father Teel's, in one part of his
double cabin; he and his family will
sleep in the other. His custom is to rise
early. As soon as ever he dresses himself he commences giving out a hymn,
sings, and then goes to prayer; he does
not even wait for his family to get up.
He serves the preachers the same way.
He never was known to wait a minute
for any preacher except Bishop Asbury.
You must rise early, dress quickly, and

go right into the other room, if you want
to be at morning prayer. I thought I
would tell you beforehand, that you
might not be taken by surprise."

I thanked him. "But," said I, "why
don't the preachers cure the old man of
this disorderly way?"

"O, he is old and set in his way," said
Brother Quinn.

"You may rest assured I will cure
him," said I.

"O, no," said he, "you cannot."

So I retired to old Father Teel's to
sleep. We had family prayer, and I
retired to rest. I had no fear about the
matter; for I was a constant early riser,
and always thought it very wrong for
preachers to sleep late and keep the
families waiting on them. Just as day
broke I awoke, rose up, and began to
dress; but had not nigh accomplished it
when I distinctly heard Teel give out his
hymn and commence singing, and about
the time I had got dressed I heard him
commence praying. He gave thanks to
God that they had been spared through
the night, and were all permitted to see
the light of a new day, and at the same
time I suppose every one of his family
were fast asleep. I deliberately opened
the door and walked out to the well,
washed myself, and then walked back
to my cabin. Just as I got to the door,
the old brother opened his door, and,
seeing me, said:—

"Good morning, sir. Why, I did not
know you were up."

"Yes," said I; "I have been up some
time."

"Well, brother," said he, "why did
you not come in to prayers?"

"Because," said I, "it is wrong to
pray of a morning in the family before
we wash."

The old brother passed on, and no
more was said at that time. That evening
just before we were about to retire to
rest, the old brother set out the book and
said to me:—

"Brother, hold prayers with us."

"No, sir," said I.

Said he: "Come, brother, take the book and pray with us."

"No, sir," said I; "you love to pray so well you may do it yourself."

He insisted, but I persistently refused, saying,—

"You are so fond of praying yourself, that you even thanked God this morning that He had spared you all to see the light of a new day, when your family had not yet opened their eyes, but were all fast asleep. And you have such an absurd way of holding prayers in your family, that I do not wish to have anything to do with it."

He then took up the book, read, and said prayers, but you may rely on it the next morning things were much changed. He waited for me, and had all his family up in order. He acknowledged his error, and told me it was one of the best reproofs he ever got. I then prayed with the family, and after that all went on well.

Our last quarterly-meeting was a camp-meeting. We had a great many tents, and a large turn-out for a new country, and, perhaps, there never was a greater collection of rabble and rowdies. They came drunk, and armed with dirks, clubs, knives, and horse-whips, and swore they would break up the meeting. After interrupting us very much on Saturday night, they collected early on Sunday morning, determined on a general riot. At eight o'clock I was appointed to preach. About the time I was half through my discourse, two very fine-dressed young men marched into the congregation with loaded whips, and hats on, and rose up and stood in the midst of the ladies, and began to laugh and talk. They were near the stand, and I requested them to desist and get off the seats; but they cursed me, and told me to mind my own business, and said they would not get down.

I stopped trying to preach, and called for a magistrate. There were two at hand, but I saw they were both afraid. I ordered them to take these men into custody, but they said they could not do it. I told them, as I left the stand, to command me to take them, and I would do it at the risk of my life. I advanced toward them. They ordered me to stand off, but I advanced. One of them made a pass at my head with his whip, but I closed in with him, and jerked him off the seat. A regular scuffle ensued. The congregation by this time were all in commotion. I heard the magistrates give general orders, commanding all friends of order to aid in suppressing the riot. In the scuffle I threw my prisoner down, and held him fast; he tried his best to get loose; I told him to be quiet, or I would pound his chest well. The mob rose, and rushed to the rescue of the two prisoners, for they had taken the other young man also. An old and drunken magistrate came up to me, and ordered me to let my prisoner go. I told him I should not. He swore if I did not, he would knock me down. I told him to crack away. Then one of my friends, at my request, took hold of my prisoner, and the drunken justice made a pass at me; but I parried the stroke, and seized him by the collar and the hair of the head, and, fetching him a sudden jerk forward, brought him to the ground, and jumped on him. I told him to be quiet, or I would pound him well. The mob then rushed to the scene; they knocked down seven magistrates, and several preachers and others.

I gave up my drunken prisoner to another, and threw myself in front of the friends of order. Just at this moment, the ringleader of the mob and I met; he made three passes at me, intending to knock me down. The last time he struck at me, by the force of his own effort, he threw the side of his face toward me. It seemed at that moment I had not power to resist temptation, and I struck a sudden blow in the burr of the ear and dropped him to the earth. Just at that moment the friends of order rushed by hundreds on the mob, knocking them down in every direction. In a few minutes, the place became too strait for the mob, and they wheeled and fled in every direction; but we secured about thirty prisoners, marched them off to a vacant tent, and put them under guard till Monday morning, when they were tried, and every man was fined to the utmost limits of the law. The aggregate amount of fines and costs was near three hundred dollars. They fined my old drunken magistrate twenty dollars, and returned him to court, and he was cashiered of his office. On Sunday, when we had vanquished the mob, the whole encampment was filled with mourning; and although there was no attempt to resume preaching till evening, yet such was our confused state, that there was not then a single preacher on the ground willing to preach, from the presiding elder, John Sale, down. Seeing we had fallen on evil times, my spirit was stirred within me. I said to the elder, "I feel a clear conscience; for under the necessity of the circumstances we have done right; and now I ask to let me preach."

"Do," said the elder; "for there is no other man on the ground can do it."

The encampment was lighted up, the trumpet blown, I rose in the stand, and required every soul to leave the tents and come into the congregation. There was a general rush to the stand. I requested the brethren, if ever they prayed in all their lives, to pray now. My voice was strong and clear, and my preaching was more of an exhortation and encouragement than anything else. My text was, "The gates of hell shall not prevail." In about thirty minutes the power of God fell on the congregation in such a manner as is seldom seen; the people fell in every direction, right and left, front and rear. It was supposed that not less than three hundred fell like dead men in mighty battle; and there was no need of calling mourners, for they were strewed all over the camp-ground; loud wailings went up to heaven from sinners for mercy, and a general shout from Christians, so that the noise was heard afar off. Our meeting lasted all night, and Monday and Monday night; and when we closed on Tuesday, there were two hundred who had professed religion, and about that number joined the Church.

CHAPTER XII
THE TRANSCENDENTALIST INTERLUDE

New England Transcendentalism was another characteristic expression of the American mind. Unsatisfied by the Enlightenment's rationalism or the religion of their own day, distrustful both of the new science and the emphasis on business and materialism, Transcendentalists sought a new faith. The result was a high romantic idealism mixed with a practical sense of social responsibility. Less a systematic philosophy than a "call" or an individual challenge, Transcendentalism sought to redefine the American ideal of individualism in terms of a romantic *Weltanschauung* and to promote the humanitarian ends that view entailed.

For their philosophical and theological views, Transcendentalists drew inspiration from many sources, especially Christianity (or more precisely, Unitarianism), Platonism, and Oriental mysticism. And though they expressed their convictions in highly individualistic ways, they did develop a core of central doctrines that defined their position. They accepted the Christian ethic and shared its belief that the world has a moral purpose and destiny. The moral law, wrote Emerson, "lies at the center of nature and radiates to the circumference." Every physical fact, he believed, is related to and expresses a moral fact: hence all reality must be viewed in moral terms. Secondly, the Transcendentalists accepted the Platonic doctrine that the world of nature is not the real world, but merely the appearance or phenomenon of a more basic spiritual reality. Since nature had no substantive reality of its own, it follows that nature is divine only as it expresses the divine spirit. Thirdly, the Transcendentalists, following Eastern mystics, believed that man has the ability to know "higher" truths directly or intuitively. Thus they believed that a philosophy limiting knowledge to the wisdom of the senses could only be partial and inadequate; it was their view that man could grasp moral and spiritual truths by direct insight. Finally, the Transcendentalists believed in the divinity and dignity of man, urging that man's free creative capacities give him the potential for higher development if he would but practice self-trust and self-reliance.

Transcendentalist humanitarianism was an outgrowth of this final point, the worth of the individual. Channing made the moral character and concerns of God and men basic in his philosophy of Unitarianism. Parker in his many writings and activities fought against privilege and social injustice from a theological vantage point; he has been called America's first "theological rebel," and was also the most distinguished metaphysician of the group. Thoreau, concerned for a true democracy that recognized the individual, wrestled with such social problems as individual rights, justice, and majority rule. All members of the group—even to some extent the remote Emerson—identified themselves with the major reform movements of the day, from abolition to labor law reforms. Thus the Transcendentalist creed combined an intense idealism with pragmatic involvement.

Transcendentalism produced the only major American philosophers to appear in the century and a half between Jonathan Edwards and the Pragmatists. (The men of the Enlightenment never realized their potential for philosophical achievement, perhaps because they were too narrowly interested in political affairs.) However, Transcendentalism itself did not develop into a major American philosophy, or even a widely held doctrine. Its idealism was philosophical and theoretical, whereas the idealism of most Americans was moral and practical. Its distrust of science and technology did not suit the temper of an industrializing nation, nor did it clearly enough define the relation between philosophic thought and social action.

Theodore Parker

1810-1860

*Parker was a leading Unitarian clergyman.
He was the son of a Lexington farmer, and
his grandfather had been captain of the
Minutemen who fought on Lexington
Common. Too poor to attend college, he was
able to earn enough by teaching school to
spend two years at Harvard Divinity School.
He was the most learned clergyman of his
time, a master of twenty languages who
was at home among both American and
European scholars. He gave Transcendentalism its most systematic philosophical
statement.*

*Parker was not merely a scholarly
theologian, however. His sermons on slavery
and his protests against injustice are moving
exhortations. Few causes of social protest
failed to gain his influential support. Parker
was thus an interesting combination of the
man of letters and the political activist.*

The selection here is from The World of
Matter and the Spirit of Man (*Boston:
Beacon Press, 1907*).

*T*his is the problem of metaphysics,—to explain the facts of human
consciousness. In metaphysics there are
and have long been two schools of
philosophers. The first is the sensational
school. Its most important metaphysical
doctrine is this: There is nothing in the
intellect which was not first in the senses. Here "intellect" means the whole
intellectual, moral, affectional and religious consciousness of man. The philosophers of this school claim to have
reached this conclusion legitimately by
the inductive method. It was at first an
hypothesis; but after analyzing the facts
of consciousness, interrogating all the
ideas and sentiments and sensations of
man, they say the hypothesis is proved
by the most careful induction. They
appeal to it as a principle, as a maxim,
from which other things are deduced.
They say that experience by one or
more of the senses is the ultimate appeal
in philosophy: all that I know is of
sensational origin; the senses are the
windows which let in all the light I
have; the senses afford a sensation. I
reflect upon this, and by reflection
transform a sensation into an idea. An
idea, therefore, is a transformed sensation. . . .

Sensationalism must have a philosophy of religion, a theology; let us see
what theology. There are two parties;
one goes by philosophy, the other mis-
trusts philosophy.

1. The first thing in theology is to
know God. The idea of God is the touchstone of a theologian. Now to know the
existence of God is to be certain thereof
as of my own existence. "Nothing in the
intellect which was not first in the
senses," says sensationalism; "all comes
by sensational experience and reflection
thereon." Sensationalism—does that
give us the idea of God? I ask the sensa-
tionalist, "Does the sensational eye see
God?" "No." "The ear hear him?"
"No." "Do the organs of sense touch or
taste him?" "No." "How then do you
get the idea of God?" "By induction
from facts of observation *a posteriori*.
The senses deal with finite things; I
reflect on them, put them all together I

193

assume that they have *cause;* then by inductive method I find out the character of that cause: that is God." Then I say, "But the senses deal with only finite things, so you must infer only a finite maker, else the induction is imperfect. So you have but a finite God. Then these finite things, measured only by my experience, are imperfect things. Look at disorders in the frame of nature; the sufferings of animals, the miseries of men; here are seeming imperfections which the sensational philosopher staggers at. But to go on with this induction: from an imperfect work you must infer an imperfect author. So the God of sensationalism is not only finite, but imperfect even at that. But am I certain of the existence of the finite and imperfect God? The existence of the outward world is only an hypothesis, its laws hypothetical; all that depends on that or them is but an hypothesis—the truth of your faculties, the forms of matter only an hypothesis: so the existence of God is not a certainty; he is but our hypothetical God. But a hypothetical God is no God at all, not the living God: an imperfect God is no God at all, not the true God: a finite God is no God at all, not the absolute God. But this hypothetical, finite, imperfect God, where is he? In matter? No. In spirit? No. Does he act in matter or spirit? No, only now and then he did act by miracle; he is outside of the world of matter and spirit. Then he is a non-resident, an absentee. A non-resident God is no God at all, not the all-present God. . . ."

But another party comes out of the same school to treat of religious matters; they give their philosophy a vacation, and to prove the existence of God they go back to tradition, and say, "Once God revealed himself to the senses of men; they heard him, they saw him, they felt him; so to them the existence of God was not an induction, but a fact of observation; they told it to others, through whom it comes to us; we can

say it is not a fact of observation but a fact of testimony."

"Well," I ask, "are you certain then? "Yes." "Quite sure? Let me look. The man to whom God revealed himself may have been mistaken; it may have been a dream, or a whim of his own, perhaps a fib; at any rate, he was not philosophically certain of the existence of the outward world in general; how could he be of anything that took place in it? Next, the evidence which relates the transaction is not wholly reliable: how do I know the books which tell of it tell the truth, that they were not fabricated to deceive me? All that rests on testimony is a little uncertain if it took place one or two thousand years ago; especially if I know nothing about the persons who testify or of that whereof they testify; still more so if it be a thing, as you say, unphilosophical and even supernatural."

So, then, the men who gave a vacation to their philosophy have slurred the philosophical argument for a historical, the theological for the mythological, and have gained nothing except the tradition of God. By this process we are as far from the infinite God as before, and have only arrived at the same point where the philosophy left us. . . .

I come now to the other school. This is distinguished by its chief metaphysical doctrine, that there is in the intellect (or consciousness), something that never was in the senses, to wit, the intellect (or consciousness) itself; that man has faculties which transcend the senses; faculties which give him ideas and intuitions that transcend sensational experience; ideas whose origin is not from sensation, nor their proof from sensation. This is the transcendental school. They maintain that the mind (meaning thereby all which is not sense) is not a smooth tablet on which sensation writes its experience, but is a living principle which of itself originates ideas when the senses present the occasion; that, as there is a body with certain senses, so there is a soul or mind with certain powers which give the man sentiments and ideas. This school maintains that it is a fact of consciousness itself that there is in the intellect somewhat that was not first in the senses; and also that they have analyzed consciousness, and by the inductive method established the conclusion that there is a consciousness that never was sensation, never could be; that our knowledge is in part *a priori;* that we know, 1, certain truths of necessity; 2, certain truths of intuition, or spontaneous consciousness; 3, certain truths of demonstration, a voluntary consciousness; all of these truths not dependent on sensation for cause, origin, or proof. Facts of observation, sensational experience, it has in common with the other school. . . .

Transcendentalism admits a religious faculty, element, or nature in man, as it admits a moral, intellectual and sensational faculty—that man by nature is a religious being as well as moral, intellectual, sensational; that this religious faculty is adequate to its purposes and wants, as much so as the others, as the eye acquainting us with light; and that this faculty is the source of religious emotions, of the sentiments of adoration, worship. Through this we have consciousness of God as through the senses consciousness of matter. In connection with reason it gives us the primary ideas of religion, ideas which transcend experience.

Now the transcendental philosophy legitimates the ideas of religion by reference to human nature. Some of them it finds truths of necessity, which cannot be conceived of as false or unreal without violence to reason; some it finds are truths of consciousness—of spontaneous consciousness, or intuition; some, truths of voluntary consciousness, or demonstration, inductive or deductive. Such ideas, capable of this legitimation, transcend experience, require and admit no further proof; as true before experience as after; true before time, after time, eternally; absolutely true. On that rock transcendentalism founds religion, sees its foundation, and doubts no more of religious truths than of the truths of mathematics. All the truths of religion it finds can be verified in consciousness today, what cannot is not religion. But it does not neglect experience. In human history it finds confirmations, illustrations, of the ideas of human nature, for history represents the attempt of mankind to develop human nature. So then as transcendentalism in philosophy legitimates religion by a reference to truths of necessity, to truths of consciousness, it illustrates religion by facts of observation, facts of testimony.

By sensationalism religious faith is a belief, more or less strange, in a probability, a credibility, a possibility. By transcendentalism religious faith is the normal action of the whole spiritual nature of man, which gives him certain knowledge of a certainty not yet attainable by experience; where understanding ends faith begins, and outtravels the understanding. Religion is natural to man, is justice, piety—free justice, free piety, free thought. The form thereof should fit the individual; hence there will be a unity of substance, diversity of form. So a transcendental religion demands a transcendental theology.

The transcendental philosophy appears in its doctrine of God. The idea of God is a fact given in the consciousness of man; consciousness of the infinite is the condition of a consciousness of the finite. I learn of a finite thing by sensation, I get an idea thereof; at the same time the idea of the infinite unfolds in me. I am not conscious of my own existence except as a finite existence, that is, as a dependent existence; and the idea of the infinite, of God on whom I depend, comes at the same time as the logical correlative to a knowledge of myself. So the existence of God is a certainty; I am as certain of that as of my own existence. Indeed without that knowledge I know nothing. Of this I am certain—I am; but of this as certain—God is; for if I am, and am finite and dependent, then this presupposes the infinite and independent. So the idea of God is *a priori;* rests on facts of necessity, on facts of consciousness.

Then transcendentalism uses the other mode, the *a posteriori.* Starting with the infinite, it finds signs and proofs of him everywhere, and gains evidence of God's existence in the limits of sensational observation; the thing refers to its maker, the thought to the mind, the effect to the cause, the created to the creator, the finite to the infinite; at the end of my arms are two major prophets, ten minor prophets, each of them pointing the transcendental philosopher to the infinite God, of which he has consciousness without the logical process of induction.

Then the character of God as given in the idea of him, given in consciousness— that represents God as a being, not with the limitations of impersonality (that is to confound God with matter); not with the limitations of personality (that confounds him with man); but God with no limitations, infinite, absolute; looked at from sensation, infinite power; from thought, infinite intellect; from the moral sense, infinite conscience; from the emotional, infinite affection; from the religious, infinite soul; from all truth, the whole human nature names him Infinite Father!

God is immanent in matter, so it is; immanent in spirit, so it is. He acts also as God in matter and spirit, acts perfectly; laws of matter or of spirit are modes of God's acting, being; as God is perfect, so the mode of his action is perfect and unchangeable. Therefore, as God is ever in matter and spirit, and where God is is wholly God active, so no intervention is possible. God cannot come where he already is, so no miracle is possible. A miracle *a parte humanâ* is a violation of what is a law to man; a miracle to God—*a parte divinâ*—is a violation of what is law to God; the most extraordinary things that have been seem miracles *a parte humanâ*—laws, *a parte divinâ.* But though God is immanent in matter and in spirit, he yet transcends both matter and spirit, has no limitations. Indeed all perfection of immanence and transcendence belong to him—the perfection of existence, infinite being; the perfection of space, immensity; the perfection of time, eternity; of power, all-mightiness; of mind, all-knowingness; of affection, all-lovingness; of will, absolute freedom, absolute justice, absolute right. His providence is not merely general, but universal, so special in each thing. Hence the universe partakes of his perfection, is a perfect universe for the end he made it for. . . .

The sensational philosophy, with all its evils, has done the world a great service. It has stood up for the body, for common sense, protested against spiritual tyranny, against the spiritualism of the middle ages which thought the senses wicked and the material world profane. To sensationalism we are indebted for the great advance of mankind in physical science, in discovery, arts, mechanics, and for many improvements in government. Some of its men are great names—Bacon, Locke, Newton. Let us do them no dishonor; they saw what they could, told it; they saw not all things that are, saw some which are not. In our day no one of them would be content with the philosophy they all agreed in then. Hobbes and Hume have done us service; the Socinians, Priestley, Collins, Berkeley, Dodwell, Mandeville, Edwards. To take the good and leave the ill is our part; but the doubts which this philosophy raises, the doubt of Hume, the doubt of Hobbes, of the English Deists in general, do not get answered by this philosophy. For this we have weapons forged by other hands, tempered in another spring.

Transcendentalism has a work to do, to show that physics, politics, ethics, religion rest on facts of necessity, facts of intuition, facts of demonstration, and have their witness and confirmation in facts of observation. It is the work of transcendentalism to give us politics which represent God's thought of a state,—the whole world, each man free; to give us morals which leave the man a complete individual, no chord rent from the human harp—yet complete in his social character, no string discordant in the social choir; to give us religion worthy of God and man,—free goodness, free piety, free thought. That is not to be done by talking at random, not by idleness, not by railing at authority, calumniating the past or the present; not by idle brains with open mouth, who outrage common sense; but the diligent toil, brave discipline, patience to wait, patience to work. Nothing comes of nothing, foolishness of fools; but something from something, wise thought from thinking men; and of the wise thought comes a lovely deed, life, laws, institutions for mankind.

The problem of transcendental philosophy is no less than this, to revise the experience of mankind and try its teachings by the nature of mankind; to test ethics by conscience, science by reason; to try the creeds of the churches; the constitutions of the states by the constitution of the universe; to reverse what is wrong, supply what is wanting, and command the just. To do this in a nation like ours, blinded still by the sensational philosophy, devoted chiefly to material interests, its politics guided by the madness of party more than sober reason; to do this in a race like the Anglo-Saxon, which has an obstinate leaning to a sensational philosophy, which loves facts of experience, not ideas of consciousness, and believes not in the First-Fair, First-Perfect, First-Good, is no light work; not to be taken in hand by such as cannot bear the strife of tongues, the toil, the heat, the war of thought; not to be accomplished by a single man, however well-born and well-bred; not by a single age and race. It has little of history behind, for this philosophy is young. It looks to a future, a future to be made; a church whose creed is truth, whose worship love; a society full of industry and abundance, full of wisdom, virtue, and the poetry of life; a state with unity among all, with freedom for each; a church without tyranny, a society without ignorance, want, or crime, a state without oppression; yes, a world with no war among the nations to consume the work of their hands, and no restrictive policy to hinder the welfare of mankind. That is the human dream of the transcendental philosophy. Shall it ever become a fact? History says, No; human nature says, Yes.

Ralph Waldo Emerson

1803-1882

Emerson was the most widely read of the Transcendentalists. He graduated from Harvard in 1821, taught school for a short time, and then attended Harvard Divinity School, where he was ordained in the Unitarian ministry. In 1829 Emerson became minister of the Old North Church in Boston; but becoming dissatisfied with formal, institutionalized religion, he resigned in 1832 and settled in Concord, where he remained for the rest of his life.

A stream of essays and addresses came from Emerson's pen, all giving expression to his romantic Platonism. Behind nature, Emerson taught, lies a higher spiritual world; and the individual personality, containing a "spark of the divine" within it, realizes itself through the individualistic virtues. In his emphasis on individualism, Transcendentalism gave expression to dominant American values.

This selection is from Emerson's essay on "Self-Reliance," in Essays, First Series *(Boston, 1883).*

I read the other day some verses written by an eminent painter which were original and not conventional. The soul always hears an admonition in such lines, let the subject be what it may. The sentiment they instill is of more value than any thought they may contain. To believe your own thought, to believe that what is true for you in your private heart is true for all men,—that is genius. Speak your latent conviction, and it shall be the universal sense; for the inmost in due time becomes the outmost, and our first thought is rendered back to us by the trumpets of the Last Judgment. Familiar as the voice of the mind is to each, the highest merit we ascribe to Moses, Plato and Milton is that they set at naught books and traditions, and spoke not what men, but what *they* thought. A man should learn to detect and watch that gleam of light which flashes across his mind from within, more than the lustre of the firmament of bards and sages. Yet he dismisses without notice his thought, because it is his. In every work of genius we recognize our own rejected thoughts; they come back to us with a certain alienated majesty. Great works of art have no more arresting lesson for us than this. They teach us to abide by our spontaneous impression with good-humored inflexibility then most when the whole cry of voices is on the other side. Else to-morrow a stranger will say with masterly good sense precisely what we have thought and felt all the time, and we shall be forced to take with shame our own opinion from another.

There is a time in every man's education when he arrives at the conviction that envy is ignorance; that imitation is suicide; that he must take himself for better for worse as his portion; that though the wide universe is full of good, no kernel of nourishing corn can come to him but through his toil bestowed on that plot of ground which is given to him to till. The power which resides in him is new in nature, and none but he knows what that is which he can do, nor does he know until he has tried. Not for nothing one face, one character, one fact, makes much impression on him, and another none. This sculpture in the memory is not without preëstablished harmony. The eye was placed where one ray should fall, that it might testify of that particular ray. We but half express ourselves, and are ashamed of that divine idea which each of us represents. It may be safely trusted as proportionate and of good issues, so it be faithfully imparted, but God will not have his work made manifest by cowards. A man is relieved and gay when he has put his heart into his work and done his best; but what he has said or done otherwise shall give him no peace. It is a deliverance which does not deliver. In the attempt his genius deserts him; no muse befriends; no invention, no hope.

Trust thyself: every heart vibrates to that iron string. Accept the place the divine providence has found for you, the society of your contemporaries, the connection of events. Great men have always done so, and confided themselves childlike to the genius of their age, betraying their perception that the absolutely trustworthy was seated at their heart, working through their hands, predominating in all their being. And we are now men, and must accept in the highest mind the same transcendent destiny; and not minors and invalids in a protected corner, not cowards fleeing before a revolution, but guides, redeemers and benefactors, obeying the Almighty effort and advancing on Chaos and the Dark. . . .

Whoso would be a man, must be a nonconformist. He who would gather immortal palms must not be hindered by the name of goodness, but must explore if it be goodness. Nothing is at last sacred but the integrity of your own mind. Absolve you to yourself, and you shall have the suffrage of the world. I remember an answer which when quite young I was prompted to make to a valued adviser who was wont to importune me with the dear old doctrines of the church. On my saying, "What have I to do with the sacredness of traditions, if I live wholly from within?" my friend suggested,—"But these impulses may be from below, not from above." I replied, "They do not seem to me to be such; but if I am the Devil's child, I will live then from the Devil." No law can be sacred to me but that of my nature. Good and bad are but names very readily transferable to that or this; the only right is what is after my constitution; the only wrong what is against it. A man is to carry himself in the presence of all opposition as if every thing were titular and ephemeral but he. I am ashamed to think how easily we capitulate to badges and names, to large societies and dead institutions. Every decent and well-spoken individual affects and sways me more than is right. I ought to go upright and vital, and speak the rude truth in all ways. If malice and vanity wear the coat of philanthropy, shall that pass? If an angry bigot assumes this bountiful cause of Abolition, and comes to me with his last news from Barbadoes, why should I not say to him, 'Go love thy infant; love thy wood chopper; be good-natured and modest; have the grace; and never varnish your hard, uncharitable ambition with this incredible tenderness for black folk a thousand miles off. Thy love afar is spite at home.' Rough and graceless would be such greeting, but truth is handsomer than the affectation of love. Your goodness must have some edge to it,—else it is none. The doctrine of hatred must be preached, as the counteraction of the doctrine of love, when that pules and whines. I shun father and mother and wife and brother when my genius calls me. I would write on the lintels of the door-post, *Whim.* I hope it is somewhat better than whim at last, but we cannot spend the day in explanation. Expect me not to show cause why I sock or why I exclude company. Then again, do not tell me, as a good man did to-day, of my obligation to put all poor men in good situations. Are they *my* poor? I tell thee thou foolish philanthropist that I grudge the dollar, the dime, the cent I give to such men as do not belong to me and to whom I do not belong. There is a class of persons to whom by all spiritual affinity I am bought and sold; for them I will go to prison if need be; but your miscellaneous popular charities: the education at college of fools; the building of meeting-houses to the vain end to which many now stand; alms to sots, and the thousand-fold Relief Societies;—though I confess with shame I sometimes succumb and give the dollar, it is a wicked dollar, which by and by I shall have the manhood to withhold.

Virtues are, in the popular estimate, rather the exception than the rule. There is the man *and* his virtues. Men do what is called a good action, as some piece of courage or charity, much as they would pay a fine in expiation of daily nonappearance on parade. Their works are done as an apology or extenuation of their living in the world,—as invalids and the insane pay a high board. Their virtues are penances. I do not wish to expiate, but to live. My life is for itself and not for a spectacle. I much prefer that it should be of a lower strain, so it be genuine and equal, than that it should be glittering and unsteady. I wish it to be sound and sweet, and not to need diet and bleeding. I ask primary evidence that you are a man, and refuse this appeal from the man to his actions. I know that for myself it makes no difference whether I do or forbear those actions which are reckoned excellent. I cannot consent to pay for a privilege where I have intrinsic right. Few and mean as my gifts may be, I actually am, and do not need for my own assurance or the assurance of my fellows any secondary testimony.

What I must do is all that concerns me, not what the people think. This rule, equally arduous in actual and in intellectual life, may serve for the whole distinction between greatness and meanness. It is the harder because you will always find those who think they know what is your duty better than you know it. It is easy in the world to live after the world's opinion; it is easy in solitude to live after our own; but the great man is he who in the midst of the crowd keeps with perfect sweetness the independence of solitude. . . .

For nonconformity the world whips you with its displeasure. And therefore a man must know how to estimate a sour face. The by-standers look askance on him in the public street or in the friend's parlor. If this aversion had its origin in contempt and resistance like his own he might well go home with a sad countenance; but the sour faces of the multitude, like their sweet faces, have no deep cause, but are put on and off as the wind blows and a newspaper directs. Yet is the discontent of the multitude more formidable than that of the senate and the college. It is easy enough for a firm man who knows the world to brook the rage of the cultivated classes. Their rage is decorous and prudent, for they are timid, as being very vulnerable themselves. But when to their feminine rage the indignation of the people is added, when the ignorant and the poor are aroused, when the unintelligent brute force that lies at the bottom of society is made to growl and mow, it needs the habit of magnanimity and religion to treat it godlike as a trifle of no concernment.

The other terror that scares us from self-trust is our consistency; a reverence for our past act or word because the eyes of others have no other data for computing our orbit than our past acts, and we are loath to disappoint them.

But why should you keep your head over your shoulder? Why drag about this corpse of your memory, lest you contradict somewhat you have stated in this or that public place? Suppose you should contradict yourself; what then? It seems to be a rule of wisdom never to rely on your memory alone, scarcely even in acts of pure memory, but to bring the past for judgment into the thousand-eyed present, and live ever in a new day. In your metaphysics you have denied personality to the Deity, yet when the devout motions of the soul come, yield to them heart and life, though they should clothe God with shape and color. Leave your theory, as Joseph his coat in the hand of the harlot, and flee.

A foolish consistency is the hobgoblin of little minds, adored by little statesmen and philosophers and divines. With consistency a great soul has simply nothing to do. He may as well concern himself with his shadow on the wall. Speak what you think now in hard words and to-morrow speak what to-morrow thinks in hard words again, though it contradict every thing you said to-day. "Ah, so you shall be sure to be misunderstood." Is it so bad then to be misunderstood? Pythagoras was misunderstood, and Socrates, and Jesus, and Luther, and Copernicus, and Galileo, and Newton, and every pure and wise spirit that ever took flesh. To be great is to be misunderstood.

I hope in these days we have heard the last of conformity and consistency. Let the words be gazetted and ridiculous henceforward. Instead of the gong for dinner, let us hear a whistle from the Spartan fife. Let us never bow and apologize more. A great man is coming to eat at my house. I do not wish to please him; I wish that he should wish to please me. I will stand here for humanity, and though I would make it kind, I would make it true. Let us affront and reprimand the smooth mediocrity and squalid contentment of the times, and hurl in the face of custom and trade and office, the fact which is the upshot of all history, that there is a great responsible Thinker and Actor working wherever a man works; that a true man belongs to no other time or place, but is the centre of things. Where he is, there is nature. He measures you and all men and all events. Ordinarily, every body in society reminds us of somewhat else, or of some other person. Character, reality, reminds you of nothing else; it takes place of the whole creation. The man must be so much that he must make all circumstances indifferent. Every true man is a cause, a country, and an age; requires infinite spaces and numbers and time fully to accomplish his design; and posterity seem to follow his steps as a train of clients. A man Cæsar is born, and for ages after we have a Roman Empire. Christ is born, and millions of minds so grow and cleave to his genius that he is confounded with virtue and the possible of man. An institution is the lengthened shadow of one man; as, Monachism, of the Hermit Antony; the Reformation, of Luther; Quakerism, of Fox; Methodism, of Wesley; Abolition, of Clarkson. Scipio, Milton called "the height of Rome;" and all history resolves itself very easily into the biography of a few stout and earnest persons. . . .

This is the ultimate fact which we so quickly reach on this, as on every topic, the resolution of all into the ever-blessed ONE. Self-existence is the attribute of the Supreme Cause, and it constitutes the measure of good by the degree in which it enters into all lower forms. All things real are so by so much virtue as they contain. Commerce, husbandry, hunting, whaling, war, eloquence, personal weight, are somewhat, and engage my respect as examples of its presence and impure action. I see the same law working in nature for conservation and growth. Power is, in nature, the essential measure of right. Nature suffers nothing to remain in her kingdoms which cannot help itself. The genesis and maturation of a planet, its poise and orbit, the bended tree recovering itself from the strong wind, the vital resources of every animal and vegetable, are demonstrations of the self-sufficing and therefore self-relying soul.

Thus all concentrates: let us not rove; let us sit at home with the cause. Let us stun and astonish the intruding rabble of men and books and institutions by a simple declaration of the divine fact. Bid the invaders take the shoes from off their feet, for God is here within. Let our simplicity judge them, and our docility to our own law demonstrate the poverty of nature and fortune beside our native riches.

But now we are a mob. Man does not stand in awe of man, nor is his genius admonished to stay at home, to put itself in communication with the internal ocean, but it goes abroad to beg a cup of water of the urns of other men. We must go alone. I like the silent church before the service begins, better than any preaching. How far off, how cool, how chaste the persons look, begirt each one with a precinct or sanctuary! So let us always sit. Why should we assume the faults of our friend, or wife, or father, or child, because they sit around our hearth, or are said to have the same blood? All men have my blood and I have all men's. Not for that will I adopt their petulance or folly, even to the extent of being ashamed of it. But your isolation must not be mechanical, but spiritual, that is, must be elevation. At times the whole world seems to be in conspiracy to importune you with emphatic trifles. Friend, client, child, sickness, fear, want, charity, all knock at once at thy closet door and say,— "Come out unto us." But keep thy state; come not into their confusion. The power men possess to annoy me I give them by a weak curiosity. No man can come near me but through my act. "What we love that we have, but by desire we bereave ourselves of the love." . . .

The populace think that your rejection of popular standards is a rejection of all standard, and mere antinomianism; and the bold sensualist will use the name of philosophy to gild his crimes. But the law of consciousness abides. There are two confessionals, in one or the other of which we must be shriven. You may fulfil your round of duties by clearing yourself in the *direct*, or in the *reflex* way. Consider whether you have satisfied your relations to father, mother, cousin, neighbor, town, cat and dog; whether any of these can upbraid you. But I may also neglect this reflex standard and absolve me to myself. I have my own stern claims and perfect circle. It denies the name of duty to many offices that are called duties. But if I can discharge its debts it enables me to dispense with the popular code. If any one imagines that this law is lax, let him keep its commandment one day.

And truly it demands something godlike in him who has cast off the common motives of humanity and has ventured to trust himself for a taskmaster. High be his heart, faithful his will, clear his sight, that he may in good earnest be doctrine, society, law, to himself, that a simple purpose may be to him as strong as iron necessity is to others!

Henry David Thoreau

1817-1862

Born in Concord, Massachusetts, Thoreau graduated from Harvard at the age of twenty but characteristically refused his diploma. He taught school for some years, and then lived in the Emerson household as handyman. From July 4, 1845, to September 6, 1847, he carried out his famous experiment in solitude at Walden Pond near Concord. His search for the essentials of individualism, and his challenge of prevailing standards he recorded in Walden, *his most widely read book.*

Throughout his life, Thoreau struggled to maintain his independence and integrity. He never married and was something of a misanthrope. He had scant respect for society's institutions, and preferred jail to taxes. His essay on "Civil Disobedience" is a fervent protest against a nation that launched an unjust war on Mexico and that seemed to crush blindly individuality. Yet Thoreau's passionate individualism was not without its contradictions, for at various times he advocated collective action to reform social conditions.

The selection here is from "Civil Disobedience," in The Writings of Henry David Thoreau, *11 vols. (Boston, 1884–1900), vol. X.*

I heartily accept the motto—"That government is best which governs least"; and I should like to see it acted up to more rapidly and systematically. Carried out, it finally amounts to this, which also I believe—"That government is best which governs not at all"; and when men are prepared for it, that will be the kind of government which they will have. Government is at best but an expedient; but most governments are usually, and all governments are sometimes, inexpedient. The objections which have been brought against a standing army, and they are many and weighty, and deserve to prevail, may also at last be brought against a standing government. The standing army is only an arm of the standing government. The government itself, which is only the mode which the people have chosen to execute their will, is equally liable to be abused and perverted before the people can act through it. Witness the present Mexican War, the work of comparatively a few individuals using the standing government as their tool; for, in the outset, the people would not have consented to this measure.

This American government—what is it but a tradition, though a recent one, endeavoring to transmit itself unimpaired to posterity, but each instant losing some of its integrity? It has not the vitality and force of a single living man; for a single man can bend it to his will. It is a sort of wooden gun to the people themselves. But it is not the less necessary for this; for the people must have some complicated machinery or other, and hear its din, to satisfy that

203

idea of government which they have. Governments show thus how successfully men can be imposed on, even impose on themselves, for their own advantage. It is excellent, we must all allow. Yet this government never of itself furthered any enterprise, but by the alacrity with which it got out of its way. *It* does not keep the country free. *It* does not settle the West. *It* does not educate. The character inherent in the American people has done all that has been accomplished; and it would have done somewhat more, if the government had not sometimes got in its way. For government is an expedient by which men would fain succeed in letting one another alone; and, as has been said, when it is most expedient, the governed are most let alone by it. Trade and commerce, if they were not made of India-rubber, would never manage to bounce over the obstacles which legislators are continually putting in their way; and, if one were to judge these men wholly by the effects of their actions and not partly by their intentions, they would deserve to be classed and punished with those mischievous persons who put obstructions on the railroads.

But, to speak practically and as a citizen, unlike those who call themselves no-government men, I ask for, not at once no government, but *at once* a better government. Let every man make known what kind of government would command his respect, and that will be one step toward obtaining it.

After all, the practical reason why, when the power is once in the hands of the people, a majority are permitted, and for a long period continue, to rule is not because they are most likely to be in the right, nor because this seems fairest to the minority, but because they are physically the strongest. But a government in which the majority rule in all cases cannot be based on justice, even as far as men understand it. Can there not be a government in which majorities do not virtually decide right and wrong, but conscience?—in which majorities decide only those questions to which the rule of expediency is applicable? Must the citizen ever for a moment, or in the least degree, resign his conscience to the legislator? Why has every man a conscience, then? I think that we should be men first, and subjects afterward. It is not desirable to cultivate a respect for the law, so much as for the right. The only obligation which I have a right to assume is to do at any time what I think right. It is truly enough said, that a corporation has no conscience; but a corporation of conscientious men is a corporation *with* a conscience. Law never made men a whit more just; and, by means of their respect for it, even the well-disposed are daily made the agents of injustice. A common and natural result of an undue respect for law is, that you may see a file of soldiers, colonel, captain, corporal, privates, powder-monkeys, and all, marching in admirable order over hill and dale to the wars, against their wills, ay, against their common sense and consciences, which makes it very steep marching indeed, and produces a palpitation of the heart. They have no doubt that it is a damnable business in which they are concerned; they are all peaceably inclined. Now, what are they? Men at all? or small movable forts and magazines at the service of some unscrupulous man in power? . . .

How does it become a man to behave toward this American government today? I answer, that he cannot without disgrace be associated with it. I cannot for an instant recognize that political organization as *my* government which is the *slave's* government also.

All men recognize the right of revolution; that is, the right to refuse allegiance to, and to resist, the government, when its tyranny or its inefficiency are great and unendurable. But almost all say that such is not the case now. But such was the case, they think, in the Revolution of '75. If one were to tell me that this was a bad government because it taxed certain foreign commodities brought to its ports, it is most probable that I should not make an ado about it, for I can do without them. All machines have their friction; and possibly this does enough good to counterbalance the evil. At any rate, it is a great evil to make a stir about it. But when the friction comes to have its machine, and oppression and robbery are organized, I say, let us not have such a machine any longer. In other words, when a sixth of the population of a nation which has undertaken to be the refuge of liberty are slaves, and a whole country is unjustly overrun and conquered by a foreign army, and subjected to military law, I think that it is not too soon for honest men to rebel and revolutionize. What makes this duty the more urgent is the fact that the country so overrun is not our own, but ours is the invading army. . . .

All voting is a sort of gaming, like checkers or backgammon, with a slight moral tinge to it, a playing with right and wrong, with moral questions; and betting naturally accompanies it. The character of the voters is not staked. I cast my vote, perchance, as I think right; but I am not vitally concerned that right should prevail. I am willing to leave it to the majority. Its obligation, therefore, never exceeds that of expediency. Even voting *for the right* is *doing* nothing for it. It is only expressing to men feebly your desire that it should prevail. A wise man will not leave the right to the mercy of chance, nor wish it to prevail through the power of the majority. There is but little virtue in the action of masses of men. When the majority shall at length vote for the abolition of slavery, it will be because they are indifferent to slavery, or because there is but little slavery left to be abolished by their vote. *They* will

then be the only slaves. Only *his* vote can hasten the abolition of slavery who asserts his own freedom by his vote. . . .

As for adopting the ways which the state has provided for remedying the evil, I know not of such ways. They take too much time, and a man's life will be gone. I have other affairs to attend to. I came into this world, not chiefly to make this a good place to live in, but to live in it, be it good or bad. A man has not everything to do, but something; and because he cannot do *everything*, it is not necessary that he should do *something* wrong. It is not my business to be petitioning the Governor or the Legislature any more than it is theirs to petition me; and if they should not hear my petition, what should I do then? But in this case the state has provided no way: its very Constitution is the evil. This may seem to be harsh and stubborn and unconciliatory; but it is to treat with the utmost kindness and consideration the only spirit that can appreciate or deserves it. So is all change for the better, like birth and death, which convulse the body.

I do not hesitate to say, that those who call themselves Abolitionists should at once effectually withdraw their support, both in person and property, from the government of Massachusetts, and not wait till they constitute a majority of one, before they suffer the right to prevail through them. I think that it is enough if they have God on their side, without waiting for that other one. Moreover, any man more right than his neighbors constitutes a majority of one already. . . .

Under a government which imprisons any unjustly, the true place for a just man is also a prison. The proper place to-day, the only place which Massachusetts has provided for her freer and less desponding spirits, is in her prisons, to be put out and locked out of the State by her own act, as they have already put themselves out by their principles.

It is there that the fugitive slave, and the Mexican prisoner on parole, and the Indian come to plead the wrongs of his race should find them: on that separate, but more free and honorable ground, where the State places those who are not *with* her, but *against* her—the only house in a slave State in which a free man can abide with honor. If any think that their influence would be lost there, and their voices no longer afflict the ear of the State, that they would not be as an enemy within its walls, they do not know by how much truth is stronger than error, nor how much more eloquently and effectively he can combat injustice who has experienced a little in his own person. . . .

I have paid no poll-tax for six years. I was put into jail once on this account, for one night; and, as I stood considering the walls of solid stone, two or three feet thick, the door of wood and iron, a foot thick, and the iron grating which strained the light, I could not help being struck with the foolishness of that institution which treated me as if I were mere flesh and blood and bones, to be locked up. I wondered that it should have concluded at length that this was the best use it could put me to, and had never thought to avail itself of my services in some way. . . .

The authority of government, even such as I am willing to submit to—for I will cheerfully obey those who know and can do better than I, and in many things even those who neither know nor can do so well—is still an impure one: to be strictly just, it must have the sanction and consent of the governed. It can have no pure right over my person and property, but what I concede to it. The progress from an absolute to a limited monarchy to a democracy, is a progress toward a true respect for the individual. Even the Chinese philosopher was wise enough to regard the individual as the basis of the empire. Is a democracy, such as we know it, the last improvement possible in government? Is it not possible to take a step further toward recognizing and organizing the rights of man? There will never be a really free and enlightened State until the State comes to recognize the individual as a higher and independent power, from which all its own power and authority are derived, and treats him accordingly. I please myself with imagining a State at last which can afford to be just to all men, and to treat the individual with respect as a neighbor; which even would not think it inconsistent with its own repose if a few were to live aloof from it, not meddling with it, nor embraced by it, who fulfilled all the duties of neighbors and fellow men. A state which bore this kind of fruit, and suffered it to drop off as fast as it ripened, would prepare the way for a still more perfect and glorious State, which also I have imagined, but not yet anywhere seen.

CHAPTER XIII

PROGRESS, REFORM, AND UTOPIA

One of the main characteristics of the romantic-democratic mind of nineteenth-century America was its impulse toward reform. Unsystematic and sometimes inconsistent in its ideology, the American response to the pressures and problems attending rapid social and economic change was the reform movements (and sometimes utopian dreams) that extended to nearly all areas of the nation's institutional life. The slavery issue, of course, soon dominated the national scene, but it should not blind one to the larger outlines of the reform pattern.

The uniqueness of America's reformers lies in the fact that they directed their efforts not so much on a class basis—classes were poorly defined and, in any case, contrary to the political ideals of the day—as toward the correction of specific institutional evils. American reformers moved to correct the institutional restraints that prevented self-realization and the pursuit of happiness promised to every individual. Freedom from these restraints seemed to many reformers a part of America's destiny; the conquest of nature suggested the possibility of the conquest of social problems as well. Thus for a variety of reasons, America became a nation of reformers, for, as Emerson put it, "What is a man born for but to be a Reformer, a Remaker of what man has made . . . , imitating that great Nature which embosoms us all, and which sleeps no moment on an old past, but every hour repairs herself, yielding us every morning a new day, and with every pulsation a new life?'' In these words, the sage of Concord expressed the spirit of the movement that inspired men and women in their efforts to uproot capital punishment, abolish slavery, end illiteracy and ignorance, and bring about an end to war. This reforming spirit also agitated for equal rights for women, preached humane treatment of the insane, and urged prison reform.

But what were the reasons for this reforming impulse? Perhaps no list can be complete, but the following reasons must certainly be mentioned. America's Enlightenment inheritance, with evangelical Christianity and Jacksonian sentiments, seemed to demand application in reform movements that freed individuals and offered them equal opportunities for full and abundant living. The idea of progress, present in the American mind and receiving support from such European reform movements as utilitarianism, held forth yet another inspiring ideal; and the social and economic tensions of an expanding nation, including the rise of the city as a factor in American culture, pressed reformers on.[1]

Beginning as informal protest, many reform movements ended with the enactment of corrective legislation—thus in fact making the state an agent of reform as well. Others, of course, were never brought to fruition. Yet whatever the outcome of its separate currents, the reform movement as a whole had a marked influence on subsequent American history.

---

[1] David Donald has advanced a provocative interpretation of the abolitionist reformers. He argues that most of them came from old-line Yankee Protestant families of middle-class backgrounds. Finding that their traditional position of leadership was being lost to the rising business class in the Northeast and disliking a life devoted to the pursuit of material ends, they turned to reform as a means of self-assertion as well as in the hope of regaining status. See David Donald, *Lincoln Reconsidered* (New York, 1956), pp. 19–36.

Horace Mann

1796-1859

The name of Horace Mann is synonymous with public education in America. Unable to afford an elementary education, Mann educated himself and was admitted to Brown University, where he graduated with highest honors in 1819. Shortly thereafter, he entered the legal profession and became a successful lawyer. In 1827, he was elected to the Massachusetts House of Representatives, where he was responsible for a number of reform measures, including the establishment of the first state-supported mental hospital in Massachusetts and the creation of a state board of education.

Mann was appointed the first secretary of the Massachusetts Board of Education in 1837 and held this position until 1848. His annual reports and his many addresses in which he explored educational philosophy, as well as matters of educational practice, occupy a commanding position in American educational history. In his later years he held a seat in Congress and, in 1853 he accepted the presidency of Antioch College. Puritan in personal outlook and a moderate Whig in politics, Mann is a representative figure of the reform movement.

This selection from Mann's lecture, "The Necessity of Education in a Republican Government," is from Life and Works of Horace Mann, *4 vols. (Boston, 1891), vol. II.*

My friends, is it not manifest to us all, that no individual, unless he has some acquaintance with the lower forms of education, can superintend even the coarsest and most common interests of life, without daily error and daily shame? The general utility of knowledge also, and the higher and more enduring satisfactions of the intellect, resulting from the discovery and contemplation of those truths with which the material and the spiritual universe are alike filled, impart to this subject a true dignity and a sublime elevation. But, in its office of attempering feelings which otherwise would blast or consume us;— in its authority to say to the clamorous propensities of our nature, "Peace, be still!"—in its auxiliary power to fit us for the endearments of domestic, for the duties of social, and for the sanctity of immortal life;—in its twofold office of enhancing the enjoyment which each one of us may feel in the virtue and happiness of all others, and of increasing the virtue and happiness of all others, to make a larger fund for common enjoyment;—in these high and sacred prerogatives, the cause of education lays claim to our mind and heart and strength, as one of the most efficient instruments prepared by the Creator for the welfare of His creatures, and the honor of Himself.

Take any individual you please, separate him from the crowd of men, and look at him, apart and alone,—like some Robinson Crusoe in a far-off island of the ocean, without any human being around him, with no prospect of leaving any human being behind him,— and, even in such a solitude, how authoritative over his actions, how decisive of his contemplations and of his condition, are the instructions he received and the habits he formed in early life! But now behold him as one of the tumultuous throng of men; observe the wide influences which he exerts upon others,—in the marts of business, in the resorts of pleasure, in the high places of official trust,—and reflect how many of all these influences, whether beneficent or malign, depend upon the education he has received, and you will have another gauge or standard whereby to estimate the importance of our theme. Look at him again, not as a being, coming, we know not whence, alighting for a brief residence upon this earth, and then making his exit through the door of the tomb, to be seen and heard of no more, and leaving no more impression upon society of his ways or works, than the sea-bird leaves upon the surface of the deep, when she stoops from the upper air, dips her breast for a moment in the wave, and then rises again to a viewless height; but look at him in his relations to posterity, as the father of a family, as a member of a generation which sows those seeds of virtue or vice, that, centuries hence, shall bear fruit or poison;—look at him as a citizen in a free government, throwing his influence and his vote into one or the other of the scales where peace and war, glory and infamy, are weighed;—look at him in these relations, and consider how a virtuous or a vicious education tends to fit or to unfit him for them all, and you will catch one more glimpse of the importance of the subject now presented to your consideration. But if we ascend to a still higher point of vision, and,— forgetting the earthly, personal career, and the wide sphere of social influences, and those acts of life which survive life,—fasten our eyes upon effects which education may throw forward into

immortal destinies, it is then that we are awed, amazed, overpowered, by the thought, that we have been created and placed in a system, where the soul's eternal flight may be made higher or lower by those who plume its tender wings and direct its early course. Such is the magnitude, the transcendence of this subject. In a philosophical view, beginning at what point we will, and following the most rigid connection and dependence of cause and effect, of antecedent and consequence, we shall find that education is intimately related to every good, and to every evil, which, as mortal, or as immortal beings, we can desire or dread. . . .

I venture, my friends, at this time, to solicit your attention, while I attempt to lay before you some of the relations which we bear to the cause of Education, because we are the citizens of a Republic; and thence to deduce some of the reasons, which, under our political institutions, make the proper training of the rising generation the highest earthly duty of the risen.

It is a truism, that free institutions multiply human energies. A chained body cannot do much harm; a chained mind can do as little. In a despotic government, the human faculties are benumbed and paralyzed; in a Republic, they glow with an intense life, and burst forth with uncontrollable impetuosity. In the former, they are circumscribed and straitened in their range of action; in the latter, they have "ample room and verge enough," and may rise to glory or plunge into ruin. Amidst universal ignorance, there cannot be such wrong notions about right, as there may be in a community partially enlightened; and false conclusions which have been reasoned out are infinitely worse than blind impulses.

To demonstrate the necessity of education in our government, I shall not attempt to derive my proofs from the history of other Republics. Such arguments are becoming stale. Besides, there are so many points of difference between our own political institutions, and those of any other government calling itself free, which has ever existed, that the objector perpetually eludes or denies the force of our reasoning, by showing some want of analogy between the cases presented.

I propose, therefore, on this occasion, not to adduce, as proofs, what has been true only in past times; but what is true at the present time, and must always continue to be true. I shall rely, not on precedents, but on the nature of things; and draw my arguments less from history than from humanity.

Now it is undeniable that, with the possession of certain higher faculties,— common to all mankind,—whose proper cultivation will bear us upward to hitherto undiscovered regions of prosperity and glory, we possess, also, certain lower faculties or propensities,— equally common,—whose improper indulgence leads, inevitably, to tribulation, and anguish, and ruin. The propensities to which I refer seem indispensable to our temporal existence, and, if restricted within proper limits, they are promotive of our enjoyment; but, beyond those limits, they work dishonor and infatuation, madness and despair. As servants, they are indispensable; as masters, they torture as well as tyrannize. Now despotic and arbitrary governments have dwarfed and crippled the powers of doing evil as much as the powers of doing good; but a republican government, from the very fact of its freedom, unreins their speed, and lets loose their strength. It is justly alleged against despotisms, that they fetter, mutilate, almost extinguish the noblest powers of the human soul; but there is a *per contra* to this, for which we have not given them credit;—they circumscribe the ability to do the greatest evil, as well as to do the greatest good.

My proposition, therefore, is simply this: If republican institutions do wake up unexampled energies in the whole mass of a people, and give them implements of unexampled power wherewith to work out their will, then these same institutions ought also to confer upon that people unexampled wisdom and rectitude. If these institutions give greater scope and impulse to the lower order of faculties belonging to the human mind, then they must also give more authoritative control and more skilful guidance to the higher ones. If they multiply temptations, they must fortify against them. If they quicken the activity and enlarge the sphere of the appetites and passions, they must, at least in an equal ratio, establish the authority and extend the jurisdiction of reason and conscience. In a word, we must not add to the impulsive, without also adding to the regulating forces.

If we maintain institutions, which bring us within the action of new and unheard-of powers, without taking any corresponding measures for the government of those powers, we shall perish by the very instruments prepared for our happiness.

The truth has been so often asserted, that there is no security for a republic but in morality and intelligence, that a repetition of it seems hardly in good taste. But all permanent blessings being founded on permanent truths, a continued observance of the truth is the condition of a continued enjoyment of the blessing. I know we are often admonished that, without intelligence and virtue, as a chart and a compass, to direct us in our untried political voyage, we shall perish in the first storm; but I venture to add that, without these qualities, we shall not wait for a storm,—we cannot weather a calm. If the sea is as smooth as glass we shall founder, for we are in a stone boat. Unless these qualities pervade the general head and the general heart, not only will republican institutions vanish amongst us, but the words *prosperity* and *happiness* will become obsolete. And all this may be affirmed, not from historical examples merely, but from the very constitution of our nature. We are created and brought into life with a set of innate, organic dispositions or propensities, which a free government rouses and invigorates, and which, if not bridled and tamed, by our actually seeing the eternal laws of justice, as plainly as we can see the sun in the heavens,—and by our actually feeling the sovereign sentiment of duty, as plainly as we feel the earth beneath our feet—will hurry us forward into regions populous with every form of evil. . . .

Our propensities have no affinity with reason or conscience. Did you ever hear two persons conversing about a third, whose ruin and infamy they agreed had come from the amount of his fortune, or from his facilities for indulgence, when, in the very breath in which they spoke of the resistless power of the temptation over him, they did not add that, in their own persons, they should be willing to run the same risk? This is the language of all the propensities. They are willing to run any risk, whether it be of health or of character, of time or of eternity. This explains how it is, that some men not wholly lost to virtue,—men who acknowledge their responsibleness to God, and their obligations to conscience,—but in whom the propensities predominate and tyrannize;—I say this explains how it is that such men, when stung and maddened by the goadings of desire, wish themselves bereft of their better attributes, that they might give full career to passion, without remorse of conscience or dread of retribution. That human depravity, which, hitherto, has made the history of our race, like the roll of the prophet, a record of lamentation and mourning and woe, has worked out through these propensities; and, if the very substance and organization of

human nature be not changed, by the eradication of these instincts, that depravity which is, to a greater or less degree, to make the future resemble the past, will pour out its agonies and its atrocities though the same channels!

Such, then, are our latent capabilities of evil,—all ready to be evolved, should the restraints of reason, conscience, religion, be removed. Here are millions of men, each with appetites capacious of infinity, and raging to be satisfied out of a supply of means too scanty for any one of them. Millions of coveting eyes are fastened on the same object—millions of hands thrust out to seize it. What ravening, torturing, destroying, then, must ensue, if these hounds cannot be lashed back into their kennel! They must be governed; they cannot be destroyed. Nature declares that the germs, the embryos, of these incipient monsters, shall not be annihilated. She reproduces them with every human being that comes into the world. Nor, indeed, is it desirable, even if it were practicable, that they should be wholly expunged and razed out of our constitution. He who made us, knew our circumstances and necessities, and He has implanted them in our nature too deep for eradication. Besides, within their proper sphere, they confer an innocent, though a subordinate enjoyment. Certainly, we would not make all men hermits and anchorites. Let us be just, even to the appetites. No man is the worse because he keenly relishes and enjoys the bountiful provisions which Heaven has made for his food, his raiment, and his shelter. Indeed, why were these provisions ever made, if they are not to be enjoyed? Surely they are not superfluities and supernumeraries, cumbering a creation which would have been more perfect without them. Let them then be acquired and enjoyed, though always with moderation and temperance. Let the lover of wealth seek wealth by all honest means, and with earnestness, if he will; let him surround himself with the comforts and the embellishments of life, and add the pleasures of beauty to the pleasures of utility. Let every honorable man indulge a quick and sustaining confidence in his own worthiness, whenever disparaged or maligned; and let him count upon the affections of his friends, and the benedictions of his race, as a part of the solid rewards of virtue. These, and kindred feelings, are not to be crushed, extinguished. Let them rouse themselves in presence of their objects, and rush out to seize them, and neigh, like a war-horse for the battle— only let them know that they have a rider, to whose eye no mist can dim the severe line they are never to pass, and whose arm can bend every neck of them, like the twig of an osier. . . . .

Let us now turn for a moment to see what means and stimulants our institutions have provided for the use of the mighty powers and passions they have unloosed. No apparatus so skilful was ever before devised. Instead of the slow and cumbrous machinery of former times, we have provided that which is quick-working and far-reaching, and which may be used for the destruction as easily as for the welfare of its possessors. Our institutions furnish as great facilities for wicked men, in all departments of wickedness, as phosphorus and lucifer matches furnish to the incendiary. What chemistry has done, in these preparations, over the old art of rubbing two sticks together, for the wretch who would fire your dwelling, our social partnerships have done for flagitious and unprincipled men. Through the right—almost universal—of suffrage, we have established a community of power; and no proposition is more plain and self-evident, than that nothing but mere popular inclination lies between a community of power and a community in every thing else. And though, in the long-run, and when other things are equal, a righteous cause always has a decisive advantage over an evil one, yet, in the first onset between right and wrong, bad men possess one advantage over the good. They have double resources—two armories. The arts of guilt are as welcome to them as the practices of justice. They can use poisoned weapons as well as those approved by the usages of war.

Again; has it been sufficiently considered, that all which has been said— and truly said—of the excellence of our institutions, if administered by an upright people, must be reversed and read backwards, if administered by a corrupt one? I am aware that some will be ready to say, "We have been unwise and infatuated to confide all the constituents of our social and political welfare to such irresponsible keeping." But let me ask of such,—of what avail is their lamentation? The irresistible movement in the diffusion of power is still progressive, not retrograde. Every year puts more of social strength into the hands of physical strength. The arithmetic of numbers is more and more excluding all estimate of moral forces, in the administration of government. And this, whether for good or for evil, will continue to be. Human beings cannot be remanded to the dungeons of imbecility, if they are to those of ignorance. The sun can as easily be turned backwards in its course, as one particle of that power, which has been conferred upon the millions, can be again monopolized by the few. To discuss the question, therefore, whether our institutions are not too free, is, for all practical purposes, as vain as it would be to discuss the question whether, on the whole, it was a wise arrangement on the part of Divine Providence, that the American continent should ever have been created, or that Columbus should have discovered it. And let me ask, further, have those who believe our institutions to be too free, and who, therefore, would go back to less liberal ones,—have they settled the question, how far back they will go? Will they go back to the dark ages, and recall an eclipse which lasted centuries long? or will they ascend a little higher for their models, to a time when our ancestors wore undressed skins, and burrowed in holes of the earth? or will they strike at once for the institutions of Egypt, where, though the monkey was a god, there was still a sufficient distance between him and his human worshipper? But all such discussions are vain. The oak will as soon go back into the acorn, or the bird into its shell, as we return to the monarchical or aristocratic forms of by-gone ages. . . .

Again, then, I ask, with unmitigated anxiety, what institutions we now possess, that can furnish defence or barrier against the action of those propensities, which each generation brings into the world as a part of its being, and which our institutions foster and stimulate into unparalleled activity and vigor? Can any Christian man believe, that God has so constituted and so governs the human race, that it is always and necessarily to be suicidal of its earthly welfare? No! the thought is impious. The same Almighty Power which implants in our nature the germs of these terrible propensities, has endowed us also with reason and conscience and a sense of responsibility to Him; and, in his providence, he has opened a way by which these nobler faculties can be elevated into dominion and supremacy over the appetites and passions. But if this is ever done, it must be mainly done during the docile and teachable years of childhood. I repeat it, my friends, *if this is ever done, it must be mainly done during the docile and teachable years of childhood.* Wretched, incorrigible, demoniac, as any human being may ever have become, there was a time when he took the first step in error and in crime; when, for the first time, he just nodded to his fall, on the brink

of ruin. Then, ere he was irrecoverably lost, ere he plunged into the abyss of infamy and guilt, he might have been recalled, as it were by the waving of the hand. Fathers, mothers, patriots, Christians! it is this very hour of peril through which our children are now passing. They know it not, but we know it; and where the knowledge is, there rests the responsibility. Society is responsible;—not society considered as an abstraction, but society as it consists of living members, which members we are. Clergymen are responsible; —all men who have enjoyed the opportunities of a higher education in colleges and universities are responsible, for they can convert their means, whether of time or of talent, into instruments for elevating the masses of the people. The conductors of the public press are responsible, for they have daily access to the public ear, and can infuse just notions of this high duty into the public mind. Legislators and rulers are responsible. In our country, and in our times, no man is worthy the honored name of a statesman, who does not include the highest practicable education of the people in all his plans of administration. He may have eloquence, he may have a knowledge of all history, diplomacy, jurisprudence; and by these he might claim, in other countries, the elevated rank of a statesman; but, unless he speaks, plans, labors, at all times and in all places, for the culture and edification of the whole people, he is not, he cannot be, an American statesman.

If this dread responsibility for the fate of our children be disregarded, how, when called upon, in the great eventful day, to give an account of the manner in which our earthly duties have been discharged, can we expect to escape the condemnation: "Inasmuch as ye have not done it to one of the least of these, ye have not done it unto me"?

William Lloyd Garrison

1805-1879

William Lloyd Garrison gained fame as the leading American abolitionist. He was born in Newburyport, Massachusetts, to a family of modest circumstances. He had little formal schooling and at fourteen he was indentured to a printer. He soon became expert in this trade and then tried his hand at writing; before long he gained recognition as an author and editor. Leaving Newburyport, he established a number of short-lived journals. Then in 1831, he founded (with his partner Isaac Knapp) the Boston Liberator, *a journal that was destined to influence the reform movement for the next thirty-five years. Though Garrison's paper backed temperance, pacifism, and opposition to capital punishment and imprisonment for debt, it was in the abolitionist cause that the* Liberator *achieved greatest fame. Garrison was a vigorous campaigner on behalf of the radical wing of the abolitionist movement, and he spoke at antislavery rallies and demonstrations in addition to his publishing efforts. After the Civil War, Garrison's interest in reform continued, and he became president of the Free Trade League, which advocated the end of all barriers to trade between the nations of the world.*

This selection is from an address given at the Park Street Church in Boston on July 4, 1829, in which Garrison, though then only twenty-four, displayed his many powers as an orator. It was printed in the National Philanthropist and Investigator *of July 22 and 29, 1829, and is taken from the first volume of* William Lloyd Garrison; The Story of His Life Told by His Children, *4 vols. (New York, 1885), vol. I.*

I speak not as a partisan or an opponent of any man or measures, when I say, that our politics are rotten to the core. We boast of our freedom, who go shackled to the polls, year after year, by tens, and hundreds, and thousands! We talk of free agency, who are the veriest machines—that merest automata—in the hands of unprincipled jugglers! We prate of integrity, and virtue, and independence, who sell our birthright for office, and who, nine times in ten, do not get Esau's bargain—no, not even a mess of pottage! Is it republicanism to say, that the majority can do no wrong? Then I am not a republican. Is it aristocracy to say, that the people sometimes shamefully abuse their high trust? Then I am an aristocrat. It is not the appreciation, but the abuse of liberty, to withdraw altogether from the polls, or to visit them merely as a matter of form, without carefully investigating the merits of candidates. The republic

215

does not bear a charmed life: our prescriptions administered through the medium of the ballot-box—the mouth of the political body—may kill or cure, according to the nature of the disease and our wisdom in applying the remedy. It is possible that a people may bear the title of freemen who execute the work of slaves. To the dullest observers of the signs of the times, it must be apparent that we are rapidly approximating to this condition. . . .

But there is another evil, which, if we had to contend against nothing else, should make us quake for the issue. It is a gangrene preying upon our vitals—an earthquake rumbling under our feet—a mine accumulating materials for a national catastrophe. It should make this a day of fasting and prayer, not of boisterous merriment and idle pageantry—a day of great lamentation, not of congratulatory joy. It should spike every cannon, and haul down every banner. Our garb should be sackcloth—our heads bowed in the dust—our supplications, for the pardon and assistance of Heaven.

Last week this city was made breathless by a trial of considerable magnitude. The court chamber was inundated for hours, day after day, with a dense and living tide which swept along like the rush of a mountain torrent. Tiers of human bodies were piled up to the walls, with almost miraculous condensation and ingenuity. It seemed as if men abhorred a vacuum equally with Nature: they would suspend themselves, as it were, by a nail, and stand upon air with the aid of a peg. Although it was a barren, ineloquent subject, and the crowd immense, there was no perceptible want of interest—no evidence of impatience. The cause was important, involving the reputation of a distinguished

citizen. There was a struggle for mastery between two giants—a test of strength in tossing mountains of law. The excitement was natural.[1]

I stand up here in a more solemn court, to assist in a far greater cause; not to impeach the character of one man, but of a whole people; not to recover the sum of a hundred thousand dollars, but to obtain the liberation of two millions of wretched, degraded beings, who are pining in hopeless bondage—over whose sufferings scarcely an eye weeps, or a heart melts, or a tongue pleads either to God or man. I regret that a better advocate had not been found, to enchain your attention and to warm your blood. Whatever fallacy, however, may appear in the argument, there is no flaw in the indictment; what the speaker lacks, the cause will supply.

Sirs, I am not come to tell you that slavery is a curse, debasing in its effect, cruel in its operation, fatal in its continuance. The day and the occasion require no such revelation. I do not claim the discovery as my own, that "all men are born equal," and that among their inalienable rights are "life, liberty, and the pursuit of happiness." Were I addressing any other than a free and Christian assembly, the enforcement of this truth might be pertinent. Neither do I intend to analyze the horrors of slavery for your inspection, nor to freeze your blood with authentic recitals of savage cruelty. Nor will time allow me to explore even a furlong of that immense wilderness of suffering which remains unsubdued in our land. I take it for granted that the existence of these evils is acknowledged, if not rightly understood. My object is to define and enforce our duty, as Christians and Philanthropists.

On a subject so exhaustless, it will be

[1] The case was that of Farnum, Executor of Tuttle Hubbard, vs. Brooks, and was heard in the Mass. Supreme Court. The "two giants" in opposition were William Wirt, ex-Attorney-General of the United States, and Daniel Webster. Wirt's eloquence made a great impression. (Boston *Traveller*, June 23, 30, 1829; *Columbian Centinel*, June 27.)

impossible, in the moiety of an address, to unfold all the facts which are necessary to its full development. In view of it, my heart swells up like a living fountain, which time cannot exhaust, for it is perpetual. Let this be considered as the preface of a noble work, which your inventive sympathies must elaborate and complete.

I assume as distinct and defensible propositions,

I. That the slaves of this country, whether we consider their moral, intellectual or social condition, are pre-eminently entitled to the prayers, and sympathies, and charities, of the American people; and their claims for redress are as strong as those of any Americans could be in a similar condition.

II. That, as the free States—by which I mean non-slaveholding States—are constitutionally involved in the guilt of slavery, by adhering to a national compact that sanctions it; and in the danger, by liability to be called upon for aid in case of insurrection; they have the right to remonstrate against its continuance, and it is their duty to assist in its overthrow.

III. That no justification plea for the perpetuity of slavery can be found in the condition of its victims; and no barrier against our righteous interference, in the laws which authorize the buying, selling and possessing of slaves, nor in the hazard of a collision with slave-holders.

IV. That education and freedom will elevate our colored population to a rank with the white—making them useful, intelligent and peaceable citizens.

In the first place, it will be readily admitted, that it is the duty of every nation primarily to administer relief to its own necessities, to cure its own maladies, to instruct its own children, and to watch over its own interests. He is "worse than an infidel" who neglects his own household, and squanders his earnings upon strangers; and the policy

of that nation is unwise which seeks to proselyte other portions of the globe at the expense of its safety and happiness. Let me not be misunderstood. My benevolence is neither contracted nor selfish. I pity that man whose heart is not larger than a whole continent. I despise the littleness of that patriotism which blusters only for its own rights, and, stretched to its utmost dimensions, scarcely covers its native territory; which adopts as its creed the right to act independently, even to the verge of licentiousness, without restraint, and to tyrannize wherever it can with impunity. This sort of patriotism is common. I suspect the reality, and deny the productiveness, of that piety which confines its operations to a particular spot—if that spot be less than the whole earth; nor scoops out, in every direction, new channels for the waters of life. Christian charity, while it "begins at home," goes abroad in search of misery. It is as copious as the sun in heaven. It does not, like the Nile, make a partial inundation, and then withdraw; but it perpetually overflows, and fertilizes every barren spot. It is restricted only by the exact number of God's suffering creatures. But I mean to say, that, while we are aiding and instructing foreigners, we ought not to forget our own degraded countrymen; that neither duty nor honesty requires us to defraud ourselves that we may enrich others.

The condition of the slaves, in a religious point of view, is deplorable, entitling them to a higher consideration, on our part, than any other race; higher than the Turks or Chinese, for they have the privileges of instruction; higher than the Pagans, for they are not dwellers in a gospel land; higher than our red men of the forest, for we do not bind them with gyves, nor treat them as chattels.

And here let me ask, What has Christianity done, by direct effort, for our slave population? Comparatively nothing. She has explored the isles of the ocean for objects of commiseration; but, amazing stupidity! she can gaze without emotion on a multitude of miserable beings at home, large enough to constitute a nation of freemen, whom tyranny has heathenized by law. In her public services they are seldom remembered, and in her private donations they are forgotten. From one end of the country to the other, her charitable societies form golden links of benevolence, and scatter their contributions like raindrops over a parched heath; but they bring no sustenance to the perishing slave. The blood of souls is upon her garments, yet she heeds not the stain. The clankings of the prisoner's chains strike upon her ear, but they cannot penetrate her heart.

I have said that the claims of the slaves for redress are as strong as those of any Americans could be, in a similar condition. Does any man deny the position? The proof, then, is found in the fact, that a very large proportion of our colored population were born on our soil, and are therefore entitled to all the privileges of American citizens. This is their country by birth, not by adoption. Their children possess the same inherent and unalienable rights as ours, and it is a crime of the blackest dye to load them with fetters.

Every Fourth of July, our Declaration of Independence is produced, with a sublime indignation, to set forth the tyranny of the mother country, and to challenge the admiration of the world. But what a pitiful detail of grievances does this document present, in comparison with the wrongs which our slaves endure! In the one case, it is hardly the plucking of a hair from the head; in the other, it is the crushing of a live body on the wheel—the stings of the wasp contrasted with the tortures of the Inquisition. Before God, I must say, that such a glaring contradiction as exists between our creed and practice the annals of six thousand years cannot parallel. In view of it, I am ashamed of my country. I am sick of our unmeaning declamation in praise of liberty and equality; of our hypocritical cant about the unalienable rights of man. I could not, for my right hand, stand up before a European assembly, and exult that I am an American citizen, and denounce the usurpations of a kingly government as wicked and unjust; or, should I make the attempt, the recollection of my country's barbarity and despotism would blister my lips, and cover my cheeks with burning blushes of shame.

Will this be termed a rhetorical flourish? Will any man coldly accuse me of intemperate zeal? I will borrow, then, a ray of humanity from one of the brightest stars in our American galaxy, whose light will gather new effulgence to the end of time. "This, sirs, is a cause that would be dishonored and betrayed if I contented myself with appealing only to the understanding. It is too cold, and its processes are too slow for the occasion. I desire to thank God that, since he has given me an intellect so fallible, he has impressed upon me an instinct that is sure. On a question of shame and honor—liberty and oppression—reasoning is sometimes useless, and worse. I feel the decision in my pulse: if it throws no light upon the brain, it kindles a fire at the heart." . . .

I come to my second proposition:—the right of the free States to remonstrate against the continuance, and to assist in the overthrow of slavery.

This, I am aware, is a delicate subject, surrounded with many formidable difficulties. But if delay only adds to its intricacy, wherefore shun an immediate investigation? I know that we, of the North, affectedly believe that we have no local interest in the removal of this great evil; that the slave States can take care of themselves, and that any proffered assistance, on our part, would be rejected as impertinent, dictatorial or meddlesome; and that we have no right to lift up even a note of remonstrance. But I believe that these opinions are crude, preposterous, dishonorable, unjust. Sirs, this is a business in which, as members of one great family, we have a common interest; but we take no responsibility, either individually or collectively. Our hearts are cold—our blood stagnates in our veins. We act, in relation to the slaves, as if they were something lower than the brutes that perish.

On this question, I ask no support from the injunction of Holy Writ, which says:—"therefore all things whatsoever ye would that men should do to you, do ye even so to them: for this is the law and the prophets." I throw aside the common dictates of humanity. I assert the right of the free States to demand a gradual abolition of slavery, because, by its continuance, they participate in the guilt thereof, and are threatened with ultimate destruction; because they are bound to watch over the interests of the whole country, without reference to territorial divisions; because their white population is nearly double that of the slave States, and the voice of this overwhelming majority should be potential; because they are now deprived of their just influence in the councils of the nation; it is absurd and anti-republican to suffer property to be represented as men, and *vice versa*.[2] Because it gives the South an injust ascendancy over other portions of territory, and a power which may be perverted on every occasion. . . .

Now I say that, on the broad system of equal rights, this monstrous inequality should no longer be tolerated. If it cannot be speedily put down—not by force, but by fair persuasion; if we are always to remain shackled by unjust Constitutional provisions, when the emergency that imposed them has long

since passed away; if we must share in the guilt and danger of destroying the bodies and souls of men, *as the price of our Union;* if the slave States will haughtily spurn our assistance, and refuse to consult the general welfare; then the fault is not ours if a separation eventually take place. . . .

It may be objected, that the laws of the slave States form insurmountable barriers to any interference on our part.

Answer. I grant that we have not the right, and I trust not the disposition, to use coercive measures. But do these laws hinder our prayers, or obstruct the flow of our sympathies? Cannot our charities alleviate the condition of the slave, and perhaps break his fetters? Can we not operate upon public sentiment, (the lever that can move the moral world,) by way of remonstrance, advice, or entreaty? Is Christianity so powerful that she can tame the red men of our forests, and abolish the Burman caste, and overthrow the gods of Paganism, and liberate lands over which the darkness of Superstition has lain for ages; and yet so weak, in her dwelling-place, that she can make no impression upon her civil code? Can she contend successfully with cannibals, and yet be conquered by her own children?

Suppose that, by a miracle, the slaves should suddenly become white. Would you shut your eyes upon their sufferings, and calmly talk of Constitutional limitations? No; your voice would peal in the ears of the taskmasters like deep thunder; you would carry the Constitution by force, if it could not be taken by treaty; patriotic assemblies would congregate at the corners of every street; the old Cradle of Liberty would rock to a deeper tone than ever echoed therein at British aggression; the pulpit would acquire new and unusual eloquence from our holy religion. The argument, that these white slaves are degraded,

[2] By the three-fifths representation clause of the Federal Constitution, Art. I., Sec. ii., 3.

would not then obtain. You would say, it is enough that they are white, and in bondage, and they ought immediately to be set free. You would multiply your schools of instruction, and your temples of worship, and rely on them for security. . . .

But the plea is prevalent, that any interference by the free States, however benevolent or cautious it might be, would only irritate and inflame the jealousies of the South, and retard the cause of emancipation. If any man believes that slavery can be abolished without a struggle with the worst passions of human nature, quietly, harmoniously, he cherishes a delusion. It can never be done, unless the age of miracles return. No; we must expect a collision, full of sharp asperities and bitterness. We shall have to contend with the insolence, and pride, and selfishness, of many a heartless being. But these can be easily conquered by meekness, and perseverance, and prayer.

Sirs, the prejudices of the North are stronger than those of the South;— they forge and rivet the chains of the nation. Conquer them, and the victory is won. The enemies of emancipation take courage from our criminal timidity. They have justly stigmatized us, even on the floor of Congress, with the most contemptuous epithets. We are (they say) their "white slaves,"[3] afraid of our shadows, who have been driven back to the wall again and again; who stand trembling under their whips; who turn pale, retreat, and surrender at a talismanic threat to dissolve the Union. . . .

It is often despondingly said, that the evil of slavery is beyond our control. Dreadful conclusion, that puts the seal of death upon our country's existence! If we cannot conquer the monster in his infancy, while his cartilages are tender and his limbs powerless, how shall we escape his wrath when he goes forth a gigantic cannibal, seeking whom he may devour? If we cannot safely unloose two millions of slaves now, how shall we bind upwards of TWENTY MILLIONS at the close of the present century? But there is no cause for despair. We have seen how readily, and with what ease, that horrid gorgon, Intemperance, has been checked in his ravages. Let us take courage. Moral influence, when in vigorous exercise, is irresistible. It has an immortal essence. It can no more be trod out of existence by the iron foot of time, or by the ponderous march of iniquity, than matter can be annihilated. It may disappear for a time; but it lives in some shape or other, in some place or other, and will rise with renovated strength. Let us, then, be up and doing. In the simple and stirring language of the stout-hearted Lundy, "all the friends of the cause must go to work, keep to work, hold on, and never give up."

If it be still objected, that it would be dangerous to liberate the present race of blacks;

I answer—the emancipation of all the slaves of this generation is most assuredly out of the question. The fabric, which now towers above the Alps, must be taken away brick by brick, and foot by foot, till it is reduced so low that it may be overturned without burying the nation in its ruins. Years may elapse before the completion of the achievement; generations of blacks may go down to the grave, manacled and lacerated, without a hope for their children; the philanthropists who are now pleading in behalf of the oppressed, may not live to witness the dawn which will precede the glorious day of universal emancipation; but the work will go on— laborers in the cause will multiply— new resources will be discovered—the victory will be obtained, worth the

[3] In Henry Adams's *Life of John Randolph* we read (p. 281): "On another occasion, he [Randolph] is reported as saying of the people of the North, 'We do not govern them by our black slaves, but by their own white slaves.' "

desperate struggle of a thousand years. Or, if defeat follow, woe to the safety of this people! The nation will be shaken as if by a mighty earthquake. A cry of horror, a cry of revenge, will go up to heaven in the darkness of midnight, and re-echo from every cloud. Blood will flow like water—the blood of guilty men, and of innocent women and children. Then will be heard lamentations and weeping, such as will blot out the remembrance of the horrors of St. Domingo. The terrible judgments of an incensed God will complete the catastrophe of republican America.

And since so much is to be done for our country; since so many prejudices are to be dispelled, obstacles vanquished, interests secured, blessings obtained; since the cause of emancipation must progress heavily, and meet with much unhallowed opposition—why delay the work? There must be a beginning, and now is a propitious time— perhaps the last opportunity that will be granted us by a long-suffering God. No temporizing, lukewarm measures will avail aught. We must put our shoulders to the wheel, and heave with our united strength. Let us not look coldly on and see our Southern brethren[4] contending single-handed against an all-powerful foe—faint, weary, borne down to the earth. We are all alike guilty. Slavery is strictly a national sin. New England money has been expended in buying human flesh; New England ships have been freighted with sable victims; New England men have assisted in forging the fetters of those who groan in bondage.

I call upon the ambassadors of Christ everywhere to make known this procla- mation: "Thus saith the Lord God of the Africans, Let this people go, that they may serve me." I ask them to "proclaim liberty to the captives, and the opening of the prison to them that are bound"— to light up a flame of philanthropy that shall burn till all Africa be redeemed from the night of moral death, and the song of deliverance be heard throughout her borders.

I call upon the churches of the living God to lead in this great enterprise.[5] If the soul be immortal, priceless, save it from remediless woe. Let them combine their energies, and systematize their plans, for the rescue of suffering humanity. Let them pour out their supplications to heaven in behalf of the slave. Prayer is omnipotent: its breath can melt adamantine rocks—its touch can break the stoutest chains. Let antislavery charity-boxes stand uppermost among those for missionary, tract and educational purposes. On this subject, Christians have been asleep; let them shake off their slumbers, and arm for the holy contest.

I call upon our New England women to form charitable associations to relieve the degraded of their sex. As yet, an appeal to their sympathies was never made in vain. They outstrip us in every benevolent race. Females are doing much for the cause at the South, let their example be imitated, and their exertions surpassed, at the North.

I call upon our citizens to assist in establishing auxiliary colonization societies in every state, county and town. I implore their direct and liberal patronage to the parent society.

I call upon the great body of newspaper editors to keep this subject con-

---

[4] An allusion to the few antislavery societies among the Friends in some of the Southern States.

[5] So Daniel Webster, in his Plymouth oration, Dec. 22, 1820, of the African slave-trade and of New England complicity with it: "I invoke the ministers of our religion, that they proclaim its denunciation of these crimes, and add its solemn sanctions to the authority of human laws. If the pulpit be silent whenever or wherever there may be a sinner bloody with his guilt within the hearing of its voice, the pulpit is false to its trust" (*Works*, 1: 46).

stantly before their readers; to sound the trumpet of alarm, and to plead eloquently for the rights of man. They must give the tone to public sentiment. One press may ignite twenty; a city may warm a State; a State may impart a generous heat to a whole country.

I call upon the American people to enfranchise a spot over which they hold complete sovereignty; to cleanse that worse than Augean stable, the District of Columbia, from its foul impurities. I ask them to sustain Congress in any future efforts to colonize the colored population of the States. I conjure them to select those as Representatives who are not too ignorant to know, too blind to see, nor too timid to perform their duty.

I will say, finally, that I despair of the republic while slavery exists therein.

If I look up to God for success, no smile of mercy or forgiveness dispels the gloom of futurity; if to our own resources, they are daily diminishing; if to all history, our destruction is not only possible, but almost certain. Why should we slumber at this momentous crisis? If our hearts were dead to every throb of humanity; if it were lawful to oppress, where power is ample; still, if we had any regard for our safety and happiness, we should strive to crush the Vampire which is feeding upon our life-blood. All the selfishness of our nature cries aloud for a better security. Our own vices are too strong for us, and keep us in perpetual alarm; how, in addition to these, shall we be able to contend successfully with millions of armed and desperate men, as we must eventually, if slavery do not cease?

Wendell Phillips

1811-1884

Born in Boston of a wealthy, well-established family, Phillips had the advantages of education and position. His father, in fact, achieved fame as the first mayor of Boston. Graduating from Harvard in 1831, Phillips entered law school and was subsequently admitted to the bar. Under the influence of Garrison, he soon came to take an active part in the antislavery movement. Leaving his legal practice, he quickly achieved fame as a reform agitator, principally as an abolitionist but also as a spokesman for other reforms. He became a skilled platform orator with a direct, brilliant, and controlled style; indeed, more than any other orator, he was responsible for introducing a colloquial style into American public speaking.

This selection is an address on the labor movement delivered late in Phillips' life. It reflects a life-long interest in labor reform as well as powerful oratory. The text is from "The Foundation of the Labor Movement," an address delivered at the Music Hall in Boston on October 31, 1871, printed in Speeches, Lectures and Letters, *Second Series (Boston, 1905).*

*L*adies and Gentlemen: We are sometimes so near an object that we cannot see it. I could place you so near the City Hall to-night that you would not know whether you were looking at a ton of granite or a wall of a large building. So it is with a fact. The men who stand the nearest to it are often the last to recognize either its breadth or its meaning. Perhaps the last men to appreciate a fact are the men nearest to whose eyes it passes; and it is just so in government. We are hardly aware of the changes that are taking place about us; our children will understand them distinctly.

There is a large class among our German fellow-citizens who advocate the abolition of the Presidency. The thoughtful in that class perceive, what the ordinary passer-by does not recognize, that we are daily abolishing the Presidency, and the movement of the country for fifty years has been toward the abolition of the Presidency. You see this tendency in a variety of circumstances. When we were first a nation, the greatest men among us were chosen President, and named for President; but now we don't think of putting up a first-rate man.

There is another feature we don't see—that the government is fast being monopolized by the House of Representatives. If we go on as we have done for half a century, there will be no government in this country except the House. Whatever defies the power of the great House will go down. Whether harmonious and beneficent results will follow our adoption of the system, depends upon whether the great mass of men and women, with universal suffrage as their sheet-anchor, can work out through these results one single tool like the House.

223

I have only gone into this statement to approach a second point; and that is, we stand on the moment when the people actually put their hands forth for power. We stand at an epoch when the nature of the government is undergoing a fundamental change. I have been speaking of machines, whether we should operate through a Senate and President, or solely through a House. I have been speaking of the spindles and wheels. Below that lies the water power. The water power of Great Britain has been the wealth of thirty thousand landholders—thirty thousand land-holding families, perhaps seven hundred thousand or a million voters. With us, the water power is to be the ballots of ten millions of adult men and women, scattered through all classes, rich and poor, educated and ignorant, prompt and conservative, radical and timid, all modes and kinds and qualities of mind. Well, that brings me to the form which this great advance of the people takes. It is the working masses that are really about to put their hands to the work of governing.

It is no accident, no caprice of an individual, nor mere shout of the political arena, that heralds today the great Labor movement of the United States.

But in the mean time, over the horizon, looming at first and now almost touching its meridian, comes up another power—I mean the power of wealth, the inordinate power of capital. Our fathers, when they prevented entail, when they provided for the distribution of estates, thought they had erected a bulwark against the money power that had killed Great Britain. They forgot that money could combine; that a moneyed corporation was like the papacy—a succession of persons with a unity of purpose; that it never died; that it never by natural proclivity became imbecile. The grandson of a king is necessarily one third an idiot; but the third generation of a money corporation is wiser for the experience of predecessors, and preserves the same unity of purpose.

This great money power looms over the horizon at the very moment when, to every thoughtful man, the power of the masses concentrating in the House of Representatives is to become the sole omnipotence of the State. Naturally so ominous a conjecture provokes resistance; naturally a peril so immediate prompts the wealthy class of the community to combine for defence.

The land of England has ruled it for six hundred years. The corporations of America mean to rule it in the same way, and unless some power more radical than that of ordinary politics is found, will rule it inevitably. I confess that the only fear I have in regard to republican institutions is whether, in our day, any adequate remedy will be found for this incoming flood of the power of incorporated wealth. No statesman, no public man yet, has dared to defy it. Every man that has met it has been crushed to powder; and the only hope of any effectual grapple with it is in rousing the actual masses, whose interests permanently lie in an opposite direction, to grapple with this great force; for you know very well that our great cities are the radiating points from which go forth the great journalism, the culture, the education, the commercial influences, that make and shape the nation. The great cities are the arsenals of great wealth, where wealth manages every thing its own way.

Now, gentlemen, to me the Labor movement means just this: It is the last noble protest of the American people against the power of incorporated wealth, seeking to do over again what the Whig aristocracy of Great Britain has successfully done for two hundred years. Thirty thousand families own Great Britain today; and if you multiply John Bright by a hundred, and double his eloquence, it seems impossible that he should save England from a violent convulsion in the great grapple between such a power and the people who have determined to have their way.

Men blame us, the representatives of the working-men of the nation, that we come into politics. The other day it was my good fortune to meet that distinguished Frenchman, Monsieur Coquerel; and he asked me what was the motto of the working-men of the United States. I said to him, "Short hours, better education, cooperation in the end, and in the mean time a political movement that will concentrate the thought of the country upon this thing."

Now, here I take issue with the best critic which the Labor movement has met: I refer to Rev. Samuel Johnson of Salem; one of the thinkers who has spread out before the people his objections to the Labor movement of this country. His first objection is, that we will hurry into politics. Well, now, our answer to him, and to the score of other scholars who have been criticizing us, is this: Gentlemen, we see the benefit of going into politics. If we had not rushed into politics, had not taken Massachusetts by the four corners and shaken her, you never would have written your criticisms. We rush into politics because politics is the safety valve. We could discuss as well as you, if you would only give us bread and houses, fair pay and leisure, and opportunities to travel. We could sit and discuss the question for the next fifty years. It's a very easy thing to discuss, for a gentleman in his study, with no anxiety about to-morrow. Why, the ladies and gentlemen of the reign of Louis XV. and Louis XVI., in France, seated in gilded saloons and on Persian carpets, surrounded with luxury, with the products of India, and the curious manufactures of ingenious Lyons and Rheims, discussed the rights of man, and balanced them in dainty phrases, and expressed them in such quaint generalizations that Jefferson borrowed the Declaration of Independence from their hands. There they sat, balancing and discussing sweetly, making out new theories, and daily erecting a splendid architecture of debate, till the angry crowd broke open the doors, and ended the discussion in blood. They waited too long, discussed about half a century too long. You see, discussion is very good when a man has bread to eat, and his children all portioned off, and his daughters married, and his house furnished and paid for, and his will made; but discussion is very bad when—

"Ye hear the children weeping, O my brothers!
Ere the sorrow comes with years;"

discussion is bad when a class bends under actual oppression. We want immediate action.

We would fain save this issue from an outbreak of actual violence. Therefore we go into politics.

Well, then, our critic goes on to say, "What do you call youselves Labor party for? All men labor. Rufus Choate labors. Daniel Webster labors. Why do you confine your party to the men that work?" Well, now, we confine it because thus there is no mistake. Now, suppose you should take up a book presenting the condition of the laboring classes of Great Britain. Mr. Gladstone works harder than any other man there; Lord Brougham did more work than any other man there; Lord Palmerston, up to his eightieth year, worked hard as any man there. But if you were to take up a book on the working-men of Great Britain, do you think you would find the condition of Lord Brougham there? If you took up a book on the British laboring class, or how much they eat, what kind of houses they live in, etc., do you think you would find Gladstone's income, and the number of rooms he had in his house, and how many children he had had the last fifty years? So if an

Englishman came here, and said, "I want to know something about your working-men. Please let me hear it from some of themselves. Whom shall I go to?" Would you send him to Daniel Webster or Rufus Choate? But Daniel Webster did as much work as any man of his day. Would you have him sent to Rufus Choate? But Rufus Choate was a hard-working man. John Marshall and Lemuel Shaw did as much work as any men in Massachusetts or Virginia; but if George Combe had come to this country, and said, "I want to see a specimen of the laboring class of the United States," I doubt whether any man would have sent him to Lemuel Shaw. I ask the critics of the Labor movement, whether any man ever misunderstood this? Every man who reads of the Labor Question knows that it means the movement of the men that earn their living with their hands; that are employed, and paid in wages; are gathered under roofs of factories; sent out on farms; sent out on ships; gathered on the walls. In popular acceptation, the working class means the men that work with their hands, for wages, so many hours a day, employed by great capitalists; that work for everybody else.

Why do we move for this class? "Why," says Mr. Johnson, "don't you move for all working-men?" Because, while Daniel Webster gets forty thousand dollars for arguing the Mexican claims, there is no need of anybody's moving for him. While Rufus Choate gets five thousand dollars for making one argument to a jury, there is no need of moving for him, or for the men that work with their brains,—that do highly disciplined and skilled labor, invent, and write books. The reason why the Labor movement confines itself to a single class is because that class of work does not get paid, does not get protection. Mental labor is adequately paid, and more that adequately pro-

tected. It can shift its channels; it can vary according to the supply and demand. If a man fails as a minister, why, he becomes a railway conductor. If that doesn't suit him, he turns out, and becomes the agent of an insurance office. If that doesn't suit, he goes West, and becomes governor of a Territory. And if he finds himself incapable of either of these positions, he comes home, and gets to be a city editor. He varies his occupation as he pleases, and doesn't need protection. But the great mass, chained to a trade, doomed to be ground up in the mill of supply and demand, that work so many hours a day, and must run in the great ruts of business,— they are the men whose inadequate protection, whose unfair share of the general product claims a movement in their behalf.

Well, the third charge brought by Mr. Johnson against us is, that we are cruel—we combine; we prevent this man from laboring there, and we won't let that man learn our trade; we form trades-unions. To be sure we do. We say to the Chinese, "Stay at home. Don't come here by importation; come by immigration." We say to the crowding millions who try to swamp our trade, "Stand aloof; we won't teach you." We say to the mills of Lowell, who have turned us out of doors, "We'll starve you into submission." Well, "it's a narrow contest. It's an unjust, it's a cruel, it's an avaricious method." So it is. Where did we learn it? Learned it of capital, learned it of our enemies.

I know labor is narrow; I know she is aggressive; I know she arms herself with the best weapon that a corrupt civilization furnishes,—all true. Where do we get these ideas? Borrowed them from capital, every one of them; and when you advance to us on the level of peace, unarmed, we'll meet you on the same. While you combine and plot and defend, so will we.

But Mr. Johnson says, "Come into

the world with the white banner of peace." Ay, we will, when you disarm. How foolish it would have been for Grant to send home his Sharp's rifles to Springfield, and garner all his cannon in New York, and put all his monitors in the harbor of Norfolk, and go down to Virginia with eighty thousand unarmed men, to look her in the face! Labor comes up, and says, "They have shotted their cannon to the lips; they have rough-ground their swords as in battle; they have adopted every new method; they have invented every dangerous machine,—and it is all planted like a great park of artillery against us. They have incorporated wealth; they have hidden behind banks; they have concealed themselves in currency; they have sheltered themselves in taxation; they have passed rules to govern us,—and we will improve upon the lesson they have taught us. When they disarm, we will—not before."

Well, then, the fourth charge is found in the *Daily Advertiser*. We had a meeting at Framingham, and passed a set of resolutions; we adopted a platform; and the next day the *Daily Advertiser* granted us the condescension of an article, criticising our action, especially mine; and they described what we had adopted. They painted its horrible tendency. They said, "If you adopt that principle, it will lead you to that (and so on to that) till the final result will be—" I held my breath. I said to myself, "What will it probably be? Perhaps the stereotyped ghost of the French Revolution; that's what's coming." "The final result will be—" Horrible! I thought probably they would paint a millionaire hanging on every lamp-post. "The final result—" Perhaps it will be Mormonism; society dissolved into its original elements. Horrible! I began to feel a faint sensation; but I concluded to read on: "The final result will be an equalization of property." Horrible, horrible! Actually, men will

be almost equal! An equalization of property! Any man that does that ought to be hanged. Well, we do mean it; we do mean just that. That's the meaning of the Labor movement,—an equalization of property. The *Advertiser* has found us out, actually discovered our plot. He's let the cat out of the bag. We didn't mean to have told you, but it is so. What we need is an equalization of property—nothing else. My ideal of a civilization is a very high one; but the approach to it is a New England town of some two thousand inhabitants, with no rich and no poor man in it, all mingling in the same society, every child at the same school, no poorhouse, no beggar, opportunities equal, nobody too proud to stand aloof, nobody too humble to be shut out. That's New England as it was fifty years ago, the horrible creature that the *Daily Advertiser* fears. That's what Framingham proposes to bring about. But why isn't Framingham contented? Because the civilization that lingers beautifully on the hillsides of New England, nestles sweetly in the valleys of Vermont, the moment it approaches a crowd like Boston, or a million of men gathered in one place like New York—rots. It cannot force the crowd; it cannot stand the great centres of modern civilization.

Our civilization cannot stand the city. One reason is, it has got some hidden disease. Another reason is, the moment it flows out into the broad, deep activity of the nineteenth century, it betrays its weakness, and copies Europe. The moment this sweet-scented, dew-smelling Vermont flows down into the slums of New York, it becomes like London. The moment the North gathers its forces, and goes down the Mississippi Valley into New Orleans, social science stands aghast. Modern civilization shrinks back at the terrible evil which she can neither fathom nor cure, just as she does in Europe.

What is our cause? It is this: there are

three hundred and fifty millions of human beings in what you call Christendom, and two hundred millions of them don't have enough to eat from January to December. I won't ask for culture, for opportunities for education, for travel, for society; but two hundred millions of men gathered under Christendom don't have even enough to eat. A hundred thousand men in the city of New York live in dwellings that a rich man wouldn't let his horse stay in a day.

But that isn't anything. You should go up to beautiful Berkshire with me, into the factories there. It shall be the day after a Presidential election. I will go with you into a counting-room—four hundred employees. The partners are sitting down, the day after a Presidential election. They take the list of workmen, and sift them out; and every man that has not voted the ticket they wanted is thrown out to starve just as if he were cattle. That's Christian civilization! that's Massachusetts! I don't like that significant fact. I leap from that town into a large mill, with five hundred employees, and say to the master, "How about the dwellings of your operatives? How many hours do they have at home?" "Well, I hope they don't have any. The best-ventilated place they are ever in is my mill. They had better stay here sixteen hours out of the twenty-four; it keeps them out of mischief better than any other place. As long as they work, they are not doing worse. I cannot attend to their houses." I say to him, "It seems to me you do the same for your ox." That's another significant fact of our civilization. I go to Lowell, and I say to a young girl, wandering in the streets, "How is this?" "Well, I worked here seven years, and I thought I would leave that mill and go to another; and the corporation won't give me my ticket. I have sued them in the Supreme Court, and I cannot get it; and here I am, penniless, in Eastern Massachusetts." That's Christian civilization. I

am picking up, not individual facts, but significant rules, that were made for labor.

You say, "What does labor need in New England?" It needs justice. Mr. Stewart, in New York, has bought a whole town; and he is going to build model houses, and house there all the labor he can get to go into them. Yet the civilization which alone can look the New Testament in the face is a civilization where one man does not depend on the pity of another man's building him a model lodging-house; the civilization which alone can look the New Testament in the face is a civilization where one man could not build, and another man would not need, that sort of refuge.

No, gentlemen, what we mean is this: the labor of yesterday, your capital, is protected sacredly. Not so the labor of to-day. The labor of yesterday gets twice the protection and twice the pay that the labor of today gets. Capital gets twice the protection and twice the pay.

Now, we mean a radical change, and in the few minutes that are left me, I want to indicate our object.

We mean certain great radical changes. I am not quite of the opinion of Mr. Secretary Boutwell, when he said here the other night, that fifty years hence the idea that a man could own land, and leave it to his children, would be ridiculous. I have not quite come to that. But then, you know there is a reason for it; he is a radical, and I have always been a conservative. There is a curious thing underlies lands. We are not quite certain that we have got the best system. Secretary Boutwell may be right. Seventy years ago a man offered to a relative of mine all the land between Federal Street and Hawley Street, between Milk Street and Franklin, for thirty-three hundred dollars. He came to him day after day, urging him to purchase; and the answer was, "I am not rich enough to have a cow-pasture at that price, and I couldn't use it for anything else,"—that tract of land which today, gentlemen, as you know, would sell for three million dollars. Now, labor goes about, like Socrates, asking questions. We don't assume anything. When we were little boys, and did our sums on the slate, and the answer came out wrong, we didn't break the slate. We went to the master; and he said, "Go back; there's a mistake somewhere; if you examine, you will find it." I come into a civilization in which two men out of three don't have enough to eat. I come into New York, where it is a rich man that supplies a lodging for houseless poverty. I say to myself, "That course isn't right; there's a mistake somewhere." Do unto others as you would have others do unto you. The end of things is New York. That doesn't cohere. Where is the mistake? It is somewhere, and the Labor movement is trying to find it out.

Again, gentlemen, we have another doubt to express. Are you quite certain that capital—the child of artificial laws, the product of society, the mere growth of social life—has a right to only an equal burden with labor, the living spring? We doubt it so much that we think we have invented a way to defeat Tom Scott, of the Pennsylvania Central. We think we have devised a little plan—Abraham Lincoln used to have a little story—by which we will save the Congress of the Nation from the moneyed corporations of the State. When we get into power, there is one thing we mean to do. If a man owns a single house, we will tax him one hundred dollars. If he owns ten houses of like value, we won't tax him one thousand dollars, but two thousand dollars. If he owns a hundred houses, we won't tax him ten thousand dollars, but sixty thousand dollars; and the richer a man grows, the bigger his tax, so that when he is worth forty million dollars he will not have more than twenty thousand dollars a year to live on. We'll double and treble and quintuple and sextuple and increase tenfold the taxes, till Stewart, out of his uncounted millions, and the Pennsylvania Central, out of its measureless income, shall not have anything more than a moderate lodging and an honest table. The corporations we would have are those of associated labor and capital—cooperation.

We'll crumble up wealth by making it unprofitable to be rich. The poor man shall have a larger income in proportion as he is poor. The rich man shall have a lesser income in proportion as he is rich. You will say, "Is that just?" My friends, it is safe. Man is more valuable than money. You say, "Then capital will go to Europe." Good heavens, let it go!

If other States wish to make themselves vassals to wealth, so will not we. We will save a country equal from end to end. Land, private property, all sorts of property, shall be so dearly taxed that it shall be impossible to be rich; for it is in wealth, in incorporated, combining, perpetuated wealth, that the danger of labor lies.

CHAPTER XIV

THE MIND OF
THE SOUTH

*T*he existence of slavery in America constituted the great challenge to American ideals of democracy, equality, and opportunity. Earlier in the century, thoughtful southerners had realized—as did Jefferson himself—that slavery was an evil and should be destroyed. Yet even in Jefferson's lifetime, the invention of the cotton gin and the subsequent rapid growth of the cotton-slave economy were making slavery profitable and even necessary to the South. The last southern emancipation effort occurred in Virginia in 1832, and thereafter antislavery sentiment all but died in the South. Southerners now came to the defense of slavery, first as a necessary evil and then, as the Civil War approached, as a positive good.

The struggle over the slavery question grew more formidable each decade. From the 1820's on, a series of compromises relating to the extension of slavery into the new territories, attempted to maintain national unity by balancing political power and sectional interests. But the conflict went deeper than a battle for political power and posed fundamental economic problems and moral issues. Indeed, it was this combination of interests in both North and South that made the impending clash between the states more inevitable and castastrophic.

The arguments for slavery were based on a variety of premises: economic need, states' rights, the Biblical sanction of slavery, and the inferior status of the Negro race. Underlying all such arguments, however, was what may be called the "plantation mind"—an image of a landed, feudal aristocracy that would counterbalance the industrial North. More imaginary than real, this mind fortified itself by repeating the arguments of Europe's reactionary spokesmen. George Fitzhugh, for example, announced that "we begin a great conservative reaction. . . . We attempt to roll back the Reformation in its political phases." And John C. Calhoun invoked a sophisticated, though dated, political philosophy to maintain the integrity of the South's sectional interests. The United States, Calhoun argued, was not an organic union; and within this structure simple majority rule did not always serve the interests of justice. From this he took his famous doctrine of "concurrent majority," which in effect would have given each section of the nation a veto power over the actions of the federal authority.

The southern mind had eloquent spokesmen in such men as Fitzhugh and Calhoun, and yet it did not escape ideological difficulties. Much of this difficulty arose from the fact that slavery did not fit into any of the traditional categories of American social thought, try as the South might to make it fit. In Calhoun these difficulties are especially clear. He destroyed Locke's state of nature and then evolved a theory of minority rights that were based squarely on the doctrine of consent; he defended slavery on the basis of the "divinity of existing coercions" and then sought to defend the South from economic enslavement by the North; and he construed the Constitution, as Professor Hartz puts it, as a compact among the states that "left nothing to tradition, nothing to force, and nothing to God."[1]

Reaction to slavery in the North, while sometimes based on economic considerations, generally sprang from deep moral conviction. Slavery was an evil, thoughtful northerners believed, and abolition was the only solution. Abolitionist literature undoubtedly exaggerated the lurid features of slavery and encouraged an emotional reaction to the problem. Yet the "peculiar institution" of slavery and the mentality that supported it were outside the main current of American development and thought, and would not survive the terrible struggle about to begin. But the romanticized picture of the antebellum South (largely a creation of the imagination) continued as a living symbol for later generations of southerners.

---

[1] On these inconsistencies and the relation of the southern mind to American liberalism, see Louis Hartz, *The Liberal Tradition in America* (New York, 1955), Part Four: The Reactionary Enlightenment.

John C. Calhoun
1782-1850

Calhoun served the nation long and ably as a Congressman from South Carolina, Secretary of War under Monroe, Vice-President under Jackson, Secretary of State under Tyler, and as Senator from South Carolina. A brilliant politician, he was also the leading political theorist of his generation.

Calhoun devoted his formidable skills to the defense of slavery as an institution essential to the survival of the South. In this effort he became the acknowledged champion of states' rights. Rejecting the principle of majority rule on the ground that majorities can be tyrannical, he developed the theory of concurrent majority as an alternative that would protect sectional interests.

This selection is from "A Disquisition on Government," The Works of John C. Calhoun, *6 vols. (New York, 1876), vol. I.*

*I*n order to have a clear and just conception of the nature and object of government, it is indispensable to understand correctly what that constitution or law of our nature is in which government originates, or to express it more fully and accurately—that law without which government would not and with which it must necessarily exist. Without this, it is as impossible to lay any solid foundation for the science of government as it would be to lay one for that of astronomy without a like understanding of that constitution or law of the material world according to which the several bodies composing the solar system mutually act on each other and by which they are kept in their respective spheres. The first question, accordingly, to be considered, What is that constitution or law of our nature without which government would not exist and with which its existence is necessary?

In considering this, I assume as an incontestable fact that man is so constituted as to be a social being. His inclinations and wants, physical and moral, irresistibly impel him to associate with his kind; and he has, accord-

ingly, never been found, in any age or country, in any state other than the social. In no other, indeed, could he exist, and in no other—were it possible for him to exist—could he attain to a full development of his moral and intellectual faculties or raise himself, in the scale of being, much above the level of the brute creation.

I next assume also as a fact not less incontestable that, while man is so constituted as to make the social state necessary to his existence and the full development of his faculties, this state cannot exist without government. The assumption rests on universal experience. In no age or country has any society or community ever been found, whether enlightened or savage, without government of some description.

Having assumed these as unquestionable phenomena of our nature, I shall, without further remark, proceed to the investigation of the primary and important question, What is that constitution of our nature which, while it impels man to associate with his kind, renders it impossible for society to exist without government?

The answer will be found in the fact

232

(not less incontestable than either of the others) that, while man is created for the social state and is accordingly so formed as to feel what affects others as well as what affects himself, he is, at the same time, so constituted as to feel more intensely what affects him directly than what affects him indirectly through others, or, to express it differently, he is so constituted that his direct or individual affections are stronger than his sympathetic or social feelings. I intentionally avoid the expression "*selfish feelings*" as applicable to the former, because, as commonly used, it implies an unusual excess of the individual over the social feelings in the person to whom it is applied and, consequently, something depraved and vicious. My object is to exclude such inference and to restrict the inquiry exclusively to facts in their bearings on the subject under consideration, viewed as mere phenomena appertaining to our nature—constituted as it is; and which are as unquestionable as is that of gravitation or any other phenomenon of the material world.

In asserting that our individual are stronger than our social feelings, it is not intended to deny that there are instances, growing out of peculiar relations—as that of a mother and her infant—or resulting from the force of education and habit over peculiar constitutions, in which the latter have overpowered the former; but these instances are few and always regarded as something extraordinary. The deep impression they make, whenever they occur, is the strongest proof that they are regarded as exceptions to some general and well-understood law of our nature, just as some of the minor powers of the material world are apparently to gravitation.

I might go farther and assert this to be a phenomenon not of our nature only, but of all animated existence throughout its entire range, so far as our knowledge extends. It would, indeed, seem to be essentially connected with the great law of self-preservation which pervades all that feels, from man down to the lowest and most insignificant reptile or insect. In none is it stronger than in man. His social feelings may, indeed, in a state of safety and abundance, combined with high intellectual and moral culture, acquire great expansion and force, but not so great as to overpower this all-pervading and essential law of animated existence.

But that constitution of our nature which makes us feel more intensely what affects us directly than what affects us indirectly through others necessarily leads to conflict between individuals. Each, in consequence, has a greater regard for his own safety or happiness than for the safety or happiness of others, and, where these come in opposition, is ready to sacrifice the interests of others to his own. And hence the tendency to a universal state of conflict between individual and individual, accompanied by the connected passions of suspicion, jealousy, anger, and revenge—followed by insolence, fraud, and cruelty—and, if not prevented by some controlling power, ending in a state of universal discord and confusion destructive of the social state and the ends for which it is ordained. This controlling power, wherever vested or by whomsoever exercised, is *Government*.

It follows, then, that man is so constituted that government is necessary to the existence of society, and society to his existence and the perfection of his faculties. It follows also that government has its origin in this twofold constitution of his nature: the sympathetic or social feelings constituting the remote, and the individual or direct the proximate, cause. . . .

But government, although intended to protect and preserve society, has itself a strong tendency to disorder and abuse of its powers, as all experience and almost every page of history testify. The cause is to be found in the same constitution of our nature which makes government indispensable. The powers which it is necessary for government to possess in order to repress violence and preserve order cannot execute themselves. They must be administered by men in whom, like others, the individual are stronger than the social feelings. And hence the powers vested in them to prevent injustice and oppression on the part of others will, if left unguarded, be by them converted into instruments to oppress the rest of the community. That by which this is prevented, by whatever name called, is what is meant by *constitution*, in its most comprehensive sense, when applied to *government*.

Having its origin in the same principle of our nature, *constitution* stands to *government* as *government* stands to *society*; and as the end for which society is ordained would be defeated without government, so that for which government is ordained would, in a great measure, be defeated without constitution. But they differ in this striking particular. There is no difficulty in forming government. It is not even a matter of choice whether there shall be one or not. Like breathing, it is not permitted to depend on our volition. Necessity will force it on all communities in some one form or another. Very different is the case as to constitution. Instead of a matter of necessity, it is one of the most difficult tasks imposed on man to form a constitution worthy of the name, while to form a perfect one—one that would completely counteract the tendency of government to oppression and abuse and hold it strictly to the great ends for which it is ordained—has thus far exceeded human wisdom, and possibly ever will. From this another striking difference results. Constitution is the contrivance of man, while government is of divine ordina-

tion. Man is left to perfect what the wisdom of the Infinite ordained as necessary to preserve the race.

With these remarks I proceed to the consideration of the important and difficult question, How is this tendency of government to be counteracted? . . .

In answering the important question under consideration it is not necessary to enter into an examination of the various contrivances adopted by these celebrated governments to counteract this tendency to disorder and abuse, nor to undertake to treat of constitution in its most comprehensive sense. What I propose is far more limited: to explain on what principles government must be formed in order to resist by its own interior structure—or to use a single term, *organism*—the tendency to abuse of power. This structure, or organism, is what is meant by constitution, in its strict and more usual sense; and it is this which distinguishes what are called "constitutional" governments from "absolute." It is in this strict and more usual sense that I propose to use the term hereafter.

How government, then, must be constructed in order to counteract, through its organism, this tendency on the part of those who make and execute the laws to oppress those subject to their operation is the next question which claims attention.

There is but one way in which this can possibly be done, and that is by such an organism as will furnish the ruled with the means of resisting successfully this tendency on the part of the rulers to oppression and abuse. Power can only be resisted by power—and tendency by tendency. Those who exercise power and those subject to its exercise—the rulers and the ruled—stand in antagonistic relations to each other. The same constitution of our nature which leads rulers to oppress the ruled—regardless of the object for which government is ordained—will, with equal strength, lead the ruled to resist when possessed of the means of making peaceable and effective resistance. Such an organism, then, as will furnish the means by which resistance may be systematically and peaceably made on the part of the ruled to oppression and abuse of power on the part of the rulers is the first and indispensable step toward *forming* a constitutional government. And as this can only be effected by or through the right of suffrage—the right on the part of the ruled to choose their rulers at proper intervals and to hold them thereby responsible for their conduct—the responsibility of the rulers to the ruled, through the right of suffrage, is the indispensable and primary principle in the *foundation* of a constitutional government. When this right is properly guarded, and the people sufficiently enlightened to understand their own rights and the interests of the community and duly to appreciate the motives and conduct of those appointed to make and execute the laws, it is all-sufficient to give to those who elect effective control over those they have elected.

I call the right of suffrage the indispensable and primary principle, for it would be a great and dangerous mistake to suppose, as many do, that it is, of itself, sufficient to form constitutional governments. To this erroneous opinion may be traced one of the causes why so few attempts to form constitutional governments have succeeded, and why of the few which have, so small a number have had durable existence. It has led not only to mistakes in the attempts to form such governments, but to their overthrow when they have, by some good fortune, been correctly formed. So far from being, of itself, sufficient—however well guarded it might be and however enlightened the people—it would, unaided by other provisions, leave the government as absolute as it would be in the hands of irresponsible rulers; and with a tend-ency, at least as strong, toward oppression and abuse of its powers. . . .

As, then, the right of suffrage, without some other provision, cannot counteract this tendency of government, the next question for consideration is, What is that other provision? This demands the most serious consideration, for of all the questions embraced in the science of government it involves a principle, the most important and the least understood, and when understood, the most difficult of application in practice. It is, indeed, emphatically that principle which *makes* the constitution, in its strict and limited sense.

From what has been said, it is manifest that this provision must be of a character calculated to prevent any one interest or combination of interests from using the powers of government to aggrandize itself at the expense of the others. Here lies the evil: and just in proportion as it shall prevent, or fail to prevent it, in the same degree it will effect, or fail to effect, the end intended to be accomplished. There is but one certain mode in which this result can be secured, and that is by the adoption of some restriction or limitation which shall so effectually prevent any one interest or combination of interests from obtaining the exclusive control of the government as to render hopeless all attempts directed to that end. There is, again, but one mode in which this can be effected, and that is by taking the sense of each interest or portion of the community which may be unequally and injuriously affected by the action of the government separately, through its own majority or in some other way by which its voice may be fairly expressed, and to require the consent of each interest either to put or to keep the government in action. This, too, can be accomplished only in one way, and that is by such an organism of the government—and, if necessary for the purpose, of the community also—as will, by dividing and distributing the powers of government, give to each division or interest, through its appropriate organ, either a concurrent voice in making and executing the laws or a veto on their execution. It is only by such an organism that the assent of each can be made necessary to put the government in motion, or the power made effectual to arrest its action when put in motion; and it is only by the one or the other that the different interests, orders, classes, or portions into which the community may be divided can be protected, and all conflict and struggle between them prevented—by rendering it impossible to put or to keep it in action without the concurrent consent of all.

Such an organism as this, combined with the right of suffrage, constitutes, in fact, the elements of constitutional government. The one, by rendering those who make and execute the laws responsible to those on whom they operate, prevents the rulers from oppressing the ruled; and the other, by making it impossible for any one interest or combination of interests, or class, or order, or portion of the community to obtain exclusive control, prevents any one of them from oppressing the other. It is clear that oppression and abuse of power must come, if at all, from the one or the other quarter. From no other can they come. It follows that the two, suffrage and proper organism combined, are sufficient to counteract the tendency of government to oppression and abuse of power and to restrict it to the fulfillment of the great ends for which it is ordained.

George Fitzhugh

1806-1881

A prominent Virginia lawyer and planter, Fitzhugh became a leading defender of slavery. Fitzhugh argued that the existence of slavery lent stability to society and reduced the amount of thievery and crime. Thus, for Fitzhugh slavery was not a necessary evil but rather a positive good, for it freed the South from the mounting social and economic problems of the rest of the world. His first important book, Sociology for the South *(1854), with its arguments against laissez-faire capitalism, attracted little attention. His next work, however, was much more vigorous and carried the argument to the enemy camp. Free society, he wrote, is a failure, and the philosophy upon which it is based—social contract, natural rights, rule by law—is false. Rather, America must return to the political theories of Aristotle that are based on the social nature of man and a hierarchical view of society.*

The selection here is from Cannibals All! *(Richmond, 1857).*

*W*e are, all, North and South, engaged in the White Slave Trade, and he who succeeds best, is esteemed most respectable. It is far more cruel than the Black Slave Trade, because it exacts more of its slaves, and neither protects nor governs them. We boast, that it exacts more, when we say, "that the *profits* made from employing free labor are greater than those from slave labor." The profits, made from free labor, are the amount of the products of such labor, which the employer, by means of the command which capital or skill gives him, takes away, exacts or "exploitates" from the free laborer. The profits of slave labor are that portion of the products of such labor which the power of the master enables him to appropriate. These profits are less, because the master allows the slave to retain a larger share of the results of his own labor, than do the employers of free labor. But we not only boast that the White Slave Trade is more exacting and fraudulent (in fact, though not in intention,) than Black Slavery; but we also boast, that it is more cruel, in leaving the laborer to take care of himself and family out of the pittance which skill or capital have allowed him to retain. When the day's labor is ended, he is free, but is overburdened with the cares of family and household, which make his freedom an empty and delusive mockery. But his employer is really free, and may enjoy the profits made by others' labor, without a care, or a trouble, as to their well-being. The negro slave is free, too, when the labors of the day are over, and free in mind as well as body; for the master provides food, raiment, house, fuel, and everything else necessary to the physical well-being of himself and family. The master's labors commence just when the slave's end. No wonder men should prefer white slavery to capital, to negro slavery, since it is more profitable, and is free from all the cares and labors of black slave-holding.

Now, reader, if you wish to know

yourself—to "descant on your own deformity"—read on. But if you would cherish self-conceit, self-esteem, or self-appreciation, throw down our book; for we will dispel illusions which have promoted your happiness, and show you that what you have considered and practiced as virtue, is little better than moral Cannibalism. But you will find yourself in numerous and respectable company; for all good and respectable people are "Cannibals all," who do not labor, or who are successfully trying to live without labor, on the unrequited labor of other people: whilst low, bad, and disreputable people, are those who labor to support themselves, and to support said respectable people besides. Throwing the negro slaves out of the account, and society is divided in Christendom into four classes: the rich, or independent respectable people, who live well and labor not at all; the professional and skillful respectable people, who do a little light work, for enormous wages; the poor hard-working people, who support every body, and starve themselves; and the poor thieves, swindlers and sturdy beggars, who live like gentlemen, without labor, on the labor of other people. The gentlemen exploitate, which being done on a large scale, and requiring a great many victims, is highly respectable—whilst the rogues and beggars take so little from others, that they fare little better than those who labor.

But, reader, we do not wish to fire into the flock. "Thou art the man!" You are a Cannibal! and if a successful one, pride yourself on the number of your victims, quite as much as any Feejee chieftain, who breakfasts, dines and sups on human flesh. And your conscience smites you, if you have failed to succeed, quite as much as his, when he returns from an unsuccessful foray.

Probably, you are a lawyer, or a merchant, or a doctor, who have made by your business fifty thousand dollars, and retired to live on your capital. But, mark! not to spend your capital. That would be vulgar, disreputable, criminal. That would be, to live by your own labor; for your capital is your amassed labor. That would be, to do as common working men do; for they take the pittance which their employers leave them, to live on. They live by labor; for they exchange the results of their own labor for the products of other people's labor. It is, no doubt, an honest, vulgar way of living; but not at all a respectable way. The respectable way of living is, to make other people work for you, and to pay them nothing for so doing—and to have no concern about them after their work is done. Hence, white slaveholding is much more respectable than negro slavery—for the master works nearly as hard for the negro, as he for the master. But you, my virtuous, respectable reader, exact three thousand dollars per annum from white labor, (for your income is the product of white labor,) and make not one cent of return in any form. You retain your capital, and never labor, and yet live in luxury on the labor of others. Capital commands labor, as the master does the slave. Neither pays for labor; but the master permits the slave to retain a larger allowance from the proceeds of his own labor, and hence "free labor is cheaper than slave labor." You, with the command over labor which your capital gives you, are a slave owner—a master, without the obligations of a master. They who work for you, who create your income, are slaves, without the rights of slaves. Slaves without a master! Whilst you were engaged in amassing your capital, in seeking to become independent, you were in the White Slave Trade. To become independent, is to be able to make other people support you, without being obliged to labor for *them*. Now, what man in society is not seeking to attain this situation? He who attains it, is a slave owner, in the worst sense. He who is in pursuit of it, is engaged in the slave trade. You, reader, belong to the one or other class. The men without property, in free society, are theoretically in a worse condition than slaves. Practically, their condition corresponds with this theory, as history and statistics every where demonstrate. The capitalists, in free society, live in ten times the luxury and show that Southern masters do, because the slaves to capital work harder and cost less, than negro slaves.

The negro slaves of the South are the happiest, and, in some sense, the freest people in the world. The children and the aged and infirm work not at all, and yet have all the comforts and necessaries of life provided for them. They enjoy liberty, because they are oppressed neither by care nor labor. The women do little hard work, and are protected from the despotism of their husbands by their masters. The negro men and stout boys work, on the average, in good weather, not more than nine hours a day. The balance of their time is spent in perfect abandon. Besides, they have their Sabbaths and holidays. White men, with so much of license and liberty, would die of ennui; but negroes luxuriate in corporeal and mental repose. With their faces upturned to the sun, they can sleep at any hour; and quiet sleep is the greatest of human enjoyments. "Blessed be the man who invented sleep." 'Tis happiness in itself—and results from contentment with the present, and confident assurance of the future. We do not know whether free laborers ever sleep. They are fools to do so; for, whilst they sleep, the wily and watchful capitalist is devising means to ensnare and exploitate them. The free laborer must work or starve. He is more of a slave than the negro, because he works longer and harder for less allowance than the slave, and has no holiday, because the cares of

life with him begin when its labors end. He has no liberty, and not a single right. We know, 'tis often said, air and water, are common property, which all have equal right to participate and enjoy; but this is utterly false. The appropriation of the lands carries with it the appropriation of all on or above the lands, *usque ad cœlum, aut ad inferos.* A man cannot breathe the air, without a place to breathe it from, and all places are appropriated. All water is private property "to the middle of the stream," except the ocean, and that is not fit to drink.

Free laborers have not a thousandth part of the rights and liberties of negro slaves. Indeed, they have not a single right or a single liberty, unless it be the right or liberty to die. But the reader may think that he and other capitalists and employers are freer than negro slaves. Your capital would soon vanish, if you dared indulge in the liberty and abandon of negroes. You hold your wealth and position by the tenure of constant watchfulness, care and circumspection. You never labor; but you are never free.

Where a few own the soil, they have unlimited power over the balance of society, until domestic slavery comes in, to compel them to permit this balance of society to draw a sufficient and comfortable living from "terra mater." Free society, asserts the right of a few to the earth—slavery, maintains that it belongs, in different degrees, to all.

But, reader, well may you follow the slave trade. It is the only trade worth following, and slaves the only property worth owning. All other is worthless, a mere *caput mortuum*, except in so far as it vests the owner with the power to command the labors of others—to enslave them. Give you a palace, ten thousand acres of land, sumptuous clothes, equipage and every other luxury; and with your artificial wants, you are poorer than Robinson Crusoe, or the lowest working man, if you have no slaves to capital, or domestic slaves. Your capital will not bring you an income of a cent, nor supply one of your wants, without labor. Labor is indispensable to give value to property, and if you owned every thing else, and did not own labor, you would be poor. But fifty thousand dollars means, and is, fifty thousand dollars worth of slaves. You can command, without touching on that capital, three thousand dollars' worth of labor per annum. You could do no more were you to buy slaves with it, and then you would be cumbered with the cares of governing and providing for them. You are a slaveholder now, to the amount of fifty thousand dollars, with all the advantages, and none of the cares and responsibilities of a master.

"Property in man" is what all are struggling to obtain. Why should they not be obliged to take care of man, their property, as they do their horses and their hounds, their cattle and their sheep. Now, under the delusive name of liberty, you work him, "from morn to dewy eve"—from infancy to old age— then turn him out to starve. You treat your horses and hounds better. Capital is a cruel master. The free slave trade, the commonest, yet the cruelest of trades. . . .

Nothing written on the subject of slavery from the time of Aristotle, is worth reading, until the days of the modern Socialists. Nobody, treating of it, thought it worth while to enquire from history and statistics, whether the physical and moral condition of emancipated serfs or slaves had been improved or rendered worse by emancipation. None would condescend to compare the evils of domestic slavery with the evils of liberty without property. It entered no one's head to conceive a doubt as to the actual freedom of the emancipated. The relations of capital and labor, of the property-holders to the non-property-holders, were things about which no one

had thought or written. It never occurred to either the enemies or the apologists for slavery, that if no one would employ the free laborer, his condition was infinitely worse than that of actual slavery—nor did it occur to them, that if his wages were less than the allowance of the slave, he was less free after emancipation than before. St. Simon, Fourier, Owen, Fanny Wright, and a few others, who discovered and proclaimed that property was not only a bad master, but an intolerable one, were treated as wicked visionaries. After the French and other revolutions in Western Europe in 1830, all men suddenly discovered that the social relations of men were false, and that social, not political, revolutions were needed. Since that period, almost the whole literature of free society is but a voice proclaiming its absolute and total failure. Hence the works of the socialists contain the true defence of slavery. . . .

In the *Liberator* of the 19th December, we observe that the editor narrows down the slavery contest to the mere question, whether "Man may rightfully hold property in man?"

We think we can dispose of this objection to domestic slavery in a very few words.

Man is a social and gregarious animal, and all such animals hold property in each other. Nature imposes upon them slavery as a law and necessity of their existence. They live together to aid each other, and are slaves under Mr. Garrison's higher law. Slavery arises under the higher law, and is, and ever must be, coeval and coextensive with human nature.

We will enumerate a few of its ten thousand modifications.

The husband has a legally recognized property in his wife's services, and may legally control, in some measure, her personal liberty. She is his property and his slave.

The wife has also a legally recognized

property in the husband's services. He is her property, but not her slave.

The father has property in the services and persons of his children till they are twenty-one years of age. They are his property and his slaves.

Children have property, during infancy, in the services of each parent.

Infant negroes, sick, infirm and superannuated negroes, hold most valuable property in the services and capital of their masters. The masters hold no property in such slaves, because, for the time, they are of no value.

Owners and captains of vessels own property in the services of sailors, and may control their personal liberty. They (the sailors) are property, and slaves also.

The services and persons, lives and liberty of soldiers and of officers, belong to the Government; they are, whilst in service, both property and slaves.

Every white working man, be he clerk, carpenter, mechanic, printer, common laborer, or what else, who contracts to serve for a term of days, months, or years, is, for such term, the property of his employer. He is not a slave, like the wife, child, apprentice, sailor or soldier, because, although the employer's right to his services be equally perfect, his remedy to enforce such right is very different. In the one case, he may resort to force to compel compliance; in the other, he is driven to a suit for damages.

Again. Every capitalist holds property in his fellow men to the extent of the profits of his capital, or income. The only income possibly resulting from capital, is the result of the property which capital bestows on its owners, in the labor of other people. . . . .

All civilized society recognizes, and, in some measure, performs the obligation to support and provide for all human beings, whether natives or foreigners, who are unable to provide for themselves. Hence poor-houses, etc.

Hence all men hold valuable property, actual or contingent, in the services of each other.

If, Mr. Garrison, this be the only difficulty to be adjusted between North and South, we are sure that your little pet, Disunion, "living will linger, and lingering will die."

When Mr. Andrews and you have quite "expelled human nature," dissolved and disintegrated society, and reduced mankind to separate, independent, but conflicting monads, or human atoms—then, and not till then, will you establish the "sovereignty of the individual," and destroy the property of man in man.

William Gilmore Simms

1806-1870

*Born in Charleston, South Carolina,
Simms began his career as a newspaper
editor. He had published five volumes of
poetry before his first novel appeared in
1833. Thereafter, a steady stream of novels
came from his pen. Like Cooper, whom he
imitated, Simms turned to social criticism
in his writings, giving emphatic statement to
the philosophy of the old, slave-holding,
aristocratic South.*

*In this selection the author is accompanying
a northerner through the South. Their
conversations with travelers are used to
define the differences that divided the two
sections.* The text is from the discussion of
the southern economy in Southward Ho!
(*New York, 1854*).

A long, and to us a comparatively interesting, conversation followed—Virginia, her resources, characteristics, scenery, and general morals, affording the principal subject. In this conversation, which occasionally ran into politics—in which some of the party showed their teeth very decidedly—the whole of our group was brought out, the ladies excepted. They had retired for the night. Most of us had rambled in Virginia at different periods; and it was in the delivery of recollections and impressions that we passed naturally into discussion. I propose to give *bits* only of this conversation, leaving out the bites—confining my report to the innocuous portions of the dialogue, and omitting certain sharp passages which occasionally followed the thoughtless or the wanton shaft. One of our "Down-East" brethren threw down the ball of provocation, dealing in a wholesale, if not wholesome, diatribe against all Southern agriculture. As his opinions are those of a somewhat numerous class, and as they are working no little mischief at the present day, it may be as well to record, with tolerable fullness, the portion of the dialogue which ensued upon their utterance.

"You pass through Virginia," said he, "as through a desert. The towns are few, and these all look old and wretched. The houses need paint, and are frequently in dilapidation. The culture is coarse and clumsy, the implements rude, and the people seem entirely ignorant of all improvements. They plough, plant, and reap precisely as their fathers did a hundred years ago, and without doing any justice to their lands. The lands have never been properly worked, and manures are but little known, and less esteemed. In favorite regions, along water-courses easily accessible, the plantations have been abandoned as entirely exhausted—sold for a song, at an average, perhaps, of a dollar an acre. The same lands, in the hands of New York farmers, have been bought up, improved, made valuable for wheat-crops, and raised to a value ranging from fifteen to seventy-five dollars per acre. Thirty bushels of wheat have been raised to the acre, on tracts which have been thrown out as barren. A like history belongs to North and South Carolina, where similar ignorance of farming, and of agricultural implements, similar coarseness and clumsiness in the cultivation of the soil, have led to similar results—the disparaged value of the lands, their abandonment, and the neglect and dilapidation of towns and houses."

"You simply know nothing about the matter," said one of the party sharply in reply—"or rather, you know just enough of the truth to involve yourself in a monstrous error. I too have travelled in the regions of which you speak, and can venture to say something on the subject, which has its bright as well as gloomy aspects. It is not all gloomy, though it is seldom that the hurrying traveller sees or suspects any other. That you see few or no towns, and that these look desolate, are the natural effects of the life of a people purely agricultural. The southern people do not live in towns if they can avoid them. The culture and command of extensive tracts of land and forest give them a distaste to city life, where they feel restrained by a sense of confinement, and by manners of artificial character—a rigid conventionalism, imposing fetters upon the ease and freedom of bearing which belongs to the forest population. Besides, public opinion in the South is unfriendly to the growth of large cities, which many of their leading minds hold to be always of the most mischievous moral tendency—as, indeed, the *North* begins also to discover. Mr. Jefferson pronounced them the *sinks* and sewers of the commonwealth, to be tolerated only as among the dirty national necessities; and the *instincts* of the great body of the agricultural population have led them rightly in the same direction. They have learned to doubt the wholesomeness of the atmosphere of city life. Regarding towns as the mere agencies of the producer, they do not desire to see them absorbing a larger population than is necessary to the actual business which they have to perform.

"You, at the North, on the contrary, look to your flourishing towns, your fine houses, great masses of brick and stone, with thousands jostling in the thoroughfares, as proofs of prosperity and civilization; though, of these thousands, thousands live by beggary, by theft, chicanery, and the constantly active exercise of a thousand evil arts— the inevitable consequence of necessities which could not arise to the community were the unnecessary members driven to an honest, healthy, industrious occupation in neglected fields of agriculture. You judge mostly by externals, which rarely show the truth—the people in cities being chiefly learned in the art of concealing their true condition, and making the best *show* to their neighbors; while the Southern agriculturists know nothing of this art, exhibit themselves precisely as they are; use no white paint to cover old boards—no stucco to make common brick look like stone; and satisfied with the real comforts of their condition, never busy themselves in the endeavor to impose upon their neighbors with the splendors of a season which would only lead to bankruptcy.

"The dilapidated Virginia farmhouse, for example, will receive more guests, at the family table, in one month, than the marble palace in Broadway or Fifth Avenue will entertain in one year. There will be always plenty and a generous welcome, though the service be of delph and not of silver.

"That we have not towns and villages is the inevitable result of staple cultivation. *Every plantation is a village*, and where it is a large one, it will be found provided with all the essential elements of progress and performance, precisely as they are to be found in a village. Here, for example, is always a blacksmith and a carpenter, possibly a wheelwright, and frequently a shoemaker; while, in place of a hotel, for the reception of the stranger, is the mansion-house of the planter—wanting in paint, I grant—of ancient fashion, uncouth architecture—the floors, perhaps, not carpeted, and the furniture of that dark, massive mahogany which the city of New York would revolt at, but which carries to my mind an idea of the dignity of an ancient race, and that reverence for the antique which is, perhaps, too much wanting in every part of our country, except the *old states of the South.*

"This ancient mansion will be found usually with its doors thrown wide—in sign of welcome. Lest you should doubt, as you approach it, you behold the planter himself descending the old brick steps to welcome you. You will be confounded to see that his costume is neither fine nor fashionable—that he wears a great broad-brimmed white hat, exceedingly ample, which may have been manufactured for his grandfather. His coat may be of white flannel, and out at the elbows; and his pantaloons will be of domestic manufacture, homespun or nankin cotton. If you are wise enough to look below the externals, you will see, perhaps, that he has learned to despise them—at all events, you will perceive that he has sacrificed for these none of the essentials of the host, the gentleman, or the patriot. His hospitality is unimpaired by his antiquity—nay, it forms a part of it—and in the retention of the one, he has retained the other as a matter of necessity. As a gentleman, he is frank and easy of manner, unaffected in his bearing, and always solicitous of your comfort and satisfaction. He does not suffer you to perceive that he would have been better pleased that you should have admired his fine house, and passed on without tasking its hospitality. These are characteristics which must be taken as an offset to those respects which you select for censure. These, I have said, are the natural consequence of staple culture. It is the farming culture which exhibits and requires much nicety of detail. In the hands of the planter of a staple, lands are held in bodies too large to be handled minutely. It is the small plot only which you can put in bandbox condition. Lands in staple countries are of less value than labor—in farming countries, of greater value than labor. In proportion as the population becomes dense, they rise in value. But few southern planters desire a dense population. One secret of their hospitality is the extensiveness of their ranges. A wealthy planter, having from fifty to five hundred slaves, will have from a hundred to a thousand head of cattle. He kills so many beeves per annum, from four to forty, according to his *force.* That he can order a *mutton* to be slaughtered, even though but a single guest claims his hospitality, is due to his extensive tracts of field and forest. He seldom sends any of his sheep, cattle, corn, or other provisions to market. These are all retained for the wants of the homestead.

"It will not do for you, recognising the peculiar characteristics of his mode of life—their elegancies, comforts, and bounties—to cavil at deficiencies, which could only be remedied by his abandonment of habits which are grateful to the virtues, and which maintain in him the essentials of all high character—dignity and reverence."

"But there must be an end to all this hospitality. The southern planter is not prosperous. His fields are failing him—his staples are no longer valuable."

"Sufficient for the day is the evil thereof. Give us time. Let time answer your prophecy; for it is prediction—not argument, not fact—which you assert. There is no need that his hospitality should be at an end. It only needs that it should be more discriminating, and that the southern planter should steadily close his door against those who come to eat his bread only to denounce the manner in which it is made, and to sleep securely beneath his roof only to leave curses rather than prayers behind them. He must only be sure that his guest, when a stranger, is a gentleman and an honest man; and he will probably, with this modification of his hospitality, never be wanting in the necessary means for satisfying it.

"But, touching his prosperity, I hold it to be the greatest mistake in the world—examining things by just and intrinsic laws—to suppose that he is not prosperous. The southern planter does not derive from his labors so large a *money* income as he formerly did, when the culture of his great staple was comparatively in few hands. It is something different, certainly, to receive twenty cents instead of one hundred for long cottons, and six cents instead of thirty for short. But, in fact, the difference does not substantially affect his prosperity, *if he be not already in debt.* In the period of high prices for his staples, he could readily abandon farming culture to his less prosperous neighbors, leaving it to other states to supply his grain, his forage, his vegetables, his cattle, mules, and horses, for which he could well afford to pay from the excess of his income. But with his resources reduced, his policy necessarily changes, and is changing hourly, in recognition of new laws and new necessities. This change effected, his property will continue as before, though actually no great amount of money passes through his hands. His fields, that *were* failing him when he addressed them wholly to the culture of a single staple, are recovering, now that he alternates his crops, and economizes, prepares, and employs his manure. He ceases to buy grain and provisions. He raises his own hogs and cattle, and his ploughs are driven by mules and horses foaled in his own pastures. He discovers that he is not worse off now, in raising the commodities themselves, for the purchase of which he simply raised the cash before; and he further discovers that, under the present system, he learns to economize land and labor,

to improve the quality of the land, and the excellence of the labor; land rises in value with the introduction of thorough tillage; and a cleanlier, more compact method of culture, increases the health of the climate as well as the prosperity of the planters. With thorough tillage he can feed his stock, and and thus lessen the extent of his ranges; and this results in a gradually increasing denseness of the settlements, which are all that is necessary to rendering the state as prosperous as the individual has been."

"What do you mean by this distinction?"

"It is one that politicians do not often make, and it constitutes the grand feature in which the southern states are deficient to a northern eye. It occasions some of the difficulties in your modes of reasoning. The wealth of the state must depend mostly upon its numbers. The wealth of the individual will depend chiefly upon himself. The people of a state may be all in the enjoyment of comfort and affluence, yet the state may be poor. This is the case with all the southern states, the government of which has a sparsely settled population on which to act. Where the population is thinly planted, the roads will be inferior, the public works infrequent and of mean appearance, and the cities (which depend wholly upon a contiguous back country for support) will stagnate in visible decline, wanting enterprise and energy. The roads, the public buildings, and the cities, by which the stranger judges of the prosperity of a people, will all depend upon the population of a state. If this be large—if the soil is well covered—the powers of taxation are necessarily enlarged, without, perhaps, growing burdensome to any; but the means of life will be correspondingly diminished in the hands of the greater number. Want and poverty will trouble thousands; a few will grow rich at the expense of the rest; with the greater number, the struggle will be incessant from morning to night, to supply the most limited wants of a painful existence. But in the southern states, where the public works are few, the public buildings humble, and the cities of difficult growth or of stagnating condition the great body of the people—nay, all the people, bond and free—live in the enjoyment of plenty always, and, in most cases, of a wondrous degree of comfort.

"To illustrate this more completely by parallels: Great Britain and France are, of course, immeasurably superior, not only to the southern states of the Union, but to *all* the states, North and South, in the wonders of art, the great thoroughfares, the noble buildings, and the gigantic cities. These are erroneously assumed to be the proofs of prosperity in a nation, when it is somewhat doubtful if they can be even regarded as just proofs of its civilization. But, in Great Britain and France, millions rise every morning, in doubt where they shall procure the daily bread which shall satisfy the hunger of nature through the next twelve hours. No such apprehension ever troubles the citizen of the rural districts of the South. Rich and poor, black and white, bond and free, are all superior to this torturing anxiety; and the beggar, who in the great cities of Europe and America is as frequent as their posts, is scarcely ever to be seen, even, in a southern city— and then he is chiefly from a northern city, whence he flies to a region, of the hospitality of which (in spite of its failing fortunes) some vague rumors have reached his ears. He flies from the proud and prosperous cities of the North seeking his bread at the hands of a people whom you profess to despise for their decline."

"With these convictions, why do you repine and complain?"

"I do neither. To do either is unmanly. That the southern people do complain,

more than is proper and needful, is surely a something to be regretted; since he who pauses to complain will probably never overtake his flying prosperity. But, that there should be gloom and despondency is but natural with a people who, without positively suffering in fortune or comfort, are yet compelled, by large transitions of fortune, to contrast their present with their past. It is not that we are ruined now, but that we remember how fortunate we were before. If we compare ourselves with other people, and not with ourselves, we shall probably congratulate ourselves rather than complain."

"With your views, you are then satisfied that your people should continue rural occupations exclusively, to the rejection of manufactures?"

"By no means. I am anxious, on the contrary, that our people should embark in every department of art and trade for which they themselves or our climate may be fitted, if only that we may be perfectly independent of our northern brethren. We have abundance of water power, all over the South; we have the operatives on the spot; and we raise all the raw materials necessary for manufactures. Our water power never congeals with frost; our operatives never work short, or strike for increased wages, for we always keep them well fed and well clothed; we pension their aged; we protect and provide for their young; and, instead of being sickly at the toils we impose—puny and perishing—they are always fat and frolicsome, and always on the increase; and cotton is every day passing into more general use, as clothing for the poorer races of mankind. But, in the introduction of manufactures, I do not propose that we should neglect or abandon any of our staples: I propose that we should only employ our surplus population and lands for the purpose. There are large tracts of territory, for example, in the Carolinas, which answer for neither cotton, tobacco, nor the smaller grains. In these very regions, there is water power in abundance; and where this is not the case, there is fuel in inexhaustible abundance, for the use of steam power. I propose to increase the wealth of the state by the application of these regions to their proper use."

"But if your whole country should become manufacturing, why not? The profits of manufactures are vastly greater than those of the cotton culture. I have seen some statistics of South Carolina, where it is estimated that seven hundred operatives will realize as large a result, in working up the cotton, as a whole district of twenty-five thousand people in making the raw material. They will work up seven thousand bales, triplicating its value, while the twenty-five thousand average but a single bale to each inhabitant."

"This is the sort of statistics which delude the world. It is perhaps true that a district of South Carolina having twenty-five thousand people will send but twenty-five thousand bags of cotton to market. It is also true, perhaps, that eight hundred operatives in a manufactory will, by their labor, increase three-fold the value of eight thousand bales,

making a total of market-values equal to the twenty-five thousand bales. But when the operatives have done this, they have done nothing more than feed and clothe themselves, while, in fact, the cotton-planter has sent nothing but his *surplus* crop into the market. Of the twenty-five thousand persons in agriculture, twelve thousand enjoy luxuries, as well as comforts, which are not common to the cities. They have more leisure; they enjoy more society; most of them ride on horseback, and the greater number of families keep carriage or buggy. Nothing is said of the variety of food which they command, or may command—the delights of their own homes, in their own grounds, their own gardens and firesides; and the ease, the independence and elasticity, which belong to him who lives in the air and sunshine; in exercises which are grateful; and retires from his toils at an early hour, to the enjoyments of his homestead and his sleep. But talking of sleep reminds me of supper. Captain, if my nose does not greatly err, we are in the latitude of the old North State. I have been smelling tar and turpentine for the last half hour."

PART IV

AMERICAN
THOUGHT IN
AN INDUSTRIAL
AGE

To the superficial observer, the acceleration in the rate of industrial growth in the last half of the nineteenth century was a clear fact that could easily be measured by the rise in productivity and the standard of living. So, too, the economic and political ascendancy of a new elite of business entrepreneurs, who almost single-handedly created vast industrial complexes, was symbolic of the times. Yet the development of an advanced industrial society brought in its wake less obvious but even more significant and disturbing changes. The phenomenal growth of cities, the rapid increase in immigration, the appearance of a modern working class, and the beginnings of industrial strife, all seemed to be undermining what men cherished most. Some Americans even questioned whether the nation's traditional and time-honored values could continue to exist in the radically new environment that was emerging. To put it another way, could the individualistic-democratic ethic of a simple agrarian society survive the advent of an urban, mechanized society where individual relationships were submerged by impersonal forces?

For the America of the late nineteenth and twentieth centuries was indeed very different, both in degree and kind, from the more simple and ordered society of an earlier era. This was so not merely because of the transition from a rural and agrarian society to an urban and industrial one. If such had been the case, perhaps men and institutions could have adapted themselves more easily to change, because their basic assumptions and presuppositions about life would have remained the same. The difficulty lay rather in the fact that the older patterns of thought no longer sufficed to meet new conditions. Increasingly, Americans found that they were unprepared to cope with the new social and economic order that was emerging. For generations they had believed in the ethic of individual responsibility, that success and achievement in this world were directly related to one's ambition, drive, and talents. In the new society, however, the older morality was not merely outmoded; it seemed simply irrelevant. Upon whom, for example, could one fix responsibility for the evils of urban slums, periodic depressions, unemployment, and the amorality of large impersonal corporations? How could one still retain faith in the idea of equality of opportunity when wealth was being concentrated into fewer and fewer hands? In brief, was it possible for America to hold to its uniqueness and serve as a model for all mankind if it was increasingly torn by the same social and economic tensions that had long wracked the European world?

But the challenges and dilemmas that America faced were not solely the results of technological and industrial changes. Equally confusing were the implications raised by the novel scientific thought that accompanied the new society and supported it. Slowly but surely science began to undermine the traditional presuppositions of the synthesis of Christianity and the philosophy of the Enlightenment, upon which American society rested. In biology, for example, the reaction to the publication in 1859 of Charles Darwin's *Origin of Species* was symbolic of the newer orientation. The doctrine of the evolution of species, for which Darwin had offered an imposing array of evidence, quickly outgrew its biological definition and inevitably began to erode the older theocentric basis of Western civilization. For evolution banished the absolute and immutable by subjecting life and institutions to the flux of constant change. It even challenged the biblical story of creation, and revealed man not as a product of beneficent purpose but as a product of a blind process of natural selection. It viewed man as a member of the animal kingdom and thus removed him from the physical universe, a place reserved for him in Christian cosmology. The inference drawn was that man and society were not proper objects for teleological examination, but rather could be considered more profitably from a purely naturalistic point of view. It is true that the scientific nauralists who asserted this radical viewpoint accepted the concept of natural law, and thus, outwardly at any rate, did not totally repudiate their intellectual ancestors. But the manner in which nineteenth-century science came to define natural law indicated the changes in the way men viewed themselves and their environment. The eighteenth century had looked upon Nature as orderly and rational, and the universe as an essentially harmonious machine, the masterpiece of a deity who had promulgated laws to govern its operation. The setting of human life was the fixed, geometrical order of Nature. In such a system time was of no consequence and processes operated in a cyclical fashion. The early nineteenth-century American Transcendentalists modified this mechanistic outlook by developing the concept of a transcendental Over-Soul and the idea that all men shared in a divine power and were capable of establishing rapport with it. Simultaneously, evangelical Protestantism reasserted itself, and religion and romanticism converged to play a dominant role in the social and intellectual history of the early national period.

The naturalists, on the other hand, developed a very different concept of nature and the universe. To them the universe was dynamic and changing, a place where beginnings were incomprehensible and ends irrelevant, for the natural law of organic evolution emphasized continuous flux and change. Even the intellect became a product of evolutionary forces, and was defined as the functioning of the brain and nervous system. The older philosophical distinction between mind and matter disappeared, and with it the Emersonian idea of the Over-Soul and the emphasis on natural rights and reason. Naturalists tended to reduce even morality and social phenomena to biological terms, and to insist upon the coercive power of natural law over men and society. Some extremists even posited a strict environmental determinism. Believing in the law of organic evolution, naturalists inevitably brought everything within their searching purview, including such hitherto sacred institutions as the church, family, and property. Even such varied disciplines as history, economics, psychology, sociology, anthropology, art, and literature were subjected to scrutiny.

One of the most significant by-products of evolutionary naturalism was the rise of a scientific spirit in American thought that permeated virtually every facet of society. No doubt the incorporation of man into the animal kingdom was a significant achievement. But in the long run the attack on a priori reasoning and the partial repudiation of the Christian-Enlightenment synthesis was to prove far more important. In developing what came to be known as the "science of man," the nineteenth century built a system of knowledge that rested squarely on the foundation of organic evolution. Repudiating the traditional theocentric world view in favor of a new methodological demigod, scientists sought a purely objective and rational explanation of human behavior and development. Regardless of the discipline involved, the emphasis was upon a search for the determinants of organic and cultural change.

Beginning with the imposing system of Herbert Spencer, which enjoyed its greatest popularity in America and which rested in the final analysis on the belief that, if the evolutionary process could proceed unhindered by artificial restraints, then inevitable upward progress would automatically follow, scientists began to explore the complexities of human society with a view toward explaining them in scientific terms. Implicit in their analysis was the belief that if one could understand the factors of human evolution that initiated change, one could either conform to them or else provide a positive goal and direction for their operation.

It might be supposed that Americans, because of their theistic inheritance, would have rejected outright the implications of naturalistic evolution. Such was not the case, however, largely because evolution appeared to buttress the optimistic doctrine of progress, a doctrine that had long been at the heart of the American democratic faith. After all, Darwin had traced the evolution of species from simple organisms to complex mammals. Therefore, might it not be possible to study man and society from the same frame of reference and thus discover the law of progress? Clearly, the formulation of such a law would make man the master of his own destiny, a not inconsiderable achievement, to say the least.

And so the search began. Among the first of the social sciences to adopt a naturalistic approach was anthropology. The pioneering work in this discipline was done by Lewis Henry Morgan, who published his important book *Ancient Society* in 1877. Adopting an evolutionary approach, Morgan attempted to outline a science of man and discover the factors of change by studying various cultures in their different stages of development. The appearance of a naturalistic approach in anthropology was immediately followed by similar developments in history and the other social sciences.

Within the ranks of the naturalists, however, there was no unanimity of opinion, and two opposing schools of thought soon appeared. The first, the conservative school, emphasized that progress was a function of evolutionary forces that eliminated the unfit and preserved the fit, thus leading to the appearance of newer and better organisms. Man's only choice, therefore, lay in submission to the iron law of evolution. Any attempt to intervene in human affairs, especially by resorting to governmental action, would have a deleterious rather than a favorable effect. In this camp were included such outstanding individuals as William Graham Sumner, Francis Amasa Walker, David A. Wells, E. A. Godkin, to cite only a few. The implications of this essentially conservative rationale were highly popular in an America that had embarked on a rapid exploitation of its material resources. Any individual, regardless of rank or background, could prove himself to be among the fit (usually defined in terms of wealth and income) by overcoming all obstacles and emerging the victor in the cutthroat competition of the jungle. Hence arose the ideology of the self-made man, which argued that society would benefit if individuals followed their own self-interest, since this would lead to a progressive betterment of the species.

However, a second group of naturalists, the reformers, denied the validity of such an approach. Like their conservative opponents, the reformers were evolutionists; but there was a fundamental distinction between the two groups. For the reformers insisted that man, possessing the ability to think, could direct the evolutionary process into socially desirable channels. Lester F. Ward, a leading reform evolutionist and the father of American sociology, asked in disbelief, "Is it true that man shall ultimately obtain dominion of the whole world except himself?" From the reform version of evolution flowed the liberal-progressive ethic of the early twentieth century, represented by such outstanding figures as Theodore Roosevelt and Woodrow Wilson in the political arena, and by John Dewey and Herbert Croly in philosophy. All of these men shared a common belief that it was possible for man to remold and transform nature and society by an intelligent application of the new knowledge being revealed by scientific naturalism.

The revolutionary philosophical implications of scientific naturalism did not, of course, go unchallenged. William Harris and the St. Louis school, advocates of a form of Hegelian idealism, continued to question naturalistic evolution. Among scientists, too, a bitter and acrimonious struggle ensued; and the outstanding scientist in the United States at that time, Louis Agassiz, led the attack on Darwinism on intellectual, metaphysical, and emotional grounds. Institutions of higher learning particularly felt the weight of the conflict, especially since the scientific and naturalistic outlook had not as yet replaced the older and still dominant scholastic modes of thought. By the 1880's however, resistance to evolutionary thought within the scientific communities had all but disappeared. The inauguration of scientist Charles W. Eliot as president of Harvard in 1869 had presaged the trend, and the younger generation of students and teachers who came to maturity after the Civil War no longer questioned the validity of evolution and naturalism.

Within organized religion, on the other hand, the situation was quite different. To many ministers and laymen reared in a tradition of Christian piety, evolution raised issues and problems that threatened the very foundations of their beliefs. Here the conflict could not be so easily resolved. While it is true that liberal Protestantism sought to accommodate itself to evolution, the more fundamentalist groups, nevertheless, staked out their opposition in no uncertain terms and even went so far as to charge the scientists with atheism and materialism. Did not evolution, its opponents argued, undercut the basis of Christian cosmology by repudiating the teleological interpretation of history? Was there even room for a deity in the evolutionary hypothesis?

But the conflict that developed between traditional religion and evolutionary science was more than simply a struggle between competing beliefs and modes of thought. In a sense it was a reflection of all the problems, uncertainties, and difficulties that Americans were experiencing. At a time when men were reexamining their social and intellectual values in the light of material changes in society, organized religion, too, had to bring its own tenets under scrutiny in order to rediscover their relevance in a new and different environment. For when *Origin of Species* first apeared, the United States was still a predominantly rural nation. The rise of industrial capitalism, mechanization, and urbanization, however, confused and baffled a people accustomed to a different way of life. These social and economic changes were reflected in the cultural and intellectual transformations of the time. Just as the formulation of the American faith had originally been stated in religious terms, so the transformation of the older America raised serious doubts concerning the validity of that faith. In its widest sense, therefore, the struggle over evolution and scientific naturalism ultimately revolved around the very concept of man and society. Historically, the United States was at least in part a product of the religious foundations of Western culture. How, therefore, could Americans accept the newer scientific orientation without surrendering their religious ideals? Even more, could these religious ideals continue to subsist if they came into conflict with the hard, cold facts of science? Finally, if there existed no higher law promulgated by an omnipresent and omnipotent deity, upon what basis could a common morality acceptable to all exist? Was Christian piety and morality simply a product of a past age, to be studied only from a historical and anthropological point of view? Did it have no relevance to the present? These were some of the issues that plagued thinkers in all fields and disciplines as they attempted to bring their cosmology into harmony with naturalistic patterns and yet not go so far as to repudiate the older theism.

As a result of social, economic, and intellectual changes, Americans in the latter part of the nineteenth century were forced to reconsider, as had many generations before them, their basic assumptions and presuppositions. And as the problems of an urban, industrial society multiplied and the unity of America fragmented, individuals everywhere sought to develop a new synthesis that would provide them with an acceptable rationale.

CHAPTER XV

EVOLUTION AND
THE RISE OF
NATURALISM

*T*he publication of Darwin's *Origin of Species* in 1859 was in many respects the culmination of a whole series of intellectual and scientific innovations that were to have a profound impact upon the American mind. When combined with the higher criticism in Biblical studies and the comparative study of religion, as well as with the advances in geology, physics, and astronomy, the idea of evolution became a methodological weapon that threatened to undermine the very foundations of traditional and cherished beliefs. No longer could it be absolutely certain that man had been created by God in His image. Indeed, the entire justification of Christianity by the idea of design seemed the vestigial belief of a bygone age.

Many proponents of evolution, however, were not content merely to attack older ideas and views. Instead they proceeded to erect their own intellectual and philosophical system, which was based upon a veneration for scientific fact as the only accurate approach to knowledge. Repudiating with a vengeance the older a priori method of arriving at truth, they insisted that only the scientific method, when focused on man, society, and the physical world, would lead to real knowledge and understanding. One of the earliest

products of evolution, consequently, was the emergence of a whole conglo-
meration of ideas that can loosely be termed "naturalism."

In the latter part of the nineteenth century, naturalistic modes of thought
seemed to predominate everywhere. Arguing that complex social phenomena
could be reduced to biological terms, and these, in turn, to simpler
physical and mechanical terms, the naturalists laid the basis for the
scientific study of man and society. Implicit in their approach was an inherent
optimism, for they assumed that a better life would inevitably result once the
accumulated myths, superstitions, and ignorance of past ages were replaced
by objective and dispassionate knowledge. But while they accepted the idea
of progress, the naturalists tended to rationalize their belief on new grounds.
Whereas ante-bellum thinkers had found the sources of progress in Christian
cosmology and the theory of individualism, the naturalists erected a scientific and, to a lesser extent, a deterministic foundation for continuous human
progress, and their synthesis became symbolic of the new intellectual and
ideological interests of their age.

All disciplines were to some degree influenced by the new scientific orientation. Anthropologists, for example, began to study the evolution of man
and society from their most primitive beginnings, in the hope of discovering
the law of progress and thus developing a true science of man. Historians also
felt the impact of scientific naturalism, and several complementary and competing schools of historical thought arose. Some historians, taking their cue
from biology, formulated the germ theory of institutional development which
traced the historical evolution of social institutions from their earliest origins
to their modern forms. Others dealt chiefly with the evolution of the social
and individual organism as influenced by environmental factors. Even
psychology, which had long remained within the province of philosophy and
religion, began to undergo a radical transformation. Prior to Darwin psychologists had generally commenced with an acceptance of consciousness, and
they had attempted to show how the mind functioned with phenomena included within the categories of knowledge and experience. To a large extent they
had dealt with the metaphysical and theological problems inherent in the idea
of free will, attempting to provide a place in the mind for the operation of this
concept. By the end of the nineteenth century, however, psychology began to
move away from its philosophical beginnings and toward the biological and
physical sciences. Psychological facts began to be explained in biological and
mechanical rather than in metaphysical and philosophical terms, and
behaviorism and instinctivism became dominant schools in the study of
mental phenomena.

Until the early part of the twentieth century, naturalists tended to be
optimistic, largely because they believed that once superstition and myth
were dethroned and replaced by the new demigod of science, the power that

flowed from knowledge could be put to desirable uses. Certainly, at the very least, the new forms of knowledge would enable man to learn what he should not do, and thus indirectly provide a basis for continued progress. As time passed, however, some of the less likable features of naturalism began to become evident. If man were simply to be studied from a thoroughgoing biological and mechanical framework, was there any room for consciousness or free will? If man was a creature of his society and a product of its folkways, mores, and institutions, was there any room for the traditional morality and the ethic of individual responsibility which had characterized American democratic thinking in past generations? Although of fundamental importance, such questions and paradoxes as these did not appreciably trouble the early naturalistic thinkers. Not until the cataclysmic events of the twentieth century were the philosophical assumptions of the naturalists brought under searching examination.

Oliver Wendell Holmes, Jr.

1841-1935

Born into a distinguished Boston family, Oliver Wendell Holmes, Jr. attended Harvard University but left in his senior year to serve as an officer in the Union Army. After the war he returned to Harvard, where he received a law degree in 1866. He then entered private practice and also began to teach law at Harvard. In 1882 he was named to the Supreme Judicial Court of Massachusetts and in 1899 became chief justice of that court. In 1902 he was elevated by Theodore Roosevelt to the United States Supreme Court, where he had a long and illustrious career until his retirement in 1932.

Like his contemporaries at the end of the nineteenth century, Holmes had imbibed Darwinian ideas and rejected ideas which claimed to represent a finished and therefore static reality. His approach to law was founded upon a naturalistic basis. In one of his most famous works, The Common Law (1881), he made the oft-quoted remark that "The life of the law has not been logic: it has been experience. The felt necessities of the time, the prevalent moral and political theories, intuitions of public policy, avowed or unconscious, even the prejudices which judges share with their fellow-men, have had a good deal more to do than the syllogism in determining the rules by which men should be governed. The law embodies the story of a nation's development through many centuries, and it cannot be dealt with as if it contained only the axioms and corollaries of a book of mathematics."

In the following selection, "The Path of the Law," Harvard Law Review, 10 (March 25, 1897), Holmes bluntly denied the possibility of avoiding judge-made-law, and he drew a sharp distinction between law and morality, thus demonstrating the influence of naturalistic evolution upon his legal approach.

When we study law we are not studying a mystery but a well-known profession. We are studying what we shall want in order to appear before judges, or to advise people in such a way as to keep them out of court. The reason why it is a profession, why people will pay lawyers to argue for them or to advise them, is that in societies like ours the command of the public force is intrusted to the judges in certain cases, and the whole power of the state will be put forth, if necessary, to carry out their judgments and decrees. People want to know under what circumstances and how far they will run the risk of coming against what is so much stronger than themselves, and hence it becomes a business to find out when this danger is to be feared. The object of our study, then, is prediction, the prediction of the incidence of the public force through the instrumentality of the courts. . . .

I wish, if I can, to lay down some first principles for the study of this body of dogma or systematized prediction which we call the law, for men who want to use it as the instrument of their business to enable them to prophesy in their turn, and, as bearing upon the study, I wish to point out an ideal which as yet our law has not attained.

The first thing for a business-like understanding of the matter is to understand its limits, and therefore I think it desirable at once to point out and dispel a confusion between morality and law, which sometimes rises to the height of conscious theory, and more often and indeed constantly is making trouble in detail without reaching the point of consciousness. You can see very plainly that a bad man has as much reason as a good one for wishing to avoid an encounter with the public force, and therefore you can see the practical importance of the distinction between morality and law. A man who cares nothing for an ethical rule which is believed and practised by his neighbors is likely nevertheless to care a good deal to avoid being made to pay money, and will want to keep out of jail if he can. . . .

The confusion with which I am dealing besets confessedly legal conceptions. Take the fundamental question, What constitutes the law? You will find some text writers telling you that it is something different from what is decided by the courts of Massachusetts or England, that it is a system of reason, that it is a deduction from principles of ethics or admitted axioms or what not, which may or may not coincide with the decisions. But if we take the view of our friend the bad man we shall find

that he does not care two straws for the axioms or deductions, but that he does want to know what the Massachusetts or English courts are likely to do in fact. I am much of this mind. The prophecies of what the courts will do in fact, and nothing more pretentious, are what I mean by the law. . . .

This is not the time to work out a theory in detail, or to answer many obvious doubts and questions which are suggested by these general views. I know of none which are not easy to answer, but what I am trying to do now is only by a series of hints to throw some light on the narrow path of legal doctrine, and upon two pitfalls which, as it seems to me, lie perilously near to it. Of the first of these I have said enough. I hope that my illustrations have shown the danger, both to speculation and to practice, of confounding morality with law, and the trap which legal language lays for us on that side of our way. For my own part, I often doubt whether it would not be a gain if every word of moral significance could be banished from the law altogether, and other words adopted which should convey legal ideas uncolored by anything outside the law. We should lose the fossil records of a good deal of history and the majesty got from ethical associations, but by ridding themselves of an unnecessary confusion we should gain very much in the clearness of our thought.

So much for the limits of the law. The next thing which I wish to consider is what are the forces which determine its content and its growth. You may assume, with Hobbes and Bentham and Austin, that all law emanates from the sovereign, even when the first human beings to enunciate it are the judges, or you may think that law is the voice of the Zeitgeist, or what you like. It is all one to my present purpose. Even if every decision required the sanction of an emperor with despotic power and a whimsical turn of mind, we should be interested none the less, still with a view to prediction, in discovering some order, some rational explanation, and some principle of growth for the rules which he laid down. In every system there are such explanations and principles to be found. It is with regard to them that a second fallacy comes in, which I think it important to expose.

The fallacy to which I refer is the notion that the only force at work in the development of the law is logic. In the broadest sense, indeed, that notion would be true. The postulate on which we think about the universe is that there is a fixed quantitative relation between every phenomenon and its antecedents and consequents. If there is such a thing as a phenomenon without these fixed quantitative relations, it is a miracle. It is outside the law of cause and effect, and as such transcends our power of thought, or at least is something to or from which we cannot reason. The condition of our thinking about the universe is that it is capable of being thought about rationally, or, in other words, that every part of it is effect and cause in the same sense in which those parts are with which we are most familiar. So in the broadest sense it is true that the law is a logical development, like everything else. The danger of which I speak is not the admission that the principles governing other phenomena also govern the law, but the notion that a given system, ours, for instance, can be worked out like mathematics from some general axioms of conduct. This is the natural error of the schools, but it is not confined to them. I once heard a very eminent judge say that he never let a decision go until he was absolutely sure that it was right. So judicial dissent often is blamed, as if it meant simply that one side or the other were not doing their sums right, and, if they would take more trouble, agreement inevitably would come.

This mode of thinking is entirely natural. The training of lawyers is a training in logic. The processes of analogy, discrimination, and deduction are those in which they are most at home. The language of judicial decision is mainly the language of logic. And the logical method and form flatter that longing for certainty and for repose which is in every human mind. But certainty generally is illusion, and repose is not the destiny of man. Behind the logical form lies a judgment as to the relative worth and importance of competing legislative grounds, often an inarticulate and unconscious judgment, it is true, and yet the very root and nerve of the whole proceeding. You can give any conclusion a logical form. You always can imply a condition in a contract. But why do you imply it? It is because of some belief as to the practice of the community or of a class, or because of some opinion as to policy, or, in short, because of some attitude of yours upon a matter not capable of exact quantitative measurement, and therefore not capable of founding exact logical conclusions. Such matters really are battle grounds where the means do not exist for determinations that shall be good for all time, and where the decision can do no more than embody the preference of a given body in a given time and place. We do not realize how large a part of our law is open to reconsideration upon a slight change in the habit of the public mind. No concrete proposition is self evident, no matter how ready we may be to accept it, not even Mr. Herbert Spencer's "Every man has a right to do what he wills, provided he interferes not with a like right on the part of his neighbors." . . .

I think that the judges themselves have failed adequately to recognize their duty of weighing considerations of social advantage. The duty is inevitable, and the result of the often proclaimed judicial aversion to deal with such considerations is simply to leave the very ground and foundation of judgments inarticulate, and often unconscious, as I have said. When socialism first began to be talked about, the comfortable classes of the community were a good deal frightened. I suspect that this fear has influenced judicial action both here and in England, yet it is certain that it is not a conscious factor in the decisions to which I refer. I think that something similar has led people who no longer hope to control the legislatures to look to the courts as expounders of the Constitutions, and that in some courts new principles have been discovered outside the bodies of those instruments, which may be generalized into acceptance of the economic doctrines which prevailed about fifty years ago, and a wholesale prohibition of what a tribunal of lawyers does not think about right. I cannot but believe that if the training of lawyers led them habitually to consider more definitely and explicitly the social advantage on which the rule they lay down must be justified, they sometimes would hesitate where now they are confident, and see that really they were taking sides upon debatable and often burning questions.

So much for the fallacy of logical form. Now let us consider the present condition of the law as a subject for study, and the ideal towards which it tends. We still are far from the point of view which I desire to see reached. No one has reached it or can reach it as yet. We are only at the beginning of a philosophical reaction, and of a reconsideration of the worth of doctrines which for the most part still are taken for granted without any deliberate, conscious, and systematic questioning of their grounds. The development of our law has gone on for nearly a thousand years, like the development of a plant, each generation taking the inevitable next step, mind, like matter, simply obeying a law of spontaneous growth. It is perfectly natural and right that it

should have been so. Imitation is a necessity of human nature, as has been illustrated by a remarkable French writer, M. Tarde, in an admirable book, *Les Lois de l'Imitation.* Most of the things we do, we do for no better reason than that our fathers have done them or that our neighbors do them, and the same is true of a larger part than we suspect of what we think. The reason is a good one, because our short life gives us no time for a better, but it is not the best. It does not follow, because we all are compelled to take on faith at second hand most of the rules on which we base our action and our thought, that each of us may not try to set some corner of his world in the order of reason, or that all of us collectively should not aspire to carry reason as far as it will go throughout the whole domain. In regard to the law, it is true, no doubt, that an evolutionist will hesitate to affirm universal validity for his social ideals, or for the principles which he thinks should be embodied in legislation. He is content if he can prove them best for here and now. He may be ready to admit that he knows nothing about an absolute best in the cosmos, and even that he knows next to nothing about a permanent best for men. Still it is true that a body of law is more rational and more civilized when every rule it contains is referred articulately and definitely to an end which it subserves, and when the grounds for desiring that end are stated or are ready to be stated in words.

At present, in very many cases, if we want to know why a rule of law has taken its particular shape, and more or less if we want to know why it exists at all, we go to tradition. We follow it into the Year Books, and perhaps beyond them to the customs of the Salian Franks, and somewhere in the past, in the German forests, in the needs of Norman kings, in the assumptions of a dominant class, in the absence of generalized ideas, we find out the practical motive for what now best is justified by the mere fact of its acceptance and that men are accustomed to it. The rational study of law is still to a large extent the study of history. History must be a part of the study, because without it we cannot know the precise scope of rules which it is our business to know. It is a part of the rational study, because it is the first step toward an enlightened scepticism, that is, toward a deliberate reconsideration of the worth of those rules. When you get the dragon out of his cave on to the plain and in the daylight, you can count his teeth and claws, and see just what is his strength. But to get him out is only the first step. The next is either to kill him, or to tame him and make him a useful animal. For the rational study of the law the black-letter man may be the man of the present, but the man of the future is the man of statistics and the master of economics. It is revolting to have no better reason for a rule of law than that so it was laid down in the time of Henry IV. It is still more revolting if the grounds upon which it was laid down have vanished long since, and the rule simply persists from blind imitation of the past. . . .

I trust that no one will understand me to be speaking with disrespect of the law, because I criticise it so freely. I venerate the law, and especially our system of law, as one of the vastest products of the human mind. No one knows better than I do the countless number of great intellects that have spent themselves in making some addition or improvement, the greatest of which is trifling when compared with the mighty whole. It has the final title to respect that it exists, that it is not a Hegelian dream, but a part of the lives of men. But one may criticise even what one reveres. Law is the business to which my life is devoted, and I should show less than devotion if I did not do what in me lies to improve it, and, when I perceive what seems to me the ideal of its future,

if I hesitated to point it out and to press toward it with all my heart.

Perhaps I have said enough to show the part which the study of history necessarily plays in the intelligent study of the law as it is to-day. In the teaching of this school and at Cambridge it is in no danger of being undervalued. Mr. Bigelow here and Mr. Ames and Mr. Thayer there have made important contributions which will not be forgotten, and in England the recent history of early English law by Sir Frederick Pollock and Mr. Maitland has lent the subject an almost deceptive charm. We must beware of the pitfall of antiquarianism, and must remember that for our purposes our only interest in the past is for the light it throws upon the present. I look forward to a time when the part played by history in the explanation of dogma shall be very small, and instead of ingenious research we shall spend our energy on a study of the ends sought to be attained and the reasons for desiring them. As a step toward that ideal it seems to me that every lawyer ought to seek an understanding of economics. The present divorce between the schools of political economy and law seems to me an evidence of how much progress in philosophical study still remains to be made. In the present state of political economy, indeed, we come again upon history on a larger scale, but there we are called on to consider and weigh the ends of legislation, the means of attaining them, and the cost. We learn that for everything we have we give up something else, and we are taught to set the advantage we gain against the other advantage we lose, and to know what we are doing when we elect.

There is another study which sometimes is undervalued by the practical minded, for which I wish to say a good word, although I think a good deal of pretty poor stuff goes under that name. I mean the study of what is called jurisprudence. Jurisprudence, as I look at it, is simply law in its most generalized part. Every effort to reduce a case to a rule is an effort of jurisprudence, although the name as used in English is confined to the broadest rules and most fundamental conceptions. One mark of a great lawyer is that he sees the application of the broadest rules. There is a story of a Vermont justice of the peace before whom a suit was brought by one farmer against another for breaking a churn. The justice took time to consider, and then said that he had looked through the statutes and could find nothing about churns, and gave judgment for the defendant. The same state of mind is shown in all our common digests and text-books. Applications of rudimentary rules of contract or tort are tucked away under the head of Railroads or Telegraphs or go to swell treatises on historical subdivisions, such as Shipping or Equity, or are gathered under an arbitrary title which is thought likely to appeal to the practical mind, such as Mercantile Law. If a man goes into law it pays to be a master of it, and to be a master of it means to look straight through all the dramatic incidents and to discern the true basis for prophecy. Therefore, it is well to have an accurate notion of what you mean by law, by a right, by a duty, by malice, intent, and negligence, by ownership, by possession, and so forth. I have in mind cases in which the highest courts seem to me to have floundered because they had no clear ideas on some of these themes. I have illustrated their importance already. If a further illustration is wished, it may be found by reading the Appendix to Sir James Stephen's *Criminal Law* on the subject of possession, and then turning to Pollock and Wright's enlightened book. Sir James Stephen is not the only writer whose attempts to analyze legal ideas have been confused by striving for a useless quintessence of all systems, instead of an accurate anatomy of one. The trouble with Austin was that he did not know enough English law. But still it is a practical advantage to master Austin, and his predecessors, Hobbes and Bentham, and his worthy successors, Holland and Pollock. Sir Frederick Pollock's recent little book is touched with the felicity which marks all his works, and is wholly free from the perverting influence of Roman models.

The advice of the elders to young men is very apt to be as unreal as a list of the hundred best books. At least in my day I had my share of such counsels, and high among the unrealities I place the recommendations to study the Roman law. I assume that such advice means more than collecting a few Latin maxims with which to ornament the discourse— the purpose for which Lord Coke recommended Bracton. If that is all that is wanted, the title *De Regulis Juris Antiqui* can be read in an hour. I assume that, if it is well to study the Roman law, it is well to study it as a working system. That means mastering a set of technicalities more difficult and less understood than our own, and studying another course of history by which even more than our own the Roman law must be explained. If any one doubts me, let him read Keller's *Der Römische Civil Process und die Actionen*, a treatise on the praetor's edict, Muirhead's most interesting *Historical Introduction to the Private Law of Rome*, and, to give him the best chance, Sohm's admirable *Institutes*. No. The way to gain a liberal view of your subject is not to read something else, but to get to the bottom of the subject itself. The means of doing that are, in the first place, to follow the existing body of dogma into its highest generalizations by the help of jurisprudence; next, to discover from history how it has come to be what it is; and, finally, so far as you can, to consider the ends which the several rules seek to accomplish, the reasons why those ends are desired, what is given up to gain them, and whether they are worth the price.

We have too little theory in the law rather than too much, especially on this final branch of study. When I was speaking of history, I mentioned larceny as an example to show how the law suffered from not having embodied in a clear form a rule which will accomplish its manifest purpose. In that case the trouble was due to the survival of forms coming from a time when a more limited purpose was entertained. Let me give now an example to show the practical importance, for the decision of actual cases, of understanding the reasons of the law, by taking an example from rules which, so far as I know, never have been explained or theorized about in any adequate way. I refer to statutes of limitation and the law of prescription. The end of such rules is obvious, but what is the justification for depriving a man of his rights, a pure evil as far as it goes, in consequence of the lapse of time? Sometimes the loss of evidence is referred to, but that is a secondary matter. Sometimes the desirability of peace, but why is peace more desirable after twenty years than before? It is increasingly likely to come without the aid of legislation. Sometimes it is said that, if a man neglects to enforce his rights, he cannot complain if, after a while, the law follows his example. Now if this is all that can be said about it, you probably will decide a case I am going to put, for the plaintiff; if you take the view which I shall suggest, you possibly will decide it for the defendant. A man is sued for trespass upon land, and justifies under a right of way. He proves that he has used the way openly and adversely for twenty years, but it turns out that the plaintiff had

granted a license to a person whom he reasonably supposed to be the defendant's agent, although not so in fact, and therefore had assumed that the use of the way was permissive, in which case no right would be gained. Has the defendant gained a right or not? If his gaining it stands on the fault and neglect of the landowner in the ordinary sense, as seems commonly to be supposed, there has been no such neglect, and the right of way has not been acquired. But if I were the defendant's counsel, I should suggest that the foundation of the acquisition of rights by lapse of time is to be looked for in the position of the person who gains them, not in that of the loser. Sir Henry Maine has made it fashionable to connect the archaic notion of property with prescription. But the connection is further back than the first recorded history. It is in the nature of man's mind. A thing which you have enjoyed and used as your own for a long time, whether property or an opinion, takes root in your being and cannot be torn away without your resenting the act and trying to defend yourself, however you came by it. The law can ask no better justification than the deepest instincts of man. It is only by way of reply to the suggestion that you are disappointing the former owner, that you refer to his neglect having allowed the gradual dissociation between himself and what he claims, and the gradual association of it with another. If he knows that another is doing acts which on their face show that he is on the way toward establishing such an association, I should argue that in justice to that other he was bound at his peril to find out whether the other was acting under his permission, to see that he was warned, and if necessary, stopped.

John Dewey
1859-1952

John Dewey was born in Burlington, Vermont, and attended the University of Vermont, where he received his bachelor's degree in 1879. Five years later he was awarded his doctorate from the Johns Hopkins University and then taught successively at the Universities of Michigan, Minnesota, and Chicago. In 1904 he went to Columbia University, where he remained for the rest of his career.

Dewey attempted in his writings to erect a system of logic and ethics on an evolutionary base. In doing so, he hoped to free philosophy from a sterile metaphysics and transform it into a form of social engineering. His treatment of ethical problems represented a radical departure from tradition, since he made ethical principles ancillary to the dominant social, economic, and political problems of the day. Dewey always defined an idea as essentially a plan of action, not a mirror of reality. Rejecting dualisms of any sort, he insisted that the nature and end of thought was to fulfill the purpose for which it had been brought into being, namely, to provide for the survival, growth, and better adjustment of the organism. He further maintained that the intelligent use of the scientific method was the best means of solving problems.

Probably more than any other person, Dewey was the philosopher of twentieth-century liberalism and progressivism. Hostile to all absolutisms, his instrumentalist approach had a varying social and economic content, but whatever its content it always retained a measure of social consciousness and a willingness to change as circumstances changed.

In the following selection, The Influence of Darwin on Philosophy (*New York: Holt, Rinehart and Winston, Inc., 1910*), *Dewey described the influences of evolutionary ideas on philosophy and methods of thinking.*

I

*T*hat the publication of the "Origin of Species" marked an epoch in the development of the natural sciences is well known to the layman. That the combination of the very words origin and species embodied an intellectual revolt and introduced a new intellectual temper is easily overlooked by the expert. The conceptions that had reigned in the philosophy of nature and knowledge for two thousand years, the conceptions that had become the familiar furniture of the mind, rested on the assumption of the superiority of the fixed and final; they rested upon treating change and origin as signs of defect and unreality. In laying hands upon the sacred ark of absolute permanency, in treating the forms that had been regarded as types of fixity and perfection as originating and passing away, the "Origin of Species" introduced a mode of thinking that in the end was bound to transform the logic of knowledge, and hence the treatment of morals, politics, and religion.

No wonder, then, that the publication of Darwin's book, a half century ago, precipitated a crisis. The true nature of the controversy is easily concealed from us, however, by the theological clamor that attended it. The vivid and popular features of the anti-Darwinian row tended to leave the impression that the issue was between science on one side and theology on the other. Such was not the case—the issue lay primarily within science itself, as Darwin himself early recognized. The theological outcry he discounted from the start, hardly noticing it save as it bore upon the "feelings of his female relatives." But for two decades before final publication he contemplated the possibility of being put down by his scientific peers as a fool or as crazy; and he set, as the measure of his success, the degree in which he should affect three men of science: Lyell in geology, Hooker in botany, and Huxley in zoology.

Religious considerations lent fervor to the controversy, but they did not provoke it. Intellectually, religious emotions are not creative but conservative. They attach themselves readily to the current view of the world and consecrate it. They steep and dye intellectual fabrics in the seething vat of emotions; they do not form their warp and woof. There is not, I think, an instance of any large idea about the world being independently generated by religion. Although the ideas that rose up like

armed men against Darwinism owed their intensity to religious associations, their origin and meaning are to be sought in science and philosophy, not in religion.

II

*F*ew words in our language foreshorten intellectual history as much as does the word species. The Greeks, in initiating the intellectual life of Europe, were impressed by characteristic traits of the life of plants and animals; so impressed indeed that they made these traits the key to defining nature and to explaining mind and society. And truly, life is so wonderful that a seemingly successful reading of its mystery might well lead men to believe that the key to the secrets of heaven and earth was in their hands. The Greek rendering of this mystery, the Greek formulation of the aim and standard of knowledge, was in the course of time embodied in the word species, and it controlled philosophy for two thousand years. To understand the intellectual face-about expressed in the phrase "Origin of Species," we must, then, understand the long dominant idea against which it is a protest.

Consider how men were impressed by the facts of life. Their eyes fell upon certain things slight in bulk, and frail in structure. To every appearance, these perceived things were inert and passive. Suddenly, under certain circumstances, these things—henceforth known as seeds or eggs or germs—begin to change, to change rapidly in size, form, and qualities. Rapid and extensive changes occur, however, in many things—as when wood is touched by fire. But the changes in the living thing are orderly; they are cumulative; they tend constantly in one direction; they do not, like the other changes, destroy or consume, or pass fruitless into wandering flux; they realize and fulfil. Each successive stage, no matter how unlike its predecessor, preserves its net effect and also prepares the way for a fuller activity on the part of its successor. In living beings, changes do not happen as they seem to happen elsewhere, any which way; the earlier changes are regulated in view of later results. This progressive organization does not cease till there is achieved a true final term, a τελὸς, a completed, perfected end. This final form exercises in turn a plenitude of functions, not the least noteworthy of which is production of germs like those from which it took its own origin, germs capable of the same cycle of self-fulfilling activity.

But the whole miraculous tale is not yet told. The same drama is enacted to the same destiny in countless myriads of individuals so sundered in time, so served in space, that they have no opportunity for mutual consultation and no means of interaction. As an old writer quaintly said, "things of the same kind go through the same formalities"—celebrate, as it were, the same ceremonial rites.

This formal activity which operates throughout a series of changes and holds them to a single course; which subordinates their aimless flux to its own perfect manifestation; which, leaping the boundaries of space and time, keeps individuals distant in space and remote in time to a uniform type of structure and function: this principle seemed to give insight into the very nature of reality itself. To it Aristotle gave the name, εἶδος. This term the scholastics translated as *species*.

The force of this term was deepened by its application to everything in the universe that observes order in flux and manifests constancy through change. From the casual drift of daily weather, through the uneven recurrence of seasons and unequal return of seed time and harvest, up to the majestic sweep of the heavens—the image of eternity in time—and from this to the unchanging pure and contemplative intelligence beyond nature lies one unbroken fulfilment of ends. Nature as a whole is a progressive realization of purpose strictly comparable to the realization of purpose in any single plant or animal.

The conception of εἶδος, species, a fixed form and final cause, was the central principle of knowledge as well as of nature. Upon it rested the logic of science. Change as change is mere flux and lapse; it insults intelligence. Genuinely to know is to grasp a permanent end that realizes itself through changes, holding them thereby within the metes and bounds of fixed truth. Completely to know is to relate all special forms to their one single end and good: pure contemplative intelligence. Since, however, the scene of nature which directly confronts us is in change, nature as directly and practically experienced does not satisfy the conditions of knowledge. Human experience is in flux, and hence the instrumentalities of sense-perception and of inference based upon observation are condemned in advance. Science is compelled to aim at realities lying behind and beyond the processes of nature, and to carry on its search for these realities by means of rational forms transcending ordinary modes of perception and inference.

There are, indeed, but two alternative courses. We must either find the appropriate objects and organs of knowledge in the mutual interactions of changing things; or else, to escape the infection of change, we *must* seek them in some transcendent and supernal region. The human mind, deliberately as it were, exhausted the logic of the changeless, the final, and the transcendent, before it essayed adventure on the pathless wastes of generation and transformation. We dispose all too easily of the efforts of the schoolmen to interpret nature and mind in terms of real essences, hidden forms, and occult faculties, forgetful of the seriousness and dignity of the ideas that lay behind. We dispose of them by laughing at the famous gentleman who accounted for the fact that opium put people to sleep on the ground it had a dormitive faculty. But the doctrine, held in our own day, that knowledge of the plant that yields the poppy consists in referring the peculiarities of an individual to a type, to a universal form, a doctrine so firmly established that any other method of knowing was conceived to be unphilosophical and unscientific, is a survival of precisely the same logic. This identity of conception in the scholastic and anti-Darwinian theory may well suggest greater sympathy for what has become unfamiliar as well as greater humility regarding the further unfamiliarities that history has in store.

Darwin was not, of course, the first to question the classic philosophy of nature and of knowledge. The beginnings of the revolution are in the physical science of the sixteenth and seventeenth centuries. When Galileo said: "It is my opinion that the earth is very noble and admirable by reason of so many and so different alterations and generations which are incessantly made therein," he expressed the changed temper that was coming over the world; the transfer of interest from the permanent to the changing. When Descartes said: "The nature of physical things is much more easily conceived when they are beheld coming gradually into existence, than when they are only considered as produced at once in a finished and perfect state," the modern world became self-conscious of the logic that was henceforth to control it, the logic of which Darwin's "Origin of Species" is the latest scientific achievement. Without the methods of Copernicus, Kepler, Galileo, and their successors in astronomy, physics, and chemistry, Darwin would have been helpless in the organic

sciences. But prior to Darwin the impact of the new scientific method upon life, mind, and politics, had been arrested, because between these ideal or moral interests and the inorganic world intervened the kingdom of plants and animals. The gates of the garden of life were barred to the new ideas; and only through this garden was there access to mind and politics. The influence of Darwin upon philosophy resides in his having conquered the phenomena of life for the principle of transition, and thereby freed the new logic for application to mind and morals and life. When he said of species what Galileo had said of the earth, *e pur se muove*, he emancipated, once for all, genetic and experimental ideas as an organon of asking questions and looking for explanations.

III

*T*he exact bearings upon philosophy of the new logical outlook are, of course, as yet, uncertain and inchoate. We live in the twilight of intellectual transition. One must add the rashness of the prophet to the stubbornness of the partizan to venture a systematic exposition of the influence upon philosophy of the Darwinian method. At best, we can but inquire as to its general bearing— the effect upon mental temper and complexion, upon that body of half-conscious, half-instinctive intellectual aversions and preferences which determine, after all, our more deliberate intellectual enterprises. In this vague inquiry there happens to exist as a kind of touchstone a problem of long historic currency that has also been much discussed in Darwinian literature. I refer to the old problem of design *versus* chance, mind *versus* matter, as the causal explanation, first or final, of things.

As we have already seen, the classic notion of species carried with it the idea of purpose. In all living forms, a specific type is present directing the earlier stages of growth to the realization of its own perfection. Since this purposive regulative principle is not visible to the senses, it follows that it must be an ideal or rational force. Since, however, the perfect form is gradually approximated through the sensible changes, it also follows that in and through a sensible realm a rational ideal force is working out its own ultimate manifestation. These inferences were extended to nature: (*a*) She does nothing in vain; but all for an ulterior purpose. (*b*) Within natural sensible events there is therefore contained a spiritual causal force, which as spiritual escapes perception, but is apprehended by an enlightened reason. (*c*) The manifestation of this principle brings about a subordination of matter and sense to its own realization, and this ultimate fulfilment is the goal of nature and of man. The design argument thus operated in two directions. Purposefulness accounted for the intelligibility of nature and the possibility of science, while the absolute or cosmic character of this purposefulness gave sanction and worth to the moral and religious endeavors of man. Science was underpinned and morals authorized by one and the same principle, and their mutual agreement was eternally guaranteed.

This philosophy remained, in spite of sceptical and polemic outbursts, the official and the regnant philosophy of Europe for over two thousand years. The expulsion of fixed first and final causes from astronomy, physics, and chemistry had indeed given the doctrine something of a shock. But, on the other hand, increased acquaintance with the details of plant and animal life operated as a counterbalance and perhaps even strengthened the argument from design. The marvelous adaptations of organ-isms to their environment, of organs to the organism, of unlike parts of a complex organ—like the eye—to the organ itself; the foreshadowing by lower forms of the higher; the preparation in earlier stages of growth for organs that only later had their functioning—these things were increasingly recognized with the progress of botany, zoology, paleontology and embryology. Together, they added such prestige to the design argument that by the late eighteenth century it was, as approved by the sciences of organic life, the central point of theistic and idealistic philosophy.

The Darwinian principle of natural selection cut straight under this philosophy. If all organic adaptations are due simply to constant variation and the elimination of those variations which are harmful in the struggle for existence that is brought about by excessive reproduction, there is no call for a prior intelligent causal force to plan and preordain them. Hostile critics charged Darwin with materialism and with making chance the cause of the universe.

Some naturalists, like Asa Gray, favored the Darwinian principle and attempted to reconcile it with design. Gray held to what may be called design on the installment plan. If we conceive the "stream of variations" to be itself intended, we may suppose that each successive variation was designed from the first to be selected. In that case, variation, struggle, and selection simply define the mechanism of "secondary causes" through which the "first cause" acts; and the doctrine of design is none the worse off because we know more of its *modus operandi*.

Darwin could not accept this mediating proposal. He admits or rather he asserts that it is "impossible to conceive this immense and wonderful universe including man with his capacity of looking far backwards and far into futurity as the result of blind chance or necessity." But nevertheless he holds that since variations are in useless as well as useful directions, and since the latter are sifted out simply by the stress of the conditions of struggle for existence, the design argument as applied to living beings is unjustifiable; and its lack of support there deprives it of scientific value as applied to nature in general. If the variations of the pigeon, which under artificial selection give the pouter pigeon, are not preordained for the sake of the breeder, by what logic do we argue that variations resulting in natural species are pre-designed?

IV

So much for some of the more obvious facts of the discussion of design *versus* chance, as causal principles of nature and of life as a whole. We brought up this discussion, you recall, as a crucial instance. What does our touchstone indicate as to the bearing of Darwinian ideas upon philosophy? In the first place, the new logic outlaws, flanks, dismisses—what you will—one type of problems and substitutes for it another type. Philosophy forswears inquiry after absolute origins and absolute finalities in order to explore specific values and the specific conditions that generate them.

Darwin concluded that the impossibility of assigning the world to chance as a whole and to design in its parts indicated the insolubility of the question. Two radically different reasons, however, may be given as to why a problem is insoluble. One reason is that the problem is too high for intelligence; the other is that the question in its very asking makes assumptions that render the question meaningless. The latter alternative is unerringly pointed to in the celebrated case of design *versus* chance. Once admit that the sole verifiable or fruitful object of knowledge is the par-

ticular set of changes that generate the object of study together with the consequences that then flow from it, and no intelligible question can be asked about what, by assumption, lies outside. To assert—as is often asserted—that specific values of particular truth, social bonds and forms of beauty, if they can be shown to be generated by concretely knowable conditions, are meaningless and in vain; to assert that they are justified only when they and their particular causes and effects have all at once been gathered up into some inclusive first cause and some exhaustive final goal, is intellectual atavism. Such argumentation is reversion to the logic that explained the extinction of fire by water through the formal essence of aqueousness and the quenching of thirst by water through the final cause of aqueousness. Whether used in the case of the special event or that of life as a whole, such logic only abstracts some aspect of the existing course of events in order to reduplicate it as a petrified eternal principle by which to explain the very changes of which it is the formalization.

When Henry Sidgwick casually remarked in a letter that as he grew older his interest in what or who made the world was altered into interest in what kind of a world it is anyway, his voicing of a common experience of our own day illustrates also the nature of that intellectual transformation effected by the Darwinian logic. Interest shifts from the wholesale essence back of special changes to the question of how special changes serve and defeat concrete purposes; shifts from an intelligence that shaped things once for all to the particular intelligences which things are even now shaping; shifts from an ultimate goal of good to the direct increments of justice and happiness that intelligent administration of existent conditions may beget and that present carelessness or stupidity will destroy or forego.

In the second place, the classic type of logic inevitably set philosophy upon proving that life *must* have certain qualities and values—no matter how experience presents the matter—because of some remote cause and eventual goal. The duty of wholesale justification inevitably accompanies all thinking that makes the meaning of special occurrences depend upon something that once and for all lies behind them. The habit of derogating from present meanings and uses prevents our looking the facts of experience in the face; it prevents serious acknowledgment of the evils they present and serious concern with the goods they promise but do not as yet fulfil. It turns thought to the business of finding a wholesale transcendent remedy for the one and guarantee for the other. One is reminded of the way many moralists and theologians greeted Herbert Spencer's recognition of an unknowable energy from which welled up the phenomenal physical processes without and the conscious operations within. Merely because Spencer labeled his unknowable energy "God," this faded piece of metaphysical goods was greeted as an important and grateful concession to the reality of the spiritual realm. Were it not for the deep hold of the habit of seeking justification for ideal values in the remote and transcendent, surely this reference of them to an unknowable absolute would be despised in comparison with the demonstrations of experience that knowable energies are daily generating about us precious values.

The displacing of this wholesale type of philosophy will doubtless not arrive by sheer logical disproof, but rather by growing recognition of its futility. Were it a thousand times true that opium produces sleep because of its dormitive energy, yet the inducing of sleep in the tired, and the recovery to waking life of the poisoned, would not be thereby one least step forwarded. And were it a thousand times dialectically demonstrated that life as a whole is regulated by a transcendent principle to a final inclusive goal, none the less truth and error, health and disease, good and evil, hope and fear in the concrete, would remain just what and where they now are. To improve our education, to ameliorate our manners, to advance our politics, we must have recourse to specific conditions of generation.

Finally, the new logic introduces responsibility into the intellectual life. To idealize and rationalize the universe at large is after all a confession of inability to master the courses of things that specifically concern us. As long as mankind suffered from this impotency, it naturally shifted a burden of responsibility that it could not carry over to the more competent shoulders of the transcendent cause. But if insight into specific conditions of value and into specific consequences of ideas is possible, philosophy must in time become a method of locating and interpreting the more serious of the conflicts that occur in life, and a method of projecting ways for dealing with them: a method of moral and political diagnosis and prognosis.

The claim to formulate *a priori* the legislative constitution of the universe is by nature a claim that may lead to elaborate dialectic developments. But it is also one that removes these very conclusions from subjection to experimental test, for, by definition, these results make no differences in the detailed course of events. But a philosophy that humbles its pretensions to the work of projecting hypotheses for the education and conduct of mind, individual and social, is thereby subjected to test by the way in which the ideas it propounds work out in practice. In having modesty forced upon it, philosophy also acquires responsibility.

Doubtless I seem to have violated the implied promise of my earlier remarks and to have turned both prophet and partizan. But in anticipating the direction of the transformations in philosophy to be wrought by the Darwinian genetic and experimental logic, I do not profess to speak for any save those who yield themselves consciously or unconsciously to this logic. No one can fairly deny that at present there are two effects of the Darwinian mode of thinking. On the one hand, there are making many sincere and vital efforts to revise our traditional philosophic conceptions in accordance with its demands. On the other hand, there is as definitely a recrudescence of absolutistic philosophies; an assertion of a type of philosophic knowing distinct from that of the sciences, one which opens to us another kind of reality from that to which the sciences give access; an appeal through experience to something that essentially goes beyond experience. This reaction affects popular creeds and religious movements as well as technical philosophies. The very conquest of the biological sciences by the new ideas has led many to proclaim an explicit and rigid separation of philosophy from science.

Old ideas give way slowly; for they are more than abstract logical forms and categories. They are habits, predispositions, deeply engrained attitudes of aversion and preference. Moreover, the conviction persists—though history shows it to be a hallucination—that all the questions that the human mind has asked are questions that can be answered in terms of the alternatives that the questions themselves present. But in fact intellectual progress usually occurs through sheer abandonment of questions together with both of the alternatives they assume—an abandonment that results from their decreasing vitality and a change of urgent interest. We do not solve them: we get over them. Old questions are solved by disappearing, evaporating, while new questions corresponding to the changed attitude of endeavor and preference take their place. Doubtless the greatest dissolvent in contemporary thought of old questions, the greatest precipitant of new methods, new intentions, new problems, is the one effected by the scientific revolution that found its climax in the "Origin of Species."

John B. Watson
1878-1958

One of the founders of behavioristic psychology, John B. Watson was born in Greenville, South Carolina. Receiving an M.A. from Furman University in 1900 and a Ph.D. from the University of Chicago in 1903, he taught at the latter institution from 1904 to 1908. From 1908 to 1920 he was professor of experimental and comparative psychology at the Johns Hopkins University. In addition to publishing many works, he also edited several major psychological journals and in 1915 served as president of the American Psychological Association. In 1920, following a divorce and quick remarriage, the trustees of Hopkins demanded his resignation. After this affair Watson entered the advertising business, never again to hold an academic position.

Earlier in his career Watson had become interested in working with animals. When his studies suggested that animals learn by trial and error, he decided to investigate the human learning process in these terms. Watson's basic problem was to determine whether instincts existed, whether there were basic unlearned reactions, and above all, if man should be considered in psychology as animals. Relegating heredity to a position of minor importance, he concluded that all learning was conditioned, and consequently demanded that the concept of consciousness be eliminated from psychology. Thus the stimulus-response relationship became the basic ingredient of behavioristic psychology, and the distinction between the human and animal world all but disappeared. In one sense behaviorism was one of the most radical products of naturalism, since it led to a determination whereby the influence of environment alone would account for human behavior and lead to a predictive and accurate science of psychology.

The following selection is from Watson's famous article, "Psychology as the Behaviorist Views It," Psychological Review, 20 (March, 1913), which aroused great controversy when it first appeared.

*P*sychology as the behaviorist views it is a purely objective experimental branch of natural science. Its theoretical goal is the prediction and control of behavior. Introspection forms no essential part of its methods, nor is the scientific value of its data dependent upon the readiness with which they lend themselves to interpretation in terms of consciousness. The behaviorist, in his efforts to get a unitary scheme of animal response, recognizes no dividing line between man and brute. The behavior of man, with all of its refinement and complexity, forms only a part of the behaviorist's total scheme of investigation.

It has been maintained by its followers generally that psychology is a study of the science of the phenomena of consciousness. It has taken as its problem, on the one hand, the analysis of complex mental states (or processes) into simple elementary constituents, and on the other the construction of complex states when the elementary constituents are given. The world of physical objects (stimuli, including here anything which may excite activity in a receptor), which forms the total phenomena of the natural scientist, is looked upon merely as means to an end. That end is the production of mental states that may be "inspected" or "observed." The psychological object of observation in the case of an emotion, for example, is the mental state itself. The problem in emotion is the determination of the number and kind of elementary constituents present, their loci, intensity, order of appearance, etc. It is agreed that introspection is the method *par excellence* by means of which mental states may be manipulated for purposes of psychology. On this assumption, behavior data (including under this term everything which goes under the name of comparative psychology) have no value *per se*. They possess significance only in so far as they may throw light upon conscious states. Such data must have at least an analogical or indirect reference to belong to the realm of psychology.

Indeed, at times, one finds psychologists who are sceptical of even this analogical reference. Such scepticism is often shown by the question which is put to the student of behavior, "what is the bearing of animal work upon human psychology?" I used to have to study over this question. Indeed it always embarrassed me somewhat. I was interested in my own work and felt that it was important, and yet I could not trace any close connection between it and psychology as my questioner understood psychology. I hope that such a confession will clear the atmosphere to such an extent that we will no longer have to work under false pretences. We must frankly admit that the facts so important to us which we have been able to glean from extended work upon the senses of animals by the behavior method have contributed only in a fragmentary way to the general theory of human sense organ processes, nor have they suggested new points of experimental attack. The enormous number of experiments which we have carried out upon learning have likewise contributed little to human psychology. It seems reasonably clear that some kind of compromise must be effected: either psychology must change its viewpoint so as to take in facts of behavior, whether or not they have bearings upon the problems of "consciousness"; or else behavior must stand alone as a wholly separate and independent science. Should human psychologists fail to look with favor upon our overtures and refuse to modify their position, the behaviorists will be driven to using human beings as subjects and to employ methods of investigation which are exactly comparable to those now employed in the animal work.

Any other hypothesis than that which admits the independent value of behavior material, regardless of any bearing such material may have upon consciousness, will inevitably force us to the absurd position of attempting to *construct* the conscious content of the animal whose behavior we have been studying. On this view, after having determined our animal's ability to learn, the simplicity or complexity of its methods of learning, the effect of past habit upon present response, the range of stimuli to which it ordinarily responds, the widened range to which it can respond under experimental conditions,—in more general terms, its various problems and its various ways of solving them,—we should still feel that the task is unfinished and that the results are worthless, until we can interpret them by analogy in the light of consciousness. Although we have solved our problem we feel uneasy and unrestful because of our definition of psychology: we feel forced to say something about the possible mental processes of our animal. We say that, having no eyes, its stream of consciousness cannot contain brightness and color sensations as we know them,—having no taste buds this stream can contain no sensations of sweet, sour, salt and bitter. But on the other hand, since it does respond to thermal, tactual and organic stimuli, its conscious content must be made up largely of these sensations; and we usually add, to protect ourselves against the reproach of being anthropomorphic, "if it has any consciousness." Surely this doctrine which calls for an analogical interpretation of all behavior data may be shown to be false: the position that the standing of an observation upon behavior is determined by its fruitfulness in yielding results which are interpretable only in the narrow realm of (really human) consciousness.

This emphasis upon analogy in psychology has led the behaviorist somewhat afield. Not being willing to throw off the yoke of consciousness he feels impelled to make a place in the scheme of behavior where the rise of consciousness can be determined. This point has been a shifting one. A few years ago certain animals were supposed to possess "associative memory," while certain others were supposed to lack it. One meets this search for the origin of consciousness under a good many disguises. Some of our texts state that consciousness arises at the moment when reflex and instinctive activities fail properly to conserve the organism. A perfectly adjusted organism would be lacking in consciousness. On the other hand whenever we find the presence of diffuse activity which results in habit formation, we are justified in assuming consciousness. I must confess that these arguments had weight with me when I began the study of behavior. I fear that a good many of us are still viewing behavior problems with something like this in mind. More than one student in behavior has attempted to frame criteria of the psychic—to devise a set of objective, structural and functional criteria which, when applied in the particular instance, will enable us to decide whether such and such responses are positively conscious, merely indicative of consciousness, or whether they are purely "physiological." Such problems as these can no longer satisfy behavior men. It would be better to give up the province altogether and admit frankly that the study of the behavior of animals has no justification, than to admit that our search is of such a "will o' the wisp" character. One can assume either the presence or the absence of consciousness anywhere in the phylogenetic scale without affecting the problems of behavior by one jot or one title; and without influencing in any way the mode of experimental attack upon them. On the other hand, I cannot for one moment assume that the paramecium responds to light; that the rat learns a problem more quickly by working at the task five times a day than once a day, or that the human child exhibits plateaux in his learning curves. These are questions which vitally concern behavior and which must be decided by direct observation under experimental conditions.

This attempt to reason by analogy from human conscious processes to the conscious processes in animals, and *vice versa*: to make consciousness, as the human being knows it, the center of reference of all behavior, forces us into a situation similar to that which existed in biology in Darwin's time. The whole Darwinian movement was judged by the bearing it had upon the origin and development of the human race. Expeditions were undertaken to collect material which would establish the position that the rise of the human race was a perfectly natural phenomenon and not an act of special creation. Variations were carefully sought along with the evidence for the heaping up effect and the weeding out effect of selection; for in these and the other Darwinian mechanisms were to be found factors sufficiently complex to account for the origin and race differentiation of man. The wealth of material collected at this time was considered valuable largely in so far as it tended to develop the concept of evolution in man. It is strange that this situation should have remained the dominant one in biology for so many years. The moment zoölogy undertook the experimental study of evolution and descent, the situation immediately changed. Man ceased to be the center of reference. I doubt if any experimental biologist today, unless actually engaged in the problem of race differentiation in man, tries to interpret his findings in terms of human evolution, or ever refers to it in his thinking. He gathers his data from the study of many species of plants and animals and tries to work out the laws of inheritance in the particular type upon which he is conducting experiments. Naturally, he follows the progress of the work upon race differentiation in man and in the descent of man, but he looks upon these as special topics, equal in importance with his own yet ones in which his interests will never be vitally engaged. It is not fair to say that all of his work is directed toward human evolution or that it must be interpreted in terms of human evolution. He does not have to dismiss certain of his facts on the inheritance of coat color in mice because, forsooth, they have little bearing upon the differentiation of the *genus homo* into separate races, or upon the descent of the *genus homo* from some more primitive stock. . . .

The time seems to have come when psychology must discard all reference to consciousness; when it need no longer delude itself into thinking that it is making mental states the object of observation. We have become so enmeshed in speculative questions concerning the elements of mind, the nature of conscious content (for example, imageless thought, attitudes, and Bewusseinslage, etc.) that I, as an experimental student, feel that something is wrong with our premises and the types of problems which develop from them. There is no longer any guarantee that we all mean the same thing when we use the terms now current in psychology. Take the case of sensation. A sensation is defined in terms of its attributes. One psychologist will state with readiness that the attributes of a visual sensation are *quality, extension, duration,* and *intensity.* Another will add *clearness.* Still another that of *order.* I doubt if any one psychologist can draw up a set of statements describing what he means by sensation which will be agreed to by three other psychologists of different training. Turn for a moment to the question of the number of isolable sensations. Is there an extremely large number of color sensations—or only four, red, green, yellow and blue? Again, yellow, while psychologically simple, can be obtained by superimposing red and green spectral rays upon the same diffusing surface! If, on the other hand, we say that every just noticeable difference in the spectrum is a simple sensation, and that every just noticeable increase in the white value of a given color gives simple sensations, we are forced to admit that the number is so large and the conditions for obtaining them so complex that the concept of sensation is unusable, either for the purpose of analysis or that of synthesis. Titchener, who has fought the most valiant fight in this country for a psychology based upon introspection, feels that these differences of opinion as to the number of sensations and their attributes; as to whether there are relations (in the sense of elements) and on the many others which seem to be fundamental in every attempt at analysis, are perfectly natural in the present undeveloped state of psychology. While it is admitted that every growing science is full of unanswered questions, surely only those who are wedded to the system as we now have it, who have fought and suffered for it, can confidently believe that there will ever be any greater uniformity than there is now in the answers we have to such questions. I firmly believe that two hundred years from now, unless the introspective method is discarded, psychology will still be divided on the question as to whether auditory sensations have the quality of "extension," whether intensity is an attribute which can be applied to color, whether there is a difference in "texture" between image and sensation and upon many hundreds of others of like character. . . . I believe we can write a psychology, define it as Pillsbury, and never go back upon our definition: never

use the terms consciousness, mental states, mind, content, introspectively verifiable, imagery, and the like. I believe that we can do it in a few years without running into the absurd terminology of Beer, Bethe, Von Uexküll, Nuel, and that of the so-called objective schools generally. It can be done in terms of stimulus and response, in terms of habit formation, habit integrations and the like. Furthermore, I believe that it is really worth while to make this attempt now.

The psychology which I should attempt to build up would take as a starting point, first, the observable fact that organisms, man and animal alike, do adjust themselves to their environment by means of hereditary and habit equipments. These adjustments may be very adequate or they may be so inadequate that the organism barely maintains its existence; secondly, that certain stimuli lead the organisms to make the responses. In a system of psychology completely worked out, given the response the stimuli can be predicted; given the stimuli the response can be predicted. Such a set of statements is crass and raw in the extreme, as all such generalizations must be. Yet they are hardly more raw and less realizable than the ones which appear in the psychology texts of the day. I possibly might illustrate my point better by choosing an everyday problem which anyone is likely to meet in the course of his work. Some time ago I was called upon to make a study of certain species of birds. Until I went to Tortugas I had never seen these birds alive. When I reached there I found the animals doing certain things: some of the acts seemed to work peculiarly well in such an environment, while others seemed to be unsuited to their type of life. I first studied the responses of the group as a whole and later those of individuals. In order to understand more thoroughly the relation between what was habit and what was hereditary in these responses, I took the young birds and reared them. In this way I was able to study the order of appearance of hereditary adjustments and their complexity, and later the beginnings of habit formation. My efforts in determining the stimuli which called forth such adjustments were crude indeed. Consequently my attempts to control behavior and to produce responses at will did not meet with much success. Their food and water, sex and other social relations, light and temperature conditions were all beyond control in a field study. I did find it possible to control their reactions in a measure by using the nest and egg (or young) as stimuli. . . . In the main, my desire in all such work is to gain an accurate knowledge of adjustments and the stimuli calling them forth. My final reason for this is to learn general and particular methods by which I may control behavior. My goal is not "the description and explanation of states of consciousness as such," nor that of obtaining such proficiency in mental gymnastics that I can immediately lay hold of a state of consciousness and say, "this, as a whole, consists of gray sensation number 350, of such and such extent, occurring in conjunction with the sensation of cold of a certain intensity; one of pressure of a certain intensity and extent," and so on *ad infinitum*. If psychology would follow the plan I suggest, the educator, the physician, the jurist and the business man could utilize our data in a practical way, as soon as we are able, experimentally, to obtain them. Those who have occasion to apply psychological principles practically would find no need to complain as they do at the present time. Ask any physician or jurist today whether scientific psychology plays a practical part in his daily routine and you will hear him deny that the psychology of the laboratories finds a place in his scheme of

work. I think the criticism is extremely just. One of the earliest conditions which made me dissatisfied with psychology was the feeling that there was no realm of application for the principles which were being worked out in content terms.

What gives me hope that the behaviorist's position is a defensible one is the fact that those branches of psychology which have already partially withdrawn from the parent, experimental psychology, and which are consequently less dependent upon introspection are today in a most flourishing condition. Experimental pedagogy, the psychology of drugs, the psychology of advertising, legal psychology, the psychology of tests, and psychopathology are all vigorous growths. These are sometimes wrongly called "practical" or "applied" psychology. Surely there was never a worse misnomer. In the future there may grow up vocational bureaus which really apply psychology. At present these fields are truly scientific and are in search of broad generalizations which will lead to the control of human behavior. . . .

The man and the animal should be placed as nearly as possible under the same experimental conditions. Instead of feeding or punishing the human subject, we should ask him to respond by setting a second apparatus until standard and control offered no basis for a differential response. Do I lay myself open to the charge here that I am using introspection? My reply is not at all; that while I might very well feed my human subject for a right choice and punish him for a wrong one and thus produce the response if the subject could give it, there is no need of going to extremes even on the platform I suggest. . . .

Will there be left over in psychology a world of pure psychics, to use Yerkes' term? I confess I do not know. The plans which I most favor for psychology lead practically to the ignoring of consciousness in the sense that that term is used by psychologists today. I have virtually denied that this realm of psychics is open to experimental investigation. I don't wish to go further into the problem at present because it leads inevitably over into metaphysics. If you will grant the behaviorist the right to use consciousness in the same way that other natural scientists employ it—that is, without making consciousness a special object of observation—you have granted all that my thesis requires.

In concluding, I suppose I must confess to a deep bias on these questions. I have devoted nearly twelve years to experimentation on animals. It is natural that such a one should drift into a theoretical position which is in harmony with his experimental work. Possibly I have put up a straw man and have been fighting that. There may be no absolute lack of harmony between the position outlined here and that of functional psychology. I am inclined to think, however, that the two positions cannot be easily harmonized. Certainly the position I advocate is weak enough at present and can be attacked from many standpoints. Yet when all this is admitted I still feel that the considerations which I have urged should have a wide influence upon the type of psychology which is to be developed in the future. What we need to do is to start work upon psychology, making *behavior*, not *consciousness*, the objective point of our attack. Certainly there are enough problems in the control of behavior to keep us all working many lifetimes without ever allowing us time to think of consciousness *an sich*. Once launched in the undertaking, we will find ourselves in a short time as far divorced from an introspective psychology as the psychology of the present time is divorced from faculty psychology.

CHAPTER XVI

PRAGMATISM: AN AMERICAN PHILOSOPHICAL ADVENTURE

*O*ne of the early fruits of the evolutionary hypothesis was the formulation and development of the philosophy of pragmatism, perhaps the most important and original American contribution to the Western philosophical tradition. Pragmatism itself represented a sharp break from the Spencerian deterministic version of evolution. Spencer and his followers had postulated the idea that men could do nothing but conform to the inevitable laws of human development. The pragmatists, on the other hand, elaborated a philosophical method or system based upon possibility and contingency, maintaining that it was possible for accidents or novelties to arise that were not predictable from a knowledge of their antecedents. The adherents of pragmatism wanted to avoid the extremes of a thoroughgoing naturalistic determinism as well as of a Hegelian idealism, both of which had been based on a monistic system.

Tracing its antecedents to Chauncey Wright, who published one of the earliest critiques of Spencer from a naturalistic point of view, pragmatism received its initial, overt formulation by Charles S. Peirce. Hoping to end the philosophers' prolonged disputes that could not be settled by recourse to facts, Peirce proposed what was for that time a radical notion. He held that the meaning of any conception is to be found in the practical consequences that might result from it—the sum of these consequences would thus constitute the meaning of the conception. In other words, Peirce was stressing the fact that statements or ideas had to be experimentally verifiable. He also attacked all mechanistic and deterministic hypotheses and viewed scientific laws as statements of probabilities rather than absolutes.

The implications of Peirce's originality went largely unheeded until William James and John Dewey took up where he had left off. James presented pragmatism as a method that would settle the sterile metaphysical debates that had long plagued philosophy. For, if in examining and comparing given metaphysical propositions one finds no difference in their empirical consequences, "then the alternatives mean practically the same thing, and all dispute is idle." To James the goal of pragmatism was to understand ideas by testing their theoretical as well as their practical consequences.

It remained for John Dewey, however, to elaborate the pragmatic view most fully. Dewey became the outstanding philosophical exponent of democracy, naturalism, and the scientific method. He defined an idea as the plan of action relative to the solution to a given problem. It therefore followed that the experimental approach to meaning led to an experimental or contingent theory of truth. Thus truth was defined as the hypothesis that best controls the conditions and consequences of experience at any given moment. Extended further, Dewey's instrumentalism (the name given to his approach) stood for a maximum use of free, critical, and experimental intelligence in the preservation of democracy. Rejecting the "spectator theory of knowledge," he came to regard knowledge as a part of nature, its end being not simply passive adjustment, but the manipulation of the environment to achieve desirable ends.

Pragmatism, in other words, was a frankly experimental philosophy that rejected what it regarded as the sterility of previous philosophy in favor of an approach that judged the validity of ideas by their results. Democratic in its orientation, humane and optimistic in its outlook, adventurous in spirit, it provided industrial America with a rationale that seemed to give its citizens a means of developing a new morality capable of dealing with problems that the older theistic-individualistic-agrarian ethic had not been able to do. Pragmatism put philosophy at the service of society and dissolved the "steel chain of ideas" implicit in Spencerian naturalistic determinism. From a social point of view pragmatism indicated that the central issue no longer revolved around individual salvation. Rather, the paramount problem was the reconstruction of society in such a manner as to provide the individual with a collective environment that dealt with the social and economic problems of an industrialized society while maintaining a framework conducive to his self-development. In pragmatism the progressive movement of the early twentieth century was to find much of its philosophical inspiration as it set about to transform American society through a democratic collectivism.

William James
1842-1910

*Born in New York City, William James
was one of the first products of the scientific
education that was emerging in America
after the Civil War. Trained at Harvard's
Lawrence Scientific School, he received an
M.D. from Harvard in 1869 and was
associated with that institution for most of
his life, first as an instructor in physiology
and later as a professor of philosophy. A
passionate believer in free will, he opposed all
deterministic philosophical systems that did
not admit the factor of chance. He also
dealt on many occasions with the competing
claims of science and religion, attempting
to erect a mode of thought that left room for
both. James was a bitter foe of Spencer,
largely because he was seeking an
experimental approach (as Spencer was not)
that emphasized active human effort
operating in an unfinished world.*

*Not only was James an outstanding
philosopher, but he also laid the foundation
for the emergence of psychology as an
independent discipline in America and
established one of the first psychological
laboratories in this country. His psychological
system was based upon the active role of the
self, and he was critical of those individuals
who looked upon the mind as a quiet
cognitive organ. Thus, the direction of
James's psychological and philosophical
inquiries led him to pragmatism as the basis
of his scientific and philosophic systems.
His emphasis on pragmatism, it must be
pointed out, was not in any way related to a
consideration merely of worldly success, for
his use of the term "practical" did not
exclude any human motive, whether aesthetic,
moral, or intellectual.*

*The following selection is from a famous
series of public lectures delivered in 1906
at the Lowell Institute in Boston and in 1907
at Columbia University, reprinted under the
title* Pragmatism (*New York, 1907*).

The pragmatic method is primarily a method of settling metaphysical disputes that otherwise might be interminable. Is the world one or many?—fated or free?—material or spiritual?—here are notions either of which may or may not hold good of the world; and disputes over such notions are un-ending. The pragmatic method in such cases is to try to interpret each notion by tracing its respective practical consequences. What difference would it practically make to any one if this notion rather than that notion were true? If no practical difference whatever can be traced, then the alternatives mean practically the same thing, and all dispute is idle. Whenever a dispute is serious, we ought to be able to show some practical difference that must follow from one side or the other's being right.

A glance at the history of the idea will show you still better what pragmatism means. The term is derived from the same Greek word πράγμα, meaning action, from which our words 'practice' and 'practical' come. It was first introduced into philosophy by Mr. Charles Peirce in 1878. In an article entitled "How to Make Our Ideas Clear," in the *Popular Science Monthly* for January of that year Mr. Peirce, after pointing out that our beliefs are really rules for action, said that, to develop a thought's meaning, we need only determine what conduct it is fitted to produce: that conduct is for us its sole significance. And the tangible fact at the root of all our thought-distinctions, however subtle, is that there is no one of them so fine as to consist in anything but a possible difference of practice. To attain perfect clearness in our thoughts of an object, then, we need only consider what conceivable effects of a practical kind the object may involve—what sensations we are to expect from it, and what reactions we must prepare. Our conception of these effects, whether immediate or remote, is then for us the whole of our conception of the object, so far as that conception has positive significance at all. . . .

There is absolutely nothing new in the pragmatic method. Socrates was an adept at it. Aristotle used it methodically. Locke, Berkeley, and Hume made momentous contributions to truth by its means. Shadworth Hodgson keeps insisting that realities are only what they are "known as." But these fore-runners of pragmatism used it in fragments: they were preluders only. Not until in our time has it generalized itself, become conscious of a universal mission, pretended to a conquering destiny. I believe in that destiny, and I hope I may end by inspiring you with my belief.

Pragmatism represents a perfectly familiar attitude in philosophy, the empiricist attitude, but it represents it, as it seems to me, both in a more radical and in a less objectionable form than it has ever yet assumed. A pragmatist turns his back resolutely and once for all upon a lot of inveterate habits dear to professional philosophers. He turns away from abstraction and insufficiency, from verbal solutions, from bad *a priori* reasons, from fixed principles, closed systems, and pretended absolutes and origins. He turns towards concreteness and adequacy, towards facts, towards action and towards power. That means the empiricist temper regnant and the rationalist temper sincerely given up. It means the open air and possibilities of nature, as against dogma, artificiality, and the pretence of finality in truth.

At the same time it does not stand for any special results. It is a method only. But the general triumph of that method would mean an enormous change in what I called in my last lecture the "temperament" of philosophy. Teachers of the ultra-rationalistic type would be frozen out, much as the courtier type is frozen out in republics, as the ultramontans type of priest is frozen out in protestant lands. Science and metaphysics would come much nearer together, would in fact work absolutely hand in hand.

Metaphysics has usually followed a very primitive kind of quest. You know how men have always hankered after unlawful magic, and you know what a great part in magic *words* have always played. If you have his name, or the formula of incantation that binds him, you can control the spirit, genie, afrite, or whatever the power may be. Solomon knew the names of all the spirits, and having their names, he held them subject to his will. So the universe has always appeared to the natural mind as a kind of enigma, of which the key must be sought in the shape of some illuminating or power-bringing word or name. That word names the universe's *principle*, and to possess it is after a fashion to possess the universe itself. "God," "Matter," "Reason," "the Absolute," "Energy," are so many solving names. You can rest when you have them. You are at the end of your metaphysical quest.

But if you follow the pragmatic method, you cannot look on any such word as closing your quest. You must bring out of each word its practical cash-value, set it at work within the stream of your experience. It appears less as a solution, then, than as a program for more work, and more particularly as an indication of the ways in which existing realities may be *changed*. *Theories thus become instruments, not answers to enigmas, in which we can rest.* We don't lie back upon them, we move forward, and, on occasion, make nature over again by their aid. Pragmatism unstiffens all our theories, limbers them up and sets each one at work. Being nothing essentially new, it harmonizes with many ancient philosophic tendencies. It agrees with nominalism for instance, in always appealing to particulars; with utilitarianism in emphasizing practical aspects; with positivism in its disdain for verbal solutions, useless questions and metaphysical abstractions.

All these, you see, are *anti-intellectualist* tendencies. Against rationalism as a pretension and a method pragmatism is fully armed and militant. But, at the outset, at least, it stands for no particular results. It has no dogmas, and no doctrines save its method. As the young Italian pragmatist Papini has well said, it lies in the midst of our theories, like a corridor in a hotel. Innumerable chambers open out of it. In one you may find a man writing an atheistic volume; in the next some one on his knees praying for faith and strength; in a third a chemist investi-

gating a body's properties. In a fourth a system of idealistic metaphysics is being excogitated; in a fifth the impossibility of metaphysics is being shown. But they all own the corridor, and all must pass through it if they want a practicable way of getting into or out of their respective rooms. . . .

You see by this what I meant when I called pragmatism a mediator and reconciler and said, borrowing the word from Papini, that she "unstiffens" our theories. She has in fact no prejudices whatever, no obstructive dogmas, no rigid canons of what shall count as proof. She is completely genial. She will entertain any hypothesis, she will consider any evidence. It follows that in the religious field she is at a great advantage both over positivistic empiricism, with its anti-theological bias, and over religious rationalism, with its exclusive interest in the remote, the noble, the simple, and the abstract in the way of conception.

In short, she widens the field of search for God. Rationalism sticks to logic and the empyrean. Empiricism sticks to the external senses. Pragmatism is willing to take anything, to follow either logic or the senses and to count the humblest and most personal experiences. She will count mystical experiences if they have practical consequences. She will take a God who lives in the very dirt of private fact—if that should seem a likely place to find him.

Her only test of probable truth is what works best in the way of leading us, what fits every part of life best and combines with the collectivity of experience's demands, nothing being omitted. If theological ideas should do this, if the notion of God, in particular, should prove to do it, how could pragmatism possibly deny God's existence? She could see no meaning in treating as 'not true' a notion that was pragmatically so successful. What other kind of truth could there be, for her, than all this agreement with concrete reality?

The following selection is from a lecture given by Dewey at Columbia University in 1908, and published in pamphlet form under the title Ethics (*New York, 1908*). [*For Dewey's career see pp. 265.*]

John Dewey
1859-1952

Since the Renaissance, moral philosophy has repeatedly reverted to the Greek ideal of natural excellence realized in social life, under the fostering care of intelligence in action. The return, however, has taken place under the influence of democratic polity, commercial expansion and scientific reorganization. It has been a liberation even more than a reversion. This combined return and emancipation, having transformed our practice of life in the last four centuries, will not be content till it has written itself clear in our theory of that practice. Whether the consequent revolution in moral philosophy be termed pragmatism or be given the happier title of the applied and experimental habit of mind is of little account. What is of moment is that intelligence has descended from its lonely isolation at the remote edge of things, whence it operated as unmoved mover and ultimate good, in order to take its seat in the moving affairs of men. Theory may therefore become responsible to the practices which have generated it; the good be connected with nature, but with nature naturally, not metaphysically, conceived, and social life be cherished in behalf of its own immediate possibilities, not on the ground of its remote connexions with a cosmic reason and an absolute end. . . .

The growth of industry and commerce is at once cause and effect of the growth in science. Democritus and other ancients conceived the mechanical theory of the universe. The notion was not only blank and repellent, because it ignored the rich social material which Plato and Aristotle had organized into their rival idealistic views; but it was scientifically sterile, a piece of dialectics. Contempt for machines as the accoutrements of despised mechanics kept the mechanical conception aloof from these specific and controllable experiences which alone could fructify it. This conception, then, like the idealistic, was translated into a speculative cosmology and thrown like a vast net around the universe at large, as if to keep it from coming to pieces. It is from respect for the lever, the pulley and the screw that modern experimental and mathematical mechanics derives itself. Motion, traced through the workings of a machine, was followed out into natural events and studied just as motion, not as a poor yet necessary device for realizing final causes. So studied, it was found to be available for new machines and new applications, which in creating new ends also promoted new wants, and thereby stimulated new activities, new discoveries and new inventions. The recognition that natural energy can be systematically applied, through experimental observation, to the satisfaction and multiplication of concrete wants is doubtless the greatest single discovery ever imported into the life of man—save perhaps the discovery of language. Science, borrowing from industry, repaid the debt with interest, and has made the control of natural forces for the aims of life so inevitable, that for the first time man is relieved from overhanging fear, with its wolflike scramble to possess and accumulate, and is freed to consider the more gracious question of securing to all an ample and liberal life. The industrial life had been condemned by Greek exaltation of abstract thought and by Greek contempt for labor as representing the brute struggle of carnal appetite for its own satiety. The industrial movement, offspring of science, restored it to its central position in morals. When Adam Smith made economic activity the moving spring of man's unremitting effort, from the cradle to the grave, to better his own lot, he recorded this change. And when he made sympathy the central spring in man's conscious moral endeavor, he reported the effect which the increasing intercourse of men, due primarily to commerce, had in breaking down suspicion and jealousy and in liberating man's kindlier impulses.

Democracy, the crucial expression of modern life, is not so much an addition to the scientific and industrial tendencies as it is the perception of their social or spiritual meaning. Democracy is an absurdity where faith in the individual as individual is impossible; and this faith is impossible when intelligence is regarded as a cosmic power, not an adjustment and application of individual tendencies. It is impossible when appetites and desires are conceived to be the dominant factor in the constitution of most men's characters, and when appetite and desire are conceived to be manifestations of the disorderly and unruly principle of nature. To put the intellectual centre of gravity in the objective cosmos, outside of men's own experiments and tests, and then to invite the application of individual intelligence to the determination of society is to invite chaos. To hold that want is mere negative flux and hence requires external fixation by reason, and then to invite the wants to give free play to themselves in social construction and intercourse is to call down anarchy. Democracy was conceivable only with a changed conception of the intelligence that forms modern science and the want that forms modern industry. It is essentially a changed psychology. The substitution, for *a priori* truth and deduction, of fluent doubt and inquiry meant trust in human nature in the concrete; in individual honesty, curiosity and sympathy. The substitution of moving commerce for fixed custom meant a view of wants as the dynamics of social progress, not as the pathology of private greed. The nineteenth century indeed turned sour on that somewhat complacent optimism in which the eighteenth century rested: the ideas that the intelligent self-love of individuals would conduce to social cohesion, and competition among individuals usher in the kingdom of social welfare. But the conception of a social harmony of interests in which the achievement by each individual of his own freedom should contribute to a like perfecting of the powers of all, through a fraternally organized society, is the permanent contribution of the industrial movement to morals—even though so far it be but the contribution of a problem.

Intellectually speaking, the centuries since the fourteenth are the true middle ages. They mark the transitional period of mental habit, as the so-called medieval period represents the petrification, under changed outward conditions, of Greek ideas. The conscious articulation of genuinely modern tendencies has yet to come, and till it comes the ethic of our own life must remain undescribed. But the system of morals which has come nearest to the reflection of the movements of science, democracy and commerce, is doubtless the utilitarian. Scientific, after the modern mode, it certainly would be. Newton's influence dyes deep the moral thought of the eighteenth century. The arrangements of the solar system had been described in terms of a homogeneous matter and motion, worked by two opposed and compensating forces: all because a method analysis, of generalization by analogy, and of mathematical deduction back to new empirical details had been followed. The imagination of the eighteenth century was a Newtonian imagination; and this no less in social than in physical matters. Hume proclaims that morals is about to become an experimental science. Just as, almost in our own day, Mill's interest in a method for social science led him to reformulate the logic of experimental inquiry, so all the great men of the Enlightenment were in search for the organon of morals which should repeat the physical triumphs of Newton. Bentham notes that physics has had its Bacon and Newton; that morals has had its Bacon in Helvétius, but still awaits its Newton; and he leaves us in no doubt that at the moment of writing he was ready, modestly but firmly, to fill the waiting niche with its missing figure.

The industrial movement furnished the concrete imagery for this ethical renovation. The utilitarians borrowed from Adam Smith the notion that through industrial exchange in a free society the individual pursuing his own good is led, under the guidance of the "invisible hand," to promote the general good more effectually than if he had set out to do it. This idea was dressed out in the atomistic psychology which Hartley built out from Locke—and returned at usurious rates to later economists.

From the great French writers who had sought to justify and promote democratic individualism, came the conception that, since it is perverted political institutions which deprave individuals and bring them into hostility, nation against nation, class against class, individual against individual, the great political problem is that reform of law and legislation, civic and criminal, of administration, and of education which will force the individual to find his own interest in pursuits which conduce to the welfare of others.

Tremendously effective as a tool of criticism, operative in abolition and elimination, utilitarianism failed to measure up to the constructive needs of the time. Its theoretical equalization of the good of each with that of every other was practically perverted by its excessive interest in the middle and manufacturing classes. Its speculative defect of an atomistic psychology combined with this narrowness of vision to make light of the constructive work that needs to be done by the state, before all can have, otherwise than in name, an equal chance to count in the common good. Thus the age-long subordination of economics to politics was revenged in the submerging of both politics and ethics in a narrow theory of economic profit; and utilitarianism, in its orthodox descendants, proffered the disjointed pieces of a mechanism, with a monotonous reiteration that if looked at aright they form a beautifully harmonious organism. . . .

Unstable equilibrium, rapid fermentation and a succession of explosive reports are thus the chief notes of modern ethics. Scepticism and traditionalism, empiricism and rationalism, crude naturalisms and all embracing idealisms, flourish side by side—all the more flourish, one suspects, because side by side. Spencer exults that natural science reveals that the rapid transit system of evolution is carrying us automatically to the goal of a perfect man in a perfect society; and his English idealistic contemporary is so disturbed by the removal from nature of its moral qualities, that he tries to show that it makes no difference, since nature in any case is known through a spiritual principle which is as permanent as nature is changing. An Amiel genteelly laments the decadence of the inner life, while his neighbor Nietzsche brandishes in rude ecstasy the banner of brute survival as a happy omen of the final victory of nobility of mind. The reasonable conclusion from such a scene is that there is taking place a transformation of attitude towards moral theory rather than mere propagation of varieties among theories. The classic theories all agree in one regard. They all alike assumed the existence of *the* end, the *summum bonum*, the final goal; and of *the* separate moral force which moves to that goal. Moralists have disputed as to whether the end is an aggregate of pleasurable state of consciousness, enjoyment of the divine essence, acknowledgment of the law of duty, or conformity to environment. So they have disputed as to the path by which the final goal is to be reached: fear or benevolence? reverence for pure law or pity for others? self-love or altruism? But these very controversies imply that there was but the one end and the one means.

The transformation in attitude, to which I referred, is the growing belief that the proper business of intelligence is discrimination of multiple and present goods and of the varied immediate means of their realization; not search for the one remote aim. The progress of biology has accustomed our minds to the notion that intelligence is not an outside power presiding supremely but statically over the desires and efforts of man, but that it is a method of adjustment of capacities and conditions within specific situations. History, as the lecturer on that subject told us, has discovered itself in the idea of process. The genetic standpoint makes us aware that the systems of the past are neither fraudulent imposture nor absolute revelations; but are the products of political, economic and scientific conditions whose change carries with it change of reflective formulations. The recognition that intelligence is properly an organ of adjustment in difficult situations makes us aware that these past theories were of value so far as they helped carry to an issue the social perplexities from which they emerged. But the chief impact of the evolutionary method is upon the present. Theory having learned what it cannot do, is made responsible for the better performance of what needs to be done, and what only a broadly equipped intelligence can do: to study the conditions out of which come the obstacles and the resources of adequate life, and to develop and test the ideas which, as working hypotheses, may be used to diminish the causes of evil and buttress and expand the sources of good. This program is indeed vague, but only unfamiliarity with it could lead one to the conclusion that it is less vague than the idea that there is a single moral ideal and a single moral motive force.

From this point of view there is no separate body of moral rules; no separate system of motive powers; no separate subject-matter of moral knowledge, and hence no such thing as an isolated ethical science. If the business of morals is not to speculate upon man's final end, and upon an ultimate standard of right, it is to utilize physiology, anthropology and psychology to discover all that can be discovered of man, his organic powers and propensities. If its business is not to search for the one separate moral motive, it is to converge all the instrumentalities of the social arts, of law, education, economics and political science upon the construction of intelligent methods of improving the common lot.

If we still wish to make our peace with the past, and to sum up the plural and changing goods of life in a single word, doubtless the term happiness is the one most apt. But we should again exchange free morals for sterile metaphysics, if we imagine that "happiness" is any less unique than the individuals who experience it; any less complex than the constitution of their capacities, or any less variable than the objects upon which their capacities are directed.

To many timid, albeit sincere, souls of an earlier century, the decay of the doctrine that all true and worthful science is knowledge of final causes seemed fraught with danger to science and to morals. The rival conception of a wide open universe, a universe without bounds in time or space, without final limits of origin or destiny, the universe with the lid off, was a menace. We now face in moral science a similar crisis and like opportunity, as well as share in a like dreadful suspense. The abolition of a fixed and final goal and causal force in nature did not, as matter of fact, render rational conviction less important or less attainable. It was accompanied by the provision of a technique of persistent and detailed inquiry in all special fields of fact, a technique which led to the detection of unsuspected forces and the revelation of undreamed of uses. In like fashion we may anticipate that the abolition of *the* final goal and *the* single motive power and *the* separate and infallible faculty in morals, will quicken inquiry into all the diversity of specific goods of experience, fix attention upon their conditions and bring to light values now dim and obscure. The change may relieve men from responsibility for what they cannot do, but it will promote thoughtful consideration of what they may do and the definition of responsibility for what they do amiss, because of failure to think straight and carefully. Absolute goods will fall into the background, but the question of making more sure and extensive the share of all men in natural and social goods will be urgent, a problem not to be escaped or evaded.

Morals, philosophy, returns to its first love; love of the wisdom that is nurse, as nature is mother, of good. But it returns to the Socratic principle equipped with a multitude of special methods of inquiry and testing; with an organized mass of knowledge, and with control of the arrangements by which industry, law and education may concentrate upon the problem of the participation by all men and women, up to their capacity of absorption, in all attained values. Morals may then well leave to poetry and to art, the task (so unartistically performed by philosophy since Plato) of gathering together and rounding out, into one abiding picture, the separate and special goods of life. It may leave this task with the assurance that the resultant synthesis will not depict any final and all inclusive good, but will add just one more specific good to the enjoyable excellencies of life.

Humorous irony shines through most of the harsh glances turned towards the idea of an experimental basis and career for morals. Some shiver in the fear that morals will be plunged into anarchic confusion—a view well expressed by a recent writer in the saying that if the *a priori* and transcendental basis of morals be abandoned "we shall have merely the same certainty that now exists in physics and chemistry"! Elsewhere lurks the apprehension that the progress of scientific method will deliver the purposive freedom of man bound hand and foot to the fatal decrees of iron necessity, called natural law. The notion that laws govern and forces rule is an animistic survival. It is a product of reading nature in terms of politics in order then to turn about and read politics in the light of supposed sanctions of nature. This idea passed from medieval theology into the science of Newton, to whom the universe was the dominion of a sovereign whose laws were the laws of nature. From Newton it passed into the deism of the eighteenth century, whence it migrated into the philosophy of the Enlightenment, to make its last stand in Spencer's philosophy of the fixed environment and the static goal.

No, nature is not an unchangeable order, unwinding itself majestically from the reel of law under the control of deified forces. It is an indefinite congeries of changes. Laws are not governmental regulations which limit change, but are convenient formulations of selected portions of change followed through a longer or shorter period of time, and then registered in those statistical forms which are amenable to mathematical manipulation. That this device of shorthand symbolization presages the subjection of man's intelligent effort to fixity of law and environment is interesting as a culture survival, but is not important for moral theory. Savage and child delight in creating bogeys from which, in concealing their origin and structure, interesting thrills and shudders may be had. Civilized man in the nineteenth century outdid these bugaboos in his image of a fixed universe hung on a cast-iron framework of fixed, necessary and universal laws. Knowledge of nature does not mean subjection to predestination, but insight into courses of change; an insight which is formulated in "laws," that is, methods of subsequent procedure.

Knowledge of the process and conditions of physical and social change by experimental science and genetic history has one result with a double name: increase of control and increase of responsibility; increase of power to direct natural change, and increase of responsibility for its equitable direction toward fuller good. Theory located within progressive practice instead of reigning statically supreme over it, means practice itself made responsible to intelligence; to intelligence which relentlessly scrutinizes the consequences of every practice, and which exacts

liability by an equally relentless publicity. As long as morals occupies itself with mere ideals, forces and conditions as they are will be good enough for "practical" men, since they are then left free to their own devices in turning these to their own account. As long as moralists plume themselves upon possession of the domain of the categorical imperative with its bare precepts, men of executive habits will always be at their elbows to regulate the concrete social conditions through which the form of law gets its actual filling of specific injunctions. When freedom is conceived to be transcendental, the coercive restraint of immediate necessity will lay its harsh hand upon the mass of men.

In the end, men do what they can do. They refrain from doing what they cannot do. They do what their own specific powers in conjunction with the limitations and resources of the environment permit. The effective control of their powers is not through precepts, but through the regulation of their conditions. If this regulation is itself to be not merely physical or coercive, but moral, it must consist of the intelligent selection and determination of the environments in which we act; and in an intelligent exaction of responsibility for the use of men's powers. Theorists inquire after the "motive" to morality, to virtue and the good, under such circumstances. What then, one wonders, is their conception of the make-up of human nature and of its relation to virtue and to goodness? The pessimism which dictates such a question, if it be justified, precludes any consideration of morals.

The diversion of intelligence from discrimination of plural and concrete goods, from noting their conditions and obstacles, and from the task of devising methods for holding men responsible for their concrete use of powers and conditions, has done more than brute love of power to establish inequality and injustice among men. It has done more, because it has confirmed with social sanctions the principle of feudal domination. All men require moral sanctions in their conduct: the consent of their kind. Not getting it otherwise, they go insane to feign it. No man ever lived with the exclusive approval of his own conscience. Hence the vacuum left in practical matters by the remote irrelevancy of transcendental morals has to be filled in somehow. It is filled in. It is filled in with class-codes, class-standards, class approvals—with codes which recommend the practices and habits already current in a given circle, set, calling, profession, trade, industry, club or gang. These class-codes always lean back upon and support themselves by the professed ideal code. This latter meets them more than half-way. Being in its pretence a theory for regulating practice, it must demonstrate its practicability. It is uneasy in isolation, and travels hastily to meet with compromise and accommodation the actual situation in all its brute unrationality. Where the pressure is greatest—in the habitual practice of the political and economic chieftains—there it accommodates the most.

Class-codes of morals are sanctions, under the caption of ideals, of uncriticized customs; they are recommendations, under the head of duties, of what the members of the class are already most given to doing. If there are to obtain more equable and comprehensive principles of action, exacting a more impartial exercise of natural power and resource in the interests of a common good, it will be because members of a class can no longer rest content in responsibility to a class whose traditions constitute its conscience, but are made responsible to a society whose conscience is its free and effectively organized intelligence.

In such a conscience alone will the Socratic injunction to man to know himself be fulfilled.

CHAPTER XVII

AMERICAN INDIVIDUALISM AND THE IDEOLOGY OF THE SELF-MADE MAN

L ong before the Civil War, the individualistic ethic had become one of the cardinal tenets of the American democratic faith. Formulated in a society unhampered by sharp feudal restrictions and articulated by a people imbued with the Protestant ethic, such a theory harmonized with the rising materialism of a nation bent on exploiting its abundant natural resources.

In the second half of the nineteenth century, however, the philosophy of individualism began to undergo a marked transformation in its intellectual and theoretical formulation. No longer was it advocated solely on religious and moral grounds, as it had been in the past. Instead, it received an impetus from the new evolutionary hypothesis, especially the version developed by Herbert Spencer.

Spencer's ideas had a special appeal to Americans, who found in them a philosophy sympathetic to the changing conditions of their society. In the first place, his imposing system, itself a product of English industrialism, provided a rationale suitable to the needs of an industrial age. Second, it seemed to rest squarely on a scientific base, built as it was on the physical law of thermodynamics and the biological notions of adaptation, selection, and evolution. Finally, it included its own version of the idea of progress, thus buttressing a faith already accepted by most Americans.

In essence, Spencer insisted that there existed a general law of organic evolution. In his view development proceeded from homogeneous to hetero-geneous, from simple to complex, and from lower to higher forms. Like his contemporary Charles Darwin, Spencer utilized two ideas: Malthusian theory, which held that population would always exceed the physical ability to sup-port itself, were it not for war, pestilence, and famine; and the notion of natural selection. He then asserted that man must conform to natural forces and could not consciously direct his own development. In fact, according to Spencer, progress could occur only if man did not attempt to impede the deterministic impact of evolution. In the final analysis, then, Spencer stood for an extreme version of laissez faire.

To a nation committed to a program of private exploitation of natural resources and the creation of a free enterprise capitalistic economy, Spencer's sociological system had an inherent attractiveness. It provided a framework by which an extreme form of individualism could be linked to a general theory of progress. It also provided an ideological and scientific justification for a conservative, laissez-faire policy. Above all, Spencer's system was in har-mony with the traditional attachment of Americans to the ideals of democracy and opportunity, since any man, regardless of his rank in society, could rise as high in life as his abilities and ambitions permitted.

To be sure, not all Americans assented to the ideology of success, with its built-in acceptance of laissez faire. Nor could its adherents always agree on a precise definition of this ideology. The Spencerian version of conservative Darwinism, for example, appealed largely to intellectuals, social scientists, and educated individuals. Businessmen, on the other hand, who had neither the benefits of a formal education nor the time and ability to master the intricacies of Spencer's system, still defended laissez faire in terms derived from the Protestant ethic and the doctrines of the classical economists. Never-theless, within broad limits, the theory of individualism and the cult of suc-cess, whatever its intellectual formulation, exerted great influence at a time when men were seeking to erect new systems of thought and mores in a changing world. Such an ideology seemed to offer fabulous rewards to those willing to test their mettle in the free and unregulated competitive arena. If the challenges were great, so too were the potential gains. And from a social point of view, society itself would ultimately be the beneficiary, since the process would ensure the progressive development of mankind to hitherto undreamed of levels.

From the Civil War to the turn of the century, this conservative faith and philosophy became the gospel of success for ambitious young Americans striving to better themselves. Even when a reaction set in, so strong was the hold of the ideology of the self-made man and the cult of success that it was destined to play an important role in subsequent decades. In our own time also, expressions of the antistate doctrine of rugged individualism in one form or another are articulated and accepted by many.

William Graham Sumner

1840-1910

Born in Paterson, New Jersey, William Graham Sumner graduated from Yale in 1863, and was ordained a minister in the Protestant Episcopal Church in 1869. His interest in social and economic matters quickly surpassed his ministerial concerns, and in 1872 he accepted a call to a newly created chair of political and social science at Yale, where he remained for the rest of his life. His fame as a scholar and teacher earned him a national reputation, as did his numerous books dealing with human society.

A disciple of Spencer, Sumner was opposed to social experimentation through governmental planning. A staunch foe of governmental regulation, he argued that such intervention could never be scientific or intelligent, and supported a laissez-faire approach based on a deterministic law of evolution. He championed big business and a sound monetary system and opposed protectionism, free silver, and inflation.

Later in life, Sumner turned from political economy to sociology. In 1906 he published Folkways, *a book destined to have an immense influence.* Folkways *was in many ways a repudiation of some of Sumner's earlier views. In this pioneering work he maintained that individual men were ultimately not governed by reason, but by the folkways and mores of the society into which they were born and lived. Such folkways and mores, Sumner argued, were not rational creations but rather by-products of the adjustment of men to their life conditions. In other words, Sumner was positing a doctrine of cultural determinism. "The mores," he commented, "can make anything right and prevent the condemnation of anything."*

The following selection is from one of Sumner's earlier works, What Social Classes Owe to Each Other *(New York, 1883), and illustrates his philosophy during that part of his career when Spencerian elements dominated his thinking.*

Certain ills belong to the hardships of human life. They are natural. They are part of the struggle with Nature for existence. We cannot blame our fellow-men for our share of these.

My neighbor and I are both struggling to free ourselves from these ills. The fact that my neighbor has succeeded in this struggle better than I constitutes no grievance for me. Certain other ills are due to the malice of men, and to the imperfections or errors of civil institutions. These ills are an object of agitation, and a subject of discussion. The former class of ills is to be met only by manly effort and energy; the latter may be corrected by associated effort. The former class of ills is constantly grouped and generalized, and made the object of social schemes. We shall see, as we go on, what that means. The second class of ills fall on certain social classes, and reform will take the form of interference by other classes in favor of that one. The last fact is, no doubt, the reason why people have been led, not noticing distinctions, to believe that the same method was applicable to the other class of ills. The distinction here made between the ills which belong to the struggle for existence and those which are due to the faults of human institutions is of prime importance.

It will also be important, in order to clear up our ideas about the notions which are in fashion, to note the relation of the economic to the political significance of assumed duties of one class to another. That is to say, we may discuss the question whether one class owes duties to another by reference to the economic effects which will be produced on the classes and society; or we may discuss the political expediency of formulating and enforcing rights and duties respectively between the parties. In the former case we might assume that the givers of aid were willing to give it, and we might discuss the benefit or mischief of their activity. In the other case we must assume that some at least of those who were forced to give aid did so unwillingly. Here, then, there would be a question of rights. The question whether voluntary charity is mischievous or not is one thing; the question whether legislation which forces one man to aid another is right and wise, as well as economically beneficial, is quite another question. Great confusion and consequent error is produced by allowing these two questions to become entangled in the discussion. Especially we shall need to notice the attempts to apply legislative methods of reform to the ills which belong to the order of Nature.

There is no possible definition of "a poor man." A pauper is a person who cannot earn his living; whose producing powers have fallen positively below his necessary consumption; who cannot, therefore, pay his way. A human society needs the active co-operation and productive energy of every person in it. A man who is present as a consumer, yet who does not contribute either by land, labor, or capital to the work of society, is a burden. On no sound political theory ought such a person to share in the political power of the State. He drops out of the ranks of workers and producers. Society must support him. It accepts the burden, but he must be cancelled from the ranks of the rulers likewise. So much for the pauper. About him no more need be said. But he is not the "poor man." The "poor man" is an elastic term, under which any number of social fallacies may be hidden.

Neither is there any possible definition of "the weak." Some are weak in one way, and some in another; and those who are weak in one sense are strong in another. In general, however, it may be said that those whom humanitarians and philanthropists call the weak are the ones through whom the productive and conservative forces of society are wasted. They constantly neutralize and destroy the finest efforts of the wise and industrious, and are a dead-weight on the society in all its struggles to realize any better things. Whether the people who mean no harm, but are weak in the essential powers necessary to the performance of one's duties in life, or those who are malicious and vicious, do the more mischief, is a question not easy to answer.

Under the names of the poor and the weak, the negligent, shiftless, inefficient, silly, and imprudent are fastened upon the industrious and prudent as a responsibility and a duty. On the one side, the terms are extended to cover the idle, intemperate, and vicious, who, by the combination, gain credit which they do not deserve, and which they could not get if they stood alone. On the other hand, the terms are extended to include wage-receivers of the humblest rank, who are degraded by the combination. The reader who desires to guard himself against fallacies should always scrutinize the terms "poor" and "weak" as used, so as to see which or how many of these classes they are made to cover.

The humanitarians, philanthropists, and reformers, looking at the facts of life as they present themselves, find enough which is sad and unpromising in the condition of many members of society. They see wealth and poverty side by side. They note great inequality of social position and social chances. They eagerly set about the attempt to account for what they see, and to devise schemes for remedying what they do not like. In their eagerness to recommend the less fortunate classes to pity and consideration they forget all about the rights of other classes; they gloss over all the faults of the classes in question, and they exaggerate their misfortunes and their virtues. They invent new theories of property, distorting rights and perpetrating injustice, as any one is sure to do who sets about the re-adjustment of social relations with the interests of one group distinctly before his mind, and the interests of all other groups thrown into the background. When I have read certain of these discussions I have thought that it must be quite disreputable to be respectable, quite dishonest to own property, quite unjust to go one's own way and earn one's own living, and that the only really admirable person was the good-for-nothing. The man who by his own effort raises himself above poverty appears, in these discussions, to be of no account. The man who has done nothing to raise himself above poverty finds that the social doctors flock about him, bringing the capital which they have collected from the other class, and promising him the aid of the State to give him what the other had to work for. In all these schemes and projects the organized intervention of society through the State is either planned or hoped for, and the State is thus made to become the protector and guardian of certain classes. The agents who are to direct the State action are, of course, the reformers and philanthropists. Their schemes therefore, may always be reduced to this type—that A and B decide what C shall do for D. It will be interesting to inquire, at a later period of our discussion, who C is, and what the effect is upon him of all these arrangements. In all the discussions attention is concentrated on A and B, the noble social reformers, and on D, the "poor man." I call C the Forgotten Man, because I have never seen that any notice was taken of him in any of the discussions. When we have disposed of A, B, and D we can better appreciate the case of C, and I think that we shall find that he deserves our attention, for the worth of his character and the magnitude of his unmerited burdens. Here it may suffice to observe that, on the theories of the social philosophers to whom I have referred, we should get a new maxim of judicious living: Poverty is the best policy. If you get wealth, you will have to support other people; if you do not get wealth, it will be the duty of other people to support you.

No doubt one chief reason for the unclear and contradictory theories of class relations lies in the fact that our society, largely controlled in all its organization by one set of doctrines, still contains survivals of old social theories which are totally inconsistent with the former. In the Middle Ages men were united by custom and prescription into associations, ranks, guilds, and communities of various kinds. These ties endured as long as life lasted. Consequently society was dependent, throughout all its details, on status, and the tie, or bond, was sentimental. In our modern state, and in the United States more than anywhere else, the social structure is based on contract, and status is of the least importance. Contract, however, is rational—even rationalistic. It is also realistic, cold, and matter-of-fact. A contract relation is based on a sufficient reason, not on custom or prescription. It is not permanent. It endures only so long as the reason for it endures. In a state based on contract sentiment is out of place in any public or common affairs. It is relegated to the sphere of private and personal relations, where it depends not at all on class types, but on personal acquaintance and personal estimates. The sentimentalists among us always seize upon the survivals of the old order. They want to save them and restore them. Much of the loose thinking also which troubles us in our social discussions arises from the fact that men do not distinguish the elements of status and of contract which may be found in our society.

Whether social philosophers think it desirable or not, it is out of the question to go back to status or to the sentimental relations which once united baron and retainer, master and servant, teacher and pupil, comrade and comrade: That we have lost some grace and elegance is undeniable. That life once held more poetry and romance is true enough. But it seems impossible that any one who has studied the matter should doubt that we have gained immeasurably, and that our farther gains lie in going forward, not in going backward. The feudal ties can never be restored. If they could be restored they would bring back personal caprice, favoritism, sycophancy, and intrigue. A society based on contract is a society of free and independent men, who form ties without favor or obligation, and cooperate without cringing or intrigue. A society based on contract, therefore, gives the utmost room and chance for individual development, and for all the self-reliance and dignity of a free man. That a society of free men, co-operating under contract, is by far the strongest society which has ever yet existed; that no such society has ever yet developed the full measure of strength of which it is capable; and that the only social improvements which are now conceivable lie in the direction of more complete realization of a society of free men united by contract, are points which cannot be controverted. It follows, however, that one man, in a free state, cannot claim help from, and cannot be charged to give help to, another. To understand the full meaning of this assertion it will be worth while to see what a free democracy is. . . .

Social improvement is not to be won by direct effort. It is secondary, and results from physical or economic improvements. That is the reason why schemes of direct social amelioration always have an arbitrary, sentimental, and artificial character, while true social advance must be a product and a growth. The efforts which are being put forth for every kind of progress in the arts and sciences are, therefore, contributing to true social progress. Let any one learn what hardship was involved, even for a wealthy person, a century ago, in crossing the Atlantic, and then let him compare that hardship even with a steerage passage at the present time, considering time and money cost. This improvement in transportation by which "the poor and weak" can be carried from the crowded centres of population to the new land is worth more to them than all the schemes of all the social reformers. An improvement in surgical instruments or in anæsthetics really does more for those who are not well off than all the declamations of the orators and pious wishes of the reformers. Civil service reform would be a greater gain to the laborers than innumerable factory acts and eight-hour laws. Free trade would be a greater blessing to "the poor man" than all the devices of all the friends of humanity if they could be realized. If the economists could satisfactorily solve the problem of the regulation of paper currency, they would do more for the wages class than could be accomplished by all the artificial doctrines about wages which they seem to feel bound to encourage. If we could get firm and good laws passed for the management of savings-banks, and then refrain from the amendments by which those laws are gradually broken down, we should do more for the non-capitalist class than by volumes of laws against "corporations" and the "excessive power of capital."

We each owe to the other mutual redress of grievances. It has been said, in answer to my argument in the last chapter about the Forgotten Women and thread, that the tax on thread is "only a little thing," and that it cannot hurt the woman much, and also that, if the women do not want to pay two cents a spool tax, there is thread of an inferior quality, which they can buy cheaper. These answers represent the bitterness and basest social injustice. Every honest citizen of a free state owes it to himself, to the community, and especially to those who are at once weak and wronged, to go to their assistance and to help redress their wrongs. Whenever a law or social arrangement acts so as to injure any one, and that one the humblest, then there is a duty on those who are stronger, or who know better, to demand and fight for redress and correction. When generalized this means that it is the duty of All-of-us

(that is, the State) to establish justice for all, from the least to the greatest, and in all matters. This, however, is no new doctrine. It is only the old, true, and indisputable function of the State; and in working for a redress of wrongs and a correction of legislative abuses, we are only struggling to a fuller realization of it—that is, working to improve civil government.

We each owe it to the other to guarantee rights. Rights do not pertain to *results*, but only to *chances*. They pertain to the *conditions* of the struggle for existence, not to any of the results of it; to the *pursuit* of happiness, not to the possession of happiness. It cannot be said that each one has a right to have some property, because if one man had such a right some other man or men would be under a corresponding obligation to provide him with some property. Each has a right to acquire and possess property if he can. It is plain what fallacies are developed when we overlook this distinction. Those fallacies run through *all* socialistic schemes and theories. If we take rights to pertain to results, and then say that rights must be equal, we come to say that men have a right to be equally happy, and so on in all the details. Rights should be equal, because they pertain to chances, and all ought to have equal chances so far as chances are provided or limited by the action of society. This, however, will not produce equal results, but it is right just because it will produce unequal results—that is, results which shall be proportioned to the merits of individuals. We each owe it to the other to guarantee mutually the chance to earn, to possess, to learn, to marry, etc., etc., against any interference which would prevent the exercise of those rights by a person who wishes to prosecute and enjoy them in peace for the pursuit of happiness. If we generalize this, it means that All-of-us ought to guarantee rights to each of us. But our modern free, constitutional States are constructed entirely on the notion of rights, and we regard them as performing their functions more and more perfectly according as they guarantee rights in consonance with the constantly corrected and expanded notions of rights from one generation to another. Therefore, when we say that we owe it to each other to guarantee rights we only say that we ought to prosecute and improve our political science.

If we have in mind the value of chances to earn, learn, possess, etc., for a man of independent energy, we can go one step farther in our deductions about help. The only help which is generally expedient, even within the limits of the private and personal relations of two persons to each other, is that which consists in helping a man to help himself. This always consists in opening the chances. A man of assured position can, by an effort which is of no appreciable importance to him, give aid which is of incalculable value to a man who is all ready to make his own career if he can only get a chance. The truest and deepest pathos in this world is not that of suffering but that of brave struggling. The truest sympathy is not compassion, but a fellow-feeling with courage and fortitude in the midst of noble effort.

Now, the aid which helps a man to help himself is not in the least akin to the aid which is given in charity. If alms are given, or if we "make work" for a man, or "give him employment," or "protect" him, we simply take a product from one and give it to another. If we help a man to help himself, by opening the chances around him, we put him in a position to add to the wealth of the community by putting new powers in operation to produce. It would seem that the difference between getting something already in existence from the one who has it, and producing a new thing by applying new labor to natural materials, would be so plain

as never to be forgotten; but the fallacy of confusing the two is one of the commonest in all social discussions.

We have now seen that the current discussions about the claims and rights of social classes on each other are radically erroneous and fallacious, and we have seen that an analysis of the general obligations which we all have to each other leads us to nothing but an emphatic repetition of old but well-acknowledged obligations to perfect our political institutions. We have been led to restriction, not extension, of the functions of the State, but we have also been led to see the necessity of purifying and perfecting the operation of the State in the functions which properly belong to it. If we refuse to recognize any classes as existing in society when, perhaps, a claim might be set up that the wealthy, educated, and virtuous have acquired special rights and precedence, we certainly cannot recognize any classes when it is attempted to establish such distinctions for the sake of imposing burdens and duties on one group for the benefit of others. The men who have not done their duty in this world never can be equal to those who have done their duty more or less well. If words like wise and foolish, thrifty and extravagant, prudent and negligent, have any meaning in language, then it must make some difference how people behave in this world, and the difference will appear in the position they acquire in the body of society, and in relation to the chances of life. They may, then, be classified in reference to these facts. Such classes always will exist; no other social distinctions can endure. If, then, we look to the origin and definition of these classes, we shall find it impossible to deduce any obligations which one of them bears to the other. The class distinctions simply result from the different degrees of success with which men have availed themselves of the chances which were presented to them. Instead of endeavoring to redistribute the acquisitions which have been made between the existing classes, our aim should be to *increase, multiply, and extend the chances.* Such is the work of civilization. Every old error or abuse which is removed opens new chances of development to all the new energy of society. Every improvement in education, science, art, or government expands the chances of man on earth. Such expansion is no guarantee of equality. On the contrary, if there be liberty, some will profit by the chances eagerly and some will neglect them altogether. Therefore, the greater the chances the more unequal will be the fortune of these two sets of men. So it ought to be, in all justice and right reason. The yearning after equality is the offspring of envy and covetousness, and there is no possible plan for satisfying that yearning which can do aught else than rob A to give to B; consequently all such plans nourish some of the meanest vices of human nature, waste capital, and overthrow civilization. But if we can expand the chances we can count on a general and steady growth of civilization and advancement of society by and through its best members. In the prosecution of these chances we all owe to each other good-will, mutual respect, and mutual guarantees of liberty and security. Beyond this nothing can be affirmed as a duty of one group to another in a free state.

Elihu Root

1845-1937

Elihu Root was descended from Puritan settlers who had migrated to America in 1639. Born in Clinton, New York, Root graduated from Hamilton College in 1865, and received his law degree from New York University School of Law in 1867. He immediately embarked upon a highly successful legal career in New York City, soon attaining a prominent place among the top rank of corporate lawyers. His associations and personal preferences drew him into the ranks of the conservative Republicans, although he himself was a moderate rather than an extreme conservative. After becoming acquainted with Theodore Roosevelt in 1886, he entered the political arena and served as Roosevelt's Secretary of War and Secretary of State, doing an outstanding job in reorganizing the War Department as well as in establishing friendly relations with Latin America. Following his years in the State Department, he served in the Senate for six years and then played an active and important role as elder statesman to the Republican party. Articulate and vocal, Root frequently expounded his brand of moderate conservatism.

The selection that follows was originally given in 1913 as one of the Stafford Little Lectures at Princeton, and is from Experiments in Government and the Essentials of the Constitution (*Princeton: Princeton University Press, 1913*).

*T*here are two separate processes going on among the civilized nations at the present time. One is an assault by socialism against the individualism which underlies the social system of western civilization. The other is an assault against existing institutions upon the ground that they do not adequately protect and develop the existing social order. It is of this latter process in our own country that I wish to speak, and I assume an agreement, that the right of individual liberty and the inseparable right of private property which lie at the foundation of our modern civilization ought to be maintained. . . .

Now, there has been a general social and industrial rearrangement. Production and commerce pay no attention to state lines. The life of the country is no longer grouped about state capitals, but about the great centers of continental production and trade. The organic growth which must ultimately determine the form of institutions has been away from the mere union of states towards the union of individuals in the relation of national citizenship. . . .

The process of devising and trying new laws to meet new conditions naturally leads to the question whether we need not merely to make new laws but also to modify the principles upon which our government is based and the institutions of government designed for the application of those principles to the affairs of life. Upon this question it is of the utmost importance that we proceed with considerate wisdom. . . .

When proposals are made to change these institutions there are certain general considerations which should be observed.

The first consideration is that free government is impossible except through prescribed and established governmental institutions, which work out the ends of government through many separate human agents, each doing his part in obedience to law. Popular will cannot execute itself directly except through a mob. Popular will cannot get itself executed through an irresponsible executive, for that is simple autocracy. An executive limited only by the direct expression of popular will cannot be held to responsibility against his will, because, having possession of all the powers of government, he can prevent any true, free, and general expression adverse to himself, and unless he yields voluntarily he can be overturned only by a revolution. The familiar Spanish-American dictatorships are illustrations of this. A dictator once established by what is or is alleged to be public choice never permits an expression of public will which will displace him, and he goes out only through a new revolution because he alone controls the machinery through which he could be displaced peaceably. A system with a plebiscite at one end and Louis Napoleon at the other could not give France free government; and it was only after the humiliation of defeat in a great war and the horrors of the Commune that the French people were able to establish a government that would really execute their will through carefully devised institutions in which they gave their chief executive very little power indeed.

We should, therefore, reject every proposal which involves the idea that the people can rule merely by voting, or merely by voting and having one man or group of men to execute their will.

A second consideration is that in estimating the value of any system of governmental institutions due regard must be had to the true functions of government and to the limitations imposed by nature upon what it is possible for government to accomplish. We all know of course that we cannot abolish all the evils in this world by statute or by the enforcement of statutes, nor can we prevent the inexorable law of nature which decrees that suffering shall follow vice, and all the evil passions and folly of mankind. Law cannot give to depravity the rewards of virtue, to indolence the rewards of industry, to indifference the rewards of ambition, or to ignorance the rewards of learning. The utmost that government can do is measurably to protect men, not against the wrong they do themselves but against wrong done by others and to promote the long, slow process of educating mind and character to a better knowledge and nobler standards of life and conduct. We know all this, but when we see how much misery there is in the world and instinctively cry out against it, and when we see some things that government may do to mitigate it, we are apt to forget how little after all it is possible for any government to do, and to hold the particular government of the time and place to a standard of responsibility which no government can possibly meet. The chief motive power which has moved mankind along the course of development that we call the progress of civilization has been the sum total of intelligent selfishness in a vast number of individuals, each working for his own support, his own gain, his own betterment. It is that which has cleared the forests and cultivated the fields and built the ships and railroads, made the discoveries and inventions, covered the earth with commerce, softened by intercourse the enmities of nations and races, and made possible the wonders of literature and of art. Gradually, during the long process, selfishness has grown more intelligent, with a broader view of individual benefit from the common good, and gradually the influences of nobler standards of altruism, of justice, and human sympathy have impressed themselves upon the conception of right conduct among civilized men. But the complete control of such motives will be the millennium. Any attempt to enforce a millennial standard now by law must necessarily fail, and any judgment which assumes government's responsibility to enforce such a standard must be an unjust judgment. Indeed, no such standard can ever be forced. It must come, not by superior force, but from the changed nature of man from his willingness to be altogether just and merciful.

A third consideration is that it is not merely useless but injurious for government to attempt too much. It is manifest that to enable it to deal with the new conditions I have described we must invest government with authority to interfere with the individual conduct of the citizen to a degree hitherto unknown in this country. When government undertakes to give the individual citizen protection by regulating the conduct of others towards him in the field where formerly he protected himself by his freedom of contract, it is limiting the liberty of the citizen whose conduct is regulated and taking a step in the direction of paternal government. While the new conditions of industrial life make it plainly necessary that many such steps shall be taken, they should be taken only so far as they are necessary and are effective. Interference with individual liberty by government should be jealously watched and restrained, because the habit of undue interference destroys that independence of character without

which in its citizens no free government can endure. . . .

The habit of undue interference by government in private affairs breeds the habit of undue reliance upon government in private affairs at the expense of individual initiative, energy, enterprise, courage, independent manhood.

The strength of self-government and the motive power of progress must be found in the characters of the individual citizens who make up a nation. Weaken individual character among a people by comfortable reliance upon paternal government and a nation soon becomes incapable of free self-government and fit only to be governed: the higher and nobler qualities of national life that makes for ideals and effort and achievement become atrophied and the nation is decadent.

A fourth consideration is that in the nature of things all government must be imperfect because men are imperfect. Every system has its shortcomings and inconveniences; and these are seen and felt as they exist in the system under which we live, while the shortcomings and inconveniences of other systems are forgotten or ignored.

It is not unusual to see governmental methods reformed and after a time, long enough to forget the evils that caused the change, to have a new movement for a reform which consists in changing back to substantially the same old methods that were cast out by the first reform.

The recognition of shortcomings or inconveniences in government is not by itself sufficient to warrant a change of system. There should be also an effort to estimate and compare the shortcomings and inconveniences of the system to be substituted, for although they may be different they will certainly exist.

A fifth consideration is that whatever changes in government are to be made, we should follow the *method* which undertakes as one of its cardinal points to hold fast that which is good . . . the great structure of British and American liberty has been built up generation after generation and century after century. Through all the seven hundred years since Magna Charta we have been shaping, adjusting, adapting our system to the new conditions of life as they have arisen, but we have always held on to everything essentially good that we have ever had in the system. We have never undertaken to begin over again and build up a new system under the idea that we could do it better. We have never let go of Magna Charta or the Bill of Rights or the Declaration of Independence or the Constitution. When we take account of all that governments have sought to do and have failed to do in this selfish and sinful world, we find that as a rule the application of new theories of government, though devised by the most brilliant constructive genius, have availed but little to preserve the people of any considerable regions of the earth for any long periods from the evils of despotism on the one hand or of anarchy on the other, or to raise any considerable portion of the mass of mankind above the hard conditions of oppression and misery. And we find that our system of government which has been built up in this practical way through so many centuries, and the whole history of which is potent in the provisions of our Constitution, has done more to preserve liberty, justice, security, and freedom of opportunity for many people for a long period and over a great portion of the earth, than any other system of government ever devised by man. Human nature does not change very much. The forces of evil are hard to control now as they always have been. It is easy to fail and hard to succeed in reconciling liberty and order. In dealing with this most successful body of governmental institutions the question should not be what sort of government do you or I think we should have. What you and I think on such a subject is of very little value indeed. The question should be:

How can we adapt our laws and the workings of our government to the new conditions which confront us without sacrificing any essential element of this system of government which has so nobly stood the test of time and without abandoning the political principles which have inspired the growth of its institutions? For there are political principles, and nothing can be more fatal to self-government than to lose sight of them under the influence of apparent expediency.

CHAPTER XVIII

THE AMERICAN
AS REFORMER

Despite the persistence of a strong and vocal laissez-faire conservative philosophy, there also emerged from the disorders and discontents of the new industrial age a reformist outlook that repudiated the determinism of conservatism and insisted that men could, at least in part, control their own destiny. Compounded of a blend of religious and humanitarian motives, the reformist mind provided the underpinnings of what later was to become known as the theory of the welfare state.

Like the conservatives, the reformers were faced with the problems that marked the advent of a society founded upon an industrial technology. They, too, desired to understand the nature of man and the nature of society, and thus to provide a framework that would ensure the progressive development of the species. They, too, considered themselves to be impartial social scientists and political philosophers seeking an objective explanation and understanding of events. They, too, wanted to assure the maximum development of each individual's potentiality, while at the same time taking into consideration the needs of an increasingly complex, industrialized society.

But if there were similarities, there were also significant differences. Unlike many conservatives, the reformers were distrustful of the thoroughgoing determinism of the followers of Spencer and Sumner. Demonstrating great respect for science, the historical or genetic method in economics and sociology, and a cultural analysis of social problems, they insisted that man through the use of critical intelligence could help to establish a more rational society. For did not man possess what animals lacked, namely, a reasoning faculty? And could he not, therefore, accept naturalistic evolution and direct the evolutionary process into such predetermined channels as he might consider ethically and socially desirable? In other words, the reformers maintained that science and evolution offered a positive justification for human intervention into the affairs of society. When they added this scientific justification to the older theistic outlook, with its emphasis on Christian morality, they established the basis for a philosophy of directed and conscious change.

Beneath the façade of the reform ideology lay certain basic assumptions. In the first place, most of the reformers assumed that man's environment was amenable to his control, and that science provided the method to achieve this aim. Second, they assumed not only the dignity and worth of the individual but also his social nature, which brought society into being. Third, they maintained that man was essentially a rational creature whose innate goodness had been corrupted in part by an improper environment. Finally, and above all, the reformers shared a vision of progress, compounded of a middle-class hope of neutralizing the growth of bigness, whether in labor or capital, and creating what Walter Weyl in *The New Democracy* (1912) called "a socialized democracy." Thus, a morally regenerate middle class, avoiding either the rapaciousness of a robber baron or the radicalism of a union organizer, would create a cooperative commonwealth of men working together in harmonious union, consciously directing progress toward the final perfection of man and society.

It is true that not all the reformers had precisely the same vision, nor did they necessarily justify themselves on the same ideological grounds. There were, after all, wide gulfs between men like Lester Frank Ward, Thorstein Veblen, Richard T. Ely, Henry Demarest Lloyd, Herbert Croly, and others who laid the basis for a philosophy of reform. All of them, however, in one way or another, took paths that eventually converged in the progressive movement of the first part of the twentieth century, a movement dominated by a middle-class version of the good society that would strike an equitable balance between the competing claims of the individual and of society. Theirs was a gentle and humane philosophy that envisioned a better world to come, a world dominated by moral and rational men. These reformers became pragmatists in philosophy; they attempted to develop a scientific ethical theory and apply the scientific method to moral, social, economic, and political problems alike; they interpreted institutions from an evolutionary and economic point of view; and occasionally they even voted Socialist. In the political arena they sought to destroy or regulate monopolies, to make government more representative and amenable to popular control, to provide a measure of social justice for all, and to mitigate the problems of urban life. Optimistic rather than pessimistic, they looked eagerly toward the more rational and humane society of the future, which they would help to create.

Henry George

1839-1897

Henry George was born in Philadelphia, the son of a middle-class family of English descent. He was brought up in a pious Episcopalian atmosphere, and his schooling was brief and uneventful. Leaving home at an early age, he tried his hand as a sailor, and then became a printer and newspaperman. His early career in journalism brought him in contact with the extreme poverty and social unrest that characterized many of America's urban centers. He was well read and his strongly religious upbringing aroused in him a warm sympathy for the plight of the less fortunate. Before long he was inquiring into the nature and causes of the poverty he saw about him.

In 1879 he published his most famous and important work, Progress and Poverty. *This book influenced an amazing number of individuals who later became prominent in the progressive movement of the early twentieth century. In his work George attacked the ideology that had grown out of the conservative Darwinian analysis, arguing that it was simply a justification and rationalization of the* status quo. *Insisting that intelligence was itself a product of evolution, he maintained that it could be used to modify an environment in which progress and poverty seemed to go hand in hand. In other words, George attempted to forge a synthesis of evolutionary concepts and Christian ethics. Although his solution to the problem of poverty—the "single tax" upon the unearned increment on the value of land—was never implemented, the ideas that George advanced proved of great importance in formulating an alternative to conservative Darwinism.*

The following selection is from Progress and Poverty *(New York, 1880), fourth edition.*

The present century has been marked by a prodigious increase in wealth-producing power. The utilization of steam and electricity, the introduction of improved processes and labor-saving machinery, the greater subdivision and grander scale of production, the wonderful facilitation of exchanges, have multiplied enormously the effectiveness of labor.

At the beginning of this marvelous era it was natural to expect, and it was expected, that labor-saving inventions would lighten the toil and improve the condition of the laborer; that the enormous increase in the power of producing wealth would make real poverty a thing of the past. Could a man of the last century—a Franklin or a Priestley—have seen, in a vision of the future, the steamship taking the place of the sailing vessel, the railroad train of the wagon, the reaping machine of the scythe, the threshing machine of the flail; could he have heard the throb of the engines that in obedience to human will, and for the satisfaction of human desire, exert a power greater than that of all the men and all the beasts of burden of the earth combined; could he have seen the forest tree transformed into finished lumber— into doors, sashes, blinds, boxes or barrels, with hardly the touch of a human hand; the great workshops where boots and shoes are turned out by the case with less labor than the old-fashioned cobbler could have put on a sole; the factories where, under the eye of a girl, cotton becomes cloth faster than hundreds of stalwart weavers could have turned it out with their hand-looms; could he have seen steam hammers shaping mammoth shafts and mighty anchors, and delicate machinery making tiny watches; the diamond drill cutting through the heart of the rocks, and coal oil sparing the whale; could he have realized the enormous saving of labor resulting from improved facilities of exchange and communication— sheep killed in Australia eaten fresh in England, and the order given by the London banker in the afternoon executed in San Francisco in the morning of the same day; could he have conceived of the hundred thousand improvements which these only suggest, what would he have inferred as to the social condition of mankind? . . .

Now, however, we are coming into collision with facts which there can be no mistaking. From all parts of the civilized world come complaints of industrial depression; of labor condemned to involuntary idleness; of capital massed and wasting; of pecuniary distress among business men; of want and suffering and anxiety among the working classes. All the dull, deadening pain, all the keen, maddening anguish, that to great masses of men are involved in the words "hard times," afflict the world to-day. This state of things, common to communities differing so widely in situation, in political institutions, in fiscal and financial systems, in density of population and in social organization, can hardly be accounted for by local causes. There is distress where large standing armies are maintained, but there is also distress where the standing armies are nominal; there is distress where protective tariffs stupidly and wastefully hamper trade, but there is also distress where trade is nearly free; there is distress where autocratic government yet prevails, but there is also distress where political power is wholly in the hands of the people; in countries where paper is money, and in countries where gold and silver are the only currency. Evidently, beneath all such things as these, we must infer a common cause.

That there is a common cause, and that it is either what we call material progress or something closely connected with material progress, becomes more than an inference when it is noted that the phenomena we class together and speak of as industrial depression are but intensifications of phenomena which always accompany material progress, and which show themselves more clearly and strongly as material progress goes on. Where the conditions to which material progress everywhere tends are most fully realized—that is to say, where population is densest, wealth greatest, and the machinery of production and exchange most highly developed—we find the deepest poverty, the sharpest struggle for existence, and the most of enforced idleness. . . .

This fact—the great fact that poverty and all its concomitants show themselves in communities just as they develop into the conditions toward which material progress tends—proves that the social difficulties existing wherever a certain stage of progress has been reached, do not arise from local circumstances, but are, in some way or another, engendered by progress itself.

And, unpleasant as it may be to admit it, it is at last becoming evident that the enormous increase in productive power which has marked the present century and is still going on with accelerating ratio, has no tendency to extirpate poverty or to lighten the burdens of those compelled to toil. It simply widens the gulf between Dives and Lazarus, and makes the struggle for existence more intense. The march of invention has clothed mankind with powers of which a century ago the boldest imagination could not have dreamed. But in factories where labor-saving machinery has reached its most wonderful development, little children are at work; wherever the new forces are anything like fully utilized, large classes are maintained by charity or live on the verge of recourse to it; amid the greatest accumulations of wealth, men die of starvation, and puny infants suckle dry breasts; while everywhere the greed of gain, the worship of wealth, shows the force of the fear of want. The promised land flies before us like the mirage. The fruits of the tree of knowledge turn as we grasp them to apples of Sodom that crumble at the touch. . . .

This association of poverty with progress is the great enigma of our times. It is the central fact from which spring industrial, social, and political difficulties that perplex the world, and with which statesmanship and philanthropy and education grapple in vain. From it comes the clouds that overhang the future of the most progressive and self-reliant nations. It is the riddle which the Sphinx of Fate puts to our civilization, and which not to answer is to be destroyed. So long as all the increased wealth which modern progress brings goes but to build up great fortunes, to increase luxury and make sharper the contrast between the House of Have and the House of Want, progress is not real and cannot be permanent. The reaction must come. The tower leans from its foundations, and every new story but hastens the final catastrophe. To educate men who must be condemned to poverty, is but to make them restive; to base on a state of most glaring social inequality political institutions under which men are theoretically equal, is to stand a pyramid on its apex.

All-important as this question is, pressing itself from every quarter painfully upon attention, it has not yet received a solution which accounts for all the facts and points to any clear and simple remedy. . . .

I propose in the following pages to attempt to solve by the methods of political economy the great problem I have outlined. I propose to seek the law which associates poverty with progress, and increases want with advancing wealth; and I believe that in the explanation of this paradox we shall find the explanation of those recurring seasons of industrial and commercial paralysis which, viewed independently of their relations to more general phenomena, seem so inexplicable. Properly commenced and carefully pursued, such an investigation must yield a conclusion that will stand every test, and as truth, will correlate with all other truth. For in the sequence of phenomena there is no accident. Every effect has a cause, and every fact implies a preceding fact. . . .

The term rent, in its economic sense— that is, when used, as I am using it, to distinguish that part of the produce which accrues to the owners of land or other natural capabilities by virtue of their ownership—differs in meaning from the word rent as commonly used. In some respects this economic meaning is narrower than the common meaning; in other respects it is wider.

It is narrower in this: In common

speech, we apply the word rent to payments for the use of buildings, machinery, fixtures, etc., as well as to payments for the use of land or other natural capabilities; and in speaking of the rent of a house or the rent of a farm, we do not separate the price for the use of the improvements from the price for the use of the bare land. But in the economic meaning of rent, payments for the use of any of the products of human exertion are excluded, and of the lumped payments for the use of houses, farms, etc., only that part is rent which constitutes the consideration for the use of the land —that part paid for the use of buildings or other improvements being properly interest, as it is a consideration for the use of capital.

It is wider in this: In common speech we speak of rent only when owner and user are distinct persons. But in the economic sense there is also rent where the same person is both owner and user. Where owner and user are thus the same person, whatever part of his income he might obtain by letting the land to another is rent, while the return for his labor and capital are that part of his income which they would yield him did he hire instead of owning the land. Rent is also expressed in a selling price. When land is purchased, the payment which is made for the ownership, or right to perpetual use, is rent commuted or capitalized. If I buy land for a small price and hold it until I can sell it for a large price, I have become rich, not by wages for my labor or by interest upon my capital, but by the increase of rent. Rent, in short, is the share in the wealth produced which the exclusive right to the use of natural capabilities gives to the owner. Wherever land has an exchange value there is rent in the economic meaning of the term. Wherever land having a value is used, either by owner or hirer, there is rent actual; wherever it is not used, but still has a value, there is rent potential. It is this capacity of yielding rent which gives value to land. Until its ownership will confer some advantage, land has no value.

Thus rent or land value does not arise from the productiveness or utility of land. It in no wise represents any help or advantage given to production, but simply the power of securing a part of the results of production. No matter what are its capabilities, land can yield no rent and have no value until some one is willing to give labor or the results of labor for the privilege of using it; and what any one will thus give depends not upon the capacity of the land, but upon its capacity as compared with that of land that can be had for nothing. I may have very rich land, but it will yield no rent and have no value so long as there is other land as good to be had without cost. But when this other land is appropriated, and the best land to be had for nothing is inferior, either in fertility, situation, or other quality, my land will begin to have a value and yield rent. And though the productiveness of my land may decrease, yet if the productiveness of the land to be had without charge decreases in greater proportion, the rent I can get, and consequently the value of my land, will steadily increase. Rent, in short, is the price of monopoly, arising from the reduction to individual ownership of natural elements which human exertion can neither produce nor increase. . . .

Nothing can be clearer than the proposition that the failure of wages to increase with increasing productive power is due to the increase of rent.

Three things unite to production— labor, capital, and land.

Three parties divide the produce—the laborer, the capitalist, and the land owner.

If, with an increase of production the laborer gets no more and the capitalist no more, it is a necessary inference that the land owner reaps the whole gain.

And the facts agree with the inference. Though neither wages nor interest anywhere increase as material progress goes on, yet the invariable accompaniment and mark of material progress is the increase of rent—the rise of land values.

The increase of rent explains why wages and interest do not increase. The cause which gives to the land holder is the cause which denies to the laborer and capitalist. That wages and interest are higher in new than in old countries is not, as the standard economists say, because nature makes a greater return to the application of labor and capital, but because land is cheaper, and, therefore, as a smaller proportion of the return is taken by rent, labor and capital can keep for their share a larger proportion of what nature does return. It is not the total produce, but the net produce, after rent has been taken from it, that determines what can be divided as wages and interest. Hence, the rate of wages and interest is everywhere fixed, not so much by the productiveness of labor as by the value of land. Wherever the value of land is relatively low, wages and interest are relatively high; wherever land is relatively high, wages and interest are relatively low. . . .

In short, the value of land depending wholly upon the power which its ownership gives of appropriating wealth created by labor, the increase of land values is always at the expense of the value of labor. And, hence, that the increase of productive power does not increase wages, is because it does increase the value of land. Rent swallows up the whole gain and pauperism accompanies progress.

It is unnecessary to refer to facts. They will suggest themselves to the reader. It is the general fact, observable everywhere, that as the value of land increases, so does the contrast between wealth and want appear. It is the universal fact, that where the value of land is highest, civilization exhibits the greatest luxury side by side with the most piteous destitution. To see human beings in the most abject, the most helpless and hopeless condition, you must go, not to the unfenced prairies and the log cabins of new clearings in the backwoods, where man single-handed is commencing the struggle with nature, and land is yet worth nothing, but to the great cities, where the ownership of a little patch of ground is a fortune. . . .

We have traced the unequal distribution of wealth which is the curse and menace of modern civilization to the institution of private property in land. We have seen that so long as this institution exists no increase in productive power can permanently benefit the masses; but, on the contrary, must tend still further to depress their condition. We have examined all the remedies, short of the abolition of private property in land, which are currently relied on or proposed for the relief of poverty and the better distribution of wealth, and have found them all inefficacious or impracticable.

There is but one way to remove an evil—and that is, to remove its cause. Poverty deepens as wealth increases, and wages are forced down while productive power grows, because land, which is the source of all wealth and the field of all labor, is monopolized. To extirpate poverty, to make wages what justice commands they should be, the full earnings of the laborer, we must therefore substitute for the individual ownership of land a common ownership. Nothing else will go to the cause of the evil—in nothing else is there the slightest hope.

This, then, is the remedy for the unjust and unequal distribution of wealth apparent in modern civilization, and for all the evils which flow from it:

We must make land common property. . . .

When it is proposed to abolish private

property in land the first question that will arise is that of justice. Though often warped by habit, superstition, and selfishness into the most distorted forms, the sentiment of justice is yet fundamental to the human mind, and whatever dispute arouses the passions of men, the conflict is sure to rage, not so much as to the question "Is it wise?" as to the question "Is it right?"

This tendency of popular discussions to take an ethical form has a cause. It springs from a law of the human mind; it rests upon a vague and instinctive recognition of what is probably the deepest truth we can grasp. That alone is wise which is just; that alone is enduring which is right. In the narrow scale of individual actions and individual life this truth may be often obscured, but in the wider field of national life it everywhere stands out.

I bow to this arbitrament, and accept this test. If our inquiry into the cause which makes low wages and pauperism the accompaniments of material progress has led us to a correct conclusion, it will bear translation from terms of political economy into terms of ethics, and as the source of social evils show a wrong. If it will not do this, it is disproved. If it will do this, it is proved by the final decision. If private property in land be just, then is the remedy I propose a false one; if, on the contrary, private property in land be unjust, then is this remedy the true one.

What constitutes the rightful basis of property? What is it that enables a man justly to say of a thing, "It is mine?" From what springs the sentiment which acknowledges his exclusive right as against all the world? Is it not, primarily, the right of a man to himself, to the use of his own powers, to the enjoyment of the fruits of his own exertions? Is it not this individual right, which springs from and is testified to by the natural facts of individual organization—the fact that each particu-

lar pair of hands obey a particular brain and are related to a particular stomach; the fact that each man is a definite, coherent, independent whole—which alone justifies individual ownership? As a man belongs to himself, so his labor when put in concrete form belongs to him.

And for this reason, that which a man makes or produces is his own, as against all the world—to enjoy or to destroy, to use, to exchange, or to give. No one else can rightfully claim it, and his exclusive right to it involves no wrong to any one else. Thus there is to everything produced by human exertion a clear and indisputable title to exclusive possession and enjoyment which is perfectly consistent with justice, as it descends from the original producer, in whom it vested by natural law. The pen with which I am writing is justly mine. No other human being can rightfully lay claim to it, for in me is the title of the producers who made it. It has become mine, because transferred to me by the stationer, to whom it was transferred by the importer, who obtained the exclusive right to it by transfer from the manufacturer, in whom, by the same process of purchase, vested the rights of those who dug the material from the ground and shaped it into a pen. Thus, my exclusive right of ownership in the pen springs from the natural right of the individual to the use of his own faculties. . . .

With what other power is man by nature clothed, save the power of exerting his own faculties? How can he in any other way act upon or affect material things or other men? Paralyze the motor nerves, and your man has no more external influence or power than a log or stone. From what else, then, can the right of possessing and controlling things be derived? If it spring not from man himself, from what can it spring? Nature acknowledges no ownership or control in man save as the result of exertion. In no other way can her treasures be drawn forth, her powers directed, or her forces utilized or controlled. She makes no discriminations among men, but is to all absolutely impartial. She knows no distinction between master and slave, king and subject, saint and sinner. All men to her stand upon an equal footing and have equal rights. She recognizes no claim but that of labor, and recognizes that without respect to the claimant. . . .

If production gives to the producer the right to exclusive possession and enjoyment, there can rightfully be no exclusive possession and enjoyment of anything not the production of labor, and the recognition of private property in land is a wrong. For the right to the produce of labor cannot be enjoyed without the right to the free use of the opportunities offered by nature, and to admit the right of property in these is to deny the right of property in the produce of labor. When non-producers can claim as rent a portion of the wealth created by producers, the right of the producers to the fruits of their labor is to that extent denied.

There is no escape from this position. To affirm that a man can rightfully claim exclusive ownership in his own labor when embodied in material things, is to deny that any one can rightfully claim exclusive ownership in land. To affirm the rightfulness of property in land, is to affirm a claim which has no warrant in nature, as against a claim founded in the organization of man and the laws of the material universe. . . .

The moment this distinction is realized, that moment is it seen that the sanction which natural justice gives to one species of property is denied to the other; that the rightfulness which attaches to individual property in the produce of labor implies the wrongfulness of individual property in land; that, whereas the recognition of the one places all men upon equal terms, securing to each the due reward of his labor,

the recognition of the other is the denial of the equal rights of men, permitting those who do not labor to take the natural reward of those who do.

Whatever may be said for the institution of private property in land, it is therefore plain that it cannot be defended on the score of justice.

The equal right of all men to the use of land is as clear as their equal right to breathe the air—it is a right proclaimed by the fact of their existence. For we cannot suppose that some men have a right to be in this world and others no right.

If we are all here by the equal permission of the Creator, we are all here with an equal title to the enjoyment of his bounty—with an equal right to the use of all that nature so impartially offers. This is a right which is natural and inalienable; it is a right which vests in every human being as he enters the world, and which during his continuance in the world can be limited only by the equal rights of others. There is in nature no such thing as a fee simple in land. There is on earth no power which can rightfully make a grant of exclusive ownership in land. If all existing men were to unite to grant away their equal rights, they could not grant away the right of those who follow them. For what are we but tenants for a day? Have we made the earth, that we should determine the rights of those who after us shall tenant it in their turn? The Almighty, who created the earth for man and man for the earth, has entailed it upon all the generations of the children of men by a decree written upon the constitution of all things—a decree which no human action can bar and no prescription determine. Let the parchments be ever so many, or possession ever so long, natural justice can recognize no right in one man to the possession and enjoyment of land that is not equally the right of all his fellows. Though his titles have been acquiesced in by generation after generation, to the landed estates of the Duke of Westminster the poorest child that is born in London to-day has as much right as has his eldest son. Though the sovereign people of the State of New York consent to the landed possessions of the Astors, the puniest infant that comes wailing into the world in the squalidest room of the most miserable tenement house, becomes at that moment seized of an equal right with the millionaires. And it is robbed if the right is denied. . . .

We have traced the want and suffering that everywhere prevail among the working classes, the recurring paroxysms of industrial depression, the scarcity of employment, the stagnation of capital, the tendency of wages to the starvation point, that exhibit themselves more and more strongly as material progress goes on, to the fact that the land on which and from which all must live is made the exclusive property of some.

We have seen that there is no possible remedy for these evils but the abolition of their cause; we have seen that private property in land has no warrant in justice, but stands condemned as the denial of natural right—a subversion of the law of nature that as social development goes on must condemn the masses of men to a slavery the hardest and most degrading.

We have weighed every objection, and seen that neither on the ground of equity or expediency is there anything to deter us from making land common property by confiscating rent.

But a question of method remains. How shall we do it?

We should satisfy the law of justice, we should meet all economic requirements, by at one stroke abolishing all private titles, declaring all land public property, and letting it out to the highest bidders in lots to suit, under such conditions as would sacredly guard the private right to improvements. . . .

It is an axiom of statesmanship, which the successful founders of tyranny have understood and acted upon—that great changes can best be brought about under old forms. We, who would free men, should heed the same truth. It is the natural method. When nature would make a higher type, she takes a lower one and develops it. This, also, is the law of social growth. Let us work by it. With the current we may glide fast and far. Against it, it is hard pulling and slow progress.

I do not propose either to purchase or to confiscate private property in land. The first would be unjust; the second, needless. Let the individuals who now hold it still retain, if they want to, possession of what they are pleased to call *their* land. Let them continue to call it *their* land. Let them buy and sell, and bequeath and devise it. We may safely leave them the shell, if we take the kernel. *It is not necessary to confiscate land; it is only necessary to confiscate rent.*

Nor to take rent for public uses is it necessary that the State should bother with the letting of lands, and assume the chances of the favoritism, collusion, and corruption this might involve. It is not necessary that any new machinery should be created. The machinery already exists. Instead of extending it, all we have to do is to simplify and reduce it. By leaving to land owners a percentage of rent which would probably be much less than the cost and loss involved in attempting to rent lands through State agency, and by making use of this existing machinery, we may, without jar or shock, assert the common right to land by taking rent for public uses.

We already take some rent in taxation. We have only to make some changes in our modes of taxation to take it all.

What I, therefore, propose, as the simple yet sovereign remedy, which will raise wages, increase the earnings of capital, extirpate pauperism, abolish poverty, give remunerative employment to whoever wishes it, afford free scope to human powers, lessen crime, elevate morals, and taste, and intelligence, purify government and carry civilization to yet nobler heights, is— *to appropriate rent by taxation.*

In this way the State may become the universal landlord without calling herself so, and without assuming a single new function. In form, the ownership of land would remain just as now. No owner of land need be dispossessed, and no restriction need be placed upon the amount of land any one could. hold. For, rent being taken by the State in taxes, land, no matter in whose name it stood, or in what parcels it was held, would be really common property, and every member of the community would participate in the advantages of its ownership.

Now, insomuch as the taxation of rent, or land values, must necessarily be increased just as we abolish other taxes, we may put the proposition into practical form by proposing—

To abolish all taxation save that upon land values.

As we have seen, the value of land is at the beginning of society nothing, but as society develops by the increase of population and the advance of the arts, it becomes greater and greater. In every civilized country, even the newest, the value of the land taken as a whole is sufficient to bear the entire expenses of government. In the better developed countries it is much more than sufficient. Hence it will not be enough merely to place all taxes upon the value of land. It will be necessary, where rent exceeds the present governmental revenues, commensurately to increase the amount demanded in taxation, and to continue this increase as society progresses and rent advances. But this is so natural and easy a matter, that it may be considered as involved, or at least understood, in the proposition to put all taxes on the value of land. That is the first step, upon which the practical struggle must be made. When the hare is once caught and killed, cooking him will follow as a matter of course. When the common right to land is so far appreciated that all taxes are abolished save those which fall upon rent, there is no danger of much more than is necessary to induce them to collect the public revenues being left to individual land holders. . . .

The poverty which in the midst of abundance pinches and embrutes men, and all the manifold evils which flow from it, spring from a denial of justice. In permitting the monopolization of the opportunities which nature freely offers to all, we have ignored the fundamental law of justice—for, so far as we can see, when we view things upon a large scale, justice seems to be the supreme law of the universe. But by sweeping away this injustice and asserting the rights of all men to natural opportunities, we shall conform ourselves to the law—we shall remove the great cause of unnatural inequality in the distribution of wealth and power; we shall abolish poverty; tame the ruthless passions of greed; dry up the springs of vice and misery; light in dark places the lamp of knowledge; give new vigor to invention and a fresh impulse to discovery; substitute political strength for political weakness; and make tyranny and anarchy impossible.

The reform I have proposed accords with all that is politically, socially, or morally desirable. It has the qualities of a true reform, for it will make all other reforms easier. What is it but the carrying out in letter and spirit of the truth enunciated in the Declaration of Independence—the "self-evident" truth that is the heart and soul of the Declaration—*"That all men are created equal; that they are endowed by their Creator with certain unalienable rights; that among these are life, liberty, and the pursuit of happiness!"*

These rights are denied when the equal right to land—on which and by which men alone can live—is denied. Equality of political rights will not compensate for the denial of the equal right to the bounty of nature. Political liberty, when the equal right to land is denied, becomes, as population increases and invention goes on, merely the liberty to compete for employment at starvation wages. This is the truth that we have ignored.

Lester Frank Ward
1841-1913

The son of a mechanic, Lester Frank Ward was born in Joliet, Illinois. He served in the Union Army during the Civil War and was wounded at the battle of Chancellorsville. In 1865 he accepted a position with the Treasury Department and held that post until 1881. Meanwhile he studied at what today is George Washington University, receiving an A.B. in 1869, an LL.B. in 1871, and an A.M. in 1872. After leaving the Treasury Department, he joined the United States Geological Survey, where he made some valuable contributions to the natural sciences. Ward's fame, however, rests upon his numerous writings in the field of sociology.

Drawing on his broad background in the modern sciences, Ward attempted to apply the concept of evolution to sociology. In his view of evolution, he carefully distinguished between physical or animal evolution, which was essentially purposeless, and human evolution, which could be modified by purposive action. The most significant factor in Ward's system was the existence of mind, which enabled man to pass from passive to active evolutionary processes, from physical to human or social evolution. Hence, Ward was a staunch advocate of rational and scientific planning in order to direct the evolutionary process into socially desirable channels, and he influenced several generations of young sociologists who took up where he had left off.

The following selection, "Mind as a Social Factor," which appeared in Mind, *9 (October, 1884), is illustrative of Ward's interpretation of evolution.*

*C*an the *laissez faire* doctrine be successfully met? That all attempts to do this have been timidly made cannot be denied. That these have been few and feeble is equally certain. While there has existed in the minds of many rational persons a vague sense of some hidden fallacy in all this reasoning, none have felt competent to formulate their objections with sufficient clearness and force to warrant pitting them against the resistless stream of concurrent science and philosophy of the nineteenth century. There has, however, been developing of late a more or less marked apprehension with regard to the possible consequences of this mode of thought. The feeling is distinct in the best minds, and to a large extent in the public mind, that the tendency of modern ideas is nihilistic. It is clear that if they become universally accepted they must work stagnation in society. The *laissez faire* doctrine is a gospel of inaction, the scientific creed is struck with sterility, the policy of resigning all into the hands of Nature is a surrender.

But this recognition is by no means

proof that the prevalent opinions are false. At best it can only suggest this on the ground that true doctrines should be progressive. But this would be a *petitio principii*. Nature is not optimistic, still less anthropocentric. For aught we know, the laws of nature are such as make a recognition of strict scientific truth a positive barrier to social advancement. The argument we have been considering must be refuted, if at all, by legitimate counter-argument.

The present attempt to meet some parts of this argument is made in full consciousness of its strength as a factor in modern thought and with due deference to the great names that stand committed to it. The scientific facts which its defenders have brought to its support are, in the main, incontestable. To answer by denying these would be to abjure science and deserve contempt. The method of nature has been correctly interpreted. The doctrines of the survival of the fittest and natural selection are perfectly true doctrines. The law of competition is the fundamental law. It is unquestionably true that progress, not only in primary organic development, but also in society, has resulted from the action of this law.

After conceding all this, the attempt, notwithstanding, to stem the tide of modern scientific thought must, indeed, seem a hopeless one. At the outset it must be frankly acknowledged that if the current views are unsound the fault is not chargeable to science. If there is any defect it must lie in the inferences drawn from the facts and not in the facts themselves. To what extent, then, is the *laissez faire* doctrine, as defined and popularly accepted, an inference? If the method of nature is correctly formulated by that doctrine, wherein lies the fallacy when it is applied to man and to society? . . .

It has always been a marvel to my comprehension that wise men and philosophers, when smitten with the specious logic of the *laissez faire* school, can close their eyes to the most obtrusive fact that civilisation presents. In spite of the influence of philosophy, all forms of which have thus far been negative and nihilistic, the human animal, with his growing intellect, has still ever realised the power that is vouchsafed through mind, and has ever exercised that power. Philosophy would have long since robbed him of it and caused his early extermination from the earth but for the persistence, through heredity, of the impulse to exercise in self-preservation every power in his possession; by which practice alone he first gained his ascendancy ages before philosophy began.

The great fact, then, to which I allude is that, in spite of all philosophy, whether mythologic, metaphysical, or naturalistic, declaring that man must and can do nothing, he *has*, from the very dawn of his intelligence, been transforming the entire surface of the planet he inhabits. No other animal performs anything comparable to what man performs. This is solely because no other possesses the developed psychic faculty.

If we analyse mind into its two departments, sense and intellect, we shall see that it is through this latter faculty that these results are accomplished. If we inquire more closely into the mode by which intellect operates, we shall find that it serves as a guiding power to those natural forces with which it is acquainted (and no others), directing them into channels of human advantage. If we seek for a single term by which to characterise with precision the nature of this process, we find this in *Invention*. The essential characteristic of all intellectual action is invention.

Glancing now at the *ensemble* of human achievement, which may be collectively called civilisation, we readily see that it is all the result of this inventive process. All practical art is merely the product of successful invention, and it requires no undue expansion of the term, nor extraordinary power of generalisation, to see in all human institutions only modified forms of arts, and true products of the intellectual, or inventive, faculty.

But what is the general result of all this? An entirely new dispensation has been given to the world. All the materials and forces of nature have been thus placed completely under the control of one of the otherwise least powerful of the creatures inhabiting the earth. He has only to know them in order to become their master. Nature has thus been made the servant of man. Thus only has man succeeded in peopling the entire globe while all other animals are restricted to narrow faunal areas. He has also peopled certain portions far more densely than any other species could have done, and he seems destined to continue multiplying his numbers for a long time yet in the future. But this quantitative proof is even less telling than the qualitative. When we confine our attention to the *élite* of mankind we do not need to have the ways specified in detail by which the powers of mind have exalted the intellectual being above all other products of creation. At the present moment the most dense and the most enlightened populations of the globe occupy what are termed temperate latitudes, which means latitudes in which for from three to five months each year vegetation ceases entirely, the waters are locked in ice, and the temperature frequently sinks far below the zero of the Fahrenheit thermometer. Imagine the thin-skinned, furless animal man subsisting in such a climate. Extinguish his fires, banish his clothing, blot out the habitations that deck the civilised landscape. How long would the puny race survive? But these are not products of nature, they are products of *art*, the wages of thought—fruits of the intellect.

When a well-clothed philosopher on a bitter winter's night sits in a warm room well lighted for his purpose and writes on paper with pen and ink in the arbitrary characters of a highly developed language the statement that civilisation is the result of natural laws, and that man's duty is to let nature alone so that untrammeled it may work out a higher civilisation, he simply ignores every circumstance of his existence and deliberately closes his eyes to every fact within the range of his faculties. If man had acted upon his theory there would have been no civilisation, and our philosopher would have remained a troglodyte.

But how shall we distinguish this human, or anthropic, method from the method of nature? Simply by reversing all the definitions. Art is the antithesis of nature. If we call one the natural method we must call the other the artificial method. If nature's process is rightly named natural selection, man's process is artificial selection. The survival of the fittest is simply the survival of the strong, which implies, and might as well be called, the destruction of the weak. And if nature progresses through the destruction of the weak, man progresses through the *protection* of the weak. This is the essential distinction.

In human society the psychic power has operated to secure the protection of the weak in two distinct ways: first, by increasing the supply of the necessities of life, and, secondly, by preventing the destruction of life through the enemies of man. The immediate instrumentality through which the first of these processes is carried on is art, the product of invention. The second process takes place through the establishment of positive institutions.

It is difficult to say which of these agencies has been most effective. Both were always indispensable, and therefore all comparison is unprofitable.

Art operates to protect the weak against adverse surroundings. It is directed against natural forces, chiefly physical. By thus defeating the destructive influences of the elements and hostile forms of life, and by forcing nature to yield an unnatural supply of man's necessities, many who would have succumbed from inability to resist these adverse agencies—the feebler members of society—were able to survive, and population increased and expanded. While no one openly denies this, there is a tendency either to ignore it in politico-economic discussions, or to deny its application to them as an answer to naturalistic arguments.

If, on the other hand, we inquire into the nature of human institutions, we shall perceive that they are of three kinds, tending to protect the weak in three ways, or ascending degrees. These three successively higher means through which this end is attained are, first, Justice, second, Morality, and third, Charity. These forms of action have been reached through the development, respectively, of the three corresponding sentiments: Equity, Beneficence, and Benevolence.

All of these altruistic sentiments are wholly unknown, or known only in the merest embryo, to all animals below man, and therefore no such means of protection exist among them. They are strictly human, or anthropic. Many evolutionists fail to recognise this. Some sociologists refuse to admit it. They look about and see so much injustice, immorality and rapacity that they are led to suppose that only natural methods are in operation in society. This is a great mistake. In point of fact, the keener the sense of justice the more conspicuous the diminishing number of violations of it come to appear, and conversely, the obviousness of injustice proves the general prevalence of justice. It is the same with morality and philanthropy.

If we consider the effect of these three codes of human conduct in the direction of enabling the weaker ones to survive we shall see that it has been immense. Out of the first has arisen government, the chief value and function of which has always been and still is such protection. Great systems of jurisprudence have been elaborated, engrossing the attention of a large portion of the population of enlightened as well as of barbaric states. To say that these have been failures because often weighted with grave defects is to misinterpret history and misunderstand society. No one could probably be found to gainsay that the moral law of society has exerted a salutary influence, yet its aim is strictly altruistic, opposed to the law of the survival of the fittest, and wholly in the direction of enabling those to survive who would not survive without its protection. Finally, the last sentiment to be developed, and doubtless the highest, is so universally recognised as peculiar to man that his very name has been given to it—the sentiment of *humanity*. Yet the mode of protecting the weak arising out of this sentiment is the one that has been most seriously called in question by the naturalistic school. It must be admitted that humanitarian institutions have done far less good than either juridical or ethical institutions. The sentiment itself is of recent origin, the product only of highly developed and greatly refined mental organisation. It exists to an appreciable degree only in a minute fraction of the most enlightened populations. It is rarely directed with judgment; no fixed, self-enforcing code of conduct, as in the other cases, having had time to take shape. The institutions established to enforce it are for the most part poorly supported, badly managed, and often founded on a total misconception of human nature and of the true mode of attaining the end in view. Hence they are specially open to attack. But if ever humanitarian sentiments become diffused throughout the body politic, become the object of deep study, as have those of justice and right, it may be confidently predicted that society will prove itself capable of caring for the most unfortunate of its members in a manner that shall not work demoralisation.

In all these ways man, through his intelligence, has laboured successfully to resist the law of nature. His success is conclusively demonstrated by a comparison of his condition with that of other species of animals. No other cause can be assigned for his superiority. How can the naturalistic philosophers shut their eyes to such obvious facts? Yet, what is their attitude? They condemn all attempts to protect the weak, whether by private or public methods. They claim that it deteriorates the race by enabling the unfit to survive and transmit their inferiority. This is true only in certain cases of hereditary diseases or mental deficiencies, which should be taken account of by man because they are not by nature. Nothing is easier than to show that the unrestricted competition of nature does not secure the survival of the fittest possible, but only of the actually fittest, and in every attempt man makes to obtain something fitter than this actual fittest he succeeds, as witness improved breeds of animals and grafts of fruits. Now, the human method of protecting the weak deals in some such way with men. It not only increases the number but improves the quality.

But "government," at least, must *laisser faire*. It must not "meddle" with natural laws. The laws of trade, business, social intercourse, are natural laws, immutable and indestructible. All interference with them is vain. The fallacy here is a *non sequitur*. It may be readily granted that these laws are immutable and indestructible. Were this not the case it would certainly be hopeless to interfere with their action. But every mechanical invention proves that nothing is easier than to interfere successfully with the operation of these uniform natural forces. They have only to be first thoroughly understood and then they are easily *controlled*. To *destroy* a force is one thing, to control its action is quite another. Those who talk in this way involve themselves in the most palpable inconsistency. They must not be allowed to stop where they do. They must go on and carry their strictures to a logical conclusion. They must deny to government the right to protect its citizens from injustice. This is a clear interference with the natural laws of society. They must deny to society the right to enforce its code of morals. Nothing is more unnatural. They must suppress the healing art which keeps the sick from dying as they do among animals. Nor is this all. They must condemn all interference with physical laws and natural forces. To dam a stream must be characterised as a "vain" attempt to overcome a natural law. The wind must be left free to blow where it will, and not be forced against the fan of a wind-mill. The vapour of heated water must be allowed to float off naturally into the air and not be pent up in a steamboiler and thence conducted into the cylinder of a steam-engine. All these things and every other device of inventive man are so many attempts to "violate" the laws of nature, which is declared impossible.

What then remains of the *laissez faire* doctrine? Nothing but this: That it is useless, and may be dangerous, to attempt to control natural forces until their character is first well understood. This is a proposition which is true for every department of force, and does not involve the surrender of the whole domain of sociology after it has been demonstrated that society is a theatre of forces.

The truth thus comes forth from a rational study of nature and human society that social progress has been due only in very slight degree to natural evolution as accomplished through the survival of the fittest, and its chief success has resulted from the reduction of competition in the struggle for existence and the protection of the weaker members. Such competition, in so far as it has been permitted to operate, has tended to lower the standard of the fittest and to check advancement. It is not, of course, claimed that the natural method has ever been fully overcome. It has always operated, and still operates, powerfully in many ways. It has been chiefly in the simpler departments of physical and mechanical phenomena that the psychic, or anthropic, method has superseded it. The inventive arts have been the result. Vital forces have yielded to some extent to the influence of mind in bringing about improved stocks of animals and vegetables, and even certain social laws have come under rational control through the establishment of institutions. Still, every step in this progress has been contested. It was not enough that the intellect was feeble and ill-fitted to grapple with such problems. It was not enough that ignorance of nature's laws should cause unnumbered failures. A still stronger barrier was presented by the intellect itself in the form of positive error embodied in philosophy. As already remarked, philosophy has always been negative and nihilistic, and has steadily antagonised the common sense of mankind. It is only quite recently that there has come into existence anything like a truly *positive* philosophy, *i.e.*, a philosophy of *action*. The intellectual power of enlightened man has at length become sufficient to grasp the problems of social life. A large body of truth has been accumulated by which to be guided in their solution. Positive error in the drawing of false conclusions from established facts is now the chief obstacle. Rational interpretation has come to prevail in all the lower departments of phenomena. It is chiefly in the complex departments of psychic and social action that error still holds sway. Nothing remains to be done but to apply the established canons of science to these higher fields of activity. Here there is still competition. Here the weaker still go to the wall. Here the strong are still the fittest to survive. Here Nature still practises her costly selection which always involves the destruction of the defenceless. The demand is for still further reduction of competition, still greater interference with the operations of natural forces, still more complete control of the laws of nature, and still more absolute supremacy of the psychic over the natural method of evolution.

These ends will be secured in proportion as the true nature of mind is understood. When nature comes to be regarded as passive and man as active, instead of the reverse as now, when human action is recognised as the most important of all forms of action, and when the power of the human intellect over vital, psychic and social phenomena is practically conceded, then, and then only, can man justly claim to have risen out of the animal and fully to have entered the human stage of development.

Herbert Croly
1869-1930

A native son of New York City, Herbert Croly entered Harvard in 1886, leaving that institution several times only to return at later dates. In 1910 he finally received his bachelor's degree, which was awarded as of the class of 1890. From 1900 to 1906 he edited the Architectural Record, *but he resigned from that post in order to write his first and most important book,* The Promise of American Life. *In 1914, with the financial backing of Willard Straight, Croly founded the* New Republic, *which quickly became one of the outstanding journals of liberal intellectuals in the United States.*

Croly was in many respects one of the outstanding philosophical spokesmen for the early twentieth-century progressive movement. He maintained that in the new industrial society the older Jeffersonian liberal ideal had to be considerably modified, that liberals had to adopt Hamiltonian means of a strong central government in order to realize their Jeffersonian democratic ends. Influenced greatly by pragmatism, he insisted that all philosophies and political theories had to be considered in the light of existing realities. Croly was also a staunch believer in the idea of progress and argued that the democratic process involved constant evolution and adjustment to meet new conditions. In his eyes only a nationalistic, democratic liberalism, which involved a greater reliance upon the powers of the central government, could help to realize the promise of America. In other words, Croly hoped to harness nationalism in order to serve the general welfare. His theories influenced a whole generation of liberal intellectuals from the progressive era through the New Deal.

The selection that follows is from Croly's The Promise of American Life *(New York: The Macmillan Company, 1909).*

*I*t is ... essential to recognize that the individual American will never obtain a sufficiently complete chance of self-expression, until the American nation has earnestly undertaken and measurably achieved the realization of its collective purpose. As we shall see presently, the cure for this individual sterility lies partly with the individual himself or rather with the man who proposes to become an individual; and under any plan of economic or social organization, the man who proposes to become an individual is a condition of national as well as individual improvement. It is none the less true that any success in the achievement of the national purpose will contribute positively to the liberation of the individual, both by diminishing his temptations, improving his opportunities, and by enveloping him in an invigorating rather than an enervating moral and intellectual atmosphere.

It is the economic individualism of our existing national system which inflicts the most serious damage on American individuality; and American individual achievement in politics and science and the arts will remain partially impoverished as long as our fellow-countrymen neglect or refuse systematically to regulate the distribution of wealth in the national interest. I am aware, of course, that the prevailing American conviction is absolutely contradictory of the foregoing assertion. Americans have always associated individual freedom with the unlimited popular enjoyment of all available economic opportunities. Yet it would be far more true to say that the popular enjoyment of practically unrestricted economic opportunities is precisely the condition which makes for individual bondage. Neither does the bondage which such a system fastens upon the individual exist only in the case of those individuals who are victimized by the pressure of unlimited economic competition. Such victims exist, of course, in large numbers, and they will come to exist in still larger number hereafter; but hitherto, at least, the characteristic vice of the American system has not been the bondage imposed upon its victims. Much more insidious has been the bondage imposed upon the conquerors and their camp-followers. A man's individuality is as much compromised by success under the conditions imposed by such a system as it is by failure. His actual occupation may tend to make his individuality real and fruitful; but the quality of the work is determined by a merely acquisitive motive, and the man himself thereby usually debarred from obtaining any edifying personal

independence or any peculiar personal distinction. Different as American business men are one from another in temperament, circumstances and habits, they have a way of becoming fundamentally very much alike. Their individualities are forced into a common mold, because the ultimate measure of the value of their work is the same, and is nothing but its results in cash.

Consider for a moment what individuality and individual independence really mean. A genuine individual must at least possess some special quality which distinguishes him from other people, which unifies the successive phases and the various aspects of his own life and which results in personal moral freedom. In what way and to what extent does the existing economic system contribute to the creation of such genuine individuals? At best it asks of every man who engages in a business occupation that he make as much money as he can, and the only conditions it imposes on this pursuit of money are those contained in the law of the land and a certain conventional moral code. The pursuit of money is to arouse a man to individual activity, and law and custom determine the conditions to which the activity must conform. The man does not become an individual merely by obeying the written and unwritten laws. He becomes an individual because the desire to make money releases his energy and intensifies his personal initiative. The kind of individuals created by such an economic system are not distinguished one from another by any special purpose. They are distinguished by the energy and success whereby the common purpose of making money is accompanied and followed. Some men show more enterprise and ingenuity in devising ways of making money than others, or they show more vigor and zeal in taking advantage of the ordinary methods. These men are the kind of individuals which the existing economic system tends to encourage; and critics of the existing system are denounced, because of the disastrous effect upon individual initiative which would result from restricting individual economic freedom.

But why should a man become an individual because he does what everybody else does, only with more energy and success? The individuality so acquired is merely that of one particle in a mass of similar particles. Some particles are bigger than others and livelier; but from a sufficient distance they all look alike; and in substance and meaning they all are alike. Their individual activity and history do not make them less alike. It merely makes them bigger or smaller, livelier or more inert. Their distinction from their fellows is quantitative; the unity of their various phases a matter of repetition; their independence wholly comparative. Such men are associated with their fellows in the pursuit of a common purpose, and they are divided from their fellows by the energy and success with which that purpose is pursued. On the other hand, a condition favorable to genuine individuality would be one in which men were divided from one another by special purposes, and reunited in so far as these individual purposes were excellently and successfully achieved.

The truth is that individuality cannot be dissociated from the pursuit of a disinterested object. It is a moral and intellectual quality, and it must be realized by moral and intellectual means. A man achieves individual distinction, not by the enterprise and vigor with which he accumulates money, but by the zeal and the skill with which he pursues an exclusive interest—an interest usually, but not necessarily, connected with his means of livelihood. The purpose to which he is devoted—such, for instance, as that of painting or of running a railroad—is not exclusive in

the sense of being unique. But it becomes exclusive for the individual who adopts it, because of the single-minded and disinterested manner in which it is pursued. A man makes the purpose exclusive for himself by the spirit and method in which the work is done; and just in proportion as the work is thoroughly well done, a man's individuality begins to take substance and form. His individual quality does not depend merely on the display of superior enterprise and energy, although, of course, he may and should be as enterprising and as energetic as he can. It depends upon the actual excellence of the work in every respect,—an excellence which can best be achieved by the absorbing and exclusive pursuit of that alone. A man's individuality is projected into his work. He does not stop when he has earned enough money, and he does not cease his improvements when they cease to bring in an immediate return. He is identified with his job, and by means of that identification his individuality becomes constructive. His achievement, just because of its excellence, has an inevitable and an unequivocal social value. The quality of a man's work reunites him with his fellows. He may have been in appearance just as selfish as a man who spends most of his time in making money, but if his work has been thoroughly well done, he will, in making himself an individual, have made an essential contribution to national fulfillment.

Of course, a great deal of very excellent work is accomplished under the existing economic system; and by means of such work many a man becomes more or less of an individual. But in so far as such is the case, it is the work which individualizes and not the unrestricted competitive pursuit of money. In so far as the economic motive prevails, individuality is not developed; it is stifled. The man whose motive is that of money-making will not make the work any more excellent than is demanded by the largest possible returns; and frequently the largest possible returns are to be obtained by indifferent work or by work which has absolutely no social value. The ordinary mercenary purpose always compels a man to stop at a certain point, and consider something else than the excellence of his achievement. It does not make the individual independent, except in so far as independence is merely a matter of cash in the bank; and for every individual on whom it bestows excessive pecuniary independence, there are many more who are by that very circumstance denied any sort of liberation. Even pecuniary independence is usually purchased at the price of moral and intellectual bondage. Such genuine individuality as can be detected in the existing social system is achieved not because of the prevailing money-making motive, but in spite thereof.

The ordinary answer to such criticisms is that while the existing system may have many faults, it certainly has proved an efficient means of releasing individual energy; whereas the exercise of a positive national responsibility for the wholesome distribution of wealth would tend to deprive the individual of any sufficient initiative. The claim is that the money-making motive is the only one which will really arouse the great majority of men, and to weaken it would be to rob the whole economic system of its momentum. Just what validity this claim may have cannot, with our present experience, be definitely settled. That to deprive individuals suddenly of the opportunities they have so long enjoyed would be disastrous may be fully admitted. It may also be admitted that any immediate and drastic attempt to substitute for the present system a national regulation of the distribution of wealth or a national responsibility for the management even of monopolies or semi-monopolies would break down and would do little to promote either individual or social welfare. But to conclude from any such admissions that a systematic policy of promoting individual and national amelioration should be abandoned is wholly unnecessary. That the existing system has certain practical advantages, and is a fair expression of the average moral standards of to-day is not only its chief merit, but also its chief and inexcusable defect. What a democratic nation must do is not to accept human nature as it is, but to move in the direction of its improvement. The question it must answer is: How can it contribute to the increase of American individuality? The defender of the existing system must be able to show either (1) that it does contribute to the increase of American individuality; or that (2) whatever its limitations, the substitution of some better system is impossible.

Of course, a great many defenders of the existing system will unequivocally declare that it does contribute effectually to the increase of individuality, and it is this defense which is most dangerous, because it is due, not to any candid consideration of the facts, but to unreasoning popular prejudice and personal self-justification. The existing system contributes to the increase of individuality only in case individuality is deprived of all serious moral and intellectual meaning. In order to sustain their assertion they must define individuality, not as a living ideal, but as the psychological condition produced by any individual action. In the light of such a definition every action performed by an individual would contribute to individuality; and, conversely, every action performed by the state, which conceivably could be left to individuals, would diminish individuality. Such a conception derives from the early nineteenth century principles of an essential opposition between the state and the individual; and it is a deduction from the common conception of democracy as nothing but a finished political organization in which the popular will prevails. As applied in the traditional American system this conception of individuality has resulted in the differentiation of an abundance of raw individual material, but the raw material has been systematically encouraged to persist only on condition that it remained undeveloped. Properly speaking, it has not encouraged individualism at all. Individuality is necessarily based on genuine discrimination. It has encouraged particularism. While the particles have been roused into activity, they all remain dominated by substantially the same forces of attraction and repulsion. But in order that one of the particles may fulfill the promise of a really separate existence, he must pursue some special interest of his own. In that way he begins to realize his individuality, and in realizing his individuality he is coming to occupy a special niche in the national structure. A national structure which encourages individuality as opposed to mere particularity is one which creates innumerable special niches, adapted to all degrees and kinds of individual development. The individual becomes a nation in miniature, but devoted to the loyal realization of a purpose peculiar to himself. The nation becomes an enlarged individual whose special purpose is that of human amelioration, and in whose life every individual should find some particular but essential function.

It surely cannot be seriously claimed that the improvement of the existing economic organization for the sake of contributing to the increase of such genuine individuals is impossible. If genuine individuality depends upon the pursuit of an exclusive interest, promoted most certainly and completely by a disinterested motive, it must be encouraged by enabling men so far as possible to work from disinterested motives. Doubtless this is a difficult,

but it is not an impossible task. It cannot be completely achieved until the whole basis of economic competition is changed. At present men compete chiefly for the purpose of securing the most money to spend or to accumulate. They must in the end compete chiefly for the purpose of excelling in the quality of their work that of other men engaged in a similar occupation. And there are assuredly certain ways in which the state can diminish the undesirable competition and encourage the desirable competition.

The several economic reforms suggested in the preceding chapter would, so far as they could be successfully introduced, promote more disinterested economic work. These reforms would not, of course, entirely do away with the influence of selfish acquisitive motives in the economic field, because such motives must remain powerful as long as private property continues to have a public economic function. But they would at least diminish the number of cases in which the influence of the mercenary motive made against rather than for excellence of work. The system which most encourages mere cupidity is one which affords too many opportunities for making "easy money," and our American system has, of course, been peculiarly prolific of such opportunities. As long as individuals are allowed to accumulate money from mines, urban real estate, municipal franchises, or semi-monopolies of any kind, just to that extent will the economic system of the country be poisoned, and its general efficiency impaired. Men will inevitably seek to make money in the easiest possible way, and as long as such easy ways exist fewer individuals will accept cordially the necessity of earning their living by the sheer excellence of achievement. On the other hand, in case such opportunities of making money without earning it can be eliminated, there will be a much closer correspondence than there is at present between the excellence of the work and the reward it would bring. Such a correspondence would, of course, be far from exact. In all petty kinds of business innumerable opportunities would still exist of earning more money either by disregarding the quality of the work or sometimes by actually lowering it. But at any rate it would be work which would earn money, and not speculation or assiduous repose in an easy chair.

In the same way, just in so far as industry became organized under national control for the public benefit, there would be a much closer correspondence between the quality of the work and the amount of the reward. In a well-managed corporation a man is promoted because he does good work, and has shown himself capable of assuming larger responsibilities and exercising more power. His promotion brings with it a larger salary, and the chance of obtaining a larger salary doubtless has much to do with the excellence of the work; but at all events a man is not rewarded for doing bad work or for doing no work at all. The successful employee of a corporation has not become disinterested in his motives. Presumably he will not do any more work than will contribute to his personal advancement; and if the standard achievement in his office is at all relaxed, he will not be kept up to the mark by an exclusive and disinterested devotion to the work itself. Still, under such conditions a man might well become better than his own motives. Whenever the work itself was really interesting, he might become absorbed in it by the very momentum of his habitual occupation, and this would be particularly the case provided his work assumed a technical character. In that case he would have to live up to the standard, not merely of an office, but of a trade, a profession, a craft, an art or a science;

and if those technical standards were properly exacting, he would be kept up to the level of his best work by a motive which had almost become disinterested. He could not fall below the standard, even though he derived no personal profit from striving to live up to it, because the traditions and the honor of his craft would not let him.

The proposed economic policy of reform, in so far as it were successful, would also tend to stimulate labor to more efficiency, and to diminish its grievances. The state would be lending assistance to the effort of the working-man to raise his standard of living, and to restrict the demoralizing effect of competition among laborers who cannot afford to make a stand on behalf of their own interest. It should, consequently, increase the amount of economic independence enjoyed by the average laborer, diminish his "class consciousness" by doing away with his class grievances, and intensify his importance to himself as an individual. It would in every way help to make the individual workingman more of an individual. His class interest would be promoted by the nation in so far as such promotion was possible, and could be adjusted to a general policy of national economic construction. His individual interest would be left in his own charge; but he would have much more favorable opportunities of redeeming the charge by the excellence of his individual work than he has under the existing system. His condition would doubtless still remain in certain respects unsatisfactory, for the purpose of a democratic nation must remain unfulfilled just in so far as the national organization of labor does not enable all men to compete on approximately equal terms for all careers. But a substantial step would be made towards its improvement, and the road marked, perhaps, for still further advance.

CHAPTER XIX

THE LIBERAL
CHALLENGE
TO EVANGELICAL
PROTESTANTISM

In the years after Appomattox, Protestantism still dominated the American religious scene. For many, it constituted the basis of American society, providing an ethical code for like-mannered men to guide their actions along morally correct lines. It was true that Protestantism by no means presented a united front, for the various sects frequently came into conflict over theological and ethical problems. Yet the similarities by and large overshadowed the differences, and it was generally accepted as a truism that the Protestant vision inspired and gave meaning to the community. Certainly, the American democratic faith, no matter how defined, ultimately rested on the foundation of Protestant morality and theology.

In the latter part of the nineteenth century, however, the rapid industrialization of the nation began to pose new issues and challenges to the fabric of institutional religion. Increasingly, ministers began to find themselves hard pressed to answer the new questions within the framework of the older theology. The Protestant ethic, after all, had developed out of the idea of individual responsibility and judgment, whereby each person ultimately faced his Maker by himself without the intercession of any institutional mechanism. In turn, this ethic had evolved a philosophy based on hard work, frugality, and stewardship, qualities that were well-adapted to a materialistic society functioning in an environment of abundance. As a result, Protestantism by the mid-nineteenth century became largely a means of justifying the status quo. Even before the Civil War, for example, it had developed arguments in support of laissez faire.

The problems of an industrialized society, nevertheless, were not so easily answered within an individualistic theological framework. Consequently, the various sects set about to reconstruct their basic tenets in such a way as to retain their essential character while at the same time making them relevant to the new issues confronting their members. Yet because of social, economic, and doctrinal diversity, Protestant theologians were unable to find a common ground acceptable to all. Those ministers coming from middle- or upper-class churches tended to reflect the more conservative views of their congregations, and they were quick to reiterate the religious case for laissez faire. Henry Ward Beecher, for example, the outstanding preacher of his day and a staunch defender of evolution, even went so far as to advocate the use of naked force against striking workers. And on the whole, most Protestant churches tended to support the conservative outlook of Beecher, even if they did not always accept his theology.

A small minority of ministers, however, cognizant of the dangers facing religion if it could not provide an adequate justification for its continued existence, attempted a restatement of essentials. Developing what became known as the social gospel, these dissenting ministers focused their efforts on resolving the growing social tensions within a society in which class conflict seemed about to erupt. Insisting that religion had a vital role to play, they reiterated their belief that the achievement of social harmony lay within the sphere of Christianity. The chief feature of the social gospel was its emphasis on the redemption of society rather than on individual salvation. To the ministers of the social gospel, it was apparent that individuals could not lead moral lives in an immoral environment. Therefore, the ministers of the social gospel became social and economic reformers as well as theologians. Emphasizing the potentialities for good in every individual, they sought the application of moral law to society and the substitution of cooperation for competition. Ultimately, they came to assert confidently that the ideal of the Kingdom of God could be partly attained only by those who followed in the footsteps of Jesus.

The social gospel, however, was only one manifestation of a liberalized Protestantism working to redefine the theistic basis of American society in the light of new conditions. Equally important were the efforts of those ministers who sought to show that there was no essential conflict between the new scientific naturalism and the older theism, and in this way sought to defend the relevance of Christianity. John Fiske, the philosopher-historian and champion of evolution, aided their cause by identifying natural law as teleological in character and by insisting that man's spiritual evolution was the goal of all development. Others, in creating what has since been called "modernism," or "liberal Protestantism," attempted to rise above all creeds and sectarian differences to establish a universal faith based on universal evolution—a faith that would complement rather than contradict science. Essentially, the modernists were working toward a new synthesis of religion and politics in terms of socialized and undogmatic Christianity whose importance in a complex world would be unquestioned.

To many reared in an atmosphere emphasizing individual piety and Christian morality, however, the liberal or modernistic version of Protestantism constituted anathema, if not heresy. Inclined to accept the Bible as the revealed truth of God, they insisted that Protestant fundamentals remain unchanged. Viewing with alarm the rise of the city with its polyglot conglomerations, its alien traditions, its apparent vices and corruption, and especially the intrusion of non-Protestant elements which would undermine American homogeneity, these rural-oriented, intellectually unsophisticated, insecure individuals reacted violently against any changes that might undermine or destroy their safe, familiar world. Seeking to conserve both their faith and way of life, they were ripe for an evangelical revival that would once more reassert the older and tested beliefs. Thus the religious awakening that swept through America in the latter part of the nineteenth and early twentieth century symbolized the repudiation of the new developments in Protestantism and marked a return to the ideal of a more simplistic society based upon the twin characteristics of independence and virtue.

There were, of course, many Protestant sects that cannot be confined so easily within a liberal or conservative framework. Christian Science, for example, founded by Mrs. Mary Baker Eddy in the 1870's, was a religion based upon a conviction that matter had no real existence, and that sin, poverty, illness, pain, and death were illusions. All of these "errors" would disappear when the mortal mind entered into a harmonious relation with the Eternal Mind. Like many other novel sects in American religious history, Christian Science became popular because it appealed in part to the American sense of mysticism. Making its strongest impact among middle-class urban groups, Christian Science provided many with a sense of serenity amidst pressing social and economic tensions and offered an alternative to the materialistic values that had become dominant in American society.

In adjusting itself to a new age, therefore, Protestantism tended to divide into a number of different and sometimes conflicting elements. One group was willing to interpret essentials anew in the hope of demonstrating their relevance and importance to the problems of an industrial age. In so doing, this group laid the groundwork for a religious version of the reform impulse that constituted an integral part of the progressive movement. Another element, however, bitterly resisted change, and insisted that theological definitions and interpretations of morality remain the same. In a sense, the conflict within Protestantism was a reflection of the changes that were transforming America as it entered a new era of its history.

Dwight L. Moody

1837-1899

Born in Northfield, Massachusetts, the son of a brickmason whose ancestors had emigrated from England in 1633, Dwight L. Moody by his early twenties was a highly successful salesman. After moving to Chicago in 1856, questions of religion and human welfare began increasingly to claim his time and interest. By 1858 he had organized a sabbath school, and developed a program of evangelical services, home visitation, and social and welfare work. In 1860 he decided to devote his entire time to this work, and became an independent city missionary.

Moody was one of the outstanding evangelists of his time, and he preached his message to millions of people, both in the United States and abroad. Like his predecessor, Charles G. Finney, Moody was concerned with the salvation of the individual's soul, arguing that a truly converted Christian was free from all sin and temptations. A premillennialist, he insisted upon the weakness of unaided human endeavor and the need to concentrate upon humility. Such being the case, Moody maintained that society could be reformed only if the individual first was able to regenerate himself. Thus, to Moody, social reform was dependent on the spiritual regeneration brought about by ancillary religious revival.

The esteem in which Moody was held by millions of his countrymen derived from the simple message of hope that he brought to them. To men caught up in a period of profound social change, the Second Coming of Christ was far more reassuring than secular plans for reforming society—though the premillennial faith was for many a form of escapism from the apparently insurmountable problems of the day. Phrasing his message in the most simple terms possible, Moody caught the imagination of nonintellectual Protestant America, and he began a period of revival that was to last over a quarter of a century.

The following selection is from one of his sermons entitled ''The Inspiration of the Bible,'' published in Moody's Latest Sermons (*Providence, Rhode Island, 1894*).

A gentleman came out to one of our meetings some time ago and said he hoped to get in that series of meetings an awakening that would last him all his life. I told he might as well try to eat enough to last him all his life. I told him he might as well try to eat enough at one time as to try to get an awakening that would last him all of his life. That is a mistake that people are making; they are running to religious meetings and they think the meetings are going to do the work. But if they don't bring you into closer contact with the word of God, the whole impression will be gone in three months. In the cx. Psalm, David prays nine times that God will quicken him according to His laws, according to His judgments, according to His precepts, according to His word. Now, if you get that kind of an awakening you have got something that is going to abide, because God's word is going to abide forever. That is substantial.

Now, another thing—you need to take the whole Bible and not a part of it. There are a great many people that are living on a few chapters and verses. They don't take the whole of the Scripture. I want to say before I forget it, that Sunday school teachers are making a woeful mistake if they don't take the whole Bible into their Sunday school classes. I don't care how young your children are, let them understand it is one book, that there are no two books—the Old Testament and the New are all one. Don't let them think that the Old Testament doesn't come to us with the same authority as the New. It is a great thing for a boy or girl to know how to handle the Bible. What is an army good for if they don't know how to handle their swords? Now, I speak very strong on this, because I was brought up in a Sabbath school that didn't have a single Bible in it. We used to have these old question books. Do you know what they are like? There are questions, and the answers are given just below; so that you don't need to study your lesson. Mother had a Bible, it was a family Bible, but she was so afraid that we would tear it that she kept it in the spare room, once in a great while we were allowed to look at it. The thing that interested me most was the family record—when Dwight was born, when father and mother were married. Those were the most interesting things to me, you know. So when I got to be a man and my beard began to come out, I was bigger then than I am now, in my own estimation. I knew it all. Oh yes! You couldn't tell me much. I was wiser than my grandfather or my great-grandfather, or all the grandsires behind me. I came down here to Boston from the country and went into a Bible class where there were a good many Harvard students. Their families belonged to the church, I suppose, and they came home to spend the Sabbath, or perhaps they came home every day. I was put into this class of young men. They handed me a Bible and told me the lesson was in John. I hunted all through the Old Testament for John, but couldn't find it. I saw the fellows hunching one another, "Ah, greenie from the country." Now, you know that is just the time when you don't want to be considered green. The teacher saw my embarrassment and handed me his Bible, and I put my thumb in the place and held on. I didn't lose my place. I said then that if I ever got out of that scrape, I would never be caught there again. Why is it that so many young men from 18 to 20 cannot be brought into a Bible class? Because they don't want to expose their ignorance. There is no place in the world that is so fascinating as a live Bible class. I believe that we are to blame that they have been brought up in the Sunday school without Bibles, and brought up with these quarterlies. The result is, the boys are growing up without knowing how to handle the Bible. They don't know where Matthew is, they don't know where the Epistle of the Ephesians is, they don't know where to find Hebrews or any of the different books of the Bible. They ought to be taught how to handle the whole Bible, and it can be done by Sunday school teachers taking the Bible into the class and going right about it at once. You can get a Bible in this country for almost a song now. Sunday schools are not so poor that they cannot get Bibles. Some time ago there came up in a large Bible class a question, and they thought they would refer to the Bible, but they found that there was not a single one in the class. So they went to the pews, but could not find one there. Finally they went to the pulpit and took the pulpit's Bible and settled the question. We are making wonderful progress, aren't we? Quarterlies are all right in their places, but if they are going to sweep the Bibles out of our Sunday schools, I think we had better sweep them out.

Now, a word about the whole Bible. I believe it is a master stroke of Satan to get us to doubt any portion of the Bible. If he can get us to doubt just one thing in that book he has accomplished a great point, and it is going to be the overthrow of many a man's and woman's faith. If I had the right to cut this out of the Bible and Mr. Sankey that and Mr. H. that it wouldn't be long before the whole Bible would be cut up. Once a gentleman took a Bible to his minister and said he wanted to show him the minister's Bible. The pastor said, "Why do you call it the minister's Bible? That isn't my Bible." Well, said the man, "I have sat under your ministry for some time, and when you have thrown anything out I have cut it out of the Bible." And he had got all of the Book of Job cut out, all Revelations, the Songs of Solomon, and about a third

of the Bible was cut out. The minister said, "I wish you would leave that Bible with me." He didn't want the people to see the book in that condition. But the man said, "Oh, no! I have got the covers and I'm going to hold on to them." And off he went holding on to the covers. If you were to hear some men preach, you wouldn't have anything but the covers in a few months. People say, "What, so you do with what you cannot understand?" I don't do anything with it. A man said to me once, "What do you do with what you don't understand?" "I don't do anything with it." "How do you understand it?" "I don't understand it." "Well, how do you interpret it?" "I don't interpret it." "What do you do with it?" "I don't do anything with it." "Don't do anything with it? Do you believe it?" "Yes, I believe it." Of course I do. I am glad there is a height I know nothing about in the Old Book, a length and a breadth we know nothing about. It makes the book all the more fascinating. I thank God it is beyond me. It is a pretty good proof that it came from God and not from the hand of man. You can take a chapter and read it for 365 days in the year, and always find something new in that chapter. Now, talk about believing in the New and Old Testament. What portion is there in the New Testament that you cannot find in the Old? In Matthew alone there are 100 quotations from the Old Testament. There are 89 chapters in the Four Gospels, and there are 142 quotations taken from the Old Testament.

There are 240 quotations in Revelations taken from the Old Testament. It is absurd for men to take one portion of the Bible and throw out the rest.

Another thing, there is not a thing in that Old Testament that men are cavilling about that God did not set His seal to when He was down here. Men say, "You don't believe in the story of those five cities being destroyed by fire,

Sodom and Gomorrah and those three others?'' Certainly. They were buying and selling until judgment came and swept them away. ''And so it shall be in the coming of the Son of God.'' Men say, ''You don't believe in the story of Elijah being fed by that widow do you?'' Certainly, Christ said there were many widows in the days of Elijah, but Elijah was fed by only one widow. Why! Christ believed it, He referred to it Himself, He set His seal to it. The Son of God believed it, and ''shall the servant be above his master?'' Men say ''do you believe the story about the Israelites being fed on manna?'' Certainly. ''As Moses lifted up the serpent in the wilderness, even so must the Son of Man be lifted up.'' He connected that with His own cross. And then at last they look as wise as owls and say, ''You certainly don't believe in the story of Jonah and the whale?'' Yes, I believe in that. When I give that up I am going to give up the resurrection. As you get along in life and you have perhaps as many friends on the other side of the river as you have on this side, you will get about as much comfort out of the story of Jonah as any other story in the Bible. May God help us to hold on to it! Jesus connected that with His own resurrection. In Matthew they said thrice, ''Show us a sign.'' And He said that the only sign should be the story of Jonah in the whale's belly. Christ believed that Jonah went into the whale's belly, and are you going to be His disciple and be wiser than He? Men say, ''It is a physical impossibility for a whale to swallow a man.'' It says, ''God prepared a great fish.'' That is enough. If God created a whale, couldn't He create a fish large enough to swallow a man? He can create a fish large enough to swallow the whole world at one swallow. It is astonishing how men are sneering and jeering at the idea that God couldn't do it. A friend of mine was going back to Scotland, and he heard a couple of these little modern philosophers discussing the Bible. One said, ''The Bible says that Balaam's ass spoke. Now, I am a scientific man, and I have taken the pains to examine an ass' mouth, and it is so formed that it couldn't speak.'' He was going to toss the whole Bible over because Balaam's ass couldn't speak. My friend said he stood it just as long as he could, and finally he said, ''Ah man you make an ass and I will make him speak.'' The idea that the God who made the ass couldn't speak through his mouth! Did you ever hear such stuff? and yet this was one of your modern philosophers!

Then there is another class of people (and I am sorry that I am now talking to those in the church, some of your modern church members, and some that profess to be Christians) who say, ''Of course I believe the Bible, but I don't believe the supernatural part.'' Well, now, if you are going to throw out that part, you might just as well burn it up and throw it away. There is no part of the Bible that doesn't teach supernatural things. You read that God went up from talking with Abraham. Now if that didn't take place, then the man that wrote Genesis knew he was telling a lie, and out goes Genesis. You go into Exodus and there are the ten plagues and Moses going through the Red Sea, the water coming out of the rock and all those supernatural things. Now if those things were not so the man that wrote it knew that he was telling a deliberate, wilful lie. Out goes Exodus. You go into Numbers, and there is Moses making a brass serpent, which is put onto a pole and the people are healed. If that didn't take place out goes that book. And so you can go into all the books of the Old Testament, and there is not one that hasn't something supernatural in it. You cannot touch Jesus Christ anywhere that there is not something supernatural about Him.

He drops down to tell the virgin that she was to be the mother of that child, and when Christ was born there came a fire down from heaven to shout His praises. That was all supernatural. His being warned and going off into Egypt was supernatural. When He commenced His ministry there was not a day when he was not doing something supernatural. One day he speaks to the leper, and he is made whole; one day He speaks to the sea and the sea obeys Him. When He died the sun refused to look upon that scene; this old world recognized Him, and the earth reeled and rocked like a drunken man. The earth knew Him. That was supernatural. And when He burst asunder the bands of death and came out of Joseph's sepulchre that was supernatural. Christmas Evans, the great Welch preacher says, "Many reformations die with the reformer, but this reformer ever lives to carry on His reformation." Thank God we don't worship a dead Jew. Do you suppose we would have this audience here today if we were worshiping a dead Christ? Not by a good deal. If he worshiped a dead Jew we wouldn't have been quickened and given life to our souls. I thank God that our Christ is a supernatural Christ, and this book a supernatural book, and I thank God that I live in a country where it is so free that all men can read it.

Now about what Christ says about Himself. He says the Scriptures cannot be broken. Let us keep in mind that the only scriptures the apostles of Christ had was the Old Testament. The New Testament wasn't written. He means every word He says. Devil or man cannot break the word of God. Why, I would as soon doubt my own existence as to doubt that book. How any man can for one moment doubt the veracity of the Bible is a mystery to me.

Now, Christ says in one place, "Heaven and earth shall pass, but not one jot or tittle of the law shall pass until the law

is fulfilled." Then, in another place, "Heaven and earth shall pass away, but my word shall not pass away." Now, I will put that as the old and new covenant. "Not one jot or tittle of the law shall pass until the law shall be fulfilled, the new covenant, and then Christ comes and adds these words, "Heaven and earth shall pass away, but my word shall not pass away." Now, notice how that has been fulfilled. There was no shorthand reporter following Him around taking down His words; there were no papers to print His sermons, and they wouldn't have printed the sermons if there had been any daily papers. The whole church and all the religious world was against Him. I can see one of your modern free thinkers standing near Him, and he hears Christ say, "Heaven and earth shall pass away, but my word shall not pass away." I see the scornful look on his face as he says, "Hear that Jewish peasant talk! Did you ever hear such conceit, such madness? He says Heaven and earth shall pass away, but His words shall not pass away." My friends, I want to ask you this question— have they passed away? Go and ask your infidels if His words have passed away. Do you know that the sun shines today on more Bibles than it has ever shone on before? Did you know that the American Bible society and the London Bible society issue 1500 Bibles every hour? Thank God the Bibles are not going out; they are just coming in! More Bibles have been printed in the last eight years than in the last 1800 years. The Bible is printed in 350 different languages—it is going to the darkest corners of the earth. "Heaven and earth shall pass away, but my word shall not pass away." Are His words passing away! No and thank God they are not going to pass away. You and I will pass away, and the world will pass away, but His word is going to live and endure. It cannot be wiped out. God broke the bands and is coming down along the ages. When they brought out the new version the American committee brought it out at the same hour as it was put out in London. It was thrown on the market on Friday morning and that would bring it out Friday afternoon. They couldn't send it to Chicago because it was so late, and so an enterprising concern set 90 different operators at work, and had the whole book telegraphed to Chicago and brought out Sunday morning. Nearly 1,900 years after Christ left the world that happened, and yet men are running around and telling us that the book is going out! But my time is up. I will take this subject up again on Tuesday, and we will go into it deeper. I have only touched it yet. Bring your Bibles along with you, and your pencils and paper. It will be a good thing to wear out your Bibles. I don't like these gilt edged Bibles that look as if they had never been used. Don't be afraid to soil them. Bring them along with you.

Walter
Rauschenbusch
1861-1918

Walter Rauschenbusch was born in Rochester, New York, the son of German immigrants who had fled to the United States following the abortive revolutions of 1848. He received his A.B. from the University of Rochester in 1884, and two years later graduated from the Rochester Theological Seminary. Ordained as a Baptist minister, he served for eleven years as a pastor of a German church in New York City before being called to the Rochester Theological Seminary in 1897.

His New York City pastorate enabled him to see firsthand the ravages of the industrial depression that began in 1893, and also gave him the opportunity to read widely in socialist and reform literature. As a result, he turned to the task of renovating a theology that had dominated Christianity for centuries and in the process became the outstanding philosopher of the social gospel in the United States. Believing that the conditions of society frequently made men evil, Rauschenbusch insisted that a moral law be substituted for the law of the jungle and he advocated a form of revisionist socialism. The new society would be brought into existence by widening the concept of the "Kingdom of God" and applying it to the social organism. A staunch advocate of democracy, which he defined in terms of cooperation among free men of good will, Rauschenbusch held out hope and a vision of a better world to come, though by no means did he believe that the Kingdom of God could be fully realized on earth.

The following selection is from Rauschenbusch's most famous and important book, A Theology for the Social Gospel *(New York: The Macmillan Company, 1917).*

The social movement is the most important ethical and spiritual movement in the modern world, and the social gospel is the response of the Christian consciousness to it. Therefore it had to be. The social gospel registers the fact that for the first time in history the spirit of Christianity has had a chance to form a working partnership with real social and psychological science. It is the religious reaction on the historic advent of democracy. It seeks to put the democratic spirit, which the Church inherited from Jesus and the prophets, once more in control of the institutions and teachings of the Church. . . .

If theology is to offer an adequate doctrinal basis for the social gospel, it must not only make room for the doctrine of the Kingdom of God, but give it a central place and revise all other doctrines so that they will articulate organically with it.

This doctrine is itself the social gospel. Without it, the idea of redeeming the social order will be but an annex to the orthodox conception of the scheme of salvation. It will live like a negro servant family in a detached cabin back of the white man's house in the South. If this doctrine gets the place which has always been its legitimate right, the practical proclamation and application of social morality will have a firm footing. . . .

In the following brief propositions I should like to offer a few suggestions, on behalf of the social gospel, for the theological formulation of the doctrine of the Kingdom. Something like this is needed to give us "a theology for the social gospel."

1. The Kingdom of God is divine in its origin, progress and consummation. It was initiated by Jesus Christ, in whom the prophetic spirit came to its consummation, it is sustained by the Holy Spirit, and it will be brought to its fulfilment by the power of God in his own time. The passive and active resistance of the Kingdom of Evil at every stage of its advance is so great, and the human resources of the Kingdom of God so slender, that no explanation can satisfy a religious mind which does not see the power of God in its movements. The Kingdom of God, therefore, is miraculous all the way, and is the continuous revelation of the power, the righteousness, and the love of God. The establishment of a community of righteousness in mankind is just as much a saving act of God as the salvation of an individual from his natural selfishness and moral inability. The Kingdom of God, therefore, is not merely ethical, but has a rightful place in theology. This doctrine is absolutely necessary to establish that organic union between religion and morality, between theology and ethics, which is one of the characteristics of the Christian religion. When our moral actions are

consciously related to the Kingdom of God they gain religious quality. Without this doctrine we shall have expositions of schemes of redemption and we shall have systems of ethics, but we shall not have a true exposition of Christianity. The first step to the reform of the Churches is the restoration of the doctrine of the Kingdom of God.

2. The Kingdom of God contains the teleology of the Christian religion. It translates theology from the static to the dynamic. It sees, not doctrines or rites to be conserved and perpetuated, but resistance to be overcome and great ends to be achieved. Since the Kingdom of God is the supreme purpose of God, we shall understand the Kingdom so far as we understand God, and we shall understand God so far as we understand his Kingdom. As long as organized sin is in the world, the Kingdom of God is characterized by conflict with evil. But if there were no evil, or after evil has been overcome, the Kingdom of God will still be the end to which God is lifting the race. It is realized not only by redemption, but also by the education of mankind and the revelation of his life within it.

3. Since God is in it, the Kingdom of God is always both present and future. Like God it is in all tenses, eternal in the midst of time. It is the energy of God realizing itself in human life. Its future lies among the mysteries of God. It invites and justifies prophecy, but all prophecy is fallible; it is valuable in so far as it grows out of action for the Kingdom and impels action. No theories about the future of the Kingdom of God are likely to be valuable or true which paralyze or postpone redemptive action on our part. To those who postpone, it is a theory and not a reality. It is for us to see the Kingdom of God as always coming, always pressing in on the present, always big with possibility, and always inviting immediate action. We walk by faith. Every human life is so

placed that it can share with God in the creation of the Kingdom, or can resist and retard its progress. The Kingdom is for each of us the supreme task and the supreme gift of God. By accepting it as a task, we experience it as a gift. By labouring for it we enter into the joy and peace of the Kingdom as our divine fatherland and habitation.

4. Even before Christ, men of God saw the Kingdom of God as the great end to which all divine leadings were pointing. Every idealistic interpretation of the world, religious or philosophical, needs some such conception. Within the Christian religion the idea of the Kingdom gets its distinctive interpretation from Christ. (*a*) Jesus emancipated the idea of the Kingdom from previous nationalistic limitations and from the debasement of lower religious tendencies, and made it world-wide and spiritual. (*b*) He made the purpose of salvation essential in it. (*c*) He imposed his own mind, his personality, his love and holy will on the idea of the Kingdom. (*d*) He not only foretold it but initiated it by his life and work. As humanity more and more develops a racial consciousness in modern life, idealistic interpretations of the destiny of humanity will become more influential and important. Unless theology has a solidaristic vision higher and fuller than any other, it can not maintain the spiritual leadership of mankind, but will be outdistanced. Its business is to infuse the distinctive qualities of Jesus Christ into its teachings about the Kingdom, and this will be a fresh competitive test of his continued headship of humanity.

5. The Kingdom of God is humanity organized according to the will of God. Interpreting it through the consciousness of Jesus we may affirm these convictions about the ethical relations within the Kingdom: (*a*) Since Christ revealed the divine worth of life and personality, and since his salvation seeks the restoration and fulfilment of even the least, it follows that the Kingdom of God, at every stage of human development, tends toward a social order which will best guarantee to all personalities their freest and highest development. This involves the redemption of social life from the cramping influence of religious bigotry, from the repression of self-assertion in the relation of upper and lower classes, and from all forms of slavery in which human beings are treated as mere means to serve the ends of others. (*b*) Since love is the supreme law of Christ, the Kingdom of God implies a progressive reign of love in human affairs. We can see its advance wherever the free will of love supersedes the use of force and legal coercion as a regulative of the social order. This involves the redemption of society from political autocracies and economic oligarchies; the substitution of redemptive for vindictive penology; the abolition of constraint through hunger as part of the industrial system; and the abolition of war as the supreme expression of hate and the completest cessation of freedom. (*c*) The highest expression of love is the free surrender of what is truly our own, life, property, and rights. A much lower but perhaps more decisive expression of love is the surrender of any opportunity to exploit men. No social group or organization can claim to be clearly within the Kingdom of God which drains others for its own ease, and resists the effort to abate this fundamental evil. This involves the redemption of society from private property in the natural resources of the earth, and from any condition in industry which makes monopoly profits possible. (*d*) The reign of love tends toward the progressive unity of mankind, but with the maintenance of individual liberty and the opportunity of nations to work out their own national peculiarities and ideals.

6. Since the Kingdom is the supreme

end of God, it must be the purpose for which the Church exists. The measure in which it fulfils this purpose is also the measure of its spiritual authority and honour. The institutions of the Church, its activities, its worship, and its theology must in the long run be tested by its effectiveness in creating the Kingdom of God. For the Church to see itself apart from the Kingdom, and to find its aims in itself, is the same sin of selfish detachment as when an individual selfishly separates himself from the common good. The Church has the power to save in so far as the Kingdom of God is present in it. If the Church is not living for the Kingdom, its institutions are part of the "world." In that case it is not the power of redemption but its object. It may even become an anti-Christian power. If any form of church organization which formerly aided the Kingdom now impedes it, the reason for its existence is gone.

7. Since the Kingdom is the supreme end, all problems of personal salvation must be reconsidered from the point of view of the Kingdom. It is not sufficient to set the two aims of Christianity side by side. There must be a synthesis, and theology must explain how the two react on each other. . . . The entire redemptive work of Christ must also be reconsidered under this orientation. Early Greek theology saw salvation chiefly as the redemption from ignorance by the revelation of God and from earthliness by the impartation of immortality. It interpreted the work of Christ accordingly, and laid stress on his incarnation and resurrection. Western theology saw salvation mainly as forgiveness of guilt and freedom from punishment. It interpreted the work of Christ accordingly, and laid stress on the death and atonement. If the Kingdom of God was the guiding idea and chief end of Jesus—as we know it was—we may be sure that every step in His life, including His death, was related to that aim and its realization, and when the idea of the Kingdom of God takes it due place in theology, the work of Christ will have to be interpreted afresh.

8. The Kingdom of God is not confined within the limits of the Church and its activities. It embraces the whole of human life. It is the Christian transfiguration of the social order. The Church is one social institution alongside of the family, the industrial organization of society, and the State. The Kingdom of God is in all these, and realizes itself through them all. During the Middle Ages all society was ruled and guided by the Church. Few of us would want modern life to return to such a condition. Functions which the Church used to perform, have now far outgrown its capacities. The Church is indispensable to the religious education of humanity and to the conservation of religion, but the greatest future awaits religion in the public life of humanity.

Edward S. Ames

1870-1958

Born in Eau Claire, Wisconsin, Edward S. Ames received his A.B. and A.M. from Drake University, a B.D. from the Yale Divinity School in 1892, and his Ph.D. from the University of Chicago in 1895. Ames spent most of his adult life as a member of the Department of Philosophy at the University of Chicago, serving as chairman until his retirement in 1935. He was also a pastor at the Church of the Disciples of Christ in Chicago from 1900 to 1940.

Author of numerous works on religion and the philosophy of religion, Ames was a leading exponent of what became known as religious modernism. Modernism, in his eyes, was the twentieth-century religion of democracy, a derivative of humanism and humanitarianism. Rejecting the idea of an incompatibility between religion and science, he started with a Jamesean study of religious experience, which he broadened into a fully empirical account of religion. Regarded as one of the most radical figures in the modernist movement, Ames's views represent the culmination of the optimistic interpretation of Protestantism that ended in a social gospel. By making good works central to religion rather than the traditional piety that had long characterized Christianity, Ames made the church an agency for the social and spiritual well-being of society as well as for the perpetuation of democratic institutions.

The following selection is from Ames' book The New Orthodoxy (*Chicago: The University of Chicago Press, 1918*).

*T*here is more reasonable hope that the great historic development of religion represented by Christianity is destined to come to a new birth of power. This cannot be expected to occur, however, through a mere emotional revival of its traditional forms and doctrines. These have outlived the order of society in which they appeared and are already transcended by the leaders of religious thought still working within their domains. Such mighty social structures do not pass away at a stroke. It required centuries to build them, and they linger on in the world just as monarchies persist long after democracy has become the accepted political ideal of the world. Christianity has lived through three marked stages and, it is believed by many, is now entering upon a fourth. The first was its earliest form, in which it was a tremendously vital impulse to a higher, freer moral life among informal intimate groups, having their common bond in allegiance to the personality and inspiring message of Jesus of Nazareth. That period is directly reflected in our New Testament. Upon its pages are the fresh imprints of the vibrant, pulsing spirit of the Master. But there is little organization. It has been impossible for the most searching scholarship to find there a model for the conduct of the modern church. No fixed ritual is established. No clear and uniform body of doctrine is presented. No provision can be traced there for economic justice and social righteousness as needed by the twentieth century. But the moral aspiration and insight are there. The clear, commanding spiritual vision of Jesus shines through it as the rays of the rising sun illumine and warm the world. That record will therefore remain a source of inspiration to the end of time.

The second stage of Christianity was that known as Catholicism. It developed by the gradual extension of the faith to great numbers of communities throughout the Roman Empire and among barbarian tribes. Contact with Greek philosophy was also a great factor in formulating the conceptions of the early church. When Christianity permeated the empire it was inevitable that it should be affected by the Latin genius for organization and by the Greek power of reflective thought. The ecclesiastical institution known to us as the Roman Catholic church may truly be regarded as deriving its impetus from the gospels, its form from the Roman Empire, and its formulations of doctrine from Greek philosophy. The official authority which characterizes it is inevitably of the quality of the system on which it was patterned. This type of Christianity was arrested in its progress by the Protestant Reformation of the sixteenth century. Its fate is sealed with the death knell of monarchy and bureaucracy in all social relations—in the family, in education, and in industry. It has produced many beautiful souls. It has adorned our human world with marvelous cathedrals and pageants. It has lifted the imagination of millions from sordid and transient things to pure and lofty visions of

faith. But it is not the form of religion for the modern man.

What then of Protestantism? It has now had four centuries of history. The celebration of the four hundredth anniversary of Luther's break with the Catholic church is being widely observed. He introduced great reforms which continue to exert a powerful influence. He gave the Bible to the people and made Christianity the religion of a book as it had never been before. He struck at the sharp separation of the sacred and the secular by opposing the celibacy of the clergy, by recognizing the state as an agency of God, and by dignifying common labor as having religious value. But the movement which he inaugurated became dogmatic and fixed and has not fulfilled his hopes. In Calvinism the doctrinal interest predominated and gave rise to creeds and confessions of faith which stand in the background of most of the evangelical churches today. Puritanism became austere and antagonistic to many natural and vital interests. It developed strength of conscience and determination of will, but lost breadth and the social graces and appreciation of the fine arts. Under all its differences Protestantism retained certain elements of Catholicism. It distrusted human nature; it emphasized the sacraments as essential means of grace; it clung to external authority, to the doctrines of the supernatural, and to a miraculous conversion of the natural human being in order to make him truly religious.

It is not impossible that future historians will regard Protestantism as coming to its close with the end of the nineteenth century as a vital, ascending type of religion. In that century several of the most characterisic principles of Protestantism were undermined by a larger knowledge of history and science. Protestantism was individualistic; the new order is social. It assumed the infallibility of the Bible, and that is no longer tenable. It exalted authority, and now there is no legitimate authority except that of experience. It denied that man is naturally religious, while it is commonly accepted today that man is incurably religious. We may well believe therefore that Christianity is entering upon a fourth great epoch, which has already been called by various names. It is referred to as the religion of the spirit, as social Christianity, and as the religion of democracy.

There is real need at the present time for statements of this latest form of Christianity created by the profound influences working through many agencies toward a richer life for all classes of men. What is this religion of the twentieth century? How shall we set forth the religious life as it appears in the light of the discoveries of the historians of religion, biblical students, natural scientists, and social psychologists? Let us think of ourselves as perfectly free souls, unawed by any authority over us or by any superstition within us, yet reverent toward the things which experience has taught us and eagerly in quest of clearer perceptions of the ideal possibilities of life. How does the religious life appear? How shall we understand its attitudes, its dramatis personae, its growing Bible, its changing goal, and its new drama of the spiritual life? Some persons have difficulty in thinking of the Christian life in this way, but no apologies are necessary for identifying it with the religious life at its best. Indeed, the Christian life may be regarded as just life itself at its best. . . .

First, then, reverence for life. We have come to have profound respect for the laws of nature, for the way she works, and for the possibility of cooperating with her. It is the scientific habit of mind to sit down quietly and observe the facts, to view patiently the processes in the growth of plants and animals and in the development of society in order to understand them and control them.

Nothing is allowed to come between the scientist and the facts. Jesus took the same unprejudiced, impartial attitude. . . .

Religion is for him the maintenance of this attitude of respect for life. The divine order is not different in principle from that which we constantly observe. God is like a good shepherd seeking his lost sheep. He is like the father receiving back his prodigal son. The analogies of seedtime and harvest hold in the moral realm. Whoever, then, in our day has this reverence for life, respects its simple principles of industry, of generosity, of persistence, and of fidelity, possesses in this respect the Christian attitude and is to that extent and by that very fact a Christian. . . .

The second conspicuous attitude of the Christian life which I mention is love, especially love of our fellow-men. We are having a great awakening in recent years with reference to social justice. This is the phrase which we have adopted to express the development in institutions, and particularly in the state, of the attitude of consideration for our fellow-men. . . .

The third attitude of the religious life is faith. Faith is that quality by which pioneers like Abraham and the Klondike adventurers go forth into new countries. It was the attitude of Columbus. It is the forward-striving, hopeful, expectant quality. To have faith means to be willing to take some risk for a cause. It is of the essence of business enterprise and of the creative spirit in science and in art. Religious faith means to have that feeling about life as a whole. No one is able to prove conclusively that human progress will continue, but no man can get the most out of life who refuses to believe in progress and in the possibility of improving the world. In spite of all the lions in the way we must go on. In spite of human frailties and weaknesses, in spite of follies and irrationalities, in spite of selfishness and greed, in spite of false ideals and paralyzing indifference, we must go on with our task whether it is our business, our science, our politics, or our religion. They are all of a piece in this respect. Everywhere we work against difficulties and in the face of discouragements which would be heartbreaking if we thought only of them. But everywhere we keep hoping and fighting and believing that improvement is to be made. When we give up that faith, we are done with life, or at least with that particular part of it concerning which we have lost faith.

One of the striking facts in the religious experience of the modern man is that while he seems to hold sacred things more lightly than did the passing generation, yet in reality he cherishes those to which he does cling with a more vital faith. He is discovering that religion does not need to be defended and protected in order to preserve it in the world. It has a surprising depth and persistence. The rationalistic mind of the eighteenth and nineteenth centuries, which still survives here and there in societies and individuals designating themselves as rationalists, assumed that religion could not survive criticism. They supposed that religion was so inextricably bound up with superstition and supernaturalism that when these were exposed and cast aside religion itself would perish. This too has been the conviction of the extreme conservatives. They must believe the Bible "from cover to cover" or reject it all. If they should relax their adherence to miracle or prophecy they could not believe in the veracity of the teaching. There is thus a significant likeness between the extremes. They agree that one must accept all or nothing. No discrimination or qualification is approved. The Bible and the Christian religion are to be defended or rejected *in toto*.

The man of the modern mind, trained in history and in the social sciences, takes a different view. He does not indorse all that has been claimed for the Bible nor does he take it to be of equal worth in all its parts. Yet he finds in it messages of greatest value. Even contradictions, discrepancies, superstitions and myths may be discovered without weakening the force of the moral ideals and precepts. Those things which are self-evidencing and verifiable in experience cannot be deprived of their validity because of accompanying errors or misconceptions. Religion is at last seen to be greater than the traditions which have grown up with it. It has deeper springs in human nature than have been suspected. Instead of being a delicate and tender growth it proves to be hardy and vigorous. Therefore it does not have to be sheltered and hidden against investigation and criticism. It cannot thrive at its best under patronizing influences nor at the hands of those who are unwilling to trust it to the free play of social forces. Certainly many men in our time have been surprised to realize how much more vital and satisfying their religious faith became the moment they began to view it with the same freedom and intelligence with which they regard art and politics. As with all other big human concerns, religion is at its best where it is close to life, unhindered by authority and open to reasonable, sympathetic criticism. Again and again in the history of Christianity its vital force has broken through old forms and doctrines and created new symbols and types of service. The dogma of biblical infallibility is one of the artificialities recently discarded, and the result has been the strengthening of religion. . . .

The Bible, like other vital books, grows by constant reinterpretation. This may be realized through the experience of anyone to whom it is a book of real religious value. . . .

The Bible thus attained makes a new and profound appeal to our time, for it is now a collection of writings reflecting the history of a religiously gifted people in their growth and aspirations. Within that history the prophetic utterances of the Old Testament and the words of Jesus mark the high peaks from which all the rest is surveyed and estimated. So aptly and searchingly do the social judgments of the prophets appeal to the social conscience of the present that in certain respects they seem like reformers of the twentieth century. At the same time the more adequate knowledge of Jesus has put him above all the prophets and given him a new hold upon the spiritual imagination and idealism of the best minds of the new social order. In this reconstruction of the biblical material and perspective the book has become a source of increasing inspiration and moral incentive.

The conception of Christianity as centering chiefly in another life is rapidly losing its hold. That which is coming into favor is the hope of Christianizing the social order itself, as Professor Rauschenbusch has phrased it. Here is taken into account the natural goodness and forward-moving tendency of human nature, its capacity for improvement, for measureless unselfishness, and for nobility and ideality of character beyond all calculation or present imagination. Many comparisons and contrasts between the old and the new are already familiar to popular thought. To state them in balanced sentences has the value of emphasis, though it is not without the dangers of brevity and exaggeration.

The old was static, the new is dynamic. The one sought perfection; the other seeks improvement. One was given; the other is to be gradually achieved. The first was prescribed; the second is to be progressively discovered. That goal depended on providence miraculously transforming the soul; this modern goal depends upon learning by experience as revealed in the lives of great men in the past and in scientific observation and experiment in the present. Religion then was apart from life, from the state, and from practical affairs; religion now is integral with life in all its forms. In the old days it lacked variety and the richness of individuality; in these days it is specialized and made concrete by the peculiar duties and relations given to each person by virtue of his place in society. The old had a separate unique literature; the new regards all noble literature as its medium. The traditional system had a special priesthood; the present order magnifies the priesthood of all true believers. The old attitude despised and feared the natural order which it called the world; the new loves the natural, especially in its service of social ideals. In the past there has been difficulty in using the fine arts in religion; at present they are means of the most impressive symbolization of the new spiritual values. For a long time Christ has been unreal and remote; at last he is becoming human and natural. God was the infinite veiled Being; he is now drawing near even at the risk of seeming finite. Transcendental mysticism was not difficult for the faith of yesterday; a natural, winsome mysticism throbs in the soul of today. The former ideal of the good man was the saintly soul, serene and at peace, withdrawn from the common struggle; the present ideal is of a man sinewy and full of courage, working in the midst of the human tasks, clear-headed and good-natured, conscious of far horizons, to which also his deeds have reference.

At last, then, religion has come to reckon with the fact that its highest quest is not for a supernatural order but just for natural goodness in largest and fullest measure. . . .

We are therefore confronted with the spectacle of life whose goal is not once for all set up and fixed, but which is put forward and lifted higher as we labor and aspire. The dream of the present is of a free society whose chief aim shall be to furnish to all its members the greatest possible power of intelligence, and will, and sympathy, and capacity for social co-operation and progress. That requires intelligence and the constant improvement of popular education. It demands a wholesome and stimulating social atmosphere of freest interaction and emulation for the energizing of the will. It means the closest comradeship and the finest sympathetic imagination, such as is now momentarily realized in times of crises, as in the Halifax disaster and in the revelations of unselfish devotion in the trenches of the Great War.

The function of the church is to make that ideal of a free and growing brotherhood of all mankind real to the experience and to the imagination of men. After all this is not so different from that which it has done for the souls of men in the past. Certainly Jesus summoned his followers into a companionship of adventure and faith on behalf of fuller friendship and deeper love. It may be said that the course of thought since the seventeenth century has been the elaboration of the value of a society in which the individual soul could come to its own in a kingdom of good-will. And surely modern social reformers would be satisfied if they could feel that adequate progress were being made in the permeation of the race with the kindliness and idealism of Jesus. That would mean the cultivation of science to understand what love really requires us to do. It would mean better organization of the state to make the ideals effective. It would mean better care of childhood, in whose plastic soul lie all the possibilities of realizing the most wonderful dreams of the sages and prophets yet to be. We cannot ignore the past nor can we be slaves to it. No more can we merely trust everything to the future; we must anticipate it and live in it as well as in the present. . . .

The new drama starts with man's life on the earth and with the upward and forward tendency within it. It shows, from the earliest records, efforts toward something better and loftier. Everywhere are temples and tombs and the signs of uplifted hands. In and around these have flowed the intense desires and aspirations of the unsatisfied soul of man, restless in his age-long quest. Often mistaken as to the source of his success, always burdened with superstitions and misconceptions of himself and his world, nevertheless he has continued to follow the gleam. At last he is finding out the immediate causes of many of his blessings and his ills. With a new joy and courage in his discovery of scientific knowledge and power he is preparing for still greater mastery and progress. With all of his old reverence for life and with greater zest he is not merely *seeking* a city which hath foundations. He is building it. He does not just sit silently listening in his worship, but he wrestles with God and, like Jacob of old, exacts his blessing. The drama which he is enacting is one of intense activity and profound thoughtfulness. This has quite changed the meaning of worship. It is now no longer the contemplation of a series of celestial events in which man beholds himself the passive recipient of divine favor or wrath. It is rather the survey of the long path of past experience and the memory of the heroic actors who have toiled there and the anticipation of the further extension of that path by labor, intelligence, and unselfish devotion. Through it all run the realization of the magnitude of the forces involved, the incalculably great scale of the events transpiring, and the tragic character of the smallest word and deed. It is this richness and inexhaustible nature of experience which constitutes its divine quality. But the divine is no more separate and aloof. It is within and organic with the human. We surrender the old contrast of the human and the divine, not by eliminating either one to retain the other, but by insisting that life as we find it has in it the warmth and intimacy of the human and also the dynamic and the outreach of the divine. Life is in this respect all of a piece, varied and intricate, but undivided.

PART V

AMERICAN THOUGHT IN A TROUBLED WORLD

Shortly after the dropping of the first atomic bomb on Hiroshima, Norman Cousins, in an editorial in the *Saturday Review of Literature*, spoke for a generation of Americans who were fearful that the coming of peace was a prelude to the extinction of man himself. The beginning of the atomic age, he remarked prophetically, has brought less hope than fear. "It is a primitive fear, the fear of the unknown, the fear of forces man can neither channel nor comprehend. . . . It has burst out of the subconscious and into the conscious, filling the mind with primordial apprehensions."[1] Thus, the coming of a new technological age brought with it not hope and expectation but fear and foreboding. For the first time in their history Americans faced a situation where they and everything they cherished were threatened with potential destruction.

Yet the recognition of fear in the American mind was not new to 1945. Over a decade earlier, Franklin Roosevelt sought to unite the nation and stir creative response by urging that "we have nothing to fear but fear itself." At the beginning of the century observers like Henry Adams and Madison Grant were expressing at least individual fears that American society was

[1] "Modern Man is Obsolete," *Saturday Review of Literature*, 28 (August 18, 1945), 5.

351

tending toward mediocrity if not extinction. In increasing numbers Americans during the first half of the twentieth century became fearful of the new social forces affecting them both at home and abroad, of the directions in which their society was going, and of the possible loss of their republican inheritance.

The nineteenth century, as we have seen, brought the industrial revolution to America and with it profound economic and social changes. In the half century before the Civil War, the introduction of the factory system marked the beginning of America's industrialization. In the last half of the nineteenth century, the American economy greatly expanded its technological base and established the basic industries and systems of national production that characterize mature industrial nations. Industrialization, urbanization, the rapid growth of the new working class, and spread of technology all reached maturity and crystallization in the 1890's, so that this decade became, as Professor Commager[2] called it, a kind of watershed that looked back to an older individualism and forward to the emergence of the New and Fair Deals. Besides these internal changes in America, events on the world scene in the twentieth century— the World Wars, the Great Depression, the struggles of the League of Nations and United Nations—made it even more difficult for Americans to retain meaning for their national existence.

The search for national meaning was complicated still further by the major intellectual currents inherited from the late nineteenth century. The evolutionary naturalism implied by Darwin's theories was extended to all human institutions, with the consequent naturalizing of such major sources of American thought as Puritanism, rationalism, and idealism. Showing that these sources did not rest on nonempirical and transcendent principles, naturalists argued that political ideals and social institutions, like the organs of an animal, must be understood as emerging within nature in man's struggle for survival. Neither transcendent, nor absolute, nor self-evident truths, America's social and moral principles were only modes of social adjustments to nature. It is significant that pragmatism, the dominant intellectual force of the first half of the twentieth century, was closely linked with evolution. Dewey in particular showed that Darwin's theory implied a view of mind and knowledge along naturalistic and pragmatic lines: ideas are interpreted as instruments for adaptation and are to be judged in terms of the quality of the results produced by the actions they direct.[3] Americans, of course, had always been a pragmatic people, distrusting abstract theory and stressing the concreteness of both

[2] Henry Steele Commager, "The Watershed of the Nineties," *The American Mind* (New Haven, 1952), Chap. II.
[3] See Dewey's essay "Charles Darwin and His Influence on Science," in his *The Influence of Darwin on Philosophy* (New York, 1910).

beliefs and gadgets. William James, in fact, was led to characterize pragmatism as but a new name for some old ways of thinking. But, with Peirce, James, Dewey, and their many disciples, pragmatism became an explicit, self-conscious philosophy, and it was systematically applied to interpretations of all areas of human activity.

Relativism and secularism were other movements that developed in the post-Darwinian and pragmatic consciousness. Holding that truths and principles are conditioned by the cultural circumstances of the individuals proposing them, relativism owed much to evolutionary theory and went hand in hand with the adoption of developmental approaches in the sciences of man. Secularization of thought and institutions also began to affect portions of the national consciousness. This development was a normal outgrowth of other trends, for if the source of political principles was not supernaturalistic religion but nature and the struggle for survival, then both principles and institutions should be cut loose from their transcendental base. Many observers of the early twentieth century pointed to a loosening of the hold of religion on the national consciousness—although Americans seemed to remain religious if not spiritual.

In their extreme form, these forces in the American mind led to expressions of skepticism and even nihilism. Skepticism cast doubt on the ability of the mind to know reality and grasp truth. The loss of virtue in the 1920's and the inability to control economic forces in the 1930's seemed to many to give experiential support to such skepticism. The attack on reason led to the cult of the irrational, with its rejection of all standards and principles in extreme cases. The "literature of revolt," with its often crushing examination of the American inheritance, gave nihilism its most forceful American expression.

Finally, America's republican system, while praised continuously through the half century, seemed to be severely threatened not only by the intellectual and literary voices of the period but also by the forces and institutions it itself had engendered. Thus, free enterprise often seemed threatened by the very persons who invoked it. Consequent upon industrialization was standardization, and the latter seemed to triumph over the individualism of the older America. Determinism mocked ideals of self-reliance; social emphases eliminated the meaning of individual guilt; and naturalism and secularism eroded the moral and religious basis of Americanism. Or so it seemed to many thoughtful persons. Perhaps the most fundamental social question of the entire period concerned the validity of the old ideas for modern and urban America.

The result of these intellectual movements and historical events was, beginning in the 1890's, the subjection of American experience to the most scrupulous examination in its history. Many persons concluded that the transcendental justifications of American experience, such as self-evident truths, natural rights, or divine sanctions, were completely unfounded. Lawyers and social scientists were finding that law—so basic in the American vision, especially the "higher law"—was not a body of fixed, eternal doctrines but was rather the rules made in the courts by very human men known as judges. Industry and technology, which promised so much in themselves and from which nineteenth-century Americans expected so much, were, as Alfred North Whitehead wrote, fulfilling the prophecies of Francis Bacon; but at the same time, "man, who at times dreamt of himself as a little lower than the angels, has submitted to become the servant and the minister of nature." Many Americans agreed with Whitehead that "it remains to be seen whether the same actor can play both parts."[4] Nineteenth-century beliefs in progress and the perfectibility of man were finding little or no basis in twentieth-century American experience. Men such as Henry Adams were linking society to the laws of physics to show the eventual decline of democratic society. By the 1950's even the American's basic character, to judge by the writings of sociologist David Riesman, had undergone fundamental change, substituting for the self-reliant, inner-directed man the socially oriented, other-directed man.

The idea of national mission, which in earlier chapters we have seen to be so basic to the American mind, was also subjected to re-examination, particularly as it seemed to be threatened by the national experience. To many observers the 1950's and the 1960's faded into history on a predominantely negative note. Politicians observed what has been called a lack of national purpose; clergymen found a loss of dedication to a moral society; historians pointed to riddles and paradoxes in America's world position; and moralists decried the low standards of personal ethics. There was in many quarters a loss of commitment to historic ideals, a sense of drift resulting from the lack of clear national purpose, and a feeling that Americans were facing the future without reserves and without a clear mandate. It had not always been so in America. In fact, almost opposite characterizations had been ascribed to past generations of Americans, such as their sense of purpose, their feeling of duty, and their drive toward the future.[5]

To see these feelings as new in the American consciousness, it is only necessary to recall something of the attitudes—among them the attitude toward history—of the period that gave birth to the Declaration of Independence. The central ideas of the period were Reason and Law and their conceptual relatives. Carl Becker summarized them thus: "In the eighteenth century

---

[4] Alfred North Whitehead, *Science and the Modern World* (New York, 1925), p. 141.
[5] This and the remaining paragraphs of the introduction are based on Robert N. Beck, "America and the Hand of History," *Social Education*, 24 (May, 1960), 197–200.

the words without which no enlightened person could reach a restful conclusion were nature, natural law, first cause, reason, sentiment, humanity, perfectibility (these last three being necessary only for the more tender-minded, perhaps.)"[6] Placing their trust in reason, the men of Enlightenment believed that eternal principles of right and justice could be grasped by human beings and subsequently made the platform of social criticism and reform.

Having discovered the truths of natural law—or most of them—the Enlightenment proceeded to make certain inferences about man and history. Voltaire, speaking for most of the men of the Enlightenment, observed that "History is little else than a picture of human crimes and misfortunes," and Americans accepted the theme. In this view, the past was a period of ignorance and superstition—and hence of unhappiness and misery—and consequently it was better to break with the old institutions and values in order to replace them with new and enlightened ones. The present, then, was the period of transition, the period of the establishment of an enlightened society in which history would renew itself.

Four dominant American characteristics—all of them involving an attitude toward history—developed from these assumptions. The first was the American sense of dynamism, expressed in many ways by many people, but by none better than Walt Whitman in a letter to Emerson: "Master, I am a man who has perfect faith. Master, we have not come through centuries, caste, heroisms, fables, to halt in this land today." Second was America's sense of mission, a belief that America is an experiment for the world—is indeed the hope of the world, if only the world will accept it. Jefferson expressed this feeling perfectly when he wrote, "It is impossible not to be sensible that we are acting for all mankind." The third characteristic was the pervasive sense of America's uniqueness. "America is different," the feeling ran—so different in fact that at times she felt constrained to turn her back on the affairs of the world. Finally, there was a persistent moralism, a tendency to see the struggles of history in absolute moral terms rather than from a relativist perspective involving power politics and human passions as well as personal values.

These characteristics might be summarized in the expression "historical Puritanism." They involved an attitude toward history in many ways not unlike the Puritan attitude toward life as a whole: activism and messianism again, but also a sense of rightness with reference to the American political code, which must be used as a judge of history but is not itself considered to be historical. To be sure, America has been involved in history in many ways, but so often her involvements have been like that typified by World War I: America enters history to make the world

[6] Carl L. Becker, *The Heavenly City of the Eighteenth Century Philosophers* (New Haven, 1932), p. 47.

"safe" for her particular political revelation. That the world has not wanted to accept that revelation, that it has at times resisted America's interventions as well as her preachments, has in past generations often been perplexing but seldom has disturbed her fundamental convictions. History for many Americans remained "bunk," even as they wrote and read histories by the score.

But America's historical Puritanism, it now appears, was already being eroded as the nation was called on to face the fateful events of the twentieth century. Earlier generations of Americans could remain aloof from the affairs of Europe but now Americans were forced to participate in them. The hostility and rejection that sometimes followed from America's new role in world affairs caused Americans to question their ability to act for mankind or to extend their ideals to the rest of the world. Many Americans, in fact, began to question the validity of those ideals even in their national context. Was, then, the conjunction of theory and daily experience so obvious to earlier generations no longer apparent? Was the American experience to issue in a kind of nihilism of action and purpose?

In the years that have followed this new American involvement, which has gradually eroded the tenets of historical Puritanism, many counsels have been offered. There have been the radical voices urging a basic reorientation for America and the adoption of new ideologies. Voices of conservatism have sought to recapture ideas of the past—European, American, and southern. The churches have responded to America's dilemmas by urging a return to faith, to transcendental justifications based on natural-law theory, and even to a neo-orthodoxy that attempts to synthesize biblical insights and forces in the modern world. And naturalists and liberals have sought to redefine American ideals within the context of their philosophical assumptions.

Yet, given the diversities, complexities, and alternative responses of the last half century of American history, the pattern that emerges has more unity and coherence than one might initially suspect. With some exceptions that pattern remains the American vision of Lockian liberalism and individualism. The critics of America throughout this period have been concerned less in rejecting that vision than in calling attention to the disparity between the ideal and the real. The literature of revolt, the New and Fair Deals, the symbolisms of the New Frontier of the 1960's, even the radical voices of the 1930's and the late 1960's—all these movements testified to the continuing vitality of the American ideal, however much experience seemed to depart from it. The time has not yet come—if ever it will—to write a concluding chapter to history.

CHAPTER XX

SHAKING OF THE FOUNDATIONS

*T*he social and intellectual ferment of the late nineteenth and early twentieth century produced a number of skeptical and pessimistic observers. Offering America new perspectives and insights into the nature of social processes, the new philosophy, pragmatism, and the new science, social science, were making inroads into the national consciousness and creating a swirl of intellectual crosscurrents that sometimes conflicted with the traditional inheritance. For many Americans, to be sure, science and pragmatism promised a great liberation, for they seemed to assure progress and to make creativity possible. Social planning and progressivism became watchwords for many Americans who believed that the phrases of Jefferson—which enjoyed a nationwide vogue in the late 1930's and 1940's— could be more fully realized by the new intellectual instruments.

Yet there were other observers who professed to see a very different picture—one indeed that was quite at variance with the traditional pattern and one that in extreme cases involved its dissolution. For example, one of the chief implications of the new social science was functionalism, or relativism, a position that viewed human ideas and institutions in particular societal settings and that denied the possibility of cross-cultural comparison. In other words, functionalists held that each culture is itself a whole, a Gestalt, and all its institutions are to be understood by reference to the culture within which they exist. Functionalism was soon applied to all areas of society—including the family, the economic system, the law, and ideologies—and it was brought to the popular consciousness by such writers as Ruth Benedict, whose *Patterns of Culture* (1934) became a scientific best seller. The analyses of the functionalists uncovered exciting and important data, but at the same time they placed in jeopardy the whole cluster of Enlightenment ideas which had served Americans in the past. Much of the recent American experience, particularly since World War II, must be understood as an attempt to overcome the eroding relativism of earlier decades.

The use of certain scientific conclusions by critics also had a disturbing effect on America. Utilizing principles taken from physics and biology, for example, Henry Adams drew not optimistic but pessimistic conclusions. Other thinkers bluntly challenged the very idea of democracy, arguing that democracy was leading America to self-destruction. Madison Grant, basing his ideas in large part upon racial premises, maintained that America's greatness was being undermined by the admission of millions of immigrants of inferior stock. Similarly, Ralph Adams Cram proclaimed that democracy reduced mankind to incapacity and led to mediocrity, both of which involved denials of human potentialities.

During the first quarter of the nineteenth century the pessimism of individuals like Adams, Grant, and Cram never gained a wide following. The depression of the 1930's, however, seemed to confirm the beliefs of those critics who had begun to question traditional values. Because of the suffering, anxiety, and despair of the 1930's, movements of the far left, such as communism, as well as those of the extreme right, including fascism, gained many converts as the depression seemed to worsen despite the efforts of the New Deal to rebuild and transform American society. Some Americans turned to the Communist party in the sincere and idealistic belief that only state ownership and control of the means of production and distribution could solve the problems of poverty and unemployment. Others, seizing upon scapegoats in the form of minority groups or radical protest movements, turned ironically to fascism in order to preserve America's cherished values.

By the 1930's, as a matter of fact, a searching critique of American society had been undertaken, and various proposals were offered. As Frederick Lewis Allen pointed out in *Only Yesterday* (1940), the common denominator of all of these movements, whether of the left, center, or right, was social-mindedness—the hope of salvation not so much for individuals, but for groups and the entire nation, to be achieved through organized group action. Through the fabric of American society also ran an undercurrent of fear—fear that the promise of America had proved an illusion. In the midst of such strong tensions and social misery, it was not surprising that radical protest movements gained a large audience.

In the long run, however, Americans on the whole avoided extreme solutions, either of the right or the left. Instead they attempted to solve their problems by invoking the national power in a nondoctrinaire, pragmatic way, and this power, in turn, was used mainly to shore up and renew traditional ideals.

Madison Grant
1865-1937

*Madison Grant was born in New York
City of a family whose roots went back to the
colonial period. He graduated from Yale in
1887 and received a law degree from
Columbia University three years later.
Though he carried on a legal practice, Grant
very early became interested in zoology.
His studies led him to write an important
series of monographs on North American
animals; he also played a leading role in
founding the New York Zoological Society in
1895 and in the movement to preserve species
threatened with extinction. Then, as a result
of his zoological interests, Grant began to
study ethnology. Fearing that a mixture of
racial strains would prove fatal to American
democracy, Grant soon became a leading
propagandist in the movement to restrict
immigration to this country. His ideas on
the subject were summed up in his major
work,* The Passing of the Great Race,
which appeared in 1916.

*Reflecting the pessimism that had begun
to trouble many native-born intellectuals
like himself, Grant urged that the Nordic
race, the ruling race of the Western world,
was declining because of its mistaken belief
in the power of environment to transform
heredity. Heredity was all-important, he
contended, and racial mixture led to racial
regression. Culture was determined by race,
and he warned that the Nordic race
(predominantly that of Western Europe
ancestry) was being threatened with
hybridization and could save itself only by
returning to rule by an aristocracy and by
maintaining the purity of its blood, and
consequently of its culture. Especially
opposed to the growing tide of immigration
from southern and eastern Europe that began
in the late 1880's, Grant mirrored the loss
of confidence in American institutions as
the nation entered an era troubled by
domestic and international problems.*

The following selection is from The
Passing of the Great Race (*New York,
1916*).

*F*ailure to recognize the clear
distinction between race and nationality and the still greater distinction
between race and language, the easy
assumption that the one is indicative
of the other, has been in the past a
serious impediment to an understanding
of racial values. Historians and philo-
logists have approached the subject
from the viewpoint of linguistics, and

as a result we have been burdened with a group of mythical races, such as the Latin, the Aryan, the Caucasian, and, perhaps, most inconsistent of all, the "Celtic" race.

Man is an animal differing from his fellow inhabitants of the globe, not in kind but only in degree of development, and an intelligent study of the human species must be preceded by an extended knowledge of other mammals, especially the primates. Instead of such essential training, anthropologists often seek to qualify by research in linguistics, religion, or marriage customs, or in designs of pottery or blanket weaving, all of which relate to ethnology alone.

The question of race has been further complicated by the effort of old-fashioned theologians to cramp all mankind into the scant six thousand years of Hebrew chronology, as expounded by Archbishop Ussher. Religious teachers have also maintained the proposition not only that man is something fundamentally distinct from other living creatures, but that there are no inherited differences in humanity that cannot be obliterated by education and environment.

It is, therefore, necessary at the outset for the reader to thoroughly appreciate that race, language, and nationality are three separate and distinct things, and that in Europe these three elements are only occasionally found persisting in combination, as in the Scandinavian nations.

To realize the transitory nature of political boundaries, one has only to consider the changes of the past century, to say nothing of those which may occur at the end of the present war. As to language, here in America we daily hear the English language spoken by many men who possess not one drop of English blood, and who, a few years since, knew not one one word of Saxon speech.

As a result of certain religious and social doctrines, now happily becoming obsolete, race consciousness has been greatly impaired among civilized nations, but in the beginning all differences of class, of caste, and of color, marked actual lines of race cleavage.

In many countries the existing classes represent races that were once distinct. In the city of New York, and elsewhere in the United States, there is a native American aristocracy resting upon layer after layer of immigrants of lower races, and the native American, while, of course, disclaiming the distinction of a patrician class, nevertheless has, up to this time, supplied the leaders of thought and the control of capital, of education, and of the religious ideals and altruistic bias of the community.

In the democratic forms of government the operation of universal suffrage tends toward the selection of the average man for public office rather than the man qualified by birth, education, and integrity. How this scheme of administration will ultimately work out remains to be seen, but from a racial point of view, it will inevitably increase the preponderance of the lower types and cause a corresponding loss of efficiency in the community as a whole.

The tendency in a democracy is toward a standardization of type and a diminution of the influence of genius. A majority must of necessity be inferior to a picked minority, and it always resents specializations in which it cannot share. In the French Revolution the majority, calling itself "the people," deliberately endeavored to destroy the higher type, and something of the same sort was, in a measure, done after the American Revolution by the expulsion of the Loyalists and the confiscation of their lands.

In America we have nearly succeeded in destroying the privilege of birth; that is, the intellectual and moral advantage a man of good stock brings into the world with him. We are now engaged in destroying the privilege of wealth; that is, the reward of successful intelligence and industry, and in some quarters there is developing a tendency to attack the privilege of intellect and to deprive a man of the advantages of an early and thorough education. Simplified spelling is a step in this direction. Ignorance of English grammar or classic learning must not be held up as a reproach to the political and social aspirant.

Mankind emerged from savagery and barbarism under the leadership of selected individuals whose personal prowess, capacity, or wisdom gave them the right to lead and the power to compel obedience. Such leaders have always been a minute fraction of the whole, but as long as the tradition of their predominance persisted they were able to use the brute strength of the unthinking herd as part of their own force, and were able to direct at will the blind dynamic impulse of the slaves, peasants, or lower classes. Such a despot had an enormous power at his disposal which, if he were benevolent or even intelligent, could be used, and most frequently was used, for the general uplift of the race. Even those rulers who most abused this power put down with merciless rigor the antisocial elements, such as pirates, brigands, or anarchists, which impair the progress of a community, as disease or wounds cripple an individual.

True aristocracy is government by the wisest and best, always a small minority in any population. Human society is like a serpent dragging its long body on the ground, but with the head always thrust a little in advance and a little elevated above the earth. The serpent's tail, in human society represented by the antisocial forces, was in the past dragged by sheer force along the path of progress. Such has been the organization of mankind from the beginning, and such it still is in older communities than ours. What progress humanity can make under the control of universal suffrage, or the rule of the average, may find a further analogy in the habits of certain snakes which wiggle sideways and disregard the head with its brains and eyes. Such serpents, however, are not noted for their ability to make rapid progress.

To use another simile, in an aristocratic as distinguished from a plutocratic, or democratic organization, the intellectual and talented classes form the point of the lance, while the massive shaft represents the body of the population and adds by its bulk and weight to the penetrative impact of the tip. In a democratic system this concentrated force at the top is dispersed throughout the mass, supplying, to be sure, a certain amount of leaven, but in the long run the force and genius of the small minority is dissipated, if not wholly lost. *Vox populi*, so far from being *Vox Dei*, thus becomes an unending wail for rights, and never a chant of duty.

Where a conquering race is imposed on another race the institution of slavery often arises to compel the servient race to work, and to introduce it forcibly to a higher form of civilization. As soon as men can be induced to labor to supply their own needs slavery becomes wasteful and tends to vanish. Slaves are often more fortunate than freemen when treated with reasonable humanity, and when their elemental wants of food, clothing, and shelter are supplied. . . .

The continuity of physical traits and the limitation of the effects of environment to the individual only are now so thoroughly recognized by scientists that it is at most a question of time when the social consequences which result from such crossings will be generally understood by the public at large. As soon as the true bearing and import of the facts are appreciated by lawmakers, a complete change in our political structure will inevitably occur, and our present reliance on the influences of education will be superseded by a readjustment based on racial values.

Bearing in mind the extreme antiquity of physical and spiritual characters and the persistency with which they outlive those elements of environment termed language, nationality, and forms of government, we must consider the relation of these facts to the development of the race in America. We may be certain that the progress of evolution is in full operation to-day under those laws of nature which control it, and that the only sure guide to the future lies in the study of the operation of these laws in the past.

We Americans must realize that the altruistic ideals which have controlled our social development during the past century, and the maudlin sentimentalism that has made America "an ayslum for the oppressed," are sweeping the nation toward a racial abyss. If the Melting Pot is allowed to boil without control, and we continue to follow our national motto and deliberately blind ourselves to all "distinctions of race, creed, or color," the type of native American of Colonial descent will become as extinct as the Athenian of the age of Pericles, and the Viking of the days of Rollo.

Henry Adams

1838-1918

Great-grandson of John Adams and grandson of John Quincy Adams, Henry Adams graduated from Harvard in 1858 and then studied law in Germany. One of the great figures in American intellectual history, Adams did not take much interest in his formal education, nor was he distinguished as a student. Rather, he found outlets for his talents by contributing to college periodicals and addressing literary societies. During the Civil War he served as secretary to his father, Charles Francis Adams, who was then ambassador to Great Britain. During these seven years in Europe, from 1861 to 1868, he read widely and was especially attracted to scientific theories. The import of these theories, he concluded, was that the American nation could never return to the absolute standards of its Puritan forebears. On his return to the United States, Adams taught medieval history for a few years at Harvard, and then devoted himself to the writing of his nine-volume History of the United States During the Administrations of Jefferson and Madison. *This and other historical writings earned him a place among the first rank of American historians.*

Following the publication of the History, *Adams experienced a severe spiritual crisis and turned to the medieval world in search of meaning. His famous study of the mind of the Middle Ages,* Mont-Saint-Michel and Chartres, *resulted from this search. His intellectual interests at this time also became centered on social theory and he set about to discover the laws governing society. These he found in the principle of the energy available to man. Since the quantity of energy man can use is rapidly accelerating, Adams predicted that the twentieth century would be a period of swift material advance and also an era of destructive war and revolution. Man, he concluded, must learn to use this available energy productively or he will perish. Indeed, Adams was by no means certain that man would not perish.*

This selection is from The Degradation of the Democratic Dogma (*New York: The Macmillan Company, 1919*).

*T*owards the middle of the nineteenth century—that is, about 1850—a new school of physicists appeared in Europe, dating from an Essay on the Motive Power of Heat, published by Sadi Carnot in 1824, and made famous by the names of William Thomson, Lord Kelvin, in England, and of Clausius and Helmholz in Germany, who announced a second law of dynamics. The first law said that Energy was never lost; the second said that it was never saved; that, while the sum of energy in the universe might remain constant—granting that the universe was a closed box from which nothing could escape—the higher powers of energy tended always to fall lower, and that this process had no known limit.

The second law was briefly stated by Thomson in a paper "On a Universal Tendency in Nature to the Dissipation of Mechanical Energy," published in October, 1852, which is now as classic as Kepler's or Newton's Laws, and quite as necessary to a scientific education. Quoted exactly from Thomson's "Mathematical and Physical Papers" (Cambridge, 1882, Vol. I, p. 514), the Law of Dissipation runs thus:

1. There is at present in the material world a universal tendency to the dissipation of mechanical energy.

2. Any restoration of mechanical energy, without more than an equivalent of dissipation, is impossible in inanimate material processes, and is probably never effected by means of organized matter, either endowed with vegetable life or subjected to the will of an animated creature.

3. Within a finite period of time past, the earth must have been, and within a finite period of time to come, the earth must again be, unfit for the habitation of man as at present constituted, unless operations have been, or are to be performed, which are impossible under the laws to which the known operations going on at present in the material world, are subject.

When this young man of twenty-eight thus tossed the universe into the ash-heap, few scientific authorities took him seriously; but after the first gasp of surprise physicists began to give him qualified support which soon became absolute. . . .

Thus, at the same moment, three contradictory laws of energy were in force, all equally useful to science: (1) The Law of Conservation, that nothing could be added, and nothing lost, in the sum of energy. (2) The Law of Dissipation, that nothing could be added, but that Intensity must always be lost. (3) The Law of Evolution, that Vital Energy could be added, and raised indefinitely in potential, without the smallest apparent compensation. . . .

Down to the end of the nineteenth century nothing greatly mattered, since the actual forces could be fairly well calculated or accounted for on either principle, but schools of applied mechanics are apt to get into trouble by using contradictory methods. One process or the other acquires an advantage. The weaker submits, but in this instance, the difficulty of naming the weaker was extreme. That the Evolutionist should surrender his conquests seemed quite unlikely, since he felt behind him the whole momentum of popular success and sympathy, and stood as heir-apparent to all the aspirations of mankind. About him were arranged in battalions, like an army, the energies of government, of society, of democracy, of socialism, of nearly all literature and art, as well as hope, and whatever was left of instinct—all striving to illustrate not the Descent but the Ascent of Man. The *hostis humani generis*, the outlaw and enemy, was the Degradationist, who could have no friends, because he proclaimed the steady and fated enfeeblement and extinction of all nature's energies; but that he should abandon his laws seemed a still more preposterous idea. Never had he asserted them so aggressively, or with such dogmatic authority. He held undisputed possession of every technical school in the world, and even the primary schools were largely under his control. His second law of thermodynamics held its place in every text-book of science. The Universities and higher branches of education were greatly, if not wholly, controlled by his methods. The field of mathematics had become his. He had no serious intellectual rival. Few things are more difficult than to judge how far a society is looking one way and working in another, for the points are shifting and the rate of speed is uncertain. The acceleration of movement seems rapid, but the inertia, or resistance to deflection, may increase with the rapidity, so that society might pass through phase after phase of speed, like a comet, without noting deflection in its thought. If a simpler figure is needed, society may be likened to an island surrounded by a rising ocean which silently floods its defences. One after another the defences have been abandoned, and society has climbed to higher ground supposed to be out of danger. So the classic Gods were abandoned for monotheism, and scholastic philosophy was dropped in favor of the Newtonian; but the classic Gods and the scholastic philosophy were always popular, and the newer philosophies won their victories by developing compulsory force. Inertia is the law of mind as well as of matter, and inertia is a form of instinct; yet in western civilization it has never held its own.

The pessimism or unpopularity of the law will not prevent its enforcement, if it develops superior force, even if it leads where no one wants to go. The proof is that the law is already enforced in every field excepting that of human history, and even human history has not wholly escaped. In physics it rules with uncontested sway. In physiology, the old army of Evolutionists have suffered defections so serious that no discipline remains. . . .

The truth or the error of the three Laws of Evolution does not properly concern the teacher. No physicist can, in these days, he expected to take oath that Dalton's atoms, or Willard Gibb's phases, or Bernouilli's kinetic gases, are true. He uses for his scholars the figure or the formula which best suits their convenience. The historian or sociologist is alone restricted in the use of formulas which shock the moral sense; yet the stoppage of discussion in the historical lecture-room cannot affect the teaching of the same young men in the physical laboratory—still less the legislation of their parents at the State capital; it would merely ruin the school of history. However much to be regretted is such a result, society cannot safely permit itself to be condemned to a lingering death, which is sure to tend towards suicide, merely to suit the convenience of school-teachers. The dilemma is real; it may become serious; in any case it needs to be understood.

The battle of Evolution has never been wholly won; the chances at this moment favor the fear that it may yet be wholly lost. The Darwinist no longer talks of Evolution; he uses the word Transformation. The historian of human society has hitherto, as a habit, preferred to write or to lecture on a tacit assumption that humanity showed upward progress, even when it emphatically showed the contrary, as was not uncommon; but this passive attitude cannot be held against the physicist who invades his territory and takes the teaching of history out of his hands. Somewhere he will have to make a stand, but he has been already so much weakened by the surrender of his defences that he knows no longer where a stand can be made. As a form of Vital Energy he is convicted of being a Vertebrate, a Mammal, a Monodelphe, a Primate, and must eternally, by his body, be subject to the second law of thermodynamics. Escape there is impossible. Science has shut and barred every known exit. Man can detect no outlet except through the loophole called Mind, and even to avail himself of this, he must follow Lapparent's advice—become a disembodied spirit and seek a confederate among such physicists or physiologists as are willing to admit that man, as an animal, has no importance; that his evolution or degradation as an organism is immaterial; that his physical force or condition has nothing to do with the subject; that the old ascetics were correct in suppressing the body; and that his consciousness is sufficient proof of his right to regard Reason as the highest potential of Vital Energy. . . .

As an Organism society has always been peculiarly subject to degradation of Energy, and alike the historians and the physicists invariably stretch Kelvin's law over all organized matter whatever. Instead of being a mere convenience in treatment, the law is very rapidly becoming a dogma of absolute Truth. As long as the theory of Degradation—as of Evolution—was only one of the convenient tools of science, the sociologist had no just cause for complaint. Every science—and mathematics first of all—uses what tools it likes. The Professor of Physics is not teaching Ethics; he is training young men to handle concrete energy in one or more of its many forms, and he has no choice but to use the most convenient formulas. Unfortunately the formula most convenient for him is not at all convenient for his colleagues in sociology and history, without pressing the inquiry further, into more intimate branches of practice like medicine, jurisprudence, and politics. If the entire universe, in every variety of active energy, organic and inorganic, human or divine, is to be treated as clockwork that is running down, society can hardly go on ignoring the fact forever. Hitherto it has often happened that two systems of education, like the Scholastic and Baconian, could exist side by side for centuries—as they exist still—in adjoining schools and universities, by no more scientific device than that of shutting their eyes to each other; but the universe has been terribly narrowed by thermodynamics. Already History and Sociology gasp for breath.

Twelve Southerners
1930

The new conservatism that developed in the South presented a very different reaction to changing America from those of the preceding selections. Embittered by the disappearance of the values of an agrarian society, by the dehumanizing effects of industrialization, and by the loss of southern culture, southern literary and intellectual figures spoke out to preserve and encourage an older, indigenous way of southern life. Among the spokesmen of this southern conservatism were the contributors to the volume from which the following selection is taken. They were John Crowe Ransom, Donald Davidson, Frank Lawrence Owsley, John Gould Fletcher, Lyle H. Lanier, Allen Tate, Herman Clarence Nixon, Andrew Nelson Lytle, Robert Penn Warren, John Donald Wade, Henry Blue Kline, and Stark Young.

This selection is comprised of several passages from a symposium of their views, I'll Take My Stand: The South and the Agrarian Tradition *(New York: Harper & Row, 1930).*

I

*W*ith the environment of the New World and the traditions of the Old, the South thus became the seat of an agrarian civilization which had strength and promise for a future greatness second to none. The life of the South was leisurely and unhurried for the planter, the yeoman, or the landless tenant. It was a way of life, not a routine of planting and reaping merely for gain. Washington, who rode daily over his farms and counted his horses, cattle, plows, and bushels of corn as carefully as a merchant takes stock of his supplies, inhaled the smell of ripe corn after a rain, nursed his bluegrass sod and shade trees with his own hands, and, when in the field as a soldier or in the city as President of the United States, was homesick at the smell of fresh-plowed earth. He kept vigil with his sick horses and dogs, not as a capitalist who guards his investments, but as one who watches over his friends.

The system of society which developed in the South, then, was close to the soil. It might be organized about the plantation with its wide fields and its slaves and self-sufficiency, or it might center around a small farm, ranging from a fifty-acre to a five-hundred-acre tract, tilled by the owner, undriven by competition, supplied with corn by his own toil and with meat from his own pen or from the fields and forests. The amusements might be the fine balls and house parties of the planter or the three-day break-down dances which David Crockett loved, or horse races, foot races, cock and dog fights, boxing, wrestling, shooting, fighting, log-rolling, house raising, or corn-shucking. It might be crude or genteel, but it everywhere was fundamentally alike and natural. The houses were homes, where families lived sufficient and complete within themselves, working together and fighting together. And when death came, they were buried in their own lonely peaceful graveyards, to await doomsday together.

II

*T*his agrarian society had its own interests, which in almost all respects diverged from the interests of the industrial system of the North. The two sections, North and South, had entered the revolution against the mother country with the full knowledge of opposing interests of their societies; knowing this difference, they had combined in a loose union under the Articles of Confederation. Finally, they had joined together under the Constitution fully conscious that there were thus united two divergent economic and social systems, two civilizations, in fact. The two sections were evenly balanced in population and in the number of states, so that at the time there was no danger of either section's encroaching upon the interests of the other. This balance was clearly understood. Without it a union would not have been possible. Even with the understanding that the two sections would continue to hold this even balance, the sections were very careful to define and limit the powers of the federal government lest one section with its peculiar interests should get control of the national government and use the powers of that government to exploit the other section. Specific powers were granted the federal government, and all not specifically granted were retained by the states.

But equilibrium was impossible under expansion and growth. One section with its peculiar system of society would at one time or another become dominant and control the national government and either exploit the other section or else fail to exercise the functions of government for its positive benefit. Herein lies the irrepressible conflict, the eternal struggle between the agrarian South and the commercial and industrial North to control the government either in its own interest or, negatively, to prevent the other section from controlling it in its interests. Lincoln and Seward and the radical Republicans clothed the conflict later in robes of morality by making it appear that the "house divided against itself" and the irrepressible conflict which resulted from this division marked a division between slavery and freedom.

Slavery, as we shall see, was part of the agrarian system, but only one element and not an essential one. To say that the irrepressible conflict was between slavery and freedom is either to fail to grasp the nature and magnitude of the conflict, or else to make use of deliberate deception by employing a shibboleth to win the uninformed and unthinking to the support of a sinister undertaking. Rob Roy MacGregor, one of the chief corruptionists of the present-day power lobby, said that the way the power companies crush opposition and win popular support is to pin the word "bolshevik" upon the leaders of those who oppose the power-lobby program. The leaders of the Northern industrial system could win popular support by tagging their opponents as *"enemies of liberty"* and themselves as "champions of freedom." This they did. Lincoln was a politician and knew all the tricks of a politician. Seward was a politician and knew every *in* and *out*. This is true of other leaders of the "party of high ideals" which assumed the name of Republican party. Doubtless, Lincoln, Seward, and others were half sincere in their idea of an irrepressible conflict, but their fundamental purpose was to win elections and get their party into power—the party of the industrial North—with an industrial program for business and a sop of free lands for the Western farmer.

The irrepressible conflict, then, was not between slavery and freedom, but between the industrial and commercial civilization of the North and the agrarian civilization of the South. The industrial North demanded a high tariff so as to monopolize the domestic markets, especially the Southern market, for the South, being agrarian, must purchase all manufactured goods. It was an exploitative principle, originated at the expense of the South and for the benefit of the North. After the South realized that it would have little industry of its own, it fought the protective tariff to the point of nullification in South Carolina and almost to the point of dissolving the Union. In this as in other cases Southerners saw that what was good for the North was fatal to the South.

The industrial section demanded a national subsidy for the shipping business and merchant marine, but, as the merchant marine was alien to the Southern agrarian system, the two sections clashed. It was once more an exploitation of one section for the benefit of the other.

The industrial North demanded internal improvements—roads, railroads, canals—at national expense to furnish transportation for its goods to Southern and Western markets which were already hedged around for the benefit of the North by the tariff wall. The South objected to internal improvements at national expense because it had less need of transporation than the North and because the burden would be heavier on the South and the benefits greater for the North—another exploitation of the Southern system. The North favored a government-controlled bank; but as corporate wealth and the quick turnover of money were confined to that section, such an institution would be for the sole benefit, the South believed, of the North. There were many other things of a positive nature

which the system of society in the North demanded of the federal government, but those mentioned will illustrate the conflict of interest between North and South. . . .

III

*A*nd now the crisis in the South's decline has been reached.

Industrialism has arrived in the South. Already the local chambers of commerce exhibit the formidable data of Southern progress. A considerable party of Southern opinion, which might be called the New South party, is well pleased with the recent industrial accomplishments of the South and anxious for many more. Southerners of another school, who might be said to compose an Old South party, are apprehensive lest the section become completely and uncritically devoted to the industrial ideal precisely as the other sections of the Union are. But reconstruction is actually under way. Tied politically and economically to the Union, her borders wholly violable, the South now sees very well that she can restore her prosperity only within the competition of an industrial system.

After the war the Southern plantations were often broken up into small farms. These have yielded less and less of a living, and it [is] said that they will never yield a good living until once more they are integrated into large units. But these units will be industrial units, controlled by a board of directors or an executive rather than a squire, worked with machinery, and manned not by farmers living at home, but by "labor." Even so they will not, according to Mr. Henry Ford, support the population that wants to live on them. In the off seasons the laborers will have to work in factories, which henceforth are to be counted on as among the charming features of Southern landscape. The Southern problem is complicated, but at its center is the farmer's problem, and this problem is simply the most acute version of that general agrarian problem which inspires the despair of many thoughtful Americans today.

The agrarian discontent in America is deeply grounded in the love of the tiller for the soil, which is probably, it must be confessed, not peculiar to the Southern specimen, but one of the more ineradicable human attachments, be the tiller as progressive as he may. In proposing to wean men from this foolish attachment, industrialism sets itself against the most ancient and the most humane of all the modes of human livelihood. Do Mr. Hoover and the distinguished thinkers at Washington see how essential is the mutual hatred between the industrialists and the farmers, and how mortal is their conflict? The gentlemen at Washington are mostly preaching and legislating to secure the fabulous "blessings" of industrial progress; they are on the industrial side. The industrialists have a doctrine which is monstrous, but they are not monsters personally; they are forward-lookers with nice manners, and no American progressivist is against them. The farmers are boorish and inarticulate by comparison. Progressivism is against them in their fight, though their traditional status is still so strong that soft words are still spoken to them. All the solutions recommended for their difficulties are really enticements held out to them to become a little more coöperative, more mechanical, more mobile—in short, a little more industrialized. But the farmer who is not a mere laborer, even the farmer of the comparatively new places like Iowa and Nebraska, is necessarily among the more stable and less progressive elements of society. He refuses to mobilize himself and become a unit in the industrial army, because he does not approve of army life.

I will use some terms which are hardly in his vernacular. He identifies himself with a spot of ground, and this ground carries a good deal of meaning; it defines itself for him as nature. He would till it not too hurriedly and not too mechanically to observe in it the contingency and the infinitude of nature; and so his life acquires its philosophical and even its cosmic consciousness. A man can contemplate and explore, respect and love, an object as substantial as a farm or a native province. But he cannot contemplate nor explore, respect nor love, a mere turnover, such as an assemblage of "natural resources," a pile of money, a volume of produce, a market, or a credit system. It is into precisely these intangibles that industrialism would translate the farmer's farm. It means the dehumanization of his life.

However that may be, the South at last, looking defensively about her in all directions upon an industrial world, fingers the weapons of industrialism. There is one powerful voice in the South which, tired of a long status of disrepute, would see the South made at once into a section second to none in wealth, as that is statistically reckoned, and in progressiveness, as that might be estimated by the rapidity of the industrial turnover. This desire offends those who would still like to regard the South as, in the old sense, a home; but its expression is loud and insistent. The urban South, with its heavy importation of regular American ways and regular American citizens, has nearly capitulated to these novelties. It is the village South and the rural South which supply the resistance, and it is lucky for them that they represent a vast quantity of inertia.

Will the Southern establishment, the most substantial exhibit on this continent of a society of the European and historic order, be completely crumbled by the powerful acid of the Great Progressive Principle? Will there be no more looking backward but only looking forward? Is our New World to be dedicated forever to the doctrine of newness?

It is in the interest of America as a whole, as well as in the interest of the South, that these questions press for an answer. I will enter here the most important items of the situation as well as I can; doubtless they will appear a little over-sharpened for the sake of exhibition.

(1) The intention of Americans at large appears now to be what it was always in danger of becoming; an intention of being infinitely progressive. But this intention cannot permit of an established order of human existence, and of that leisure which conditions the life of intelligence and the arts.

(2) The old South, if it must be defined in a word, practiced the contrary and European philosophy of establishment as the foundation of the life of the spirit. The ante-bellum Union possessed, to say the least, a wholesome variety of doctrine.

(3) But the South was defeated by the Union on the battlefield with remarkable decisiveness, and the two consequences have been dire; the Southern tradition was physically impaired, and has ever since been unable to offer an attractive example of its philosophy in action; and the American progressive principle has developed into a pure industrialism without any check from a Southern minority whose voice ceased to make itself heard.

(4) The further survival of the Southern tradition as a detached local remnant is now unlikely. It is agreed that the South must make contact again with the Union. And in adapting itself to the actual state of the Union, the Southern tradition will have to consent to a certain industrialization of its own.

(5) The question at issue is whether the South will permit herself to be so industrialized as to lose entirely her historic identity, and to remove the last substantial barrier that has stood in the way of American progressivism; or will accept industrialism, but with a very bad grace, and will manage to maintain a good deal of her traditional philosophy. . . .

IV

*I*f anything is clear, it is that we can never go back, and neither this essay nor any intelligent person that I know in the South desires a literal restoration of the old Southern life, even if that were possible; dead days are gone, and if by some chance they should return, we should find them intolerable. But out of any epoch in civilization there may arise things worth while, that are the flowers of it. To abandon these, when another epoch arrives, is only stupid, so long as there is still in them the breath and flux of life. In our American life today good things are coming in, which we should try to understand and to share, so far as our natures allow. But it is just as obvious that good things are going out. There was a Southern civilization whose course was halted with those conventions of 1867 by which the negro suffrage in the South—not in the North—was planned, and the pillaging began. But that does not imply that this Southern civilization, once the fine flower of men's lives, is wholly dead; for the core of our humanity lies in the belief that the essence of the soul is its mockery of death. It would be childish and dangerous for the South to be stampeded and betrayed out of its own character by the noise, force, and glittering narrowness of the industrialism and progress spreading everywhere, with varying degrees, from one region to another. . . .

To arrive, then, at some conception of the end of living, the civilization, that will belong to the South, is our great, immediate problem. But in this case, as always in life, alongside a man's open course there moves a mystery, to him dark and shining at once. The mystery here is change, whose god is Mutability. In the shifting relation between ourselves and the new order lies the profoundest source for our living. I mean change in that almost mystical sense by which, so long as we are alive, we are not the same and yet remain ourselves. All things hate steadfastness and are changed, Spenser wrote, and yet, being rightly weighed:

They are not changed from their first estate;
But by their change their being do dilate:
And turning to themselves at length again,
Do work their own perfection so by fate.
Then over them change doth not rule and
　reign,
But they rule over change and do themselves
　maintain.

That a change is now in course all over the South is plain; and it is as plain that the South changing must be the South still, remembering that for no thing can there be any completeness that is outside its own nature, and no thing for which there is any advance save in its own kind. If this were not so, all nature by now would have dissolved in chaos and folly, nothing in it, neither its own self nor any other.

Lawrence Dennis

1893-

After service with the American Expeditionary Force in World War I, Lawrence Dennis graduated from Harvard College in 1920. He then spent seven years in the United States Diplomatic corps, serving in Haiti, Roumania, Nicaragua, Honduras and France. He resigned in 1927 to enter the banking and brokerage fields and then, in 1930, he turned to writing. Concerned about the menace of communism as well as the apparent breakdown of American capitalism, he became convinced that fascism offered the best hope for the survival of American society. Dennis's fascism was akin to the views articulated by Hitler, Mussolini, and later Franco, but it was not simply an imitation of them. He believed that within the context of American society fascism had validity primarily in the economic field, but not in the cultural sphere where, as in Europe, fascism would result in totalitarianism. Dennis wrote a number of books and articles on political problems and edited and published two journals, The Weekly Foreign Letter *and* Appeal to Reason.

This selection is from an article entitled "Fascism for America," in The Annals of the American Academy of Political and Social Science, *180 (1935).*

Conservatives like Messrs. Hoover and Ogden Mills have repeatedly warned us of the fascist danger implicit in the trends of the Roosevelt New Deal. Only this week a group of moderate socialists, rendering a report in the name of the Methodist Federation for Social Service, admonished the Nation that Senator Long, Father Coughlin, and General Johnson, all of whom either now are or recently have been supporters of the New Deal, constitute a serious fascist menace. Moderate socialists generally will be found to concur in the generalization that present trends in this country are towards fascism. As for the orthodox Communists, any one who is familiar with their current writings and utterances is aware that one of their dogmas is that the reign of a fascist antichrist is likely to be the culminating phase of the decline of capitalism and the prelude to the opening of the communist millennium. Indeed, about the only important leaders who do not openly express this fundamental agreement as to the imminence of fascism, and even as to its actuality in a modified form, are our three outstanding leaders—President Roosevelt, Senator Long, and Father Coughlin—and their followers, these leaders being charged by the conservative and liberal critics with fascist tendencies.

The Liberal Diagnosis

Now, I entirely agree with the Hoovers, the Norman Thomases, and the

Communists that our three foremost political and spiritual leaders are moving in fascist directions. But I do not agree with the critics of these leaders that fascism is per se something to be feared or fought. It appears to me that prevailing social forces the world over make a fascist trend the inevitable alternative to chaos or communism. I cannot be sure at present whether our momentarily outstanding leaders will lead us on to fascism or to chaos. They are not clear in their own minds, as yet, as to ends and means. Therefore it seems to me that instead of denouncing a trend we are clearly powerless to arrest, those of us who can think and still have a chance to think out loud ought to try to clarify the issues so that the wills of the leaders and their followings may be clarified as to choices of ends and means. It is significant that I, an apologist for the authoritarian state and a critic of liberal democracy, should be trying to fix the thought of constructive minds on the analysis of present trends with a view to creating informed judgments and making enlightened choices, while the rabble of the liberal intelligentsia is largely occupied with organizing emotional demonstrations and unloosing floods of impassioned words against the fascist trend which is sweeping the world.

Now, although I agree with the diagnosis by Messrs. Hoover and Mills that we are moving towards fascism under the leadership of Messrs. Roosevelt, Long, and Coughlin, I cannot accept their prescription of a fight to preserve and reinvigorate the old system. Believing it doomed, I see no sense in fighting for it. Fighting for lost causes imposes on mankind the most futile and criminal sort of warfare. British mercantilism which was doomed in 1775, and the Southern planter system with its accompaniment of Negro slavery which was doomed by 1850, each fought on American soil two futile wars for two doomed or lost causes. Why? Well, largely because certain sincere and worthy people felt it to be a matter of duty and honor loyally to fight for a system under which they had been fairly well off.

Most of us here today, quite as much as Mr. Hoover and Mr. Mills, have been fairly well off under the liberal-capitalist system. Like all the other doomed systems of the past, it has glorious traditions which can be made to evoke dynamic responses from large numbers of people. But if it is an order doomed by the irresistible trend of prevailing social forces, why fight for it?

Every time I read an utterance of Mr. Hoover or exponents of his orthodox and traditional liberal capitalism, I think of the British loyalists of the Stuart dynasty since 1688. It is pathetic and romantic to want a boat to row you over to bonny Prince Charlie, and a constitution in distress can be almost as full of pathos as an exiled prince in distress. All that is needed now for the loyalists of the liberal American Constitution is a few good ballads. I offer this suggestion to the Republican National Committee. But I see the captains of industry, along with the realistic leaders of radical reaction to prolonged depression, climbing on the fascist band wagon.

The Communist Diagnosis

As for the communist diagnosis of the present phase of capitalist decline, particularly as to the proposition that it obviously indicates fascism in the interest of the elite of the present order, I am in substantial agreement. The Hoover conservatives say that we are going fascist and that it will be the end of liberal capitalism. To this I say "Check." The Communists say that we are going fascist because it will be the only salvation of the élite of the present order. To this I say "Double check."

With the rest of the communist thesis as to fascism, I disagree. The communist contention that any possible fascist formula will be doomed to early disaster, I find utterly unprovable. I also deny the communist assertion that any fascist formula would necessarily prove detrimental to the welfare of the people. This latter proposition, of course, raises issues of ultimate values rather than of facts, so it cannot be argued out. Naturally, I reject many of the communist values, one of the most important of which is that human welfare demands the liquidation of the élite of the old order. Liquidation, as you know, is a euphemism for experiences like being stood up before a Communist firing squad.

I find the bourgeoisie of this country too numerous and too strong to be liquidated except in one of the bloodiest and most prolonged civil wars the world has ever known. Aside from the consideration that I should not like to be liquidated, I cannot but feel that the liquidation of so large and useful a group of persons would be a greater loss to the rest of the community than the advantages any dictatorship of triumphant proletarian revolutionary leaders could possibly vouchsafe to the community.

So I am against the Marxian class struggle. I am in favor of a middle-class revolution and against a proletarian revolution. The middle-class revolution has already begun. I call it fascist. I hope it can be more productive of human values than the middle-class revolutions of England in 1648 and 1688, of America from 1776 to 1825, or of France from 1789 to 1815.

I am prepared to make a concession to the communist thesis which I cannot make to the liberal thesis. I am prepared to admit that, given a conceivable combination of circumstances and events, the radicalism of Lenin, as it might be made explicit and effective by a régime of competent, professional, power-hungry, revolutionary leaders, having a high order of military and administrative genius, could be made to work. I am unable to see how the radicalism of Adam Smith, John Locke, and John Stuart Mill, now the conservatism of Herbert Hoover, can possibly be made to work in the world of Mussolini, Hitler, and Stalin. I consider any one of the last three named leaders fitter to survive in the present struggle for existence. I would remind any who may not be clear on this that fitness to survive is not an ethical quality.

Failure of the Present System

The reason why my money is not on the liberals and why my sympathies are not with their ideologies is due to a complex of facts implicit in the present situation and of personal preferences. I find the liberal theory and practice inadequate both to what I consider to be social requirements and to my own personal requirements. I am wholly uninterested in explanations of its failures or in prescriptions for its recovery. It has failed. It has proved inadequate. Therefore, by the inexorable law of the survival of the fittest, it is doomed.

In the present crisis of liberalism which began in 1914, the exponents, the theorists, and the practitioners of liberalism have had their innings. They and their system have failed. I cannot and do not have to prove that a new system will work better. For a new system inevitably to emerge out of the crisis of the present system, it is necessary only to have it established that the present system is inadequate. The growing ranks of the recipients of state relief and of the frustrated élite of the middle classes are going to be more and more swayed in their emotional reactions and impulses to action by the simple logic I have just stated: When a system fails or proves inadequate, a new one is indicated. There is only one argument that can defeat that logic, and that argument is turning the failure or the inadequacy of the system challenged into success and adequacy.

The liberal leaders have had their chance since 1914. They have been slipping one by one into the abyss. They have failed. The people are not interested in their excuses or sympathetic to pleas for a second chance. They have ears now only for leaders who promise a new system. New leaders will enjoy power only as long as they move in the direction of a new system. Mr. Roosevelt can hold his prestige only as long as people believe in the New Deal.

Let me emphasize the fact that we face the situation of a system which has been giving increasing signs since 1914 that it no longer works tolerably well. It came out of all the wars of the nineteenth century stronger than it went in. It is therefore nonsense to say that war is the cause of the depression or the world crisis of liberal capitalism. Liberalism won the Napoleonic wars but lost the late World War. Liberalism in England, America, and continental Europe had won innumerable wars up to 1814.

Government Financing of the System

Need I run over a bill of particulars to substantiate the proposition that the present system no longer works, and that the changes now being inaugurated in this country are not reforms calculated to restore the system to normal operating efficiency? The banks could not reopen and they could not now stay open without Government intervention. Public order could not be maintained if the state failed to increase public expenditure to provide work and relief for the growing number of the destitute and unemployed. Although surplus bank reserves are over two and a quarter billion dollars, or enough to support an expansion of commercial loans in excess of twenty billion dollars, bank loans to industry and commerce have been almost steadily shrinking during the past two years. Banks do not lend and investors do not put idle funds into new enterprises or construction because under present conditions the prospects of getting a return are not good enough.

The measure of recovery from the panicky lows of 1933 which we momentarily enjoy in the lull before the next crash is proportionate to and dependent on the amount of Government money actually being disbursed to prevent banks from being closed, to pay for labor that private enterprise will not hire, and to give money to farmers and other producers which they could not obtain in the open market. Not only the unemployed, but the banks, the railroads, agriculture, and industry are on the dole. Profits are being obtained by certain producers through the Government financing of curtailment of production. But for this Government financing on credit of curtailment of production, prices would have continued their fall until every bank, insurance company, and large debtor in the country would have gone into insolvency.

Two things are certain: (1) The Government cannot go on financing a curtailment of production without lowering the national standard of living and without thereby increasing the violence of popular discontent; (2) the Government cannot go on financing curtailment of production, the maintenance of artificial price levels, the solvency of insolvent railroads and financial institutions, and a growing army of destitute unemployed all by the process of borrowing.

The orderly processes of the liberal-capitalist system call for adjustment of the financial difficulties through bankruptcy, mortgage foreclosures—putting the country through the legal wringer, in other words. The system calls for adjustment of market, price, and wage difficulties by letting prices and employment be determined by the free play of supply and demand without Government subsidy to production curtailment or to subsistence of the unemployed. There is not a serious-minded man in the country who would long keep his head on if he tried to put the country through the wringer of orderly capitalist readjustment. Therefore I say the system is doomed and no longer works. The plea of the conservatives for a return to the Constitution is absurd when the strict enforcement of constitutional property rights would precipitate civil war.

Every economic adjustment today rests on Government interventions in new and innumerable forms. Therefore I say we are headed towards fascism, communism, or chaos. It is not yet fascism or communism because the bases of Government intervention do not at present constitute a system which can be rationally defined or successfully maintained. In other words, the underlying scheme of Government intervention does not constitute a stable system of social administration. It seems to work only because the scheme of Government intervention now in operation is a sort of toboggan—the toboggan slide of the dollar and national credit to the vanishing point. When we hit bottom, we shall have chaos or fascism. I should like to see fascism before we hit bottom.

Briefly, there is no recovery of the orderly capitalist sort, here, in England, in France, or in Canada. There cannot be such recovery without a revival of private investment in adequate volume. There cannot be a revival of private investment in adequate volume under present conditions of closed world markets, artificial maintenance of prices, and colossal government expenditures for relief. Liberalism can stand off the final crash only as long as strong liberal governments like those of the United States, England, and France can coast along down the toboggan of inflation. But on that route, liberalism will have a one-way ride.

Liberalism in Germany survived the postwar inflationary ride only as long as the financially sound liberal countries like the United States and England could support the international financial structure. When liberalism in America, England, and France takes this last ride, there will be no other financially sound liberal countries to maintain the integrity of liberal-capitalistic institutions with the aid of foreign loans and financial arrangements. As I see it, liberalism in America is on its last ride down the dollar toboggan.

Liberalism cannot achieve a governmental pattern of intervention which can be stabilized and made permanently to work, and there's the rub. Granted this generalization which I think I have sufficiently established, we have the alternatives of some form of authoritarian state to do a job of economic or social planning, or chaos. I do not have to prove that state planning will succeed; I have only to prove that without state planning, conditions are intolerable.

Ends and Means

Broadly summarized, the issues are matters of ends and means. The ends of the liberal-capitalist state are mainly those of good policing, the protection of life and property, and the enforcement of contracts, with a little welfare in the form of education, sanitation, and traffic regulation thrown in, all on the broad assumption that individuals can best plan their economic activities without other government intervention. The ends of the authoritarian state are some sort of planned social order, made explicit and effective by the state.

There is a plan under both the liberal and the authoritarian scheme of things. But the plan of the liberal scheme of things results mostly from the play of individual and competitive initiatives in a relatively free market and field of economic choices. The plan of the authoritarian scheme of things has to result from the planning of a central authority, which must always be really a council of *persons*, charged with this function. Hence the epithet "dictatorship" attaches so easily to the planned state.

Now fascism, as a term, differs from communism, as a term, for the purposes of this discussion, largely in the following respect: The communist plan is, for the moment, whatever the Communist council of elders or cardinals of the international Communist faith, assembled in Moscow, decide and promulgate; while the fascist plan is whatever the fascist council in a given nation decides.

As yet there is no fascist council planning government intervention in this country. Consequently, any fascist plan for America which I might offer you would of necessity have to be largely the creation of my imagination. A Communist, on the other hand, could give you a plan for America fresh from the pigeonholes of the Moscow Communist Party bureaucracy. The ends of a planned society can be many and different societies. The means of an authoritarian state, are always essentially governmental. Therein communism and fascism are alike. But in this connection "governmental" must be understood as referring to everything that enters into the enterprise of achieving a centrally planned scheme of social organization. Hence, both the communist and the fascist states are properly called totalitarian.

I shall try briefly to lay down certain broad generalizations as to both ends and means of an ideal fascist authoritarian state for this country.

Public Welfare

The fundamental ends of government and public administration, whether under fascism, liberalism, communism, or any other "ism," are obviously public order and the realization of some idealized scheme of public welfare. I have little patience with those liberal, fascist, or communist critics of other political systems who assume that those systems are conceived and operated by wicked and insane leaders whose chief motivation in the exercise of political power is the gratification of irrational personal caprices at the expense of the welfare of the people they govern. Order and public welfare, I believe, are the ends of every government in operation today. But there are different schemes of maintaining order, and there are different values and hierarchies of values to make up the content of any scheme of public welfare. The ideologies and the methodologies of welfare differ.

The weakness of the liberal scheme is that it can no longer maintain order without concerning itself with economic government in ways which are admittedly incompatible with the basic tenets of liberalism. And the trouble with the liberal scheme of welfare is obviously that too many people are dissatisfied with it. Liberalism stands condemned, not of an indifference to welfare, but of failure to work out its ideologies and methodologies of welfare. As I have already stated, this amounts to saying that the liberal plan no longer works. The alternatives are chaos or an authoritarian plan. . . .

The Sphere of Control

Control, of course, is not bounded by the confines of the economic interests. The fascist state, however, is concerned mainly with effective control of capital and labor. A type of fascism could well arise to seek control in the field of cultural interests and activities not affected with important economic interest. I should deplore the growth of such a type of fascism. I am not prepared to delimit the functions of the state as the liberals are—in theories which strangely differ from practices.

Broadly stated, the individual can and should be left a large field of choices in respect to occupations, uses of leisure time, and uses of resources not required for public ends. The field in which the state has to be most authoritarian and restrictive of liberty is a field which will only affect seriously two or three thousand corporations and the five or ten thousand men who have hitherto had too much freedom of choice of policies for self-enrichment.

The point I want to stress is that so far as the millions of stockholders, bondholders, depositors, and insured having an interest in corporate affairs are concerned, fascism will not materially modify their rights or liberties, for the very good reason that, as it is, they have *de facto* no rights or liberties to be modified except the rights to sell their rights of ownership if they can find a buyer and to take what management gives them. These rights will undoubtedly be left to them.

State intervention, of course, will often penalize owners under fascism. Mistakes and rascality of management have done the same under liberal capitalism. Wherein would the right of an insuree in the Metropolitan Insurance Company have been modified if the state had told its managers that they could not put $25,000,000 into a office building in New York at a high rate of interest

but that they must put that sum into slum clearance projects at a low rate of interest? There must be much state interference with corporate management under fascism, and there should be little state interference with personal habits. Economic and not sumptuary control is the need. But economic control must not mobilize cultural instruments of the control, like radio, press, school, and church, against the state. The state must have a monopoly of those uses of power which can make or break successful social planning.

This leads me briefly to speak of the problems of means under a fascist authoritarian state. The ends, as we have already seen, are order and welfare, which I would express more concretely by saying as high a standard of living as the people want to pay for with their labor and available resources. The means, however, are the more characteristically fascist features of the new system. I can only run over certain important fundamentals.

Concentration of Power

As to the political or governmental scheme of things, the keynote is concentration of power, or centralization of control. This means scrapping the principle of separation of power. Government is no longer a matter of checking and balancing or playing a game of the individual versus a state which is constantly suspected of having designs on his liberty and welfare. Individuals who have been beaten by the depression in the free market do not want liberal liberties to do things they cannot as a practical matter do, and liberal liberties for others to do things to them which the others can and actually do, and which the victims do not like to have done to them.

The liberal critics of fascism are apt to stress the question of liberty. With a curious lack of historical sense and of a sense of humor, they forget that the cry for liberty has always been the cry of the leaders of the "outs." Our liberal critics can be quite sure that any successful revolution will leave a lot of people with more liberty than they had before. Our liberal friends can also be sure that the people who want a new Deal or a new system are not entirely enchanted with their present liberties. Liberty is a word to be used by people fighting for something they do not have; it is not a good propaganda word for people to play with who are fighting to keep something they have and which their opponents are after.

Senator Long's followers really want to share other people's liberties by sharing their wealth. Every social revolution is a fight for liberty. The members of the Liberty League are on the defensive, and the leaders of the Long and Coughlin forces are on the offensive. My money is usually on the offensive. The élite of the present order can assure their leadership or liberties only by giving up the defensive and joining the offensive on the technological problems of social organization and production.

The political instrument of government must be directed by an executive council representing a mandate from the people to do a managing job. This means the end of the parliamentary or congressional system, under which governmental decisions and policies are the results of power group pressures. . . .

The Mind of the Masses

Many of the conservatives believe or seem to believe that the American people are attached to a given system and ideology. This is a delusion peculiar to the lawyers and the instructed classes. Ninety per cent of the American people have no grasp whatever of the ideological content of the system. They have not read the Federalist papers, Rousseau, Montesquieu, Adam Smith, or Blackstone. If they are moved by words or symbols, like "Constitution," "liberty," "democracy," "representative government," and so forth, it is purely a result of early emotional conditioning and the association of a given feeling with a given word, without the occurrence of any understanding process. All these words or symbols can be incanted by any demagogue committed to any enterprise. A fascist dictatorship can be set up by a demagogue in the name of all the catchwords of the present system, just as a Communist dictatorship was set up in Russia in October 1917 in the name of democracy and other catchwords of the liberals.

It is also a mistake to suppose that the American people are averse to government regimentation, or orderly organization and procedure. We are the most organized, standardized, regimented, and docile people in the world so far as the processes of mass direction and management are concerned. People who fall into this erroneous generalization about the American people fail to see that most of our government is now done by large corporations and cultural associations rather than by the state. The state can easily include the corporation and most of the cultural associations within its scheme of social control without having the masses of the people notice the difference. The $25,000-a-year vice-president of a big bank or a big university is as much the yes-man of the power hierarchy on which his job depends as any communist or fascist party official, and he has about the same liberty of basic dissent.

I am not showing a contempt but a high respect for the masses in advancing these heterodox generalizations about them. The people have too much sense to take symbols and verbalisms, like the "Constitution" and "liberty," as seriously as our educated liberals and lawyers do. Both Senator Long and Father Coughlin, in harping on the calamities of our present situation and in clamoring for changes, are in far closer harmony with the logic of mass needs than are our intellectual exponents of liberalism, or conservatism, as you may care to call it, who are invoking symbols and verbalisms not as instruments of action but as deterrents to revolutionary action. The people want public order and the elements of subsistence. Liberty with these, yes; liberty without them is nonsense.

Character of Coming Fascism

Revolutionary change is indicated. It is beginning. Its velocity and momentum will accelerate. The élite of the present order have their chance now to reform their thinking and lead the trend. Whether our coming fascism is more or less humane and decent will depend largely on the contributions our humane élite can make to it in time. There need be no acute class struggle, if the élite of the present order in both parties will but recognize that a planned economy can best be planned in the interests of the dominant élite, if it is also planned to give the masses the maximum output of human satisfactions. The larger the total product, the larger the cut for ownership and management. The problem can be that of organizing for the maximum social income as a part of organization for class advantage. It can also be a class struggle between the "ins" fighting to defend their liberties, and the "outs" fighting to capture them. It will depend largely on the decision of the "ins" during the next few months.

Thurman Arnold
1891-1969

Thurman Arnold had a distinguished career as lawyer, teacher, and public servant. Educated at Princeton and Yale, he received a law degree from Harvard and practiced law in Wyoming until 1927. He then accepted a professorship in the Yale Law School, following which he held a series of positions in the federal government, including service as Assistant Attorney General and Associate Justice of the United States Court of Appeals.

Politically, Arnold gave full support to the New and Fair Deals. He believed, as the selection indicates, that an elaborate mythology had grown up around American capitalism, and that this agreed-upon fiction had long ceased to reflect the reality of the American economic system. His observations strike at the heart of many of the inherited economic ideas of America.

This selection is from his best-known book, The Folklore of Capitalism *(New Haven: Yale University Press, 1937).*

*T*he confusion in political thinking which we have just described arose out of the gradual decay of an old legal and economic religion. The difficulty with the religion was that it had become an obstacle to the organizing ability of the American people. It was producing phobias instead of inspiration. Economic principles had become an arsenal of weapons used against new organizations instead of for them. Governmental morality had become an excuse for government not to meet obvious demands.

In a period when rational philosophies of government were necessary for our comfort, everyone was demanding a new creed; yet every new creed advanced violated the old ideals which were still sacred. This is usual in times of social change. It is one of the inevitable symptoms of progress from one form of social organization to another. The literature of the time is typical of any similar age which is experiencing a conflict between its ideals and its needs.

The most obvious conflict of 1937 was that in which the creeds accepted by respectable people described social organizations in the language of personally owned private property, when as a matter of fact the things which were described were neither private, nor property, nor personally owned. The complete failure of the language of law and economics as a means of communication of sensible ideas created the endless debate about principle and the exhortations to heed the lessons of history which we have been observing in courts, in colleges, and in the editorial pages of newspapers. Before analyzing the failure of our economic and legal language as a means of communication of practical ideas it is first necessary, at the risk of repetition, to discover why old gods always thrash around so violently before they die, and why most respectable people become so uncomfortable in the process.

383

The Discomfort of a Changing Mythology

The reason for this confusion which attends the growth of new organizations in society lies deep in the psychology which concerns the effects of words and ceremonies on the habits of men in groups. Men always idealize these habits and the structure they give to society. The idealizing is done by magic words which at first are reasonably descriptive of the institutions they represent. At least they represent the dreams which men have of those institutions. When the institutions themselves disappear, the words still remain and make men think that the institutions are still with them. They talk of the new organizations which have come to take the place of the old in the terms of these old words. The old words no longer fit. Directions given in that language no longer have the practical results which are expected. Realists arise to point this out and men who love and reverence these old words (that is, the entire God-fearing, respectable element of the community) are shocked. Since the words are heavily charged with a moral content, those who do not respect them are immoral. The respectable moral element of society will have nothing to do with such immorality. They feel compelled to turn the power over to nonrespectable people in order to reserve the right to make faces at them. Yet they recognize that those immoral people are doing something which has to be done. This fact can only be explained under the curious age-old concept of sin. No religion ever got along without this concept. It is useful because everyone can continue to work to abolish it, knowing full well their objective will never be reached. Thus, in these times of confusion, everyone believes that human character is disintegrating. This happens whenever the rising generation thinks differently from the old.

By this process the formulas become more important than facts. They cease to be tools and become objectives in themselves. Legal and economic literature (or whatever other ceremony is current in such times) becomes more important than life. And in the confusion which results from this conflict respectable men become angry, sad, romantic, cynical, disillusioned, last-ditch defenders of a faith. They do not become cheerful, practical technicians dealing with the facts before them.

In such times men get to talking about the decline and fall of civilization and worrying about Greece and Rome. A vast literature of explanation and exhortation pours forth. This is a symptom that the class which produces that literature is becoming uneasy and impotent and needs a great deal of printed matter in order to prove to itself that it still represents the only sound type of organization. The blame for that uneasiness is all ascribed to the immorality of a society which has perversely and sinfully become unlike the little ideal pictures which represent what a proper society should be like. At such times men predict Fascism, Communism, and all sorts of similar catastrophes. They prove this by putting it on the printed page, because they have more faith in the printed page than in the spoken word.

The result of this uneasiness may be war, or may be only a lot of oratory, poetry, and romantic economics. What happens depends on whether the kindly, tolerant, respectable elements of society are able to emerge from this mood of impotence before less kindly and tolerant people seize the reins of power. The mood does little harm if it is only a temporary escape from reality, like being in love, or mourning for the dead. Indeed, it would be a drab human race which did not shed a tear over departed institutions. Romantic lovers and inconsolable widows are both very lovely dramatizations of important ideals and the writer would not abolish them if he could. Nevertheless, it is an incontestable fact that they are hard people to put up with outside of books and when there is a job to be done.

The Mythology of Private Property in an Age of Organization

Why has the literature of law and economics become today more like a funeral service than the pep talk for salesmen which it should be to promote organization? The reason is that it is using the little pictures of private property and profit motive to describe a society which is much more like an army than the group of horse traders which it is supposed to be. Against the background of such a society the terms do not make sense. Men believe that a society is disintegrating when it can no longer be pictured in familiar terms. Unhappy is a people that has run out of words to describe what is going on.

It is obvious today that private property has disappeared. The writer, for example, owns some furniture which he can use without the assistance of any large organization, though not to the extent his parents could, because he is unable to repair it as his father was. For transportation he has an automobile, but he does not know what is going on under the hood and could not run it without a great organization to assist him. His father owned a western ranch and raised his own horses. These horses burned hay, but the hay did not come from a filling station, which in turn required a still larger organization to supply it. Yet today furniture and automobiles are the nearest we come to private property generally owned by any large group of our population.

The other things the writer "owns" are all claims to rank or privilege in an organizational hierarchy. He is a professor at the Yale Law School and hopes that Yale will feed and lodge him. He has a piece of paper from an insurance company which he hopes will induce that organization to take care of his wife if he dies. He has other pieces of paper from other organizations operating buildings and railroads and manufacturing plants which give him precarious privileges in those industrial governments. Wealth today consists in nothing any one individual can use. The standards of wealth are simply current expectations of how the individual stands with the rulers of industrial baronies coupled with a guess as to the strength of those principalities. . . .

The reason why old myths create such a problem in times when old institutions are not functioning effectively is that they induce men to act in direct contradiction to observed facts. Such conduct is of course one of the great cohesive forces of society, for when institutions are functioning effectively it is the power of superstition rather than the power of reason that holds them together. However, when the institutions have become impotent to meet social needs, these same superstitions have the effect of throwing respectable, moderate, and kindly people out of power because they cannot free themselves of the old myths long enough to be effective leaders. . . .

One of the essential and central notions which give our industrial feudalism logical symmetry is the personification of great industrial enterprise. The ideal that a great corporation is endowed with the rights and prerogatives of a free individual is as essential to the acceptance of corporate rule in temporal affairs as was the ideal of the divine right of kings in an earlier day. Its exemplification, as in the case of all vital ideals, has been accomplished by ceremony. Since it has been a central ideal in our industrial government, our judicial institutions have been particularly concerned with its celebration. Courts, under the mantle of the Constitution, have made a living thing out of this fiction. Men have come to believe that their own future liberties and dignity are tied up in the freedom of great industrial organizations from restraint, in much the same way that they thought their salvation in the future was dependent on their reverence and support of great ecclesiastical organizations in the Middle Ages. . . .

This book is not concerned with the unsolvable problem of whether America would have progressed faster or slower under some other set of myths. It does not attack the use of the corporate personality in folklore. The results have been the creation of one of the greatest productive machines that the world has ever known, and this perhaps is justification enough if anyone is interested in justifying what has happened. This book is concerned only with diagnosing the present difficulties which have come upon us now that the industrial feudalism is no longer protecting large groups of our citizens who demand security, and with trying to explain the ideological difficulties which prevent the creating of organizations which will give that protection. We cannot be practical about social problems if we are under the illusion that we can solve them without complying with the taboos and customs of the tribe. The corporate personality is part of our present religion. We must continue to refer to corporations as individuals in public discourse so long as the words have emotional relevance. Since, however, we must use the words and ceremonies, it becomes important that we be able to use them intelligently. . . .

Therefore, if one wishes to guess the social philosophy of the future, he must guess first what class will come into control of the organizations which make and distribute the goods and, second, whether the change will be violent or slow. If it is violent, a whole new set of terms will dramatize the sudden rise of the new organization to power. The old terms will flow back gradually during a period of confusion, while the new organizations fumble and fail as organizations always must fail to live up to the promises of their creed. And finally a note of positive affirmation will be heard which, like Lincoln's "Gettysburg Address," seems to link the new organizations to some heroic event in the past, to express the contradictory notions and ideals of the people, and to fill them with the pride and morale necessary for expansion.

If the rise of the new organization is slow, the terms will change their meaning, rather than be supplanted by new terms. Capitalism will become "socialistic" in a slow revolution. In a more violent one, "Capitalism" will be supplanted by "Socialism" and then in the period of stabilization "Socialism" will gradually become "capitalistic." This is what is happening in Russia. We can note today the charge being constantly made by those who were most idealistic about Socialism in Russia that the Communists are abandoning their ideals and "reverting" to Capitalism. In contrast to this we heard speeches *ad nauseam* in the last campaign that the New Deal was in devious and hidden ways making our capitalistic system socialistic. The observer who watches this process should never be alarmed about the "stupidity" of the so-called intelligent people who make speeches of this kind. It is part of the process of change in a rational world. All he needs to worry about is the character of the people who are gradually coming into power. Does he think that they are good organizers and at the same time tolerant and humanitarian? If he reaches this conclusion, he need not worry about "failure to balance the budget." All "balancing the budget" ever can mean is that an institution has achieved public acceptance of its objectives. If it has, there will never be any difficulty about balancing its budget.

CHAPTER XXI

THE RESPONSE
OF THE
CHURCHES

*T*o a people accustomed to a belief in the beneficence of divine providence and a faith in their historic mission and destiny, the momentous events that marked the twentieth century—including a world-wide
depression and two global wars—were a bewildering challenge. In the
midst of such a threatening world, men once more began to seek universal
and unshakable standards of truth, justice, and morality to which they could
hold fast.

In such an atmosphere it was perhaps not surprising that an increasing
number of Americans began to examine anew the religious heritage of their
society. The problem they faced, however, was not simply to restate and
emphasize established religious truths. Had that been so, religion would
have faced no serious crisis. But the fact that many elements in the traditional
faith of Americans seemed peculiarly outmoded and obsolete. Liberal Protestantism, for example, with its belief in the innate goodness of man, its ideal of
social betterment (even utopianism), and its acceptance of a theology of
immanence, appeared outdated by the monstrous evils that marked the
world in these decades. Even the older fundamentalist Protestantism seemed
an anachronism, especially following the failure of one of its major goals—

prohibition—an objective that had promised the eradication of evil but had helped instead to spread crime and corruption in American life.

Yet the dilemmas of religion were not simply internal in nature but were intimately related to developments within American culture. For as the older individualistic ethic declined, to be replaced by a social and organizational ethic, the role and function of religion in the United States also underwent a drastic transformation. To many individuals the appeal of religion was based not so much on its intrinsic truths as on the sustenance it could provide for "the American way of life." One attended a house of worship not necessarily out of reverence for a deity and his revealed truths, but because attendance was expected. In addition, institutional affiliation provided the individual with a means of identification with a particular social grouping—an identification based increasingly on religion as the older ethnic identification declined with the end of mass immigration.

Recognizing the weakness of organized religion, virtually all religious leaders agreed on the need for a revitalized Christianity that would once again restore meaning and significance to the life of man. However, it was apparent that a simple reiteration of older themes was insufficient, and many churchmen began to seek new ways of presenting and interpreting the message of Christianity.

The quest for a theology that would provide a meaningful perspective for contemporary man became noticeable initially in Protestantism. Influenced by the crisis theology of such philosophers as Karl Barth and Paul Tillich, Protestant theologians began to undertake a searching examination of the optimistic hopes and dreams that had characterized liberal Christianity and the social gospel. Rejecting the emphasis on the innate goodness of human nature, these ministers began to resurrect the older doctrine of original sin, arguing that the dilemmas and paradoxes that mankind faced were perennial and could not be solved on a permanent basis by man. As Reinhold Niebuhr, the outstanding spokesman for Protestant neo-orthodoxy put it, the human race had little hope for redemption if it relied solely on the potentialities of human nature or the processes of history. Only a religion of grace or a gospel that held out hope of a transcendent source of redemption could bring comfort to the human spirit in its inevitable defeat in the world of nature and history. The theologians of the new orthodoxy thus propounded a religious faith that restored the transcendental significance of Christian belief. In so doing they developed a Christianity that was quite unlike that of the past— one that at times was even "post-Christian" in its sources and meanings.

Neo-orthodox Protestantism, nevertheless, was too sophisticated and intellectual a creed to have immediate effect on the lives of millions who had neither the training nor patience to master its intricacies or difficulties. Yet the need for a faith was so great that soon after the end of World War II the older evangelical-fundamentalist tradition began to reassert itself. Speaking in terms easily understood by the masses of people, evangelical ministers like Billy Graham insisted that salvation at a revival meeting not only offered man hope of divine forgiveness but also freed him from all future temptation. Thus the major prerequisite for the solution both of the problem of the individual and of national and international problems was an unreserved acceptance of Jesus. In an era when America seemed to be moving away from liberalism toward conservatism, the simple message of the evangelists struck a responsive chord in the hearts of millions who dreamed of a return to the imagined simplicities of the past.

The problems faced by Protestantism in recent decades have by no means been unique to that group alone. The Catholic Church in the United States also has had to face similar difficulties growing out of the secularization of American culture. In the 1930's, the Catholic hierarchy and prominent lay philosophers responded to this challenge by embarking on a militant crusade on behalf of the Thomistic version of natural law. Insisting upon the ability of man's reason to fathom the eternal law of God, Catholics argued that the eighteenth- and nineteenth-century world had collapsed largely because of its atheism, its materialism, and its secularism that raised "progress" to the level of divine truth. Only by returning to the natural law and the traditional truths of Christianity as interpreted by the Catholic Church, they insisted, could modern man find significance and meaning in his life.

The neo-Thomistic movement within the Catholic Church tended to reflect the traditional authoritarian conservatism of that body. After the Second World War, however, Catholicism, like Protestantism, began to find many of its cherished tenets challenged at key points by younger critics who argued that the Church, largely because of its authoritarian and bureaucratic character, had lost contact with the spiritual needs of its members. The convening of the Second Vatican Council by Pope John XXIII encouraged younger dissidents and reformers to express their dissatisfaction with traditional beliefs and practices and to offer their own plans for reform. The result was a period of turmoil and strain within the Catholic Church that seemed, by the late 1960's, to border on what some conservatives regarded as outright heresy. The response of the critics, on the other hand, was to point out that even religious structures must be periodically reformed if they were not to become bastions of irrelevant conservatism.

Despite the apparent strength of religious faith at mid-century, it was still questionable whether Christianity in any form could triumph over the increasing secularization of American life, a trend that affected all denominations. Christianity also was hard-pressed by critics who attacked its supernatural beliefs and its otherwordliness, which they argued had led to a passive acceptance of evil. These critics pointed to the deliberate slaughter of six million Jews by a supposedly Christian nation as well as the barbarism of total warfare devised by men who claimed the sanction of the church. Even within the churches a small dissenting minority challenged their co-religionists to apply religious and ethical principles to such contemporary issues as race and poverty.

Whether or not religion could ever again exercise the influence it had in the past, or even become a vital force in itself rather than a means to an end—for to most Americans religion was good and desirable because it reinforced the American way of life which was regarded as *the* ultimate good—remained for the future to answer.

Reinhold Niebuhr

1892-

One of the outstanding Protestant theologians and philosophers of our time, Reinhold Niebuhr was born in Wright City, Missouri. After studying at a theological seminary in St. Louis, he received a B.D. from Yale in 1914 and an M.A. in 1915. In the latter year he accepted a call to a struggling, working-class church in Detroit and, as a result, became interested in the problems of an industrialized society. Slowly but surely Niebuhr came to the recognition that the advocates of liberal Christianity and the social gospel had misread the nature and potentialities of man—that the liberal church, like the orthodox church, was preaching the good life in terms irrelevant to the problems of modern society. He then turned to the task of developing an outlook suitable to the contemporary world. In 1928 Niebuhr was called to Union Theological Seminary in New York City.

The leading advocate of Protestant neo-orthodoxy, Niebuhr has consistently emphasized the concept of original sin— the frank recognition of the essentially sinful and tragic nature of man. Defining original sin in terms of a historical situation that never permits a choice between absolute good and absolute evil, he rejected the notion of the perfectibility of man and the idea of progress in its eighteenth-century sense. Holding that Christianity, properly understood, has a relevance to the dilemmas of modern man, Niebuhr has attempted to formulate a more realistic philosophy that takes into account the limitations of man. He has argued that man, though capable of imposing achievements, is yet a finite being, driven by a sinful pride to claim a dignity and eminence that no man possesses and to affirm a finality for his convictions that no relative human judgment deserves. But it should be noted that while emphasizing the limitations of man, Niebuhr has always taken a liberal or radical position on social and economic issues.

The following selections are representative of Niebuhr's thinking. The first is from "The Dilemma of Modern Man," The Nation, *164 (February 22, 1947), and the second from* The Children of Light and the Children of Darkness: A Vindication of Democracy and a Critique of Its Traditional Defence (*New York: Charles Scribner's Sons, 1944*).

*W*e are living in an age in which our social and historical imperatives may be fairly simply defined but not easily achieved. Our task is to create and re-create community within the terms set by a technical civilization. The constant elaboration of man's technical skills has created a potential world community, but this community cannot be actualized as easily as modern men had hoped. The same technical skills have created abundance in modern industrial communities; yet these communities all suffer from great social insecurity because they find it difficult to distribute the new wealth equitably enough to guarantee harmony and stability.

In such a historical situation the average person still interprets the faith by which he lives primarily in sociopolitical terms. He has faith in this or that social objective. Usually in the United States and in the Western world generally the objective is defined as "the democratic way of life." I do not believe that such a purely political objective constitutes an adequate "faith." It may define our primary moral obligation, or at least the social dimension of that obligation, but it does not define the meaning of our existence. Any adequate sense of the meaning of life must be able to comprehend not only what we ought to do but what we are. It must explain why we are creatures who do not find it easy, or even possible, to fulfil our highest obligation.

At the present moment the popular definition of our political ideal as the "democratic way of life" hides a very great dilemma, which is also a part of the total human situation. For the world is divided between different types of "democrats," between those who would sacrifice freedom, or have already sacrificed it, for the sake of an equalitarian and collectivist democracy and those who would make no sacrifice of any freedom in the interest of justice. In the international community this cleavage may result in a world conflict between two cohorts of world-savers holding contradictory views of democracy. In national communities it may still lead to the most tragic internecine conflicts. The truth obviously lies somewhere between these two creeds; but it is difficult to find, precisely because political creeds have been invested with a religious aura by a supposedly irreligious age. This whole development rather refutes John Dewey's hope, expressed some years ago in his "Common Faith," that men of good-will would agree on social and moral objectives, once modern culture had dissolved the irrelevant loyalties of historical religions. We have, as Americans, a particularly embarrassing position in this debate or conflict between contradictory conceptions of democracy. For America in general, and the American plutocracy in particular, has a more uncritical confidence in the organic relation between "free enterprise" and democracy than any other nation; and this type of bigotry may do more damage to the world community and the cause of justice than any religious bigotry ever did.

Even if this contradiction in the definition of our democratic objectives did not exist, it would still be impossible to define the meaning of human existence purely in terms of some social and political objective—partly because no human life can be completely contained within the bounds of the social and historical dimension of life, and partly because we do not either individually or collectively move as easily or surely toward ideal goals as past generations have assumed. Our age is secular, either non-Christian or anti-Christian, in the main outlines of its basic creed. It has disavowed the historical religious faiths partly because their symbols seem outmoded in an age of science but chiefly because modern men find the tragic view of life implicit in religion unacceptable and the old theories of redemption irrelevant. A message of redemption which offered men and nations life only through death and declared that men could be saved only through repentance seemed completely irrelevant to an age which saw history moving forward to ever more impressive elaborations of human power and freedom. There was nothing the matter with human life which historical growth could not cure.

The implicit faith of the past two centuries has hardly prepared us for the kind of frustration through which we must live in the next century or two. For we have been given the task of creating community in larger dimensions than any one or two centuries can accomplish. The frustrations of our age become pathetic rather than tragic when we have no means of either anticipating or comprehending the character of our present experiences. The one unifying element in all strands of modern culture was the idea of progress. We had faith in a redemptive history. This faith, which supposedly made all other interpretations of life completely incredible, is now progressively disclosing itself as the most incredible of all interpretations of life. This refutation of the culture of modern man by contemporary history may be regarded as the real spiritual crisis of our day.

When the atomic bomb fell upon Hiroshima it brought more than one chapter in both political and cultural history to a symbolic conclusion. It particularly concluded that chapter of Western spiritual history, beginning in the Renaissance, which regarded history as a kind of God and time as a kind of Christ. It was an age which assumed that technical progress, which continually increased man's power over nature and freedom from natural limitations, would inevitably contribute to human welfare and happiness. It was an age which assumed that man's increased mobility and the wider range of his eyes, ears, and voice, transfigured by microscope and telescope, telegraph and radio, would inevitably lead to the enlargement of the human community. Actually mechanical advances have only created a potential, and not an actual, world community, and have meanwhile destroyed many of the organic forms of community which gave life sanity and stability in older cultures.

We have had to learn that history is neither a God nor a redeemer. The real fact is that while history solves many problems, it ·aggravates rather than mitigates the basic incongruities of human existence. Man is a finite and contingent creature, with some sense of universal value transcending his own existence but unfortunately inclined to endow the contingent values of his life or culture, of his truth or loyalty, with an absolute significance which it does not deserve. He thereby finds community with his fellow-men as difficult as it is necessary; particularly since his fellow-men are engaged in the same idolatrous process. Man can neither live alone, not being self-sufficient, nor easily come to terms with his fellow-men. The same instruments which extend the range of possible community also extend the range of man's impulse to domination over his fellows. Thus history pitches the drama of life on continually higher levels, but the essentials of the drama remain the same.

The fact that history is endlessly creative but not redemptive might have been more apparent to modern man had it not been for another illusion in modern culture. This other illusion is closely related to the idea of progress and is indeed frequently the basis for it. It is the illusion that the so-called "methods of science" or "impartial scientific inquiry" or "scientific objectivity" are actually the instruments by which mankind rises to higher and higher degrees of perfection. There are forms of the idea of progress which trust primarily in the extension of the evolutionary process of biology into the realm of history. But more frequently historical progress is assumed to depend upon the ability of man gradually to rise from his position as a creature of natural and historical forces to become their master. The instrument by which this is to be accomplished is science. By scientific impartiality man presumably rises from finite to universal perspectives, from interested to disinterested appraisal of problems of justice, from prejudice and passion to god-like serenity and impartiality. Science will not only unlock the mysteries of existence which have remained closed to the poetic and religious imagination and to the speculations of philosophy but will redeem man from the fragmentary and partial character of his life and actions and guarantee action of universal validity.

Sometimes it is assumed that the methods of science will make men moral merely by making them rational. Sometimes it is believed that science should be used to control the dark and irrational forces in human nature, "that the same science which has altered the face of nature can change the habits of men." Sometimes the continued egotism and irrationality of individuals are assumed, but it is believed that a "scientific" politics will be able to manage social forces as readily as man now manages the forces of nature. The end product of these illusions is the type of rationalism which dreams of setting up a world government containing scientifically tested constitutional instruments for equilibrating all the vitalities of a community of nations and for arbitrating or, if necessary, suppressing every political conflict.

A simple fact has been obscured by this cult of redemption through science. Man is a creature whose rational and vital processes are in organic unity, and there is no "scientific method" by which he can escape from the hopes, fears, ambitions, and anxieties of his own individual existence or those of his nation, civilization, or ethnic group. In all problems pertaining to the security or the meaning of his own life or the justice of his conflict with some competing life or vitality, he is never the disinterested observer but an interested participant. In so far as impartiality is possible, it is a moral and religious as much as a scientific achievement. A contrite recognition of the interested character of our views and actions must always lie behind the achievement of relative disinterestedness. The achievement involves the whole of the personality and is therefore not purely intellectual or scientific.

Modern culture has wittingly or unwittingly followed the thought of Comte, who believed that the history of the world could be divided into three ages—the theological, the metaphysical, and the scientific—and who saw the possibility of solving all human problems in the third and final stage of human development by the application of the scientific method to man's social existence. Actually the ability of science to achieve impartial and universally valid judgments rests partly upon the sharply circumscribed fields of inquiry in which science looks for causal relations and partly upon the fact that a natural science, which investigates the determined sequences of nature, is under no temptation to weigh evidence or make hazardous judgments on such imponderables as human motives.

But the wider the field of inquiry becomes, the more plainly will even the natural sciences betray themselves to be under the guidance of presuppositions, implicit or explicit metaphysical assumptions, which are not the consequence but the basis of the inquiry. If it is historical rather than biological or geological sequence which is under inquiry, there is no strictly "scientific" method of judging the motives which prompt human actions or of comparing competing vitalities in history. Every judgment of fact is also a value judgment, presupposing a norm. The norm is itself historically conditioned, and the application of the norm to the stuff of history is twice conditioned.

This fact does not invalidate the social and historical sciences or prove that they ought to be reduced to statistical proportions in order to become purer sciences. Both the logical and the analytical powers of reason remain instruments by which partial and particular points of view are corrected, and the whole stuff of historical reality is brought under examination. We must continue to seek to understand what things are and how they came to be what they are in history as well as in nature. But there is no magic in either logic or the scientific method which will coerce men or nations to subordinate the particular to the universal interest or to correct the partial by a more universal insight. Reason in history remains permanently ambiguous, being both the servant and the master of all of history's vitalities.

There is, for instance, no "scientific method" which could guarantee that statesmen who must deal with the social and political consequences of atomic energy could arrive at the kind of "universal mind" which operated in the discovery of atomic energy. Statesmen who deal with this problem will betray "British," "American," or "Russian" bias, not because they are less intelligent than the scientists but because they are forced to approach the issue in terms of their responsibility to their respective nations. Their formulation of a solution is intimately and organically related to the hopes, fears, and ambitions of nations. They must deal with history as a vital and not a rational process. As a vital process it is always something less and something more than reason. It is less than rational in so far as the power impulses of nations express themselves as inexorably as the force of a stampeding herd of cattle. It is something more than rational in so far as human beings have aspirations and loyalties transcending both impulse and prudence. Man is a heaven-storming creature whose highest ideals are curiously compounded with his immediate and mundane interests. The Marxist dream of a universal classless society, mixed with the power impulses of a Russian state and the anxieties of a precarious dictatorship, is a nice symbol of what historical reality is like. Our so-called democratic world is a little more rational; but the mixture of democratic idealism and the quest for profits of a vast American economic machine must be almost as bewildering to the outside observer as the Russian mixture.

The collective mixtures of ideals and interests are more vivid than individual expressions of human spirituality, but every individual life is governed less by prudence and rationality and more by what lies below the level of reason and rises above the level of rational calculation than a scientific culture understands. One may be grateful for the fact that poets and novelists continued to bear testimony to these dimensions of life even in a scientific age, if they dealt at all authentically with the human scene. Because man in his grandeur and in his misery, in his high aspirations and in their egoistic corruption, is and always will be a more complex creature than modern culture has understood, his history is more tragic and his redemption from self-seeking, whether individual or collective, more difficult and always less final than we have assumed.

Old cultures and civilizations, reigning oligarchies and traditional social systems and structures do not quietly yield to the logic of a new historical development. They refuse to die in bed. They take the field, ostensibly to defend their "ideals" against some new barbarism, but also to preserve established interests against new vitalities. That is why we must march through any number of world wars before we can achieve world community; and why the world community which is within the grasp of human powers will be less stable and secure than our calculating world planners can realize. History presents us with constantly enlarged responsibilities. We must meet these responsibilities if we would remain human. The Nazis have shown us the perverse consequences of any effort to turn the clock back and "return to the womb" of tribal primitivism. We must move on. But there are neither securities nor fulfilments in history in which the heart can rest.

Since we are free spirits who transcend the historical process, as well as creatures who are involved in it, we crave for some ultimate security and fulfilment. But since history remains as fragmentary and as full of contradictions as our individual life-adventures, we can have such security and fulfilment only in an ultimate sense and only by faith. The kind of faith which adequately completes the temple of meaning will also reveal that our own egotism, and that of our nation, and not merely the egotism of competitor or foe is responsible for the tragic aspects of history. Thus contrition and faith go hand in hand.

In Christian piety the devout soul always beholds itself in a double relation to Christ. The perfect love, of which the Cross is the symbol, is regarded as the final norm of human goodness and defines what man ought to be. But man also knows himself to be the crucifier of the Christ. This expresses our understanding of the fact that life can only be brought to completion by a love in which the self is not concerned for itself but only for its fellows. But we also know that as individuals and as groups we seek our own. The justice we have achieved in history is a compromise between these two impulses; and the compromise is not achieved simply by calculation and prudence. Such pity and mercy as are insinuated into the cruelties and inhumanities of human life are the fruits of the contrition, which recognizes that the egotism we abhor in others is in us also. Fanaticism is always the product of self-righteousness. Religion has produced as much fanaticism as contrition, because religion is never a good force per se, but merely the final conflict between human self-esteem and divine mercy. And the one is as frequently victorious as the other.

A secular age imagined that it could exorcise fanaticism by disavowing religion. But an age which prides itself upon its scientific objectivity has actually sunk to new levels of cruelty, for the man who knows himself to be absolutely right through the benefit of science is as cruel as those who achieved this fanaticism by religious revelation. Not only Marxist fanatics are involved in the cruelties of our age, but democratic idealists also. The ancients were certainly not more merciless to their foes than we; no one has been so merciless to a vanquished foes as we since the Assyrians. We are pitiless because we do not know ourselves to be pitiable.

A secular age thought it would be sufficient to disavow the other-worldliness of religion in order to achieve a consistent and humane sense of responsibility for the commonweal. But the disavowal of an incredible heaven led to the avowal of incredible utopias; incredible because they defined an unconditioned good amid the conditions of nature [and] history. This persistent utopianism has generated fanatical furies of our day, for if the heaven of a classless society could be established on earth, would it be worth the price which the Communists are ready to pay? It is also responsible for the alternate fits of illusion and disillusion which distract us from our historic responsibilities.

Life is never completed, either individually or collectively; and it is never completely freed from chaos or from contradictions to its essential meaning. An adequate faith must understand this quality of life; but that is impossible without an explicit or implicit belief that a divine mercy can complete what we cannot complete. Such a faith may of course be corrupted and may beguile men from their pressing responsibilities; but the alternative secular idealism also leads to deep corruptions. It tempts men to seek in others, and never in themselves, the root of human misery. And if they finally find it in themselves, their optimism gives way to despair. The mood of this century compared with the optimism of the nineteenth century looks very much like the despair which all false optimism generates. . . .

*D*emocracy, as every other historic ideal and institution, contains both ephemeral and more permanently valid elements. Democracy is on the one hand the characteristic fruit of a bourgeois civilization; on the other hand it is a perennially valuable form of social organization in which freedom and order are made to support, and not to contradict, each other.

Democracy is a "bourgeois ideology" in so far as it expresses the typical viewpoints of the middle classes who have risen to power in European civilization in the past three or four centuries. Most of the democratic ideals, as we know them, were weapons of the commercial classes who engaged in stubborn, and ultimately victorious, conflict with the ecclesiastical and aristocratic rulers of the feudal-medieval world. . . .

Since bourgeois civilization, which came to birth in the sixteenth to eighteenth centuries and reached its zenith in the nineteenth century, is now obviously in grave peril, if not actually in *rigor mortis* in the twentieth century, it must be obvious that democracy, in so far as it is a middle-class ideology, also faces its doom.

This fate of democracy might be viewed with equanimity, but for the fact that it has a deeper dimension and broader validity than its middle-class character. Ideally democracy is a permanently valid form of social and political organization which does justice to two dimensions of human existence: to man's spiritual stature and his social character; to the uniqueness and variety of life, as well as to the common necessities of all men. Bourgeois democracy frequently exalted the individual at the expense of the community; but its emphasis upon liberty contained a valid element, which transcended its excessive individualism. The community requires liberty as much as does the individual; and the individual requires community more than bourgeois thought comprehended. Democracy can therefore not be equated with freedom. An ideal democratic order seeks unity within the conditions of freedom; and maintains freedom within the framework of order. . . .

If democracy is to survive it must find a more adequate cultural basis than the philosophy which has informed the building of the bourgeois world. The inadequacy of the presuppositions upon which the democratic experiment rests does not consist merely in the excessive individualism and libertarianism of the bourgeois world view; though it must be noted that this excessive individualism prompted a civil war in the whole western world in which the rising proletarian classes pitted an excessive collectivism against the false individualism of middle-class life. This civil conflict contributed to the weakness of democratic civilization when faced with the threat of barbarism. Neither the individualism nor the collectivism did justice to all the requirements of man's social life, and the conflict between half-truth and half-truth divided the civilized world in such a way that the barbarians were able to claim first one side and then the other in this civil conflict as their provisional allies.

But there is a more fundamental error in the social philosophy of democratic civilization than the individualism of bourgeois democracy and the collectivism of Marxism. It is the confidence of both bourgeois and proletarian idealists in the possibility of achieving an easy resolution of the tension and conflict between self-interest and the general interest. . . .

According to the scripture "the children of this world are in their generation wiser than the children of light." This observation fits the modern situation. Our democratic civilization has been built, not by children of darkness but by foolish children of light. It has been under attack by the children of darkness, by the moral cynics, who declare that a strong nation need acknowledge no law beyond its strength. It has come close to complete disaster under this attack, not because it accepted the same creed as the cynics; but because it underestimated the power of self-interest, both individual and collective, in modern society. The children of light have not been as wise as the children of darkness.

The children of darkness are evil because they know no law beyond the self. They are wise, though evil, because they understand the power of self-interest. The children of light are virtuous because they have some conception of a higher law than their own will. They are usually foolish because they do not

know the power of self-will. They underestimate the peril of anarchy in both the national and the international community. Modern democratic civilization is, in short, sentimental rather than cynical. It has an easy solution for the problem of anarchy and chaos on both the national and international level of community, because of its fatuous and superficial view of man. It does not know that the same man who is ostensibly devoted to the "common good" may have desires and ambitions, hopes and fears, which set him at variance with his neighbor.

It must be understood that the children of light are foolish not merely because they underestimate the power of self-interest among the children of darkness. They underestimate this power among themselves. The democratic world came so close to disaster not merely because it never believed that Nazism possessed the demonic fury which it avowed. Civilization refused to recognize the power of class interest in its own communities. It also spoke glibly of an international conscience; but the children of darkness meanwhile skilfully set nation against nation. They were thereby enabled to despoil one nation after another, without every civilized nation coming to the defence of each. . . .

Our modern civilization, on the other hand, was ushered in on a wave of boundless social optimism. Modern secularism is divided into many schools. But all the various schools agreed in rejecting the Christian doctrine of original sin. It is not possible to explain the subtleties or to measure the profundity of this doctrine in this connection. But it is necessary to point out that the doctrine makes an important contribution to any adequate social and political theory the lack of which has robbed bourgeois theory of real wisdom; for it emphasizes a fact which every page of human history attests. Through it one may understand that no matter how wide the perspectives which the human mind may reach, how broad the loyalties which the human imagination may conceive, how universal the community which human statecraft may organize, or how pure the aspirations of the saintliest idealists may be, there is no level of human moral or social achievement in which there is not some corruption of inordinate self-love.

This sober and true view of the human situation was neatly rejected by modern culture. That is why it conceived so many fatuous and futile plans for resolving the conflict between the self and the community; and between the national and the world community. Whenever modern idealists are confronted with the divisive and corrosive effects of man's self-love, they look for some immediate cause of this perennial tendency, usually in some specific form of social organization. One school holds that men would be good if only political institutions would not corrupt them; another believes that they would be good if the prior evil of a faulty economic organization could be eliminated. Or another school thinks of this evil as no more than ignorance, and therefore waits for a more perfect educational process to redeem man from his partial and particular loyalties. But no school asks how it is that an essentially good man could have produced corrupting and tyrannical political organizations or exploiting economic organizations, or fanatical and superstitious religious organizations.

The result of this persistent blindness to the obvious and tragic facts of man's social history is that democracy has had to maintain itself precariously against the guile and the malice of the children of darkness, while its statesmen and guides conjured up all sorts of abstract and abortive plans for the creation of perfect national and international communities.

The confidence of modern secular idealism in the possibility of an easy resolution of the tension between individual and community, or between classes, races and nations is derived from a too optimistic view of human nature. This too generous estimate of human virtue is intimately related to an erroneous estimate of the dimensions of the human stature. The conception of human nature which underlies the social and political attitudes of a liberal democratic culture is that of an essentially harmless individual. The survival impulse, which man shares with the animals, is regarded as the normative form of his egoistic drive. If this were a true picture of the human situation man might be, or might become, as harmless as seventeenth- and eighteenth-century thought assumed. Unfortunately for the validity of this picture of man, the most significant distinction between the human and the animal world is that the impulses of the former are "spiritualized" in the human world. Human capacities for evil as well as for good are derived from this spiritualization. There is of course always a natural survival impulse at the core of all human ambition. But this survival impulse cannot be neatly disentangled from two forms of its spiritualization. The one form is the desire to fulfil the potentialities of life and not merely to maintain its existence. Man is the kind of animal who cannot merely live. If he lives at all he is bound to seek the realization of his true nature; and to his true nature belongs his fulfilment in the lives of others. The will to live is thus transmuted into the will to self-realization; and self-realization involves self-giving in relations to others. . . .

On the other hand the will-to-live is also spiritually transmuted into the will-to-power or into the desire for "power and glory." Man, being more than a natural creature, is not interested merely in physical survival but in prestige and social approval. Having the intelligence to anticipate the perils in which he stands in nature and history, he invariably seeks to gain security against these perils by enhancing his power, individually and collectively. Possessing a darkly unconscious sense of his insignificance in the total scheme of things, he seeks to compensate for his insignificance by pretensions of pride. The conflicts between men are thus never simple conflicts between competing survival impulses. They are conflicts in which each man or group seeks to guard its power and prestige against the peril of competing expressions of power and pride. . . .

Since the survival impulse in nature is transmuted into two different and contradictory spiritualized forms, which we may briefly designate as the will-to-live-truly and the will-to-power, man is at variance with himself. The power of the second impulse places him more fundamentally in conflict with his fellowman than democratic liberalism realizes. The fact he cannot realize himself, except in organic relation with his fellows, makes the community more important than bourgeois individualism understands. The fact that the two impulses, though standing in contradiction to each other, are also mixed and compounded with each other on every level of human life, makes the simple distinctions between good and evil, between selfishness and altruism, with which liberal idealism has tried to estimate moral and political facts, invalid. The fact that the will-to-power inevitably justifies itself in terms of the morally more acceptable will to realize man's true nature means that the egoistic corruption of universal ideals is a much more persistent fact in human conduct than any moralistic creed is inclined to admit.

Democratic theory therefore has not squared with the facts of history. This grave defect in democratic theory was comparatively innocuous in the heyday of the bourgeois period, when the youth and the power of democratic civilization surmounted all errors of judgment and confusions of mind. But in this latter day, when it has become important to save what is valuable in democratic life from the destruction of what is false in bourgeois civilization, it has also become necessary to distinguish what is false in democratic theory from what is true in democratic life.

The preservation of a democratic civilization requires the wisdom of the serpent and the harmlessness of the dove. The children of light must be armed with the wisdom of the children of darkness but remain free from their malice. They must know the power of self-interest in human society without giving it moral justification. They must have this wisdom in order that they may beguile, deflect, harness and restrain self-interest, individual and collective, for the sake of the community. . . .

The reason this final democratic freedom is right, though the reasons given for it in the modern period are wrong, is that there is no historical reality, whether it be church or government, whether it be the reason of wise men or specialists, which is not involved in the flux and relativity of human existence; which is not subject to error and sin, and which is not tempted to exaggerate its errors and sins when they are made immune to criticism.

Every society needs working principles of justice, as criteria for its positive law and system of restraints. The profoundest of these actually transcend reason and lie rooted in religious conceptions of the meaning of existence. But every historical statement of them is subject to amendment. If it becomes fixed it will destroy some of the potentialities of a higher justice, which the mind of one generation is unable to anticipate in the life of subsequent eras. . . .

Another and contrasting justification

for a free society must be added. Sometimes new truth rides into history upon the back of an error. An authoritarian society would have prevented the new truth with the error. The idea that economic life is autonomous and ought not to be placed under either moral or political control is an error, for reasons which we have previously discussed. The self-regulating and self-balancing forces in economic life are not as strong as Adam Smith supposed. The propagation of this error has caused great damage in modern life. But a seed of truth was contained in the error. The intricacies of modern commerce and industry could not have developed if the medieval moral and political controls had been maintained; and even now when we know that all economic life must submit to moral discipline and political restraint, we must be careful to preserve whatever self-regulating forces exist in the economic process. If we do not, the task of control becomes too stupendous and the organs of control achieve proportions which endanger our liberty. . . .

The freedom of society is thus made necessary by the fact that human vitalities have no simply definable limits. The restraints which all human communities place upon human impulses and ambitions are made necessary by the fact that all man's vitalities tend to defy any defined limits. But since the community may as easily become inordinate in its passion for order, as may the various forces in the community in their passion for freedom, it is necessary to preserve a proper balance between both principles, and to be as ready to champion the individual against the community as the community against the individual. Any definition of a proper balance between freedom and order must always be at least slightly colored by the exigencies of the moment which may make the peril of the one seem greater and the security of the other therefore preferable. Thus even the moral and social principle which sets limits upon freedom and order must, in a free society, be subject to constant reexamination.

William F. (Billy) Graham

1918-

Born in Charlotte, North Carolina, Billy Graham was brought up a strict Presbyterian by parents who hoped that he would enter the ministry. He briefly attended Bob Jones College and then transferred to the fundamentalist Florida Bible Institute. In 1939 he enrolled at Wheaton College, another fundamentalist institution, where he received his B.A. in 1943. The following year he became associated with the Youth for Christ movement in Chicago, gaining valuable experience in revival techniques. The turning point in Graham's career came in 1949, when his tent revival in Los Angeles received national publicity. Since that time he has become America's most famous evangelist. His well-organized and well-financed revivals have attracted millions.

Graham's popularity derives essentially from his easily-understood message. Reducing faith to an all-embracing panacea for the ills of the world, he has in effect asserted that conversion produces a radical transformation in human nature. Since the sinfulness of human nature is at the root of all of man's problems, conversion is regarded as the key to peace and human happiness. Thus, mankind's problems are to be dealt with in terms of the individual; social action or collectivist solutions are futile. Consequently, Graham has criticized many features of modern society and has espoused an ultraconservative point of view in politics and economics. He has warned against deficit spending, the United Nations, the evils of big government, corruption in organized labor, and the intrusion of communists and fellow travelers into all areas of American life.

Graham's appeal has been largely to those unsophisticated people who seek a return to the imagined simplicity of the past. While Graham's and indeed the enduring influence of revivalism in general is still a debatable issue, there seems little doubt that the popularity of the movement has resulted from a spiritual void and the sense of frustration in American life.

The following selection is from Graham's Peace With God *(New York: Doubleday & Company, 1953), which has sold over half a million copies.*

*A*ll humanity is seeking the answer to the confusion, the moral sickness, the spiritual emptiness that oppresses the world. All mankind is crying out for guidance, for comfort, for peace.

We are told that we live in the "age of anxiety." Historians point out that there have been few times in all history when man has been subject to so much fear and uncertainty. All the familiar props seem to have been swept away. We talk of peace but are confronted by war. We devise elaborate schemes for security but have not found it. We grasp at every passing straw and even as we clutch, it disappears.

For generations we have been running like frightened children, up first one blind alley and then another. Each time we have told ourselves: "This path is the right one, this one will take us where we want to go." But each time we have been wrong.

One of the first paths we chose was labeled "political freedom." Give everyone political freedom, we said, and the world will become a happy place. Let us select our own government leaders and we shall have the kind of government that will make life worth living. So we achieved political freedom, but we did not achieve our better world. Our daily newspapers give us reports of corruption in high places, of favoritism, of exploitation, of hypocrisy equal to and sometimes surpassing the despotism of ancient kings. Political freedom is a precious and important thing, but it alone cannot give us the kind of world we long for.

There was another very hopeful path marked "education," and many put their whole faith in it. Political freedom coupled with education will do the trick, they said, and we all rushed madly along the educational path. It seemed a bright, well-lighted, sensible path for a long time, and we traveled it with eager, expectant feet, but where has it led us?

You know the answer. We are the most informed people in the history of civilization—and yet the most miserable. Our high school students know more about the physical laws of the universe than the greatest scientist in the days of Aristotle. But though our heads are crammed with knowledge, our hearts are empty.

The brightest, most inviting path of all was the one marked "higher standards of living." Almost everyone felt he could trust this one to carry him automatically into that better and more joyful world. This was felt to be the sure route. This was the "press the button and you're there" route! This was the path that led through the beautiful full-color magazine advertisements, past all the shining new cars, past the gleaming rows of electric refrigerators and automatic washing machines, past all the fat chickens cooking in brand-new copper-bottomed pots. We knew we'd hit the jackpot this time! The other paths might have been false leads, but this time we had it!

All right, look around you right this minute. At this very moment in history you see in America a country that has political freedom to an extent that is undreamed of in many parts of the civilized world. You see the greatest and most far-reaching public education system that man has ever created, and we are eulogized at home and abroad for our high standard of living. "The American way of life" we like to call this fully electrified, fully automatic, chrome-plated economy of ours—but has it made us happy? Has it brought us the joy and satisfaction and the reason for living that we were seeking?

No. As we stand here feeling smug and proud that we have accomplished so much that generations before us only dreamed about; as we span our oceans in hours instead of months; as we produce miracle drugs that wipe out some of man's most dread diseases; as we erect buildings that make the Tower of Babel seem an anthill; as we learn more and more of the mysterious secrets that lie in the depths of the sea, and peer further and further into outer space, do we lose one iota of that empty feeling within us? Do all these modern wonders bring us a sense of fulfillment, do they help to explain why we are here, do they point out what we are supposed to learn?

Or does that awful feeling persist? Does every further discovery of the magnitude of the universe comfort you or make you feel more alone and helpless than ever? Does the antidote for human fear and hatred and corruption lie in some laboratory test tube, or in an astronomer's telescope?

We cannot deny that science has given man many things he thought he wanted. But this same science has now presented us the most dreaded gift ever bestowed upon humanity. The life and future of every living being on this planet is affected by this gift of science. It stands like a somber shadow behind our waking thoughts. It stalks like a specter of horror through our children's dreams. We pretend it isn't there. We try to pretend that we haven't received this gift, that it's all a joke, and that some morning we'll wake up and find that the H-bomb hasn't really been invented and that the A-bomb has never been made—but our morning newspaper tells us different.

There are other paths, of course, and many are traveling them this very moment. There are the paths of fame and fortune, of pleasure and power. None of them leads anywhere but deeper into the mire. We are ensnared in the web of our own thinking, trapped so cleverly and so completely that we can no longer see either the cause or the cure of the disease that is inflicting such deadly pain.

If it is true that "for every illness there is a cure," then we must make haste to find it. The sand in civilization's hourglass is rapidly falling away, and if there is a path that leads to the light, if there is a way back to spiritual health, we must not lose an hour! . . .

So that is where we stand today—a nation of empty people. We have tried to fill ourselves with science and education, with better living and pleasure, with the many things we thought we wanted, but we are still empty. Why are we empty? Because the Creator made us for Himself; and we shall never find completeness and fullness apart from fellowship with Him.

Jesus told us long ago that "Man shall not live by bread alone," but we have paid no heed. We have gone on stuffing ourselves with bread of every description. We have stuffed until we are sick.

We cannot stand the terrible emptiness of ourselves, we cannot look at the lonely desolate road that lies ahead. We are desperately weary of the hatred and greed and lust that we know are within us, but we are helpless to be rid of it and filled with something better.

Time is of the essence. The tools of total annihilation have been placed within our reach. We cannot scurry up any more false paths, we cannot explore any more unknown roads, we cannot afford to be trapped in any more blind alleys. We don't have that much time! For our generation has accomplished what other generations only *tried* to do, or dreamed of doing in their most insane moments of power and ruthlessness! We have achieved a weapon of total destruction. We are witnessing the climax of man's madness—the atom cleaved!

How the demons must have laughed as some of the most brilliant men on earth worked furiously for years to achieve this horror! The atom cleaved! Divide and conquer! Split apart, destroy, shatter, crush, crumble! He of the cloven hoof has done his work, and men have been avid to aid him. We see before us Satan's masterpiece, his clever counterfeit of the cloven tongues of divine fire. For this satanic fire and the pentecostal flames both fall from above, both are cloven, both illuminate, both instantly transform everything they touch—but with such a difference. The difference of heaven and hell!

We are living in a topsy-turvy world, where all is confusion. But you may be sure that it is confusion with a plan— Satan's plan! The Bible tells us that Satan is the great deceiver and he has devoted himself to the cause of our great self-deception and to the deceptions that lie between nations all over this world. He has led us to believe that things were getting better, when they are really getting worse. . . .

Christ came to give us the answers to the three enduring problems of sin, sorrow, and death. It is Jesus Christ, and He alone, who is also enduring and unchanging, "the same yesterday, and today and forever."

All other things may change, but Christ remains unchangeable. In the restless sea of human passions, Christ stands steadfast and calm, ready to welcome all who will turn to Him and accept the blessings of safety and peace. For we are living in an age of grace, in which God promises that whosoever will may come and receive His Son. But this period of grace will not go on indefinitely. We are even now living on borrowed time. . . .

Since you have made your decision for Christ and have begun studying the Bible, you find yourself confronted with various social obligations and problems. You have made your peace with God. You are no longer at war and at enmity with God. Sin has been forgiven. You have new horizons for your thinking—new perspectives for your life. The whole world has changed. You now begin to see others through the eyes of Jesus. Old ideas and ideals have changed. Prejudices that you once held

are beginning to slip away. Selfishness that was once characteristic of you in many areas of your life has now gone. . .

Christians, above all others, should be concerned with social problems and social injustices. Down through the centuries the church has contributed more than any other single agency in lifting social standards to new heights. Child labor has been outlawed. Slavery has been abolished. The status of woman has been lifted to heights unparalleled in history, and many other reforms have taken place as a result of the influence of the teachings of Jesus Christ. The Christian is to take his place in society with moral courage to stand up for that which is right, just, and honorable.

First: *the Christian should be a good citizen.* The Bible teaches that the Christian should be law-abiding. The Bible also teaches loyalty to country. A loyalty and love of country does not mean that we cannot criticize certain unjust laws that may discriminate against special groups. The Bible says that God is no respecter of persons. All should have equal opportunities. The government of God is to be our model.

The Bible also teaches that we are to co-operate with the government. Jesus was asked, "Is it lawful to give tribute?" Jesus set the example forever by paying taxes. It takes money to run a government and to maintain law and order. The tax dodger is a civic parasite and an actual thief. No true Christian will be a tax dodger. Jesus said, we are to "render to Caesar the things that are Caesar's." We ought to be more than taxpayers. To be simply law-abiding is not enough. We ought to seek and work for the good of our country. Sometimes we may be called upon to die for it. We are to do it gladly—as unto God. We are to be conscientious in our work as good citizens.

We should be philanthropic and give to charitable organizations that are doing good for the betterment of mankind. We should enter in to various activities such as the Community Chest, the Red Cross, the Salvation Army, and other good, constructive, and helping-hand organizations. Christians should be interested in orphanages, hospitals, asylums, prisons, and all social institutions. Jesus said, "Love thy neighbor as thyself." Think of a country without any philanthropic enterprises whatever! No one would want to live in it. We want to live where neighborly love prevails. We are to take our place in the community. Those in positions of responsibility are entitled to respect, support, and co-operation. "Let every soul be subject unto the higher powers. For there is no power but of God: the powers that be are ordained of God."

Second: *Christians should be "given to hospitality."* The Bible teaches that our homes should be open to all and that those who come in and out of our homes should sense the presence of Christ. That which God has given to us should be shared with others. In doing so God will bless and prosper our homes.

Third: *we should have the Christian attitude toward sex.* Nowhere does the Bible teach that sex in itself is a sin, although many interpreters of the Bible would try to make it appear so. The Bible teaches that the *wrong use* of sex is sinful. For sex, the act by which all life on this earth is created, should be the most wonderful, the most meaningful, the most satisfying of human experiences. . . .

Fourth: it follows naturally that *those who take a Christian view of sex will take a Christian view of marriage.* Before you enter into a marriage, consider the real spiritual implications that make an earthly marriage binding in heaven. Little by little as we grow toward maturity, we learn to love, first our parents and our friends and later the one person who is to share our life. We have already seen how difficult this

process is, for it is hate and not love that comes naturally to the unregenerate sinner. . . .

Fifth: *we are to take the Christian attitude in labor-management relationships.* The Bible says, "Whatever you do, put your whole heart and soul into it, as into work done for God, and not merely for men—knowing that your real reward, a heavenly one, will come from God, since you are actually employed by Christ, and not just by your earthly master. But the slacker and the thief will be judged by God himself, Who naturally has no distinction to make between master and man. Remember, then, you employers, that your responsibility is to be fair and just towards those whom you employ, never forgetting that you yourselves have a Heavenly Employer."

If Christ could prevail in all labor-management relations we would not have any strikes. There would not be these long drawn-out arguments in which both sides are unwilling to concede the rights of the other. Management would treat employees with generosity, and employees would be eager to put in a full day's work for their hire—for they would not only be working for their wages, they would be working for God.

The Bible teaches that there is dignity in all types of honest labor, and the Christian should be the most faithful, the most willing and efficient worker of all. He should stand out in a factory or shop as one who wants justice, but who would not stoop to take unfair advantage.

By the same token, the Christian employer should treat his employees with a respect and generosity that will become an example for other employers. A man of real Christian concepts cannot help being concerned about safety precautions, good working conditions, and the well-being of those in his employ. He will not only see his workers as "man power," but also as human beings.

Both management and labor should remember that the improved conditions and better understanding they now enjoy had their beginnings as the result of a great spiritual revival. The heritage of labor unions comes from the church and the mighty Wesleyan revivals of the eighteenth century. Social liberty for the working classes began when a Christian leader, Lord Shaftsbury, in the face of bitter family opposition, led a lifelong crusade for better working conditions, shorter hours, more pay, and fair treatment for the working man.

Had it not been for the spiritual revival of the eighteenth century, the gains that labor has made might not have been achieved, or might have been delayed until much later in our history. When some labor leaders talk of outlawing religion, disregarding God, the Bible, and the church, they should remember how much of what they have today is due to the power of the gospel of Christ.

Some labor leaders have grown haughty, proud, rich, self-satisfied, and power-seeking. Many industrialists have done the same. All of them should humble themselves before God, seek to recognize the needs of each other, their extreme dependence on each other, and above all, try to apply the Golden Rule in its practical and realistic sense.

Sixth: *the Christian looks through the eyes of Christ at the race question* and admits that the church has failed in solving this great human problem. We have let the sports world, the entertainment field, politics, the armed forces, education and industry outstrip us. The church should have been the pacesetter. The church should voluntarily be doing what the federal courts are doing by pressure and compulsion. But in the final analysis the only real solution will be found at the foot of the cross where we come together in brotherly love. The closer the people of all races get to Christ and His cross, the closer they will get to one another. . . .

Seventh: *the Christian attitude should prevail in the matter of economics.* Jesus said a man's life does not consist in the abundance of the things which he possesses. Money is a good slave but a bad master. Property belongs in the purse or the bank but not in the heart. Wealth has its place and its power, but it is not entitled to occupy the throne or sway the scepter. Covetousness puts money above manhood. It shackles its devotee and makes him its victim. It hardens the heart and deadens the noble impulses and destroys the vital qualities of life.

Beware of covetousness in every phase and form! All of us should keep ourselves from it through vigilance, prayer, self-control, and discipline. Life is not a matter of dollars and cents, houses and lands, earning capacity and financial achievement. Greed must not be allowed to make man the slave of wealth. . .

Eighth: *a Christian will be concerned about suffering humanity around him.* The great slum areas of your own country will become a burden to you. The poverty and suffering of thousands of people in your own neighborhood will become a concern to you. You will join with organizations and associations to help alleviate the suffering of humanity around you. Many people spend so much time in lofty enterprises that they make no contribution to suffering immediately at hand. . . .

Ninth: *the Christian has a special obligation to fellow Christians.* Fellow Christians are in a special class. We are *to have supernatural love* for them. "We know that we have passed from death unto life, because we love the brethren. He that loveth not his brother abideth in death."

We are to love our enemies. We are even to love those who persecute us and say "all manner of evil against us, falsely."

But the greatest of our human love is for those other Christians. Jesus said, "This is my commandment, that ye love one another, as I have loved you.". . .

These are just a few of the scores of things that could be mentioned that are the social obligations of the Christian. He cannot withdraw himself as a hermit and live a solitary life. He is a member of society. Therefore, the teachings of Jesus are full of our attitudes toward our fellow men.

Study the Bible, read it—and then live by it. Only then can you demonstrate to a confused world the transforming power of the indwelling Christ.

Michael Novak

1933-

Born in 1933, Michael Novak graduated from Stonehill College in 1956 and received an S.T.B. from Gregorian University in Rome in 1958. He later attended Harvard University, where he studied the history and philosophy of religion. Since then he has been a member of the faculty at Stanford University.

Novak has been one of the younger and more articulate critics within the Catholic Church. In a number of books, including Belief and Unbelief: A Philosophy of Self-Knowledge (1965) *and* A Time to Build (1967), *he has dealt with the issue of God in a postreligious age. His book,* The Open Church, Vatican II, Act II (1964), *also dealt with the contemporary issues facing the Church. Novak's criticisms (which have been echoed by other Catholics), while expressed in a sympathetic vein, have nevertheless created serious problems for a Church unaccustomed to dissent.*

The selection is from Novak's article "American Catholicism After the Council," in Commentary, *XL (August, 1965).*

The city of Rome rests placidly in the crystalline Italian sun, century by century, and generations of men appear within her walls and disappear. There are men today, on all continents, who shed tears when they confront her beauty and her seeming eternality. But today the city is the symbol of crisis, not of peace.

Countless Roman Catholics of the present generation are challenging, not the essential truths of the Catholic faith, and not even the role of the bishop of Rome, but the mystical hold which the limited traditions of the city of Rome have long exercised upon the Catholic world. It is inevitable that a Church be secular. How else could a Church live in history, except by entering into the historical forms of its time and place? But if a Church must in any case be secular, many Catholics in the middle of the 20th century are asking: why must its secularism be Roman and of the baroque Italian period?

Hardly a conflict at the Second Vatican Council has not been colored by this fundamental issue: whether the Church shall be Latin or Catholic. The fundamental opposition is between a party of nostalgia on the one hand, and a party of the present and the real on the other. Yet it would be a serious mistake to underestimate the intelligence, seriousness, conviction, and past successes of the party of nostalgia. The Church over which that party has presided has for generations captured the imagination and the intellectual allegiance of legions of talented men. Through most difficult and disturbing times, defended and guided by the party of nostalgia, the Church has come to the threshold of a new age intact and robust.

It is a remarkable fact that although anti-Catholicism has long been the anti-Semitism of the intellectuals, and although the atheist has appropriated to himself all the moral pro-words which attract the young—honesty, courage, integrity, and the rest—the Catholic Church is at the present moment more intellectually fit than she has been for centuries. There have seldom been so many first-rate artists, writers, theologians, philosophers, and men of affairs who are also Catholic. It is true that countless young people of sensitivity and intelligence have left the Church in these centuries, and continue to do so at a high rate. But her present health is a direct result of the imagination and intelligence and energy of those many who have remained within.

For some ninety years and longer, an intellectual underground has been building up in Roman Catholicism. Small at first, centering in groups of writers, theologians, and philosophers, now in Paris, now in Tübingen, now at Munich, London, Louvain, Milan, or even Rome, this underground has self-consciously labored for the renewal and reform of Roman Catholicism from within.

Since early in the last century, young theologians like Johann Möhler of Tübingen (d. 1838) have been working for the reunion of the churches, and writers in France and Germany have strained every nerve to draw Catholicism out of her isolation from the contemporary world. A curious phenomenon all these years is that outsiders writing or speaking of Catholicism have often been as Roman, hierarchical, and monolithic in their view of the Church as the most conservative Catholics. Such outsiders called "Catholic" only those manifestations which bore the stamp of curial and official Rome; perhaps 95 per cent of their utterances about Catholicism had the curial hierarchical pyramid, not the living underground, in mind. Hence the great sense of surprise, shock, and at first hesitant pleasure which nearly everywhere greeted the "new" attitudes of Pope John and the Council.

To be sure, this preoccupation with the outward appearance of pre-Johannine Catholicism was in large measure justified. "Every time one of us succeeds in stirring a little flame in the ashes," François Mauriac once wrote, "someone from curial Rome comes and crushes it." Nevertheless, the unpreparedness of most professional commentators on Catholicism (H. Stuart Hughes is one notable exception) for what has come to the surface since 1962 is the symptom of a sickness in contemporary intellectual life. The antipathy and prejudice which have in the main prevented sympathetic studies of the role of Catholicism in Western civilization are something of a scandal. All too often, especially in the United States, intelligent Catholics, under questioning, have stated what they believe their faith to involve, only to be faced with the rejoinder: "But you can't be in good standing and hold that, can you?" The stereotype is a burden, and the Catholic, like the Negro and the Jew, would like to be taken for what he is, not for what Cardinal Spellman, Graham Greene, Charles de Gaulle, and other assorted Catholics are.

The present turmoil in the Catholic Church has been occasioned by the official recognition at the Vatican Council of the fact that there are in the Church countless styles of Catholic life, many competing theologies, many philosophies of man, and many conceptions of freedom and law. Italian Catholics and Irish Catholics live in quite different emotional worlds. When the French say *liberté* they do not mean what Americans mean by freedom; Englishmen and Spaniards speaking of law have different concrete experiences in mind; a German and a Latin American mean different things by order; some Catholics in Africa understand spontaneously the notion "people of God," since they are still living a tribal life which is more like that of biblical peoples than is Western life today.

"Catholic" does not mean universal and the same, but universal and diverse.

Moreover, it is impossible to make sense out of the current restlessness among Roman Catholics without recalling that, after 1789, nearly every major Catholic institution of learning in Northern Europe—and often in the South as well—was seized by the state. Originality and imagination in Catholic studies were at a low ebb in the 18th century; but in the 19th, Catholic studies were virtually wiped out. Moral theology, for example, as a recent book by John T. Noonan, Jr.,[1] intimates, endured a gap in scholarship for almost the entire first two generations of the 19th century. Only toward mid-century were libraries reassembled, eclectic surveys of previous scholarship organized, seminary manuals hastily put together. Too early to benefit by the fruits of historical scholarship just being organized, but cut off by two generations from a living tradition, 19th century Catholic moral theology had virtually to be begun from scraps. Into the vacuum rushed the canon lawyers; about four-fifths of the material in standard textbooks on moral theology used in Catholic seminaries (Regatillo-Zalba, for example) is borrowed from canon law. Here lie the roots of the present Catholic dilemma on birth control.

In 1870, the First Vatican Council articulated the faith of Catholics in the infallibility of the Church, in which the pope shares; marching armies drove the Council from Rome before the complementary role of the bishops could be discussed. Theologically, the chief effect of what the Council did was to establish stringent conditions upon papal teaching, so that the line between the pope's personal opinions and his articulation of the faith of all is now clearly marked. Nevertheless, the chief psychological effect was a heightening of the baroque monarchical view of the papacy dear to certain Roman hearts.

Worse still, modern means of communication were shortly to change the impact and universality of papal teaching; the stage was set for the most pyramidal period in the history of the Church. The pope would be seen as the peak of the pyramid, the papal curia as an intermediary between him and the bishops; below the bishops would come priests and religious, and, like an iceberg nine-tenths of which is under water, laymen would be left by canon law with hardly a mention. (Even now when laymen speak about the Church, they speak of "they." "When will the Church do something about birth control?" means "When will *they. . . .*")

This same period marked the Celtic ascendancy in the Church: not only did Ireland gain political independence from England and ecclesiastical subservience at home, but Irish bishops multiplied in the United States, in Australia, in England, and throughout the mission lands of the British Empire. The Celtic bishops have maintained a theological tradition largely isolated from the life of our times, unfertilized by dissent or pluralism, greatly inclined to viewing the Church as a pyramid and seriously vulnerable to establishing a personality cult around the pope. On the other side of the ledger, the Celtic bishops are in the main excellent organization men, whose primary virtue is loyalty.

In an era of radio, teletype, and television, meanwhile, papal teaching suddenly became not merely the theology of the bishop of Rome, distant and localized, but the ordinary teaching of the Church spread through the world—particularly wherever the non-intellectual Irish were in charge. The whole system of checks and balances in Roman Catholicism was upset. Now, because

---

[1] *Contraception* (Cambridge, Mass.: Harvard University Press, 1965).

of radio and the daily press, and a heretofore unheard-of deference to Rome, the "ordinary teaching" of the bishops had lost its crucial theological role. *Whatever* the pope said was now known everywhere, on the instant, and was much more gravely discussed than hitherto. It has become a serious, novel, and yet common misconception among some Catholics to accept all papal opinions as if they were gospel truth.

Three amusing ironies are at work here. The first is that the hyperpapalists often try to comfort non-Catholics by noting that the exercise of papal infallibility is, necessarily, a most rare occurrence. But before their own people, they endow nearly every papal instruction with some subtle measure of infallibility: "near to being infallible" or the like. (Their opponents retort that infallibility, like pregnancy, is or isn't; there's no in-between.)

The second irony is that most of the hyperpapalists, in practice, are selective in their attitude toward Rome; they discount the instructions they don't like—Pius XI on social reconstruction and the sins of capitalism, for example, or Pius XII on liturgical reform.

The third irony is that since 1878 and the pontificate of Leo XIII most of the popes, skipping over the heads of the bishops, have been in alliance with the intellectual underground. The popes have been "liberal," the bishops in the main have not. Leo's *Rerum Novarum*, for example, was a belated effort to awaken the baroque apathies of Roman Catholics to the magnitude of the social reconstruction required in our time; it was a response to the challenge of socialism. Even Leo's choice of Thomas Aquinas as special teacher of the Church was an appeal to historical studies— Leo well knew the low estate of Catholic scholarship in the 19th century, and Thomas Aquinas was infinitely better than the manuals then so recently

scraped together (and misleadingly purporting to be "Thomistic").

The popes since Leo XIII have been an extraordinary series of leaders. Fr. Gustav Weigel, S.J., said once, not long before his death: "We've had good popes for too long; nothing would be better for the faith than a bad one." Fr. Weigel had a horror of Christians who put their faith not in God but in men; and he seemed to believe that overemphasis on the pope was a characteristic vice of the Catholicism of our time. Others, less gentle than Fr. Weigel, call this vice the Celtic heresy.

Yet every heresy contains a portion of truth, and its error is usually by exaggeration. The Second Vatican Council has set in motion the elaboration of a more authentic view of the role of the bishop of Rome. The distinguishing mark of God's covenanted people is its service to others, and the relationships which unite that people are also relations of service. Bishops and priests are chosen from among the people to represent them before God, to minister to their needs, to preside at their worship, to teach, to govern. They are clearly warned not to rule as the rulers of the Gentiles, but by service. And the servant of these servants of God, the center of unity among them, is the bishop of Rome.

The pope has two special services to offer the Catholic people. In the first place, he is a focal point of unity—one of the college of bishops, and yet not merely one among equals, because also the central focus of the others. (The relations between pope and college are not yet thoroughly worked out in history; a great deal remains to be learned through future developments.) In the second place, he offers a single clear voice by which, in time of need, the conscience of the Church can be articulated—in exceptional cases, even without consulting the bishops. Hochhuth's play testifies to the usefulness of such a ministry in Christianity; he does not single out the World Council of Churches or the Catholic bishops for equal blame with Pius XII.

Just before the opening of the Second Vatican Council, one of the outstanding theologians of the Catholic underground, later to become the chief light of the Council, voiced his pessimism. "The Council is coming fifty years too soon; if only we had more time!" Everywhere the men working for renewal and reform were hitching their belts for another long siege; they knew renewal would win in the end, but a retrogressive Council might postpone the day. They feared that the many hundreds of Italian bishops, the Spanish and Latin American bishops, and the Celtic bishops would rubber-stamp the seminary theology of the last three generations. "We thought we would come in October, say yes, and be home for good by Christmas," one American bishop later confessed.

Pope John's opening address to the Council on October 11, 1962, was the beginning of the end of the Roman style in the Church. The Pope called for a *pastoral* Council—a realistic Council, a Council attending to the needs of men. No condemnations. No definitions. No subtleties. Traditional *Romanità* could not thrive on that sort of ground.

There is no need to recapitulate here the story of the Council thus far.[2] As to its repercussions in America, however, from 1962 on, pioneering ecumenical gatherings in city after city, attracting thousands, have been electric in their impact. In 1964, Cardinal Cushing urged Boston Catholics for their spiritual profit to listen to Billy Graham. Nuns from St. Louis marched in Selma, Alabama, in 1965; and in quiet defiance of orders from the chancery (while Cardinal Cushing was ill and in the hospital) hundreds of priests and seminarians then marched with the Catholic Interracial Council in the South Boston St. Patrick's Day parade. All of a sudden, things which long ago should have happened are happening. The distance covered between 1962 and 1965 is little short of amazing.

But the distance covered is only, let us say, from 1789 to 1945. Pope John wanted an *aggiornamento* that would bring the Church "up to today." The Council has, in the end, let him down. The Council has hardly begun to cope with the world of the coming era on which we have already embarked. Looking backward, the Council is an astonishing success. But looking forward, the Council is in many ways a failure. Perhaps a Council—an unwieldy organ of more than two-thousand men— must inevitably work twenty years or so behind the time, dealing with issues that are ripe for institutional resolution. Perhaps it is enough that the Council has established the *principle* of renewal and reform, and that the old Roman will to eternality and changelessness appears to be broken. The Church is an historical, ever-changing institution, as the Council has recognized; that very fact liberates the energies of the Church to meet the future on its own terms, to enter the coming secular culture as enthusiastically, though in an entirely new manner, as she entered the secular culture of ancient Greece, or Rome, or the early Northern countries of Europe.

But a vision of the secular civilization of the future hardly seems to have entered the minds of many of the bishops. Too many of them are more concerned about the "confusions" which the recent changes are causing among their previously undisturbed flocks. Some of the bishops are of an appallingly rigid and frightened cast of mind: Bishop Hannon of Scranton has

[2] See, e.g., the reports by the pseudonymous Xavier Rynne, published by Farrar, Straus & Giroux, New York.

forbidden his people to take part in Bible vigils (a danger to their faith); Bishop Topel of Spokane has called 1964 "a year of shame" because the newly awakened Catholic press has been calling spades spades, and naming bishops by name for what they do or don't do. Unaccustomed to being held to account for their actions like other men, some bishops may be forgiven for sighing after the good old days.

Nevertheless, the world in which we live is a serious world, not a toy for timid bishops. Between thirty and fifty million people in Europe have been killed by violence since this century began, and the same moral, political, social, and economic factors which contributed to this bloodshed are still operative. A new civilization, as Albert Camus saw in *The Rebel*, is rising on the rubble heap left by the Second World War, a civilization technical beyond any ever known, international in scope, and secularist in attitude. The Church has no time to worry about how deeply a bishop's feelings may be hurt. The question for her is whether the yeast of religious faith will be able to penetrate this technical world at all.

Pope John XXIII was sufficiently sensitive to feel the malaise which after the Second World War gripped Europe and the world: old traditions have been discredited, old beliefs are mere words on the lips even to many who hold them, and for values like justice, human dignity, and liberty it is very difficult to give an intellectual justification. From a coldly scientific point of view, the planet Earth is insignificant; among men, the species is of more significance than the individual; the natural course of history treats men cruelly. It is difficult, as Albert Camus found, to argue one's way out of the nihilism which facts seem to force upon us.

In the United States, few saw dramatized in fire and in pain the depths of modern nihilism; besides, the more limited illusions of the pragmatist live longer. Anglo-American life has always maintained amenities of fair play, liberty, and law, for which no creditable account is to be found in Anglo-American philosophy. Such amenities are a part of the Anglo-American inheritance, part of our acquired fund of sentiment which David Hume extolled and which is not yet bankrupt. So long as this inheritance lasts, many philosophers will be able to continue their games with words. But one day they will have to resume the hard work of articulating why we value individual persons more than things, why persons are valuable beyond their usefulness or beyond the contributions they make to the economy, and what, in short, a man is.

These are questions in which believers and non-believers have an equal stake, and which are absolutely fundamental for the future. The Council convened by Pope John has barely touched these questions, having become deeply involved in ecclesiastical problems. Thus, as Cardinal Lercaro of Bologna recently warned in Rome, there is a grave danger that the Council will not have lived up to the vision of Pope John. In no case are the documents approved by the Council representative of the best that Catholic theology has to offer. In every case, compromise with the men of *Romanità* or with the bishops who lacked theological sophistication was required. The Council was, under the leadership of Roman minds, badly prepared. It was snatched from disaster only by the ardent hopes and example of Pope John, assisted by the energy, intelligence, and determination of a score of leaders among the cardinals and bishops of the world.

It seems that the bishops, particularly those of the United States, have hardly grasped the extent to which not only the Middle Ages but also the modern age are at an end; a new, technical, secular, urban, pluralistic age has begun. Language appropriate for an agricultural society no longer conveys meaning; even the word "father" means something different for the human spirit after Freud, not to mention what it means in "broken" homes or in those millions of families whose lives center not on parents but on teenagers.

"Secularism" for many of the American bishops is a dirty word; they blame on it virtually every ill that plagues society, from racial discrimination to lurid advertising. The bishops hardly ever recognize their own complicity in the evils of modern life; one seldom hears them, as a group, confess their own sins. There are, after all, bishops who have in the name of prudence compromised their professed moral code in the matter of race (but who even in the name of the same prudence brook no compromise in the matter of birth control). But most of all, the bishops have yet to come to grips with the fact that atheism and agnosticism represent a noble way of life, a way of life which is more attractive than Celtic folk religion to many young, educated Catholics.

A fourteen-year-old girl was recently overheard to say on a campus where she had come to attend a Newman Club meeting: "They're talking about Scripture and liturgy. But I came here to find out *whether there's a God.*" The Catholic people have changed in character under the system of universal education the atheists of the Enlightenment saw fit to pioneer, and under the system of parochial schools the German and Irish bishops of the United States insisted on providing for them. Catholics in the United States constitute the largest body of college-educated Catholics in the history of the Church.

In the last few years, partly under the release granted them by Kennedy's election, partly under the impact of the Council, partly by the ripeness of time, Catholics in the United States have "aged" remarkably. In the schools and universities, in the Catholic and secular press, and in Church meeting rooms, the atmosphere is charged with questions, criticisms, and initiatives. The drive to understand, the drive of inquiry and personal appropriation, has clearly been awakened, and pupils from the schools the bishops took such pains to build are, as it were, turning around to bite the bishops' hands. Teachers of the old style hardly know how to cope. The defensive speak of a "breakdown in the spirit of obedience." But in reality nothing has broken down but the image of the pyramid; the questioners and the doers are obeying the Council's directives and following the Council's example.

It is in this sense that the Council has had its greatest success. Catholics now want the whole Church, every day and everywhere, to be one large Council: full of free speech, argument, dissent, respect for diversity, and the slow search for consensus. Not all the bishops are like Pope John; not all like this kind of Church. But who, then, are the better Catholics, those of the Church of silence, conformity and comfort, or those of the Church of freedom and dissent?

In fact, the spirit of faith and obedience among Catholics has seldom been more alert; but this faith is directed toward the whole Church rather than toward the local pastor or diocesan bishop. Catholics listen now with two ears; one for the local voice, one for the voice of renewal and reform which is stirring in many other places, including the Council, if not locally. It is difficult for some pastors to be reminded, perhaps for the first time, that they are stewards and not masters of the faith. In the old days, the great ideal of many a pastor was to let nothing disturb the waters; now such a man hesitates, for fear the disturbance might be the Holy Spirit.

But if the newer Catholics have two ears, they also have three eyes. That, at least, is the claim of Daniel J. Callahan's new collection, *The Generation of the Third Eye*.[3] The title is taken from a phrase of John Courtney Murray's, about the introspective, analytic temper of the times, and the contributors are writers, artists, and scholars who are under forty. John Cogley, who at forty-eight finds himself untimely placed in an older generation, adds an "afterword" which shows, if anything can, that there is a difference between the generations.

Two points emerge from this collection. One is that for nearly every contributor the ordinary parish life of the Church in America has been virtually bankrupt. The sermons are abominable, both in theology and in culture; the churches are run as "parish plants" rather than as praying and believing communities. The financial strain of building and maintaining parochial schools seems to have made practical materialists out of the Catholic community.

Secondly, nearly every one of the writers represented has found his nourishment as a Catholic not from the ecclesiastical structure but from the intellectual Catholic underground. Years ago, this one discovered Bernanos and Bloy, or that one Simone Weil. Through a friendship here, a prophetic book there, they developed against the stream of unintellectual Catholicism. It seems likely that the next generation of such Catholics, now in the colleges, will number in the scores of thousands; for the Council has made the underground official.

To be sure, some members of the underground are reacting as if the war were still on; everyone is anticipating a backlash among the bishops. It is perfectly plain that the bishops of the United States, especially those along

the Eastern seaboard (Cardinal Spellman and the two recent Apostolic Delegates purportedly share a large responsibility for their nomination) were unprepared for the Council. Many of them for years strenuously opposed liturgical reform, did little to publish the social encyclicals of the popes, treated the new theology of Rahner, Congar, Danièlou, and others as vaguely heretical, and knew almost nothing of the intellectual revolution in contemporary biblical studies. It would be too much to expect that all of these bishops, after a brief "graduate school" exposure at the Council to what has been going on in Catholicism these last ninety years, will be able to relay their discoveries to the often unread, firmly set monsignors and pastors who preside over the daily life of their dioceses.

Still, most of the bishops of the United States appear not only to have benefited immeasurably by the Council, but also to have begun to win over their clergy and their Waugh-like laymen. One of the touching aspects of the Council was the sight of old men changing the ideas of a lifetime, and voting—for the good of the Church—for ideas they had many long years opposed. "If you had told me last week that I would vote yes this morning, I'd have said you were crazy," one Archbishop from the Midwest told a reporter at the Council, "but I did."

What, then, of the future? The fact that the underground is now official has temporarily brought a wavering in the sense of direction. Since their inception, journals like *The Commonweal* and *Cross Currents* had been saying that reform and renewal are required; suddenly Pope John and the Council have concurred. Now what?

There are enormous institutional problems to be dealt with in Roman Catholicism. There are too few places

[3] New York: Sheed & Ward, 1965.

in which the insight, experience, and concern of the laymen are made institutionally effective. Laymen are given no responsibility; in the business world and in government they are treated as adults, but in the Church as children. The extreme spiritual poverty of parish and diocesan community life seems to be due chiefly to this enforced childlikeness.

One of the brightest spots is the fact that the nearly two hundred thousand nuns in the United States, especially those from the Midwest and the West, are moving swiftly into 20th-century and secular American life; the example of the six from St. Louis who marched at Selma was a shot heard round the country; even in Boston.

Serious sectional problems are also involved. The Catholic cities of the Eastern seaboard are depressingly dead; the Celtic heresy has killed them. Sister Marie Augusta Neal's thesis for Harvard, *Values and Interests in Social Change*,[4] a study of the Boston clergy, indicates that the future in Boston, at least, is hopeful. But the Boston Catholic paper, *The Pilot*, often has to be ecclesiastically careful, and, when the Cardinal is out of the office, the chancery can be as narrow, complacent, and restrictive as any in the country. Let us not speak of Providence, New York, the major sees of New Jersey, or Philadelphia.

Wherever one visits in America, one finds again and again that the fundamental problem of American Catholicism lies in the bureaucratic minds who hover like flies around many of the bishops, the nervous Nellies of the chancery offices who censor books, discourage talks with Protestants, fear that the Council has caused "confusion" among the faithful, and build (as in one diocese) $400,000 and (in another) $90,000 rectories for the use of no more

than four priests. Such men may be loyal administrators and genial golf companions and they may often think of themselves as the most select group in the world; but many of them should recognize that they are among the most unenlightened, mediocre, and complacent men who ever represented the gospels of Jesus Christ.

This problem is formally like that which afflicts civil government and even universities: how can a living institution make effective in its midst not only bureaucrats but also prophets? How do you get, and keep, open minds and free spirits in administrative posts?

The problem is only exacerbated by the tradition of authoritarianism in the Church and by the tradition of celibacy. The fact is commonly discussed among Catholics that too many of those who advance in the hierarchy seem attracted to these traditions because of their own emotional disturbances. It is probable that some manifestations of ecclesiastical power reveal deep personal insecurity. There are very few checks-and-balances in Church structure to minimize the potential dangers of such disequilibrium.

St. Augustine, that great bishop, once wrote in self-reflection that bishops are the enemies of the Church, and surely it is true that every blindness of the local bishop injures the life of the diocese he serves. The Catholic people, and the clergy, need institutional safeguards against abuses. The monsignori in Chicago who resisted Cardinal Meyer's every effort to integrate the parochial schools—for fear those who form the economic base of their huge, brick parish plants would move away— and some among the clique who form a purple guard around Cardinal Spellman are by their impenetrable complacency scandals to every alert man who encounters them.

---

[4] Englewood Cliffs, N.J.: Prentice-Hall, 1965.

Connected with this issue are several others. The ordinary parish priests, particularly the assistant pastor, are at the present time the least free members of the Church. In canon law, they have almost no protection for what may be called in imitation of Thoreau "evangelical disobedience." How can the gospels be preached when those of sensitive conscience are forbidden by administrative prudence to avoid disturbing the present order? Many a priest finds himself saying one thing in private, another in public. What is the use of giving one's life to the service of the gospels if one is made to serve, instead, the timidity of those who, with whatever good intentions, flatter the rich, the powerful, the secure?

Besides, the Catholic people have, until recently, been unwilling to let a priest speak in his own name; he is taken much too seriously as speaking for the entire Church. Consequently, many priests do not speak their own minds; they mouth accepted conventions which will "disturb" no one. Their acquiescence has entangled them in spiderwebs of their own weaving, and only their own courage will free them and the gospels to which they are dedicated.

Thirdly, the descendants of Europe's peasants are only now beginning to lift their eyes from the vulgar and aggressive search for dollars which they found to be the obvious requirement for coping with the Protestant Establishment of the United States. No one is deceived into thinking that "the emerging laymen" (a descriptive phrase for the religiously and intellectually alert) in this country number more than a few score thousand, perhaps a few hundred thousand. Apathy, indifference to religion except as a vague and ultimate comfort, and docility in early assimilating the pyramidal view of the Church mark the vast majority of American Catholics. Here, again, the situation faced by Catholicism in the United States is formally similar to that of the life of general culture and the intellect: the vast majority of the people belong spiritually to the hucksters of Hollywood, Madison Avenue, and the thoughtless pulpit.

But these are largely intramural issues. The internal political structure of the Church as it exists at present inhibits spiritual and intellectual development; and it is the business of laymen, nuns, priests, and bishops who care about such things to reform the structure and practices of the institution they love.

On a wider front, there are a whole host of issues of concern to all Americans in which the Church is more or less "officially" involved: education, for example. An increasing number of educated Catholics are critical of the parochial schools not so much because these are intellectually inferior to the public schools (often they aren't), but because their graduates do not seem noticeably different in behavior and attitudes from those who go to the public schools. Why put millions of dollars into a program of such meager religious fruitfulness?

The younger Catholic intellectuals— often products of the Catholic schools— are the most vociferous critics of the schools. But in many new suburbs, the people of the parish rather than the clergy insist on the building of a Catholic school. Many parents seem to feel incompetent to educate their own children in religious matters; they seem to need the feeling of security which comes from placing their children under the moral protection of priests and nuns. Meanwhile, those who teach in the schools, trying valiantly to reach new standards both in secular disciplines and in the "new theology" of Vatican II, become increasingly sensitive to criticism, whose truth they are often willing to admit but whose practicality they sometimes question.

Three relatively modest propositions appear to be developing as a feasible and widespread attitude toward this question: (1) At some period in their education, Catholic children ought to have *some* formal Catholic education; otherwise, their theological education will fall below their general education. But they should spend part of their career also in public and secular schools; (2) At least one important part of religious education can best be given in the home, through public prayer in church, and through personal reading and organized discussion groups; (3) The maintenance of an independent Catholic school system, for part of the education of at least part of the Catholic population, contributes to the diversity and richness of American education.

On a second important public issue, racial justice, only a year ago the inactivity of Catholics threatened to dissipate the trust and good feeling of the then just budding ecumenical movement. For the very Jews and Protestants who were most apt to be open to new dialogue with Catholics were among the first to become sensitive to the moral demands of the racial revolution; and they were scandalized by Catholic inactivity. But gradually, through the lonely witness of such men as the Berrigan brothers (one a Jesuit, one a Josephite), and through the pressure of other active spirits who increasingly allowed themselves to be diverted from the work of Vatican II and other intramural matters, more and more Catholic consciences were touched. An institutional mark of sorts was reached when the well-known Paulist Center on Boston Common threw open its doors, in May 1965, to an ecumenically sponsored teach-in on the emotionally charged issue of racial imbalance in the Boston public schools.

Several important traits of the American Catholic community came to light in these developments; and these traits illuminate Catholic attitudes on other problems. In America more than in Europe, many Catholics are victims of the serious flaws in late scholastic philosophy and theology; many interpret reality through eyes blinded to certain important features. For example, American Catholics commonly interpret a generalization as a normative statement; they register the descriptive mode only with difficulty. If a psychologist or a sociologist describes what frequently happens, they take him to be recommending a course of action; detached analysis is seldom credited. "Is" (in the tradition of the Aristotelian final cause) is taken as an "ought."

Again, many American Catholics are fond of verbal solutions to concrete problems. If the American bishops *said*, in 1957 that racial discrimination is immoral, and said it solemnly in their annual proclamation, many Catholics feel the problem has been solved.

Again, if the essential position of the Church is once enunciated, then many American Catholics believe it is illegitimate to blame the Church for the concrete, individual actions or attitudes of the Catholic clergy or people. Thus, if Pius XII in (as Albert Camus sadly noted) an obscure encyclical condemned Nazism, then the *Church* was not involved in Hitler's wars, only errant individuals were. In fact, even if Pius XII had not spoken, the *Church* would have "spoken," silently. For the *Church* is a pure, immaculate, spotless Platonic ideal, not to be confused with the sinners who give her flesh in history. The Church, for example, has always believed in religious liberty, never persecuted Jews or Protestants, always fostered truth and scientific inquiry, ever championed the rights of man, never approved racial discrimination.

Again, the upper blade of Platonic unreality in late scholasticism makes necessary a lower blade of Machiavellian "prudence" in dealing with actual complexities in history. The very bishop who believes most in the sinlessness of the Platonic Church is apt to have a finger in many deals involving local real estate; another is warning the local newspaper not to print a certain story; another is pressuring politicians in this direction or in that. Italian and Irish bishops, in particular, seem to have mastered the regular swing of the pendulum from the rhetoric of sermons on the sinless beauty of the Church to the vigorous use of power for the worldly needs of the Church.

Finally, many American Catholics still seem to prefer group loyalty to truth; self-congratulation to honesty. There is at present a vogue of criticism and self-accusation, to be sure; but many are still untouched by it, and many who voice it seem surprised at the new possibility of speaking out; like Edward M. Keating of *Ramparts*, they sound not a little strident.

This group loyalty has largely blinded American Catholics to the needs of other groups. The oscillation between idealism and cynical prudence has led American Catholics to believe in racial justice while tolerating racial injustice. The emphasis on essential definition rather than on personal appropriation and responsibility, and the confusion of the normative with the descriptive, have enabled American Catholics to be blind to concrete realities in the name of "unchanging principles."

These same traits of mind characterize the usual American Catholic foray into American social or political life, on the censorship of movies, on birth control clinics, on aid to parochial schools, etc. Often the values which Catholics wish to uphold in these matters are commendable in themselves; but the political and social techniques for defending them smack of Italian or Irish scholasticism. Essentialistic, non-historical, and abstract ideals are voiced on the one hand,

and ecclesiastical prestige is wielded as political power on the other.

Increasingly, this mental scholasticism is yielding to the sunshine of American liberties and the brisk winds of American realities. Cardinal Cushing has recently recognized that the Catholic conscience need not be articulated in public law, and tentatively approved the amendment of the birth control laws of Massachusetts so that they would be more in conformity with the general public conscience. Catholics can maintain their stricter views in private; the domain of public law is distinguishable from the domain of personal conscience.

Pope John XXIII, Cardinal Cushing's closest ecclesiastical model, made another important distinction in *Mater et Magistra*, concerning Communism: the original ideology is one thing, the reality which has evolved under historical pressures is another. Late scholasticism pure and simple was unable to make such a distinction; in its purview, only logic and essential definitions mattered.

In proportion as American Catholics learn to distinguish essences from existents, norms from descriptions, logic from history, their political and social actions will become increasingly more nuanced, reasoned, and appropriate to a democratic society. Catholics will ever have a moral code more strict in certain matters than many other Americans, but their way of defending the values they cherish can become both more effective from their own point of view and less repugnant to others. A more historically minded and concrete philosophy and theology, already gaining in acceptance, will gradually make this transition in intellectual style possible.

Many of the younger Catholic intellectuals, however, are involved neither in the intramural problems of the Church nor in the problems of the "official"

Church and American culture. They are getting their degrees or are teaching in the whole spectrum of academic studies, are entering political life or the professions, are active in urban renewal or journalism or the arts. They have little or no interest in ecclesiastical matters; they often resent the ecclesiastical establishment as vaguely stupid, or narrow, or merely professional. They have never had a conversation with a bishop and, except with a personal friend or relative, rarely with a priest. They often remain practicing Catholics, faithful to the sacraments. But the world of the spirit in which they live is that of the general secular world rather than that of the Catholic community at large.

They are concerned about the fact that automobiles are choking our cities; that the very poor continue to suffer gravely in our society; that our complex democracy requires the replacement of venal-minded and unintelligent politicians with men of talent, or some vision, and of suitably thick skin. They are worried about the inequalities suffered by women in our society. They are disturbed to the depths of their consciences by the risks of wider warfare the U.S. is courting. As Christians, they may feel they have a special stake in these problems, and special emphases in defining and attacking them. But they receive little enlightenment in how they might cope with such problems in church on Sunday morning.

Thus the great irony of American Catholicism is that, after decades of ecclesiastical warnings about the dangers of "secularism," the most sensitive and inquiring young Catholics are presently finding the spiritual values represented by American secularism more compelling than the spiritual attitudes of the Catholic clerical establishment. The secular world has little to say, of course, about God, about ultimate questions of hope, destiny, and

conscience; for such matters, and for the Eucharist which is their communal symbol, many young Catholics maintain their ties with the historic Church and its spiritual tradition. But they find a broadly conceived pragmatism to be a more adequate philosophical language for dealing with reality than late scholasticism. And they find contemporary political, economic, and social theory more morally relevant than most of the sermons they suffer through on Sunday mornings.

The future of American Catholicism will probably manifest an increasing secularization of the thought patterns of clergy and people, to the benefit of the religious faith they cherish. For though most varieties of American secularism appear to be agnostic, few appear to be absolutely closed to religious values. Consequently, many more Catholics will probably adopt some version of pragmatism, with an existentialist emphasis upon self-appropriation and self-criticism, as their basic philosophical and theological language. Given this language, they will add to the pluralistic values usually championed by secular philosophers, special religious values of their own. And their fundamental ethical and political decisions will involve balancing one of these values against another, in establishing what is best to do here and now on each occasion.

If this prediction is correct, American Catholics will in a sense be recovering the Aristotelian tradition of *phronesis* and the short-lived Thomistic tradition of concrete *prudentia* and *caritas*, which were swallowed up in the abstract, essentialistic "Reason" of late scholasticism. Neither Aristotle nor Thomas Aquinas, however, shared what would today be called "historical consciousness." Thus, the contribution of modern secularism to the wisdom which can be assimilated by the Church is above all an acute awareness of the historical and contingent factors which characterize human history and the development of human intelligence.

American Catholics have little to fear, and much to gain, from the critical assimilation of secular wisdom in their attempt to understand the meaning of their faith at this moment in human history. In so doing, from their own treasury they also bring their own special contribution to the general wisdom of our culture. Their tradition of contemplative life will have much to say to a world of greater leisure; their tradition of emptiness and abandonment in prayer will have much to say to those, like the Anglican Bishop J. A. T. Robinson, who suddenly discover that God cannot be imagined nor, strictly, conceived.

American culture and American Catholicism benefit by the mutual criticism and guarded but respectful cooperation they lend to one another. American Catholicism is becoming, and ought to become, different from any other form of Catholicism in history, because it is *American*. And America, without its minority groups and their special values, is homogenized and vulgar.

Each man who cherishes the needs of the human spirit is a precious asset in a land of buyers and sellers. Every analysis of the life of the spirit in the United States leads to the same conclusion: the real war, the bitter war which lies ahead, is for the soul of the American people. Who will get there first, the huckster and the demagogues, or men of reality and statesmen? On every corner there are barkers who desire, for a fee, to cover up the realities of the world of bloodshed in which we live. There are too few who speak with honesty, with reverence for human personality, with compassion for the weak, with restraining intelligence for the strong, with realism in action. Secular intellectuals and religious men who value such things need each other —and that is why American Catholicism needs soon to be making its intellectual and artistic contributions to American culture.

Walter Kaufmann
1921-

German-born Walter Kaufmann came to the United States in 1939. He received his B.A. from Williams College in 1941, and then entered military service. After the war he continued his graduate studies at Harvard and was awarded his doctorate in philosophy in 1947, Since 1947 he has taught philosophy at Princeton University.

The author of numerous works on philosophy and the philosophy of religion—including Nietzsche *(1950) and* Critique of Religion and Philosophy *(1958)—Kaufmann has emerged as one of the leading modern critics of traditional religion, especially Christianity. Insisting that theologians as well as philosophers often have deliberately avoided subjecting their opinions and beliefs to searching examination, he has attempted to point out the myths, inconsistencies, and illogical beliefs that have remained embedded in the religious heritage of Western society. He has even questioned whether traditional religion should indeed play* any *role in modern society.*

In the introduction to a recent book Kaufmann remarked: "Of faith and morals, one cannot speak honestly for long without hurting feelings. Therefore, most people speak dishonestly of the most important subjects. . . . The starting point is not a set of premises that I refuse to question. This book is based not on the all-too-widespread will to believe, but on the will to be honest."[1] Kaufmann's position is probably representative of a widespread skepticism and agnosticism that has presented institutional religion with one of its most serious intellectual challenges.

The following selection is from his article "The Faith of a Heretic," Harper's Magazine, 218 (February 1959). The point of view presented in this article was elaborated much more fully in his book bearing the same title, The Faith of a Heretic *(New York: Doubleday & Company, 1961).*

---

[1] Walter Kaufmann, *The Faith of a Heretic* (New York: Doubleday & Company, 1961), pp. 9, 24. This book has been brought out in an Anchor Book paperback edition (1963).

423

*W*hen I was eleven, I asked my father: "What really is the Holy Ghost?" The articles of faith taught us in school—in Berlin, Germany—affirmed belief in God, Christ, and the Holy Ghost, and I explained to my father: "I don't believe that Jesus was God, and if I can't believe in the Holy Ghost either, then I am really not a Christian."

At twelve, I formally left the Protestant church to become a Jew. Having never heard of Unitarianism, I assumed that the religion for people who believed in God, but not in Christ or the Holy Ghost, was Judaism.

A few months after my conversation with my father, but before I left the church, Hitler came to power. Warned of the persecution that my decision might entail, I replied that one certainly could not change one's mind for a reason like that. I did not realize until a little later that all four of my grandparents had been Jewish; and none of us knew that this, and not one's own religion, would be decisive from the Nazis' point of view. My decision had been made independently of my descent and of Nazism, on religious grounds.

I took my new religion very seriously, explored it with enormous curiosity and growing love, and gradually became more and more orthodox. When I arrived in the United States in January 1939, I was planning to become a rabbi. A lot of things happened to me that winter, spring, and summer; and when the war broke out I had what, but for its contents, few would hesitate to call a mystical experience. In the most intense despair I suddenly saw that I had deceived myself for years: I had believed. At last the God of tradition joined the Holy Ghost and Christ.

Of course, I could maintain my old beliefs by merely giving them a new interpretation; but that struck me as dishonest. Ikhnaton, the monotheistic Pharaoh—as I explained in a letter to my family who were by now in England —could also have reinterpreted the traditional polytheism of Egypt, but was a fanatic for the truth. He taught his court sculptor to make life masks of people to see how they really looked, and in one of the heads which the sculptor had then done of Ikhnaton, his hunger for the truth had become stone. I had loved that head for years. Should I now do what I admired him for not doing?

You may say that Ikhnaton was wrong and that it is the essence of religion to pour new wine into old skins, reading one's current insights into ancient beliefs. But if you do this, disregarding Jesus' counsel not to do it, you should realize that you could do it with almost any religion. And it is less than honest to give one's own religion the benefit of every possible doubt while imposing unsympathetic readings on other religions. Yet this is what practically all religious people do. Witness the attitude of Protestants and Catholics toward each other. . . .

The autobiographical sketch with which I have begun may do more harm than good. Some amateur psychologists may try to explain "everything" in terms of one or two experiences; some Protestants may say. "If only he had come to *me* about the Holy Ghost!" while some Catholics may feel that it all shows once again how Protestantism is merely a way-station on the road to Hell.

This is the kind of gambit that the shut-ins pull on travelers. As if I had buried the Holy Ghost beyond recall when I was eleven, and God when I was eighteen! I merely started relatively early to concern myself with such questions—and have never stopped since. Let the shut-in explore Judaism and Protestantism, Catholicism and Buddhism, atheism and agnosticism, mysticism, existentialism, and psychology, Thomas and Tillich. Let him consult the lot and not just his own present prejudice; let him subject his thoughts about religion to the candid scrutiny of those who differ with him and to his own ever-new re-examination; let him have a host of deep experiences, religious and otherwise, and think about them. That is the ground on which a genuine conversation can take place: it need not make a show of erudition, if only it has grown out of a series of open-hearted encounters. But as long as one is content to gloat over the silver lining of one's own religion, one bars any serious conversation and merely makes the first move in a game of skill.

To an even moderately sophisticated and well-read person it should come as no surprise that any religion at all has its hidden as well as its obvious beauties and is capable of profound and impressive interpretations. What is deeply objectionable about most of these interpretations is that they allow the believer to say Yes while evading any No. The Hebrew prophets represent a notable exception. When interpreting their own religious heritage, they were emphatically not conformists who discovered subtle ways in which they could agree with the religion of their day. Nor was it their point that the cult was justifiable with just a little ingenuity. On the contrary.

Let those who like inspiring interpretations be no less forthright in telling us precisely where they stand on ritual and immortality, on the sacraments and Hell, on the Virgin Birth and Resurrection, on the Incarnation and the miracles, and on: "Resist not evil." And: "Let him who would sue you in court for your coat have your cloak, too." And: "No one comes to the Father but through Me."

If you must pour new wine into old skins, you should at least follow one of Jesus' other counsels and let your Yes be Yes, and your No, No.

When considering Christianity, it is easy to get lost in the changing fashions of thought that have been read into it or reconciled with it—from Neoplatonism (Augustine) and Aristotelianism (Aquinas) to romanticism (Schleiermacher), liberalism (Harnack), and existentialism (Tillich, Bultmann, and others). There is no room here to cross swords with a dozen apologists; in any case, dozens more would remain.

The central question about Christianity concerns Jesus Christ. If he was God in a sense in which no other man has been God, then Christianity is right in some important sense, however Christendom may have failed. To decide whether Jesus was God in some such unique sense, a philosopher cannot forbear to ask just what this claim might mean. If, for example, it does not mean that Jesus of Nazareth knew everything and was all-powerful, it is perplexing what is meant. But a large part of what most Christians mean is surely that Jesus was the best and wisest man of all time; and many Protestants mean no more than that.

Millions of Christians agree on this claim and back it up by citing Gospel passages they like; but different people pick different passages. To some Jesus looks like St. Francis, to others like John Calvin, and to many more the way a man named Hofmann painted him. Pierre van Paassen's Jesus is a Socialist and Fosdick's a liberal, while according to Reinhold Niebuhr Jesus' ethic coincides, not surprisingly, with Niebuhr's. To use a political term: almost everybody gerrymanders, carving an idealized self-portrait from the Gospels and much less attractive straw men from the literatures of other faiths. A great deal of theology is like a jigsaw puzzle: the verses of Scripture are the pieces, and the finished picture is prescribed by each denomination, with a certain latitude allowed. What makes the game so pointless is that not all pieces have to be used, and any piece that does not fit may be reshaped, provided one says first, "this means." That is called exegesis.

In *The Literature of the Christian Movement*, Morton Scott Enslin, one of the outstanding New Testament scholars of our time, remarks that the Jesus of the Fourth Gospel is really not very attractive, and that if it were not for the other three Gospels and the fact that readers create for themselves "a conflate," the Jesus of St. John would lose most of his charm. Surely, the same consideration applies to all four Gospels.

Those who consider Jesus the best and wisest of men should reread the Gospels and ponder at the very least these five points.

First: Are they prepared to maintain their claim regarding the Jesus of any one of the four Gospels—and, if so, which? Or is it their point that the evidence warrants the assumption that the historical Jesus, however inadequately understood by the Evangelists, was a wiser and better man than Socrates and Jeremiah, Isaiah and the Buddha, Lao-tze and Hillel?

Secondly: Although Jesus is widely considered mankind's greatest moral teacher, the greatest Christians, not to speak of scholars, have never been able to agree what his moral teachings were. Matthew, and he alone, reports that Jesus said: "Let your Yes be Yes, and your, No, No." But the four Evangelists agree in ascribing to Jesus evasive and equivocal answers to plain questions, not only those of the high priest and Pilate; and quite generally the Jesus of the New Testament avoids straightforward statements, preferring parables and hyperboles. Some of the parables are so ambiguous that different Evangelists, not to speak of later theologians, offer different interpretations. Nor have Christians ever been able to agree on the import of the hyperboles of the

Sermon on the Mount. Luther, for example, taught that Christ's commandments were intended to teach man his utter incapacity for doing good: man must throw himself on the mercy of God, believing that Christ died for our sins. On concrete moral issues, Jesus can be, and has been, cited on almost all sides. The Buddha and the Hebrew prophets were not so equivocal.

Third: One of the few things about Jesus' moral teachings that seems fairly clear is that he was not greatly concerned about social justice. This makes his ethic much less impressive than the prophets'.

Fourth: Albert Schweitzer has argued in considerable detail that this lack of concern was due to the fact that Jesus predicated his entire message on a false belief: namely, that the world was about to come to an end. If Schweitzer is right, as I think he is, Jesus was surely not the wisest of men. And can we call him the greatest moralist unless we accept his radical depreciation of *this* life and his belief in Heaven and Hell?

Finally, the Jesus of the New Testament believed, and was not greatly bothered by his belief, that God would damn and torment the mass of mankind in all eternity. According to all three Synoptic Gospels, he actually reassured his disciples:

"If any one will not receive you or listen to your words, shake off the dust from your feet as you leave that house or town. Truly, I say to you, it shall be more tolerable on the day of judgment for the land of Sodom and Gomorrha than for that town."

This is no isolated dictum; the Sermon on the Mount, for example, is also punctuated by threats of Hell.

Augustine, Aquinas, and Calvin stressed Hell, but many Christian apologists today simply ignore all such passages. A few insist that in a couple of intertestamentary apocalypses we find far more detailed visions of Hell. They do not mention that these apocalypses would not be known today if it had not been for the esteem in which the early Christians held them. For the Jews rejected them while accepting the humane teachings of men like Hillel and Akiba. Rabbi Akiba, a contemporary of Paul and the Evangelists, taught that "only those who possess no good deeds at all will descend into the netherworld"; also that "the punishment of the wicked in Gehinnom lasts twelve months."

Of course, Jesus also stressed love, citing—or agreeing with a Pharisee who cited—Moses. But this as well as the fact that he said some lovely things and told some fine parables is hardly sufficent to establish the Christian claims about him: that much he has in common with Moses, Micah, and Hosea, with the Buddha, Confucius, and Laotze, to name a mere half-dozen teachers who preceded him by a few centuries.

It might be countered that the story of Jesus is the best possible symbol of love. But is it? Consider the story the way it looks to people not committed to, and prejudiced in favor of, Christianity: God caused a virgin, betrothed to Joseph, to conceive His Own Son, and this Son had to be betrayed, crucified, and resurrected in order that all those— and only those—might be saved who should both believe this story and be baptized and eat and drink on regular occasions what they themselves believe to be the flesh and blood of this Son (or, in some denominations, merely the symbols of His flesh and blood); meanwhile, the rest of mankind suffer eternal torment, and according to many Christian creeds and teachers, they were predestined for damnation by God Himself from the beginning.

One might choose to be a Christian in spite of all this if one could intensely admire the great Christians who came after Jesus. But Peter and Paul, Athanasius and Augustine, Luther and Calvin, seem far less admirable to me, for all their admitted virtues, than Hosea and Micah, Isaiah and Jeremiah, Hillel and Akiba; or the Buddha, Socrates, and Spinoza. Maimonides, unlike Aquinas whom he influenced, did not believe in eternal damnation or that heretics should be executed. Some recent Protestant writers have been wonderfully forthright about Luther's and Calvin's shortcomings; but for candid portraits of the saints one must on the whole turn to non-Catholic writers—with at least one notable exception. In 1950, Malcolm Hay, a Catholic, published one of the most moving books of our time, *The Foot of Pride*, which is admirably frank about some of the most celebrated saints.

In an essay published in Germany in 1939—or rather in a book seized barely before publication by the Gestapo and destroyed except for about half-a-dozen copies—Leo Baeck, probably the greatest rabbi of our time, said something profoundly relevant:

A good deal of church history is the history of all the things which neither hurt nor encroached upon this piety, all the outrages and all the baseness which this piety was able to tolerate with an assured and undisturbed soul and an untroubled faith. And a spirit is characterized not only by what it does but, no less, by what it permits. . . . The Christian religion, very much including Protestantism, has been able to maintain silence about so much that it is difficult to say what has been more pernicious in the course of time: the intolerance which committed the wrongs or the indifference which beheld them unperturbed.

This thought may diminish even one's affection for St. Francis, but not one's admiration for the prophets.

The world's other religions remain. If we apply the same criteria, only two issue a real challenge to us, or at least to me: Judaism and Buddhism. I admire Genesis and Job, the Book of Jonah and the Dhammapada far above any book in the New Testament. But popular Buddhism with its profuse idolatry, its relics, and its superstitions repels me, and I have reservations even about the teachings of the Buddha. I admire much of his profound analysis of man's condition: the world has no purpose; it is up to us to give our lives a purpose; and we cannot rely on any supernatural assistance. Life is full of suffering, suffering is rooted in desire and attachment, and much desire and attachment are rooted in ignorance. By knowledge, especially of the Buddha's teachings, it is possible to develop a pervasive detachment, not incompatible with a mild, comprehensive compassion—and to cease to suffer. But consider the Old Testament and Sophocles, Michelangelo and Rembrandt, Shakespeare and Goethe: the price for the avoidance of all suffering is too high. Suffering and sacrifice can be experienced as worthwhile: one may find beauty in them and greatness through them.

Much of the appeal of Christianity is due to the fact that it contains at least intimations—but really no more than that—of this tragic ethos. But the story of Christ remains uncomfortably similar to the saga of the boss's son who works very briefly in the shop, where he makes a great point of his home and is cruelly beaten by some of his fellow workers, before he joins his father as co-chairman of the board and wreaks horrible revenge. This "happy" end makes most of the Christian martyrs, too, untragic figures. These observations may strike believers as blasphemous, but they might do well to reflect on the manner in which they pass judgment on other religions, and there may be some point in considering how one's own religion must strike those who don't accept it.

Probably the only great religion in which genuine self-sacrifice and tragedy have occupied a central place is Judaism, especially prior to the introduction of belief in any after life. Moses is the very incarnation of humane devotion, wearing himself out in the service of God and men, expecting, and receiving, no reward whatever, but finding his reward in his work. He asks God to destroy him rather than his people and intercedes for them again and again. In the prophets, from Hosea to the songs of the suffering servant, we find the same outlook.

Why, then, do I not accept Judaism? In view of all the things I do not believe, I have no wish to observe the six-hundred-odd commandments and prohibitions that define the traditional Jewish way of life, or to participate in religious services. With most so-called orthodox Jews I have much less in common than with all kinds of other people, Jews and Gentiles. Reform Judaism seems to me to involve compromise, conformism, and the wish to be innocuous. To that extent, it, too, stands opposed to the ethos of the prophets. And if a succession of great Jews should equal the boldness of the prophets, who repudiated the ritual of their day, and go a step further by also renouncing, and denouncing, all kinds of belief—would not this amount to giving up religion?

What remains if you give up the great religions? Many people think: only Communism, Nazism, and immorality. But the morality of Socrates, Spinoza, and Hume compares favorably with Augustine's, Luther's, and Calvin's. And the evil deeds of Communism and Nazism are not due to their lack of belief but to their false beliefs, even as the evils deeds of the Crusaders, Inquisitors, and witch hunters, and Luther's exhortation to burn synagogues and Calvin's decision to burn Servetus, were due to *their* false beliefs. Christianity, like Islam, has caused more wars than it has prevented; and the Middle Ages, when Europe was Christian, were not a period of peace and good will among men. Does it make sense that those who refuse to let their Yes be Yes and their No, No—those who refuse to reject false beliefs, those who would rather stretch them and equivocate—should have a monopoly on being moral?

Renouncing false beliefs will not usher in the millennium. Few things about the strategy of contemporary apologists are more repellent than their frequent recourse to spurious alternatives. The lesser lights inform us that the alternative to Christianity is materialism, thus showing how little they have read, while the greater lights talk as if the alternative were bound to be a shallow and inane optimism. I don't believe that man will turn this earth into a bed of roses either with the aid of God or without it. Nor does life among the roses strike me as a dream from which one would not care to wake up after a very short time.

Some evils and some kinds of suffering can be abolished, but not all suffering can be eliminated; and the beauty, goodness, and greatness that redeem life on earth are inseparable from suffering. Nietzsche once said: "If you have an enemy, do not requite him evil with good, for that would put him to shame. Rather prove that he did you some good." If life hurts you, the manly thing is neither to whine nor to feel martyred, but to prove that it did you some good.

No one way is the best way of life for all. To me the *Apology* of Socrates, as immortalized by Plato in less than thirty pages, presents a challenge from which I cannot, and have no wish to, get away. Here is part of Socrates' answer to the charges of impiety and corruption of the Athenian youth, on which he was convicted and put to death:

I am better off than he is—for he knows nothing but thinks he knows, while I neither know nor think I know. . . . If you say to me, . . . you shall be let off, but upon one condition, that you are not to inquire . . . in this way any more, and that if you are caught doing so again you shall die—if this was the condition on which you let me go, I should reply: . . . while I have life and strength I shall never cease from the practice and teaching of philosophy, exhorting any-one whom I meet. . . . Are you not ashamed of heaping up the greatest amount of money and honor and reputation, and caring so little about wisdom and truth? . . . The unexamined life is not worth living. . . . If you suppose that there is no consciousness, but a sleep like the sleep of him that is undisturbed even by dreams, death will be an unspeakable gain. . . . Eternity is then only a single night.

It would be folly to wish to foist this outlook on everybody. Professors of philosophy discourage and fail a large percentage even of their graduate students and are assuredly not eager to turn all men into philosophers. In philosophy, as in religion, teaching usually involves a loss of dimension; and the Socratic fusion of philosophy and life, critical acumen and passion, laughter and tragic stature is almost unique.

One need not believe in Pallas Athena, the virgin goddess, to be overwhelmed by the Parthenon. Similarly, a man who rejects all dogmas, all theologies, and all religious formulations of beliefs may still find Genesis the sublime book *par excellence*. Experiences and aspirations of which intimations may be found in Plato, Nietzsche, and Spinoza have found their most evocative expression in some sacred books. Since the Renaissance, Shakespeare, Rembrandt, Mozart, and a host of others have shown that this religious dimension can be experienced and communicated apart from any religious context. But that is no reason for closing my heart to Job's cry, or to Jeremiah's, or to the Second Isaiah. I do not read them as mere literature; rather, I read Sophocles and Shakespeare with all my being, too.

Moreover, I am so far quite unable to justify one of my central convictions: that, even if it were possible to make all men happy by an operation or a drug that would stultify their development, this would somehow be an impious crime. This conviction is ultimately rooted in the Mosaic challenge: "You shall be holy; for I the Lord your God am holy."

To communicate to others some feeling for man's religious quest, to arouse an aspiration in them which nothing but death can quell, and to develop their critical powers—that is infinitely more important to me than persuading anybody that Shakespeare was right when he wrote these lines:

The cloud-capp'd towers, the gorgeous
    palaces,
The solemn temples, the great globe itself,
Yea, all which it inherit, shall dissolve:
And, like this insubstantial pageant faded,
Leave not a rack behind. We are such stuff
As dreams are made on, and our little life
Is rounded with a sleep.

I do not believe in any after life any more than the prophets did, but I don't mind living in a world in which people have different beliefs. Diversity helps to prevent stagnation and smugness; and a teacher should acquaint his students with diversity and prize careful criticism far above agreement. His noblest duty is to lead others to think for themselves.

Oddly, millions believe that lack of belief in God, Christ, and Hell leads to inhumanity and cruelty while those who have these beliefs have a monopoly on charity—and that people like myself will pay for their lack of belief by suffering in all eternity. I do not believe that anybody will suffer after death nor do I wish it.

Some scientists tell us that in our own galaxy alone there are probably hundreds of thousands of planets with living beings on them, more or less like those on the earth, and that there are about 100 million galaxies within the range of our telescopes. Man seems to play a very insignificant part in the universe, and my part is surely negligible. The question confronting me is not, except perhaps in idle moments, what part might be more amusing, but what I wish to make of my part. And what I want to do and would advise others to do is to make the most of it: put into it all you have got, and live and, if possible, die with some measure of nobility.

CHAPTER XXII

THE
CONSERVATIVE
STANCE

I n 1945 the power of the German and Japanese war machines had been
smashed, and Americans looked forward to an era of peace and prosperity, dominated by a concert of nations determined to see that the tragedies
of the 1930's would not be repeated. Yet only a few short years later
these dreams had been rudely shattered, and men were forced to face the
terrifying possibility that the technology they had created might yet be used
to bring about their own destruction.

But the dilemmas facing Americans at mid-century were not simply the
problems of an advanced technological society. The fear of destruction was
only an outward symptom of a deeper problem that ultimately concerned
fundamental moral and philosophical issues. What Americans were most
concerned about was their own undefined future in a world where the processes of change and transformation had been sharply accelerated and often
seemed to be beyond their effective control. Ever since the days of the Puritans, Americans had enjoyed the psychological security of their firm faith in
America and its destiny, a faith that revolved around a core of religious
doctrines and a belief in a fundamental moral law. Indeed, the nation's
history from the seventeenth through the early twentieth century seemed to

offer convincing evidence that America was truly fulfilling its divine mission both in material and spiritual aspects. Because of their fortunate past, few Americans in these years appeared to be very much troubled by ideological issues. Conservatives and liberals alike, despite their wide differences, were united in an optimistic prognosis of their country's future.

The rise of Nazism and fascism in the 1930's, the worldwide threats to democracy in the 1940's, and the continued expansion of communism in the 1950's, however, forced Americans to reconsider traditional assumptions about themselves and their society. Some even attempted to formulate a new political philosophy they deemed more suited to the needs of a changing world. The result was the rise of a self-conscious conservatism.

This New Conservatism was an amalgam of many political forces and different ideological premises. It enrolled in its support those who had once had kinship with radical discontent as well as those who were concerned with maintaining the nation's great political traditions. Some who spoke out were angry young men, others were scholars of international reputation; some embraced the "radical Right" while others were "middle-of-the-roaders."

To the question, what is conservatism? there is no easy answer. The traditions of political discussion are not always consistent, and frequently in fact what is "liberal" to one generation is "conservative" to another. For Americans these terms are especially difficult, for they are lacking in a clearly defined liberal or conservative tradition, and the American electorate has seldom had an opportunity to choose officials in terms of such positions. Both conservatives and liberals have, in fact, invoked America's past and its traditions to justify and define their position. And Americans have been interested more in results than in theory. Consequently they have borrowed frequently from European sources and adapted these ideas to the American experience in a way that further blurred ideological lines and distinctions.

The conservative, one spokesman has said, "is full of harsh doubts about the goodness and equality of men, the wisdom and possibilities of reform, and the sagacity of the majority."[1] To the conservative, man is a composite of good and evil—not perfect, not perfectible. Equality has meaning only in a spiritual sense; politically, society must recognize classes and respect aristocracies. Society is a living organism, a unity, that has a status of primacy. Society cannot be static, but it must be stable, for its ideal is ordered liberty. Government is natural not artificial, good not evil. Nevertheless, government cannot serve all purposes, and it is limited in its potentialities for good. The theory of natural law becomes the basis of the limitation of government as well as of legitimate authority. Religion usually has a central role in the conservative philosophy and the conservative often assigns a

[1] Clinton Rossiter, *Conservatism in America* (New York, 1955), p. 17.

prominent place in his ideal society to institutionalized religion. Finally, the conservative respects history and reveres tradition, believing them both to be man's most reliable teachers.

Such is the mood, if not the total philosophy, of the conservative. How pervasive did the conservative mood become in America? Some observers believe the new conservatism became more widespread than, for example, political choices would indicate. The search for consensus, for agreement on fundamental ideals and purposes, as well as pressures for conformity were among the forces producing an extension of the conservative mind. Adlai E. Stevenson, in the presidential campaign of 1952, observed in a speech at Columbus, Ohio, that "the strange alchemy of time has somehow converted the Democrats into the truly conservative party of this country—the party dedicated to conserving all that is best, and building solidly and safely on these foundations." The conservative sentiment he expressed was shared by wide segments of the American people.

Peter Viereck
1916-

Born in New York City, Peter Viereck was educated at Harvard, where he received the Ph.D degree in 1942. He then taught at several schools, including Mount Holyoke College. One of the creators of the New Conservatism, Viereck is also one of the ablest spokesmen for this conservative viewpoint. He has been influenced by a host of conservative thinkers of the past— Aristotelian, feudal, Burkean—but he writes in and for the American scene. He has also consistently opposed the "idiot conservatism" of radical right-wing groups, and has supported many social welfare programs as essential to the well-being of society.

Viereck's conservatism finds expression in many articles and in such books as Conservatism Revisited (*1949*), The Unadjusted Man (*1956*), Conservatism: From John Adams to Churchill (*1956*), *and the volume from which the following selection is taken*, Shame and Glory of the Intellectuals (*Boston, 1953*).

"*A*ll political systems," observed the poet Paul Valéry, "imply (and are generally not aware that they do imply) a certain conception of man, and even an opinion about the destiny of the species, an entire metaphysic." We should all try to achieve an awareness of what it is we are implying. "Metaphysically" (to use a "conservative" word despised by Enlightened Progressives), the difference between a democratic leftist and a democratic conservative is as follows: The conservative, politically descended from Burke, distrusts human nature and believes (politically speaking) in Original Sin, which must be restrained by the ethical traffic lights of traditionalism. The leftist and the liberal, descended from Rousseau, unconsciously assume the natural goodness of man—the less restrained in power the better.

If human nature were naturally good, then I would join the left-liberals and democratic socialists of the west in trusting a party power-machine to regiment a country's economy without eventually creating a political dictatorship to enforce such vast controls. Both Christianity and Dr. Freud teach a different view of human nature.

Conservatism and *liberalism*, as here used, are not clear or primary criteria for the American electoral scenes of 1952–56 (least of all while both parties are under such similarly middle-of-the-road, anti-extremist amalgams of liberal and conservative motifs as Stevenson and Eisenhower). *Conservative* and *liberal* are long-run "metaphysical" and psychological terms, not short-run practical terms. They cannot suffice to help us choose between electing a Democrat or Republican as village fire chief. In that sense they are "useless" terms of pragmatic activists. In that sense I even *intend* them to be "useless," being interested only in social and psychological speculations, not at all in political propaganda tracts for any particular party or candidate.

But in their "useless," impractical

way, the terms *liberal* and *conservative* do enrich our understanding of an important split in human nature, a psychological and literary as well as political split. This is the split between those who trust the "natural goodness" of man and primarily want to release it from *outer* restraints, and those who fear his natural caveman propensities and primarily want to check them with *inner* restraints.

A sense of man's limitations—a sense of his precariousness and mystery—is the necessary corrective against megalomaniac efforts to remake the world by force. The brilliant communist atomic spy, Klaus Fuchs, wrote in his court confession that the reading of Karl Marx meant to him, above all, the overcoming of human limitations; this overweening self-assertion of man, ruthlessly remaking society regardless of moral limitations, was (he confessed) the basis of his communist faith: "The idea which gripped me most was . . . that now, for the first time, man understands the historical forces and he is able to control them, and that therefore for the first time he will be really free. I carried this idea over into the personal sphere. . . ."

There are Lenins of religion, as there are Torquemadas of atheism; both equally lack this sense of human limitation. Christianity, rightly understood, teaches it the most wisely and truly. But the formula of "Christianity or communism," high-pressured with the same techniques as a campaign for Ivory Soap instead of God, is much too pat without qualification. What about the Red Dean of Canterbury and communism's Christian "peace" fronts? The formula holds true only if you add "Christianity rightly understood," thereby opening an un-pat debate that would fill volumes. How often is Christianity understood and practiced spiritually rather than as a sociological convention? May not its spiritual ethics

sometimes work through decent unbelievers (God "works in mysterious ways") while being betrayed not so much by open godlessness as by drab, leaden-eyed, uninspired lip service?

This Burkean (or today perhaps Niebuhrian) sense of human limitation and frailty, as opposed to the megalomaniac faith in limitless progress through mass-movements and material reforms, is a basic distinction between the conservative temperament and the progressive temperament. I say "temperament," not "political party" or "economic program." This Burkean sense is more basic a test of your outgrowing the illusions of liberalism than your position on the economic laws (introduced by the Republican party) against child labor or the economic laws (introduced by the Democratic party) for minimum wages. If such humane reforms, over the centuries, were a monopoly of liberalism, then who wouldn't be a liberal? What is left to debate if you beg the question by making one -ism synonymous with decency and the other with evil? What decent person today doesn't favor such laws?

No, social reform by itself is no criterion for conservative versus progressive (though the motives behind reform, whether motives of class-war-incitement or class-war-prevention, are obvious criteria). I cannot for a minute take seriously the assertions of America's superficial (merely economic) "conservatives" that they would abolish "all New Deal laws," most of which are the mildest, revolution-preventing reforms, passed by *both* parties. All that is shadow-boxing and campaign oratory. The genuine differences between the conservative and progressive outlooks on life are in the ethical and psychological realm, cutting across the lines of political party, economic class, or nationality.

There is no single shiny object to be peddled as *"the* new conservatism."

That only raises the question: which kind and conserving what? Let author and reader subordinate labels to contents. I don't care what the views here presented are labeled, in case you prefer to define conservatism differently. One writer suggests, "Instead, call these views the *true* liberalism, which the totalitarian and Popular Front liberals have betrayed." Less dramatic and more pedantic than that, I'd settle for being labeled simply "a value-conserving classical humanist." What difference does it make anyway? Here is the real point: after twenty years of hackneyed liberal conformism in high places and of a cult of revolt-for-its-own-sake among writers and intellectuals, it is time to work out a more human view of humanity. And by "human" I mean a view of society based on ethics and psychology, in contrast with an ethically-relativist and psychologically-superficial view of society based on economics.

Economics, economic determinism, and their nonexistent Economic Man are superannuated Marxist-and-capitalist fads. They reflect the temporarily overwhelming impact—the impact of novelty and of crisis—made upon the nineteenth century by the industrial revolution. In America after the Civil War, this industrial impact corrupted and narrowed the broader and more idealistic conservatism of our founding fathers. Hence, the pejorative misuse of the word today; hence, the need . . . to distinguish at considerable length between the true value-conserving kind and the contemporary degenerate kind, which conserves merely economic greed. For the more independent students and younger professors, the new conservatism (in its value-conserving sense) is rapidly becoming the only escape from the stultifying standardization of their cynical, value-denying elders. . . .

Though diverse subjects have been treated in these pages, their unity is basic because it reflects two underlying themes. The one unifying theme has been negative, the other positive. Negative theme: to examine the ethical, artistic, and political dangers of the new philistinism. Positive: a humanistic conservatism to meet the danger in these three fields.

At its best, the new conservatism may be defined as the rediscovery of values. This is what makes conservatism so fresh and exciting today, unlike the earlier Colonel Blimp, as cartooned by Low. A generation of pompous, Laski-indoctrinated leftists has intervened, a generation of Comrade Blimps, to whom conservatism is a subversive Dirty Word from the wrong side of the intellectual railroad tracks. No wonder the British Labor Government was so philistine and boring: on European unity uncreative and without Churchillian vision, in economics more skilled at afflicting the comfortable than comforting the afflicted. Conservatism is the rediscovery of tradition, the daring search for that lost Grail, the value code of Western man.

Society is in a bad way when too many people reject every ancient value in ethics and politics and art because thereby they can show off better at cocktail parties. Civilization is an infinitely fragile bundle of accumulated habits and restraints. The necessary conservative function of any generation is not just to enjoy itself but to pass on this bundle in good condition to the next generation.

Radicalism and revolt are just as valuable as conservatism so long as they really do correct social defects. But not when their insurgency accentuates, instead of corrects, social defects. In the past, when society had too much *laissez faire*, the thunder from the left was a valuable corrective to social defects. Today, when the world is afflicted by too much statism, the left accentuates, rather than corrects, social defects. Because society has changed. Today Bohemia and Left Bank and Left Wing, all the dully "daring" defiance of bourgeois conventions, have become the rheumatic jitterbugging of aging *enfants terribles*.

In the Victorian and Coolidgean ages, civilization was stuffy and stodgy, conservatism at its worst. It was dull to have only law and tradition; it was healthy and useful for obscure and surrealist poems and paintings to stir up placid reality with a nightmare art. It was healthy and useful to have the young rebel poke dull old civilization in its stuffed shirt; the *enfant terrible* served a real purpose.

Today the whole world is *terrible*. The whole world has become a surrealist painting. What was shocking in early surrealist painting was: legs and arms strewn about, buildings torn open. This contrasted with an unstrewn and untorn Victorian and Coolidgean reality. Today, however, reality is strewn all over the place. To us who were soldiers in Italy, strewn limbs and buildings became the norm. If the Babbitt is he who kowtows to fashionable conventions, then it is the wilfully obscure poet and the surrealist artist and the *enfant terrible* Greenwich Village genius who is the philistine; *he* is accentuating society's defects. The traditional moralist, the conservative in politics and in poetry, is correcting the defects. When reality is itself a nightmare, then an art which is lucid and calm and ennobling—an eighteenth-century neo-classical art—is more helpful, more original, and more exciting.

For a generation brought up not under Queen Victoria but under Princess Rita Hayworth, with not Bishop Wilberforce but Dr. Kinsey as Father Confessor, for such a generation Flaming Youth is not exciting but a bore. The only way to shock your reader in a modern non-Victorian novel—if that's what you want to do—would be to use the word "limbs" instead of "legs." That would shock them more than all the boring four-letter words of our war novelists.

But an affectation of archiepiscopal reactionary stodginess would be just as tiresome as the present rebel stodginess. In both art and politics one pendulum extreme is as bad as the other. Why have any affectations, either reactionary or revolutionary? Why not be yourself? Integrity may be the dullest platitude in the preaching of old Polonius, but integrity is the two-plus-two that does make four. A reverence for integrity, not because it's fashionable but because it's true, such a reverence would work a moral revolution deeper and more helpful than all the shallow artistic and political and economic revolts of our panting apostles of progress. It would be a moral revolution against that inner smirk which prefers cleverness to love and prefers statistics to wisdom. . . .

Unlike the ancient conservatism of Great Britain, the young American conservatism is still primarily a cultural, ethical, and educational movement, not primarily political.

The proper start for a new American conservatism, aiming not at success but at truth, not at activism but at long-range education, is in the world of literature, the arts and sciences, intellectual history, the universities, the humanities. Starting there and slowly osmosing into more "practical" spheres of American life, such a movement will eventually affect politics and economics by raising in both parties the *level of insight* into historical and ethical processes. By being more contemplative than activist, by asking all those basic questions the activists ignore rather than by too glibly answering them, a conservative return to values will transform politics and economics indirectly. If instead it tries to start by being directly and actively political and economic, it will at best fail and transform nothing at all. At worst it will lend itself to unscrupulous material exploitation. The thoughtfulness here recommended to new conservatives is not a flight from practical action but an inner prelude to practical action. The most successful political conservatism in history, the Tory party of Disraeli and Churchill, derived to a surprising extent from sources that were almost entirely literary, like Coleridge.

Our civilization is very old, very broad; we Americans are only a very young, very small part of it. Its essentials, its truth and its beauty, together with a deep understanding of human nature, are transmitted more through the humanities than through that up-to-date journalism of the academic world, the courses in current politics, economics, and other uselessly "useful" techniques. Not that the latter are unworthy—call them the Good Housekeeping of American education—but they happen not to be the main value transmitters and insight transmitters. Values and insights are transmitted by saturating yourself in the Elizabethan and Greek plays, the Aeneid and the Song of Roland, the poetry of Dante and Hölderlin, the psychological insight of Augustine, Pascal and the nineteenth-century Russian novelists.

The American conservative can transform his country more by teaching these value transmitters, and by raising their status above the media of mass-entertainment in public esteem, than by any directly political action. (It should be evident that courses in practical technical training and in the humanities can both be happily combined, wherever economic need so dictates.)

Saturation in the value transmitters of literature is an intimately personal part of every free citizen's growth. It is achieved not by streamlined public lectures on Great Books Predigested but by lonely reverie. It is aided not at all by our mechanized and progressive "teaching aids," replete with loudspeakers, with tape-recorders, and even with thinking-brain machines for grading multiple-choice questions. There is no

substitute for the traditional, even sentimental Abraham Lincoln picture of the young boy brooding alone by candlelight over the dog-eared open book. Only such daily individual reverie can think through—to its future implications—every exciting idea of the past. This does more than inane loyalty oaths and patriotic propaganda to prevent two kinds of disloyalty:

1. The constant unconscious echoing of fellow-traveler clichés in intellectual circles.

2. On a more frivolous plan, the daily cultural betrayal of our past in the mass-entertainment—the Don't Think Clubs—of the air waves and the celluloid.

Neither form of value betrayal can be compromised with even slightly. It is not enough to apologize, "I only tune in on the better programs." It is true that already today a television set can serve what its ads call "your beautiful American way of life." But only when chopped up into firewood and blazing merrily.

The new conservatism—meaning: a fresh and creative traditionalism—never admires the past passively in sterile escapism. It must daily and actively re-experience, as if for the first time, the aspirations of the past—and then fulfil them in the future. . . .

In the 1930's Edmund Wilson, agonizing over the contrast between radical ideals and Soviet realities, implored intellectuals to "take communism away from the communists." And, indeed, one of the finest achievements of the New Deal era, now drawing to a close, is that it achieved many humanitarian ideals of the so-called left without the murderous police-state practices of the far left. In the 1950's, to reverse the slogan of the 1930's, our more responsible leaders ought to take anticommunism away from the anticommunists. And to take conservatism away from the wrong—the solely economics-minded—conservatives. It will be as important to keep the present era of *pause* under humane conservatives as it was to keep the past era of *change* out of the hands of the leftist version of terrorists and thought controllers.

Youth has been called too wonderful a thing to waste on the the the young. Conservatism, which ought to mean the freshness and zest of rediscovery, is too wonderful to waste on the old-in-spirit. . . .

The discrediting of the Soviet fraud has made it a lot easier for intellectuals to become American traditionalists without being howled down as "reactionaries," "flag wavers," or "fascists." Recognition of the blood-stained nature of the Soviet banner makes it seem less deliciously clever to trample on the American banner at every possible occasion. This swing from the outworn poses of revolt is releasing a burst of creative new thinking.

But the same change brings new dangers as well as new blessings. In time the new traditionalism may degenerate into a new white-wash of pretentious philosophy for what has always been unpretentious: the old robber baronism of public-be-damned. At least those endearingly unshaved and candid old pirates did not try to be smoothie "philosophers" of "conservatism." Genuine giants of our dinosaur era of chaotic expansion, like crusty Commodore Vanderbilt, swashbuckling Dan Drew carelessly trailing seminaries and suicides, or old J. P. Morgan, would have puffed their black cigars scornfully at such fancy nonsense. If this white-wash takes place, then the American flag, rightly saved from the muddy boots of fellow-traveler liberals, would be saved in vain. Or is it a patriotic triumph if the dawn's early glare reveals our flag progressing from being a door mat to being a fig leaf?

Such patriots, reaping unjustified fruits from our justified revulsion against communism, now have their grand opportunity. They can now suddenly seem the Great Oaks of the American Dream instead of the parasitic vines. History itself seems beckoning us toward their comforting shade, those stalwart "uncommunistic" pillars both of profit system and of God-fearingness.

But what if there be a contradiction between these two supposedly equal pillars? What if the essence of the patriotic American tradition, along with the tradition of the whole Christian Hellenic-Judaic world, is an awareness of this contradiction between our profits and our prophets?

Lay not up for yourselves treasures upon earth . . . for where your treasure is, there will your heart be also. . . . No man can serve two masters . . . ye cannot serve God and mammon.

I have faith in American capitalism because I believe its profit system has been sufficiently modified by ethics—and because I believe it can continue to be revised peacefully, without need of socialism, when it does violate the demands of humanity. Defending it on this basis, we can create faith in our system in Europe, in India, and at home. But if we adopt the un-American principle of putting profits above humanity and ethics, we shall discredit American capitalism and aid Moscow. This will have two results, the first abroad and the second at home:

1. Abroad we will find ourselves fatally without allies, a fate not displeasing to some of the "go it alone" isolationists. In that case, the American Adam Smith will produce Cain and Abel Smith in Europe, a fratricidal destruction of the free world for Stalin's benefit.

2. More ironically, we will at home be *behaving exactly as Marxism says we behave:* namely, putting our capitalist profit motive over all religious, ethical, and cultural ties. By combating Marxism in the wrong way, we would for the first time in our history become Marxist economic determinists in our behavior.

Can anything happen that would prove Marx right? Though he was steeped in enough Western humanism to make him preferable to the Soviet terror, yet his doctrinaire Hegelianism and Prussian statism produced a dogma seemingly impossible to justify. Here is the achievement of our Old Guarders: their triumph would accomplish the dazzling feat of justifying the following passage of Marx and Engels, which our past history had gloriously disproved:

> The bourgeoisie has played an extremely revolutionary role. . . . It has destroyed all feudal, patriarchal, and idyllic relationships. It has ruthlessly torn asunder the motley feudal ties that bound men to their "natural superiors;" it has left no other bond betwixt man and man but crude self-interest and unfeeling "cash payment." It has drowned religious ecstasy, chivalrous enthusiasm, and humdrum sentimentalism in the ice-water of selfish calculation. It has degraded personal dignity to the level of exchange value; and in place of countless dearly-bought chartered freedoms, it has set up one solitary unscrupulous freedom—freedom of trade.

Capitalism has many other merits but happens not to be a sacred religion. The current ambitious attempt to make it one in our textbooks is being incorrectly denounced as "fascism" by New Deal liberals and incorrectly hailed as "free individualism" by Republican conservatives. It is neither. It is a return to that Sahara of inhuman aridity: the belief in Economic Man. It is a return to the incomplete liberties—merely top-of-the-iceberg—of private economic liberty. It ignores the nine-tenths of human liberties beneath the top of the brain: the nine-tenths of imagination and art and religion. . . .

The cause of democratic socialism, opposing both fascism and communism, contains more good will than most -isms of our time. Why is most of that good will squandered without producing more than High-minded Editorials? Why, to put it cruelly, is democratic socialism ultimately a failure?

Social democracy has an attractive social program for both the masses and the intellectuals. Then why has it so frequently failed to stop either communism or fascism in Europe? Why has it failed to summon forth the energy and enthusiasm to keep itself in power firmly and long? The Weimar Republic is a classic case of such failure.

The answer is not only economic but psychological. Surely it is an obvious answer, though perhaps not normally stated in just that way. The answer is simply that an inherent inner conflict condemns all social democrats to be Hamlets. An innate schizophrenia paralyzes—(with great but rare exceptions like Reuter)—their ability to *take action* in any crisis or to stay firmly in power against aggressive enemies who know what they want.

The source of their paralyzing inner conflict is that they want incompatibles. They want economic collectivism and political individual rights at the same time. With what consequences? Their *economic* wish for collectivism requires *political* dictatorship to enforce. Their sincere *political* wish for individual liberty requires some individualism also in all the nonpolitical fields, *economics* not excluded.

But the very phrase "free enterprise" —here their conditioning makes them inflexible—the very phrase "free enterprise" horrifies all socialists and also the less moderate wing of New Dealers. Their conditioned response is to dismiss it as some Wall Street plot, some insincere propaganda slogan for selfish undemocratic interests. This it is—sometimes and superficially. But not always and not basically. Nobody is speaking of total laissez faire nor of materialistic profit worship; but basically the economy healthiest for democracy is most certainly the free market and free consumer choice, that encourager of individual diversities.

The humiliating failure of Weimar and

the social democrats to prevent Germans from voting Nazi tempts one to misquote Churchill: never has so little been achieved with so much effort by so many. "But what about Scandinavia?" a socialist asks. The success of Scandinavian social democrats, insofar as it is really a success, proves my point. Where they do well, they are not democrats-plus-socialists but democrats-period. Being democratic includes social reform; "democrat" by itself already means "social-reform democrat." But social reform—Christian humanitarianism or nineteenth-century "Tory socialism"—does not at all mean the statist "socialism" of present American and European socialists.

Here I am using "socialism" not in any watered-down sense. I use it to mean a statism that socializes the economic and industrial life of the country. Socialism is a statism that nationalizes not merely a post office here, a public utility there, but the main means of production.

Full socialist control of press and radio by the government, even if indirectly via newsprint, control of most economic power by government and lack of economic power by any kind of opposition, will make democracy impossible. Impossible not in theory but in actual practice, even if sincerely maintaining every one of the outward democratic forms in theory. After becoming emperor, Augustus maintained the sovereignty of the Roman Senate in theory; did that mean Rome was still a republic?

But though democratic socialism is a contradiction, it is not one that necessarily leads to ruin. That depends on which half of the contradiction your social democrat stresses. In Europe, America can and should work with democratic socialists against communism wherever they are democrats first, as they are in the case of Reuter, Attlee, and most French and Scandinavian socialists. Europe's unsocialist social-

ism and America's classless, democratized capitalism are both in practice—never in theory—living in thoroughly mixed-up economy, flexible and undoctrinaire, and doing very well, thank you.

All this does not change the fact that, in the long run, the Hamlet wavering between freedom and statism will continue to enfeeble the socialists themselves. It will also enfeeble and demoralize any country under them. In the long run they will have to face the need of shifting their position: from the outward leftist fringe of society toward the more conservative center. They will have to say quite brutally to themselves, "Come, come, no nonsense now!" and throw out their "revolutionary" dogmas. Those dogmas are a hang-over from an earlier century, before history established beyond challenge the unrevolutionary nature of freedom. . . .

Not yet daring to breathe aloud the heresy of sobriety, some socialists tacitly have reached these centrist, mixed-economy conclusions already. Still a minority, these more reasonable souls are found with increasing frequency in England and Scandinavia; perhaps by the time of his death the wise French socialist Léon Blum had also evolved to this stage. At this stage, the ambiguous word "socialist" becomes —like Disraeli's Tory socialism or maybe Niebuhr's Christian synthesis—a sound sense of the organic ties between free individuals. It becomes a sound rebuke to the laisser-faire atomism and anarchism of the more doctrinaire capitalists, yet without crossing the fatal statist line.

But while many social democrats are democrats first, let us not optimistically overlook the fact that many others still are socialists first. The Marxist, the Bevanites, and the Schumacher wing of German socialists really "mean business" with their socialism. This does credit to their sincerity.

It does not do credit to their capacity for preserving liberties. The Achilles heel of even the wisest democratic socialists is that they recognize no statist margin, limiting the usefulness of even the wisest social legislation beyond a certain point. Instead they put their faith (that same old Rousseau-istic faith) in counterbalancing the superstate by the mass-electorate, via its theoretical "democratic controls." The "natural goodness" of the Ortegan mass-man is somehow to prevent an all-powerful bureaucracy from abusing politically its excessive economic power. Well, it can't be done.

Walter Lippmann
1889-

*Born in New York City, Lippmann
graduated from Harvard College and then
spent a year doing graduate study there in
philosophy. Lippmann thought of becoming
a teacher but decided instead to turn to
writing. He then entered upon a long and
distinguished career as editor, author,
and columnist. Over the years he has
developed a reputation as one of America's
most important commentators.*

*At Harvard, Lippmann espoused socialist
ideas, and early in his career he associated
himself with many liberal and radical
causes. One of his first posts was that of
associate editor of the* New Republic. *But
the debacle of Versailles forced Lippmann
to reconsider his fundamental assumptions.
His subsequent disillusionment with liberal
ideas found partial expression in his book*
Public Opinion, *published in 1922. In the
years that followed, Lippmann gradually
adopted more conservative ideas, if not the
whole mantle of conservatism. Of special
importance is Lippmann's support of the
resurgence of the natural-law theory of
society.*

*This selection, which discusses the theory of
natural law, is from* The Public Philosophy
(*Boston: Little, Brown and Company, 1955*).

I should say that I am a liberal
democrat and have no wish to disen-
franchise my fellow citizens. My hope is
that both liberty and democracy can be
preserved before the one destroys the
other. Whether this can be done is the
question of our time, what with more
than half the world denying and des-
pairing of it. Of one thing we may be
sure. If it is to be done at all, we must be
uninhibited in our examination of our
condition. And since our condition is
manifestly connected with grave errors
in war and peace that have been committed by democratic governments, we
must adopt the habit of thinking as
plainly about the sovereign people as
we do about the politicians they elect.
It will not do to think poorly of the politicians and to talk with bated breath
about the voters. No more than the
kings before them should the people be
hedged with divinity. Like all princes
and rulers, like all sovereigns, they are
ill-served by flattery and adulation. And
they are betrayed by the servile hypocrisy which tells them that what is true
and what is false, what is right and
what is wrong, can be determined by
their votes.

If I am right in what I have been saying, there has developed in this century
a functional derangement of the relationship between the mass of the people
and the government. The people have
acquired power which they are incapable of exercising, and the governments they elect have lost powers which
they must recover if they are to govern.
What then are the true boundaries of
the people's power? The answer cannot
be simple. But for a rough beginning
let us say that the people are able to
give and to withhold their consent to

443

being governed—their consent to what the government asks of them, proposes to them, and has done in the conduct of their affairs. They can elect the government. They can remove it. They can approve or disapprove its performance. But they cannot administer the government. They cannot themselves perform. They cannot normally initiate and propose the necessary legislation. A mass cannot govern. . . .

Where mass opinion dominates the government, there is a morbid derangement of the true functions of power. The derangement brings about the enfeeblement, verging on paralysis, of the capacity to govern. This breakdown in the constitutional order is the cause of the precipitate and catastrophic decline of Western society. It may, if it cannot be arrested and reversed, bring about the fall of the West. . . .

There is a principle which, if it can be applied deeply enough, gets at the root of the disorder of modern democracy. It is that though public officials are elected by the voters, or are appointed by men who are elected, they owe their primary allegiance not to the opinions of the voters but to the law, to the criteria of their professions, to the integrity of the arts and sciences in which they work, to their own conscientious and responsible convictions of their duty within the rules and the frame of reference they have sworn to respect.

The implied principle may be defined in other terms by saying that while the electors choose the ruler, they do not own any shares in him and they have no right to command him. His duty is to the office and not to his electors. Their duty is to fill the office and not to direct the office-holder. I realize that, as I have stated it, the principle runs counter to the popular view that in a democracy public men are the servants (that is, the agents) of the people (that is, of the voters). . . .

We are living in a time of massive popular counter-revolution against liberal democracy. It is a reaction to the failure of the West to cope with the miseries and anxieties of the Twentieth Century. The liberal democracies have been tried and found wanting—found wanting not only in their capacity to govern successfully in this period of wars and upheavals, but also in their ability to defend and maintain the political philosophy that underlies the liberal way of life.

If we go back to the beginnings of the modern democratic movements in the eighteenth century, we can distinguish two diverging lines of development. The one is a way of progress in liberal constitutional democracy. The other is a morbid course of development into totalitarian conditions. . . .

Although the two ways of evolution appear to have the same object—a society with free institutions under popular government—they are radically different and they arrive at radically different ends.

The first way, that of assimilation, presumes the existence of a state which is already constitutional in principle, which is under laws that are no longer arbitrary, though they may be unjust and unequal. Into this constitutional state more and more people are admitted to the governing class and to the voting electorate. The unequal and the unjust laws are revised until eventually all the people have equal opportunities to enter the government and to be represented. Broadly speaking, this has been the working theory of the British movement towards a democratic society at home and also in the Commonwealth and Empire. This, too, was the working theory of the principal authors of the American Constitution, and this was how—though few of them welcomed it—they envisaged the enfranchisement of the whole adult population.

The other way is that of the Jacobin

revolution. The people rise to power by overthrowing the ruling class and by liquidating its privileges and prerogatives. This is the doctrine of democratic revolution which was developed by French thinkers in the eighteenth century and was put into practice by the Jacobin party in the French Revolution. In its English incarnation the doctrine became known as Radicalism. In America, though it had its early disciples, notably Tom Paine, not until the era of the Founding Fathers was over, not until the era of Andrew Jackson, did the Jacobin doctrine become the popular political creed of the American democracy. . . .

Of the two rival philosophies, the Jacobin is almost everywhere in the ascendant. It is a ready philosophy for men who, previously excluded from the ruling class, and recently enfranchised, have no part in the business of governing the state, and no personal expectation of being called upon to assume the responsibilities of office. The Jacobin doctrine is an obvious reaction, as de Tocqueville's observation explains, to government by a caste. When there is no opening for the gradualness of reform and for enfranchisement by assimilation, a revolutionary collision is most likely.

The Jacobin doctrine is addressed to the revolutionary collision between the inviolable governing caste and the excluded men claiming the redress of their grievances and their place in the sun. Though it professes to be a political philosophy, the doctrine is not, in fact, a philosophy of government. It is a gospel and also a strategy for revolution. It announces the promise that the crusade which is to overthrow the ruling caste will by the act of revolution create a good society.

The peculiar essence of the dogma is that the revolution itself is the creative act. Towards the revolution as such, because it is the culmination and the climax, all the labor and the sacrifice of the struggle are to be directed. The revolutionary act will remove the causes of evil in human society. Again and again it has been proved how effective is this formula for arousing, sustaining and organizing men's energies for revolution: to declare that evil in society has been imposed upon the many by the few—by priests, nobles, capitalists, imperialists, liberals, aliens—and that evil will disappear when the many who are pure have removed these few who are evil. . . .

We live long enough after the new gospel was proclaimed to have seen what came of it. The post-revolutionary man, enfranchised and emancipated, has not turned out to be the New Man. He is the old Adam. Yet the future of democratic society has been staked on the promises and the predictions of the Jacobin gospel.

For the Jacobin doctrine has pervaded the theory of mass education in the newly enfranchised mass democracies. In America and in most of the newer liberal democracies of the Western world, the Jacobin heresy is, though not unchallenged and not universal, the popular and dominant theory in the schools. . . .

The Jacobin doctrine does not solve this problem of mass education—as it does not solve or even throw light upon the problem of how to construct and govern the utopian society which is to exist when the revolution has taken place. What it does is to provide an escape from these unsolved problems. It affirms that in politics the state will wither away and then there will be no problems of how to govern it. . . .

In the Jacobin gospel of the eighteenth century, and even in the Marxist gospel of the nineteenth century, the new man would be there when the artificial garments were removed—when once he was emancipated by the revolutionary act from the deformation imposed upon him by the clergy, the nobility and the bourgeoisie. A hundred years later the new man was nowhere in sight. So the early and softer gospel gave way to a later and infinitely harder one. The new man and the new heaven on earth demanded the remaking of pre-Leninist and pre-Hitlerian man. The decrees of history as revealed to Marx, and the decrees of nature as revealed to Hitler, had to be carried out.

But in order to do that, the human species had first to be transformed— or failing that, exterminated. Destiny called upon the mortal god to make surviving mankind "an active unfailing carrier," as Hannah Arendt says, "of a law to which human beings would otherwise only passively and reluctantly be subject."

In the eyes of its devotees, this is not an inhuman and satanic doctrine. It is above and beyond humanity. It is for the superman that its gospel announces. The ruthlessness, the arbitrariness, the cruelty are not monstrous wickedness. They are natural and necessary, predestined like the fall of a sparrow, in the sublime construction of the earthly paradise. . . .

To speak of a public philosophy is, I am well aware, to raise dangerous questions, rather like opening Pandora's box. . . .

The founders of our free institutions were themselves adherents of this public philosophy. When they insisted upon excluding the temporal power from the realm of the mind and the spirit, it was not that they had no public philosophy. It was because experience had taught them that as power corrupts, it corrupts the public philosophy. It was, therefore, a practical rule of politics that the government should not be given sovereignty and proprietorship over the public philosophy.

But as time went on, there fell out of fashion the public philosophy of the founders of Western institutions. The rule that the temporal power should be excluded from the realms of the mind and of the spirit was then subtly transformed. It became the rule that ideas and principles are private—with only subjective relevance and significance. Only when there is "a clear and present danger" to public order are the acts of speaking and publishing in the public domain. All the first and last things were removed from the public domain. All that has to do with what man is and should be, or how he should hold himself in the scheme of things, what are his rightful ends and the legitimate means, became private and subjective and publicly unaccountable. And so, the liberal democracies of the West became the first great society to treat as a private concern the formative beliefs that shape the character of its citizens.

This has brought about a radical change in the meaning of freedom. Originally it was founded on the postulate that there was a universal order on which all reasonable men were agreed: within that public agreement on the fundamentals and on the ultimates, it was safe to permit and it would be desirable to encourage, dissent and dispute. But with the disappearance of the public philosophy—and of a consensus on the first and last things—there was opened up a great vacuum in the public mind, yawning to be filled. . . .

I believe there is a public philosophy. Indeed there is such a thing as the public philosophy of civility. It does not have to be discovered or invented. It is known. But it does have to be revived and renewed.

The public philosophy is known as *natural law*, a name which, alas, causes great semantic confusion. This philosophy is the premise of the institutions of the Western society, and they are, I believe, unworkable in communities that do not adhere to it. Except on the premises of this philosophy, it is impossible to reach intelligible and workable

conceptions of popular election, majority rule, representative assemblies, free
speech, loyalty, property, corporations
and voluntary associations. The founders
of these institutions, which the recently
enfranchised democracies have inherited, were all of them adherents of some
one of the various schools of natural
law.

For over two thousand years, says
Barker, European thought has been
acted upon by the idea that the rational
faculties of men can produce a common
conception of law and order which
possesses a universal validity. This
conception was first formulated as a
theory by Zeno and the Stoics. It was
absorbed by the Roman lawyers, was
adopted by the Christian fathers, was
reestablished and reworked by Saint
Thomas Aquinas, and in a new formulation, after the Renaissance and Reformation, it provided the philosophy of the
English Revolution of 1688 and of the
American Revolution of 1776. The long
life of this idea and, above all, the recurring revival of the idea in all ages,
would seem to indicate that it reflects a
wide and recurring human need—that
it is involved with practical questions of
policy in the face of recurring political
problems. . . .

They are the laws of a rational order
of human society—in the sense that all
men, when they are sincerely and lucidly
rational, will regard them as self-evident. The rational order consists of the
terms which must be met in order to
fulfill men's capacity for the good life
in this world. They are the terms of the
widest consensus of rational men in a
plural society. They are the propositions
to which all men concerned, if they are
sincerely and lucidly rational, can be
expected to converge. . . .

As the bitter end has become visible
in the countries of the total revolution,
we can see how desperate is the predicament of modern men. The terrible events
show that the harder they try to make

earth into heaven, the more they make it
a hell.

Yet, the yearning for salvation and for
perfection is most surely not evil, and it
is, moreover, perennial in the human
soul. Are men then doomed by the very
nature of things to be denied the highest
good if it cannot be materialized in this
world and if, as so large a number of
modern men assume, it will not be
materialized in another world?

The answer to this question is known.
It can be had by recognizing the difference between the realm of existence
where objects are materialized to our
senses, and the realm of essence, where
they are present to the mind. I am using
the ambiguous but irreplaceable word
"essence" as meaning the true and
undistorted nature of things. The understanding of our relation to these two
realms of being is exceedingly difficult
to communicate, so difficult that, as a
matter of fact, it has remained an eso-
teric wisdom.

Yet if there is a way out of the modern
predicament, it begins, I believe, where
we learn to recognize the difference
between the two realms. For the radical
error of the modern democratic gospel is
that it promises, not the good life of this
world, but the perfect life of heaven. The
root of the error is the confusion of the
two realms—that of this world where
the human condition is to be born, to
live, to work, to struggle and to die,
and that of the transcendent world in
which men's souls can be regenerate
and at peace. The confusion of these
two realms is an ultimate disorder. It
inhibits the good life in this world. It
falsifies the life of the spirit. . . .

In the traditions of civility, the
prevailing view has been that the two
realms are inseparable but disparate,
and that man must work out his destiny
in the balance, which is never fixed
finally between the two. . . .

I believe that the public philosophy
can be revived, and the reconnaissance

which we have made has been a demonstration that when it is applied to such central concepts as popular sovereignty, property, freedom of speech, and education, the public philosophy clarifies the problems and opens the way towards rational and acceptable solutions. The revival of the public philosophy depends on whether its principles and precepts—which were articulated before the industrial revolution, before the era of rapid technological change, and before the rise of the mass democracies—depends on whether this old philosophy can be reworked for the modern age. If this cannot be done, then the free and democratic nations face the totalitarian challenge without a public philosophy which free men believe in and cherish, with no public faith beyond a mere official agnosticism, neutrality and indifference. There is not much doubt how the struggle is likely to end if it lies between those who, believing, care very much—and those who, lacking belief, cannot care very much. . . .

I do not contend, though I hope, that the decline of Western society will be arrested if the teachers in our schools and universities come back to the great tradition of the public philosophy. But I do contend that the decline, which is already far advanced, cannot be arrested if the prevailing philosophers oppose this restoration and revival, if they impugn rather than support the validity of an order which is superior to the values that Sartre tells each man "to invent."

What the prevailing philosophers say about religion is not itself, in Tillich's terms, religion as an ultimate concern of worship and of love. But if the philosophers teach that religious experience is a purely psychological phenomenon, related to nothing beyond each man's psychic condition, then they will give educated men a bad intellectual conscience if they have religious experiences. The philosophers cannot give them

religion. But they can keep them away from it.

Philosophers play the same role in relation to the principles of the good society. These require, as we have seen, the mastery of human nature in the raw by an acquired rational second nature. In the literal sense, the principles of the good society must be unpopular until they have prevailed sufficiently to alter the popular impulses. For the popular impulses are opposed to public principles. These principles cannot be made to prevail if they are discredited,—if they are dismissed as superstition, as obscurantism, as meaningless metaphysics, as reactionary, as self-seeking rationalizations.

The public philosophy is in a large measure intellectually discredited among contemporary men. Because of that, what we may call the terms of discourse in public controversy are highly unfavorable to anyone who adheres to the public philosophy. The signs and seals of legitimacy, of rightness and of truth, have been taken over by men who reject, even when they are not the avowed adversaries of, the doctrine of constitutional democracy.

If the decline of the West under the misrule of the people is to be halted, it will be necessary to alter these terms of discourse. They are now set overwhelmingly against the credibility and against the rightness of the principles of the constitutional state; they are set in favor of the Jacobin conception of the emancipated and sovereign people.

I have been arguing, hopefully and wishfully, that it may be possible to alter the terms of discourse if a convincing demonstration can be made that the principles of the good society are not, in Sartre's phrase, invented and chosen—that the conditions which must be met if there is to be a good society are there, outside our wishes, where they can be discovered by rational inquiry, and developed and adapted and refined by rational discussion.

If eventually this were demonstrated successfully, it would, I believe, rearm all those who are concerned with the anomy of our society, with its progressive barbarization, and with its descent into violence and tyranny. Amidst the quagmire of moral impressionism they would stand again on hard intellectual ground where there are significant objects that are given and are not merely projected, that are compelling and are not merely wished. Their hope would be re-established that there is a public world, sovereign above the infinite number of contradictory and competing private worlds. Without this certainty, their struggle must be unavailing.

Friedrich A. von Hayek

1899-

Hayek is one of the few foreign-born thinkers included in this volume. Nevertheless, he merits inclusion because the position he has developed is an important one in the Western community of nations, and is attractive to many Americans.

Born in Vienna, Hayek received his doctorate from the University of Vienna in 1923. Shortly thereafter, he settled in England, where he taught at the University of London. He became a naturalized British citizen in 1938. In 1950 he went to the University of Chicago as professor of social and moral science.

Hayek's political and economic views are clearly not in agreement with those of modern liberals. He maintains—in the spirit of the dominant trends of nineteenth-century social thought—that individual liberty is the most precious of political values. At the same time, he believes that conservatives can learn valuable lessons from the liberal's valid criticisms of conservatism. Searching for a name for his position, he accepts "Whiggism" as perhaps the best descriptive term he can find—though he notes that earlier generations might well have used the term "liberal" to designate his views.

The selection here is from the Postscript "Why I Am Not a Conservative" to his book The Constitution of Liberty (*Chicago: The University of Chicago Press, 1960*).

*A*t a time when most movements that are thought to be progressive advocate further encroachments on individual liberty, those who cherish freedom are likely to expend their energies in opposition. In this they find themselves much of the time on the same side as those who habitually resist change. In matters of current politics today they generally have little choice but to support the conservative parties. But, though the position I have tried to define is also often described as "conservative," it is very different from that to which this name has been traditionally attached. There is danger in the confused condition which brings the defenders of liberty and the true conservatives to-gether in common opposition to developments which threaten their different ideals equally. It is therefore important to distinguish clearly the position taken here from that which has long been known—perhaps more appropriately—as conservatism.

Conservatism proper is a legitimate, probably necessary, and certainly widespread attitude of opposition to drastic change. It has, since the French Revolution, for a century and a half played an important role in European politics. Until the rise of socialism its opposite was liberalism. There is nothing corresponding to this conflict in the history of the United States, because what in Europe was called "liberalism" was here the common tradition on which the American polity had been built: thus the defender of the American tradition was a liberal in the European sense. This already existing confusion was made worse by the recent attempt to transplant to America the European type of conservatism, which, being alien to the American tradition, has acquired a somewhat odd character. And some time before this, American radicals and socialists began calling themselves "liberals." I will nevertheless continue for the moment to describe as liberal the position which I hold and which I believe differs as much from true conservatism as from socialism. Let me say at once, however, that I do so with increasing misgivings, and I shall later have to consider what would be the appropriate name for the party of liberty. The reason for this is not only that the term "liberal" in the United States is the cause of constant misunderstandings today, but also that in Europe the predominant type of rationalistic liberalism has long been one of the pacemakers of socialism.

Let me now state what seems to me the decisive objection to any conservatism which deserves to be called such. It is that by its very nature it cannot offer an alternative to the direction in which we are moving. It may succeed by its resistance to current tendencies in slowing down undesirable developments, but, since it does not indicate another direction, it cannot prevent their continuance. It has, for this reason, invariably been the fate of conservatism to be dragged along a path not of its own choosing. The tug of war between conservatives and progressives can only affect the speed, not the direction, of contemporary developments. But, though there is need for a "brake on the vehicle of progress," I personally cannot be content with simply helping to apply the brake. What the liberal must ask, first of all, is not how fast or how

far we should move, but where we should move. In fact, he differs much more from the collectivist radical of today than does the conservative. While the last generally holds merely a mild and moderate version of the prejudices of his time, the liberal today must more positively oppose some of the basic conceptions which most conservatives share with the socialists. . . .

Before I consider the main points on which the liberal attitude is sharply opposed to the conservative one, I ought to stress that there is much that the liberal might with advantage have learned from the work of some conservative thinkers. To their loving and reverential study of the value of grown institutions we owe (at least outside the field of economics) some profound insights which are real contributions to our understanding of a free society. However reactionary in politics such figures as Coleridge, Bonald, De Maistre, Justus Möser, or Donoso Cortés may have been, they did show an understanding of the meaning of spontaneously grown institutions such as language, law, morals, and conventions that anticipated modern scientific approaches and from which the liberals might have profited. But the admiration of the conservatives for free growth generally applies only to the past. They typically lack the courage to welcome the same undesigned change from which new tools of human endeavors will emerge.

This brings me to the first point on which the conservative and the liberal dispositions differ radically. As has often been acknowledged by conservative writers, one of the fundamental traits of the conservative attitude is a fear of change, a timid distrust of the new as such, while the liberal position is based on courage and confidence, on a preparedness to let change run its course even if we cannot predict where it will lead. There would not be much to object to if the conservatives merely disliked too rapid change in institutions and public policy; here the case for caution and slow process is indeed strong. But the conservatives are inclined to use the powers of government to prevent change or to limit its rate to whatever appeals to the more timid mind. In looking forward, they lack the faith in the spontaneous forces of adjustment which makes the liberal accept changes without apprehension, even though he does not know how the necessary adaptations will be brought about. It is, indeed, part of the liberal attitude to assume that, especially in the economic field, the self-regulating forces of the market will somehow bring about the required adjustments to new conditions, although no one can foretell how they will do this in a particular instance. There is perhaps no single factor contributing so much to people's frequent reluctance to let the market work as their inability to conceive how some necessary balance, between demand and supply, between exports and imports, or the like, will be brought about without deliberate control. The conservative feels safe and content only if he is assured that some higher wisdom watches and supervises change, only if he knows that some authority is charged with keeping the change "orderly."

This fear of trusting uncontrolled social forces is closely related to two other characteristics of conservatism: its fondness for authority and its lack of understanding of economic forces. Since it distrusts both abstract theories and general principles, it neither understands those spontaneous forces on which a policy of freedom relies nor possesses a basis for formulating principles of policy. Order appears to the conservatives as the result of the continuous attention of authority, which, for this purpose, must be allowed to do what is required by the particular circumstances and not be tied to rigid rule. A commitment to principles presupposes an understanding of the general forces by which the efforts of society are co-ordinated, but it is such a theory of society and especially of the economic mechanism that conservatism conspicuously lacks. So unproductive has conservatism been in producing a general conception of how a social order is maintained that its modern votaries, in trying to construct a theoretical foundation, invariably find themselves appealing almost exclusively to authors who regarded themselves as liberal. Macaulay, Tocqueville, Lord Acton, and Lecky certainly considered themselves liberals, and with justice; and even Edmund Burke remained an Old Whig to the end and would have shuddered at the thought of being regarded as a Tory.

Let me return, however, to the main point, which is the characteristic complacency of the conservative toward the action of established authority and his prime concern that this authority be not weakened rather than that its power be kept within bounds. This is difficult to reconcile with the preservation of liberty. In general, it can probably be said that the conservative does not object to coercion or arbitrary power so long as it is used for what he regards as the right purposes. He believes that if government is in the hands of decent men, it ought not be too much restricted by rigid rules. Since he is essentially opportunist and lacks principles, his main hope must be that the wise and the good will rule—not merely by example, as we all must wish, but by authority given to them and enforced by them. Like the socialist, he is less concerned with the problem of how the powers of government should be limited than with that of who wields them; and, like the socialist, he regards himself as entitled to force the value he holds on other people.

When I say that the conservative lacks principles, I do not mean to suggest that he lacks moral conviction. The typical conservative is indeed usually a man of very strong moral convictions. What I mean is that he has no political principles which enable him to work with people whose moral values differ from his own for a political order in which both can obey their convictions. It is the recognition of such principles that permits the coexistence of different sets of values that makes it possible to build a peaceful society with a minimum of force. The acceptance of such principles means that we agree to tolerate much that we dislike. There are many values of the conservative which appeal to me more than those of the socialists; yet for a liberal the importance he personally attaches to specific goals is no sufficient justification for forcing others to serve them. I have little doubt that some of my conservative friends will be shocked by what they will regard as "concessions" to modern views that I have made in Part III of this book. But, though I may dislike some of the measures concerned as much as they do and might vote against them, I know of no general principles to which I could appeal to persuade those of a different view that those measures are not permissible in the general kind of society which we both desire. To live and work successfully with others requires more than faithfulness to one's concrete aims. It requires an intellectual commitment to a type of order in which, even on issues which to one are fundamental, others are allowed to pursue different ends.

It is for this reason that to the liberal neither moral nor religious ideals are proper objects of coercion, while both conservatives and socialists recognize no such limits. I sometimes feel that the most conspicuous attribute of liberalism that distinguishes it as much from conservatism as from socialism is the view that moral beliefs concerning matters of conduct which do not directly interfere with the protected sphere of other persons do not justify coercion. This may also explain why it seems to be so much easier for the repentant socialist to find a new spiritual home in the conservative fold than in the liberal.

In the last resort, the conservative position rests on the belief that in any society there are recognizably superior persons whose inherited standards and values and position ought to be protected and who should have a greater influence on public affairs than others. The liberal, of course, does not deny that there are some superior people—he is not an egalitarian—but he denies that anyone has authority to decide who these superior people are. While the conservative inclines to defend a particular established hierarchy and wishes authority to protect the status of those whom he values, the liberal feels that no respect for established values can justify the resort to privilege or monopoly or any other coercive power of the state in order to shelter such people against the forces of economic change. Though he is fully aware of the important role that cultural and intellectual elites have played in the evolution of civilization, he also believes that these elites have to prove themselves by their capacity to maintain their position under the same rules that apply to all others.

Closely connected with this is the usual attitude of the conservative to democracy. I have made it clear earlier that I do not regard majority rule as an end but merely as a means, or perhaps even as the least evil of those forms of government from which we have to choose. But I believe that the conservatives deceive themselves when they blame the evils of our time on democracy. The chief evil is unlimited government, and nobody is qualified to wield unlimited power. The powers which modern democracy possesses would be even more intolerable in the hands of some small elite.

Admittedly, it was only when power came into the hands of the majority that further limitation of the power of government was thought unnecessary. In this sense democracy and unlimited government are connected. But it is not democracy but unlimited government that is objectionable, and I do not see why the people should not learn to limit the scope of majority rule as well as that of any other form of government. At any rate, the advantages of democracy as a method of peaceful change and of political education seem to be so great compared with those of any other system that I can have no sympathy with the anti-democratic strain of conservatism. It is not who governs but what government is entitled to do that seems to me the essential problem.

That the conservative opposition to too much government control is not a matter of principle but is concerned with the particular aims of government is clearly shown in the economic sphere. Conservatives usually oppose collectivist and directivist measures in the industrial field, and here the liberal will often find allies in them. But at the same time conservatives are usually protectionists and have frequently supported socialist measures in agriculture. Indeed, though the restrictions which exist today in industry and commerce are mainly the result of socialist views, the equally important restrictions in agriculture were usually introduced by conservatives at an even earlier date. And in their efforts to discredit free enterprise many conservative leaders have vied with the socialists. . . .

What I have said should suffice to explain why I do not regard myself as a conservative. Many people will feel, however, that the position which emerges is hardly what they used to call "liberal." I must, therefore, now face the question of whether this name is today the appropriate name for the party of liberty. I have already indicated

that, though I have all my life described myself as a liberal, I have done so more recently with increasing misgivings— not only because in the United States this term constantly gives rise to misunderstanding, but also because I have become more and more aware of the great gulf that exists between my position and the rationalistic Continental liberalism or even the English liberalism of the utilitarians.

If liberalism still meant what it meant to an English historian who in 1827 could speak of the revolution of 1688 as "the triumph of those principles which in the language of the present day are denominated liberal or constitutional" or if one could still, with Lord Acton, speak of Burke, Macaulay, and Gladstone as the three greatest liberals, or if one could still, with Harold Laski, regard Tocqueville and Lord Acton as "the essential liberals of the nineteenth century," I should indeed be only too proud to describe myself by that name. But, much as I am tempted to call their liberalism true liberalism, I must recognize that the majority of Continental liberals stood for ideas to which these men were strongly opposed, and that they were led more by a desire to impose upon the world a preconceived rational pattern than to provide opportunity for free growth. The same is largely true of what has called itself Liberalism in England at least since the time of Lloyd George.

It is thus necessary to recognize that what I have called "liberalism" has little to do with any political movement that goes under that name today. It is also questionable whether the historical associations which that name carries today are conducive to the success of any movement. Whether in these circumstances one ought to make an effort to rescue the term from what one feels is its misuse is a question on which opinions may well differ. I myself feel more and more that to use it without long explanations causes too much confusion and that as a label it has become more of a ballast than a source of strength.

In the United States, where it has become almost impossible to use "liberal" in the sense in which I have used it, the term "libertarian" has been used instead. It may be the answer; but for my part I find it singularly unattractive. For my taste it carries too much the flavor of a manufactured term and of a substitute. What I should want is a word which describes the party of life, the party that favors free growth and spontaneous evolution. But I have racked my brain unsuccessfully to find a descriptive term which commends itself.

We should remember, however, that when the ideals which I have been trying to restate first began to spread through the Western world, the party which represented them had a generally recognized name. It was the ideals of the English Whigs that inspired what later came to be known as the liberal movement in the whole of Europe and that provided the conceptions that the American colonists carried with them and which guided them in their struggle for independence and in the establishment of their constitution. Indeed, until the character of this tradition was altered by the accretions due to the French Revolution, with its totalitarian democracy and socialist leanings, "Whig" was the name by which the party of liberty was generally known.

The name died in the country of its birth partly because for a time the principles for which it stood were no longer distinctive of a particular party, and partly because the men who bore the name did not remain true to those principles. The Whig parties of the nineteenth century, in both Britain and the United States, finally brought discredit to the name among the radicals. But it is still true that, since liberalism took the place of Whiggism only after the movement for liberty had absorbed the crude and militant rationalism of the French Revolution, and since our task must largely be to free that tradition from the overrationalistic, nationalistic, and socialistic influences which have intruded into it, Whiggism is historically the correct name for the ideas in which I believe. The more I learn about the evolution of ideas, the more I have become aware that I am simply an unrepentant Old Whig—with the stress on the "old."

To confess one's self an Old Whig does not mean, of course, that one wants to go back to where we were at the end of the seventeenth century. It has been one of the purposes of this book to show that the doctrines then first stated continued to grow and develop until about seventy or eighty years ago, even though they were no longer the chief aim of a distinct party. We have since learned much that should enable us to restate them in a more satisfactory and effective form. But, though they require restatement in the light of our present knowledge, the basic principles are still those of the Old Whigs. True, the later history of the party that bore that name has made some historians doubt where there was a distinct body of Whig principles; but I can but agree with Lord Acton that, though some of "the patriarchs of the doctrine were the most infamous of men, the notion of a higher law above municipal codes, with which Whiggism began, is the supreme achievement of Englishmen and their bequest to the nation"—and, we may add, to the world. It is the doctrine which is at the basis of the common tradition of the Anglo-Saxon countries. It is the doctrine from which Continental liberalism took what is valuable in it. It is the doctrine on which the American system of government is based. In its pure form it is represented in the United States, not by the radicalism of Jefferson, nor by the conservatism of Hamilton or even of John Adams, but by the ideas of James Madison, the "father of the Constitution."

I do not know whether to revive that old name is practical politics. That to the mass of people, both in the Anglo-Saxon world and elsewhere, it is today probably a term without definite associations is perhaps more an advantage than a drawback. To those familiar with the history of ideas it is probably the only name that quite expresses what the tradition means. That, both for the genuine conservative and still more for the many socialists turned conservative, Whiggism is the name for their pet aversion shows a sound instinct on their part. It has been the name for the only set of ideals that has consistently opposed all arbitrary power.

It may well be asked whether the name really matters so much. In a country like the United States, which on the whole still has free institutions and where, therefore, the defense of the existing is often a defense of freedom, it might not make so much difference if the defenders of freedom call themselves conservatives, although even here the association with the conser-

vatives by disposition will often be embarrassing. Even when men approve of the same arrangements, it must be asked whether they approve of them because they exist or because they are desirable in themselves. The common resistance to the collectivist tide should not be allowed to obscure the fact that the belief in integral freedom is based on an essentially forward-looking attitude and not on any nostalgic longing for the past or a romantic admiration for what has been.

The need for a clear distinction is absolutely imperative, however, where, as is true in many parts of Europe, the conservatives have already accepted a large part of the collectivist creed—a creed that has governed policy for so long that many of its institutions have come to be accepted as a matter of course and have become a source of pride to "conservative" parties who created them. Here the believer in freedom cannot but conflict with the conservative and take an essentially radical position, directed against popular prejudices, entrenched positions, and firmly established privileges. Follies and abuses are no better for having long been established principles of policy.

CHAPTER XXIII

THE
RESTATEMENT
OF LIBERALISM

*T*o the degree that the conservative mood gained in strength and importance, the older pragmatic, secular, democratic liberalism that had
played such an important role in American life and thought since the
1880's came increasingly under attack. Vernon L. Parrington, the
author of a classic history and defense of the American liberal tradition,
caught the beginnings of the newer mood of disillusionment and doubt
when he wrote shortly before his death in 1929:

> Liberals whose hair is growing thin and the lines of whose figures are no longer what they
> were, are likely to find themselves today in the unhappy predicament of being treated as
> mourners at their own funerals. When they pluck up heart to assert that they are not yet
> authentic corpses, but living men with brains in their heads, they are pretty certain to be
> gently chided and led back to the comfortable armchair that befits senility. Their counsel is
> smiled at as the chatter of a belated post-Victorian generation that knew not Freud, and if
> they must go abroad they are bidden take the air in the garden where other old-fashioned
> plants—mostly of the family *Democratici*—are still preserved.[1]

And yet Parrington himself was unwilling to abandon his liberal faith, so
strongly did he believe in its validity. As he concluded: "Yet it is perhaps conceivable that our current philosophy—the brilliant coruscations of our youn-

[1] Vernon L. Parrington, *Main Currents in American Thought* (New York, 1930), vol. III, p. 401.

457

ger intelligentsia—may indeed not prove to be the last word in social philosophy. Perhaps—is this *lèse-majesté*—when our youngest liberals have themselves come to the armchair age they will be smiled at in turn by sons who are
still cleverer and who will find their wisdom as foolish as the wisdom of 1917
seems to them today."[2]

Parrington proved to be a wiser prophet than he perhaps realized, for
in the 1930's and afterwards it became fashionable to accuse liberals of espous-
ing a shallow optimism based on the faulty premise of the innate goodness of
man. The liberal belief in reason, science, and critical intelligence as weapons
in the construction of a better world was not founded on historical reality,
these critics argued, and they went so far as to contend that the liberal vision
of progress had proved a disastrous illusion, which had left mankind unprepared to cope with such evils as Nazism and communism. The attack on liberalism was widespread and drew sustenance from such varied sources as Protestant neo-orthodoxy as well as fundamentalism, Catholic neo-Thomism, and
others who advanced various forms of philosophical and political conservatism. Indeed, many who had once been associated with the liberal philosophy
and liberal causes demonstrated a hostility born of disillusionment toward the
older ideological underpinnings of their faith.

But despite the sharpness of the conservative attack, liberalism in one
form or another is still perhaps the prevailing belief of a majority of Americans.
And defenders of liberalism continue to insist that their philosophy, with
certain modifications, still can and should play a vital and important role in
American life. These modern liberals refuse to speak in terms of absolutes.
They are critical of the revival of a prescriptive interpretation of natural law
and theories of original sin, and they are opposed to a community of fixed
hierarchies. They maintain that liberalism and democracy—defined in terms of
science, critical intelligence, tolerance, and a belief in the possibility of
progress—still possess an attractiveness that other philosophies lack.
Democratic liberalism, they have argued, is the one system that by rejecting
authoritarian absolutes (whether religious, political, or intellectual) provides
its own self-correctives. In the tradition of John Dewey, many liberals have
continued to fight for an ideology they deem worthy of defense. Often they
have accepted as valid some of the criticisms levied against the older liberalism—especially its utopian optimism and its reluctance to confront the
totalitarian challenges of the 1930's and afterwards—and have attempted to
reformulate the liberal philosophy by introducing a greater degree of realism
and by pointing out the danger of accepting a view of man that omits a recognition of his potential for evil.

Whether or not American liberalism, however defined, can continue to
exist among the vicissitudes and dangers of the modern world remains an

[2] Vernon L. Parrington. *Main Currents in American Thought* (New York, 1930), vol. III, p. 413.

unanswered question. Daniel Bell, himself active in numerous liberal causes during the New Deal, spoke for a whole generation of disillusioned liberals and radicals whose hopes were shattered in the gas chambers of Dachau and Auschwitz and on the leveled streets of Nagasaki and Hiroshima when he remarked that "Ours, a 'twice-born' generation, finds its wisdom in pessimism, evil, tragedy, and despair."[3] In seeking the explanation for the inadequacy of liberalism, Bell concluded that

> In the end, the generation failed. Not because the idealistic impulses became exhausted; this is the inevitable trajectory, perhaps, of any radical generation. Not because events had belied the predictions; this is a healthier America. But because this may well have been the *last* radical generation for a time—the last because it was the first that tasted power and became corrupt. (Yet it is not only that power corrupts, for, as Alex Comfort once said, corrupt men seek power.) But the seed of the corruption was the *hubris* of the "possessed." Generous of impulse, it sought the end of injustice, but in the single vision the dogmatism grew hard and the moral sense cynical, so that, when reality proved the vision false, all that was left was the hardness, or the despair.[4]

And yet, as a leading exponent of the liberal philosophy has remarked in an eloquent defense of liberalism, "Our disappointments are real. But they are real because our powers are great and our expectations legitimately high"[5]

[3] Daniel Bell, *The End of Ideology: On the Exhaustion of Political Ideas in the Fifties* (Glencoe, Ill., 1960), p. 287.
[4] *Ibid.*, pp. 291–292.
[5] Charles Frankel, *The Case for Modern Man* (New York, 1955), p. 209.

Lewis Mumford
1895-

A native of New York City, Lewis Mumford attended the City College of New York, Columbia, and New York University, although he never received an academic degree. For most of his career he has been one of America's most important social critics. His major work has been a multivolumed study of the philosophy of civilization, of which five books have been published (Technics and Civilization, The Culture of Cities, The Condition of Man, The Conduct of Life, The City in History), *all of them concerned with the weaknesses and disintegrations of modern society.*

In the classical humanist tradition, Mumford has argued persuasively and effectively for a greater degree of rational planning in our urban society, pointing out with brilliant insights the disintegrative tendencies inherent in most of our cities and the threat this poses to our culture.

The following selection was written by Mumford in 1940 when he resigned as an editor of the New Republic. *This move was occasioned by his disillusionment with those pragmatic liberals who, he felt, would not take a firm stand against the menace of Nazi totalitarianism. In this article he argued against pragmatic liberalism as a political philosophy for Americans, and offered instead his own version of the liberal philosophy. The text is from "The Corruption of Liberalism,"* New Republic, *102 (April 29, 1940).*

As an economic creed, liberalism was undermined by imperialism and monopoly before the nineteenth century closed. But as a personal and social philosophy, liberalism has been dissolving before our eyes only during the past decade. The liberal lacks confidence in himself and in his vision of life. He has shown in every country where the attacks on liberalism have been forceful that he either does not possess stable convictions, or that he lacks the insight and the courage that would enable him to defend them. Continually hoping for the best, the liberal remains unprepared to face the worst; and on the brink of what may turn out another Dark Ages,

he continues to scan the horizon for signs of dawn. . . .

The Romans used to say that the worst results come about through the corruption of what is good; and one may say this about the present state of liberalism. But the defects of liberalism are not due to isolated mistakes of judgment that individual liberals have made; they are due to fatal deficiencies that go to the very roots of liberal philosophy. Unfortunately, liberalism's weaknesses are so debilitating that they not merely undermine its own will-to-survive, but they may also give up elements in a longer human tradition, on whose maintenance our very civilization depends.

460

Liberalism is a very mixed body of doctrine. So it is important that, in discussing its errors, we should detach its essential and enduring values from those which have characterized a particular age, class or group. . . .

Now the universal elements in liberalism, the moralizing elements are the real objects of the fascist attacks. These universal elements arose long before modern capitalism: they were part of the larger human tradition, embodied in the folkways of the Jews, in the experimental philosophy of the Greeks, in the secular practices of the Roman Empire, in the sacred doctrines of the Christian Church, in the philosophies of the great post-medieval humanists. The Marxian notion that ideas are always the shadows of the existing economic institutions runs bluntly against facts precisely at this point. For although a culture forms a related organic whole, a residue is left in each period and place which tends to become part of the general heritage of mankind. This residue is relatively small in amount but infinitely precious; and no single class or people can create it or be its sole keeper.

The effort to equate Manchester liberalism with the humanist traditions of personal responsibility, personal freedom and personal expression is sometimes shared by the defenders of capitalistic privilege; that is the gross fallacy of those who try to tie together private capitalism and "the American way." But these notions are false, whether held by the absolutists of private property or by the absolutists who would challenge the regime of private property. The most important principles in liberalism do not cling exclusively to liberalism: what gives them their strength is their universality and their historic continuity. Confucius, Socrates, Plato, Aristotle, testify to them no less than Jefferson and Mill. Liberalism took over this humanist tradition, revamped

it, and finally united it to a new body of hopes and beliefs that grew up in the eighteenth century.

This second element in liberalism, which seems to many people as important as the first, rests upon a quite different set of premises. Liberalism in this sense was symbolically a child of Voltaire and Rousseau: the Voltaire who thought that the craft of priests was responsible for the misery of the world, and the Rousseau who thought that man was born naturally good and had been corrupted only by evil institutions. It was likewise a by-product of the inventors and industrialists of the period, who, concentrating upon the improvement of the means of life, thought sincerely that the ends of living would more or less take care of themselves.

This pragmatic liberalism, which I shall here distinguish from the ideal liberalism, was vastly preoccupied with the machinery of life. It was characteristic of this creed to overemphasize the part played by political and mechanical invention, by abstract thought and practical contrivance. And accordingly it minimized the role of instinct, tradition, history; it was unaware of the dark forces of the unconscious; it was suspicious of either the capricious or the incalculable, for the only universe it could rule was a measured one, and the only type of human character it could understand was the utilitarian one. That there are modes of insight into man and into the cosmos which science does not possess, the liberal did not suspect; he took for granted that the emotional and spiritual life of man needs no other foundation than the rational, utilitarian activities associated with the getting of a living. Hence, finally, liberalism's progressive neglect of the fields of esthetics, ethics and religion: these matters were left to traditional thinkers, with the confident belief that they would eventually drop out of existence, mere vestiges of the race's childhood. On the whole most liberals today have produced no effective thought in any of these fields; and they live, as it were, on the debris of past dogmas and buried formulations. Unconscious, for example, of the sources of their ethical ideas, they pick up more or less what happens to be lying around them, without any effort at consistency or clarity, still less at creativeness: here a scrap left over from childhood, there a fragment of Kant or Bentham, or again a dash of Machiavelli, pacifist Quakers one moment and quaking Nietzscheans the next.

In short, it is not unfair to say that the pragmatic liberal has taken the world of personality, the world of values, feelings, emotions, wishes, purposes, for granted. He assumed either that this world did not exist, or that it was relatively unimportant; at all events, if it did exist, it could be safely left to itself, without cultivation. For him men were essentially good, and only faulty economic and political institutions—defects purely in the mechanism of society—kept them from becoming better. That there might be internal obstacles to external improvement seemed to him absurd. That there was as large a field for imaginative design and rational discipline in the building of a personality as in the building of a skyscraper did not occur to him. Unfortunately, immature personalities, irrational personalities, demoralized personalities are as inevitable as weeds in an uncultivated garden when no deliberate attempt is made to provide a constructive basis for personal development.

Behind this failure to establish, on a fresh basis, a normative discipline for the personality was a singular optimism —the belief that it was not needed. Did not liberalism imply an emancipation from the empty institutional religion, from the saws, precepts, moralizings of the past? Did this not mean that "science," which confessedly despised norms, would eventually supply all the guidance necessary for human conduct? Such was the innocence of the liberal that those who were indifferent to ethical values thought of themselves as realists. They could hardly understand William James when he called emotionality the *sine qua non* of moral perception. But the fact was that the most old-fashioned theologian, with a sense of human guilt and human error, was by far the better realist. Though the theologian's view of the external world might be scientifically weak, his view of the internal world, the world of value and personality, included an understanding of constant human phenomena —sin, corruption, evil—on which the liberal closed his eyes.

Pragmatic liberalism did not believe in a world where the questions of good and evil were not incidental but of radical importance. Its adherents thought that they would presently abolish the evils inherent in life by popularizing anesthetics and by extending the blessing of the machine. They did not believe in the personal life. That was outmoded. Esthetic interests, moral discipline, the habits of contemplation and evaluation, all this seemed mere spiritual gymnastics: they preferred more physical exercises. By activity (busy work) pragmatic liberals kept their eyes manfully on the mere surface of living. They did not believe that any sensible man would, except when he made his will, face the more ultimate facts of existence. For them, the appraisal of death was a neurotic symptom; happily, science's steady advances in hygiene and medicine might postpone further and further that unpleasant occasion itself. . . .

Is it any wonder, then, that pragmatic liberalism has been incapable of making firm ethical judgments or of implementing them with action? Its color-blindness to moral values is its most serious weakness today; hence it cannot distinguish between barbarism and civilization. Indeed, it is even inclined to pass a more favorable verdict on barbarism when it shows superiority in material organization. Refusing to recognize the crucial problem of evil, those who follow this creed are incapable of coping with the intentions of evil men: they look in vain for merely intellectual mistakes to account for the conduct of those who have chosen to flout man's long efforts to become civilized. Evil for the pragmatic liberal has no positive dimensions: he conceives it as a mere lack of something whose presence would be good. Poverty is an evil, because it indicates the lack of a good, namely riches. For this kind of liberal, the most heinous fact about a war is not the evil intentions and purposes that one or both sides may disclose: it is mainly the needless waste of material, the unbearable amount of human suffering, the premature deaths.

Lacking any true insight into these stubborn facts of human experience—corruption, evil, irrational desire—liberals also fail to understand that evil often lies beyond purely rational treatment, that a mere inquiry into causes, mere reasonableness and sweetness in one's attitude, may not only fail to cure an evil disposition but may aggravate it. Now, unfortunately, there are times when an attitude of intellectual humility and sympathy is entirely inappropriate to the press of a particular situation. There are times when active resistance or coercion is the only safeguard against the conduct of men who mean ill against human society. The alternative to coercion is what the religious call conversion, salvation, grace, on the part of the offender. That, too, is essentially a pre-rational process, not hostile to reason, but proceeding by a short cut into an area that reason cannot directly touch. Liberals tend to minimize the

effectiveness of both coercion and conversion, both force and grace; but it is hard to point to any large and significant social change in which both elements did not play a part.

Coercion is, of course, no substitute for intelligent inquiry and no cure in itself for anti-social conduct. But just as there are maladies in the human body which call for surgery rather than diet—though diet, if applied at an early stage, might have been sufficient—so there are moments of crisis in society when anti-social groups or nations that resist the ordinary methods of persuasion and compromise must be dealt with by coercion. In such moments, to hesitate, to temporize, only gives the disease a deeper hold on the organism; and to center one's efforts upon changing the mind of one's opponent, by opposing reason to his irrationality, and to overlook the elementary precaution of depriving him of his weapons for attacking one, is to commit a fatal offense against the very method one seeks to uphold.

The liberal's notion that reasoning in the spirit of affable compromises is the only truly human way of meeting one's opponent overlooks the important part played by force and grace. And his unctuous notion that evil must not seriously be combated because the person who attempts to oppose it may ultimately have to use physical force, and will become soiled by the act of fighting, is a gospel of despair. This belief is the core of his defeatist response to Nazism; it means in practice turning the world over to the rule of the violent, the brutal and the inhuman, who have no such fine scruples, because the humane are too dainty in their virtue to submit to any possible assault on it. Now the dangers are real: force *does* brutalize the users of it; when blood is spilt, anger rises and reason temporarily disappears. Hence force is not to be used daily in the body politic, like food or exercise; it is only to be used in an emergency, like medicine or the surgeon's knife. Fascism is barbarous, not because it uses force, but because it *prefers* force to rational accommodation: it deliberately turns mental and physical coercion into human nature's daily food. . . .

The essential moral weakness of liberalism, which I have only glanced at here, is coupled with a larger weakness in the liberal philosophy. Along with liberalism's admirable respect for rational science and experimental practice, goes an overvaluation of intellectual activities as such, and an undervaluation of the emotional and affective sides of life. In the liberal theology, emotions and feelings have taken the place of a personal devil. Now as every good psychologist knows, and as Court Korzybski has ably demonstrated, emotions and feelings, associated with the most devious and remote body processes, are involved in all thought. Reason and emotion are inseparable: their detachment is a practical device of limited use. Thought that is empty of emotion and feeling, that bears no organic relation to life, is just as foreign to effective reason as emotion that is disproportionate to the stimulus or is without intellectual foundations and references. The body, the unconscious, the prerational are all important to sound thought. But because the liberal has sought no positive discipline for emotion and feeling, there is an open breach between his affective life and his intellectual interests. His first impulse in any situation is to get rid of emotion because it may cause him to go wrong. Unfortunately for his effort to achieve poise, a purely intellectual judgment, eviscerated of emotional reference, often causes wry miscalculations. The calmness and sang-froid of Ber. ɜ was perhaps his most serious weakness during the long period before the Munich crisis; ominously, it repeated the self-defeating mood of Bruening, in the days preceding

his removal. Instead of priding himself on not being "carried away by his emotions," the liberal should rather be a little alarmed because he often has no emotions that could, under any conceivable circumstances, carry him away. . . .

Closely allied with the liberal's emotional anesthesia is his incurable optimism—a wrinkled smile left over from the eighteenth century, when, in the first flush of confidence, the possibilities of human advance seemed boundless. This optimism belonged to a constructive and expanding age: in its inception, it was a healthy reaction against the moldering institutions and precedents of the past. But it has become an unfortunate handicap in a period when destructive forces are gaining the upper hand, and when, in the approaching stabilization of population and industry, the malevolence of the human will, on the part of the propertied classes, may at critical moments—as already in Germany and Italy—give unlimited power to those who represent barbarism. Destruction, malice, violence, hold no temptation for the liberal; and in the kindness of his heart, he cannot bring himself to believe that they may viciously influence the conduct of any large part of mankind. The liberals could not understand that the gift of Czecho-Slovakia to Nazi Germany could not appease Hitler: that one might as well offer the carcass of a dead deer in a butcher store to a hunter who seeks the animal as prey—the meat being valued chiefly as a symbol of his prowess. And that is why the talk of mere economic adjustments that would enable the fascist states to live at peace with the rest of the world is muddled nonsense; it assumes, contrary to fact, that fascism springs out of rational motives and pursues concrete utilitarian ends. The bad arrangements of the peace of Versailles did not by themselves create fascism, nor will the best results of a magnanimous peace conference be able at once to wipe out its destructive impulses and undermine its irrational philosophy. Unfortunately it is not in Ricardo or Marx or Lenin, but in Dante and Shakespeare and Dostoevsky, that an understanding of the true sources of fascism are to be found. Economic explanations reflected a reality in the nineteenth century; they disguise a reality—the claim to barbaric conquest —today.

During the last ten years, the optimism of the liberals has remained unshaken. The incurable tendency of the liberal is to believe the best about everybody: to hope when there is no reason to hope, and to exhibit the nicest moral qualms, the most delicate intellectual scruples, in situations that demand that he wade in and coarsely exert his utmost effort. We now face a world that is on the brink, perhaps of another Dark Age; and because a Dark Age is not included in the liberal chronology, liberalism glibly refuses to accept the evidence of its sense. Like the sun-dial, it cannot tell time on a stormy day. So, habitually, the pragmatic liberals brand those whose eyes are open to the human devastation around them as "hysterical," "mystical," "having concealed fascist tendencies," or—taking a leaf from the Hitlerites—as "warmongers."

Now one must remember that liberalism has two sides. There is an ideal liberalism, deeply rooted in the example and experience of humanity: a doctrine that commands the allegiance of all well disposed men. And there is a transient doctrine of liberalism, the pragmatic side, which grew up in the eighteenth century out of a rather adolescent pride in the scientific conquest of nature and the invention of power machinery: this is the side that emphasizes the utilitarian aspects of life, that concentrates on purely intellectual issues, and that, in its exclusive concern for tolerance and "open-mindedness" is ready to extend its benevolent protection to those who

openly oppose the very purposes of civilization. What is important in ideal liberalism are elements like the great Roman notion of *Humanity*, united in the pursuit of freedom and justice, embracing all races and conditions. This ideal is radically opposed at every point to the autarchy advocated by the fascists; and it is no less opposed to the isolationism, moral and physical and political, advocated by most American liberals —a passive milk-and-water version of the fascist's contemptuous attitude toward the rest of the human race. . . .

To achieve a new basis for personal development and communal action, the liberal need not abandon his earlier concern for science, mechanism, the rational organization of society. But he can no longer regard the world that is embraced by these things as complete or all-sufficient. The world of political action must transcend that of the Economic Man: it must be as large as the fully developed human personality itself. No mere revision of Marxism, no mere ingenious political program with a few socialistic planks added or taken away, no attempt to make five disparate economic systems produce profit in a community where new social motives must take the place of dwindling or absent profits—none of these shallow dodges will suffice. What is demanded is a recrystallization of the positive values of life, and an understanding of the basic issues of good and evil, of power and form, of force and grace, in the actual world. In short: the crisis presses toward a social conversion, deep-seated, organic, religious in its essence, so that no part of personal or political existence will be untouched by it: a conversion that will transcend the arid pragmatism that has served as a substitute religion. For only the living—those for whom the world has meaning—can continue to live, and willingly make the fierce sacrifices and heroic efforts the present moment demands.

Sidney Hook
1902-

Born in New York City, Sidney Hook received his B.S. from the City College of New York and his M.A. and Ph.D. from Columbia University. In 1927 he joined the department of philosophy and later became chairman of the graduate division of philosophy and psychology at New York University. He served also as president of the American Philosophical Association.

A student and disciple of John Dewey, Hook has been an ardent advocate of the pragmatic philosophy as a means of clarifying contemporary social, cultural, and political problems. A prolific writer of books and articles on determinism and dialectical materialism, he has also been a frequent commentator on contemporary issues. He has consistently defended democracy against its critics, and has dealt with the difficult problem involved in granting freedom to those individuals and groups who would destroy it in the event they attain power. Critical of metaphysical speculation, Hook has argued effectively for a pragmatic, secular, democratic liberalism as a way of life.

The following selection, "Naturalism and Democracy," appeared in Yervant H. Krikorian, ed., Naturalism and the Human Spirit *(New York: Columbia University Press, 1944). In it Hook describes the possible justifications of democracy, and concludes by rejecting any idealistic philosophy and by reaffirming the validity of the pragmatic tradition.*

*W*e now come to the problem which is of primary concern to philosophers. What are the grounds upon which acceptance of democracy in contradistinction to other modes of social life can be justified? So far as I can see, there are four generic types of justification which have been or can be offered.

The first asserts that the rational foundation of democratic belief consists in a set of supernatural religious truths in the sense that there can be no intelligent ground for choosing between democracy and other forms of society which does not logically commit us to some kind of theology.

The second asserts the same thing about metaphysics understood as a theory of "reality." Usually these two approaches go hand in hand.

The third maintains that the choice of democracy is a nonrational preference rooted in the constitution of our natures and brought to flower by nurture and education.

The fourth affirms that the belief in democracy is an hypothesis controlled by the same general pattern of inquiry which we apply to any scientific hypothesis, but referring to different subject matter, that is, our evaluations.

1. *Democracy and religion.* Does demo-

cracy as a way of life rest upon belief in supernatural religious truths in the sense that if the latter are denied, the former must necessarily be denied? It is becoming increasingly fashionable to maintain this. Were historical considerations relevant here, I think it could be conclusively established that the great institutional religions, with the possible exception of some forms of Protestantism, have tended in fact to support theocratic forms of government. Nor is this surprising if the Kingdom of Heaven be taken as a model or inspiration for the Kingdom of Earth. Whoever heard of a democratically organized Paradise? Walt Whitman in heaven would meet with the same fate as Lucifer, but for different reasons. Not only is the notion of a democratically organized heaven blasphemous, but the proposal to reform along democratic lines a hierarchically organized church would lead to excommunication. If we examine the actual behavior which has been sanctified by the maxim: "Render unto Caesar what is Caesar's and to God what is God's," we will discover that historical, institutional religion has always been able to adapt itself to any form of government or society which will tolerate its existence.

But our concern is not with historical questions, fascinating as they are, but with the logic of the position. We must consequently rephrase the question to read: Does belief in democracy logically rest upon any theological propositions in the sense that the denial of the second entails the denial of the first? And for this discussion I shall take as illustrative of theological propositions the two cardinal propositions of natural theology, namely, "God exists" and "Man has an immortal soul." To assert that whoever has no grounds for affirming the existence of God and immortality has no grounds for affirming the validity of democracy is to claim that the former are at least necessary conditions of the latter. I shall argue that they constitute neither necessary nor sufficient conditions.

a. Before examining this claim, let us note the tremendous risk it involves. Were those who advance it ever compelled to admit that these theological propositions are indemonstrable or false, they would have to surrender their belief in democracy. But this, I submit, very few of them are prepared to do. They would search for other reasons and grounds. Like those who would make the validity of moral judgments dependent upon the existence of God and immortality, the theological defenders of democracy shift from a problem in which, although difficult, it is possible to reach an agreement on the basis of some empirical evidence, to one in which the nature of the terms and sphere of discourse makes such agreement much more difficult. Confirmed democrats, it seems to me, are much more convinced of the validity of the democratic ideal than they are of the theological propositions upon which it presumably depends. They would no more exonerate from the obligation of accepting the democratic ideal an atheist or agnostic who pleads that he has no reason to believe in God and the hereafter than they would exempt him from the obligation of living honestly.

b. Aside from the difficulties of establishing God's existence, how can we get from the fact of his existence to the desirability of the democratic way of life? None of the attributes of God, save the moral attributes, can serve as a premise justifying one way of life rather than another. And if the moral attributes of God can serve as premises, necessary or sufficient, for the democratic way of life, it is only because *we* regard them as worthy, that is, as truly moral. Obviously any theology which makes God's power the justification or source of his goodness is worse than useless for purposes of deriving democracy. The attribution of moral qualities to God is an expression of what we think his qualities ought to be. And this is a problem of precisely the same order as that which we are called upon to answer when we ask for the grounds of our democratic allegiance.

c. The situation is the same if we grant that human beings have immortal souls. In what way is this a necessary or sufficient presupposition of democracy? The brotherhood of man may be a theological fact as it is a biological fact, but what makes it wrong for Cain to kill his brother Abel and right, under certain circumstances, for us to kill Cain is a moral principle which can no more be derived from theology than from biology —unless, of course, the moral principle is one of the premises of our theological (or biological) system. In this case we are no further along than we were when we raised the question about the democratic way of life. In passing it should be observed that belief in the immortality of the soul can be, and has been, used (in the Hindu doctrines of *samtra* and *karma*) to sanctify the tightest system of antidemocratic social stratification the world has ever seen.

2. *Democracy and metaphysics.* The problem of the metaphysical foundation of democracy is more difficult because of varying conceptions of metaphysics. By "metaphysics" I shall understand the discipline designated by the term "ontology" or any theory of "being *überhaupt.*" The evidence seems to me to be overwhelming that there is a definite historical connection between the social movements of a period and its dominant metaphysical teachings; furthermore, I am prepared to defend as a historically true proposition that systems of idealistic metaphysics, because of the semiofficial roles they have played in their respective cultures, have been more generally employed to bolster antidemocratic social movements than systems of empirical or materialistic

metaphysics. Whether there is *always* an intrinsic personal or psychological relation between a philosopher's metaphysics and his ethics or politics is a more difficult question, but one which seems to me to require an answer in the negative. More germane to our present concern is my contention that there is no necessary logical connection between a theory of being or becoming and any particular theory of ethics or politics. Stated more accurately, it seems to me demonstrable that no system of metaphysics *univocally* determines a system of ethics or politics. There may be certain facts about man and nature which might have a bearing upon our judgment about what social system is of the highest worth, but, as I shall argue later, these are facts concerning which the empirical sciences are qualified to report without benefit of metaphysics.

Two species of metaphysics are most often invoked in behalf of democracy. One asserts that the value of democracy or the values from which it may be derived are "grounded in reality," a phrase which is interpreted to mean that the universe "justifies" or "guarantees" both the validity and the ultimate supremacy of basic human ideals. I must confess that it is difficult for me to understand this view except as a shamefaced kind of theology. However that may be, there is no agreed-upon denotation of *the* universe. There are many universes. Nor is there any one basic human ideal, but there are many human ideals which are often in conflict with one another, even though they all invoke the universe as a ground of their validity and as a guaranty of their triumph. Finally, and most important, no matter what character the universe is alleged to have, no matter what the nature of the far-off event toward which it is moving, no matter who wins or loses, nothing logically compelling in the way of judgment follows unless *we* have already morally evaluated the character of events. For most metaphysics the very word "reality" is an implicit value term. To be sure, history may be conceived as a struggle between the Prince of Darkness and the Prince of Light, but the latter is so named because he carries *our* moral flag.

The second metaphysical view to which resort is often made is at the same time a kind of rejoinder to our position. It distinguishes between a metaphysical realm of being and a metaphysical realm of values and grounds the democratic way of life in the latter. Just as the spectrum of colors is there to be beheld by all who are not color blind and would still be there even if man's ancestors had climbed no higher than the mole in the tree of evolution, so the spectrum of values is there to be beheld by all who are not value blind and would still be there even if human beings had never existed at all. The view that colors would still be there even if human beings had no eyes is not without its difficulties. But they do not begin to compare in difficulty with the view that values are essentially unrelated to an evaluator and his interests. Santayana has quite aptly remarked of this doctrine that there is much sense in saying that whiskey "is pervaded as it were, by an inherent intoxication, and stands dead drunk in its bottle."

The subject is vast, but it is enough to show that this view is question-begging in precisely the same way as other theological and metaphysical derivations. The existence of these absolute norms is presumably certified or authenticated at some point by an act of immediate intuition. If the testimony of the intuition is construed not merely from what individuals *say* they intuit but also from the conduct that flows from their intuition—and conduct counts more in any moral scheme than mere words—then it is clear that individuals intuit or "see" *different* values.

The "great" visions are not all compatible with one another in what they command, not to mention the visions that we do not call great. Which visions are the authentic ones? Prior to every conclusion that these are the objective values of all eternity, or even of all time and existence, is the assumption that *this* is the trustworthy seer. In a dispute between two men, one of whom asserts that the other is color blind and the other that the first is "just seeing things," there are definite ways of determining who is right. In a dispute between two seers whose immediate intuitions report conflicting news about the nature and hierarchy of absolute values, there is no rational way of reaching a consensus. The true prophet cannot be distinguished from the false by invoking absolute values whose validity depends upon a prior assumption of the reliability of prophetic testimony. The complacency with which some writers have cut the Gordian knot by introducing reference to the intuitions of "the best people" or "the most cultured people" or "the saving remnant" is evidence either of parochialism or of snobbery.

The record of human error and cruelty shows what ghastly consequences often result from the conviction that one's moral insight cannot possibly be wrong and that it needs no further justification than its own incandescent purity. No more than a solipsist can make plausible on his own assumptions the existence of another solipsist, can an absolutist find a rightful place for another absolutist who disagrees with him. Absolutists face each other over an abyss which cannot be bridged even by their weapons of war.

3. *Democracy and preferences.* The view that an acceptance of democracy is an expression of a preference does not carry us far until the kind of preference is indicated. A preference may express a passing whim or a deep natural bent;

it may be impulsive or reflective. Preferences are rooted in our natures. Their forms, occasions, and objects are supplied by education, that is, broadly speaking, by social habits and intelligence. But either our natures can be changed or the educators can be re-educated. If neither is possible, then the fact of moral choice becomes unintelligible. If we can offer no justification of a preference except that it is ours, obviously no point of intellectual or moral issue is raised; nor, a fortiori, can any be settled by the trial of arms. If we offer a justification of a preference, it will take one of the generic forms already discussed or about to be discussed.

4. *Democracy as a hypothesis.* When democracy is taken strictly as a form of political government, its superiority over other forms of government can be established to the extent to which it achieves more security, freedom, and co-operative diversity than any of its alternatives. If we test the workings of political democracy by Paul's scheme of virtues or by Nietzsche's, we may perhaps reach another conclusion. So long as there is no dispute about observable effects and so long as we raise no question about the moral ideals by which we evaluate these effects, we have clear sailing.

But, as has already been made plain, by democracy as a way of life we mean a way of organizing human relationships which embodies a certain complex of moral ideals. Can these ideals be treated as hypotheses? The conventional reply has always been that no moral principle can be regarded as a hypothesis, for we must already have certain knowledge of what is good before we can evaluate the consequences of acting upon it. If any position is question-begging, surely this seems to be.

Were this a symposium on value theory, I would devote all my time to developing the general theory of moral ideals as hypotheses. But here I can only

barely indicate that the notion is not viciously circular. A moral ideal is a prescription to act in a certain situation or class of situations in determinate ways that will organize the human needs and wants involved so as to fulfill a set of other values which are postulated as binding in relation to the problem in hand. No more than in other cases of inquiry do we start with an empty head. The cluster of values we bring to the situation is the result of prior experience and reflection. *They are not arbitrarily postulated.* The consequences of acting upon the hypothesis may lead us to challenge a postulated or assumed value. This in turn can become the subject of a similar investigation. Terminal values are always related to specific contexts; there is no absolute terminal value which is either self-evident or beyond the necessity of justifying itself if its credentials are challenged. There is no vicious infinite regress involved if we take our problems concretely and one at a time. Nor is the procedure narrowly circular. For if after a long history of raising and solving moral problems we postulate as a value in solving a later problem a value which had itself to be certified in an earlier problem, this would testify to the presence of a fruitful set of systematically related values in the structure of our moral behavior. New values would emerge or be discovered in the course of our attempt to act upon our ideals and from the necessity of mediating the conflict between the postulated values as they bear on concrete human needs in specific situations.

I should like, however, to make the general position take form out of the discussion of the theme before us. That theme is: *Why should we treat individuals of unequal talents and endowments as persons who are equally entitled to relevant consideration and care?* Short of a treatise, I can state only the reasons, without amplification of the concrete needs of the social situation which democracy seeks to meet and the institutional practices by which it must meet them.

1. This method of treating human beings is more successful than any other in evoking a maximum of creative, voluntary effort from all members of the community. Properly implemented, it gives all persons a stake in the community and elicits a maximum of intelligent loyalty.

2. It enlarges the scope of our experience by enabling us to acquire insight into the needs, drives and aspirations of others. Learning to understand how life is organized by other centers of experience is both a challenge and a discipline for our imagination. In aiding the growth of others, we aid our own growth.

3. The willingness to understand another man's point of view without necessarily surrendering to it makes it more likely that different points of view may negotiate their differences and learn to live peacefully with one another. A democratic community cannot be free from strife in a world where inequalities will always exist, but its ethics, when intelligently acted upon, makes more likely the diminution of strife or its transference to socially harmless forms than is the case when its principle of equality is denied. The consequences are less toadying, less fear, and less duplicity in the equalitarian community than there are in the non-equalitarian society.

4. In nurturing the capacities of each individual so that they may come to their greatest fulfillment we can best share our existing stores of truth and beauty and uncover new dimensions in these realms. How can anyone dedicated to the values of science and art consistently oppose a policy which maximizes the possibility of the discovery and widest dispersion of scientific truths and artistic meanings?

5. Regard for the potentialities of all individuals makes for less cruelty of man toward man, especially where cruelty is the result of blindness to, or ignorance of, the needs of others. A community organized along democratic lines is guilty of cruelty only at those points where it has failed to live up to its own ideals. A totalitarian community is systematically insensitive to the personal needs not only of members of the outlawed scapegoat group but also of the majority of its subjects who are excluded from policy-making discussions. At best, there is no way of determining these personal needs except by the interpretation of the dictator and his experts who act on the fateful dogma that they know the true interests of their subjects better than the subjects themselves. At worst, the dictator assumes not only that he speaks for his subjects but that in some mystic way he feels and thinks for them too. Despite the great limitations—limitations from the point of view of their own ideals—under which the nineteenth- and twentieth-century democracies of the Western world suffered, I think it is indisputable, on the evidence, that by and large their social life, in so far as this was the consequence of policy, displayed less cruelty than the social life of any other historical period.

6. Reasonableness of conclusions, where attitudes and interests conflict, depends upon the degree of mutual consultation and free intellectual communication between the principals involved. The democratic way of life makes possible the widest forms of mutual consultation and communication. Conclusions reached by these processes have a quality that can never be found where conclusions are imposed by force or authority—even if they are our own. Let me illustrate what I mean by taking as an example an enterprise represented by a community of scholars, let us say the American Philosophical

Association. Who among us, desirous as we may be of the possibility of philosophical agreement, would forego the methods of public discussion, criticism, argument, and rejoinder for a philosophical consensus imposed by a Gestapo or a G.P.U., even if by a strange quirk of affairs, it was *our* philosophic position that the goon squads of orthodoxy sought to make the way of salvation? Who among us, knowing that outside the threshold of our meetings there stood an individual of foreign country, color, or faith, capable of making a contribution to our deliberations, would not open the door to him? These are not rhetorical questions framed to discover philosophical fifth columnists. They are designed to show that the procedures of critical discussion and discovery, which are pre-eminently exhibited in the work of a scientific community, take for granted that national, racial, or religious origins are irrelevant to the logic of the method by which reasonable conclusions are reached. Democracy as a way of life differs from its alternatives in that it makes possible the extension of this method of reaching reasonable conclusions from the fields of professional science and philosophy to all areas of human experience in which genuine problems arise.

There are other grounds that may be offered in justification of democracy as the most adequate social philosophy for our times. Every one of them, like the foregoing, postulates implicitly or explicitly values or desiderata. But I repeat: these postulates are ultimate only for the problem in hand. They may require justification. When we undertake such justification, we have undertaken a new inquiry into a new problem. Much is assumed on the basis of previously tested evidence: nothing is logically begged.

There are two important consequences of approaching democracy in this way. The first is that we avoid the temptation,

which is rapidly gaining vogue, of making democracy absolutely valid in and for itself. There are many today who write as if they believe that democracy should prevail even though the heavens fall and say in so many words that "to question the validity of democracy is to disbelieve in it" and that we can meet the blind fanatical faith of fascism only with a faith in democracy which is at least just as fanatical. This temptation, it seems to me, must be avoided, because, by counterposing subrational dogma to subrational dogma, we prepare the ground for an acceptance of a "might makes right" morality. Secondly, those who make of democracy an absolute value, which requires no justification but its inherent rightness, tend to identify this absolute democracy with whatever particular democratic *status quo* exists. On the other hand, the natural tendency of those who cannot distinguish between social philosophies on the ground of their inherent rightness is to test a social philosophy by the social institutions in which it is embodied. They are, therefore, more attentive to the actual workings and effects of democracy, more historical minded, and less likely to gloss over existing imperfections.

To those who say that human beings will not fight wholeheartedly except for certainties, and emphatically not for a hypothesis which is only probable, the reply must be made that this empirical proposition is highly dubious. Men have fought and do fight vigorously for causes on the basis of preponderant evidence. Vigorous action, indeed, is only desirable in troubled situations when we have first decided what *is* intelligent action. And intelligent action does not result when we assume that our ideas or ideals simply cannot be wrong. That both intelligence and resoluteness are compatible is clear in fields as far apart as military science and medicine. Once it is decided that the chances of one military action are relatively better than another or once it is decided that an operation gives a patient a better chance of surviving than no operation, wisdom demands that the best warranted alternative be pursued with all our heart and all our soul. Let us remember that when we are called upon to fight for democracy we are not asked to fight for an ideal which has just been proposed as a *merely possible* valid ideal for our times; we already have considerable evidence in its behalf, the weight of which, unfortunately too often, is properly evaluated by some critics only when democracy is lost or imperiled.

Morris Raphael Cohen
1880-1947

Born in Minsk, Russia, Morris Cohen came to the United States at the age of twelve. After receiving his B.S. degree from the City College of New York in 1900 and his Ph.D. from Harvard University in 1906, he returned to City College until his retirement in 1938. At City College he helped to shape the thinking of several generations of students, many of whom subsequently achieved prominence in their own right. Cohen gained a reputation as one of America's most prominent philosophers, and received many professional honors, including election as president of the American Philosophical Association in 1929.

The embodiment of the spirit of intelligent and critical dissent, Cohen was never associated with any party or cult. Although his writings touched on many other subjects, legal philosophy was his specialty. In fact, Cohen spent most of his career in a search for an adequate philosophical basis for justice, for, as he saw it, any commentator on the law as it existed also had the duty to formulate a philosophy of what the law ought to be. Consequently, Cohen attempted to apply pragmatism in such a way as to justify metaphysical speculation, and his legal philosophy sought a reconciliation of naturalism and idealism.

The following selection, taken from a collection of his essays entitled The Faith of a Liberal *(New York, 1946), illustrates Cohen's conception of liberalism as a way of life.*

*T*o affirm a faith in liberalism may seem quixotic at a time when the word "liberalism" is commonly associated either with an outmoded individualistic theory of economics or with a political trend that shuns clear thinking and seems to offer a special haven to those mushy-minded persons who, rather than make a definite choice between Heaven and Hell, cheerfully hope to combine the best features of each. But liberalism and liberal civilization may be conceived more generously. For my part I prefer to think of the liberal temper as, above all, a faith in enlightenment, a faith in a process rather than in a set of doctrines, a faith instilled with pride in the achievements of the human mind, and yet colored with a deep humility before the vision of a world so much larger than our human hopes and thoughts. If there are those who have no use for the word "faith" they may fairly define liberalism as a rationalism that is rational enough to envisage the limitations of mere reasoning.

Liberalism is too often misconceived as a new set of dogmas taught by a newer and better set of priests called "liberals." Liberalism is an attitude rather than a set of dogmas—an attitude that insists upon questioning all plausible and self-evident propositions, seeking not to reject them but to find out what evidence there is to support them rather than their possible alternatives. This open eye for possible alternatives which need to be scrutinized before we can determine which is the best grounded is profoundly disconcerting to all conservatives and to almost all revolutionaries. Conservatism clings to what has been established, fearing that, once we begin to question the beliefs that we have inherited, all the values of life will be destroyed. The revolutionary, impressed with the evil of the existing order or disorder, is prone to put his faith in some mighty-sounding principle without regard for the complications, compromises, dangers, and hardships that will be involved in the adjustment of this principle to other worthy principles. Revolutionaries and reactionaries alike are irritated and perhaps inwardly humiliated by the humane temper of liberalism, which reveals by contrast the common inhumanity of both violent parties to the social struggle. Liberalism, on the other hand, regards life as an adventure in which we must take risks in new situations, in which there is no guarantee that the new will always be the good or the true, in which progress is a precarious achievement rather than an inevitability. . . .

Liberalism has been viewed historically as that philosophy which regards the exercise of human energy as in itself a good, which becomes evil only when it becomes self-defeating. It is opposed to the view that regards the natural desires of the flesh as inherently evil and justified only under certain restricted and properly sanctioned conditions. Liberalism is thus a reaction against all views which favor repression or which regard the denial of natural desires as in itself a good.

Liberalism so conceived is concerned with the liberation of the mind from the restraints of authoritarianism and fan-aticism. As opposed to the policies of fear and suppression, based on the principle that nature is sin and intellect the devil, the aim of liberalism is to liberate the energies of human nature by the free and fearless use of reason. Liberalism disregards rules and dogmas that hinder the freedom of scientific inquiry and the questioning of all accepted truths. Prophets, priestly hierarchies, sacred books and sanctified traditions must submit their claims to the court of human reason and experience. In this way mankind wins freedom from superstitious fears, such as that of magic or witchcraft, and from arbitrary and cruel restraints on human happiness. Liberalism in general thus means the opening up of opportunities in all fields of human endeavor, together with an emphasis on the value of deliberative rather than arbitrary forces on the governance of practical affairs. . . .

We are now entering into the world arena, and the question is no longer that of the special type of liberal civilization which once existed in the United States, but whether any type of liberal civilization can exist in our America. Liberal civilization has existed in many forms in many nations. What is its essence? Here again it is safer to indicate realities and let the result coin its own definition.

Liberal civilization came to the fore in Europe in the middle of the eighteenth century. It was a movement which banished the Inquisition, abolished the despotic power of kings, and broke up the system of censorship and of political and economic privilege in relation to taxation, trade, and obedience to oppressive laws. It was necessary to wage a long fight before monopoly privileges were taken away from the old aristocracy. The movement to extend education to everybody came to full force only in the nineteenth century. It was the nineteenth century that saw the removal of limitations on the suffrage as well as those on holding public office: property qualifications, religious affiliations, and the like. The liberal movement was directed to the wiping out of such restraints. The emancipation of women and their final admission to the privilege of the suffrage has occurred within our own day.

If a formula is necessary for all this, I would suggest that liberalism means a pride in human achievement, a faith in human effort, a conviction that the proper function of government is to remove the restraints upon human activity. The philosophy back of that is summed up in two great faiths or beliefs: the belief in progress, and the belief in toleration. I think those are the two fundamental ideas of liberalism.

The idea of progress can hardly be understood unless we have in mind the ideas against which the idea of progress was a reaction. The people who were in favor of progress had some definite objective. They were opposed to the old attitude which we associate with Calvinism, but which existed even in large sections of the Catholic Church, as well as in non-Christian groups. This was the view that human nature is profoundly and radically sinful and corrupt. Therefore human beings cannot be trusted to fulfill their natural inclination. Nature is sin. To indulge our natural impulses is sinful. That is an idea which is easily recognized; it has not yet died.

As a consequence of the idea that the human flesh is corrupt and our nature sinful, there was the necessity of relying upon authorities and magistrates, rules and blue laws. The excessive regulation of life by governments, such as we had in some of the Puritan colonies, was a natural consequence of that belief.

The belief in progress was a reaction against such a point of view. The believers in progress said: "No, human flesh is not originally corrupt. To be sure, man commits sins and crimes. You cannot deny that. But that is due to the bad institutions under which we live. If you could only wipe out the evil institutions under which man has lived, human nature would assert itself." This is the idea that underlies almost all of Shelley's writings—an idea that he got from Godwin.

There is something very beautiful and noble about that idea. There are, to my knowledge, few parallels in human history to the nobility of Condorcet in the shadow of the guillotine. He was hiding in a garret in Paris; his life was hanging on a thread; and yet he was writing a marvelously enthusiastic sketch of the progress of the human race, anticipating for the human race an indefinite advance towards perfection.

The only fit parallel that I can find to the nobility of that act is Socrates discussing the immortality of the soul, just before drinking the hemlock, or Jesus saying, "Father, forgive them, for they know not what they do," during the crucifixion.

The idea of progress took root as a creed of hope and a fighting faith. In the course of time, however, progress came to be a shibboleth for a fatalistic optimism or meliorism. The notion that man inevitably progresses through the centuries came to claim the support of science under the name of evolution. But there is no evidence in science or history for the assumption that human nature is bound to become perfect as it develops in time.

There is no proof that human history is a simple straight line upward and onward, and there can be no such proof. For one thing, there are no clear meanings that can be assigned to the terms "upward" and "onward." Upward, of course, was a very definite idea under the old Ptolemaic astronomy. But under modern conditions one has to define "upward" with regard to standards. Unfortunately, people who talk glibly about progress and evolution generally have no very definite conception of any final goal or standard, or even of any definite direction. . . .

Belief in gradual and inevitable progress becomes more and more difficult to maintain, in the face of the carnage and destruction of two world wars and the failure of two victories to achieve the high objectives upon which so many wartime hopes were pinned. The kind of liberalism that was associated with this faith in progress through piecemeal cumulative reform has little appeal today and may well have less tomorrow. But is the liberal attitude necessarily dependent upon confidence in the inevitable success of our efforts? Many stout champions of the liberal cause have been frank to admit their inability to predict the future. Why can we not risk our lives in struggles of uncertain outcome? I am inclined to think that the faith in progress which is essential to the liberal attitude is not a faith in the inevitability of progress but rather a faith in its possibility.

That faith requires us to admit that we do not already possess the absolute truth. Such an admission runs counter to the religious, political, or economic convictions of many men and women. But it may be that the same catastrophes and failures which are destroying the faith in inevitable and gradual progress may also undermine the absolutisms that block the development of a liberalism fitted to the problems of our American future. . . .

Liberalism can move forward, like science, because it embraces self-correcting principles which permit the correction of error and partial truth without an overthrow of the system that makes such correction possible. Like science, liberalism is based on the faith that other human beings can carry forward, by rational methods, the gains that we have won in human understanding. The faith of the liberal, as of the scientist, grows out of a deep humility which recognizes the limitations of

mortal finitude and acknowledges the impossibility of any individual's attaining correct answers to all the problems that he faces. But this humility is combined with a hope that, through rational communication and collaboration among individuals, a living body of common thought may be created which will more adequately answer the problems of an age or society than can any individual, whether he be a scientist or a dictator. In the long run, liberal democracy may outlast any form of dictatorship because the strength of a liberal democracy is not bounded by the prowess of any one man or party. The strength of liberalism lies in the fact that it enables each of us to rise above the limitations of our hereditary class prejudices and to contribute toward a body of *ideas and aspirations in action* that may incorporate more understanding than is vouchsafed to any single mortal. In the end, there is no way in which people can live together decently unless each individual or group realizes that the whole of truth and virtue is not exclusively in its possession. This is a hard lesson to learn, but without it there can be no humane civilization.

Let us take the other great belief of liberalism: the belief in tolerance. This is very closely connected with scientific method. Unless one has a certain amount of skepticism in one's system, one cannot possibly believe in tolerance. What does tolerance mean? Tolerance means that we shall give our enemies a chance. If we are secure and we know that our enemies cannot hurt us, we may be willing to give them a chance. But suppose that we believe in a certain sacred truth—say the truth of the Messiah, or the truth of a certain economic order, or the truth of certain constitutional doctrines—and some scalawag preaches that these are not true. Shall we be tolerant to untruth? That seems to me to be the crux of the whole question of liberalism. The true liberal has a certain amount of skepticism. The true liberal, being impressed with scientific method, says: "Certainly we should, for, although I am convinced that what I believe to be truth is the truth, the other man may have something to say which I haven't heard yet, or the other man may have a point of view which is worth investigating. On the whole, in the conflict of opinions, more truth will thus come out than if there is suppression."

This attitude involves a number of things which are generally not recognized. It involves not only a certain amount of skepticism in our own fundamental conviction, but a certain amount of detachment which very few people have. It is a rare gift to be able to be tolerant in that sense, because if we are pressed, if the enemy has the sword at our throats, we are not tempted to play fair and play according to the rules. We will do anything in our power to kill our assailant—or, at any rate, to get the sword away. And in general, people are not tolerant under stress, in periods of great passion, in periods of compulsion. Tolerance is a virtue that seems to thrive only in a certain leisure, in a certain cultivation. The people who show it best are the philosophers, because they thrive on diversity; or scientists, who also thrive upon the skepticism that is inherent in scientific methods. . . .

The hasty conclusion that liberalism is dead has been given currency by the passionate and uncompromisingly ruthless war spirit, common to Communists and Fascists. But I do not believe that liberalism is dead, or that it has outlived its day. There still seems to me enough human reason left to which to appeal against reckless fanaticism.

Fanaticism is prone to belittle the gains that have come to mankind from the spirit of free inquiry, free discussion, and rational accommodation. So long as human beings lack omniscience, society can only suffer serious loss when one group suppresses the opinions and criticisms of all others. Liberalism, conceived as the spirit of free inquiry, free discussion, and rational accommodation, can continue to appeal to the conscience of men as long as the world offers visible proofs of the blindness of all illiberal power philosophies.

Liberalism, so conceived, may take forms very different from those with which the word has been traditionally associated in the popular mind. Traditionally, liberalism has been conceived as a form of individualism. Liberalism in economics has been associated with opposition to collective controls over production and distribution. In politics liberalism has been historically associated with the supremacy of individual rights. Neither of these beliefs has a very bright future. . . .

My own belief is that increased governmental participation in our economic life is desirable and necessary if we are to avoid the greater evils of economic anarchy and corporate despotism. And such an approach to the problem of economic controls can be made entirely within the framework of liberalism. I do not challenge the right of those who oppose this tendency to invoke the name of liberalism. Liberals may disagree with each other on all kinds of vital issues. But if liberal individualists and liberal collectivists disagree with each other they do not need to resort to guns to settle their differences. Like scientists they can argue and exchange evidence and arrange crucial experiments; and, though these methods cannot be relied upon to produce immediate unanimity on all issues, they do, in the long run, bring substantial agreement on most issues which have been examined in a scientific spirit over a considerable period. And the problems that have been thus solved, whether in the field of mathematics or in the field of penology, are more likely to stay solved than those settled by guns. . . .

There remains the inevitable question: Is it worth while to try to perpetuate liberal civilization? Perhaps most people, if pressed to state their real attitude, would say it is not. For liberal civilization, after all, is based upon (or can be expressed in) the Greek motto: "What is important is not life, but the good life." Many of our current opinions seem to me to be contrary to that. They seem to assume that life as such is more important than the good life. That seems to me the real issue, and one of the most fundamental issues we can face. The reasons that lead the Catholic Church to condemn birth-control; the reasons that make so many lovely, sentimental people condemn the death penalty for criminals—all these reasons seem to me to go upon the assumption that life as such is sacred, and the human beings must not lay their hands upon the gates of life and death. If you really believe that, then the question of liberalism is a minor matter. The important thing is: "Keep your hands off from the gates of life and death."

The real liberal takes a very different attitude. He believes that life is important only as the condition or opportunity for the good life, and prefers not to live at all if he must live as a slave or in degradation.

History has no end, and I do not pretend to be able to predict the future. But I do think it worth while to reiterate my general disbelief in the doctrine that history is just one continuous line of progress onward and upward; or even in the more ancient view of Aristotle, the Hindus, Vico, and Nietzsche, that history is a series of repeatable cycles. I accept neither of these views because I do not believe history is as simple as that. In fact, I do not believe that if we take the whole complex of history we can form any adequate symbol for it. What we can do is to consider certain phases of it.

Suppose we stood outside of the earth and actually saw its motion. It would appear even more irregular than that of the other planets. We obtain some clarity by decomposing the concrete reality into elements. So it is, I think, with regard to history. We have to decompose the various elements which enter into history, and trace each one of them separately. When we do that it seems to me that we have to fall back upon a general view which may be called the polarity of nature, i.e., the two-sidedness of things. In the physical realm there is always action and reaction. There is no one force acting, but always many forces acting in opposite directions. So, in life, there is growth and decay. In human history there are ups and downs. There are periods of flowering and periods of decay. There is no use, it seems to me, in thinking that any one movement of history, or of human life, will continue forever.

So I come back to the notion of Goethe —that if you could say to one moment, "O stay, thou art so fair," that would be the end.

Arthur M. Schlesinger, Jr.
1917-

Born in Columbus, Ohio, the son of a distinguished American historian, Arthur Schlesinger, Jr., graduated from Harvard in 1938. The following year his honors thesis was published under the title Orestes A. Brownson: A Pilgrim's Progress. While a Junior Fellow at Harvard, he wrote The Age of Jackson (1945), for which he received a Pulitzer Prize. To date he has also published three volumes of a multi-volume work on the New Deal entitled The Age of Roosevelt.

Approaching the study of history from a liberal framework, Schlesinger has seen American history as alternating between periods of liberal reform and conservative consolidation, with social conflict the generating force behind this cycle. Not only has he championed the forces of liberal reform in his historical studies, but he has taken an active role in political affairs. He served first as an advisor to Adlai E. Stevenson during the presidential campaigns of 1952 and 1956, and then became a member of John F. Kennedy's administration as a special assistant to the President.

Schlesinger has been deeply concerned with preserving liberal democratic values against their many detractors. He is thoroughly familiar with the criticisms levied against American liberalism from the progressive era through the New Deal. Consequently, Schlesinger has worked to revive liberal theory in order to make it a functional philosophy that recognizes the darker side of man's nature, and yet preserves the idea of man as the master of his own destiny who is able, within certain limits, to direct the course of society and to promote the well-being of members of that society. To develop a more realistic ideology, he has attempted to synthesize the theory of original sin as expounded by Reinhold Niebuhr with the older democratic liberalism, thus providing a philosophy relevant to the challenges of contemporary life.

The following selection is from Schlesinger's The Vital Center: The Politics of Freedom (Boston: Houghton Mifflin Company, 1949).

*W*estern man in the middle of the twentieth century is tense, uncertain, adrift. We look upon our epoch as a time of troubles, an age of anxiety. The grounds of our civilization, of our certitude, are breaking up under our feet, and familiar ideas and institutions vanish as we reach for them, like shadows in the falling dusk. Most of the world has reconciled itself to this half-light, to the reign of insecurity. Even those peoples who hastily traded their insecurities for a mirage of security are finding themselves no better off than the rest. Only the United States still has buffers between itself and the anxieties of our age: buffers of time, of distance, of natural wealth, of national ingenuity, of a stubborn tradition of hope.

A nation which has made a religion of success ought to find it hard to acclimate itself to the middle of the twentieth century. For frustration is increasingly the hallmark of this century—the frustration of triumphant science and rampant technology, the frustration of the most generous hopes and of the most splendid dreams. Nineteen hundred looked forward to the irresistible expansion of freedom, democracy and abundance; 1950 will look back to totalitarianism, to concentration camps, to mass starvation, to atomic war. Yet for the United States the world tragedy still has the flickering unreality of a motion picture. It grips us as we see it; but, lingering over the familiar milk-shake in the bright drugstore, we forget the nightmare in the resurgence of warmth and comfort. Anxiety is something we hear about. It is not yet part of our lives—not of enough of our lives, anyway, to inform our national decisions. . . .

Since progressives, on the whole, create our contemporary climate of opinion, the impression exists that the present perils to free society result exclusively from the failure of the conservatives. In a sense, this is true—in the sense that the conservatives have had the power, notably in the period between the wars, and have failed to use it intelligently. Yet one reason for their failure, as D. W. Brogan has reminded us, is the failure of their critics, whose hearts were in the right place, but whose heads were too often "muddled, full of sentiment, empty of knowledge, living on slogans and clichés, unwilling to realize how complicated is the modern world and that the price of liberty is eternal intellectual vigilance." Compared with the conservatives, the progressives were indeed innocent; but is innocence enough?

During the years of plutocratic stagnation, why did not progressivism have strong faith and lucid purposes? And, in the cases where progressives were sure of their diagnosis and of their remedy, why has that certitude now vanished? Let us concede at once the relative superiority in practice of left-wing governments—at least of the pragmatic left, though not of the doctrinaire left. The New Deal government of Franklin D. Roosevelt, for all its confusions and defects, kept its eye more steadily on the ball than any other government of our time, conservative, socialist, Communist or fascist. Yet history has discredited the hopes and predictions of doctrinaire progressivism about as thoroughly as it has those of conservatism. The progressive "analysis" is today a series of dry and broken platitudes, tossed out in ash-heaps (where they are collected and dusted off by the editors of the liberal weeklies).

What is the progressive? The defining characteristic of the progressive, as I shall use the word, is the sentimentality of his approach to politics and culture. He must be distinguished, on the one hand, from the Communist; for the progressive is soft, not hard; he believes himself genuinely concerned with the welfare of individuals. He must be distinguished on the other, from the radical democrat; for the progressive, by refusing to make room in his philosophy for the discipline of responsibility or for the danger of power, has cut himself off from the usable traditions of American radical democracy. He has rejected the pragmatic tradition of the men who, from the Jacksonians to the New Dealers, learned the facts of life through the exercise of power under conditions of accountability. He has rejected the pessimistic tradition of those who, from Hawthorne to Reinhold Niebuhr, warned that power, unless checked by accountability, would corrupt its possessor.

The type of the progressive today is the fellow traveler or the fellow traveler of the fellow traveler: see the Wallace movement or (until fairly recently) the columns of the *New Republic* and the *Nation*. His sentimentality has softened up the progressive for Communist permeation and conquest. For the most chivalrous reasons, he cannot believe that ugly facts underlie fair words. However he looks at it, for example, the USSR keeps coming through as a kind of enlarged Brook Farm community, complete with folk dancing in native costumes, joyous work in the fields and progressive kindergartens. Nothing in his system has prepared him for Stalin.

This is not a new breed in American history. A century ago, after Jacksonian democracy had split over the slavery question, one wing of northern Jacksonians under Martin Van Buren went into the Free Soil Party. The other wing refused to turn against the South. Many of this pro-southern group retained a Jacksonian desire for social reform; they certainly held no brief for slavery; yet as men implicated in the industrial evils of the north, who were they, they would cry, to pronounce judgment on the social system of the South? "The only difference between the negro slave

of the South, and the white wages slave of the North," as one member of this group put it, "is, that the one has a master without asking for him, and the other has to beg for the privilege of becoming a slave. . . . The one is the slave of an individual; the other is the slave of an inexorable class."

The members of this group were known as Doughfaces—that is, "northern men with southern principles." The infiltration of contemporary progressivism by Communism had led to the same self-flagellation, the same refusal to take precautions against tyranny. It has created a new Doughface movement—a movement of "democratic men with totalitarian principles."

The core of Doughface progressivism is its sentimental belief in progress. The belief in progress was the product of the Enlightenment, cross-fertilized with allied growths, such as science, bourgeois complacency, Unitarianism and a faith in the goodness of man. It dispensed with the Christian myths of sin and atonement. Man's shortcomings, such as they were, were to be redeemed, not by Jesus on the cross, but by the benevolent unfolding of history. Tolerance, free inquiry and technology, operating in the framework of human perfectibility, would in the end create a heaven on earth, a goal much more wholesome than a heaven in heaven. . . .

Optimism gave the progressives a soft and shallow conception of human nature. With the aggressive and sinister impulses eliminated from the equation, the problem of social change assumed too simple a form. The corruptions of power—the desire to exercise it, the desire to increase it, the desire for prostration before it—had no place in the progressive calculations. As a result, progressivism became politically inadequate: it could neither persuade nor control the emotions of man. And it became intellectually inadequate: it could not anticipate nor explain the tragic movements of history in the twentieth century. Ideologies which exploited the darker passions captured men by appeals unknown to the armory of progressivism. . . .

Conservatism in its crisis of despair turns to fascism: so progressivism in its crisis of despair turns to Communism. Each in a sober mood has a great contribution to make to free society: the conservative in his emphasis on law and liberty, the progressive in his emphasis on mass welfare. But neither is capable of saving free society. Both, faced by problems they cannot understand and fear to meet, tend to compound their own failure by delivering free society to its totalitarian foe. To avoid this fate, we must understand as clearly as possible the reasons for the appeal of totalitarianism. . . .

As organization towers higher and higher above him, man grows in forlornness, impotence and fear. As monopoly or state capitalism enlarges its power, the outlets in economic enterprise dwindle. Man longs to escape the pressures beating down on his frail individuality; and, more and more, the surest means of escape seems to be to surrender that individuality to some massive, external authority. Dostoievsky remarks, "Man is tormented by no greater anxiety than to find some one quickly to whom he can hand over that gift of freedom with which the ill-fated creature is born." The psychological stigmata of the fugitives from freedom, Erich Fromm finds in his remarkable analysis, are the strivings for submission and for domination, the losing of self in masochism or sadism.

The totalitarian state, which has risen in specific response to this fear of freedom, is an invention of the twentieth century. It differs essentially from old-style dictatorship, which may be bloody and tyrannical but yet leaves intact most of the structure of society. Totalitarianism, on the contrary, pulverizes the social structure, grinding all independent groups and diverse loyalties into a single amorphous mass. The sway of the totalitarian state is unlimited. This very fact is a source of its profound psychological appeal. On an economic level, it seeks to supply the answer to the incoherence and apparent uncontrollability of industrial society. On the political and psychological level, it holds out hope of allaying the gnawing anxieties; it offers institutional outlets for the impulses of sadism and masochism. As a system of social organization, it purports to invest life with meaning and purpose. Against the loneliness and rootlessness of man in free society, it promises the security and comradeship of a crusading unity, propelled by a deep and driving faith. . . .

The independent left everywhere in the world has been in a state of moral paralysis at least since 1917. The commanding personality of Lenin and the unanswerable fact of the Russian Revolution gave Western radicalism a fatal complex of inferiority. Under the spell of that complex, the left committed itself to the long and corrupting enterprise of accepting in the Soviet Union crimes much worse than those it attacked in its own countries. Just as the left gained moral strength when it protested against Amritsar or the judicial murder of Sacco and Vanzetti, so it lost moral strength when it kept its silence before the anonymous victims of the Soviet despotism. . . .

If the distinguishing moral commitment of the new radicalism is its faith in freedom and the unconditional rejection of totalitarianism, the distinguishing political commitment is its belief in the limited state. The Soviet experience has caused a revaluation of the politics of Marxism—a revaluation which questions in particular the total concentration of all political and economic power in the apparatus of the single-party state. For the Soviet experience has proved, if it has proved anything, that concentration of power creates classes whatever the system of ownership—classes under Communism as well as under capitalism. Who whom? remains the crucial question; and in every system, as history has finally taught us, the tendency of the ruling class toward oppression can be checked only by the capacity of the other classes for resistance.

And resistance requires essentially an independent base from which to operate. It requires privacy, funds, time, newsprint, gasoline, freedom of speech, freedom of assembly, freedom from fear; it requires resources to which its own access is secure and which remain relatively inaccessible to the ruling class. Resistance is possible, in short, only when the base is clearly separate from the state. Under a system of total state ownership, the sinews of resistance are doled out to the opposition only by the charity of the ruling class. . . .

The failure of nerve is over. The new radicalism need not invoke Marx at every turn in the road, or point its prayer-rug every morning to Moscow. It has new confidence in its own insights and its own values. It has returned in great part to the historic philosophy of liberalism—to a belief in the integrity of the individual, in the limited state, in due process of law, in empiricism and gradualism. Man in its estimate is precious but not perfect. He is intoxicated by power and hence most humane in a society which distributes power widely; he is intimidated by industrialism and thus most secure in a society which will protect him from want and starvation. We conclude with Pascal: "Man is neither angel nor brute, and the unfortunate thing is that he who would act the angel acts the brute."

As the old order crumbles through the world, we know that any path which can preserve peace and freedom is narrow and hazardous. Our instruments must be as precise as possible, our analysis as dispassionate, our conclusions as honest and objective as we can make them. One false step may plunge the world into atomic war or deliver it into totalitarian darkness. The new radicalism seeks to fight for honesty and clarity in a turbulent and stricken society, to restore a serious sense of the values of facts, of the integrity of reason, of devotion to truth. Its final success will depend upon its immediate success in shaping the policy of the only one of the two great powers accessible to it: the United States. . . .

Today, finally and tardily, the skeptical insights are in process of restoration to the liberal mind. The psychology of Freud has renewed the intellectual's belief in the dark, slumbering forces of the will. The theology of Barth and Niebuhr has given new power to the old and chastening truths of Christianity. More than anything else, the rise of Hitler and Stalin has revealed in terms no one can deny the awful reality of the human impulses toward aggrandizement and destruction—impulses for which the liberal intellectual had left no room in his philosophy. The conceptions of the intellectual are at last beginning to catch up with the instincts of the democratic politician.

When the challenge of Communism finally forced American liberals to take inventory of their moral resources, the inventory resulted in the clear decision that freedom had values which could not be compromised in deals with totalitarianism. Thus America found itself reaching much the same conclusion as the non-Communist left of Europe. In the years after the Second War Americans began to rediscover the great tradition of liberalism—the tradition of Jackson and Hawthorne, the tradition of a reasonable responsibility about politics and a moderate pessimism about man. . . .

The people as a whole are not perfect; but no special group of the people is more perfect: that is the moral and rationale of democracy. Consistent pessimism about man, far from promoting authoritarianism, alone can inoculate the democratic faith against it. "Man's capacity for justice makes democracy possible," Niebuhr has written in his remarkable book on democratic theory; "but man's inclination to injustice makes democracy necessary."

The image of democratic man emerges from the experience of democracy; man is a creature capable of reason and of purpose, of great loyalty and of great virtue, yet he is vulnerable to material power and to spiritual pride. In our democratic tradition, the excessive self-love which transforms power into tyranny is the greatest of all dangers. But the self-love which transforms radicalism from an instrument of action into an expression of neurosis is almost as great a danger. If irresponsible power is the source of evil, and irresponsible impotence, the source of decadence, then responsible power—power held for limited terms under conditions of strict accountability—is the source of wisdom. . . .

The fight on the part of the "humble members of society" against business domination has been the consistent motive of American liberalism. Far from importing subversive European ideas when he renewed this theme, Franklin Roosevelt was only returning to the political doctrine of the hallowed past. Nor is there anything specifically Marxist about class conflict. "As far as I am concerned," Marx himself wrote, "the honour does not belong to me for having discovered the existence either of classes in modern society or of the struggle between the classes. Bourgeois historians a long time before me expounded the historical development of this class struggle." "To limit Marxism to the teaching of the class struggle," added Lenin, "means to curtail Marxism—to distort it, to reduce it to something which is acceptable to the bourgeoisie. A Marxist is one who *extends* the acceptance of the class struggle to the acceptance of the *dictatorship of the proletariat.*" It is precisely this extension which American radicalism has refused to make.

The problem of classes is this: Class conflict is essential if freedom is to be preserved, because it is the only barrier against class domination; yet class conflict, pursued to excess, may well destroy the underlying fabric of common principle which sustains free society.

I cannot imagine a free society which has eliminated class conflict. So long as there is inequality in the distribution of property and variety in the nature of economic interests, so long will politics center on economic issues; and so long the insurgency of the discontented will provide the best guarantee against the tyranny of the possessors.

Yet this conflict must be kept within bounds, if freedom itself is to survive. The differences among classes in a capitalist democracy are often wide and bitter; but they are much less impassable than the differences between capitalist democracy and authoritarianism; and sometimes in the heat of the battle the warring classes tend to forget their family relationship. It is perhaps fortunate for the continuity of the American development that the Civil War came along to heal the social wounds opened up in the age of Jackson; that one world war closed the rifts created by the New Freedom and another those of the New Deal. But external war is an expensive means of making antagonistic classes suddenly realize how much their agreement outweighs their differences. . . .

The lesson of the experiments with democratic socialism is plainly that the state should aim at establishing conditions for economic decisions, not at making all the decisions itself. It should create an economic environment favorable to private business policies which increase production; and then let the free market carry the ball as far as it can. Keynes, not Marx, is the prophet of the new radicalism.

The function of the state, in other words, is to define the ground rules of the game; not to pitch, catch, hit homers or (just as likely) pop up or throw to the wrong base. The state may acquire total economic power for the most benevolent of motives; but benevolence is no guarantee of wisdom. The danger of the total planner is, first, that his almost inevitable blunders may convulse the entire economy, and, second, that in a panic-stricken effort to cover up his blunders he may multiply his controls till they destroy the initiative and free movement of men and finally the free play of political criticism.

The state can do a great deal to set the level of economic activity by policies which at once will be stable enough to create an atmosphere favorable to private investment and adequate consumption and effective enough to prevent economic breakdown. Keynes and his followers have pointed out the great resources of fiscal and monetary policy. When a sag in spending or in demand threatens the economy, then the government through tax reduction and compensatory spending can maintain high levels of employment and production. Taxation and subsidies can be potent means of directing private investment to under-developed industries and regions; and a whole range of general incentives can be used to draw labor and capital into socially beneficial undertakings. . . .

Free society cannot survive unless it defeats the problems of economic stagnation and collapse. But economic success can only create the conditions for the survival of freedom; it can make no guarantees. The preservation of freedom requires a positive and continuing commitment. Specifically the maintenance of the United States as a free society confronts the American people with an immediate responsibility in two areas in particular: civil rights and civil liberties. . . .

World destiny has belatedly thrust upon the United States the necessity for having a real foreign policy—a policy that is, which exists in terms of day-to-day operations, not in terms of Fourth of July oratory. Webster's reply to Hülsemann served too long as the model for American diplomacy: "The power of this republic at the present moment is . . . of an extent in comparison with which the possessions of the House of Hapsburg are but as a patch on the earth's surface." Americans today, both conservative and liberal, still tend to think of foreign policy in terms of such ringing defiances of European tyrants— foreign policy as a means of expressing sentiments, in other words, not of influencing events. . . .

A little American efficiency, accompanied by a policy of support for native progressive movements, would go far to counter the appeal of the Russian revolutionary spirit in the underdeveloped areas. We have to accept the fact that we must apply this efficiency selectively in Asia. The reconstruction/containment formula stretches our resources in Europe alone, and we can hardly undertake a program of comparable scope for all the peoples of Asia and Africa. We must choose our spots— Japan, perhaps, the Philippines, Indonesia, India, Israel, Turkey—concentrate on exporting technology rather than commodities, and seek to make those nations the leaders of a progressive Asian civilization along democratic lines. A confused and mistaken policy has lost us the battle in China. But, if we learn from the Chinese failure, we may be able to help build a pro-democratic alternative to Communism in the other crucial areas of the Orient. We must pursue our Asian objectives with as much determination as we have pursued our objectives in Europe. Europe's mighty industrial capacity undoubtedly gives it top priority in the Soviet plan of expansion; but in the long run, the loss of either Europe or Asia would be fatal to the democratic position.

The present design of our foreign policy, then, is to carry out the reconstruction/containment policy in Europe and to develop some more complex and limited equivalent in the underdeveloped lands. These policies cannot succeed, however, unless the United States itself does things we have not done in the past. First, we must stay out of a depression and thereby show the world that our strength is solid and stable. Second, we must revise our commercial expectations, reduce our tariffs and open our gates wide to foreign goods. Our efforts to increase production through the world will have little effect in ending the dollar gap unless we are willing to accept foreign goods in exchange for our own. Third, we must reform our own racial practices—not only repeal such insulting symbols as the Oriental exclusion laws, but demonstrate a deep and effective concern with the racial inequities within the United States. Fourth, we must not succumb to demands for an anti-Soviet crusade or a preventive war, nor permit reactionaries in the buffer states to precipitate conflicts in defense of their own obsolete prerogatives. . . .

Through this century, free society has been on the defensive, demoralized by the infection of anxiety, staggering under the body blows of fascism and Communism. Free society alienates the lonely and uprooted masses; while totalitarianism, building on their frustrations and cravings, provides a structure of belief, men to worship and men to hate and rites which guarantee salvation. The crisis of free society has assumed the form of international collisions between the democracies and the totalitarian powers; but this fact should not blind us to the fact that in its essence this crisis is internal.

Free society will survive, in the last resort, only if enough people believe in it deeply enough to die for it. However reluctant peace-loving people are to recognize that fact, history's warning is clear and cold; civilizations which cannot man their walls in times of alarm are doomed to destruction by the barbarians. We have deeply believed only when the issue of war has reduced our future to the stark problem of self-preservation. Franklin Roosevelt read the American people with his usual uncanny accuracy when he named the Second War, not the "war for freedom," but the "war for survival." Our democracy has still to generate a living emotional content, rich enough to overcome the anxieties incited by industrialism, deep enough to rally its members to battle for freedom—not just for self-preservation. Freedom must become, in Holmes's phrase, a "fighting faith."

Why does not democracy believe in itself with passion? Why is freedom not a fighting faith? In part because democracy, by its nature, dissipates rather than concentrates its internal moral force. The thrust of the democratic faith is away from fanaticism; it is toward compromise, persuasion and consent in politics, toward tolerance and diversity in society; its economic foundation lies in the easily frightened middle class. Its love of variety discourages dogmatism, and its love of skepticism discourages hero-worship. In place of theology and ritual, of hierarchy and demonology, it sets up a belief in intellectual freedom and unrestricted inquiry. The advocate of free society defines himself by telling what he is against: what he is for turns out to be certain *means* and he leaves other people to charge the means with content. Today democracy is paying the price for its systematic cultivation of the peaceful and rational virtues. "Many a man will live and die upon a dogma; no man will be a martyr for a conclusion."

Democracy, moreover, has not worn too well as a philosophy of life in an industrial age. It seemed more solid at the high noon of success than it does in the uncertainties of falling dusk. In its traditional form, it has pre-supposed emotional and psychological stability in the individual. It has assumed, much too confidently, that the gnawing problems of doubt and anxiety would be banished by the advance of science or cured by a rise in the standard of living. The spectacular reopening of these problems in our time finds the democratic faith lacking in the profounder emotional resources. Democracy has no defense-in-depth against the neuroses of industrialism. When philosophies of blood and violence arise to take up the slack between democracy's thin optimism and the bitter agonies of experience, democracy by comparison appears pale and feeble.

Yet it seems doubtful whether democracy could itself be transformed into a political religion, like totalitarianism, without losing its characteristic belief in individual dignity and freedom. Does this mean that democracy is destined to defeat, sooner or later, by one or another of the totalitarian sects?

The death pallor will indeed come over free society, unless it can recharge the deepest sources of its moral energy. And we cannot make democracy a fighting faith merely by exhortation nor by self-flagellation; and certainly not by renouncing the values which distinguish free society from totalitarianism. Yet we must somehow dissolve the anxieties which drive people in free society to become traitors to freedom. We must somehow give the lonely masses a sense of individual human function, we must restore community to the industrial order. . . .

The essential strength of democracy as against totalitarianism lies in its startling insight into the value of the individual. Yet, as we have seen, this insight can become abstract and sterile; arrogant forms of individualism sometimes discredit the basic faith in the value of the individual. It is only as far as that insight can achieve a full social dimension, so far as individualism derives freely from community, that democracy will be immune to the virus of totalitarianism. . . .

Democracy requires unremitting action on many fronts. It is, in other words, a process, not a conclusion. However painful the thought, it must be recognized that its commitments are unending. The belief in the millennium has dominated our social thinking too long. Our utopian prophets have always supposed that a day would come when all who had not worshiped the beast nor received his mark on their foreheads would reign for a thousand years. "And God shall wipe away all tears from their eyes; and there shall be no more death, neither sorrow, nor crying, neither shall there be any more pain: for the former things are passed away." . . .

So we are forced back on the reality of struggle. So long as society stays free, so long will it continue in its state of tension, breeding contradiction, breeding strife. But we betray ourselves if we accept contradiction and strife as the total meaning of conflict. For conflict is also the guarantee of freedom; it is the instrument of change; it is, above all, the source of discovery, the source of art, the source of love. The choice we face is not between progress with conflict and progress without conflict. The choice is between conflict and stagnation. You cannot expel conflict from society any more than you can from the human mind. When you attempt it, the psychic costs in schizophrenia or torpor are the same.

The totalitarians regard the toleration of conflict as our central weakness. So it may appear to be in an age of anxiety. But we know it to be basically our central strength. The new radicalism derives its power from an acceptance of conflict —an acceptance with a determination to create a social framework where conflict issues, not in excessive anxiety, but in creativity. The center is vital; the center must hold. The object of the new radicalism is to restore the center, to reunite individual and community in fruitful union. The spirit of the new radicalism is the spirit of the center— the spirit of human decency, opposing the extremes of tyranny. Yet, in a more fundamental sense does not the center itself represent one extreme? while, at the other, are grouped the forces of corruption—men transformed by pride and power into enemies of humanity.

The new radicalism, drawing strength from a realistic conception of man, dedicates itself to problems as they come, attacking them in terms which best advance the humane and libertarian values, which best secure the freedom and fulfillment of the individual. It believes in attack—and out of attack will come passionate intensity.

Can we win the fight? We must commit ourselves to it with all our vigor in all its dimensions: the struggle within the world against Communism and fascism; the struggle within our country against oppression and stagnation; the struggle within ourselves against price and corruption: nor can engagement in one dimension exclude responsibility for another. Economic and political action can help restore the balance between individual and community and thereby reduce one great source of anxiety. But even the most favorable social arrangements cannot guarantee individual virtue; and we are far yet from having solved the social problem.

The commitment is complex and rigorous. When has it not been so? If democracy cannot produce the large resolute breed of men capable of the climactic effort, it will founder. Out of the effort, out of the struggle alone, can come the high courage and faith which will preserve freedom.

B. F. Skinner
1904-

*Born in Susquehanna, Pennsylvania,
B. F. Skinner received his bachelor's degree
from Hamilton College in 1926 and a Ph.D.
from Harvard five years later. Between 1933
and 1936 he held one of the prized
appointments as a Junior Fellow at Harvard.
After teaching at the Universities of
Minnesota and Indiana, he returned in
1948 to Harvard as professor of psychology.*

*Widely known for his experiments in the
control of behavior, Skinner has also dealt
with the difficult problem of the relationship
between democracy, science, and ethics.
Holding steadfastly to the validity of the
scientific approach in the study of the
individual as well as of society, he has
insisted that such knowledge could be used
to evolve a community marked by peace and
order, peopled by brave, healthy, intelligent,
and happy individuals. In 1948, he published
a utopian novel,* Walden Two, *in which he
sketched out in detail his ideal, to be
achieved through scientific control and
manipulation of human beings.*

*Although skeptical of particular answers
to the dilemmas posed by ethical questions,
Skinner has remained loyal to the pragmatic
tradition of John Dewey. He is a supporter
of the view that the scientific method provides
the only means for the discovery of truth,
including ethical truth. In this sense he is
within the democratic liberal tradition and
a foe of those philosophers and theologians
who would erect systems that deprive man
of effective control of his own destiny.*

*The following selection is from Skinner's
article "Freedom and the Control of Men"
in* The American Scholar, *25 (Winter,
1955–1956); this article was also reprinted
in his book* Cumulative Record: Enlarged
Edition *(New York, 1961).*

*T*he second half of the twentieth
century may be remembered for its
solution of a curious problem. Although
Western democracy created the conditions responsible for the rise of
modern science, it is now evident that
it may never fully profit from that
achievement. The so-called "democratic
philosophy" of human behavior to
which it also gave rise is increasingly in
conflict with the application of the
methods of science to human affairs.
Unless the conflict is somehow resolved,
the ultimate goals of democracy may be
long deferred.

Just as biographers and critics look
for external influences to account for
the traits and achievements of the men
they study, so science ultimately explains behavior in terms of "causes" or
conditions which lie beyond the individual himself. As more and more

causal relations are demonstrated, a practical corollary becomes difficult to resist: it should be possible to *produce* behavior according to plan simply by arranging the proper conditions. Now, among the specifications which might reasonably be submitted to a behavioral technology are these: Let men be happy, informed, skillful, well behaved and productive.

This immediate practical implication of a science of behavior has a familiar ring, for it recalls the doctrine of human perfectibility of eighteenth- and nineteenth-century humanism. A science of man shares the optimism of that philosophy and supplies striking support for the working faith that men can build a better world and, through it, better men. The support comes just in time, for there has been little optimism of late among those who speak from the traditional point of view. Democracy has become "realistic," and it is only with some embarrassment that one admits today to perfectionistic or utopian thinking.

The earlier temper is worth considering, however. History records many foolish and unworkable schemes for human betterment, but almost all the great changes in our culture which we now regard as worthwhile can be traced to perfectionistic philosophies. Governmental, religious, educational, economic and social reforms follow a common pattern. Someone believes that a change in a cultural practice—for example, in the rules of evidence in a court of law, in the characterization of man's relation to God, in the way children are taught to read and write, in permitted rates of interest, or in minimal housing standards—will improve the condition of men: by promoting justice, permitting men to seek salvation more effectively, increasing the literacy of a people, checking an inflationary trend, or improving public health and family relations, respectively. The underlying hypothesis is always the same: that a different physical or cultural environment will make a different and better man.

The scientific study of behavior not only justifies the general pattern of such proposals; it promises new and better hypotheses. The earliest cultural practices must have originated in sheer accidents. Those which strengthened the group survived with the group in a sort of natural selection. As soon as men began to propose and carry out changes in practice for the sake of possible consequences, the evolutionary process must have accelerated. The simple practice of making changes must have had survival value. A further acceleration is now to be expected. As laws of behavior are more precisely stated, the changes in the environment required to bring about a given effect may be more clearly specified. Conditions which have been neglected because their effects were slight or unlooked for may be shown to be relevant. New conditions may actually be created, as in the discovery and synthesis of drugs which affect behavior.

This is no time, then, to abandon notions of progress, improvement or, indeed human perfectibility. The simple fact is that man is able, and now as never before, to lift himself by his own boot straps. In achieving control of the world of which he is a part, he may learn at last to control himself. . . .

Designing a new cultural pattern is in many ways like designing an experiment. In drawing up a new constitution, outlining a new educational program, modifying a religious doctrine, or setting up a new fiscal policy, many statements must be quite tentative. We cannot be sure that the practices we specify will have the consequences we predict, or that the consequences will reward our efforts. This is in the nature of such proposals. They are not value judgments—they are guesses. To confuse and delay the improvement of cultural practices by quibbling about the word *improve* is itself not a useful practice. Let us agree, to start with, that health is better than illness, wisdom better than ignorance, love better than hate, and productive energy better than neurotic sloth. . . .

With a world of their own making almost within reach, men of good will have been seized with distaste for their achievement. They have uneasily rejected opportunities to apply the techniques and findings of science in the service of men, and as the import of effective cultural design has come to be understood, many of them have voiced an outright refusal to have any part in it. Science has been challenged before when it has encroached upon institutions already engaged in the control of human behavior; but what are we to make of benevolent men, with no special interests of their own to defend, who nevertheless turn against the very means of reaching long-dreamed-of goals?

What is being rejected, of course, is the scientific conception of man and his place in nature. So long as the findings and methods of science are applied to human affairs only in a sort of remedial patchwork, we may continue to hold any view of human nature we like. But as the use of science increases, we are forced to accept the theoretical structure with which science represents its facts. The difficulty is that this structure is clearly at odds with the traditional democratic conception of man. Every discovery of an event which has a part in shaping a man's behavior seems to leave so much the less to be credited to the man himself; and as such explanations become more and more comprehensive, the contribution which may be claimed by the individual himself appears to approach zero. Man's vaunted creative powers, his original accomplishments in art, science and

morals, his capacity to choose and our right to hold him responsible for the consequences of his choice—none of these is conspicuous in this new self-portrait. Man, we once believed, was free to express himself in art, music and literature, to inquire into nature, to seek salvation in his own way. He could initiate action and make spontaneous and capricious changes of course. Under the most extreme duress some sort of choice remained to him. He could resist any effort to control him, though it might cost him his life. But science insists that action is initiated by forces impinging upon the individual, and that caprice is only another name for behavior for which we have not yet found a cause.

In attempting to reconcile these views it is important to note that the traditional democratic conception was not designed as a description in the scientific sense but as a philosophy to be used in setting up and maintaining a governmental process. It arose under historical circumstances and served political purposes apart from which it cannot be properly understood. In rallying men against tyranny it was necessary that the individual be strengthened, that he be taught that he had rights and could govern himself. To give the common man a new conception of his worth, his dignity, and his power to save himself, both here and hereafter, was often the only resource of the revolutionist. When democratic principles were put into practice, the same doctrines were used as a working formula. This is exemplified by the notion of personal responsibility in Anglo-American law. All governments make certain forms of punishment contingent upon certain kinds of acts. In democratic countries these contingencies are expressed by the notion of responsible choice. But the notion may have no meaning under governmental practices formulated in other ways and would certainly have no place in systems which did not use punishment.

The democratic philosophy of human nature is determined by certain political exigencies and techniques not by the goals of democracy. But exigencies and techniques change; and a conception which is not supported for its accuracy as a likeness—is not, indeed, rooted in fact at all—may be expected to change too. No matter how effective we judge current democratic practices to be, how highly we value them or how long we expect them to survive, they are almost certainly not the *final* form of government. The philosophy of human nature which has been useful in implementing them is also almost certainly not the last word. The ultimate achievement of democracy may be long deferred unless we emphasize the real aims rather than the verbal devices of democratic thinking. A philosophy which has been appropriate to one set of political exigencies will defeat its purpose if, under other circumstances, it prevents us from applying to human affairs the science of man which probably nothing but democracy itself could have produced.

Perhaps the most crucial part of our democratic philosophy to be reconsidered is our attitude toward freedom—or its reciprocal, the control of human behavior. We do not oppose all forms of control because it is "human nature" to do so. The reaction is not characteristic of all men under all conditions of life. It is an attitude which has been carefully engineered, in large part by what we call the "literature" of democracy. With respect to some methods of control (for example, the threat of force), very little engineering is needed, for the techniques or their immediate consequences are objectionable. Society has suppressed these methods by branding them "wrong," "illegal" or "sinful." But to encourage these attitudes toward objectionable forms of control,

it has been necessary to disguise the real nature of certain indispensable techniques, the commonest examples of which are education, moral discourse, and persuasion. The actual procedures appear harmless enough. They consist of supplying information, presenting opportunities for action, pointing out logical relations, appealing to reason or "enlightened understanding," and so on. Through a masterful piece of misrepresentation, the illusion is fostered that these procedures do not involve the control of behavior; at most, they are simply ways of "getting someone to change his mind." But analysis not only reveals the presence of well-defined behavioral processes, it demonstrates a kind of control no less inexorable, though in some ways more acceptable, than the bully's threat of force. . . .

The methods of education, moral discourse, and persuasion are acceptable not because they recognize the freedom of the individual or his right to dissent, but because they make only *partial* contributions to the control of his behavior. The freedom they recognize is freedom from a more coercive form of control. The dissent which they tolerate is the possible effect of other determiners of action. Since these sanctioned methods are frequently ineffective, we have been able to convince ourselves that they do not represent control at all. When they show too much strength to permit disguise, we give them other names and suppress them as energetically as we suppress the use of force. Education grown too powerful is rejected as propaganda or "brain-washing," while really effective persuasion is decried as "undue influence," "demagoguery," "seduction," and so on.

If we are not to rely solely upon accident for the innovations which give rise to cultural evolution, we must accept the fact that some kind of control of human behavior is inevitable. We cannot use good sense in human affairs unless someone engages in the design and construction of environmental conditions which affect the behavior of men. Environmental changes have always been the condition for the improvement of cultural patterns, and we can hardly use the more effective methods of science without making changes on a grander scale. We are all controlled by the world in which we live, and part of that world has been and will be constructed by men. The question is this: Are we to be controlled by accident, by tyrants, or by ourselves in effective cultural design?

The danger of the misuse of power is possibly greater than ever. It is not allayed by disguising the facts. We cannot make wise decisions if we continue to pretend that human behavior is not controlled, or if we refuse to engage in control when valuable results might be forthcoming. Such measures weaken only ourselves, leaving the strength of science to others. The first step in a defense against tyranny is the fullest possible exposure of controlling techniques. A second step has already been taken successfully in restricting the use of physical force. Slowly, and as yet imperfectly, we have worked out an ethical and governmental design in which the strong man is not allowed to use the power deriving from his strength to control his fellow men. He is restrained by a superior force created for that purpose—the ethical pressure of the group, or more explicit religious and governmental measures. We tend to distrust superior forces, as we currently hesitate to relinquish sovereignty in order to set up an international police force. But it is only through such counter-control that we have achieved what we call peace—a condition in which men are not permitted to control each other through force. In other words, control itself must be controlled.

Science has turned up dangerous processes and materials before. To use the facts and techniques of a science of man to the fullest extent without making some monstrous mistake will be difficult and obviously perilous. It is no time for self-deception, emotional indulgence, or the assumption of attitudes which are no longer useful. Man is facing a difficult test. He must keep his head now, or he must start again—a long way back.

Those who reject the scientific conception of man must, to be logical, oppose the methods of science as well. The position is often supported by predicting a series of dire consequences which are to follow if science is not checked. A recent book by Joseph Wood Krutch, *The Measure of Man*, is in this vein. Mr. Krutch sees in the growing science of man the threat of an unexampled tyranny over men's minds. If science is permitted to have its way, he insists, "we may never be able really to think again." A controlled culture will, for example, lack some virtue inherent in disorder. We have emerged from chaos through a series of happy accidents, but in an engineered culture it will be "impossible for the unplanned to erupt again." But there is no virtue in the accidental character of an accident, and the diversity which arises from disorder can not only be duplicated by design but vastly extended. The experimental method is superior to simple observation just because it multiplies "accidents" in a systematic coverage of the possibilities. Technology offers many familiar examples. We no longer wait for immunity to disease to develop from a series of accidental exposures, nor do we wait for natural mutations in sheep and cotton to produce better fibres; but we continue to make use of such accidents when they occur, and we certainly do not prevent them. Many of the things we value have emerged from the clash of ignorant armies on darkling plains, but it is not therefore wise to encourage ignorance and darkness.

It is not always disorder itself which we are told we shall miss but certain admirable qualities in men which flourish only in the presence of disorder. A man rises above an unpropitious childhood to a position of eminence, and since we cannot give a plausible account of the action of so complex an environment, we attribute the achievement to some admirable faculty in the man himself. But such "faculties" are suspiciously like the explanatory fictions against which the history of science warns us. We admire Lincoln for rising above a deficient school system, but it was not necessarily something *in him* which permitted him to become an educated man in spite of it. His educational environment was certainly unplanned, but it could nevertheless have made a full contribution to his mature behavior. He was a rare man, but the circumstances of his childhood were rare too. We do not give Franklin Delano Roosevelt the same credit for becoming an educated man with the help of Groton and Harvard, although the same behavioral processes may have been involved. The founding of Groton and Harvard somewhat reduced the possibility that fortuitous combinations of circumstances would erupt to produce other Lincolns. Yet the founders can hardly be condemned for attacking an admirable human quality.

Another predicted consequence of a science of man is an excessive uniformity. We are told that effective control —whether governmental, religious, educational, economic or social—will produce a race of men who differ from each other only through relatively refractory genetic differences. That would probably be bad design, but we must admit that we are not now pursuing another course from choice. In a modern school, for example, there is usually a syllabus which specifies what every student is to learn by the end of each year. This would be flagrant regimentation if anyone expected every student to comply. But some will be poor in particular subjects, others will not study, others will not remember what they have been taught, and diversity is assured. Suppose, however, that we someday possess such effective educational techniques that every student will in fact be put in possession of all the behavior specified in a syllabus. At the end of the year, all students will correctly answer all questions on the final examination and "must all have prizes." Should we reject such a system on the grounds that in making all students excellent it has made them all alike? Advocates of the theory of a special faculty might contend that an important advantage of the present system is that the good student learns *in spite* of a system which is so defective that it is currently producing bad students as well. But if really effective techniques are available, we cannot avoid the problem of design simply by preferring the status quo. At what point should education be deliberately inefficient?

Such predictions of the havoc to be wreaked by the application of science to human affairs are usually made with surprising confidence. They not only show a faith in the orderliness of human behavior; they presuppose an established body of knowledge with the help of which it can be positively asserted that the changes which scientists propose to make will have quite specific results—albeit not the results they foresee. But the predictions made by the critics of science must be held to be equally fallible and subject also to empirical test. We may be sure that many steps in the scientific design of cultural patterns will produce unforeseen consequences. But there is only one way to find out. And the test must be made, for if we cannot advance in the design of cultural patterns with absolute certainty, neither can we rest completely confident of the superiority of the status quo. . . .

Far from being a threat to the tradition of Western democracy, the growth of a science of man is a consistent and probably inevitable part of it. In turning to the external conditions which shape and maintain the behavior of men, while questioning the reality of inner qualities and faculties to which human achievements were once attributed, we turn from the ill-defined and remote to the observable and manipulable. Though it is a painful step, it has far-reaching consequences, for it not only sets higher standards of human welfare but shows us how to meet them. A change in a theory of human nature cannot change the facts. The achievements of man in science, art, literature, music and morals will survive any interpretation we place upon them. The uniqueness of the individual is unchallenged in the scientific view. Man, in short, will remain man. (There will be much to admire for those who are so inclined. Possibly the noblest achievement to which man can aspire, even according to present standards, is to accept himself for what he is, as that is revealed to him by the methods which he devised and tested on a part of the world in which he had only a small personal stake.)

If Western democracy does not lose sight of the aims of humanitarian action, it will welcome the almost fabulous support of its own science of man and will strengthen itself and play an important role in building a better world for everyone. But if it cannot put its "democratic philosophy" into proper historical perspective—if, under the control of attitudes and emotions which it generated for other purposes, it now rejects the help of science—then it must be prepared for defeat. For if we continue to insist that science has nothing to offer but a new and more horrible form of tyranny, we may produce just such a result by allowing the strength of science to fall into the hands of despots. And if, with luck, it were to fall instead to men of good will in other political communities, it would be perhaps a more ignominious defeat; for we should then, through a miscarriage of democratic principles, be forced to leave to others the next step in man's long struggle to control nature and himself.

Morton White

1917-

A native son of New York City, Morton White received a B.S. from the City College of New York in 1936 and his M.A. and Ph.D. in philosophy from Columbia University in 1938 and 1942, respectively. After teaching at Columbia and the University of Pennsylvania, he went to Harvard in 1948 as a professor of philosophy.

The author of a number of philosophical studies and inquiries, including The Origins of Dewey's Instrumentalism (*1943*) *and* Toward Reunion in Philosophy (*1956*), *White has been concerned with preserving the values associated with the pragmatic democratic liberalism of twentieth-century America. In 1949, as a matter of fact, he published* Social Thought in America, *a critical though highly sympathetic analysis of five important intellectual figures (John Dewey, Oliver Wendell Holmes, Jr., Thorstein Veblen, Charles A. Beard, James Harvey Robinson) who had contributed much to the liberal philosophy. Admitting that at mid-century the views of these men were coming more and more under attack by the adherents of the right as well as by numerous theologians, White insisted nevertheless that these early twentieth-century liberals had provided a sound foundation on which to erect a social and political ideology. White has been sharply critical of detractors of liberalism, particularly Reinhold Niebuhr and Walter Lippmann—the former for emphasizing the doctrine of original sin and the latter for going back to the Aristotelian-Thomistic version of natural law.*

The following selection is from an abridged version to the "Epilogue for 1957" of Social Thought in America (*Boston: Beacon Press, 1957*), *which appeared under the title "Original Sin, Natural Law, and Politics" in* Partisan Review, 23 (*Spring, 1956*).

I will consider the views of two distinguished critics of the liberal tradition: Reinhold Niebuhr, the most democratic and courageous opponent of secular liberalism on the American scene, and Walter Lippmann, who has bemoaned the disappearance of "The Public Philosophy" in a vein distinctly antithetical to the outlook of Dewey and Holmes. In criticizing Lippmann and Niebuhr I mean to align myself spiritually with Dewey and Holmes, even though I am not always prepared to defend the actual letter of their texts. I

497

do not share Niebuhr's faith, not do I admire his Hegelian way of dealing with contradictions: I cannot accept the historical inevitability of sin which is such an important part of his view; I deplore Lippmann's revival of the ancient and obscure theory of essences and natural law. And, in general, it seems to me a sad commentary on the thought of 1956 that two of our most popular social thinkers can produce nothing more original or natural than original sin and natural law as answers to the pressing problems of this age.

Niebuhr, Dewey and Human Nature. It has been maintained that Niebuhr's reflections on human nature have provided a new generation of liberals with insights that transcend the limitations of Dewey. On the one hand Dewey is pictured as a disciple of the Enlightenment, confident of the intrinsic goodness of human nature, one of the latter-day *illuminati* who see man everywhere in the chains of ignorance and who hold that scientific knowledge will usher in a millennial era of social happiness through democratic planning. On the other hand Niebuhr is seen as a shrewd Pauline, aware of man's selfishness, and his inevitable incapacity to free himself from the effects of original sin through his own unassisted efforts. Supplied with this more accurate picture of human nature, Niebuhr is supposed to see the folly of placing too much trust in any central group of social planners, while Dewey, it is argued, was ineffectually innocent, a child of light in Niebuhr's biblical phrase, but unable to illuminate this wicked world of gas chambers and mushroom clouds. Niebuhr becomes the symbol of tough, Christian realism, while Dewey represents soft-headed, complacent, dreamy secular liberalism.

What we must consider, then, is the relation between Dewey's and Niebuhr's views of human nature, the grounds offered for them, and their political consequences.

Dewey is presumably a child of light, but what is a child of light in Niebuhr's view? He is defined by contrast to children of darkness "who know no law beyond their will and interest." By contrast "those who believe that self-interest *should* be brought under the discipline of a higher law could then be termed 'the children of light' "; the children of light "may thus be defined as those who *seek* to bring self-interest under the discipline of a more universal law and in harmony with a more universal good." [My italics.]

Surely there is nothing wrong with being a child of light, then. To believe that one should bring self-interest under a more universal law and in harmony with a more universal good, is to act morally; and surely the effort to act morally is not being attacked by Niebuhr. One can hardly believe that he opposes the effort to bring self-interest under law, in spite of his grotesquely false statement that "nothing that is worth doing can be achieved in our lifetime." Therefore one seeks for a more plausible explanation of what he means.

As we push on we see that Niebuhr may escape absurdity, but only at the expense of making it silly to say that Dewey is a child of light and at the risk of making the whole distinction between the two kinds of children useless. In the last analysis Niebuhr may mean by a child of light either (a) one who thinks that it is *easy* to bring self-interest under law, or (b) one who thinks that we can bring self-interest *completely* under a higher law, that we will reach a time when men will *always* act so as to give only limited weight to their own desires. But on either view of a child of light, it is preposterous to suppose that Dewey is a child of light and doubtful to suppose that the contrast between children of light and children of darkness can illuminate the ideological struggles of our time. It is almost ridiculous for Niebuhr to present his own version of the Christian view as the only one to navigate between idiotic optimism and equally idiotic pessimism, as if all rationalists and naturalists said that men were gods, while their extreme opponents maintained that they were devils, and only Niebuhr knew the middle way.

To get back to Dewey and his position in Niebuhr's scheme. Dewey has never supposed that the way to social happiness would be *easy*, nor has he ever said that a time would come when *all* human action would be morally right and all tensions resolved. . . .

It must be said in Niebuhr's behalf that there is an awful lot in Dewey's writing which suggests that the way to a better society *is* easy. For it is true that Dewey in his later writings tended to identify the intelligent solution of a social problem as one that dispenses with the use of force, and therefore seemed to imply that it was never desirable to apply force. If Niebuhr criticizes Dewey on this count, I can understand Niebuhr, but I reject another aspect of Niebuhr's attack on Dewey's attitude toward intelligence. Once we distinguish between the relatively specific conclusion that all political problems can be solved without the appeal to force, and the more general philosophical thesis that no conclusion about the ways of achieving certain ends should be arrived at except by the use of intelligence or scientific method, we see a far more profound issue between Dewey and Niebuhr. In other words, if one identifies the use of intelligence with the use of absolutely peaceful methods, one is accepting a dubious thesis within political technology itself, but if one identifies the use of intelligence with the use of what is commonly called scientific method in the evaluation of judgments of political technology, one can only ask: What

other ways are there? One must remember, of course, that we are thinking of political technology as the discipline in which we ask about the best ways of achieving certain social and political ends, and that the answers to such questions take the form of statements to the effect that a certain kind of action is most likely to achieve a certain kind of result.

Human Nature and Politics. So far, I see no reason to think of Niebuhr as having demolished or replaced Dewey as a social or political philosopher. But we have not yet dealt with what is thought to be Niebuhr's chief distinction: his deeply "realistic" vision of man's state by comparison with Dewey's supposedly idle dreams. What can we say about this contrast after our earlier conclusions about Dewey's relations to the children of light?

Here it seems necessary to say, as one must so frequently say when one is bound by neither formula nor prejudice, that the differences which Niebuhr magnifies so dramatically and misleadingly are differences in degree of emphasis on the part of thinkers who see that man is not perfect. Some think that the resolution of social tension is extremely difficult and some are more optimistic; in short, there are disputes as to how heavenly earth can be. But can this bare, unqualified, banal dichotomy, if it is the real dichotomy between the children of light and the children of darkness, help us divide the intellectual or political globe in an interesting way? All we have here is the recognition that men are somewhere between the serpent and the dove, and while Niebuhr puts us closer to the serpent, Dewey puts us closer to the dove. But the serious question for political action is "How close?" in either case. Niebuhr's more recent reflections lead him to answer: "Too close to the serpent to allow for successful central planning," and for this reason some of our younger liberals who reject socialism in favor of Keynesianism now think of Niebuhr as one of the deepest political thinkers in America: for example, Arthur Schlesinger, Jr.

It should be remembered, however, that Niebuhr has not always held his present political position. He defended socialism in his earlier work, when he held the same Pauline and Augustinian doctrine of man. What has happened since then is that Niebuhr's skepticism about man's power to help himself has deepened; Niebuhr has learned things about man and society which were not previously encapsulated in the view of man he inherited from Augustine and Paul. That view is consistent with a variety of political positions, and it's absurd to suppose that Niebuhr only recently began to wake up to "implications" that he should have seen in his salad days. Niebuhr saw Stalin, Hitler, Mussolini, and Franco in operation, and this, more than any theological speculation about man, must have brought home to him the dangers of limiting political freedom. In this respect he is like Dewey and all human beings who learn by experience. It is therefore absurd to say that while Niebuhr has a theory which permits him to see that man is not perfect, Dewey is tied to a philosophy preventing him from seeing the same obvious fact. The difference between Niebuhr and Dewey must be put in more concrete terms and once we put it in this way we shall be leaving relatively empty "theories of human nature" for the solid ground of politics.

The contemporary liberal's fascination with Niebuhr, I suggest, comes less from Niebuhr's dark theory of human nature and more from his actual political pronouncements, from the fact that he is a shrewd, courageous, and right-minded man on many political questions. Those who applaud his politics are too liable to turn then to his theory of human nature and praise it as the philosophical instrument of Niebuhr's

political agreement with themselves. But very few of those whom I have elsewhere called "atheists for Niebuhr," follow this inverted logic to its conclusion: they don't move from praise of Niebuhr's theory of human nature to praise of its theological ground. We may admire them for drawing the line somewhere, but certainly not for their consistency.

Historical Inevitability and Original Sin. Precisely because of the emergence of Niebuhr as an influence on so many distinguished liberals of the present generation, there is a greater need for some of Dewey's methodological exhortations. Dewey is committed to the use of empirical methods in discovering what man is or is not likely to achieve, while Niebuhr is, in the last analysis, a devotee of the a priori road that begins with a theology based on faith. Furthermore, Niebuhr is committed to a view of history which in its own way is as rigid as any promulgated by Marx or the more dogmatic theorists of the Enlightenment. Niebuhr constantly speaks of "the perennial and persistent character of human egotism in any possible society," "the vast forces of historical destiny," "inexorable historical developments," and of social conflict as an "inevitability in human history," in a way that leaves him open to all the arguments so powerfully deployed by Isaiah Berlin in his essay, *Historical Inevitability.*

It is true that Niebuhr often shows a fondness for citing historical evidence in support of his conclusions; he says, for example, that the doctrine of original sin "emphasizes a fact which every page of human history attests." But such evidence as he does offer is surely not enough to establish the thunderous statement that man *cannot* conquer his selfish interests to the point of establishing a planned society. His dark view of man's estate is, in his own mind, a corollary of his doctrine of original sin and that is a view of man which, as he says in his *Nature and Destiny of Man*, transcends the canons of rationality. If history should fail to support his view, or if it should at any moment appear to go against it, Niebuhr's attitude toward his own doctrine would not be seriously affected, since his own conviction rests on faith. In this respect it resembles all of the interpretations of history, like Augustine's and Hegel's, which are demolished in Berlin's essay. But the matter should stand differently with those of Niebuhr's admirers who have not yet been persuaded of the theology underlying Niebuhr's reflections on history. How can those who are sober historians and who reject the pretensions of inevitability and necessity that they find in Toynbee or Marx, react to the block historical universe that Niebuhr portrays when he speaks of inexorable historical developments, vast forces of historical destiny, and inevitability in human history?

From Kierkegaard to Hegel. I have said little about the details of Niebuhr's theology, except to point out that it rests on faith and that it implies the inevitability of sinfulness in history. And although there is hardly space for dealing with the labyrinth of Niebuhr's theology, it is desirable to say something, however brief, about the inevitability of sin in Niebuhr's view, if only to remind some of his more agnostic admirers once again of what he says in his more theological writings. It is to Niebuhr's credit that he recognizes that "the Christian doctrine of sin in its classical form offends both rationalists and moralists by maintaining the seemingly absurd position that man sins inevitably and by a fateful necessity, but that he is nevertheless to be held responsible for actions which are prompted by an ineluctable fate." . . .

Niebuhr says that none of this is to be taken "literalistically," though one should suppose that it is to be taken literally. He criticizes literalistic distortions of Christian doctrine, such as the view that we inherit corruption. This is connected with Niebuhr's belief that we are not doomed to sin by *natural* causes, with the opposition to the Pelagian notion that original sin is a force of inertia in nature, and with his constant rejection of the view that man's *finitude* is solely responsible for his sinning. All of this Niebuhr expresses by saying that "evil in man is a consequence of his *inevitable though not necessary* unwillingness to acknowledge his dependence, to accept his finiteness and to admit his insecurity," and so it is important to say a few words on this contrast between the necessary and the inevitable, especially in the light of what was said earlier about Niebuhr's views on history.

The problem of necessity is one of the most difficult philosophical problems, and therefore one can never be sure of understanding even what the most clear-headed philosophers say on this subject. But there is a usage according to which what happens necessarily happens inevitably. Thus Webster, when he explains the meaning of "inevitable," quotes Burke as saying: "It was inevitable; it was necessary; it was planted in the nature of things." That is to say, we sometimes take "inevitable" and "necessary" as interchangeable, even if as philosophers we are not altogether sure of what they mean. What, then, does Niebuhr want to bring out by distinguishing them? So far as I can see, that we do not sin necessarily in the sense of being determined by what he calls *natural* or physical causes, because we transcend nature. But Niebuhr says that we cannot avoid sinning. His point is that we are driven to sin, not by physical events, but by other things which are equally beyond our control. Niebuhr is therefore free to demarcate a certain kind of unavoidable act, namely that which is caused physically, and call it a *necessary* one, which he calls another kind of unavoidable act—the kind produced by our finitude, freedom, and lack of faith—*inevitable*. The important point is, however, that he believes (a) that we commit certain evil acts which are unavoidable, and (b) that we are morally responsible for them, that is, subject to blame for them.

Now there have been philosophers who have tried to make the inevitability of an act consistent with praising or blaming it. And there are others, like Mr. Berlin in the essay I have cited, who think that inevitability and blame are incompatible. But Niebuhr is a very different kind of thinker. He agrees that there is a contradiction between them but, in his Hegelian and Whitmanesque way, accepts it. The doctrine of original sin, he says, "remains absurd from the standpoint of a pure rationalism, for it expresses a relation between fate and freedom which cannot be fully rationalized, unless the paradox be accepted as a rational understanding of the limits of rationality and as an expression of faith that a rationally irresolvable contradiction may point to a truth which logic cannot contain. Formally there can be, of course, no conflict between logic and truth. The laws of logic are reason's guard against chaos in the realm of truth. They eliminate contradictory assertions. But there is no resource in logical rules to help us understand complex phenomena, exhibiting characteristics which seem to require that they be placed into contradictory categories of reason." Some readers may appreciate what Niebuhr means when he adds that "loyalty to all the facts may require a provisional defiance of logic, lest complexity in the facts of experience be denied for the sake of a premature logical consistency," but how long does he want us to wait? With such a modest remark Niebuhr may disarm some of the most logically hardened of his readers, but he can't help making

them wince when he calls on Hegel's dialectic in his defense: "Hegel's 'dialectic' is a logic invented for the purpose of doing justice to the fact of 'becoming' as a phenomenon which belongs into [*sic*] the category of neither 'being' nor 'non-being.' The Christian doctrine of original sin, with its seemingly contradictory assertions about the inevitability of sin and man's responsibility for sin, is a dialectical truth which does justice to the fact that man's self-love and self-centredness is inevitable. . . ." How easy it is for the extremes to meet and what an irony of history it is that a follower of Kierkegaard—the great enemy of Hegel—should have to appeal to Hegel to save himself at the most vital point in his argument.

Enter Lippmann and Locke. In turning from the thought of Niebuhr to the recent writing of Walter Lippmann we find a similar preoccupation with human deficiency, selfishness, and ineptitude, only this time the fault is said to lie not in power-mad leaders who plan us into totalitarianism but rather with the people, the masses who have secured so much power over government and turned statesmen into lackeys. In one respect, therefore, Lippmann and Niebuhr appear at opposite poles of the social thinking that has gained prominence since the work of Dewey and Holmes went into eclipse. Lippmann fears the masses and Niebuhr fears the leaders, so that while Niebuhr has replaced Dewey as the hero of some liberals who have abandoned socialism, Lippmann has come to replace Justice Holmes as the hero of the more conservative young men. The Augustinian doctrine of original sin in Niebuhr is neatly matched by the Thomistic concept of natural law in Lippmann.

The doctrine of natural law is one of the oldest and most debated doctrines in the history of moral and political philosophy. It is the central theory of the Catholic Church on moral and political matters; it was adopted by John Locke; it influenced the language and thought of the Declaration of Independence; it was rejected by Dewey, Holmes, and Veblen; it has recently been revived by many thinkers who, like Lippmann, cannot bear the absence of a set of moral principles which are universally binding, certain, rationally established by the inspection of universals, essences, or meanings, depending on which outmoded epistemology or ethics is adopted. . . .

Mr. Lippmann is eager to revive the notion of self-evident natural law and to put it in the hands of wise statesmen who will not be so tied to the demands of the people. Presumably with the approval of Mr. Mortimer J. Adler, who is thanked in the preface of *The Public Philosophy* and who has expressed similar views in a less winning way, Mr. Lippmann chastises positivist professors who have subverted natural law through a refusal to recognize that there is a realm of essences in addition to a realm of existence. It is ironical, therefore, that positivists like Rudolf Carnap have in recent times been the most active defenders of the notion of analyticity (the sister notion of self-evidence, as we have seen) as well as supporters of the view that meanings and universals exist. Positivists, of course, have used the notions of analyticity and meaning quite differently. They are mainly interested in showing that mathematical propositions are analytic, that is to say, true by virtue of the meanings of their component terms, and they vehemently (and laudably) deny that the principles of morality may be so viewed. But it is certainly wrong to say, as Lippmann does, that all of them deny the existence of the universals or meanings which are so essential for the philosopher of natural law.

In opposition to Lippmann, Locke, Aquinas, and the positivists, to say nothing of a vast number of the other philosophers like Bertrand Russell and G. E. Moore in some of their writings, I think that the notion of an analytic statement, the notion of a self-evident statement as conceived by Aquinas and Locke, and the meanings so dear to all of them and Lippmann, are first of all obscure in themselves and secondly incapable of sustaining the philosophical load which has been put upon them. I shall concentrate on the significance of this contention for the doctrine of natural law, though I can at best outline only part of my view here.

Very few philosophers have taken the existence of meanings, conceived as universals, for granted. The usual pattern of philosophical argument is to assume that the reader believes in the existence of physical objects—the tables and chairs of epistemology books—but that he is too dull to see that universals like the attribute of being a table also exist. And so it is frequently pointed out that we couldn't understand the general word "chair" unless it had a meaning quite distinct from every individual chair in the universe. In this way the existence of meanings construed as properties of things is supposedly proven. But then a new move must be made, for the ordinary man has a rather limited conception of existence; in other words he uses the word "exists" narrowly, as applying only to physical objects which exist in space and time, and this won't do.

Having begun with a tolerance and a garden-variety understanding of the word "exist," the ordinary man has now been led to the point where he must see that there are at least two meanings of "exist" and that this is the solution to the problem of understanding. But can any one suppose that this postulation of Platonic meanings really illuminates the notion of understanding? We think immediately, and rightly so, of dormitive virtues "explaining" why opium puts people to sleep.

The situation is even worse when we examine Lippmann's introduction of essences. The Platonic theorist of understanding has the comparatively easy job of showing how understanding is *possible*, whereas Lippmann must show that a belief in self-evident principles of natural law is *necessary*. In other words the philosopher who offers the theory of understanding outlined above can at least assume that the man he is trying to persuade understands *some* words, and after having found out what those words are, the philosopher may begin to crank his machines and grind out his universals in order to "explain" how the understanding the man has is possible. But a theorist of natural law will frequently have to face people who don't believe that there are self-evident moral principles to begin with. How can he get the machinery rolling then? Where can he begin? What premises can the theorist of natural law start with? Surely it is not self-evident that *there are* self-evident principles of natural law and therefore we must be shown that there are.

It may be said in reply that the theorist of natural law *can* deal with the man who has not quite made up his mind, the man who is at most doubtful about whether there are self-evident principles of morality. But this is *par excellence* a situation in which the philosopher of natural law appeals to things which are at least dubious and at least as obscure as that which is to be defended or explained. Does Lippmann suppose that he is likely to persuade such a doubtful man that there are essences which if properly unpacked make the truth of moral principles evident? Even if he were to accomplish the first bit of required persuasion—that is to say, even if the public should be persuaded of the existence of essences—Lippmann will fail to show them that the principles

of political morality are self-evident statements about men in which, as Aquinas says, "the predicate is contained in the notion of the subject," or logically deducible therefrom. . . .

We all have deep moral convictions: we firmly believe certain moral principles which we try to act on to the best of our ability. They make up, along with others, the foundations of our whole structure of belief; they constitute our terminal beliefs. We want them to be consistent with each other and to fit in harmoniously and simply with other, less confidently held beliefs; we want this structure to mesh with experience and feeling. But individuals and societies have surrendered many beliefs which they once accepted as terminal, and some of these beliefs are moral beliefs. What, then, is the purpose of inventing a mysterious realm of essence *of which* our terminal beliefs are supposed to be true? Wouldn't it be saner to recognize that we all have our ultimate convictions at any moment, that they are not absolutely immune to change (though we can resolve, at our own peril, to make them permanently immune), that some people adopt the same beliefs as terminal and others don't? Who are the people we get along with? Very often the people with whom we have a great deal of agreement on these fundamental beliefs. Who are the people we quarrel with? Very often those with whom we don't share these beliefs. The point is that we and those whose lines end up at the same terminal shouldn't need the kind of mutual encouragement that comes from inventing a realm of essences beneath (or above) the terminal: and those who go in different directions are the last people in the world who are likely to use essences in the same way even if they agreed that such things existed.

CHAPTER XXIV

RADICALISM IN
THE SIXTIES

America has experienced many voices which were judged to be radical by the generations who heard them. The Populists of the late nineteenth century, the socialists of the twentieth century, and critics like Niebuhr and Mumford are only a few examples. In general, protest movements in America have centered on the theme of social-mindedness and reform of existing institutions. Relatively few movements or individual critics have seriously challenged the basic framework of American society.

In the 1960's, however, a series of events, including the maturing of the civil rights movement and the protest against American involvement in Vietnam, led to the rise of a form of radical protest that seemed to challenge many, if not most, of the values that Americans had held for three centuries. Before discussing this new radicalism, it is important to emphasize the fact that its adherents remained in the minority. Though aware of the presence of such unfamiliar forms of criticism and often deeply affected by its manifestations, Americans on the whole continued to embrace the reinstated liberalism discussed in the preceding chapter. Many spokesmen for that liberalism—Arthur Schlesinger is but one illustration—though recognizing the defects of American society, nevertheless rejected the radical critique.

Though radicals remained in the minority, few Americans could avoid confronting the conditions and experiences that had embittered many of America's younger idealists. An unpopular war drained the nation and divided its people. Civil rights crusades and movements among black people sought to achieve self-identity and full citizenship for all minority groups. Poverty, so to speak, was discovered—a cruel paradox in the midst of plenty, but partly a product of developing affluence itself. The urban ghetto became the focal point of protest, since it was the center of so many social ills. America's youth became progressively separated from the preceding generation, leading to the formation of such fringe groups as the hippies and Students for a Democratic Society. But, whatever their particular political views, Americans rather broadly felt the threat (if not the actuality) of alienation, of violence, of the equation of liberalism—in a few quarters now a dirty word—with the Establishment, and insensitivity with social evil.

Three writers have been selected to express the meaning of the movement. Supporter and organizer of the New Left, Michael Harrington urges a radical reorganization of America's institutions by way of a planned economy and participatory democracy. The New Deal, he believes, has become conservative, and American capitalism still reflects an old greed, however new the setting. Social and economic planning is the key to a new civilization. Herbert Marcuse is perhaps more radical, feeling that liberal America with its ideas of freedom and tolerance has actually become a totalitarian organization. Its formal tolerance leads to inactivity and, by the neutralization of opponents, the elimination of protest and change. Through this analysis, Marcuse is led to the conclusion that tolerance must be withdrawn from regressive and repressive opinions and movements. The third author, Nathan Glazer, expresses a series of concerns about the New Left shared by many Americans as the sixties drew to a close. Protest movements, he believes, did have some successes, particularly in the areas of civil rights, poverty, and education. But three flaws are apparent in the premises of the New Left: the assumption that social betterment is primarily a matter of power (it involves as much technological questions), the belief that politicizing issues will lead to reform (reform is less, not more, a matter of politics in modern society), and the expectation of more freedom (contemporary problems—population, pollution, and so on—necessitate more regulation).

Some readers may sense a submerged but liberal table of values even in the radical critique, while others may find a disenchantment with traditional America. The 1960's closed, however, with America's liberal institutions largely intact and, for most Americans, still supple enough to serve as a basis of social and political life, however rapidly technological change was affecting the very fabric of human life.

Michael Harrington

1928-

Actively associated with many socialist organizations, Michael Harrington was born in St. Louis Missouri. After graduation from college, he attended Yale Law School and later received a master's degree from the University of Chicago. A brief editorial career was followed by years of work in a variety of labor, youth, and political organizations, both national and international. His books and papers have expressed convictions that have helped formulate the ideology of the New Left in America. Their central themes are a planned economy and participatory democracy.

The selection is from Harrington's book, Toward a Democratic Left (*New York: The Macmillan Company, 1968*).

So the pragmatic, anti-ideological United States of America is in the embarrassing position of having to take some steps toward a new civilization, or else.

Washington has meticulously defined intolerable problems and then officially proposed inadequate solutions to them. The New Deal has, in many ways, become conversative, and business is incapable of resolving a public crisis in which it has a vested interest. Obviously, there is no individual or movement with finished answers to these complex challenges. Yet it is possible to suggest the broad outlines of a hope which, if it is vaguer than blueprint, is much more precise than the rhetoric of the Great Society.

Even in a society based on private economic power, the Government can be an agency of social, rather than corporate, purpose—if a vast popular mobilization forces it to do so. This does not require a fundamental transformation of the system which, unfortunately, the people will probably not want during the next twenty years in any case. It does, however, mean that the society will democratically plan "uneconomic" allocations of significant resources. This should shake up the *status quo* even if it doesn't revolutionize it.

Under such conditions it would be possible to realize full—and meaningful—employment for all those ready and able to work. Going beyond the quantities of the New Deal, the economy could be stimulated by promoting the affluence of the public sector rather than by tax cuts, and in the process millions of creative jobs can be designed to better the nation's education, health, leisure and the like. Within twenty years such a policy of social investments should end all poverty, eradicate the slums and erode the economic and social basis of racism. And those people who are unable to work could be provided with a guaranteed annual income instead of shoddy, uncoordinated and inadequate welfare payments.

Now it is obvious that the accomplishment of these goals requires important structural changes in the system even if they do not demand a totally new society. Yet it is wrong to think that this can be done technocratically, by the very best intentioned of experts. Democracy, it must be emphasized, is a practical necessity and not just a philosophic

507

value. For the people cannot possibly take charge of their own destiny unless there is a political revolution in knowledge and government is forced to let the governed know what is going on.

It will even be necessary to take America's most cherished conservative myth seriously: that the "grass roots" should be a spontaneous, natural locus of political life. To make this old saw come true will take a radical reorganization of local and regional government in America—and therefore a frontal attack on a bastion of undemocratic, conservative power. . . .

The only way to get resources allocated to satisfy the people's needs is to let the people determine what these needs are.

If the people are thus going to impose their own priorities on the political spending of their money, there must be new institutions. To begin with, there must be a political revolution in knowledge so that society is actually provided with intelligible information about the basic choices before it. . . .

There is, however, one main locus of comprehensive planning: the Bureau of the Budget. All of the various programs must compete with one another for available funds, and there is, therefore, a cost-oriented overview of the Government. The decisions of the Budget Director on the legislative shopping list are, as Andrew Shonfeld put it, the "closest that any member of an American Government gets to the power exercised by the leader of the House of Commons in England."

The Government must certainly be limited by the availability of resources. But if it also looked at the economy from the grand perspective of need—if it kept social, and not just cost, accounts —it could carry out its budgeting function more humanely and probably more efficiently. There is even a place for visionary planning that would look into the far distance and estimate what

should be done in the name of imponderables like justice. Once the $1 trillion GNP is reached in the Seventies and begins to compound, there could well develop a gap between the nation's ability to spend money speedily, effectively and ingeniously and the fiscal drag created by the automatic increase in Federal revenue from taxing higher and higher incomes. It would be too bad if the shape of a new civilization were mainly debated in the Bureau of the Budget. . . .

The following scenario should illustrate the kind of reforms that are needed. The imagined law is not presented as a guidepost for legislative draftsmen, and none of its details is sacred. It simply dramatizes a principle. For I am convinced that if there is a democratic will to action, a way will be found to act. . . .

The President shall be obliged to make to the nation a periodic Report on the Future.

The report shall project the basic choices and different futures before the country and estimate both the economic and the social costs of alternate programs. It shall specify what groups stand to make particular gains from the various possible courses of action.

The report shall state a Social Consumption Criterion which will clearly measure the impact of every department of public expenditure on the social standard of living. In particular, it shall explain exactly how the major areas of spending are contributing toward the abolition of poverty and racial discrimination.

The report shall be presented to a Joint Congressional Committee on the Future, which shall hold public hearings on it. Staff funds will be provided to any significant group of legislators, whether they are on the committee or not, so that they can write a substitute report or propose major amendments to the President's draft.

The House and Senate will then debate, and vote on, the general economic and social orientation of the American Government during the next period. (I am deliberately vague about the time span. Whether it should be geared to a four-year Presidential political cycle or to a period determined by economic considerations hardly need be settled now. The important point is that the report's horizon be set in the middle distance where the historic options begin to take shape.)

The focal point of the Report on the Future is the Office of the President. Yet truly democratic planning obviously cannot be simply centralized in Washington, in the White House or even on Capitol Hill. The decisions to be made are not technical and cannot be determined by the most idealistic expert. They will, among other things, inevitably provoke conflict. Moreover, if there is even a hope that the people will have a meaningful role to play, the democratic Left will have to take the conservative myth of the grass roots much more seriously than conservatives have ever done.

To begin with, then, the Government must encourage difference at least as much as it seeks consensus. . . .

Rather than deploring this fact of conflict, it should be brought out into the full light of day. Concealing it in the name of consensus rhetoric does not end the power struggle but simply drives it underground, which is where the democratic forces are at a disadvantage and money talks so persuasively. That is why the scenario of the Report on the Future contains positive encouragement for minority statement of opinion. And even more to the point, the Government must subsidize dissent at every level of American life.

At this point, then, one of the most dialectical aspects of a modern society comes to the fore: that it will take resolute Federal action in order to make it possible for the grass roots to grow.

According to the national romance, Washington is a distant, inhuman and bureaucratic place which has somehow usurped the rights of the folks in the towns and neighborhoods. In point of political fact, the poor, the workers, the Negroes and even significant sections of the middle class have found that the Federal Government is closer to them than City Hall or the State House. And even while rightists argued for decentralization they understood this reality. This explains the irony, noted by Edward C. Banfield and James Q. Wilson in *City Politics*, of conservative insistence on planning in the housing programs of the Fifties. Banfield and Wilson write that the conservatives "thought that local planning commissions, which in most cities had always been closely allied with real estate, and other business interests, would afford some kind of check on the liberals who (as it seemed to the conservatives) dominated the housing and urban renewal programs."

There are many reasons for this undemocratic conservative strength at the so-called grass roots. The energies of the liberal-labor movement have been directed toward Washington, where they have the greatest impact; municipal reliance on property taxes has given the small property owners a passionate interest in city politics; and the incredible fragmentation of local government, with its 80,000 separate units, has created a bewildering network of vested bureaucratic interests. Whatever was the case on the frontier or in the town meeting, the seemingly libertarian demand to return power to the people is often a disguised way of proposing minority rule.

It was precisely this structural conservatism of local and state government that forced the nationalization of so many government functions in Washington. As the business-oriented Committee for Economic Development put the paradox in a 1966 policy report, either there will be "a revolutionary readjustment" at the lower levels of politics or else the Federal power will grow even greater. This would mean, the CED said, an 80 percent reduction in the number of local governing bodies and a consolidation of jumbled sovereignties into metropolitan and county units large enough to provide a functional economic basis for their tasks. This rather radical perception on the part of sophisticated executives is clearly relevant to the central problem of this chapter: how to get democratic participation in national economic planning.

Indeed, one of the CED proposals is an excellent point of departure for structuring dissent and debate into the nation's political life. There should be, the CED report said, neighborhood units of about 50,000 people throughout the society. These would be excellent places to focus the political revolution in knowledge. In New York City in the fall of 1967 the report of a commission on school decentralization headed by McGeorge Bundy provoked vigorous controversy on all sides. But, with the exception of the central education bureaucracy itself, every party in the dispute—Bundy, parents organizations, civil-rights groups and the teachers' union—recognized that local control would be possible only if the people involved could ask their own questions, make their own studies and check their own statistics. Earlier, in 1966, Albert Shanker, president of the United Federation of Teachers, was one of the first to argue that a community school board would have to have its own, independent research funds in order to interpret, and even controvert, the facts as represented by the Board of Education.

This idea should be generalized. No group in a modern society can play a serious political role unless it has access to expert information. In France, for instance, trade-unionists told me that they often did not even take the seats assigned to them on various planning commissions because they did not have the technical competence to deal with the issues (the labor federations in that country are, of course, much less centralized than in America, a fact which doubled this particular disadvantage). And, as a rule in this technological civilization, policies are deduced from data and the data are profoundly influenced by the questions that are asked. Boards of education and national economic planners in Washington want to ask their questions and get their answers. They should have the right to do so. And the grass roots, if they are to be taken seriously and even have the chance to be democratic, should have the same right.

So these creative suggestions from capital and labor should be merged. The Federal Government should provide research funds for neighborhood institutions and functionally organized metropolitan areas. And, so that the consequent agony of officials being forced to pay their critics not become intolerable, this should be done under automatic, objective formulas and not through administrative discretion. In addition a Federal trust should be established—a sort of National Institute of Social and Economic Health parallel to the present Institutes of Health—to grant money to private, voluntary organizations and individuals.

However, Federal action to make neighborhood political life possible is only a first step in making planning democratic. In addition, new, unheard-of governmental units must be created.

Economic and social problems do not conform to the state and municipal lines the nation inherited from the accidents of its history. The Tennessee Valley Authority constituted an isolated, enormously successful recognition of this fact, which now must become a norm rather than an exception. It seemed for a while in 1964 that anti-poverty sentiment would lead to the creation of a second, multistate region called Appalachia. That did happen on paper, but the new structure was primarily devoted to the ancient rite of highway building, which was hardly an exercise in democratic creativity. And while *ad hoc* crises, like the Northeastern drought, periodically force governors to co-operate, nothing really fundamental is changed by the event.

The problems of BosWash, ChiPitts and San San (the nicknames respectively, of the Northeastern, Midwestern and West Coast megalopolises of the next generation) require regional authorities even more than those of the Tennessee Valley did in the Thirties. This is obviously true in functional, economic terms, but it is also relevant to the issue of democracy. For, once again, the problem is to make the decision process as transparent as possible, and this can be done only when political units stand in some reasonable relationship to social reality. . . .

There is a marvelous Federal instrument for persuading all these autonomous political authorities to consent to their own regionalization: money. As part of the Social Consumption Criterion for Government programs described earlier, Washington should insist on the creation of functional units to receive funds. In his tax-sharing proposal for assigning a specified portion of Federal revenue to local government, Walter Heller admitted that the problem was so acute that he had thought of putting strings in the grants to force the establishment of area-wide bodies. But he turned down the idea on the grounds that keeping the whole program flexible was a paramount consideration. I do not think that one should thus so easily surrender so persuasive an argument for convincing

the middle class of its basic responsibility. . . .

But this is not to say that the private sector has no role to play in dealing with these problems. The danger, as it was described in the chapter on the social-industrial complex, is that businessmen would use the criteria of profit to make decisions which are essentially "uneconomic" and a matter for democratic determination. However, as long as the companies simply execute the contracts drawn up through the political process, instead of dictating them, the $1.3 trillion of corporate assets in the United States are obviously quite relevant to what must be done.

Here the basic tactic is not direct Federal spending but indirect, though often not very subtle, Federal persuasion. In Europe it is called "indicative" planning.

There are many ways in which government can motivate industry to act in a given way. A national economic plan is, from a businessman's point of view, a free piece of market research, a sophisticated guide for his investments in the future. As it is now, American executives are extremely sensitive to shifts in the "public market." If they had a really developed perspective—a ten-year projection in a Freedom Budget, an even more speculative description of trends and priorities in a Report on the Future —their self-interest could be directed toward the common good. In this case, unlike that of the social-industrial complex, that self-interest would not determine the common good but be subordinated to it.

One of the most important means of government persuasion is, of course, tax policy. This is true even though it is precisely in this area that so many discreetly anti-social subsidies have been made. Suburban middle-class home building has been encouraged to the detriment of people in the slums; the Kennedy-Johnson cuts reduced the most progressive levy in the land, the Federal income tax, but increased regressive deductions for Social Security; and, as Philip Stern documented in *The Great Treasury Raid*, an incredible series of loopholes has been bored into the law so that there are actually millionaires who pay no tax at all. Indeed, the very concept of taxable income in the United States has been rigged so as to exclude a great deal of the money taken in by the middle class and the rich. The organized workers and the working poor, on the other hand, pay as they go and have no such benefits.

And yet, tax policy could be a powerful weapon for accomplishing justice. As Joseph Pechman described the extraordinary range of policy alternatives it can serve, "The tax structure may encourage consumption or saving, help to raise or lower private investment in general or in particular industries, stimulate or restrain the outflow of investment funds to foreign countries, and subsidize or discourage particular expenditures by individuals and business firms." If this enormous power were utilized to further the democratically determined goals of America's future, it could help to motivate business to make a social contribution.

Indeed, there is probably no better example in all of government of the need for transparency in administration. Tax laws have served so many clandestine reactionary purposes precisely because they have been the work of experts and special pleaders. And a major function of the President's Report on the Future—and, even before such a planning perspective is adopted, of the presidency with its present values— should be to translate the hidden social priorities of the tax system into plain English. All of the subsidies to particular groups in the name of the common good should be clearly labeled so that the laymen can understand them. Congress should mandate the Executive to

do this, but private-sector foundations and universities might seek to make an even more candid statement of the situation.

Eventually, I suspect it would be well to think of an America in which there would be only a progressive income tax and no other. There is an immediate case for financing Social Security out of general revenues in this fashion and doing away with the actuarial fictions which allow that system to redistribute income from the poor to the rich (a married man with four children and $5,000 a year pays a 3.9 percent tax. A $50,000-a-year bachelor pays .5 percent of his income). Moreover, the Federal Government might make various grants contingent on the reduction, or abolition of state sales taxes, which are also reactionary in effect. It must be remembered that, particularly if military spending were to level off, this society is going to have to work hard to spend money in the future. As Walter Heller computes it, there will be a "fiscal drag" (the revenues automatically generated by a fast growing GNP even without an increase in taxes) of $20 billion in 1970, assuming that defense expenditures stay at the 1967 level. Heller makes out an excellent case for returning a portion of this bonanza to the states and cities but, as I noted earlier, is much too rigid about making these grants without any strings.

If there were a basic national economic and social orientation, Federal tax sharing could be a means of creating viable local and regional governments and promoting the social goals of the entire society.

Government purchases are another important Federal lever for moving the corporations to action. In 1964, as Leonard Lecht of the National Planning Association, estimated the figures, Washington bought more than 19 percent of GNP and local governments paid for about 11 percent. With allowances for double counting, the combined governmental expenditure at all levels amounted to 28 percent of GNP. That makes the nation its own biggest customer. And the 1967 Manpower Report computed that no less than 21 million jobs were directly or indirectly dependent on Federal spending, a figure which extended to approximately a third of the non-agricultural work force. . . .

In anticipation of these various skepticisms, the argument of this book in no way rests on philosophic premises about the nature of man. Instead, every accusation made against Washington has been confirmed by Washington. The case for radical innovation in the United States today is, in short, available to the public at the Government Printing Office.

The democratic Left should thus use all of these Government-certified catastrophes to show why a certain humanization of the life of man has become a practical necessity. It should be willing to cajole, and even frighten, the society into minimal decency, and the Federal card file of social tragedies can be a valuable tool of the visionary's trade. But as a movement with the conviction that there is more to people than greed and fear, the Left must also speak in the name of the historic idealism of the United States.

For America, even this actual America without a democratic Left, is also the most radical country in the world.

As the Sixties come to an end, this seems a preposterous statement. This country appears to have degenerated into a war of each against all, of black against white, lower class against lowest class, suburbanites against metropolis, and the whole relatively fat, smug, complacent nation against the millions of Asia, Africa and Latin America. There are violence and racism everywhere, and perhaps never before has there been less of a mood of social solidarity.

And yet these reactionary hatreds are vicious expressions of that very impulse which, in other circumstances, makes America so radical. There have never been fixed hierarchies in this country, and a man therefore had to assert his worth and establish his identity for himself. When there was hope, people joined together for militant action which proclaimed their dignity. This was the way of the original revolutionists, of the Abolitionists, the Populists, the trade-unionists, the civil-rights activists and all the others who constitute the living tradition of the American Left. But when fear predominates, as today, this very same independence of spirit drives a man to defend his own equality by attacking his neighbor's. American fraternity and fratricide both derive from the national conviction that a man must stand up on his own two feet.

So it was that workers poured into the unions authorized by the National Recovery Act in 1933—and poured right out of them. It was a time of layoffs, and once the new unionists saw that the law did not really protect them from management retaliation, it was every man for himself. But in 1935 and after there were hirings rather than firings and a national sense that something could be done. There was renewed hope, and the very same workers moved with courage and audacity and permanently altered the social relationships of the society.

In some ways it is precisely this fierce knowledge of the individual's own value that has kept the American labor movement from class consciousness on a European model. The worker on the automobile assembly line has always known that Henry Ford is more privileged than he is and not because of any personal accomplishment. Yet he has also felt that he is just as good as Henry Ford. It was this pride, rather than passivity, that kept him from adopting a philosophy based on the inherent differences between classes. And the left-wing character of the American social experience has been one of the greatest obstacles to the emergence of a consciously left-wing political movement.

I say this sociologically but I have also seen it with my own eyes. The American worker, even when he waits on table or holds open a door, is not servile; he does not carry himself like an inferior. That openness, frankness and democratic manner which Tocqueville described in the last century persists to this very day. They have been a source of rudeness, contemptuous ignorance, anti-intellectualism, violence—and of a creative self-confidence among great masses of people. It was in this latter spirit that the CIO was organized and the black freedom movement marched.

So the American character is complex and dialectical, and it would be a mistake to generalize from only the present demoralization. Moreover, it is the larger social context that determines which aspect of the national personality will come to the fore. A brief sketch of some recent history should make this point clearer.

Somewhere in the 1950s—the Montgomery bus boycott of 1955 is probably the best date—the United States began to recover from McCarthyism. In the 1958 elections there was a liberal sweep, and the 1960 sit-ins helped create a dynamic movement in the South. With John F. Kennedy's victory there was a new sense of optimism even though the Dixiecrat-Republican coalition thwarted most progressive legislation. Kennedy's death hallowed many of his proposals, and the first, neo-New Dealish days of the Johnson Administration saw more Congressional action than at any time in a generation.

Throughout this period the ugly American emotions were still very much

alive, yet the country was too hopeful for them to dominate. In the vocabulary of the 1964 elections, "front-lash" solidarity prevailed over "back-lash" prejudice. But in 1965 the war in Vietnam took over American politics, and by 1966 Lyndon Johnson had run out of the New Deal, Fair Deal and New Frontier. The reactionaries seized on both these opportunities, and the mood of the nation was transformed. There then appeared what Bayard Rustin has called the "politics of fear and frustration." As the possibilities for significant change declined, Negroes, whose hopes had been raised on high, desperately and unsuccessfully demanded their just due. This frightened whites, who became more repressive, and new gains were thereby made even more difficult and the Negroes even more frustrated. By the summer of 1967 each side was arming.

There is one consolation in this sorry narrative. Today pessimism reinforces pessimism, but tomorrow, were the nation to move but one inch toward the democratic Left, hope would corroborate hope, and the best in the American character would once again be liberated. Something like that happened during the tragically brief Presidency of John Kennedy. The 1960 margin of victory was barely perceptible, yet it tipped an historic balance. The country somehow did understand that it was necessary to get moving again. And even after the defeats and retreats of the recent years, that popular idealism which Kennedy touched is still among us. When the moment comes, it could take the nation beyond the New Deal.

So the democratic Left does not simply deduce the practical necessity of change from the official figures. It also has, in Silone's phrase, a sense of the seed beneath the snow, of the radicalism of the American experience.

Being economical is a luxury America and the world can no longer afford.

Keynes, as brilliant an economist as he was, looked forward to the relative obsolescence of his own discipline. He believed that "the day is not far off when the Economic Problem will take the back seat where it belongs, and that the arena of the heart and head will be occupied, or reoccupied, by our real problems—the problems of life and human relations, of creation and behaviour and religion." But what Keynes did not realize was that, within a generation, America would have no alternative but to take advantage of these utopian opportunities. The old traditions—the calculus of loss and gain, the cult of efficiency, the assumption that the most profitable use of a resource is the best use—are not only unnecessary. They are profoundly anti-social as well.

According to these economic criteria, it is utterly rational for the world market to redistribute wealth from the poor to the rich and for aid and trade policies to facilitate this abomination. In the global system of injustice created by the nineteenth-century West, it is logical that the Third World perform the most brutal tasks for the least possible remuneration. It also follows quite rigorously that the most costly items in this whole process are not even entered in the ledger: violence, instability and the constant threat of World War III.

Within the United States, whatever the social industrialists may think, justice is not a sound business investment. The poor *are* a bad financial risk, and so are the Negroes, central cities, beauty, civility, clean air and all the rest. The new society—that second America which the Government tells us must be built within little more than three decades—cannot be designed according to the commercial priorities which brought the first America to crisis.

So there must be many more planned, social investments, both nationally and internationally.

The scandalous and dangerous gap between the rich and poor nations can be closed only if the advanced economies contract, on a regular and progressive basis, to supply billions of dollars for world economic planning and to restructure the world market in favor of the developing lands. And here at home the physical and spiritual torment of the other America and the fear and discontent of the well-off require democratic investments and imagination.

There are, however, powerful institutional forces in the United States that do not want such changes. The men who articulate them are doubtlessly sincere and honest and even genuinely moved by starving Asians or rat-bitten children in a Northern ghetto. It is not that they are personally evil but that they are the agents of the old, and disastrous, economics. To them oil profits are more important than the domestic Peace Corps of Peru; a good price for fertilizer takes precedence over food shipments to India; and a real-estate windfall weighs more in the balance than the fate of black America.

There is no consensus possible with such men as long as they hold to their institutional values. The Left must therefore attack their power democratically and non-violently and thereby widen the areas in which people organizing themselves politically are stronger than money. For when a free society avoids conflict, that is not an act of civic prudence but a surrender to the manipulative elites which work behind the façade of unanimity.

All this, one will be told, is un-American. For a long time all kinds of people—from the conscious friends of injustice defending their privileges to the sincere academics—have said that the Left is either a foreign conspiracy or a mawkish day-dream or perhaps both. Sometimes they were aided in their work by Leftists who allowed their libertarian ideals to be identified with totalitarian movements. But now the old caricatures of the Left are even more unreal than ever before.

For America has indicted America. We have meticulously documented the fact that by acting in the old ways we shall increasingly betray our ideals. To redeem our own promises to ourselves, Americans must move toward the democratic Left.

Herbert Marcuse
1898-

Another of the few foreign-born authors represented in this volume, Herbert Marcuse in his writings has stirred youth not only in America but throughout the world. Born in Berlin, he studied at the universities of Berlin and Freiburg. He had earned a reputation as a scholar on Hegelian and post-Hegelian thought before immigrating to the United States in 1934. After serving with the State Department from 1941 to 1950, he held a number of academic appointments in American universities and wrote many distinguished books on social philosophy. Though varied in focus, they all point toward the need of a truly nonrepressive society as the essential instrument for liberating human energies. His attention to the problem of tolerance in the following selection continues this emphasis by concentration on a theme associated with liberalism since the days of the Enlightenment. Marcuse's major observation is that "liberal" tolerance has become an instrument whereby the Establishment silences opposition and thus retains its repressive power. In the crises of present-day America, such tolerance must be rejected.

The selections are Marcuse's "Repressive Tolerance" and "Postscript 1968" from Wolff, Moore, and Marcuse, A Critique of Pure Tolerance *(new ed., Boston: Beacon Press, 1969).*

*T*his essay examines the idea of tolerance in our advanced industrial society. The conclusion reached is that the realization of the objective of tolerance would call for intolerance toward prevailing policies, attitudes, opinions, and the extension of tolerance to policies, attitudes, and opinions which are outlawed or suppressed. In other words, today tolerance appears again as what it was in its origins, at the beginning of the modern period—a partisan goal, a subversive liberating notion and practice. Conversely, what is proclaimed and practiced as tolerance today, is in many of its most effective manifestations serving the cause of oppression.

The author is fully aware that, at present, no power, no authority, no government exists which would translate liberating tolerance into practice, but he believes that it is the task and duty of the intellectual to recall and preserve historical possibilities which seem to have become utopian possibilities—that it is his task to break the concreteness of oppression in order to open the mental space in which this society can be recognized as what it is and does.

Tolerance is an end in itself. The elimination of violence, and the reduction of suppression to the extent required for protecting man and animals from cruelty and aggression are preconditions for the creation of a humane society. Such a society does not yet exist; progress toward it is perhaps more than before arrested by violence and suppression on a global scale. As deterrents against nuclear war, as police action against subversion, as technical aid in the fight against imperialism and communism, as methods of pacification in neo-colonial massacres, violence and suppression are promulgated, practiced, and defended by democratic and authoritarian governments alike, and the people subjected to these governments are educated to sustain such practices as necessary for the preservation of the status quo. Tolerance is extended to policies, conditions, and modes of behavior which should not be tolerated because they are impeding, if not destroying, the chances of creating an existence without fear and misery.

This sort of tolerance strengthens the tyranny of the majority against which authentic liberals protested. The political locus of tolerance has changed: while it is more or less quietly and constitutionally withdrawn from the opposition, it is made compulsory behavior with respect to established policies. Tolerance is turned from an active into a passive state, from practice to nonpractice: laissez-faire the constituted authorities. It is the people who tolerate the government, which in turn tolerates opposition within the framework determined by the constituted authorities.

Tolerance toward that which is radically evil now appears as good because it serves the cohesion of the whole on the road to affluence or more affluence. The toleration of the systematic moronization of children and adults alike by publicity and propaganda, the release of destructiveness in aggressive driving, the recruitment for and training of special forces, the impotent and benevolent tolerance toward outright deception in merchandising, waste, and planned obsolescence are not distortions and aberrations, they are the essence of a system which fosters tolerance as a means for perpetuating the struggle for existence and suppressing the alternatives. The authorities in education, morals, and psychology are vociferous against the increase in juvenile delinquency; they are less vociferous against the proud presentation, in word and deed and pictures, of ever more powerful missiles, rockets, bombs—the mature delinquency of a whole civilization.

According to a dialectical proposition it is the whole which determines the truth—not in the sense that the whole is prior or superior to its parts, but in the sense that its structure and function determine every particular condition and relation. Thus, within a repressive society, even progressive movements threaten to turn into their opposite to the degree to which they accept the rules of the game. To take a most controversial case: the exercise of political rights (such as voting, letter-writing to the press, to Senators, etc., protest-demonstrations with a priori renunciation of counterviolence) in a society of total administration serves to strengthen this administration by testifying to the existence of democratic liberties which, in reality, have changed their content and lost their effectiveness. In such a case, freedom (of opinion, of assembly, of speech) becomes an instrument for absolving servitude. And yet (and only here the dialectical proposition shows its full intent) the existence and practice of these liberties remain a precondition for the restoration of their original oppositional function, provided that the effort to transcend their (often self-imposed) limitations is intensified. Generally, the function and value of tolerance depend on the equality prevalent in the society in which tolerance is practiced. Tolerance itself stands subject to overriding criteria: its range and its limits cannot be defined in terms of the respective society. In other words, tolerance is an end in itself only when it is truly universal, practiced by the rulers as well as by the ruled, by the lords as well as by the peasants, by the sheriffs as well as by their victims. And such universal tolerance is possible only when no real or alleged enemy requires in the national interest the education and training of people in military violence and destruction. As long as these conditions do not prevail, the conditions of tolerance are "loaded": they are determined and defined by the institutionalized inequality (which is certainly compatible with constitutional equality), i.e., by the class structure of society. In such a society, tolerance is *de facto* limited on the dual ground of legalized violence or suppression (police, armed forces, guards of all sorts) and of the privileged position held by the predominant interests and their "connections."

These background limitations of tolerance are normally prior to the explicit and judicial limitations as defined by the courts, custom, governments, etc. (for example, "clear and present danger," threat to national security, heresy). Within the framework of such a social structure, tolerance can be safely practiced and proclaimed. It is of two kinds: (1) the passive toleration of entrenched and established attitudes and ideas even if their damaging effect on man and nature is evident; and (2) the active, official tolerance granted to the Right as well as to the Left, to movements of aggression as well as to movements of peace, to the party of hate as well as to that of humanity. I call this non-partisan tolerance "abstract" or "pure" inasmuch as it refrains from taking sides—but in doing so it actually protects the already established machinery of discrimination.

The tolerance which enlarged the range and content of freedom was always partisan—intolerant toward the protagonists of the repressive status quo. The issue was only the degree and extent of intolerance. In the firmly established liberal society of England and the United States, freedom of speech and assembly was granted even to the radical enemies of society, provided they did not make the transition from word to deed, from speech to action.

Relying on the effective background limitations imposed by its class structure, the society seemed to practice general tolerance. But liberalist theory had already placed an important condition on tolerance: it was "to apply only to human beings in the maturity of their faculties." John Stuart Mill does not only speak of children and minors, he elaborates: "Liberty, as a principle, has no application to any state of things anterior to the time when mankind have become capable of being improved by free and equal discussion." Anterior to that time, men may still be barbarians, and "despotism is a legitimate mode of government in dealing with barbarians, provided the end be their improvement, and the means justified by actually effecting that end." Mill's often-quoted words have a less familiar implication on which their meaning depends: the internal connection between liberty and truth. There is a sense in which truth is the end of liberty, and liberty must be defined and confined by truth. Now in what sense can liberty be for the sake of truth? Liberty is self-determination, autonomy—this is almost a tautology, but a tautology which results from a whole series of synthetic judgments. It stipulates the ability to determine one's own life: to be able to determine what to do and what not to do, what to suffer and what not. But the subject of this autonomy is never the contingent, private individual as that which he actually is or happens to be; it is rather the individual as a human being who is capable of being free with the others. And the problem of making possible such a harmony between every individual

liberty and the other is not that of finding a compromise between competitors,
or between freedom and law, between
general and individual interest, common
and private welfare in an *established*
society, but of *creating* the society in
which man is no longer enslaved by
institutions which vitiate self-determination from the beginning. In other
words, freedom is still to be created
even for the freest of the existing
societies. And the direction in which it
must be sought, and the institutional and
cultural changes which may help to attain the goal are, at least in developed
civilization, *comprehensible*, that is to
say, they can be identified and projected,
on the basis of experience, by human
reason.

In the interplay of theory and practice,
true and false solutions become distinguishable—never with the evidence
of necessity, never as the positive, only
with the certainty of a reasoned and
reasonable chance, and with the persuasive force of the negative. For the
true positive is the society of the future
and therefore beyond definition and
determination, while the existing positive is that which must be surmounted.
But the experience and understanding of
the existent society may well be capable
of identifying what is *not* conducive to a
free and rational society, what impedes
and distorts the possibilities of its
creation. Freedom is liberation, a specific historical process in theory and
practice, and as such it has its right
and wrong, its truth and falsehood.

The uncertainty of chance in this
distinction does not cancel the historical
objectivity, but it necessitates freedom
of thought and expression as preconditions of finding the way to freedom
—it necessitates *tolerance*. However, this
tolerance cannot be indiscriminate and
equal with respect to the contents of
expression, neither in word nor in deed;
it cannot protect false words and wrong
deeds which demonstrate that they contradict and counteract the possibilities
of liberation. Such indiscriminate tolerance is justified in harmless debates, in
conversation, in academic discussion; it is
indispensable in the scientific enterprise,
in private religion. But society cannot
be indiscriminate where the pacification
of existence, where freedom and happiness themselves are at stake: here, certain things cannot be said, certain ideas
cannot be expressed, certain policies
cannot be proposed, certain behavior
cannot be permitted without making
tolerance an instrument for the continuation of servitude.

The danger of "destructive tolerance"
(Baudelaire), of "benevolent neutrality" toward *art* has been recognized:
the market, which absorbs equally
well (although with often quite sudden
fluctuations) art, anti-art, and non-art,
all possible conflicting styles, schools,
forms, provides a "complacent recep-
tacle, a friendly abyss" (Edgar Wind,
Art and Anarchy (New York: Knopf,
1964), p. 101) in which the radical impact of art, the protest of art against the
established reality is swallowed up.
However, censorship of art and literature is regressive under all circumstances. The authentic oeuvre is not and
cannot be a prop of oppression, and
pseudo-art (which can be such a prop)
is not art. Art stands against history,
withstands history which has been the
history of oppression, for art subjects
reality to laws other than the established
ones: to the laws of the Form which
creates a different reality—negation of
the established one even where art
depicts the established reality. But in
its struggle with history, art subjects
itself to history: history enters the
definition of art and enters into the
distinction between art and pseudo-art.
Thus it happens that what was once
art becomes pseudo-art. Previous forms,
styles, and qualities, previous modes of
protest and refusal cannot be recap-
tured in or against a different society.

There are cases where an authentic oeuvre carries a regressive political message—Dostoevski is a case in point. But then, the message is canceled by the oeuvre itself: the regressive political content is absorbed, *aufgehoben* in the artistic form: in the work as literature.

Tolerance of free speech is the way of improvement, of progress in liberation, *not* because there is no objective truth, and improvement must necessarily be a compromise between a variety of opinions, but because there *is* an objective truth which can be discovered, ascertained only in learning and comprehending that which is and that which can be and ought to be done for the sake of improving the lot of mankind. This common and historical "ought" is not immediately evident, at hand: it has to be uncovered by "cutting through," "splitting," "breaking asunder" (*discutio*) the given material—separating right and wrong, good and bad, correct and incorrect. The subject whose "improvement" depends on a progressive historical practice is each man as man, and this universality is reflected in that of the discussion, which a priori does not exclude any group or individual. But even the all-inclusive character of liberalist tolerance was, at least in theory, based on the proposition that men were (potential) *individuals* who could learn to hear and see and feel by themselves, to develop their own thoughts, to grasp their true interests and rights and capabilities, also against established authority and opinion. This was the rationale of free speech and assembly. Universal toleration becomes questionable when its rationale no longer prevails, when tolerance is administered to manipulated and indoctrinated individuals who parrot, as their own, the opinion of their masters, for whom heteronomy has become autonomy.

The telos of tolerance is truth. It is clear from the historical record that the authentic spokesmen of tolerance had more and other truth in mind than that of propositional logic and academic theory. John Stuart Mill speaks of the truth which is persecuted in history and which does *not* triumph over persecution by virtue of its "inherent power," which in fact has no inherent power "against the dungeon and the stake." And he enumerates the "truths" which were cruelly and successfully liquidated in the dungeons and at the stake: that of Arnold of Brescia, of Fra Dolcino, of Savonarola, of the Albigensians, Waldensians, Lollards, and Hussites. Tolerance is first and foremost for the sake of the heretics—the historical road toward *humanitas* appears as heresy: target of persecution by the powers that be. Heresy by itself, however, is no token of truth.

The criterion of progress in freedom according to which Mill judges these movements is the Reformation. The evaluation is *ex post*, and his list includes opposites (Savonarola too would have burned Fra Dolcino). Even the ex post evaluation is contestable as to its truth: history corrects the judgment—too late. The correction does not help the victims and does not absolve their executioners. However, the lesson is clear: intolerance has delayed progress and has prolonged the slaughter and torture of innocents for hundreds of years. Does this clinch the case for indiscriminate, "pure" tolerance? Are there historical conditions in which such toleration impedes liberation and multiplies the victims who are sacrificed to the status quo? Can the indiscriminate guaranty of political rights and liberties be repressive? Can such tolerance serve to contain qualitative social change?

I shall discuss this question only with reference to political movements, attitudes, schools of thought, philosophies which are "political" in the widest sense—affecting the society as a whole, demonstrably transcending the sphere of privacy. Moreover, I propose a shift in the focus of the discussion: it will be concerned not only, and not primarily, with tolerance toward radical extremes, minorities, subversives, etc., but rather with tolerance toward majorities, toward official and public opinion, toward the established protectors of freedom. In this case, the discussion can have as a frame of reference only a democratic society, in which the people, as individuals and as members of political and other organizations, participate in the making, sustaining, and changing policies. In an authoritarian system, the people do not tolerate—they suffer established policies.

Under a system of constitutionally guaranteed and (generally and without too many and too glaring exceptions) practiced civil rights and liberties, opposition and dissent are tolerated unless they issue in violence and/or in exhortation to and organization of violent subversion. The underlying assumption is that the established society is free, and that any improvement, even a change in the social structure and social values, would come about in the normal course of events, prepared, defined, and tested in free and equal discussion, on the open marketplace of ideas and goods.[1] Now in recalling John Stuart Mill's passage, I drew attention to the premise hidden in this assumption: free and equal discussion can fulfill the function attributed to it only if it is *rational*—expression and development of independent thinking, free from indoctrination, manipulation, extraneous authority. The notion of pluralism and countervailing powers is no substitute for this requirement. One might in

theory construct a state in which a multitude of different pressures, interests, and authorities balance each other out and result in a truly general and rational interest. However, such a construct badly fits a society in which powers are and remain unequal and even increase their unequal weight when they run their own course. It fits even worse when the variety of pressures unifies and coagulates into an overwhelming whole, integrating the particular countervailing powers by virtue of an increasing standard of living and an increasing concentration of power. Then, the laborer, whose real interest conflicts with that of management, the common consumer whose real interest conflicts with that of the producer, the intellectual whose vocation conflicts with that of his employer find themselves submitting to a system against which they are powerless and appear unreasonable. The ideas of the available alternatives evaporates into an utterly utopian dimension in which it is at home, for a free society is indeed unrealistically and undefinably different from the existing ones. Under these circumstances, whatever improvement may occur "in the normal course of events" and without subversion is likely to be improvement in the direction determined by the particular interests which control the whole.

By the same token, those minorities which strive for a change of the whole itself will, under optimal conditions which rarely prevail, be left free to deliberate and discuss, to speak and to assemble—and will be left harmless and helpless in the face of the overwhelming majority, which militates against qualitative social change. This majority is

[1] I wish to reiterate for the following discussion that, *de facto*, tolerance is *not* indiscriminate and "pure" even in the most democratic society. The "background limitations" stated on page 518 restrict tolerance before it begins to operate. The antagonistic structure of society rigs the rules of the game. Those who stand against the established system are a priori at a disadvantage, which is not removed by the toleration of their ideas, speeches, and newspapers.

firmly grounded in the increasing satisfaction of needs, and technological and mental coordination, which testify to the general helplessness of radical groups in a well-functioning social system.

Within the affluent democracy, the affluent discussion prevails, and within the established framework, it is tolerant to a large extent. All points of view can be heard: the Communist and the Fascist, the Left and the Right, the white and the Negro, the crusaders for armament and for disarmament. Moreover, in endlessly dragging debates over the media, the stupid opinion is treated with the same respect as the intelligent one, the misinformed may t ɪk as long as the informed, and propaganda rides along with education, truth with falsehood. This pure toleration of sense and nonsense is justified by the democratic argument that nobody, neither group nor individual, is in possession of the truth and capable of defining what is right and wrong, good and bad. Therefore, all contesting opinions must be submitted to "the people" for its deliberation and choice. But I have already suggested that the democratic argument implies a necessary condition, namely, that the people must be capable of deliberating and choosing on the basis of knowledge, that they must have access to authentic information, and that, on this basis, their evaluation must be the result of autonomous thought.

In the contemporary period, the democratic argument for abstract tolerance tends to be invalidated by the invalidation of the democratic process itself. The liberating force of democracy was the chance it gave to effective dissent, on the individual as well as social scale, its openness to qualitatively different forms of government, of culture, education, work—of the human existence in general. The toleration of free discussion and the equal right of opposites was to define and clarify the different forms of dissent: their direction, content, prospect. But with the concentration of economic and political power and the integration of opposites in a society which uses technology as an instrument of domination, effective dissent is blocked where it could freely emerge: in the formation of opinion, in information and communication, in speech and assembly. Under the rule of monopolistic media—themselves the mere instruments of economic and political power—a mentality is created for which right and wrong, true and false are predefined wherever they affect the vital interests of the society. This is, prior to all expression and communication, a matter of semantics: the blocking of effective dissent, of the recognition of that which is not of the Establishment which begins in the language that is publicized and administered. The meaning of words is rigidly stabilized. Rational persuasion, persuasion to the opposite is all but precluded. The avenues of entrance are closed to the meaning of words and ideas other than the established one—established by the publicity of the powers that be, and verified in their practices. Other words can be spoken and heard, other ideas can be expressed, but, at the massive scale of the conservative majority (outside such enclaves as the intelligentsia), they are immediately "evaluated" (i.e. automatically understood) in terms of the public language—a language which determines "a priori" the direction in which the thought process moves. Thus the process of reflection ends where it started: in the given conditions and relations. Self-validating, the argument of the discussion repels the contradiction because the antithesis is redefined in terms of the thesis. For example, thesis: we work for peace; antithesis: we prepare for war (or even: we wage war); unification of opposites: preparing for war *is* working for peace. Peace is redefined as necessarily, in the prevailing situation, including preparation for war (or even war) and in this Orwellian form, the meaning of the word "peace" is stabilized. Thus, the basic vocabulary of the Orwellian language operates as a priori categories of understanding: preforming all content. These conditions invalidate the logic of tolerance which involves the rational development of meaning and precludes the closing of meaning. Consequently, persuasion through discussion and the equal presentation of opposites (even where it is really equal) easily lose their liberating force as factors of understanding and learning; they are far more likely to strengthen the established thesis and to repel the alternatives.

Impartiality to the utmost, equal treatment of competing and conflicting issues is indeed a basic requirement for decision-making in the democratic process—it is an equally basic requirement for defining the limits of tolerance. But in a democracy with totalitarian organization, objectivity may fulfill a very different function, namely, to foster a mental attitude which tends to obliterate the difference between true and false, information and indoctrination, right and wrong. In fact, the decision between opposed opinions has been made before the presentation and discussion get under way—made, not by a conspiracy or a sponsor or a publisher, not by any dictatorship, but rather by the "normal course of events," which is the course of administered events, and by the mentality shaped in this course. Here, too, it is the whole which determines the truth. Then the decision asserts itself, without any open violation of objectivity, in such things as the make-up of a newspaper (with the breaking up of vital information into bits interspersed between extraneous material, irrelevant items, relegating of some radically negative news to an obscure place), in the juxtaposition of gorgeous ads with unmitigated horrors, in the introduction and interruption of the broadcasting of facts by overwhelming commercials. The result is a *neutralization* of opposites, a neutralization, however, which takes place on the firm grounds of the structural limitation of tolerance and within a preformed mentality. When a magazine prints side by side a negative and a positive report on the FBI, it fulfills honestly the requirements of objectivity: however, the chances are that the positive wins because the image of the institution is deeply engraved in the mind of the people. Or if a newscaster reports the torture and murder of civil rights workers in the same unemotional tone he uses to describe the stockmarket or the weather, or with the same great emotion with which he says his commercials, then such objectivity is spurious—more, it offends against humanity and truth by being calm where one should be enraged, by refraining from accusation where accusation is in the facts themselves. The tolerance expressed in such impartiality serves to minimize or even absolve prevailing intolerance and suppression. If objectivity has anything to do with truth, and if truth is more than a matter of logic and science, then this kind of objectivity is false, and this kind of tolerance inhuman. And if it is necessary to break the established universe of meaning (and the practice enclosed in this universe) in order to enable man to find out what is true and false, this deceptive impartiality would have to be abandoned. The people exposed to this impartiality are no *tabulae rasae*, they are indoctrinated by the conditions under which they live and think and which they do not transcend. To enable them to become autonomous, to find by themselves what is true and what is false for man in the existing society, they would have to be freed from the prevailing indoctrination (which is no longer recognized as indoctrination). But this means that the trend would have to be reversed: they would have to get information slanted in the opposite direction. For the facts are never given immediately and never accessible immediately; they are established, "mediated" by those who made them; the truth, "the whole truth" surpasses these facts and requires the rupture with their appearance. This rupture—prerequisite and token of all freedom of thought and of speech—cannot be accomplished within the established framework of abstract tolerance and spurious objectivity because these are precisely the factors which precondition the mind *against* the rupture.

The factual barriers which totalitarian democracy erects against the efficacy of qualitative dissent are weak and pleasant enough compared with the practices of a dictatorship which claims to educate the people in the truth. With all its limitations and distortions, democratic tolerance is under all circumstances more humane than an institutionalized intolerance which sacrifices the rights and liberties of the living generations for the sake of future generations. The question is whether this is the only alternative. I shall presently try to suggest the direction in which an answer may be sought. In any case, the contrast is not between democracy in the abstract and dictatorship in the abstract.

Democracy is a form of government which fits very different types of society (this holds true even for a democracy with universal suffrage and equality before the law), and the human costs of a democracy are always and everywhere those exacted by the society whose government it is. Their range extends all the way from normal exploitation, poverty, and insecurity to the victims of wars, police actions, military aid, etc., in which the society is engaged—and not only to the victims within its own frontiers. These considerations can never justify the exacting of different sacrifices and different victims on behalf of a future better society, but they do allow weighing the costs involved in the perpetuation of an existing society against the risk of promoting alternatives which offer a reasonable chance of pacification and liberation. Surely, no government can be expected to foster its own subversion, but in a democracy such a right is vested in the people (i.e. in the majority of the people). This means that the ways should not be blocked on which a subversive majority could develop, and if they are blocked by organized repression and indoctrination, their reopening may require apparently undemocratic means. They would include the withdrawal of toleration of speech and assembly from groups and movements which promote aggressive policies, armament, chauvinism, discrimination on the grounds of race and religion, or which oppose the extension of public services, social security, medical care, etc. Moreover, the restoration of freedom of thought may necessitate new and rigid restrictions on teachings and practices in the educational institutions which, by their very methods and concepts, serve to enclose the mind within the established universe of discourse and behavior—thereby precluding a priori a rational evaluation of the alternatives. And to the degree to which freedom of thought involves the struggle against inhumanity, restoration of such freedom would also imply intolerance toward scientific research in the interest of deadly "deterrents," of abnormal human endurance under inhuman conditions, etc. I shall presently discuss the question as to who is to decide on the distinction between liberating and repressive, human and inhuman teachings and practices; I have already suggested that this distinction is not a matter of value-preference but of rational criteria.

While the reversal of the trend in the

educational enterprise at least could conceivably be enforced by the students and teachers themselves, and thus be self-imposed, the systematic withdrawal of tolerance toward regressive and repressive opinions and movements could only be envisaged as results of large-scale pressure which would amount to an upheaval. In other words, it would presuppose that which is still to be accomplished: the reversal of the trend. However, resistance at particular occasions, boycott, non-participation at the local and small-group level may perhaps prepare the ground. The subversive character of the restoration of freedom appears most clearly in that dimension of society where false tolerance and free enterprise do perhaps the most serious and lasting damage, namely, in business and publicity. Against the emphatic insistence on the part of spokesmen for labor, I maintain that practices such as planned obsolescence, collusion between union leadership and management, slanted publicity are not simply imposed from above on a powerless rank and file, but are *tolerated* by them—and by the consumer at large. However, it would be ridiculous to speak of a possible withdrawal of tolerance with respect to these practices and to the ideologies promoted by them. For they pertain to the basis on which the repressive affluent society rests and reproduces itself and its vital defenses—their removal would be that total revolution which this society so effectively repels.

To discuss tolerance in such a society means to re-examine the issue of violence and the traditional distinction between violent and non-violent action. The discussion should not, from the beginning, be clouded by ideologies which serve the perpetuation of violence. Even in the advanced centers of civilization, violence actually prevails: it is practiced by the police, in the prisons and mental institutions, in the fight against racial minorities; it is carried,

by the defenders of metropolitan freedom, into the backward countries. This violence indeed breeds violence. But to refrain from violence in the face of vastly superior violence is one thing, to renounce a priori violence against violence, on ethical or psychological grounds (because it may antagonize sympathizers) is another. Non-violence is normally not only preached to but exacted from the weak—it is a necessity rather than a virtue, and normally it does not seriously harm the case of the strong. (Is the case of India an exception?) There, passive resistance was carried through on a massive scale, which disrupted, or threatened to disrupt, the economic life of the country. Quantity turns into quality: on such a scale, passive resistance is no longer passive—it ceases to be non-violent. The same holds true for the General Strike.) Robespierre's distinction between the terror of liberty and the terror of despotism, and his moral glorification of the former belongs to the most convincingly condemned aberrations, even if the white terror was more bloody than the red terror. The comparative evaluation in terms of the number of victims is the quantifying approach which reveals the man-made horror throughout history that made violence a necessity. In terms of historical function, there is a difference between revolutionary and reactionary violence, between violence practiced by the oppressed and by the oppressors. In terms of ethics, both forms of violence are inhuman and evil—but since when is history made in accordance with ethical standards? To start applying them at the point where the oppressed rebel against the oppressors, the have-nots against the haves is serving the cause of actual violence by weakening the protest against it.

Comprenez enfin ceci: si la violence a commencé ce soir, si l'exploitation ni l'oppression n'ont jamais existé sur terre, peut-être la non-violence affichée peut apaiser la querelle. Mais si le régime tout entier et jusqu'à vos non-violentes pensées sont conditionnées par une oppression millénaire, votre passivité ne sert qu'à vous ranger du côté des oppresseurs. (Sartre, Preface to Frantz Fanon, *Les Damnés de la Terre*, Paris: Maspéro, 1961, p. 22).

The very notion of false tolerance, and the distinction between right and wrong limitations on tolerance, between progressive and regressive indoctrination, revolutionary and reactionary violence demand the statement of criteria for its validity. These standards must be prior to whatever constitutional and legal criteria are set up and applied in an existing society (such as "clear and present danger," and other established definitions of civil rights and liberties), for such definitions themselves presuppose standards of freedom and repression as applicable or not applicable in the respective society: they are specifications of more general concepts. By whom, and according to what standards, can the political distinction between true and false, progressive and regressive (for in this sphere, these pairs are equivalent) be made and its validity be justified? At the outset, I propose that the question cannot be answered in terms of the alternative between democracy and dictatorship, according to which, in the latter, one individual or group, without any effective control from below, arrogate to themselves the decision. Historically, even in the most democratic democracies, the vital and final decisions affecting the society as a whole have been made, constitutionally or in fact, by one or several groups without effective control by the people themselves. The ironical question: who educates the educators (i.e. the political leaders) also applies to democracy. The only authentic alternative and negation of dictatorship (with respect to this question) would be a society in which "the people" have become autonomous individuals, freed

from the repressive requirements of a struggle for existence in the interest of domination, and as such human beings choosing their government and determining their life. Such a society does not yet exist anywhere. In the meantime, the question must be treated *in abstracto*—abstraction, not from the historical possibilities, but from the realities of the prevailing societies.

I suggested that the distinction between true and false tolerance, between progress and regression can be made rationally on empirical grounds. The real possibilities of human freedom are relative to the attained stage of civilization. They depend on the material and intellectual resources available at the respective stage, and they are quantifiable and calculable to a high degree. So are, at the stage of advanced industrial society, the most rational ways of using these resources and distributing the social product with priority on the satisfaction of vital needs and with a minimum of toil and injustice. In other words, it is possible to define the direction in which prevailing institutions, policies, opinions would have to be changed in order to improve the chance of a peace which is not identical with cold war and a little hot war, and a satisfaction of needs which does not feed on poverty, oppression, and exploitation. Consequently, it is also possible to identify policies, opinions, movements which would promote this chance, and those which would do the opposite. Suppression of the regressive ones is a prerequisite for the strengthening of the progressive ones.

The question, who is qualified to make all these distinctions, definitions, identifications for the society as a whole, has now one logical answer, namely, everyone "in the maturity of his faculties" as a human being, everyone who has learned to think rationally and autonomously. The answer to Plato's educational dictatorship is the democratic educational dictatorship of free men. John Stuart Mill's conception of the *res publica* is not the opposite of Plato's: the liberal too demands the authority of Reason not only as an intellectual but also as a political power. In Plato, rationality is confined to the small number of philosopher-kings; in Mill, every rational human being participates in the discussion and decision —but only as a rational being. Where society has entered the phase of total administration and indoctrination, this would be a small number indeed, and not necessarily that of the elected representatives of the people. The problem is not that of an educational dictatorship, but that of breaking the tyranny of public opinion and its makers in the closed society.

However, granted the empirical rationality of the distinction between progress and regression, and granted that it may be applicable to tolerance, and may justify strongly discriminatory tolerance on political grounds (cancellation of the liberal creed of free and equal discussion), another impossible consequence would follow. I said that, by virtue of its inner logic, withdrawal of tolerance from regressive movements, and discriminatory tolerance in favor of progressive tendencies would be tantamount to the "official" promotion of subversion. The historical calculus of progress (which is actually the calculus of the prospective reduction of cruelty, misery, suppression) seems to involve the calculated choice between two forms of political violence: that on the part of the legally constituted powers (by their legitimate action, or by their tacit consent, or by their inability to prevent violence), and that on the part of potentially subversive movements. Moreover, with respect to the latter, a policy of unequal treatment would protect radi-

calism on the Left against that on the Right. Can the historical calculus be reasonably extended to the justification of one form of violence as against another? Or better (since "justification" carries a moral connotation), is there historical evidence to the effect that the social origin and impetus of violence (from among the ruled or the ruling classes, the have or the have-nots, the Left or the Right) is in a demonstrable relation to progress (as defined above)?

With all the qualifications of a hypothesis based on an "open" historical record, it seems that the violence emanating from the rebellion of the oppressed classes broke the historical continuum of injustice, cruelty, and silence for a brief moment, brief but explosive enough to achieve an increase in the scope of freedom and justice, and a better and more equitable distribution of misery and oppression in a new social system—in one word: progress in civilization. The English civil wars, the French Revolution, the Chinese and the Cuban Revolutions may illustrate the hypothesis. In contrast, the one historical change from one social system to another, marking the beginning of a new period in civilization, which was *not* sparked and driven by an effective movement "from below," namely, the collapse of the Roman Empire in the West, brought about a long period of regression for long centuries, until a new, higher period of civilization was painfully born in the violence of the heretic revolts of the thirteenth century and in the peasant and laborer revolts of the fourteenth century.[2]

With respect to historical violence emanating from among ruling classes, no such relation to progress seems to obtain. The long series of dynastic and imperialist wars, the liquidation of Spartacus in Germany in 1919, Fascism

[2] In modern times, fascism has been a consequence of the transition to industrial society *without* a revolution. See Barrington Moore's *Social Origins of Dictatorship and Democracy* (Boston: Beacon Press, 1966).

and Nazism did not break but rather tightened and streamlined the continuum of suppression. I said emanating "from among ruling classes": to be sure, there is hardly any organized violence from above that does not mobilize and activate mass support from below; the decisive question is, on behalf of and in the interest of which groups and institutions is such violence released? And the answer is not necessarily ex post: in the historical examples just mentioned, it could be and was anticipated whether the movement would serve the revamping of the old order or the emergence of the new.

Liberating tolerance, then, would mean intolerance against movements from the Right, and toleration of movements from the Left. As to the scope of this tolerance and intolerance: . . . it would extend to the stage of action as well as of discussion and propaganda, of deed as well as of word. The traditional criterion of clear and present danger seems no longer adequate to a stage where the whole society is in the situation of the theater audience when somebody cries: "fire." It is a situation in which the total catastrophy could be triggered off any moment, not only by a technical error, but also by a rational miscalculation of risks, or by a rash speech of one of the leaders. In past and different circumstances, the speeches of the Fascist and Nazi leaders were the immediate prologue to the massacre. The distance between the propaganda and the action, between the organization and its release on the people had become too short. But the spreading of the word could have been stopped before it was too late: if democratic tolerance had been withdrawn when the future leaders started their campaign, mankind would have had a chance of avoiding Auschwitz and a World War.

The whole post-fascist period is one of clear and present danger. Consequently, true pacification requires the withdrawal of tolerance before the deed, at the stage of communication in word, print, and picture. Such extreme suspension of the right of free speech and free assembly is indeed justified only if the whole of society is in extreme danger. I maintain that our society is in such an emergency situation, and that it has become the normal state of affairs. Different opinions and "philosophies" can no longer compete peacefully for adherence and persuasion on rational grounds: the "marketplace of ideas" is organized and delimited by those who determine the national and the individual interest. In this society, for which the ideologists have proclaimed the "end of ideology," the false consciousness has become the general consciousness—from the government down to its last objects. The small and powerless minorities which struggle against the false consciousness and its beneficiaries must be helped: their continued existence is more important than the preservation of abused rights and liberties which grant constitutional powers to those who oppress these minorities. It should be evident by now that the exercise of civil rights by those who don't have them presupposes the withdrawal of civil rights from those who prevent their exercise, and that liberation of the Damned of the Earth presupposes suppression not only of their old but also of their new masters.

Withdrawal of tolerance from regressive movements *before* they can become active; intolerance even toward thought, opinion, and word, and finally, intolerance in the opposite direction, that is, toward the self-styled conservatives, to the political Right—these antidemocratic notions respond to the actual development of the democratic society which has destroyed the basis for universal tolerance. The conditions under which tolerance can again become a liberating and humanizing force have still to be created. When tolerance mainly serves the protection and preservation of a repressive society, when it serves to neutralize opposition and to render men immune against other and better forms of life, then tolerance has been perverted. And when this perversion starts in the mind of the individual, in his consciousness, his needs, when heteronomous interests occupy him before he can experience his servitude, then the efforts to counteract his dehumanization must begin at the place of entrance, there where the false consciousness takes form (or rather: is systematically formed)—it must begin with stopping the words and images which feed this consciousness. To be sure, this is censorship, even precensorship, but openly directed against the more or less hidden censorship that permeates the free media. Where the false consciousness has become prevalent in national and popular behavior, it translates itself almost immediately into practice: the safe distance between ideology and reality, repressive thought and repressive action, between the word of destruction and the deed of destruction is dangerously shortened. Thus, the break through the false consciousness may provide the Archimedean point for a larger emancipation —at an infinitesimally small spot, to be sure, but it is on the enlargement of such small spots that the chance of change depends.

The forces of emancipation cannot be identified with any social class which, by virtue of its material condition, is free from false consciousness. Today, they are hopelessly dispersed throughout the society, and the fighting minorities and isolated groups are often in opposition to their own leadership. In the society at large, the mental space for denial and reflection must first be re-created. Repulsed by the concreteness of the administered society, the effort of emancipation becomes "abstract"; it is reduced to facilitating the recognition of what is going on, to freeing language from the tyranny of the Orwellian syntax and logic, to developing the concepts that comprehend reality. More than ever, the proposition holds true that progress in freedom demands progress in the *consciousness* of freedom. Where the mind has been made into a subject-object of politics and policies, intellectual autonomy, the realm of "pure" thought has become a matter of *political education* (or rather: counter-education).

This means that previously neutral, value-free, formal aspects of learning and teaching now become, on their own grounds and in their own right, political: learning to know the facts, the whole truth, and to comprehend it is radical criticism throughout, intellectual subversion. In a world in which the human faculties and needs are arrested or perverted, autonomous thinking leads into a "perverted world": contradiction and counter-image of the established world of repression. And this contradiction is not simply stipulated, is not simply the product of confused thinking or phantasy, but is the logical development of the given, the existing world. To the degree to which this development is actually impeded by the sheer weight of a repressive society and the necessity of making a living in it, repression invades the academic enterprise itself, even prior to all restrictions on academic freedom. The pre-empting of the mind vitiates impartiality and objectivity: unless the student learns to think in the opposite direction, he will be inclined to place the facts into the predominant framework of values. Scholarship, i.e. the acquisition and communication of knowledge, prohibits the purification and isolation of facts from the context of the whole truth. An essential part of the latter is recognition of the frightening extent to which history was made and recorded by and for the victors, that is, the extent to which history was the development of oppression. And this oppression is in the facts themselves which it establishes; thus they themselves carry a negative value as part and aspect of their facticity. To treat the great crusades *against* humanity (like that against the Albigensians) with the same impartiality as the desperate struggles *for* humanity means neutralizing their opposite historical function, reconciling the executioners with their victims, distorting the record. Such spurious neutrality serves to reproduce acceptance of the domination of the victors in the consciousness of man. Here, too, in the education of those who are not yet maturely integrated, in the mind of the young, the ground for liberating tolerance is still to be created.

Education offers still another example of spurious, abstract tolerance in the guise of concreteness and truth: it is epitomized in the concept of self-actualization. From the permissiveness of all sorts of license to the child, to the constant pyschological concern with the personal problems of the student, a large-scale movement is under way against the evils of repression and the need for being oneself. Frequently brushed aside is the question as to what has to be repressed before one can be a self, oneself. The individual potential is first a negative one, a portion of the potential of his society: of aggression, guilt feeling, ignorance, resentment, cruelty which vitiate his life instincts. If the identity of the self is to be more than the immediate realization of this potential (undesirable for the individual as human being), then it requires repression and sublimation, conscious transformation. This process involves at each stage (to use the ridiculed terms which here reveal their succinct concreteness) the negation of the negation, mediation of the immediate, and identity is no more and no less than this process. "Alienation" is the constant and essential element of identity, the objective side of the subject—and not, as it is made to appear today, a disease, a psychological condition. Freud well knew the difference between progressive and regressive, liberating and destructive repression. The publicity of self-actualization promotes the removal of the one and the other, it promotes existence in that immediacy which, in a repressive society, is (to use another Hegelian term) bad immediacy (*schlechte Unmittelbarkeit*). It isolates the individual from the one dimension where he could "find himself": from his political existence, which is at the core of his entire existence. Instead, it encourages non-conformity and letting-go in ways which leave the real engines of repression in the society entirely intact, which even strengthen these engines by substituting the satisfactions of private and personal rebellion for a more than private and personal, and therefore more authentic, opposition. The desublimation involved in this sort of self-actualization is itself repressive inasmuch as it weakens the necessity and the power of the intellect, the catalytic force of that unhappy consciousness which does not revel in the archetypal personal release of frustration—hopeless resurgence of the Id which will sooner or later succumb to the omnipresent rationality of the administered world—but which recognizes the horror of the whole in the most private frustration and actualizes itself in this recognition.

I have tried to show how the changes in advanced democratic societies, which have undermined the basis of economic and political liberalism, have also altered the liberal function of tolerance. The tolerance which was the great achievement of the liberal era is still professed and (with strong qualifications) practiced, while the economic and political process is subjected to an ubiquitous and effective administration in accordance with the predominant interests. The result is an objective contradiction between the economic and political structure on the one side, and the theory and practice of toleration on the other. The altered social structure tends to weaken the effectiveness of tolerance toward dissenting and oppositional movements and to strengthen conservative and reactionary forces. Equality of tolerance becomes abstract, spurious. With the actual decline of dissenting forces in the society, the opposition is insulated in small and frequently antagonistic groups who, even where tolerated within the narrow limits set by the hierarchical structure of society, are powerless while they keep within these limits. But the tolerance shown to them is deceptive and promotes coordination. And on the firm foundations of a coordinated society all but closed against qualitative change, tolerance itself serves to contain such change rather than to promote it.

These same conditions render the critique of such tolerance abstract and academic, and the proposition that the balance between tolerance toward the Right and toward the Left would have to be radically redressed in order to restore the liberating function of tolerance becomes only an unrealistic speculation. Indeed, such a redressing seems to be tantamount to the establishment of a "right of resistance" to the point of subversion. There is not, there cannot be any such right for any group or individual against a constitutional government sustained by a majority of the population. But I believe that there is a "natural right" of resistance for oppressed and overpowered minorities to use extralegal means if the legal ones have proved to be inadequate. Law and order are always and everywhere the law and order which protect the established hierarchy; it is nonsensical to invoke the absolute authority of this law and this order against those who suffer from it and struggle against it—

not for personal advantages and revenge, but for their share of humanity. There is no other judge over them than the constituted authorities, the police, and their own conscience. If they use violence, they do not start a new chain of violence but try to break an established one. Since they will be punished, they know the risk, and when they are willing to take it, no third person, and least of all the educator and intellectual, has the right to preach them abstention.

Postscript 1968

*U*nder the conditions prevailing in this country, tolerance does not, and cannot, fulfill the civilizing function attributed to it by the liberal protagonists of democracy, namely protection of dissent. The progressive historical force of tolerance lies in its extension to those modes and forms of dissent which are not committed to the status quo of society, and not confined to the institutional framework of the established society. Consequently, the idea of tolerance implies the necessity, for the dissenting group or individuals, to become illegitimate if and when the established legitimacy prevents and counteracts the development of dissent. This would be the case not only in a totalitarian society, under a dictatorship, in one-party states, but also in a democracy (representative, parliamentary, or "direct") where the majority does not result from the development of independent thought and opinion but rather from the monopolistic or oligopolistic administration of public opinion, without terror and (normally) without censorship. In such cases, the majority is self-perpetuating while perpetuating the vested interests which *made* it a majority. In its very structure this majority is "closed," petrified; it repels "a priori" any change other than changes within the system. But this means that the majority is no longer justified in claiming the democratic title of the best guardian of the common interest. And such a majority is all but the opposite of Rousseau's "general will": it is composed, not of individuals who, in their political functions, have made effective "abstraction" from their private interests, but, on the contrary, of individuals who have effectively identified their private interests with their political functions. And the representatives of this majority, in ascertaining and executing its will, ascertain and execute the will of the vested interests which have formed the majority. The ideology of democracy hides its lack of substance.

In the United States, this tendency goes hand in hand with the monopolistic or oligopolistic concentration of capital in the formation of public opinion, i.e., of the majority. The chance of influencing, in any effective way, this majority is at a price, in dollars, totally out of reach of the radical opposition. Here too, free competition and exchange of ideas have become a farce. The Left has no equal voice, no equal access to the mass media and their public facilities—not because a conspiracy excludes it, but because, in good old capitalist fashion, it does not have the required purchasing power. And the Left does not have the purchasing power because it is the Left. These conditions impose upon the radical minorities a strategy which is in essence a refusal to allow the continuous functioning of allegedly indiscriminate but in fact discriminate tolerance, for example, a strategy of protesting against the alternate matching of a spokesman for the Right (or Center) with one for the Left. Not "equal" but *more* representation of the Left would be equalization of the prevailing inequality.

Within the solid framework of pre-established inequality and power, tolerance is practiced indeed. Even outrageous opinions are expressed, outrageous incidents are televised; and the critics of established policies are interrupted by the same number of commercials as the conservative advocates. Are these interludes supposed to counteract the sheer weight, magnitude, and continuity of system-publicity, indoctrination which operates playfully through the endless commercials as well as through the entertainment?

Given this situation, I suggested in "Repressive Tolerance" the practice of discriminating tolerance in an inverse direction, as a means of shifting the balance between Right and Left by restraining the liberty of the Right, thus counteracting the pervasive inequality of freedom (unequal opportunity of access to the means of democratic persuasion) and strengthening the oppressed against the oppressors. Tolerance would be restricted with respect to movements of a demonstrably aggressive or destructive character (destructive of the prospects for peace, justice, and freedom for all). Such discrimination would also be applied to movements opposing the extension of social legislation to the poor, weak, disabled. As against the virulent denunciations that such a policy would do away with the sacred liberalistic principle of equality for "the other side," I maintain that there are issues where either there is no "other side" in any more than a formalistic sense, or where "the other side" is demonstrably "regressive" and impedes possible improvement of the human condition. To tolerate propaganda for inhumanity vitiates the goals not only of liberalism but of every progressive political philosophy.

I presupposed the existence of demonstrable criteria for aggressive, regressive, destructive forces. If the final democratic criterion of the declared opinion of the majority no longer (or rather not yet) prevails, if vital ideas, values, and ends of human progress no longer (or rather not yet) enter, as competing equals, the formation of public opinion, if the people are no longer (or rather not yet) sovereign but "made" by the real sovereign powers— is there any alternative other than the dictatorship of an "elite" over the people? For the opinion of people (usually designated as The People) who are unfree in the very faculties in which liberalism saw the roots of freedom: independent thought and independent speech, can carry no overriding validity and authority—even if The People constitute the overwhelming majority.

If the choice were between genuine democracy and dictatorship, democracy would certainly be preferable. But democracy does not prevail. The radical critics of the existing political process are thus readily denounced as advocating an "elitism," a dictatorship of intellectuals as an alternative. What we have in fact is government, representative government by a non-intellectual minority of politicians, generals, and businessmen. The record of this "elite" is not very promising, and political prerogatives for the intelligentsia may not necessarily be worse for the society as a whole.

In any case, John Stuart Mill, not exactly an enemy of liberal and representative government, was not so allergic to the political leadership of the intelligentsia as the contemporary guardians of semi-democracy are. Mill believed that "individual mental superiority" justifies "reckoning one person's opinion as equivalent to more than one":

Until there shall have been devised, and until opinion is willing to accept some mode of plural voting which may assign to education as such the degree of superior influence due to it, and sufficient as a counterpoise to the numerical weight of the least educated class, for so long the benefits of completely universal suffrage cannot be obtained without bringing with them, as it appears to me, more than equivalent evils.[3]

"Distinction in favor of education, right in itself," was also supposed to preserve "the educated from the class legislation of the uneducated," without enabling the former to practice a class legislation of their own.[4]

Today, these words have understandably an antidemocratic, "elitist" sound—understandably because of their dangerously radical implications. For if "education" is more and other than training, learning, preparing for the existing society, it means not only enabling man to know and understand the facts which make up reality but also to know and understand the factors that establish the facts so that he can change their inhuman reality. And such humanistic education would involve the "hard" science ("hard" as in the "hardware" bought by the Pentagon?), would free them from their destructive direction. In other words, such education would indeed badly serve the Establishment, and to give political prerogatives to the men and women thus educated would indeed be anti-democratic in the terms of the Establishment. But these are not the only terms.

However, the alternative to the established semi-democratic process is *not* a dictatorship or elite, no matter how intellectual and intelligent, but the struggle for a real democracy. Part of this struggle is the fight against an ideology of tolerance which, in reality, favors and fortifies the conservation of the status quo of inequality and discrimination. For this struggle, I proposed the practice of discriminating tolerance. To be sure, this practice already presupposes the radical goal which it seeks to achieve. I committed this *petitio principii* in order to combat the pernicious

---

[3] *Considerations on Representative Government* (Chicago: Gateway Edition, 1962), p. 183.
[4] *Ibid.*, p. 181.

ideology that tolerance is already institutionalized in this society. The tolerance which is the life element, the token of a free society, will never be the gift of the powers that be; it can, under the prevailing conditions of tyranny by the majority, only be won in the sustained effort of radical minorities, willing to break this tyranny and to work for the emergence of a free and sovereign majority—minorities intolerant, militantly intolerant and disobedient to the rules of behavior which tolerate destruction and suppression.

Nathan Glazer

1923-

*Writer and sociologist Nathan Glazer
was born in New York City. After receiving
a master's degree from the University of
Pennsylvania in 1944, he began an editorial
career that spanned more than a decade.
This was followed by a series of academic
appointments and a Columbia University
doctorate in 1962. Since that time, he has
been professor of sociology at the University
of California at Berkeley.*

*Glazer has many important publications
to his credit, and as is expected of a
sociologist, they frequently center on social
issues in America. In the following
selection, Glazer treats critically the
assumptions of the New Left and its
proposals for social change. He finds those
assumptions untenable, even if it be granted
that the New Left has had some success in
such areas as poverty and education. His
own position suggests that, as America
faces the overburdening problems of a mass
technological society, solutions must be
found that may run beyond such
traditional political distinctions as left and
right, conservative and liberal.*

*The selection is from his article, "The
New Left and Its Limits,"* in Commentary,
XLVI (July, 1968).

*F*or the last few years I have looked
with increasing skepticism on the analyses and the actions of the radical Left in
America. By the radical Left I mean
those who believe there is something
fundamentally and irredeemably wrong
with our society, and who think the
chief way of righting it lies in mobilizing
the power of all the disadvantaged
groups among us behind a drive for
radical change, change going to the
roots. My own skepticism in the face of
so much passion and indeed accomplishment often troubles me, and it will
certainly annoy radicals. They may
say that to have been radical or liberal
in one's youth, and to become relatively
conservative in one's middle years, is so
common an experience that it needs
hardly any explanation at all. However,
just as I would not explain the radical
mood or outlook on psychological or

temperamental grounds, so I would hope
that radicals might suspend such easy
judgments on my own outlook. There
have been, after all, young conservatives and old radicals, even if not as
many as the other way around. And just
as I would accord the radical outlook
full respect—as a perspective on the
world that has its own rationale, its
own roots, its own great thinkers, its
own successes—so I would hope that
radicals might for a while consider the
point of view that is skeptical of their
analyses, their programs, and their
hopes.

There are three principal areas in
which the new radicalism expresses
itself: the problem of the Vietnam war,
and by extension the whole question of
the role of the United States in world
affairs, and in the development of the
poorer countries; the problem of achiev-

ing equality for Negroes, which now centers in the crisis of the great urban ghettos; and the problem of higher education—in particular the role of youth in the administration of the campus and the shaping of the curriculum. In none of these three areas can we point to much to be happy about. I need not describe the sense of catastrophe that hangs over us whether we consider the war, or the black-white conflict. I would not apply so grand a term as catastrophe to the campus situation, and yet there is a growing sense of the triviality of much of mass higher education; and while I would hesitate to go so far as to say that the hearts and minds of our young people are being destroyed, I think the crisis in the universities is as serious in its own right for American youth as are Vietnam and race for the larger society.

In all three areas, radicalism, true to the term, wishes to go to the roots because, it says, what is wrong in each case is wrong at the roots. To find a half-million Americans in Vietnam, killing and being killed, burning villages and destroying crops, is sufficiently outrageous to make it plausible that there is a horror within the bowels of our society which has called those outer horrors forth. To find in the ghettos vast numbers of poverty-stricken people who have lost all faith in society, their fellow man, and their own power, who present a picture of disinheritance that no other advanced industrial society can show us; and to find on the other hand among many whites a ferocious hatred of these unfortunates that again no other advanced society can show us—this too is sufficient cause to assume that the roots are poisoned. To confront, finally, in the colleges and universities a host of petty demands and restrictions irrelevant to understanding and education, makes it easy enough to believe that something very basic is the operative cause.

Faced with these evils, and the general sense that something fundamental is wrong, the radical chooses between two broad general approaches to getting at the roots. One is the whole grand scheme of Marxism, in its various modern formulations. Capitalism is too old-fashioned a term to arouse much interest—it is now replaced by imperialism. Similarly, the increasing misery of the working class is replaced by the increasing misery of the underdeveloped world, and by that of our own "colonials" at home, the Negroes and other minority groups. The machine presumed to be at the heart of the misery has also been modernized, but fundamental to it still is the selfishness of a ruling class which cannot or will not give up its power and which therefore must be smashed. The mechanisms of a better society are still not studied much—they fall under the ban Marx and Engels imposed on utopianism and reformism. Thus the Communist country where the most serious effort to establish such mechanisms has been made, Yugoslavia, is of no great interest to today's radicals. They are more concerned with Cuba and China, which still maintain a pre-institutional—or a post-institutional?—revolutionary vigor, in which the thought and decisions of the central leader of the revolution are capable of overturning the new and barely established social structures every other day.

The most attractive aspect of the new radicalism is that it has developed a second and more popular approach to getting at the roots—more pragmatic and empirical, more humanist, less mechanical and dogmatic. This is the approach suggested in the Port Huron statement of 1962, a document characteristic of the early spirit of Students for a Democratic Society (SDS). But the candid and open stance of the New Left in its first phase of development—that something deep was wrong but no one quite knew precisely what it was or what would change it—could not be maintained forever as a basis for action. Thus an explanation began to emerge. The simple analysis of the Old Left, that capitalism or imperialism is at the root of the matter, was not very satisfactory, if only because it was too easy to point to the example of capitalist countries like Sweden and England on the one side and Communist ones like Soviet Russia and East Germany on the other to prove that no necessary causal relation exists between oppression and the institutions of capitalism. Referring to real experience—"where am *I* bugged?, where do *I* feel the pinch?"—the New Left began to decide that the problem lies not in the institutions of capitalism as such but rather in all types of fixed and formal institutions. The university administrator is not involved in the search for private profit, nor is the indifferent slum school teacher, the insensitive social worker, the hypocritical mayor, the technologically minded general. Rather —so goes the new argument—they are all small men trapped into serving big and powerful institutions that have grown hopelessly distant from immediate human needs and satisfactions. The institutions nevertheless draw on strong personal motivations to achieve their inhuman ends—the desire for money and power and advancement, for security, for a comfortable home-life in suburbia. In the view of the New Left, the minor and more benign motivations of men emerge as having greater potentialities for evil than the grander ones. It is the man who wants to do his best for his wife and children, keep up the mortgage and buy a new car—it is this man who also releases the gas in the chambers and who makes the napalm containers. He may even be a good union member and vote Democratic.

When one sees institutions themselves as the source of our present evils, and when one sees these institutions fed not by the limited and distorted motivations of rampant capitalism, but by such ancient and wellrooted human impulses as the drives for comfort, security, and family, then one has forged an analysis which is indeed powerful.

Nevertheless, the New Left has an answer—a conception of democracy in which our traditional mix of civil liberties and elected legislatures and officials is supplemented or supplanted by new rights and new forms of democratic intervention in the process of decision-making and administration. Thus attempts have been made to establish such rights as those of the poor to direct representation in the institutions that affect their lives, to financial support with dignity, to legal counsel. These new conceptions have already scored remarkable successes. We have seen formerly unshakable Boards of Education begin to bow to demands that only a year or two ago may have seemed extremist and irrational—for example, the demand for community control of ghetto schools. We have seen "student power" in higher education reach levels that were inconceivable four years ago. To be sure, the forging of foreign policy still appears to lie beyond the reach of New Left ideas. And yet is it? In recent demonstrations we have seen revolutionary techniques employed that are justified less by resort to the traditional rhetoric of revolution than by the argument that new forms of "representation" of minority points of view are required in a democratic polity.

The question of how enduring these new developments will be still remains open, but it is clear that they already serve as extremely effective weapons to advance the argument that something fundamental is wrong with American society. Of course, the argument that something fundamental is wrong leads easily to the conclusion that something grand and apocalyptic is required to set it straight. And indeed, the two positions reinforce each other: given the inclination toward some tremendous change, some tremendous flaw must be found to justify it (just as the reverse is true). But a powerful analysis of what is wrong with society may be too powerful. The radical Left explains what is wrong by the tendency of men to act within institutions which develop their own dynamic, and a dynamic which may become irrelevant or positively subversive of the ends they are set up to realize. As instances, they point to the tendency of educational institutions to act in such ways as to inhibit education, welfare institutions in such ways as to reduce competence, defense institutions in such ways as to increase the likelihood and the ferocity of war. When I say that this analysis may be too powerful, I mean to raise the question: what alternative is there to institutions designed to deal with problems, calling upon the more common and everyday motivations, and developing their own rigidities and blinders?

There is an answer on the New Left even to that—and the answer is to release man's natural creativity and spontaneity, whether through revolution, or through participatory democracy, or through the smashing of the old institutions, and to hope that these newly released forces will finally lead to the overcoming of ancient social dilemmas. For the New Left believes that man is good by nature, and corrupted by institutions; that the earth and its riches are sufficient to maintain all men in comfort and happiness, and that only human selfishness and blindness prevent the emergence of this ideal state. One can appeal to the early Marx, who is so popular today, and his vision of a society in which man can fish in the morning, work in the afternoon, and criticize the arts in the evening, just as he will, and entirely according to the rhythms of his own being. Some on the

New Left believe that only a violent overthrow of the institutions of society can bring such a world to birth; others believe that a steady and determined and unyielding pressure on power elites and power holders, if applied long enough, ingeniously enough, unflinchingly enough, will force these groups to give up their power and their goods and to desist in their willful obstruction of those who wish to create a better and more beautiful world.

There are, in my opinion, three serious flaws in this position.

The first is the assumption that the problems of bringing a better society into being are fundamentally problems of power. This has become a matter of gospel, and not only with the New Left. Yet the fact is that only certain basic problems can be settled, and even those only to a limited degree, by direct clashes between conflicting interests; and in advanced societies, the number of such problems grows progressively smaller and smaller. The natural history of social problems seems to involve an initial stage in which a selfish power monopoly must be defeated or overthrown. But clear evils to fight against are rapidly succeeded by increasingly ambiguous evils, whose causes and solutions are equally unclear. The minute we move to this later stage, we confront one important limitation of the radical perspective.

Let me be concrete. In the South not long ago, the resistance to equality for Negroes was centered in an irrational and inhuman racist ethos that denied to Negroes the most elementary rights of man in a democratic society, such as the right to a fair trial, to the security of life and property, and to the vote. The task of confronting these evils was simply to fight them, to organize to fight them, to insist that the Constitution be obeyed—even, if one was heroic enough, to die or risk death in the process.

But this was the initial state of reform: equivalent in its moral clarity to earlier battles like those aimed at extending the franchise, banning child labor, establishing labor's right to organize, setting up systems of unemployment insurance and social security. After the principle has been established there comes a second stage, in which the problems are more complex, often more technical. It is in part for this reason that the administrators and the experts now take over, together with those whose interests are directly concerned, while the army of reformers moves off to issues in which the conflict between good and evil is still clear cut. This is precisely what happened after the victories of the civil-rights movement in the South and the shift of the movement to the North.

We are often very sympathetic to cynical explanations of human behavior, including our own, and we are thus attracted to the belief that when Southern whites only were affected by Negro demands, Northern whites could be staunchly militant in defense of Negro rights, but that when the Northerners themselves were affected, they fell silent or slunk off the battlefield. But something rather more important occurred as the battleground of the civil-rights movement shifted from the South to the North. In the South, the issues were civic equality and the vote; in the North, because both these goals had long been attained, the issues became employment and upgrading in jobs, income, education, housing. These are all highly complex matters that no simple law can settle. It cannot be decreed that Negroes and whites should have the same income regardless of their skills and education, or that they should have the same education regardless of their home backgrounds, or that they should have the same home backgrounds, regardless of their history, their culture, their experience.

Of course it is possible, even in this later stage of reform when the key element has ceased to be the obdurate political power of a selfish interest group, to insist that nothing has really changed. Thus, many who argue that it is "white racism" which is keeping the Negro down—an idea strongly encouraged by the Report of the National Advisory Commission on Civil Disorders—are in effect trying to cast the enormous problems of creating a true and widespread equality for American Negroes in the pattern of the heroic battles to change the cruel social structure of the South. Yet this interpretation flies in the face of the fact that racist attitudes have been in steady decline in this country for two decades. And if "white racism" refers to practices, it contradicts the reality that most of the major institutions in American life—government, big business, higher education, the foundations—have been engaged for years in a variety of efforts to increase and upgrade Negro participation in every area of American life. Paradoxically, "white racism" has become a rallying cry precisely at a moment when it has never been milder.

The truth is that it is not white racism but the difficulty of the problems which has so far frustrated us in finding satisfying jobs for the hard-core unemployed, or improving education and housing in the ghettos and slums. Not even the enactment of such legislative proposals as are being put forward by the Poor People's March on Washington would by itself settle matters—as, in its time, the enactment of the right to collective bargaining did. If the government were to become the "employer of last resort," there would still be thorny questions concerning rates of pay (certainly minimal wages would no longer be a solution, as they were with WPA in the depression), civil-service protection for these workers, and policies for dealing with incompetence and absenteeism—for after all we are speaking of people who cannot get jobs or will not take those which are available in a fairly brisk labor market.

If we consider education, no reform has yet been proposed or envisaged that can reasonably promise better education for ghetto youth, though we can passionately support community control of schools as a measure which *might* at least help to affect the tricky factor of the child's motivation. And even when we speak of housing and neighborhoods, where simple physical facilities alone are important, we have no easy solutions—as becomes evident once the question is raised of how much happier the poor have proved to be in public housing projects than in slums. In none of these major areas is there a major reform that can promise what social security or the right to collective bargaining promised. This is only an index to the increasing complexity of our problems, themselves the result of the increasing sophistication of social demands—not *any* job, but a good and meaningful job with security and promise of advancement; not merely free education, but education with certain effects; not just a minimally adequate dwelling, but one located within a network of social supports that we can often scarcely divine, let alone set out to create.

Even the demands for a guaranteed annual income, or a negative income tax, or a family allowance—demands that are, it is clear enough, pressed because there is no rapid and easy path to equality through good jobs—raise further technical questions that will not be solved by the passionate insistence that Congress decree an end to poverty or that communities do away with white racism. The guaranteed annual income or negative income tax would have serious and undetermined effects on those who work for rates at or near the

legal minimum. If such workers (maids, messenger boys, janitors, hotel employees, restaurant employees, etc.) are to retain any incentive to work, the guaranteed annual income or negative income tax return must be set below the minimum wage—at which point we are back to welfare and the painful issues it involves (who qualifies, for how much, etc.?). The family allowance is less problematic, but as generally proposed it is too small to permit the abolition of the welfare system; nor can we be happy over the inevitable support it entails for population growth at a time when for other good reasons we might want to discourage large families.

At the moment it is fashionable among radicals to ignore these details and to justify their indifference by an assault on the idea that work is necessary to society. But anyone who looks concretely at what human beings in this country want, and what radicals feel is the least they should have (good housing, good education, various social services, good health care, recreational opportunities, etc.), and then simply adds up what that requires in the way of material and human resources, would soon be disabused of the notion that we can ignore the effects of various social measures on the incentive to work. Quite characteristically, the radical wants it both ways—he wants services that are enormously costly in manpower, and he wants social measures that will encourage fewer people to work.

If the issues become thus complex, when there are no simple slogans to proclaim—or, when such slogans are proclaimed, there are no visible routes to their immediate realization—then understandably the fervor and commitment of many reformers and radicals fall off. This is in part what happened when the issue of civil rights for Negroes in the South was replaced by the issue of achieving effective equality for the

Negro throughout the nation. We can trace much the same development in all the earlier areas of reform; indeed, the advancement of a society can almost be measured by the extent to which political issues are transformed into technical issues—when this happens it is generally a sign that the central power struggle is over. In Scandinavia and England the provision of good medical care, for example, has come to involve such questions as how many doctors and nurses are needed, how they should be trained, how they can be kept from going to America or induced to move to small towns and distant rural areas, what kind of hospitals should be built, etc. Of course, politics enters into all this, with parties taking positions according to their class composition, their history, and their ideology. Yet such differences are relatively marginal, and only one element of many—among which they are by no means the most important—going into the framing of solutions.

To my mind, there are fewer and fewer major areas of American domestic policy in which the old-fashioned conflict between interests representing clearly reactionary forces, and the interests of the society in general, still remains central. One is the continued Southern resistance to legislation aimed at bettering the lot of the Negro; another is the continued resistance of organized medicine to an adequate program of medical care. In most other areas, I would argue, complex technical issues have superseded the crude power struggle between the forces of reaction and the forces of progress. This is not to deny that self-serving interests still operate throughout the political sphere, but so long as care is taken to pay them off, they do not constitute serious roadblocks in the way of improving our society. The drive for security is a massive one—in farmers, in businessmen in workers—and I am not sure that our special interests are so much stronger than their counterparts in other societies which manage their problems pretty well, or in any imaginable future society.

A second argument against the perspective of radical leftism follows from this general point that in an industrially advanced society, whatever its background and history, social problems become more and more complex, more technical, and less political: Because change is continuous in such societies, no solution is ever complete or final, and consequently there is no alternative to bureaucracies, administrators, and experts. Of course, certain issues are on occasion structured so that solutions really can have a once-and-for-all character—in particular those issues which can be posed in strictly political or legal terms. Thus, the right to organize, when put into law and upheld by the courts, finally ended one great battle in American history. But most of the problems we face are not so simple and require continuous expert attention.

Consider, for example, public housing. No directly political measure, like a huge appropriation of money, could solve the problem of housing in this country; nor could the introduction of some new principle, like the once-new principle of public housing itself. For no matter what we might do on the political front, we would still have to decide what kind of housing to build, where to build it, in what size developments and at what scale; we would need to know the effect of setting different income limits, of excluding or not excluding those with criminal records, of accepting this proportion or that from the relief rolls; and we would have to determine the further effect of these and many other decisions on the balance of integration and segregation. There is no way of reaching such decisions from any large political position, radical or conservative: indeed, these questions (and they are increasingly becoming the ones that any advanced society must settle) make those very distinctions irrelevant. A few years ago I visited Warsaw and spoke to researchers in the field of housing and other social services. The problems we spoke about, that troubled them, were not very different from those of anyone dealing with housing in New York or Chicago, or, I would hazard, in Stockholm and Moscow.

Public welfare is another example. In the 1930's the basic issue was raised: is the government responsible for providing subsistence to those unable to earn it themselves? And the answer, after a struggle, was given: yes. It was, as is common in this politically complex nation, not as good or sharp an answer as other nations have given, but in the more advanced states of the Union, at any rate, public services of a standard commensurate with that of Northwestern Europe were established for the widowed and orphaned and abandoned and aged and disabled. The battle was over; reformers and radicals rested, or moved off to other fields. Twenty years later they were back, in force, denouncing the social workers, organizing the clients against them. What had happened? Had welfare services deteriorated or been cut back? Quite the contrary. More was being spent on them and they were probably being run more efficiently. Yet where it had once seemed the achievement of a generous society that those without income were no longer required to beg or to depend on private charity, but now received as of right some minimal level of subsistence, it seemed to the society of twenty years later an outrage that they were maintained on a dignity-destroying dole, that they were not rehabilitated, turned into productive and self-respecting citi-

zens. Let me suggest that it is much easier to give someone money than to turn him into a productive and self-respecting citizen. The first task is also a much easier one to place on the banners of a political movement or to write into legislation than the second.

Or consider the poverty program. Within Congress, Left and Right both agree that something should be done about poverty, and that training the unemployed or the not-yet employed is a good idea; in consequence we have now developed a large range of training programs, of varying kinds, under varying auspices. When any one of these programs comes up for renewal, the technical people running it will always argue that theirs is the most important and should be maintained or expanded, and will try to convince their friends in Congress. Now it is true that congressmen, faced with conflicting expert opinion and pressure from differing interests, will tend to fall back on old prejudices and old political commitments—the liberals will generally say, spend more, the conservatives, spend less. But the combat takes place in a surprisingly restricted area. It is not yet as restricted as the area of political combat in England and Sweden, but it is much narrower than it was in this country twenty years ago.

Admittedly the overall scale of expenditures on housing or welfare or work-training programs is still an important political question in America, but this is not really what many on the radical Left are concerned about. For even if we were to spend twice as much in each of these areas as we do now, things would not really change that much, and no one—least of all the radical Leftists themselves—would believe that the millennium awaited by the radical Left had arrived.[1] But as a matter of

[1] New York City spends twice as much per child in its public schools as most other large cities do, yet these schools hardly serve as a model for the solution of the problems of urban education.

fact, even the scope of politics as regards the scale of expenditure is remarkably restricted. In all advanced countries, taxes are very high and not easily increased; similar proportions of the GNP are devoted to social welfare; and in increasing competition among equally worthy programs—health, education, welfare, work-training, scientific research, and the like—poses similarly perplexing decisions. We may come to a better understanding of these matters, but scarcely by following the assumptions and perspectives of the radical Left.

If, then, the need for reform and change is continuous, and depends on the expert knowledge of technicians continuously applied, there can be no alternative to institutionalization, the permanent bodies devoted to permanent problem areas, with all its consequences. I do not see how any sensible man can still think, as Lenin did in *State and Revolution*, that institutions and the state will wither away to the point where they can be run on a part-time and unspecialized basis by—in his term—cooks. Yet this is the vague, if not always expressed, hope of the New Left. Knowing that institutions corrupt, they hope to do away with them. One of the major grounds for my skepticism is my belief that, even though they corrupt, there is no chance of doing away with them.

I am aware, of course, of the common wisdom that to put education in the hands of the educators, housing in the hands of the professional housers, welfare in the hands of the social workers is to ensure that traditional practices will become institutionalized, that reformers will be fought, and that difficulties will pile up and get worse. But the fact is that judicious, flexible, creative people are always in short supply. Not every problem can be placed in the hands of the best men in the society—though this often seems to

be what we are asked to achieve when we are told that our doctors must be better, our teachers must be better, our social workers must be better. Where after all are we to find a place for the people in our society who are less than the most imaginative, the most energetic, the most effective? The great majority of men, whether or not they lead lives of quiet desperation, certainly hope to lead lives of minimal security and moderate gratification. While we take it for granted that this is a reasonable and humane objective for Vietnamese peasants or Indian city-dwellers, we consider it reprehensible that most American doctors, teachers, social workers, and the like are of the same sort. No doubt this common human tendency seems reprehensible when viewed in the context of the suffering we are called upon to alleviate. But what solution is there? As far as I can see, only the normal political one—when the problems become bad enough, and enough people get angry and protest, new programs are started, new men and new ideas flow in, and hopefully all this leads to a new level of achievement, itself to become institutionalized in its turn, and to require at some later time another infusion of ideas, money, and innovators from the outside.

The New Left's main answer to the problem of institutionalization is participatory democracy, a concept derived from the Paris Commune in which, according to Marx's account, the people, permanently politicized, permanently in arms, met every day to settle their fate. This is a grand vision and one which makes it possible to argue that all established institutions, even if formally democratic, are actually undemocratic because they do not reflect the desires of the people at any given moment. I cannot imagine, however, how one can ever overcome the danger raised by a direct dependence on the people, permanently in session. For it inevitably means depending on that part of the people that is willing, for one reason or another, to stay permanently in session.

Participatory democracy is suited to truly revolutionary movements and moments—but only moments. No people as a whole has ever been ready to make a primary commitment to political action over a long period of time. Those who assert that formal democracy cannot be true democracy because many do not vote, many who vote do not know, the candidates do not reflect the full range of opinion and possibility, etc., ignore the fact that this limited interest on the part of most people most of the time is actually among the greatest defenses of democracy. It means, as Aaron Wildavsky has pointed out, that there are always enormous reserves to be mobilized whenever significant interests are affected. Wildavsky contends that one of the most critical resources in politics is time—time for talking, electioneering, canvassing—and the poor have as much of this resource as anyone else. Perhaps money decides only unimportant things, such as which of two not very different candidates will carry an election. But if important issues arise, reserves are available that can be brought into battle. Is it not such reserves that the organizers in the slums are now trying to mobilize? If they fail, as they sometimes do, it may be because they have not correctly diagnosed what is really troubling people in the slums, because they have been unable to convince them that the potential gains are worth their sacrifice of time and energy. And if issues are indeed becoming increasingly complex, it also becomes harder and harder to isolate and sloganize action that, if demanded and then taken, will result in a clear improvement of conditions.

In response to all these realities, we find new and astonishing doctrines coming into vogue. Herbert Marcuse,

for example, attacks democracy and tolerance as themselves being barriers to the actions required for the overthrow of a monstrous society. In the past, even the Leninists, whatever their actual practices—the suppression of free speech and the murder of political opponents—usually tried to cover them up with such terms as "peoples' democracy" and with such justifications as the paramount need to defend the revolution from the violence of others. But lip service to the virtues of democracy and tolerance are now, it seems, to be abandoned by radicals on the ground that democracy and tolerance only protect an evil society—protect it precisely because they can be displayed as its virtues! We have come to such twisted arguments as one recently given by an American professor against accepting a Fulbright fellowship: he agreed that he was free to attack American foreign policy abroad, but by so doing he would mislead his foreign audience into believing that the United States was a free society and worthy of support by men of good will.

In the universities, participatory democracy has now been replaced by a new doctrine which decrees that when democratic procedures either do not exist (as indeed they do not in many sectors of many universities) or when a democratic system fails to respond to deeply felt needs (as with the Vietnam war) then it is quite legitimate to engage in disruption and disorder to bring about change. This argument has attracted the support of substantial minorities of students and even of faculties, though it has been less effective among the American people at large.

The new doctrine, which we see exemplified at Nanterre and Columbia, is a far cry from the ideals of participatory democracy, especially in the early days of the new Left when meetings were open to all, when discussions to gain consensus went on endlessly, when there was deep soul-searching about the morality of engaging in activity that provoked the violence of political opponents and police. Under the auspices of the new doctrine, the rights of the majority are held in derision, and political opponents are prevented from speaking or being heard. Tactics are worked out to strip authorities of dignity through staged confrontations, to arrange matters so that violence will erupt for the benefit of the press and television, to win over basically unsympathetic students who, owing to their commitment to fairmindedness, will almost always be "radicalized" by exposure to police intervention. In effect, we have moved from the ideal of the politicized masses with direct control over their fate—an unlikely form of organization in any case—to the quite cynical manipulation of the masses by those who themselves object to "formal" democracy and to the public order and tolerance that are its foundation. That small minorities are able to get so far with these tactics is attributable to two circumstances: first that they operate in an environment (the university) which is in fact undemocratic and which is also totally incapable of handling confrontation, disruption, and provocation; and second, that we have in the Vietnam war a case in which democratic processes most certainly do not work well, any more than they do in less explosive sectors of foreign policy in this country.

I think some good has and will come out of these tactics—university constitutions are being revised, and probably for the better—balanced by a good deal of evil. Alongside the wrong of university administrations which are unresponsive to faculty and student opinion, we now have the new wrong of groups of students who can impose their will on the university, regardless of what the majority of their colleagues and teachers want or think. Just recently, the students of Stanford University voted 70 per cent

in favor of allowing the government agencies and Dow Chemical to recruit on campus—but on how many other campuses has policy been made by an aggressive minority, without a student vote to determine majority sentiment? The fact that our universities are not democratically organized has made it possible for small groups to instigate change and reform—and this is to the good. But the ultimate end of these changes and reforms will still have to be something on the order of formal democracy—universal suffrage, free discussion, free balloting, all of which seem remote from the affections of the passionate on the New Left. For when these democratic forms prevail, leftists can claim no greater rights than others, regardless of how strongly they feel they are right.

Through these changes in attitude and tactics, an anti-institutional bias remains at the heart of the New Left position; and at the heart of my own critique of that position is my belief that there can be no substitute for institutions, even though they may become tired, bureaucratic, and corrupt. Yet no more, in my view, can there be any substitute for the organized and aroused people when the institutions become, as they ineluctably will, inadequate to their task. At that point, they must be supplemented or supplanted by new institutions, which will hopefully respond more sensitively to the needs of their clients. I think in the host of proposals and experiments of the past six or seven years there have been many good ones—but then they eventually will become part of the institutionalized system too. We now have neighborhood law firms, which some people around the poverty program saw as the guarantor of a determinedly antagonistic and suspicious attitude toward all institutions. But why? How can they escape becoming institutions themselves? They will have to recruit staff, set limits to their work load, accept some cases and reject others, arrive at a modus vivendi with the rest of the institutionalized world, give security to their employees. And would we want it otherwise? Do we want to devote, each of us, full time to every problem—welfare, education, housing, legal rights, and what have you—or are we prepared to accept the subdivisions of a complex society, leaving some of our resources in reserve, to be called out against the worst problems, the most serious scandals?

One does feel rather like a Scrooge in insisting that spontaneity and feeling can never replace the institutions, with their bureaucrats, clerks, secretaries, forms, computers, regulations, and—hopefully—appeal boards. But there are to my mind more serious reasons than any I have yet suggested for thinking that this dream of the New Left must remain a limited one, and this brings me to the third major failing of the radical perspective. As I look to the future, I see that the expectation of more freedom, of more spontaneity, must be disappointed. Kenneth Boulding has pointed to three factors pushing us inexorably toward a more rather than a less organized society: one is the existence of the terribly destructive atomic weapons, the second is the growth of population, the third the exhaustion of natural resources. To these three might be added a fourth: the pollution of the environment.

The interesting thing about all these problems is that they take on roughly the same character in all advanced societies, and in each case the answer seems to come down to greater controls. Thus, once the atomic weapons emerge, there is no way of sweeping them under the rug. They are a reality, and to deal with them involves a species of considerations which makes the radical perspective all but entirely irrelevant. Perhaps I am wrong. Perhaps one can envisage the masses raging through the streets of Moscow and Washington demanding the absolute destruction of these horrible weapons, and with full faith in the good will of the other side. But even if we were to get this far, can anyone imagine the same thing happening in the streets of Peking, or Tel Aviv, or Cairo?

The population explosion—and I assume we are all frightened at the projections—constitutes a similar trap, for it means that the most basic of all forms of human spontaneity will have to be subjected to elaborate institutional controls if the world is ever to arrive at anything like the good life, or the good-as-possible life, that radicals so mistakenly tie to the overthrow of organized society. So too the gradual exhaustion of natural resources—which we are less concerned about today but which we will soon be forced to worry about constantly—sets another inexorable limit to the kind of society in which freedom is maximized and controls put at a minimum. As to environmental pollution, it is a more immediate concern, and one ironically linked to higher standards of living, in the form of insecticides, soaps, fertilizers, automobiles. Here too we can only foresee greater and more intrusive controls being imposed—not only in America but in all advanced countries, and not only under capitalism but under Communism (as a glance at the Russian response to these same problems quickly reveals). The radicals have offered no alternative to these imperatives, except the return to smaller communities, and lower standards of living. This I would regard as wholly consistent with their outlook, and one that makes sense in its own terms. Relatively few people, however, are willing to adopt it, and in the underdeveloped world it makes no sense at all.

My discussion up to now has concentrated solely on domestic affairs. Perhaps many might agree that our domestic problems are complex, require continuous and expert attention, and in large measure transcend or make irrelevant traditional political distinctions. But what about Vietnam? It is on this issue, after all, that the radical Left now principally expresses itself. Does not Vietnam point to some horrible illness in the American system—a sick reliance on technology as the solution to all problems, an outrageous view of the American role and prerogatives in the world, a suppressed violence which will out in the most grisly forms, an inhumanly narrow view of other societies and other peoples? I would agree that just as domestic politics stops at the water's edge, so my analysis in large measure is relevant only to our domestic problems. Many people look at the war and conclude, as I said at the beginning, that the roots are poisoned, that radical change is needed. Many other people— and this is a constant in the history of radicalism—begin with the idea that the roots are poisoned, and take the war as proof of their original conviction. Like the Talmudic scholar in the old story, they once ran through the streets shouting, "I have an answer! Does anyone have a question?" But now Vietnam has given them a very good question, too.

Nevertheless, I cannot accept the idea that the fundamental character of American society, its political or economic life, is the prime cause of the horrors of Vietnam. In the end, I cannot help believing, the Vietnam war must be understood as the result of a series of monumental errors. The key point to me is this: *America would not have had to be very different from what it now is for some President to have gotten us out of Vietnam rather than deeper and deeper into it.* Was America so much different or so much better under Eisenhower than it has been under Johnson? And yet all it took was a simple decision by Eisen-

hower to keep us from intervening in Vietnam in 1954.

The Vietnam war does to my mind point to something basically wrong with the American political system, but it is less apocalyptic than the analyses of the radical Left suggest. I believe—along with Senator Fulbright—that foreign policy, which was relatively marginal for the United States until the late 1930's, has become, or has remained, too exclusively the province of the President and his closest advisers. Whereas in domestic affairs the President must answer constantly to Congress, he has become literally irresponsible in the area of foreign affairs, where he must answer only to the electorate and only once every four years. If he is stubborn or stupid or makes mistakes and insists on sticking with them—and his position as head of a political party gives him every incentive to do so—he can destroy the country before being called to account. Since, moreover, we are still relatively insulated in our day-to-day national life from the world outside, the President can deceive the people as to the extent of his errors in foreign affairs much more effectively than he can in domestic affairs. This is a very serious matter indeed and the United States may be fatally damaged before we find a way out. But I cannot easily reconcile my own understanding as to how we have come to this terrible position with the basic perspectives and criticisms of the New Left. Nor are those perspectives particularly helpful in figuring out what we can do to repair the political system against a defect of this character and magnitude.

Ultimately, my disagreement with the radical Left comes down to this: I see no Gordian knot to be cut at a single stroke, the cutting of which would justify the greatest efforts (as in the past it has seemed to justify great horrors). Nationalizing the means of production, as Socialist countries have discovered, is no all-embracing answer; nor is permanent mobilization of the people, which is in any case fantastically difficult to accomplish, and which, if it were to be accomplished, as it has for a time in China, would create a society that we would find repulsive; nor is the destruction of the upper classes—in the advanced countries at any rate, whatever value such destruction might yield in underdeveloped nations—for the upper classes now consist of the managers, the organizers, and the highly skilled professionals, whom we would inevitably have to re-create.

From the point of view of the heroisms of the past, it is a gray world we are entering, in which technicians and interest groups, neither of whom can be said to bear the banner of humanity in its noblest form, will be the determining forces. The best we can do is to ensure that as things go wrong—and they inevitably will—the people will have an opportunity to protest. They will rarely know, I am afraid, quite what to do to set things right, but their complaints and their occasional rebellious fury will be important "inputs," to use the dreary language of the future, in setting the matter right. The logic of the situation—the size of our population, the number of our organizations, the extent of our problems, the interrelations among the different parts of our society, the development of science and technology—all point to this outcome. Under the circumstances, even reform and its traditions become part of the system. How much protest do we need to keep the system straight and keep it correcting itself? At what point will protest wreck the institutions altogether and prevent them from functioning? The system is necessary; not this system exactly, but some system, and one which, given the external forces that govern our lives, will turn out to be not so significantly different.

I view radicalism as a great reservoir of energy which moves the establishment to pay attention to the most serious and urgent problems, and tells it when it has failed. To a more limited degree, it is also a reservoir of potential creativity— a reaching for new solutions and new approaches. What radicalism is not, and what it can no longer be, is the great sword of vengeance and correction which goes to the source of the distress and cuts it out. There is no longer a single source, and no longer a single sword.

SUGGESTIONS FOR
FURTHER READING

The literature dealing with American intellectual history is extensive. The following list, therefore, is not intended to be definitive. Most of the works selected for inclusion in this section simply represent a cross section of some of the more important books dealing with various aspects of American intellectual development. For a more complete bibliography the reader can consult Oscar Handlin and others, eds., *Harvard Guide to American History* (Cambridge, Mass.: Harvard University Press, 1954); Library of Congress, *A Guide to the Study of the United States of America: Representative Books Reflecting the Development of American Life and Thought* (Washington, D.C.: United States Government Printing Office, 1960), and the bibliography in Merle Curti, *The Growth of American Thought* (3rd ed., New York: Harper & Row, 1964), pp. 797–900.

I. General Works

Aaron, Daniel, *Men of Good Hope: A Story of American Progressives* (New York: Oxford University Press, 1951).

Baritz, Loren, *City on a Hill: A History of Ideas and Myths in America* (New York: John Wiley & Sons, 1964).

Beard, Charles A. and Mary R., *The American Spirit: A Study of the Idea of Civilization in the United States* (New York: The Macmillan Company, 1942).

Beard, Charles A. and Mary R., *The Rise of American Civilization* (New York: The Macmillan Company, 1927).

Boorstin, Daniel, *The Genius of American Politics* (Chicago: University of Chicago Press, 1953).

Bowers, David F., ed., *Foreign Influences in American Life* (Princeton, N.J.: Princeton University Press, 1944).

Burns, Edward M., *The American Idea of Mission: Concepts of National Purpose and Destiny* (New Brunswick, N.J.: Rutgers University Press, 1957).

Cash, Wilbur J., *The Mind of the South* (New York: Alfred A. Knopf, 1941).

Cohen, Morris Raphael, *American Thought: A Critical Sketch* (New York: The Free Press of Glencoe, 1954).

Curti, Merle, *The Growth of American Thought* (3rd ed., New York: Harper & Row, 1964).

Curti, Merle, *The Roots of American Loyalty* (New York: Columbia University Press, 1946).

Curti, Merle, *The Social Ideas of American Educators* (New York: Charles Scribner's Sons, 1935).

Dorfman, Joseph, *The Economic Mind in American Civilization* (5 vols., New York: The Viking Press, 1946–1959).

Dorson, Richard M., *American Folklore* (Chicago: University of Chicago Press, 1959).

Egbert, Donald D., and Persons, Stow, eds., *Socialism and American Life* (2 vols., Princeton, N.J.: Princeton University Press, 1952).

Ekirch, Arthur, *The Decline of American Liberalism* (New York: Oxford University Press, 1955).

Ellis, John T., *American Catholicism* (Chicago: University of Chicago Press, 1956).

Gabriel, Ralph H., *The Course of Ameri-*

can Democratic Thought (2nd ed., New York: The Ronald Press Company, 1956).

Glazer, Nathan, American Judaism (Chicago: University of Chicago Press, 1957).

Gossett, Thomas F., Race: The History of an Idea in America (Dallas: Southern Methodist University Press, 1963).

Greene, Evarts B., Religion and the State: The Making and Testing of an American Tradition (New York: New York University Press, 1941).

Hartz, Louis, The Liberal Tradition in America: An Interpretation of American Political Thought Since the Revolution (New York: Harcourt, Brace and Company, 1955).

Higham, John, et al., History: The Development of Historical Studies in the United States (Englewood Cliffs, N.J.: Prentice-Hall, 1965).

Hofstadter, Richard, The American Political Tradition and the Men Who Made It (New York: Alfred A. Knopf, 1948).

Hofstadter, Richard, Anti-intellectualism in American Life (New York: Alfred A. Knopf, 1963).

Hudson, Winthrop S., American Protestantism (Chicago: University of Chicago Press, 1961).

Hurst, James Willard, The Growth of American Law (Boston: Little, Brown and Company, 1950).

Jones, Howard Mumford, The Pursuit of Happiness (Cambridge, Mass.: Harvard University Press, 1953).

Kohn, Hans, American Nationalism (New York: The Macmillan Company, 1957).

Kraus, Michael, The Writing of American History (Norman, Okla.: University of Oklahoma Press, 1953).

Lerner, Max, America as a Civilization: Life and Thought in the United States Today (New York: Simon and Schuster, 1957).

Lynd, Staughton, Intellectual Origins of American Radicalism (New York: Pantheon Books, 1968).

McLoughlin, William G., Jr., Modern Revivalism: Charles Grandison Finney to Billy Graham (New York: The Ronald Press Company, 1959).

Merriam, Charles E., A History of American Political Theories (New York: The Macmillan Company, 1920).

Mosier, Richard D., The American Temper: Patterns of Our Intellectual Heritage (Berkeley, Calif.: University of California Press, 1952).

Mott, Frank L., Golden Multitudes: The Story of Best Sellers in the United States (New York: The Macmillan Company, 1947).

Mott, Frank L., A History of American Magazines (5 vols., Cambridge, Mass.: Harvard University Press, 1938–1968).

Niebuhr, H. Richard, The Kingdom of God in America (New York: Harper and Brothers, 1937).

Niebuhr, H. Richard, The Social Sources of Denominationalism (New York: Holt, Rinehart and Winston, 1929).

Nye, Russell B., This Almost Chosen People: Essays in the History of American Ideas (East Lansing: Michigan State University Press, 1966).

Parrington, Vernon L., Main Currents in American Thought (3 vols., New York: Harcourt, Brace and Company, 1927–1930).

Perry, Ralph Barton, Puritanism and Democracy (New York: The Vanguard Press, 1944).

Persons, Stow, American Minds: A History of Ideas (New York: Holt, Rinehart and Winston, 1958).

Persons, Stow, ed., Evolutionary Thought in America (New Haven, Conn.: Yale University Press, 1950).

Potter, David M., People of Plenty: Economic Abundance and the American Character (Chicago: University of Chicago Press, 1954).

Rossiter, Clinton, Conservatism in America (New York: Alfred A. Knopf, 1955).

Schlesinger, Arthur M., and White, Morton, eds., Paths of American Thought (Boston: Houghton Mifflin Company, 1963).

Schneider, Herbert W., A History of American Philosophy (New York: Columbia University Press, 1946).

Skotheim, Robert A., American Intellectual Histories and Historians (Princeton, N.J.: Princeton University Press, 1966).

Smith, Henry Nash, *Virgin Land: The American West as Symbol and Myth* (Cambridge, Mass.: Harvard University Press, 1950).

Smith, James Ward, and Jamison, Albert Lelands, eds., *Religion in American Life* (4 vols., in 5 parts, Princeton, N.J.: Princeton University Press, 1961).

Smith, T. V., *The American Philosophy of Equality* (Chicago: University of Chicago Press, 1927).

Spencer, Benjamin T., *The Quest for Nationality: An American Literary Campaign* (Syracuse, N.Y.: Syracuse University Press, 1957).

Spiller, Robert E., et al., eds., *Literary History of the United States* (3 vols., New York: The Macmillan Company, 1948).

Stokes, Anson P., *Church and State in the United States* (3 vols., New York: Harper & Row, 1950).

Strout, Cushing, *The American Image of the Old World* (New York: Harper & Row, 1963).

Sweet, William W., *The Story of Religion in America* (2nd ed., New York: Harper & Row, 1950).

Wecter, Dixon, *The Hero in America* (New York: Charles Scribner's Sons, 1941).

Weinberg, Albert K., *Manifest Destiny* (Baltimore: The Johns Hopkins Press, 1935).

Weisberger, Bernard A., *They Gathered at the River: The Story of the Great Revivalists and Their Impact upon Religion in America* (Boston: Little, Brown and Company, 1958).

Welter, Rush, *Popular Education and Democratic Thought in America* (New York: Columbia University Press, 1962).

White, Morton, and White, Lucia, *The Intellectual Versus the City: From Thomas Jefferson to Frank Lloyd Wright* (Cambridge: Harvard University Press and the M.I.T. Press, 1962).

Wiltse, Charles M., *The Jeffersonian Tradition in American Democracy* (Chapel Hill, N.C.: University of North Carolina Press, 1935).

Wish, Harvey, *The American Historian: A Social-Intellectual History of the Writing of the American Past* (New York: Oxford University Press, 1960).

Wright, Benjamin, *American Interpretations of Natural Law* (Cambridge, Mass.: Harvard University Press, 1931).

II. The Puritan and Enlightenment Minds

Adams, James Truslow, *Provincial Society, 1690–1763* (New York: The Macmillan Company, 1927).

Adams, Randolph G., *Political Ideas of the American Revolution* (Durham, N.C.: Trinity College Press, 1922).

Bailyn, Bernard, *The Ideological Origins of the American Revolution* (Cambridge, Mass.: Harvard University Press, 1967).

Beard, Charles A., *An Economic Interpretation of the Constitution of the United States* (New York: The Macmillan Company, 1913).

Becker, Carl L., *The Declaration of Independence* (New York: Alfred A. Knopf, 1922).

Boorstin, Daniel J., *The Americans: The Colonial Experience* (New York: Random House, 1958).

Brown, Robert E., *Charles Beard and the Constitution: A Critical Analysis of "An Economic Interpretation of the Constitution"* (Princeton, N.J.: Princeton University Press, 1956).

Colbourn, H. Trevor, *The Lamp of Experience: Whig History and the Intellectual Origins of the American Revolution* (Chapel Hill, N.C.: University of North Carolina Press, 1965).

Craven, Wesley F., *The Legend of the Founding Fathers* (New York: New York University Press, 1956).

Davis, Richard Beale, *Intellectual Life in Jefferson's Virginia, 1790–1830* (Chapel Hill, N.C.: University of North Carolina Press, 1964).

Dietze, Gottfried, *The Federalist: A Classic on Federalism and Free Government* (Baltimore: The Johns Hopkins Press, 1960).

Gaustad, Edwin S., *The Great Awakening in New England* (New York: Harper & Row, 1957).

Gay, Peter, *A Loss of Mastery: Puritan Historians in Colonial America* (Berkeley, Calif.: University of California Press, 1966).

Gewehr, Wesley M., *The Great Awakening in Virginia, 1740–1790* (Durham, N.C.: Duke University Press, 1930).

Greene, Evarts B., *The Revolutionary Generation, 1763–1790* (New York: The Macmillan Company, 1943).

Gunmere, Richard M., *The American Colonial Mind and the Classical Tradition: Essays in Comparative Culture* (Cambridge, Mass.: Harvard University Press, 1963).

Handler, Edward, *America and Europe in the Political Thought of John Adams* (Cambridge, Mass.: Harvard University Press, 1964).

Hawke, David, *A Transaction of Free Men: The Birth and Course of the Declaration of Independence* (New York: Charles Scribner's Sons, 1964).

Heimert, Alan, *Religion and the American Mind: From the Great Awakening to the Revolution* (Cambridge, Mass.: Harvard University Press, 1966).

Hindle, Brooke, *The Pursuit of Science in Revolutionary America, 1735–1789* (Chapel Hill, N.C.: University of North Carolina Press, 1956).

Humphrey, Edward F., *Nationalism and Religion in America, 1774–1789* (Boston: Chipman Law Publishing Company, 1924).

Koch, Adrienne, *The Philosophy of Thomas Jefferson* (New York: Columbia University Press, 1943).

Koch, G. Adolph, *Republican Religion: The American Revolution and the Cult of Reason* (New York: Henry Holt and Company, 1933).

Kraus, Michael, *The Atlantic Civilization: Eighteenth-Century Origins* (Ithaca, N.Y.: Cornell University Press, 1949).

Kraus, Michael, *Intercolonial Aspects of American Culture on the Eve of the Revolution* (New York: Columbia University Press, 1928).

McDonald, Forrest, *We the People: The Economic Origins of the Constitution* (Chicago: University of Chicago Press, 1958).

Malone, Dumas, *Jefferson and His Time* (2 vols., Boston: Little, Brown and Company, 1948–1951).

Maxson, Charles H., *The Great Awakening in the Middle Colonies* (Chicago: University of Chicago Press, 1920).

Miller, Perry, *The New England Mind: The Seventeenth Century* (New York: The Macmillan Company, 1939), and *The New England Mind: From Colony to Province* (Cambridge, Mass.: Harvard University Press, 1953).

Miller, Perry, *Orthodoxy in Massachusetts, 1630–1650* (Cambridge, Mass: Harvard University Press, 1933).

Morais, Herbert M., *Deism in Eighteenth-Century America* (New York: Columbia University Press, 1934).

Morgan, Edmund S., *The Puritan Dilemma: The Story of John Winthrop* (Boston: Little, Brown and Company, 1958).

Morison, Samuel Eliot, *The Founding of Harvard College* (Cambridge, Mass.: Harvard University Press, 1935), and *Harvard College in the Seventeenth Century* (2 vols., Cambridge, Mass.: Harvard University Press, 1936).

Morison, Samuel Eliot, *The Intellectual Life of Colonial New England* (New York: New York University Press, 1956).

Murdock, Kenneth B., *Literature and Theology in Colonial New England* (Cambridge, Mass.: Harvard University Press, 1949).

Rossiter, Clinton, *Seedtime of the Republic: The Origin of the American Tradition of Political Liberty* (New York: Harcourt, Brace and World, 1953).

Savelle, Max, *Seeds of Liberty: The Genesis of the American Mind* (New York: Alfred A. Knopf, 1948).

Schlesinger, Arthur M., *Prelude to Independence: The Newspaper War on Britain, 1764–1776* (New York: Alfred A. Knopf, 1957).

Schneider, Herbert W., *The Puritan Mind* (New York: Henry Holt and Company, 1930).

Simpson, Alan, *Puritanism in Old and New England* (Chicago: University of Chicago Press, 1955).

Sweet, William W., *Religion in Colonial*

America (New York: Charles Scribner's Sons, 1942).

Tyler, Moses Coit, *The Literary History of the American Revolution, 1763–1783* (2 vols., New York: G. P. Putnam's Sons, 1897).

Van Doren, Carl, *Benjamin Franklin* (New York: The Viking Press, 1938).

Wertenbaker, Thomas J., *The First Americans, 1607–1690* (New York: The Macmillan Company, 1927).

Wertenbaker, Thomas J., *The Golden Age of Colonial Culture* (2nd ed., New York: New York University Press, 1949).

Wright, Conrad, *The Beginnings of Unitarianism in America* (Boston: The Beacon Press, 1955).

Wright, Louis B., *The Cultural Life of the American Colonies, 1607–1763* (New York: Harper & Row, 1957).

Wright, Thomas C., *Literary Culture in Early New England, 1620–1730* (New Haven, Conn.: Yale University Press, 1920).

III. The Early National and Romantic Period

Arieli, Yehoshua, *Individualism and Nationalism in American Ideology* (Cambridge, Mass.: Harvard University Press, 1964).

Barnes, Gilbert H., *The Antislavery Impulse, 1830–1844* (New York: D. Appleton-Century Company, 1933).

Billington, Ray A., *The Protestant Crusade, 1800–1860* (New York: The Macmillan Company, 1938).

Blau, Joseph L., ed., *Social Theories of Jacksonian Democracy* (New York: Hafner Publishing Company, 1947).

Bode, Carl, *The American Lyceum* (New York: Oxford University Press, 1956).

Bode, Carl, *The Anatomy of American Popular Culture, 1840–1861* (Berkeley, Calif.: University of California Press, 1959).

Boorstin, Daniel J., *The Americans: The National Experience* (New York: Random House, 1965).

Branch, Edward Douglas, *The Sentimental Years, 1836–1860* (New York: D. Appleton-Century Company, 1934).

Brooks, Van Wyck, *The Flowering of New England* (New York: E. P. Dutton and Company, 1936); *The Times of Melville and Whitman* (New York: E. P. Dutton and Company, 1947); and *The World of Washington Irving* (New York: E. P. Dutton and Company, 1944).

Carpenter, Jesse T., *The South as a Conscious Minority, 1789–1861* (New York: New York University Press, 1930).

Cole, Arthur C., *The Irrepressible Conflict, 1850–1865* (New York: The Macmillan Company, 1934).

Cross, Whitney R., *The Burned-Over District* (Ithaca, N.Y.: Cornell University Press, 1950).

Davies, John D., *Phrenology: Fad and Science: A 19th-Century American Crusade* (New Haven, Conn.: Yale University Press, 1955).

Davis, David B., *The Problem of Slavery in Western Culture* (Ithaca, N.Y.: Cornell University Press, 1966).

Eaton, Clement, *The Mind of the Old South* (Baton Rouge, La.: Louisiana State University Press, 1964).

Ekirch, Arthur A., *The Idea of Progress in America, 1815–1860* (New York: Columbia University Press, 1944).

Fish, Carl R., *The Rise of the Common Man* (New York: The Macmillan Company, 1927).

Frederickson, George M., *The Inner Civil War: Northern Intellectuals and the Crisis of the Union* (New York: Harper & Row, 1965).

Frothingham, Octavius B., *Transcendentalism in New England* (New York: G. P. Putnam's Sons, 1876).

Griffin, Clifford S., *Their Brothers' Keepers: Moral Stewardship in the United States, 1800–1865* (New Brunswick, N.J.: Rutgers University Press, 1960).

Jenkins, William S., *Proslavery Thought in the Old South* (Chapel Hill, N.C.: University of North Carolina Press, 1935).

Johnson, Charles A., *The Frontier Camp Meeting* (Dallas, Texas: Southern Methodist University Press, 1955).

Krout, John A., and Fox, Dixon R., *The Completion of Independence,*

1790–1830 (New York: The Macmillan Company, 1944).

Matthiessen, F. O., *American Renaissance: Art and Expression in the Age of Emerson and Whitman* (New York: Oxford University Press, 1941).

Meyers, Marvin, *The Jacksonian Persuasion: Politics and Belief* (Stanford, Calif.: Stanford University Press, 1957).

Miller, Perry, *The Life of the Mind in America: From the Revolution to the Civil War* (New York: Harcourt, Brace and World, 1965).

Nagel, Paul, *One Nation Indivisible: The Union in American Thought, 1776–1861* (New York: Oxford University Press, 1964).

Nye, Russell B., *The Cultural Life of the New Nation, 1776–1830* (New York: Harper & Row, 1960).

Rusk, Ralph L., *The Life of Ralph Waldo Emerson* (New York: Charles Scribner's Sons, 1949).

Rusk, Ralph L., *The Literature of the Middle Western Frontier* (2 vols., New York: Columbia University Press, 1925).

Smith, Timothy L., *Revivalism and Social Reform in Mid-Nineteenth-Century America* (New York: Abingdon Press, 1957).

Somkin, Fred, *Unquiet Eagle: Memory and Desire in the Idea of American Freedom, 1815–1860* (Ithaca, N.Y.: Cornell University Press, 1967).

Sweet, William W., *Religion in the Development of American Culture, 1765–1840* (New York: Charles Scribner's Sons, 1952).

Taylor, William R., *Cavalier and Yankee: The Old South and the American National Character* (New York: George Braziller, 1961).

de Tocqueville, Alexis, *Democracy in America*, Phillips Bradley, ed. (2 vols., New York: Alfred A. Knopf, 1946).

Tyler, Alice F., *Freedom's Ferment* (Minneapolis: University of Minnesota Press, 1944).

IV. Industrial and Modern America

Aaron, Daniel, *Writers on the Left: Episodes in American Literary Communism* (New York: Harcourt, Brace and World, 1961).

Abell, Aaron I., *American Catholicism and Social Action* (Garden City, N.Y.: Hanover House, 1960).

Abell, Aaron I., *The Urban Impact on American Protestantism, 1865–1900* (Cambridge, Mass.: Harvard University Press, 1943).

Auerbach, Morton, *The Conservative Illusion* (New York: Columbia University Press, 1959).

Boller, Paul F., Jr., *American Thought in Transition: The Impact of Evolutionary Naturalism, 1865–1900* (Chicago: Rand McNally and Company, 1969).

Bremner, Robert H., *From the Depths: The Discovery of Poverty in the United States* (New York: New York University Press, 1956).

Brooks, Van Wyck, *The Confident Years: 1885–1915* (New York: E. P. Dutton and Company, 1952), and *New England: Indian Summer, 1865–1915* (New York: E. P. Dutton and Company, 1940).

Buck, Paul H., *The Road to Reunion, 1865–1900* (Boston: Little, Brown and Company, 1937).

Cargill, Oscar, *Intellectual America* (New York: The Macmillan Company, 1941).

Carter, Paul A., *The Decline and Revival of the Social Gospel: Social and Political Liberalism in American Protestant Churches, 1920–1940* (Ithaca, N.Y.: Cornell University Press, 1956).

Chugerman, Samuel, *Lester F. Ward: The American Aristotle* (Durham, N.C.: Duke University Press, 1939).

Commager, Henry S., *The American Mind: An Interpretation of American Thought and Character Since the 1880's* (New Haven, Conn.: Yale University Press, 1950).

Cremin, Lawrence A., *The Transformation of the School: Progressivism in American Education, 1876–1957* (New York: Alfred A. Knopf, 1961).

Cross, Robert D., *The Emergence of Liberal Catholicism in America* (Cambridge, Mass.: Harvard University Press, 1958).

Curti, Merle, ed., *American Scholarship*

in the Twentieth Century (Cambridge, Mass.: Harvard University Press, 1953).

Destler, Chester M., *American Radicalism, 1865–1901* (New London, Conn.: Connecticut College, 1946).

Dorfman, Joseph, *Thorstein Veblen and His America* (New York: The Viking Press, 1934).

Faulkner, Harold U., *The Quest for Social Justice, 1898–1914* (New York: The Macmillan Company, 1931).

Filler, Louis, *Crusaders for American Liberalism* (New York: Harcourt, Brace and Company, 1939).

Fine, Sidney, *Laissez Faire and the General-Welfare State: A Study of Conflict in American Thought, 1865–1901* (Ann Arbor, Mich.: University of Michigan Press, 1956).

Forcey, Charles, *The Crossroads of Liberalism: Croly, Weyl, Lippmann, and the Progressive Era, 1900–1925* (New York: Oxford University Press, 1961).

Foster, Frank H., *The Modern Movement in American Theology* (New York: Fleming H. Revell Company, 1939).

Fullinwider, S. P., *The Mind and Mood of Black America: 20th Century Thought* (Homewood, Ill.: Dorsey Press, 1969).

Furniss, Norman F., *The Fundamentalist Controversy, 1918–1931* (New Haven, Conn.: Yale University Press, 1954).

Ginger, Ray, *Altgeld's America* (New York: Funk and Wagnalls Company, 1958).

Goldman, Eric F., *Rendezvous With Destiny: A History of Modern American Reform* (New York: Alfred A. Knopf, 1952).

Gurko, Leo, *The Angry Decade* (New York: Dodd, Mead and Company, 1947).

Haller, Mark H., *Eugenics: Hereditarian Attitudes in American Thought* (New Brunswick, N.J.: Rutgers University Press, 1963).

Handlin, Oscar, *Race and Nationality in American Life* (Boston: Little, Brown and Company, 1950).

Herberg, Will, *Protestant-Catholic-Jew:*

An Essay in American Religious Sociology (Garden City, N.Y.: Doubleday and Company, 1955).

Higham, John, *Strangers in the Land: Patterns of American Nativism, 1860–1925* (New Brunswick, N.J.: Rutgers University Press, 1955).

Hoffmann, Frederick J., *The Twenties* (New York: The Viking Press, 1955).

Hofstadter, Richard, *The Age of Reform: From Bryan to F.D.R.* (New York: Alfred A. Knopf, 1955).

Hofstadter, Richard, *Social Darwinism in American Thought, 1860–1915* (Philadelphia: University of Pennsylvania Press, 1944).

Hopkins, Charles H., *The Rise of the Social Gospel in American Protestantism 1865–1915* (New Haven, Conn. Yale University Press, 1940).

Jordy, William H., *Henry Adams: Scientific Historian* (New Haven, Conn.: Yale University Press, 1952).

Kazin, Alfred, *On Native Grounds* (New York: Reynal and Hitchcock, 1942).

Kirkland, Edward C., *Dream and Thought in the Business Community, 1860–1900* (Ithaca, N.Y.: Cornell University Press, 1956).

McCloskey, Robert G., *American Conservatism in the Age of Enterprise* (Cambridge, Mass.: Harvard University Press, 1951).

Madden, Edward H., *Civil Disobedience and Moral Law in Nineteenth-Century American Philosophy* (Seattle: University of Washington Press, 1968).

May, Henry F., *The End of American Innocence: A Study of the First Years of Our Own Time, 1912–1917* (New York: Alfred A. Knopf, 1959).

May, Henry F., *Protestant Churches and Industrial America* (New York: Harper & Row, 1949).

Meier, August, *Negro Thought in America, 1880–1915* (Ann Arbor: University of Michigan Press, 1963).

Meyer, Donald B., *The Protestant Search for Political Realism, 1919–1941* (Berkeley, Calif.: University of California Press, 1960).

Miller, Robert M., *American Protestantism and Social Issues, 1919–1939* (Chapel Hill, N.C.: University of North Carolina Press, 1958).

Moore, Edward C., *American Pragmatism: Peirce, James, and Dewey* (New York: Columbia University Press, 1961).

Nevins, Allan, *The Emergence of Modern America, 1865–1878* (New York: The Macmillan Company, 1927).

Newman, William J., *The Futilitarian Society* (New York: George Braziller, 1961).

Noble, David W., *The Paradox of Progressive Thought* (Minneapolis: University of Minnesota Press, 1958).

Paul, Arnold M., *Conservative Crisis and the Rule of Law: Attitudes of Bar and Bench, 1887–1895* (Ithaca, N.Y.: Cornell University Press, 1960).

Perry, Ralph Barton, *The Thought and Character of William James* (2 vols., Boston: Little, Brown and Company, 1935).

Prothero, James W., *The Dollar Decade: Business Ideas in the 1920's* (Baton Rouge, La.: Louisiana State University Press, 1954).

Quint, Howard H., *The Forging of American Socialism: Origins of the Modern Movement* (Columbia, S.C.: University of South Carolina Press, 1953).

Rader, Benjamin G., *The Academic Mind and Reform: The Influence of Richard T. Ely in American Life* (Lexington, Ky.: University of Kentucky Press, 1966).

Resek, Carl, *Lewis Henry Morgan: American Scholar* (Chicago: University of Chicago Press, 1960).

Riesman, David, et al., *The Lonely Crowd: A Study of the Changing American Character* (New Haven, Conn.: Yale University Press, 1950).

Rogin, Michael Paul, *The Intellectuals and McCarthy: The Radical Specter* (Cambridge, Mass.: M.I.T. Press, 1967).

Rumble, Wilfred E., Jr., *American Legal Realism: Skepticism, Reform, and the Judicial Process* (Ithaca, N.Y.: Cornell University Press, 1968).

Russett, Cynthia E., *The Concept of Equilibrium in American Social Thought* (New Haven, Conn.: Yale University Press, 1966).

Schlesinger, Arthur M., *The Rise of the City, 1878–1898* (New York: The Macmillan Company, 1933).

Schneider, Herbert W., *Religion in 20th Century America* (Cambridge, Mass.: Harvard University Press, 1952).

Slosson, Preston W., *The Great Crusade and After, 1914–1928* (New York: The Macmillan Company, 1931).

Spitz, David, *Patterns of Anti-Democratic Thought* (New York: The Macmillan Company, 1949).

Starr, Harris, E., *William Graham Sumner* (New York: Henry Holt and Company, 1925).

Strout, Cushing, *The Pragmatic Revolt in American History: Carl Becker and Charles Beard* (New Haven, Conn.: Yale University Press, 1958).

Wecter, Dixon, *The Age of the Great Depression, 1929–1941* (New York: The Macmillan Company, 1948).

White, Edward A., *Science and Religion in American Thought: The Impact of Naturalism* (Stanford, Calif.: University of California Press, 1952).

White, Morton, *Social Thought in America: The Revolt Against Formalism* (New York: The Viking Press, 1949).

Wiener, Philip P., *Evolution and the Founders of Pragmatism* (Cambridge, Mass.: Harvard University Press, 1949).

Wilkins, Burleigh T., *Carl Becker* (Cambridge, Mass.: M.I.T. Press, 1961).

Wilson, R. Jackson, *In Quest of Community: Social Philosophy in the United States, 1860–1920* (New York: John Wiley & Sons, 1968).

Wyllie, Irvin G., *The Self-Made Man in America: The Myth of Rags to Riches* (New Brunswick, N.J.: Rutgers University Press, 1954).

INDEX

DATE DUE

DEC 1 '80			
NO 20 '82			
DE 4 '82			
MAY 4 '87			
GAYLORD			PRINTED IN U.S.A.